The Langhorne Sisters

James Fox was born in Washington DC in 1945. He worked as a journalist in Africa, and later on the *Sunday Times*. He is the author of the bestselling *White Mischief*.

D0124414

Also by James Fox

White Mischief

The Langhorne Sisters

James Fox

Granta Books
London

Granta Publications, 2/3 Hanover Yard, London N1 8BE

First published in Great Britain by Granta Books 1998
This edition published by Granta Books 1999

Copyright © 1998 by James Fox

Extracts from unpublished letter by Joyce Grenfell. Copyright © Joyce Grenfell
Extracts from *Darling Ma — Letters to her Mother 1932–1944*, edited and introduced by James
Roose Evans. London: Hodder and Stoughton, 1988. Copyright © 1998 by Reginald
Grenfell and James Roose Evans
Extract from *Joyce Grenfell Requests the Pleasure*. London: Macmillan, 1976.
Copyright © Joyce Grenfell 1976
Extract from *The Crack-Up* by F. Scott Fitzgerald. Copyright © 1945 by New Directions
Publishing Corp. Reprinted by permission of New Directions Publishing Corp: UK rights
by permission of David Higham Associates Ltd.
Excerpts from *The Price Was High: The Last Uncollected Stories of F. Scott Fitzgerald*, edited by
Matthew J. Bruccoli, copyright © 1979 by Francis Scott Fitzgerald Smith, reprinted by
permission of Harcourt Brace & Company and in the UK by David Higham Associates.
Extracts (various) from Scott Fitzgerald reprinted by permission of Harold Ober Associates
Incorporated. Copyright as indicated in various books.
Letters from Bernard Shaw to Nancy Astor reprinted by permission of The Society of
Authors on behalf of the Bernard Shaw Estate.
Extracts from letters by Hilaire Belloc reprinted by permission of the
Peters Fraser & Dunlop Group Ltd.
Verse from 'The D-Day Dodgers' by permission of Hamish Henderson.
Excerpt from 'Novelists of the Post-War South: Albion W. Tourgée, George W. Cable,
Kate Chopin, Thomas Nelson Page' from *Patriotic Gore: Studies in the Literature
of the American Civil War* by Edmund Wilson. Copyright © 1962 by Edmund Wilson.
Copyright renewed © 1990 by Helen Miranda Wilson. Reprinted by
permission of Farrar, Straus & Giroux, Inc.
Excerpt from *Over the Rim of the World* by Freya Stark. London: John Murray, 1988 by
permission of John Murray (Publishers) Ltd.

James Fox has asserted his moral right under the Copyright, Designs and Patents Act,
1988, to be identified as the author of this work.

All rights reserved. No reproduction, copy or transmissions of this publication may be
made without written permission. No paragraph of this publication may be reproduced,
copied or transmitted save with written permission or in accordance with the
provisions of the Copyright Act 1956 (as amended). Any person who does any
unauthorized act in relation to this publication may be liable to criminal
prosecution and civil claims for damages.

A CIP catalogue record for this book is available from the British Library.

3 5 7 9 10 8 6 4 2

Typeset by M Rules
Printed and bound in Great Britain by Mackays of Chatham PLC

Contents

For Francis Wyndham
and
In loving memory of my mother,
Dinah Bridge, 1920–1998

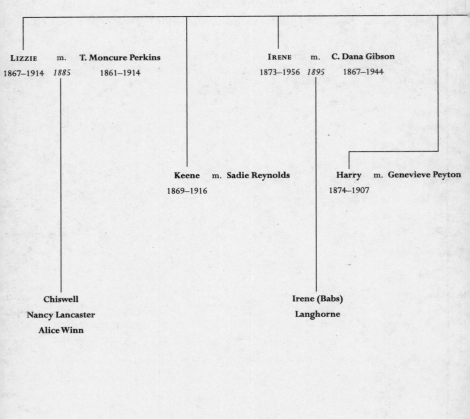

CHISWELL DABNEY LANGHORNE
1843–1919

LIZZIE m. **T. Moncure Perkins**
1867–1914 *1885* 1861–1914

IRENE m. **C. Dana Gibson**
1873–1956 *1895* 1867–1944

Keene m. Sadie Reynolds
1869–1916

Harry m. Genevieve Peyton
1874–1907

Chiswell
Nancy Lancaster
Alice Winn

Irene (Babs)
Langhorne

THE LANGHORNE
FAMILY TREE

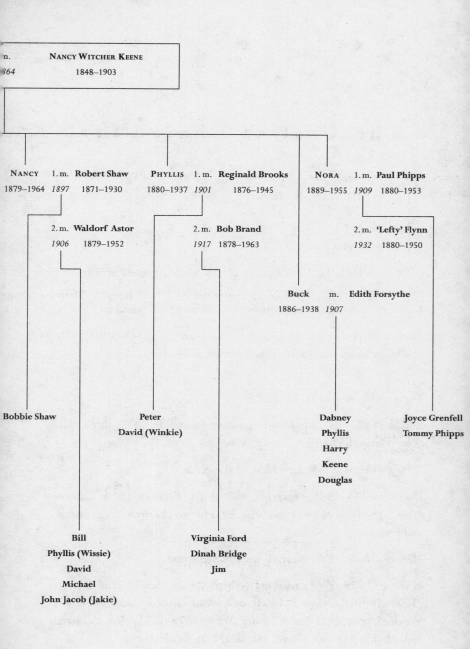

n.
864

NANCY WITCHER KEENE
1848–1903

NANCY 1. m. **Robert Shaw**
1879–1964 *1897* 1871–1930

2. m. **Waldorf Astor**
1906 1879–1952

PHYLLIS 1. m. **Reginald Brooks**
1880–1937 *1901* 1876–1945

2. m. **Bob Brand**
1917 1878–1963

Buck m. **Edith Forsythe**
1886–1938 *1907*

NORA 1. m. **Paul Phipps**
1889–1955 *1909* 1880–1953

2. m. **'Lefty' Flynn**
1932 1880–1950

Bobbie Shaw

Peter
David (Winkie)

Dabney
Phyllis
Harry
Keene
Douglas

Joyce Grenfell
Tommy Phipps

Bill
Phyllis (Wissie)
David
Michael
John Jacob (Jakie)

Virginia Ford
Dinah Bridge
Jim

The Cast of Characters

CHISWELL DABNEY LANGHORNE (1843–1919), known as 'Chillie', pronounced 'Shilly'; patriarch of the Langhorne family; railroad entrepreneur, sometime tobacco auctioneer. Husband of Nanaire.

NANCY WITCHER KEENE LANGHORNE, 'Nanaire' (1848–1903), wife of Chillie Langhorne, whom she married in 1864.

Their children in order of age:

LIZZIE (1867–1914) married Moncure Perkins in 1885; three children: Chiswell (Chillie), Nancy, Alice.

KEENE (1869–1916) married Sadie Reynolds.

IRENE (1873–1956) married the artist Charles Dana Gibson (1867–1944), creator of the Gibson Girl; two children: Irene (Babs) and Langhorne.

HARRY (1874–1907) married Genevieve Peyton.

NANCY (1879–1964) married Robert Gould Shaw 2nd of Boston (1871–1930), divorced 1903; one child: Bobbie Shaw. Married Waldorf Astor, later 2nd Viscount Astor (1879–1952); five children: Bill, Phyllis (Wissie), David, Michael, John Jacob (Jakie).

PHYLLIS (1880–1937) married Reginald (Reggie) Brooks November 1901; two children: Peter and David (Winkie); separated in 1912, divorced 1915. Married Robert Henry Brand (Bob) in 1917; three children: Virginia, Dinah, Jim.

WILLIAM (Buck) (1886–1938) married Edith Forsythe; five children: Dabney, Phyllis, Harry, Keene, Douglas.

NORA (1889–1955) married Paul Phipps in 1909; two children: Joyce (later Grenfell) and Tommy; divorced 1931. Married Maurice Bennet Flynn ('Lefty') in 1932.

Other main characters, in the order that their names first appear in the book:

ALICE WINN (b. 1902), younger daughter of Lizzie.

BOB BRAND (Robert Henry Brand) (1878–1963), later 1st Lord Brand of Eydon. Member of Milner's Kindergarten and the Round Table, economist and banker, married Phyllis in 1917. Grandfather of the author.

BOBBIE SHAW (Robert Gould Shaw) (1898–1970), only son of Nancy and Robert ('Bob') Shaw of Boston.

CHARLES DANA GIBSON (1867–1944), artist and illustrator, creator of the Gibson Girl, married Irene in 1895.

DAVID ASTOR (b. 1912), Nancy and Waldorf's second son, later editor of the *Observer*.

DINAH BRIDGE (1920–1998), younger daughter of Phyllis; mother of the author.

HENRY DOUGLAS PENNANT (1876–1915), the 'Captain'. Soldier and trophy shooter, younger son of Baron Penrhyn.

JIM BRAND (1924–1945), only son of Phyllis and Bob Brand.

LEFTY FLYNN (1880–1950), former Yale football star, silent screen actor and Nora's second husband.

MICHAEL ASTOR (1916–1980), Nancy and Waldorf's third son, author of *Tribal Feeling*.

MONCURE PERKINS (1861–1914), Lizzie's husband, father of Nancy Lancaster and Alice Winn.

NANCY LANCASTER (1897–1994), Lizzie's eldest daughter, gardener and decorator, who married 1. Henry Field, 2. Ronnie Tree and 3. Juby Lancaster.

PAUL PHIPPS (1880–1953), Nora's first husband, father of Joyce Grenfell and Tommy Phipps.

PETER BROOKS (1902–1944), eldest son of Phyllis and her first husband, Reggie Brooks.

PHILIP KERR (1882–1940), later 11th Marquis of Lothian. Member of Milner's Kindergarten and the Round Table; British Ambassador to the United States, 1939–1940.

REGGIE BROOKS (1876–1945), Phyllis's first husband; father of Peter and Winkie Brooks.

WINKIE BROOKS (1910–1936), Phyllis's second son with Reggie Brooks.

WISSIE (PHYLLIS) ASTOR, later Countess of Ancaster (1909–1975), only daughter of Nancy and Waldorf.

1

The Argument

One summer day, when I was eight, I was sitting at lunch with my great-aunt Nancy Astor in her house by the sea at Sandwich in Kent. It was a heady affair, with the clatter of grown-up talk, the butler and the footman, the dazzle of white linen and glass in the sun and the many guests. I was placed, since I had come late, between two grown-ups; at the end of the table sat the dangerous, exciting figure of Nancy, aged seventy-five.

This was 1954 and it would have been the second half of August because grouse was served, dark red and gamey. It was one of my first transfers from the nursery — the one here at Rest Harrow was at the back of the house with an indoor sand-pit *en suite* — to the dining room, and I had brought with me the idea that all food had to be eaten without question. I couldn't bring myself to swallow this foul-tasting bird. One whiff of it put it in the league of acquired taste, as alien as whisky or olives: an impossible initiation. Despite the vigilant butler, I began to offload all the bird and its sauce into my starched napkin for future disposal in my pocket. In my first term at boarding school I had already lined the entire underside of a long table (we moved one place sideways each week) with slivers of mousetrap cheese, carved to fit a running groove in the carpentry. I had not eaten a single piece of mousetrap in my career so far. Had I done so I would have been sick;

had I not I would have been forced to sit alone looking at the plate. These were the old days. The stale, rancid smell of those institutions was often, I am sure, the result of bad food secreted over many years by the inmates. But this grouse disposal was too reckless a move and the butler gave me away. Children can be ignored until they blow their own protection.

Nancy had by now alarmed two generations of children with her sudden wheeling attacks. Her son Michael wrote of the trick of survival he had learned during his childhood at Cliveden, the house by the Thames where Nancy had ruled since 1906: always to keep the battle fluid when it was launched unexpectedly, above all to avoid being cornered. There was no question that she enjoyed reducing single children to tears as much as driving them, *en masse*, to a frenzy of excitement. Her tactic, with grown-ups too, was to strike at the exposed nerve, the one that only she could see with her uncanny instinct, and then to sting again before the victim had time to react. As they were ready to walk off, she would often wheedle and charm them into what would turn into enslaved, long-term friendship. Now it was my turn, and I was already off my balance.

Some minutes earlier she had fiercely challenged my late arrival. 'Where've you bin? What have you bin doin'?' The Langhorne sisters' Virginian accent was light and resonant, a chime not a drawl, but still with the declamatory southern cadence suited to storytelling. (This was not the case with their brothers. In the Waldorf Astoria Buck Langhorne's next-door neighbour heard raucous black voices in the next room and complained to the manager, to be told that the gentleman was Lady Astor's brother and she owned the hotel.) Nancy was commanding; always listened to. She would talk down the table, singling out targets to liven up her act, to keep a general conversation going between thirty people. In this instance it was less an attack than a desire to get the child to perform and play to her rules, but I couldn't know that. I had mumbled in reply, my eyes fixed in concentration at my interrogator – the blank schoolboy defence – then slipped, flustered, into my chair. All morning I had caddied for the golfers on the great course at Royal St George's, its boundary a few steps from the house. I watched a grown-up cousin losing his temper, throwing and breaking clubs, swearing and stamping as his ball bounced out of sight behind the dunes. At a moment of high tension in this game the handle of the golf cart I was tending slipped from its tubular pipe and began rolling downhill towards a bunker. I had chased it, hurling myself onto it like the midshipman on the deck, impaling my stomach on the handleless tube and somersaulting with all the equipment into the sand. The short-tempered cousin now used up what remained of his rage on me and my golf cart. 'What the *hell* are you doing?' I wandered off, contemplating this injustice, and somehow, in my daydream, I arrived late for lunch.

And now with the grouse off the plate and in the napkin, Nancy turned on me once more. 'What are you doin'?' There was a rush of words and then, 'You're just as bad as that terrible father of yours. If you take after your father . . .' My American father was in disgrace for his divorce and was struggling against alcohol – so embodying two of Nancy's most fervent and lifelong denouncements. I was very fond of my father and sensed his ostracism although I didn't understand our being coupled in this way, and I don't remember the rest of the verbal attack. I felt exposed and shamed in a dining room now silent except for Aunt Nancy's voice, with dead bird and gravy halfway under the table, the blood drumming in my head, blackness behind the eyes, going under to a place without air.

I had come for this holiday with my sister and my recently divorced mother Dinah, a favourite niece of Nancy's and daughter of her closest sister, Phyllis. Five years earlier we had crossed the Atlantic on a boat called the SS *Media* to make a life in England and each summer we would visit Rest Harrow in Kent. There were many cousins of my age and it was a holiday we eagerly anticipated: bicycles on the empty flat roads, evening cricket, the beach only a few yards from its deeply pebbled front door, the night sound of waves from the dormitory bedrooms, the drama of ships stranded quite close to the shore on the treacherous Goodwin Sands, whose distress could be examined through binoculars from the balcony. The Goodwin lightship wailed all night in the fog. It was the cleanest house I had ever visited – the smell of polish and wax and Jeyes fluid on the brown linoleum of the back stairs, the flowers in the sitting rooms. Above all there was the presence of Aunt Nancy, who controlled everybody's lives. She was small and neat, with a sprig of lemon-scented verbena pinned to her brooch, and almost always holding a golf club. She gave out dark caramels from America (rationing was still in force) and would slip into imitations and mockeries, putting in false teeth, inventing wild games. In the morning we would go to her bedroom to be given her version of a Christian Science lesson. Bibles were strewn about the bed, the text for the day marked and ready. I remember the rapid, repetitive delivery, her face covered in cold cream: 'Man is made in the image and likeness of God.' 'Hold up your shoulders,' was a frequent order from Nancy, often a form of greeting, and 'Hold on to the Truth' or 'Hold the Right Thought' her parting cautions. She radiated excitement and protection. She could also make you cry, quickly and brutally. Visiting children were often startled. One of my playmates, introduced to Lady Astor, was lightly poked in the chest with the greeting, 'I hear you're a horrible little boy.' He turned against her forever.

When the parental swap-over came, my father, now working in London as a lawyer for the US Navy, came to visit, he was not allowed to sleep in the house. He would walk over from the glamorous Guilford Hotel – a luxury place for golfers with a sun terrace of blue wicker chairs and a real American bar, isolated on the shore a few yards down the private roadway. He was known as 'The Lollipop Man'. He brought a large box of lollipops from the US Navy 'PX' in London, a cave of plenty, of diplomatic duty-free whose austerity-busting goods made me popular at school. He was popular too; he might have been Glenn Ford. He had, after all, been a Commander in the US Navy and nobody was to know that he had never been to sea. Occasionally I would sleep in the Guilford Hotel and luxuriously and vengefully wet its beds in my sleep.

My father, Lyttleton Fox, despite social and academic distinctions at Yale and Harvard Law School, was eccentric, abstracted, fitting awkwardly with the tribal English upper class, although they noticed it more than he. Nancy, too, had been a somewhat proud outsider from England and its class system, and she made a point of welcoming Americans in her houses. My father arrived from the Guilford Hotel one day in a pair of coral-coloured trousers. 'Go and change those disgustin' red pants,' Nancy commanded him, as I stood at his side, 'You're not in the Virgin Islands now.' I held this phrase in my memory for many years before I understood it. I could tell it had a devastating effect on my father. His spirit had been crushed by his divorce. Some technicality had required him to spend six miserable weeks in the British Virgin Islands, a few years back, to help my mother obtain it. There was no adultery, merely incompatibility. Nancy was tactlessly, cruelly rubbing salt in his wound. At the same time she offered him more friendliness and generous support than anyone else in England. Savile Row suits were ordered for him, she invited him to stay later on, wrote him letters and telephoned. He ended up her devoted admirer and ally, learning that the attacks were part of her terrible drive to improve everybody and everything around her, employing, quite often, the roughest techniques. He became, eventually, an amused connoisseur of her *mauvais mots*. If she could sense a nerve to attack, Nancy could also empathize with suffering almost to the point of feeling it herself. Then she would act – an engine of kindness – putting into gear the vast resources at her disposal of money and secretaries. There appeared to be no limit to her generosity.

But by the mid-1950s things had changed for Nancy. She had lost her touch. She had begun to develop a monstrous streak in her behaviour. The wit and speed that had carried her into Parliament, the first woman MP ever to sit there, through successive turbulent elections and public life for over twenty-five years as a politician, were disappearing, leaving a blunt weapon in their place. Like a damaged prize-fighter, the fearlessness, after all those years of holding her corner against a battery of male resentment, was giving way to cantankerousness. The generosity was still there, but now she would write out cheques to strangers (cheques for £500 would flutter down from the balcony of her Eaton Square flat to the milkman below, to be intercepted by the butler); the power of money had become random and indiscriminate. And still she was driven by a furious energy. Her son Jakie, taking her face in both hands, said to her, 'The trouble with you, Mama, is that the engine works perfectly but the steering has gone.' Having been a champion of the causes of women and children, often siding with her Labour opponents, she had become reactionary and quirky in her views. She was mystified that her grown-up children had become estranged from her, and wouldn't visit. She had pushed them away with her overweening possessiveness and need for control, which she had always confused with love. Now she raged against them, and occasionally tried to sabotage their careers. By the late 1950s she would be at unilateral war with most of her family, 'blaming and quarrelling', and her family was in a loveless state, fractured by her personality. Bobbie Shaw, the child of her first marriage, the one she loved the most, had never been able to tear himself away. But even their extraordinary closeness was now often expressed in raw antagonism.

At the height of her powers, she had been the most famous woman in the world. In Britain there had never been an MP with a more intimate relationship with her constituency than Nancy had had with Plymouth for thirty-five years – including the ten years in which her millionaire second husband, Waldorf Astor, had been MP there. The voting record, in this largely working class constituency, proved it. She had lost her political reputation in the days of appeasement leading up to Munich when, following Chamberlain's nationally popular policy of peace-seeking, she and the 'Cliveden Set' became the scapegoats when it turned to disaster, branded unfairly as pro-Germany, or worse. Her performance in Parliament had by then become garrulous and open to ridicule. She was getting badly knocked about by the incoming socialists and Waldorf prevented her from returning to the House of Commons in the 1945 election, believing she would suffer a humiliating defeat. She never forgave him, treating him as a leper until his death in 1952. She was unaware, because Waldorf never told her, that all her political friends agreed with him but hadn't dared to face her with it.

She had been the supreme entertainer, funny, original, socially fearless, a brilliant hostess, a keeper of long-term friendships, a fairy godmother; as well as prejudiced, bullying, deliberately tactless. Even this could be exciting in the way that it could instantly transform situations; her behaviour was always a guarantee against boredom, pomposity, convention. The positive side of her volcanic nature, the sheer force of her personality, her humour, her high spirits, her attractiveness, above all her courage, had greatly outweighed the negative. She had got away with it all, like a comedian, through speed and timing, an instinctive brilliance. No one who knew her well, even the children who suffered from her appalling record as a parent, put the score against her. She had long and loyal friendships with Arthur Balfour, George Bernard Shaw, Sean O'Casey and T. E. Lawrence, who were not bullyable types needing her patronage. It was to Nancy that Harold Macmillan came to discuss his marital problems. Having wanted to be like her saintly mother Nanaire, she had ended up like her father, the irascible, tempestuous Chillie Langhorne, who had brought them all out of poverty, but whose bullying ways she had always despised. His full name was Chiswell Dabney Langhorne, known and pronounced 'Shilly Langan'.

Watching the documentary on Muhammad Ali and his fight with George Foreman in Zaïre, *When We Were Kings*, I suddenly heard and saw Nancy in the verbal performances of the greatest boxer of all time. When doling out righteousness, which they both liked doing, Ali, like Nancy, used the high warble of the Southern preacher – of which they both had a touch – as a chiding and a warning, the 'ooooooweee' of the train whistle. There were so many similarities: the commanding of attention through shock and surprise, the moral courage, the wit veering into verbal cruelty against opponents, and the jokes themselves. Nancy, of course, never used rhymes but Ali's comeback to a doubting sportswriter before the 'Rumble in the Jungle' was pure Nancy. 'He says I'm not the man I was ten years ago,' Ali said to the television camera. 'I talked to his wife. She says he's not the man he was *two* years ago.' Nancy said to a pompous British Cabinet Minister at Cliveden, having got the attention of the whole table, 'I know your wife thought you were a bore when she married you, because she told me so, but nobody could have thought you'd be as bad as this.' The rest of her guests, who had been saying this behind his back, were convulsed with laughter. And the Minister's vanity was flattered by this apparent display of intimacy.

Both had converted to a religion – Nancy's based on a Protestant fundamentalism, Ali's on a Muslim equivalent – which they preached with every other breath and which led them into frequent ill-judged and intolerant remarks on religion and race. And because of their fame all of these remarks were quoted. Both aired their prejudices in the cause, as they saw it, of truth and 'freedom'. Nancy talked as patronizingly about men as did Ali, after his conversion, about women. Like Ali, sparring a few rounds in the local gym on a sudden whim years later, dressed in a suit and slowed by Parkinson's disease, there was enough in Nancy's verbal sparring late in her life to remind one of the old magic, the footwork, the anticipation, the speed and timing. Unlike Ali, who retired into his sickness with remarkable grace and humanity, Nancy would continue to throw punches without the artistry, often with severe consequences. She would fight, as it were, unwise, reckless exhibition bouts and still draw audiences on both sides of the Atlantic.

Nancy had ten more years to live after the summer of 1954 when I visited Rest Harrow. Just before she died, the sweetness returned to her nature. She imagined herself back in the Virginia of her youth at Mirador, her father's house in the Blue Ridge Mountains, riding along the red clay roads, with her sisters and brothers, Harry, and Keene and Buck and their playmates 'The Goodloe Boys'. 'Am I dying, or is it my birthday?' she asked her son Jakie, surprised to be suddenly visited by so many of her children. 'A bit of both,' he gently informed her.

Nancy outlived all the other Langhorne sisters, the glamorous, high-spirited sisterhood that had been famous in Virginia and then in America long before Nancy married Waldorf Astor in 1906: Lizzie, the eldest, twelve years older than Nancy; Irene, the next elder sister;

Phyllis and Nora, the youngest. She had also long outlived her two older brothers, Harry and Keene, and her younger brother Buck, who had spent a great deal of their time – outmatched by their formidable sisters – going on sprees in the mountains and had succumbed variously to drink and tuberculosis as the years went by. She had survived the violent deaths of Phyllis's three sons, her nephews, Peter and Winkie Brooks, and Jim Brand, my mother's half-brothers and her full brother respectively.

'Nothing could be quite as lovely as that,' Nancy wrote about the Virginia of her youth some years before she died and after a lifetime in some of the finest houses in England. It was the Virginia of better days that she was remembering; the years of her teens when her father Chillie Langhorne had struck his bonanza collaborating with the Yankees in railroad construction, rescuing his family from their twenty-five years of poverty following the war between the states. He had bought Mirador with this quite sudden wealth, as a summer place – a colonnaded colonial red-brick house with a farm, near Charlottesville, whose back porch looked across apple orchards and up a long gentle slope towards the Blue Ridge Mountains. It had box hedges along its paths, smokehouses for the hams, dark green shutters on its Georgian windows, a fine cobbled stableyard. In Mirador Chillie Langhorne had re-created a world belonging to the sentimental novels of the 1830s, years after the war that had devastated Virginia. None of the sisters ever quite got over the idyllic idea of Mirador and yet they abandoned it, despite the communal wealth at their disposal. But like many families with a sense of themselves they had invested it with a symbolic importance beyond its natural beauty. Its importance was that it had produced, perhaps invented, the Langhorne sisters.

Their fame had already begun by the time Chillie bought Mirador in 1892, when Nancy was twelve, and Irene had emerged as the last Southern Belle – a fame comparable now only to that of super-models and movie stars. The Golden Age of the Belle lasted for thirty years from the end of the civil war to the moment when Irene, aged sixteen, 'bewitching' to look at, was led by a beau on to the dance floor at

White Sulphur Springs and declared a Belle in her own right — a Cinderella-like transformation. The Belle system was taken immensely seriously in Virginia. It was a highly institutionalized fantasy, a means of foiling the memory of defeat, of ignoring poverty, of turning the clock back to some imagined 1840, of defending the inviolable purity of the white Southern girl in the face of forced emancipation and reconstruction. It was a lifeline of self-esteem. Irene capped this by taking herself north — Mr Langhorne was glad to bury the hatchet — and leading the New York balls, the first Southern girl to do so since the war and then by marrying the famous illustrator Charles Dana Gibson. In 1890 he had created the 'Gibson Girl'. Her image — the upturned nose, what the poet Thom Gunn called her 'sporty jaw', the slender waist, the slightly disdainful look of the new emancipated woman — looked remarkably like Irene. Gibson had created the first nationwide fashion frenzy and he had become a cult figure himself, mobbed for his autograph. Their wedding in Richmond was an affair of American royalty and was seen as another symbolic end to the North/South hostilities. Irene became the Gibson Girl, the icon of the young American woman that gripped magazine readers for two more decades. She had turned the vanishing Southern Belle into a modern media fantasy. She then settled down with Dana Gibson to be immortal, fixed in the moment of her fame, as the world changed about her.

The eldest sister Lizzie, born soon after the surrender at Appomattox in 1865, was left behind when Chillie Langhorne's circus took to the road. With her parents, she had borne the brunt of those twenty years since the war and resented the Yankee beaux coming down in droves, in private railroad cars, to get a fashionable taste of the South and to propose to Irene. In Lizzie's time no one went north from Virginia, it was unheard of. When Nancy and Phyllis, the sister she was always closest to, were children, the family had lived in a one-storey clapboard house on a street in Danville, with eight children and destitute relations crammed into four rooms. Their mother Nanaire had eleven children, most of them born under these harsh conditions. Three died in infancy after Lizzie was born. Later Lizzie helped Nanaire to raise the remaining four unruly children. In contrast to Nanaire she did it severely and was forever resented for it by her siblings. She never enjoyed the pleasures of a Mirador childhood. Before the Langhorne fortunes had changed, she married a Virginian, Moncure Perkins – an option all of the others avoided in these hard times, and was the only one to remain there, despite the mystical attachment to it that the other sisters claimed all their lives. Lizzie belonged to the old Richmond of reconstruction, of black-veiled war widows, drunken husbands, winter mud and summer dust, of obsession with genealogy and, above all, with talk. It was a place rebuilt out of rubble in late Victorian style, of mahogany furniture and gas lamps, of deep conservatism, of cultivation and shabbiness, and close-knit pride where everybody knew everyone else on the ten blocks where they all lived. Lizzie became saddened, somewhat embittered by the way her sisters treated her, and ended up fatally dependent on Nancy's controlling purse strings.

In Irene's wake, Nancy, Phyllis and later Nora, the youngest sister, began to exercise what their mother called, 'the right of every Langhorne daughter to become a Belle'. They became famous quickly and in succession. Chillie had taught Nancy and Phyllis to ride, bareback at first, to jump the steep Virginia snake fences, to break and train yearlings, to be fearless, to take 'excessive' risks. The combination of beauty and brilliance on the hunting field – Phyllis became the best rider of her generation – gave them an advantage of mobility never lost on the sisters in later, more difficult times. They were helped too by the wave of admiration and forgiveness towards the South that followed Reconstruction, and the Northern fantasies of an old and gracious world, 'distinguished', and 'aristocratic', beyond the Mason Dixon line. Industrialists and carpetbaggers were sending their daughters to the spas in white flannel blazers to teach them how to be Belles, imagining a pageant of southern chivalry. By the time they had bought out 'Belledom,' and taken over the spas, it was all over. The Langhorne sisters had gone north where every appearance at a horse show or a ball and certainly each engagement or marriage was a sensation reported in the *New York Times*.

There was nothing self-conscious about the way the Langhornes carried on at Mirador. In the Republican political imagination during Reconstruction Virginians especially were looked on with suspicion as Tories and aristocrats. And the Langhornes had taken effortlessly and naturally to this new wealth, reverting to the old simplicities of rural life, to the squirearchy of Chillie's boyhood, of horses and hunting, quail shooting and leisurely farming. Country Virginia was no cotton-growing Georgia with great plantations and labour gangs. It was Anglophile, gentle, enclosed. It was almost unchanged since the days of Thomas Jefferson at Monticello a hundred years earlier; cultivated, unpretentious, with good food and endless hospitality, and a preoccupation with gardens. Mirador was not furnished with the Victorian mahogany of the Richmond bourgeoisie, but with old Georgian furniture bought cheaply, with mixed cretonne, unfashionable chintz – the walls painted different shades of grey. They danced waltzes and two-steps in the parlour to the fiddle and banjo played by black musicians and sang in close harmony. They lived closely with their servants, treating them – some of them former slaves – as they would their subordinate relations, calling their nurses 'Aunt', hugging them, in the photographs, like their own sisters. They lived closely enough to inherit the religious feelings and diurnal superstitions of their black staff, and to adopt their particular humour and sense of the ridiculous. It was built in to the Langhorne style. They liked performing, too – especially Chillie, the tempestuous, all-protecting patriarch 'who kept them all in stitches with his plantation songs, his dancing and inspired high jinks', as it was reported in a newspaper. 'The Langhornes are like street musicians,' a Chicago psychiatrist who knew the family said some years later. 'They entertain you whether you ask them to or not.' Together they were clannish, quick-witted, verbally merciless with each other, battering out vanities with their cruel games of 'truth' that, to the amazement of visitors, brought sounds of terrible weeping from behind closed doors, followed by hysterical laughter. 'We were fitted for battling in our family,' Phyllis wrote. The 'M' in Mirador, she said stood for misery as well as mirth.

The Langhornes seemed to have invented themselves through this collective mystique of sisterhood. To outsiders they were fascinating *en masse*, and impenetrable, giving the impression that no one would ever get as close to them as they were to each other. It was this relationship that anchored their lives, that produced the glamour and excitement for the strings of admirers who fell in love with each or all of them. They gave off the sense that they were set apart, even unique. They were thought of in the plural long after their separate careers were a matter of history. They produced this effect in part because each of them had such a strong sense of her own identity. They were starkly different types: Lizzie, the strict pioneer figure, of stern elegance and puritan disapproval; Irene, Chillie's favourite, passive and golden, the image of what men expected from women of that era – unintellectual, chaste but flirtatious, stately and amusing, the eternal Belle and the most ready victim of her sisters' wit. Nancy, the most flamboyant of the sisters, represented power – an irresistible force of nature, bred in the Blue Ridge Mountains. It was turned loose initially on the stuffy Edwardian ruling class of England and then on the House of Commons and finally, with devastating effect, on her own family.

Nora, the youngest, mother to the famous English comedienne and actress Joyce Grenfell, was the wayward sister, the eternal child. Dreamy, disorganized, and unschooled, she was talented – a brilliant mimic, with a romantic, smoky singing voice. She was physically the most attractive and the kindest-hearted of them all. She was also free with her favours, unable to tell the truth and chronically irresponsible with money. Her life, punctuated with seductions and boltings, debts and broken appointments, was a charmed one, until her last years, successfully devoted to making sure everyone had a good time. She said of herself that she had 'a heart like a hotel'. One of her beaux added 'and every room was full'. Of all the sisters she was considered the best company, the cosiest and most reassuring, and to children she was enchanting. 'If you had half an hour to spend on earth, you'd spend it with Aunt Nora,' said one of her nieces. 'Then,' she added, breaking the metaphor, 'you wouldn't see her for a year.'

But the sister who had the greatest effect on those around her, particularly on men, was Phyllis, eighteen months younger than Nancy. When the beaux were courting them, Nancy remembered, 'They liked me but it was Phyllis they always fell in love with.' Such charm as she had is indefinable, but clearly she possessed charm to a great degree. Feminine, sympathetic, there was a luminous quality to her beauty, a melancholy in her nature, a 'minor key' as her sisters called it, and a streak of introversion so foreign to her father and her siblings. She radiated some mixture of love and goodness along with the connecting Langhorne gaiety. She was musical, a brilliant horsewoman and huntress. She was also the most popular within her family, although not with her father, who disliked her reticence and her need for solitude, and liked to watch the tears swell 'like diamonds' in her eyes when he made her cry.

Of all her contemporaries, including husbands and admirers, Phyllis was the only person Nancy loved her entire life. She loved her with such a passionate longing that at times it seemed as if Nancy's other attachments were an exhausting duty and challenge. It was to Phyllis that Nancy confided, in her early letters from Cliveden, the panic she felt having married into the Astor clan, the longing to be back at Mirador, and her grief, which lasted for twenty years, for her mother's death. Only Nancy knew, for some years, of Phyllis's great and secret romance with a captain in the Grenadier Guards, and the many intimate sadnesses of her life. Phyllis and Nancy, whose lives are the centre of this story, appear at first to represent opposite, complementary forces. If Nancy represented elemental power, Phyllis, at least in Nancy's eyes, stood for the inner life Nancy had always longed for and never achieved, despite her fanatical, and to Phyllis, incomprehensible devotion to Christian Science. These were the qualities Nancy missed after the death of their mother Nanaire, her idol of long-suffering selflessness and the driving force for the great crusade of 'goodness' that dominated her life. Despite her bountiful compassionate heart Nancy never acquired the gift of selfless love, a virtue that she hammered out in repetition, exhorted on others, and carried as her banner. She never understood why Nanaire's rewards – total devotion from her children – had eluded her. She had assumed exclusive rights of ownership over them, for many years with a clear conscience, believing she was doing God's work, and that they were better off under her improving wing. She tried to exercise these rights over her sisters, too, particularly Phyllis.

Nancy and Phyllis, inseparable as children and apparently so different in temperament, nevertheless had similarities of character which led them into parallel mistakes in their family lives. Both made the same damaging move, with their parents' encouragement, of marrying northern millionaires, by whom they had children, and whom they then divorced. Chillie Langhorne's instructions were contradictory: to be a Belle but also to make your own destiny. Both sisters reinvented their lives as far away from their first husbands as possible. Having burned their boats in America, these two great beauties shipped their horses across the Atlantic and tried their luck again on the hunting fields of Leicestershire.

Given their sex, their origins and the time they lived in, they ended up in quite unforeseeable circumstances, at the heart of English political life and close to the problems of Europe, substituting one changing and vanishing world for another. The men they married or drew into their orbit in England were, this time, the brightest and the best, high-minded reformers and idealists closely connected with power, who saw their great task as nothing less than federating the old Empire, and forging an imagined Pax Americana–Britannica, a civilizing, global rule of law that would end nationalism, the arms race, war itself. They belonged to the generation from before 1914, brought up in public schools and Oxford quadrangles, the last to believe that they were dealing with a rational, perfectible world, ready to stabilize itself into an ordered system under British guidance. Their plans were swept away by two world wars and economic collapse, tragedies that deeply affected their own lives.

I grew up, for much of my holiday childhood, in the house of my grandfather, Bob Brand. He had married Phyllis, my grandmother, in

1917. In 1928 they bought Eydon Hall, an elegant Palladian house with an *ante bellum* feel, in the heart of Northamptonshire. It was bought to remind Phyllis of Mirador, and to put her in the best hunting country, or what my grandfather, brought up in Hertfordshire, called 'a real grass country': she was subject to bouts of melancholy, for which hunting was her one sure antidote. Her premature death in 1937 was a catastrophe for my grandfather, whose marriage had been a love affair sustained for twenty years, a love hard won and the only one in his life. In the twenty-five years he still had to live, he never got over his grief, and wrote in the pages he filled trying to make sense of it that when she died 'everything lovely had left my life'. He had been living, since, 'in a spiritual half world'.

Very little in the house had changed – he had kept it that way, seeing no point in doing otherwise. The house in some ways was a shrine to Phyllis – her saddles and bridles were locked in a tackroom in the stableyard, untouched and unused after her death. Her boudoir, a pretty room in a bow on the side of the house, with a desk, an Adam fireplace, armchairs, was also kept locked and unused, the plain silk curtains gradually falling apart. Elsewhere the décor hadn't changed since she created it, and the lightness and grace of the architecture still reflected her southern taste, her furniture and paint. It was unlike any other house in the district, and one of the prettiest I have seen in England, to this day. My grandfather lived alone here, with a few members of the pre-war staff, including the retired butler, My Blyth, a man of eccentric informality compared to his peers in that formal profession. Phyllis had employed him in 1922 and had written to Bob Brand 'he is the greatest treasure we have got'. Nancy discovered that Phyllis had found the only butler in England who had the natural familiarity of the black staff at Mirador. Mr Blyth could hardly move when I knew him and I acted as his bicycle courier, riding to the pub for his cigarettes.

Except when his grandchildren returned for the school holidays, Bob Brand would often eat alone in the Palladian dining room, surrounded by portraits of his Dacre ancestors. He divided his time between Eydon, London, where he made occasional speeches in the

House of Lords, and All Souls at Oxford where he had rooms. From his study he would send letters to *The Times* on currency and economic matters, or prepare speeches for the House of Lords. 'The Wisest Man in the Empire' as he was labelled at the age of thirty — and which would furnish the headline for his obituary — was a man of great sweetness of nature and benevolence, who looked at you through what appeared to be the same rimless glasses he had worn to the Paris Peace Conference of 1919. I remember as a child his heavy corduroys, the thistle-cutter he carried, the black beret he wore. If nothing had changed in the house, little had changed on the land or in the village since the nineteenth century or earlier. His farm was only semi-mechanical even in the 1950s. I would work on it in the summer, turning the 'swaff', a word used by the farm workers for the sheaths of hay they cut by hand scythe — a word so ancient that the *OED* calls it obsolete — or 'stooking' the corn upright in bundles in the fields, waiting to be threshed. He wrote to my mother before the summer holidays, although I needed no enticement, 'Tell James we are v. short of labour.'

Both Bob Brand and my Aunt Nancy were still alive when I was old enough to take in the Langhorne sisters' myth. 'Gaiety, laughter, high spirits, spontaneity,' was what they were said to have had in such abundance. Bob Brand wrote of 'an exceptional fascination and charm which I have never known equalled in any family'. They seemed to have set an unmatchable standard for it. And there was the sense of Mirador — pictures of it abounded — as a lost paradise from where we all came. The legacy of Phyllis having chosen Northamptonshire for foxhunting was that we, her grandchildren, were brought up in a world of hunter trials, point to points and pony club balls, where little had changed across three generations. This was just before teenage rebellion and rock and roll when adolescents still tried to emulate their parents in their dress and their pastimes. Horse talk was the only conversation I remember with any outsider, particularly with girls at the orange-juice balls in the draughty town halls of the Cotswolds. It was a very conventional world. Nobody hugged their servants in Northamptonshire or sang in close harmony, as far as I knew. Most of my relations with Langhorne blood in England did seem refreshingly different, even exotic compared with the stiff English landed gentry. At Haseley there was Nancy Lancaster, Lizzie's daughter, a decorating and gardening genius, no less, who flew the Confederate flag from the pediment, and once threatened a bringer of divorce writs with a shotgun through an upper window. In her semi-dotage Nancy Astor would stay with her and make uncoordinated remarks to visitors such as 'Do ring my niece often. She adores men,' or, conversely, 'Pay no attention to my niece. She lies for pleasure.' (Nancy Lancaster, née Perkins, was married successively to Henry Field, Ronnie Tree and Juby Lancaster. To avoid confusion I have called her by her last married name throughout the story; the name by which she is best known posthumously and which furnished the title of her biography.)

One day my housemaster at Eton burst into my room for one of his surprise communications and asked me if I was descended from the Ziegfeld Follies. I wrote to my grandfather who replied, 'Your grandmother would have been amused by this remark. Possibly Nora her sister might have added to the gaiety of the Z.F. though not your grandmother tho she had every wonderful quality. I don't know if I have ever shown you the letters I collected on her death here, which was the greatest disaster for me.'

I didn't take up his offer until twenty years after he died. In the meantime the stories of this southern Langhorne legend had settled into an orthodoxy of repetition, partly to do with the Virginian way of oral history – where you can predict the next sentence if you have heard them often enough. Relations wrote privately published books of hagiography. There was an endless looking-back. I began to wonder about the perfection of it all. The rough side of life didn't seem to bite into the story. I had heard other tales, more shadowy ones: disasters never much discussed. Of my two uncles, Phyllis's sons from her first marriage, one had fallen or jumped to his death from a hotel bedroom in New York; the other had shot himself in a garage in Miami. As a schoolboy I would catch glimpses of Bobbie Shaw. I was fascinated and shocked by his appearance at lunch with Nancy in Eaton Square in

1960. Podgy and creased-looking, he was dressed in a sub-Teddy-boy mix: a long jacket, thick crepe suede shoes, narrow trousers, his hair slicked back and dyed jet-black, his fingers covered in rings, a Cartier watch on his wrist. He smoked Woodbines, the cheapest cigarettes you could obtain, which he kept in a Fabergé cigarette case. He made everybody laugh a great deal, even more than the other relations, and he was startlingly rude to his mother, able to say, apparently with impunity, in what sounded like a cockney accent, 'Oh mother do *shut up*.' He had once been an officer in the Blues – the Royal Horse Guards – and a famous steeplechase rider. He was unlike any other grown-up I had ever met, exotic and extraordinary. Where did he fit into the story?

I first saw the letters Bob Brand had mentioned, some years before I started working on them, on one of my return visits to Eydon in the early 1980s to stay with my aunt Virginia and uncle Edward Ford who had inherited the house when Bob Brand died. They directed me to the disused servants' hall and to a large black trunk covered in Cunard and White Star steamship stickers. When I first opened it, I saw what looked like two or three thousand envelopes, all neatly packaged and tied with string or with disintegrating rubber bands. Some were dated and sorted; a great quantity lay in random piles. They were letters between the Langhorne sisters, but mostly between Nancy and Phyllis, telling the story of their progress through the century. They included Bob Brand's entire correspondence with Phyllis from the day they met. They also contained correspondence of another great love affair – that of Phyllis and the Grenadier Captain, which Bob Brand had generously preserved in the collection. He had added some pages of memoir to the collection and, it seemed, instructions to a future storyteller. The letters, he said, would tell the story. He had tried – he had made some attempts – but found that he could go no further. 'It is only now that I realise intensely the limitations of the common plain Englishman,' he wrote. 'I have no visual imagination, no power of describing what is perhaps indescribable, only a wound in my heart which never seems to heal.'

Since he had kept everything, the letters in the trunk also contained the story of the next generation, of the children who belonged to the first marriages in America, outsiders to the new lives Phyllis and Nancy created in England. They describe, in their own words, the price these sisters paid for crossing the Atlantic. In different ways it was their past lives in America, which they had tried to excise from history, that came back to haunt Nancy and Phyllis, particularly their relationships with these American children. Like a classical drama, a chain of events begun in Boston in the early 1900s led to an outcome that Bob Brand couldn't possible predict, but which destroyed his family life and his happiness. This theme dominates the second half of this story, since it was central to the lives of Nancy and Phyllis — and their relationship lies at the core of the narrative. In Nancy's case I have drawn on correspondence between herself and her first child Bobbie Shaw that was not in the trunk, and indeed for the rest of the story I have collected material from other archives, as well as from private collections, documents and many interviews and memoirs.

The real voices in this book belong to the characters themselves. Most of the letters were not available to Nancy Astor's biographers and many not gleaned — perhaps on account of her illegible handwriting — from the archives. It is rare to discover such a huge, personal communication between so many close relatives. It could only come out of an age where not only were there two or three posts a day, and this still the preferred form of communication, but also where a convention existed of returning collections of letters to the senders in times of grief. The process whereby my grandfather managed to collect so many in one place will surely never happen again. They contain the intimate stories of these famous sisters and of the men whose lives they changed, told in their own voices to each other.

2

Mr Langhorne's Rock

In 1890, the year Irene had been formally unveiled as a Belle at White Sulphur Springs, aged sixteen – changing from a schoolgirl into a local figure of royalty – Chillie Langhorne finally went bust, after all the years of hustling and trying to get ahead in the rock-bottom economy after Reconstruction. One traumatic day, when Nancy was aged eleven and Phyllis ten, they were sitting with their younger siblings on packing cases in Grace Street, in Richmond, their mother in tears preparing to retreat to the country to stay with a cousin near Mechum's River. Chillie, now getting on for fifty, would board in Richmond and look for work. The house – the best they had in several moves – would be sold, the servants they had grown up with dismissed. It was a dire move even for Richmond where nobody had any money and Nanaire, nursing Nora, her eleventh and youngest child, was almost at breaking point. It was the first time they would be homeless since the war, twenty-three years ago. That was the day General Henry T. Douglas, a friend of Chillie's, who already had a concession with the Chesapeake & Ohio (C & O) railroad company, gave him a contract and he burst into the house in Grace Street shouting 'Hold everything. Hold everything.'

The fortune-changing moment was told with variations down the years but the two events always occurred on the same day. Nancy told it again on BBC television when she was eighty-three. It had become a catechism by then, with a touch of the book of Genesis. 'And General Douglas said, "Chillie what are you doing?" And my Father said, "I'm starving . . ."' And so on. Chillie Langhorne knew General Douglas from the Maryland club in Baltimore, where even in lean times he would go looking for company and good food and where the younger men especially would seek him out for entertainment. He was already well known and immensely popular, from Lynchburg to Baltimore, long before this moment, as a storyteller, a formidable poker player, a star at the Confederate reunions. In Danville as a young man he had become a legend as a tobacco auctioneer, turning the business of selling two bales a minute into a comedy routine, pulling the crowds to his act. At the age of ninety-six Mrs Beatty Moore, who knew the Langhorne sisters when she was a young girl, remembered her father and the older people talking about him. 'Mr Langhorne was an auctioneer of *tabaccer*,' she told me, sitting on her porch, looking over the Chesapeake Bay. 'And there was a big rock in Danville on which he stood. It was known as Langhorne's Rock. Mr Langhorne was a remarkable man and he was a most amusing man and somebody always had a story on Mr Langhorne. He wasn't a tobacco auctioneer for very long but he was a cracking good one.' Nevertheless this was for many years barely a living.

Railroading, meanwhile, had been booming in Virginia since 1880. The old lines, four of which touched on Richmond from before the war, were expanding, financed by Northern money and a riot of corrupt privatization in the Virginia legislature; the selling off of the state's pre-war railroad stock. Rich coal deposits had been found in the south-west of the state which resulted in a new line being constructed from Richmond to Newport News, a small town about to be transformed into one of the world's biggest coal ports. Northern investors were pouring money into Virginia and exporting the profits.

The key to the meeting with General Douglas — omitted from family accounts — was the labour problem. Chillie Langhorne had an advantage over the opposition, the Yankee managers, whatever his ignorance of railroads: he was a skilled employer. He knew how to 'kid along', as he called it, the black labour force, which was both nomadic, after the war and emancipation, and in a state of near mutiny at their barely improved conditions as wage-earners. The occasional labour riots and clashes since the war had been directed mostly at the occupying Union invaders, the former abolitionists, and now Douglas was having trouble with his Northern investors wanting better results. Chillie had the background: a paternalistic touch that Nancy – who rarely lost an employee – later used to great effect, a mixture of wit and brusque intimacy. It could deploy, too, the connecting quasi insult that both of them knew how to get away with, without causing offence.

Chillie Langhorne was also 'kind and tremendously honest', according to his sister, Liz Lewis, an early Virginian suffragette, as well as 'irascible, yes, impetuous, impulsive, bit big'. He elicited loyalty and radiated confidence through his birth-given assumption that he could do anything better than anybody else, despite twenty-five years back and forth from the breadline. Years after his retirement black employees would seek him out on the strength of his old record.

The fact that it had taken him twenty-five years to succeed, given these entrepreneurial skills, said as much about his will, his desire not to sink into the cult of Virginia's tragic decline – which began long before the war and absorbed so many of his surviving compatriots – as about the condition in which Generals Sherman and Sheridan had left Virginia. 'They must be left with nothing,' as Sheridan had put it, as he set about plundering the Shenandoah Valley 'except their eyes to weep with over the war'. The photographs of the sacked Richmond show a scale of damage unimaginable without aerial bombardment. The rest of the economy was not fully restored until the end of the Second World War. To have money was a rarity among Virginians and it had happened to Chillie in less than two years.

Before the war, his father owned a farm and a flour mill near Lynchburg, and had one of the largest houses outside town, overlooking the James River. Chillie, the eldest of two sons, ended the civil war in

Danville, a veteran of twenty-two years old. He had joined up with the
11th Virginia Infantry, foot-marched the length and breadth of
Virginia, in and out of the Blue Ridge Mountains and into Maryland in
that dire atmosphere of death, sickness, and near starvation for most of
the war. He was invalided out of the action with 'feverish boils' soon
before Gettysburg. It became a fixation not to have fought; to have
survived his companions. Children and grandchildren were taken on
solemn walks across the valley floor where his entire regiment had
been wiped out, walking into the cannon fire in rigid formation.

In Danville, in the last grim days of the Confederacy, he met
Nancy Witcher Keene – Nanaire – whose family of Irish descent
were burghers connected to local Danville, and state politics. She
was a beauty of delicate but striking classical looks, sharply blue eyes
and a trim figure, who would have been a Danville Belle but she
never had her moment. She was sixteen when she married Chillie.
They spent the first months of the marriage in a tented camp in
Danville where Nanaire was a nurse. When the war was over Chillie
and Nanaire took his father and mother, his brother Tom and his sister
Liz into their care. They lived in four small rooms in a house in
Danville that still stands, now with a storey added and a plaque com-
memorating the fame of Nancy Astor and Irene Gibson. Nanaire bore
eleven children in twenty years, nine of them born in the Danville
house. It was there, too, that Nanaire lost three of them, Chillie,
Mary and 'Litttle Jack' and buried them in her family graveyard at
Chestnut Hill.

Chillie was always fiercely loyal to the memory of the
Confederacy, always wore the stars and bars in his lapel. He was the
first to break into 'Dixie' in his fine tenor voice at the despondent
Confederate reunions. Nancy claimed that it wasn't until she went
north for the first time that she realized that 'Damyankee' was two
words. But, unlike others of his generation, many of whom were
worn down by despair, or went off to South America rather than lose
face by taking menial jobs, he had the ability to mix this patriotic
sentiment with realism. That included the possibility of collaborating

with the invading, occupying army of 'Yankees, Carpetbaggers and Scalawags'.

He had already tried his luck on the margins of the railroad business before he got his main break. By the time the Atlantic and Danville and the Virginia Central were being reconstructed on his doorstep he knew the men who were fixing the deals and talked his way into some piece-work contracts: masonry, signals, supplies. Hoping to ride the boom, he had moved his family to Richmond in 1885 but couldn't get in on the fancier contracts, on the bribery and political pocket-lining, and the greater technical expertise in the capital. Tobacco production was in recession; a coal mine he was involved in had a cave-in and his luck ran out.

Once he had the entrée and the backing, he could talk and charm anybody into anything. The key to railroading, he discovered, was to get the terms of the contract right and that, he said, took 'personality'. 'Then you can always find some damn fool who likes hard work to build the railway.' The sheer force and attraction of his personality – his assumption of being instantly at the top of the pile – is reflected in the guest list of the party he gave at White Sulphur Springs in 1892 only two years after he had put up his plaque 'C. D. Langhorne & Co.': Mr Reinhart, President of the Atchison Topeka and Santa Fe Railroad; Mr Scott, President of the Pennsylvania Railroad, President George Stevens of the C & O. Chillie bought Mirador the following year.

He had always wanted to get back to the landscape he had visited and loved as a boy before the war, in Albemarle County, near Monticello. Mirador, with its shutters and breeze-gathering porches and its red-brick walls, lay at the foot of the Blue Ridge, eighteen miles from Charlottesville. It was built in 1825, in what, until 1800, had been Indian territory and it was still remote. Even in the 1920s you had to open farm gates to get to Charlottesville on the main road. The magic of the place was this part of the Blue Ridge itself, so perfectly named.

In May when I first saw this landscape – the time of dogwood and honeysuckle which scents the whole countryside – it was a vivid mix of pure blues and greens, hazy grass meadows and apple orchards. The hills that seemed to slide down into the fields appeared, after a bout of rain, as flat paper cut-outs of different pale blues, stacked flat against each other, marking the heights and outlines of the ridge. It is the scale of these low-lying, tree-covered hills that is so beautiful, so intimate and reassuring.

At 1,500 feet Mirador is cooler than Richmond in summer, perfect for horses and hunting – the surviving local culture – and in Chillie's day good for shooting quail. It was only three miles from a branch line of the C & O railway at Greenwood, a crucial communication. The country roads were worse than before the war; the journey to Charlottesville by horse took four hours. That was another sound that, as Phyllis put it later on, 'makes me long for I know not what', – the train whistle echoing off the hills as it approached Crozet's tunnel, morning and evening, two long blasts and two short. This was the train that brought the guests from Washington and New York to visit the Langhornes in their prosperity, and through Irene, their fame.

After all these years of struggling and trying to make ends meet, obeying her husband, dealing with his impulsive and 'rampageous' ways, Nanaire now had to cope with his furious hospitality; the impromptu meals, always a mark of status in Virginia, particularly in these still impoverished times; and Chillie's stag parties and reunions, which became more expansive, more meticulously prepared. Nor did Nanaire particularly like the country after the dangers and scares of the war outside Danville. But she was proud of Irene's success and kept a scrapbook of her progress. Eighteen ninety-three was the year Irene broke all records for a Southern Belle by leading the Patriarch's Ball in New York – the great, exclusive event in the social calendar of Mrs Astor's '400'. Irene was the first Southern girl to be given such an honour. She had become famous at the age of twenty, through print, through word of mouth.

In these early Mirador days Nancy and Phyllis were at school in Richmond. Chillie had kept the house there in Grace Street, and would come to Mirador for holidays and weekends. Keene, born in 1865, the eldest, handsomest and funniest son, his father's favourite, was helping him on the contracts, when he wasn't on protracted sprees with his friends in the mountains, escaping from his father's dominating strictness. Harry, the second son, was drinking his way through Charlottesville university. Mr Langhorne had made the mistake of preventing his sons from drinking at home, where mint juleps were forced on anyone else who came by. Both boys had acquired a great love of bourbon and 'spreeing' and both had contracted tuberculosis at a young age. Buck and Nora were, at this moment, still in the nursery.

Only Lizzie, the eldest sister, born in 1867, lived outside her father's all-encompassing protection. In 1885, when she married Moncure Perkins, she had left the family home and moved to a small house in Richmond. On paper Moncure's family had been grander, more landed, better connected in Virginian terms than the Langhornes. Their daughter, Alice Winn, indefatigable genealogist of the Langhorne family forebears, maintained that Moncure was related to 'every President' from Virginia, that his mother was a cousin of Robert E. Lee, that his family's flour mill was one of the biggest in the south and had fed Lee's army. But it was all gone. The Haxall flour mill — belonging to his mother's side of the family — had made the biggest blaze of all when Richmond was set on fire by the Yankees. And unfortunately, Moncure 'wasn't really interested in money', according to Alice Winn. 'He had no ambition whatsoever,' she said. 'He was only interested in going to the Commonwealth Club in Richmond which he loved, and you know, general life.' The Perkinses still had some land in Buckingham County, but Moncure 'wouldn't go to it. He would never go up. He hated the country.' He would leave it to Lizzie to take their children to Mirador to stay in the guest cottage, unchaperoned, and exposed to her unpopularity within the family.

Lizzie was slender and trim when she first married, with green eyes and a lot of long black hair. 'She had beautiful legs,' said her other daughter, Nancy Lancaster, 'and tremendous chic.' But she also had her own idea of her position in the family. Lizzie thought of Nanaire almost as an older sister; they had had babies at the same time. She remembered all the hard times and the exhaustion of bringing up her many siblings. She had helped Nanaire to bury the three young children at Chestnut Hill. To the other sisters, and even to Nanaire, she seemed to come from a different, older generation. She had a sense of correctness, a severe side to her that belonged with the elaborate funereal conventions of Richmond. She would try to dictate to her younger sisters on matters of dress and on the old-fashioned etiquette for which she was a great stickler. She was shocked that they didn't wear 'dull headed black pins' and tried to forbid them from wearing brown shoes in the country. She even thought Nanaire 'unsuitably young and gay'. But Lizzie also had a high temper and she was confrontational. She fought Chillie as if he was her own husband and he, in turn, treated Lizzie as another wife though, as Alice Winn put it, 'one he wanted to divorce, if you see what I mean'.

When Lizzie was in charge, if Nanaire was away or ill, Nancy remembered her 'looking very matronly and important' and administering spankings far more liberally than the children's parents. Once when Nancy came home singing a song she'd learned in the street Lizzie made her wash her mouth out with turpentine 'to remove the contamination'. Nancy was never to forget, or forgive, the humiliation.

When he was at Mirador, Chillie, in his bowler hat with the high crown, his cigar-cutter dangling on a watch chain, would dominate the daily proceedings, hunting people down, shouting his orders to the stables through a bullhorn. He was an impressive figure, stocky, erect, his hair still curly, always elegantly dressed in clean linen and three-piece suits, even on the hottest days, smelling of lavender and cologne and usually holding a cigar in his right hand – when he wasn't chewing plug tobacco. Most of his pronouncements were preceded by the word 'Dammit', including requests to his children to close the door. His granddaughter Nancy Lancaster remembered 'the fresh good-smelling cleanliness of him – he was the cleanest man in the world. Nanaire said he put on clean linen every day of his life. I mean even when he had no money.'

In the winter, as soon as they were old enough, the children hunted with the Deep Run Hunt of Richmond. The long weekends in the summer also centred around riding – the highly competitive horse shows at Richmond and Charlottesville – tennis parties and endless visitors. Chillie now had the right to stop the train at Greenwood with a telephone call to the station. A field line had been rigged up on poles across the apple orchards. The conductor looked after the supplies for the Mirador table – soft shell crabs, oyster crabs, spot and shad roe up from Norfolk and Chesapeake Bay, terrapins from Baltimore, kept in the basement at Mirador for the making of soup. Nancy and Phyllis would go down into the cool basement, with its smell of kerosene and damp, to play with them, and would weep for their pets on their day of reckoning. Terrapin soup was a favourite along with batter bread and roe herring; home cured ham, watermelon from the ice house and their nightly supper of corn bread and eggs, raw tomatoes, beaten biscuits and molasses. It was the way of life Chillie knew as a boy in Lynchburg before the war – a luxurious simplicity. Only Harry, 'the only mean Langhorne', objected to his parents' sharing of all these goods with friends and neighbours, calling it churlishly 'a new miracle of the loaves and fishes'.

Chillie would ride around the district in the mornings, often followed by his children on their ponies, or he'd take them on the wagon to get the mail from Greenwood. Before lunch, coming up the steps, he would feel for the cellar key on his watch chain, and go to prepare his mint juleps, doing a shuffle and singing a rhyme as he mixed the sugar and mint, the bourbon and ice. He spent much time thinking about food and its preparation. According to Nancy, a woman once said to Nanaire, 'Oh Mrs Langhorne your husband has such lovely eyes,' and she replied: 'Don't be fooled by that. He looks just the same way at a batter cake.' After lunch he would have his nap, in the Virginian style, on a black horsehair sofa in the cool stone hall of the house, or in some unexpected place from where, woken by noise or laughter, he would erupt in fury. The children would then be obliged to fan the flies from his face until he dropped off again. 'Damn it. Go in the porch and finish your laughter. Then come back,' he would tell them. Nancy liked the danger, delicately touching the end of his nose with the fan just as he was dropping off. On the back porch was a bucket of spring water and a dipper. When he came back from all that performing in New York or Baltimore, Chillie would drink a bucket a day to restore himself.

On Sundays the family would go to the Episcopalian Emmanuel Church at Greenwood. Chillie Langhorne sat in the third pew from the front, with a spittoon beside him, into which he aimed his tobacco juice. This concession was won after a hard battle with the pastor, who apparently tolerated Chillie's gesture of pretending to wind a barrel organ when he judged the sermon was taking too long. Irene, who had a beautiful voice, would sing in the choir and her father would watch her, watery-eyed with adoration. Irene had become a local musical star. She sang in a husky alto, sitting at the piano and throwing her head back romantically. 'Goodnight Beloved' was one of her best. She had made a hit in Richmond playing 'Germaine' in a French opera called *Chimes of Normandy*.

With the combination of their prosperity, Mr Langhorne's personality, and the fame of Irene's beauty, the Langhorne family fitted uniquely, if fantastically, into the Northerners' myth of the Old South, into what Edmund Wilson called their 'historical optical illusion'. 'Having devastated the feudal South, the Northerners wanted to be told of its glamor, of its old time courtesy and grace,' wrote Edmund Wilson in *Patriotic Gore*. 'A rush of industrial development had come at the end of the war,' he wrote, 'and the cities of the North and the West, now the scene of so much energetic enterprise which rendered them uglier and harsher, were losing their old amenities; and the Northerners wanted, besides, a little to make it up to the South for their wartime vituperation. They took over the Southern myth and themselves began to revel in it.' Since the late 1880s, Northern readers had developed an insatiable taste for tales of gallantry, of quaint and picturesque darkies, and gracious living in the South, particularly from the fiction of the Virginian writer Thomas Nelson Page, who knew the Langhornes quite well and must have been delighted that his magnolia-scented fiction appeared to have some echo in real life. (It is unlikely that Chillie was familiar with Page's work. He was never seen to read a book. His basic education – cut short by the war – revealed itself in his perfunctory handwriting. Nanaire, however, was an avid reader, played the piano by ear and painted watercolours.) Page managed to bring plantation paternalism back into fashion in the North, with no acknowledgement of slavery or the causes of the war, and ignoring the fact that the intention – the origin – of the war had been to destroy a way of life and an imagined set of attitudes. It was a fashion that was to reach its zenith with *Gone with the Wind* in 1936. Page rhapsodized about the pre-war Virginian world of the 1830s, mixed it with the eighteenth century, and described 'for all its faults . . . the purest sweetest life ever lived which made men noble, gentle and brave, and women tender, pure and true', in stories such as *In Ole Virginia*, as well as social studies like *Social Life in Old Virginia Before the War*. His bestselling *Red Rock*, published in 1898, praised Virginians for resisting Reconstruction. They were often written in Negro dialect with an invented demotic vocabulary – the word 'Massa' became proof of the loving faithfulness of the household staff. Former abolitionists publicly recanted, rubbed their eyes, admitted that they might have been wrong all along. Perhaps slavery had never actually existed. Virginians themselves played up to the myth, at least in Richmond, where they were deliberately trying to recreate an atmosphere of leisure and elegance, greater even than that before the war, to help soften the hurt and the poverty.

To the romantic Yankee eye, the Langhornes were not far off this image. Outside Mirador, though, the state was littered with ghost towns with their abandoned and overgrown mansions, including the Lees house at Stratford, often squatted in by sallow-complexioned, undernourished families of poor whites. Chillie had, in fact, bought Mirador and the land cheaply; it had barely recovered its post-war price of $2 an acre, compared to $150 before the war. But to the social reporter from New York Chillie Langhorne seemed like proper antiquity, the English Squire from the Tidewater with his mint juleps, his storytelling, his fine manners and his hospitality. Margaret Mitchell might well have used him as the model for Scarlett's father, Gerald

O'Hara, with his 'tempers and his roarings', but who 'beneath his choleric exterior had the tenderest of hearts', and in whom there was also something, as Scarlett saw, 'vital, earthy and coarse'. Nanaire, too, seemed to revive the image of the old plantation matriarch from the sentimental novels of the 1830s, justifying the Southern institutions. She was the one who really ran the place: resourceful, a fount of goodness and virtue, a paragon of Christian values, on whom everyone depended, black and white, whose daughters were warrior-pioneers in the making or, in their new incarnation, 'Gibson Girls'. The Mirador servants, with their quaint old names completed the picture. Phyllis later had a nurse called Mrs Virgil Homer Brown; there was an ancient former slave called Fountain Winston who lived in a shack in the garden and dressed in top hat and tails. Nancy and Phyllis's nurse, Aunt Liza Pie, smoked a pipe and spoke directly to Jesus. 'I cannot remember a time when I did not love some coloured man or woman just as much as anyone in the family,' Nancy wrote in her memoir notes, 'Only those who have lived in the South in the old days will understand this.'

The Northern beaux came down in their railroad cars to investi-gate this extraordinary household, and Nancy kept a list of them: lawyers, literary men, budding politicians, rich bankers, foreigners. They came to get a touch of, and to buy up if possible, this simple Southern charm, to find a little *ante bellum* romance and an antidote to the rich and regimented tedium of Bar Harbor and Newport – but mostly to court Irene.

Mr Langhorne didn't care much for appearances. He would pick up Irene, even after she was famous, in a ramshackle wagon with a mad-looking coloured boy in the seat beside him. When he finally built a tennis court he left a large cherry tree growing on the back line, claim-ing that, according to the law of dammits, if it was a game of skill they could play around the tree. It was embarrassing for Irene when her father slapped the butler's pockets to see if he was concealing pancakes, or recycled the butter left on their plates. One survivor remembered him roaring at a rich suitor from Philadelphia, 'Dammit, McFadden, you've been here for two days eating my hog and hominy, and you haven't said a word to Irene.' Nora later claimed, perhaps fancifully, that her father had laid down: 'Etiquette is for people with no breeding, fashion for people with no taste.'

In the social columns Chillie soon became a 'gentleman of the Old Virginia School', then 'Colonel' Langhorne, and finally the Langhornes were upgraded in the *New York Times* to a 'First Family of Virginia', although everyone in genealogically obsessed Virginia knew this not to be quite true. The Langhornes had been distinguished soldiers and landed gentry in Wales. Some had fought for Cromwell, others against him, one of them had changed sides midstream. The first Langhorne then came to Virginia in 1672 – officially ten years too late to qualify as a 'First Family'; or to be one of the hundred or so inter-marrying families that dominated public life for two centuries. Chillie's maternal grandfather was a lawyer called Chiswell Dabney, whose immigrating ancestor was a little grander, having come over in 1649 – the year of the Cavalier exodus from Cromwell. Chillie Langhorne's ancestors mixed not with the old nobility but with the middle class, the merchants and husbandmen, the backbone of the settlement. Surviving letters from Chillie's father, John Scaisbrooke Langhorne, show that the family couldn't depend on the land, even though they had a surplus of slaves. He wrote home to his father from Nashville in 1834, where he was a clerk in a cotton company, sneering at the *nouveau riche* traders and later immigrants there: 'You wd be amused to see the airs that these gentry put on. They consider themselves lords of the forest when upon enquiring you find the generality of them to have commenced the world a blacksmith or stonemason divested of every quality that is req-uisite for a gentleman and by unparalleled labour have acquired wealth which here is considered without any accomplishment, a passport to all society.' His cousin John Langhorne was a clerk in a steamboat com-pany plying the Missouri. But with cousinage, after five generations, you could attach yourself to any family you liked in Virginia. This was what everybody talked about after the war – lateral family trees and past recollections – 'There was nothing else to do.' An irreverent American cousin, irritated by the dogged attempts by other cousins to upgrade the Langhornes in the league tables told me, 'If you go down to Virginia and scratch around you'll discover that the Langhornes were *only just* not black. Only just.'

Phyllis and Nancy were inseparable as children, running wild, preferring to play in the streets, making a name for themselves in the neighbourhood. Nancy, a fierce-eyed tomboy, preferred boys' games, including baseball. She was the fastest runner on the block, never to be upstaged, and fearlessly took the lead in the fights. Phyllis was her more passive accomplice, and under her protection. They turned cartwheels and somersaults; a street boy called Blind Willie had taught them to tap dance. Nancy was to perform once more, this time for the movie camera on her eightieth birthday, shuffling her golfing shoes on the Cliveden gravel.

The years in Richmond before this — the privations, the lack of space, the uprooting from one house to another, her mother's 'continual domestic trials' — made a seminal impression on Nancy. Thirty years later she was still describing them to Phyllis in her letters, remembering, for example, how Nanaire had dreaded Christmas. 'Small wonder,' she wrote to Phyllis, 'her great heart ached to buy every soul a present & a good one & her small purse emptying so fast. Oh for a chance to fill that purse & see her empty it to her hearts desire.' She remembered how Nanaire would answer obediently, 'Yes Dab' — her patronymic nickname for Chillie when he gave an order.

As they grew older Nancy and Phyllis developed an ever-sharper sense of Nanaire's predicament; and of their own childhood callousness, as they saw it, towards her. Phyllis wrote to Nancy in 1909, six years after their mother's death, remembering her 'sighing for romance & the delicate polite touches of life. Pour soul, how my heart aches for her sometimes now, think of the grind she had & really mighty few pleasures but I do believe she had real satisfaction out of her daughters, except me who was so unsociable and curious!! If only we could have her back now when we could be more sympathetic & less hateful than we were.' Nancy was haunted by the expedition they took with Nanaire to her childhood home in Chestnut Hill where she had buried three of her children. The house and garden were in ruins after the war, she couldn't find the gravestones and broke down in tears on the front steps. Nancy had gone on playing, not understanding what she was crying about.

The children also lived under the domestic tyranny of their father, with his cussing, his roaring commands, and unpredictable, often unexplained spankings. They tried to shine to please him on their Sunday walks, where he talked to them like grown-ups and they called him 'Sir'. He addressed most children as 'You little devil' (and referred to any of his male contemporaries as 'that damn rascal'). 'No-one dared argue with him at home; his temper was ungovernable,' Nancy wrote later, 'His word was law. There was no talking back. We took it out on Mother.' They were fond of Chillie but they were delighted when he went away, and they had Nanaire to themselves.

Nancy was unforgiving, in later years, of the dominating, controlling traits of her father's character. 'Very early in my life,' she wrote, in her notes for a memoir, 'I sensed that she had the finer sense of values and the stronger character. But Father had the power. He held the purse strings. He was often bad tempered and unreasonable. I felt if Mother had independent means she would not have had to stand that. I felt that men put women in this position for this very reason, that it rendered them helpless. They had no kind of independence.' Men, she said, had logic, women humanity and spiritual values. One had the purse strings, the other the emptying purse. It was a lesson she never forgot, a driving force. Her heroines at this time – Joan of Arc, Mary Queen of Scots and the markswoman Annie Oakley – were not models of domestic tranquillity.

In the circumstances Nancy might have forgiven Chillie: she recognized his force and his courage, which she inherited too, and the feeling of safety he generated when his children saw him deal with the outside world. But it was her early perceptions of her father's attitude to her mother that she said turned her later into 'an ardent suffragette', that gave her a sense of basic differences in values between the sexes, hardened into a lifelong conviction that women could be apolitical and get things done together while the men bickered and postured among themselves.

Yet Nancy could see that Chillie adored Nanaire, that he was never unfaithful to her, although his 'lunacy' prevented him from showing his affection. But she also saw his unfairness, his temper, and 'the common male weakness of making one dollar do the work of two', even when he had money. It was one key to Nancy's counterweighted personality that far from being able to integrate the qualities of these two parents, she turned them into an unbridgeable division, in her mind, between God and Mammon, in which worldly ambition was evil and selfish, a 'tragedy' in God's eyes. The only thing God could 'see' was the striving for good and in this respect Nanaire became, in her imagination, a deity.

3

Mrs Langhorne's
Violet Lunch

Whatever the state of their finances, the Langhornes went each summer to White Sulphur Springs, the most fashionable of the hot water spas across the Blue Ridge in the Allegheny Mountains. The spas had been the centre of Southern glamour and the marriage market since 1830, particularly 'The White' which to Nancy and Phyllis was a place of outlandish fantasy. It was their only contact with the outside world: a gigantic doll's house dedicated to beaux and belles, to highly organized courtly activity.

To get to the Springs, to lead a masked ball or a 'German Cotillion' (a form of Vienna ballroom parade), to be a reigning Belle, was the only ideal in life worth pursuing for a Southern débutante, even more so after the war. Your life could be transformed overnight by one appearance at a ball. In the meantime you were surrounded by stiff and deeply bowing beaux who carried your satin dancing shoes to the ballroom entrance in little bags. If a mother couldn't scrape the funds to go, she sent her daughter in a chaperoned group, and then, Richmond style, drew down the blinds to feign absence. For Nancy, aged eleven, and Phyllis, aged ten, these trips under Irene's mantle in 1890 were a sensation.

The White looked its part as a Southern metropolis. It was a great stretched classical façade of white wood, with tiers of elevated balconies 200 yards long, called 'piazzas', suspended on rows of Ionic columns. This giant, creaking construction was set in acres of lawns, surrounded by low hills in incongruously remote country. Before the railroads were extended up to their front doors, the spas were reached by river, canal and stagecoach, from New Orleans, the Carolinas, Washington – an arduous Southern migration. It was a matter of honour to make the journey, even for the hardest hit families; a tribal affirmation. The White itself was a place of bare, carpetless discomfort inside, like some rustic Versailles; chaotic, overbooked, the ballrooms badly ventilated, the sanitation primitive, the linen dirty and flearidden. Families would sleep in the halls, divided from each other by sheets pinned up between them. The waters were said to have aphrodisiac properties, part of the reason for The White's popularity. They were prescribed for dyspepsia, but produced a violent craving for food, prolonging the treatment cycle indefinitely and straining the manners of the guests as they barged their way into the canteen-like dining rooms at meal times.

But Virginian pride was focused on these ramshackle wooden hotels. They had flourished before the war and even functioned during it, until they were shot at and wrecked or turned into field hospitals. Before the railroad money came it was a purely Southern affair, a return to pre-war isolation, a way to forget the war itself, and the poverty. The lavishness of the pre-war days had been replaced, from 1868, by 'Calico Balls' and 'Starvation Parties'. It was a way, too, to counter the shock of emancipation. The Belles became the pure white maidens of Provençal romance, antidotes to the surrounding blackness, whose honour was, literally, worth dying for. The cause of the last duel in Virginia, fought in 1868 between two penniless journalists, in which one was killed, was the honour of Mary Triplett, one of the top three Belles, and the charge that she had been insulted in a poem.

The adulation of the Belles had a direct relation to Virginia's sense of defeat, the sense of injustice that could hardly be addressed in conversation. They had an electrifying effect on Richmond society.

Greatest of all, until Irene ousted her, was Miss May Handy, who undoubtedly possessed star quality. Nancy and Phyllis knew everything about her; how she was schooled and watched over like an athlete; how her diet was prescribed; how, exceptionally for Richmond, she lived alone with her maid for company; how she was too grand for any beau to approach her. That was the crucial, misleading lesson: that love could only be pure and good if unsatisfied – the Provençal romance. 'Yearning' and 'loyalty' were the key words. The little girls of Richmond would rush out into Franklin Street to see her pass, wearing her bunch of 'May Handy violets' and 'smelling delicious', then ran around the block to meet her again. They chanted a skipping rhyme:

> 5 cents for cake
> 5 cents for candy
> 15 cents kiss May Handy

The Belles had similar looks. They were round and placid, with prominent busts and full hips, their faces not beautiful in the classic sense. May Handy was photographed on a throne, with a shining aureole rising behind her, and with a look of unreachable remoteness on her face.

The Langhornes were reported at The White in 1889 – a year before Irene's elevation – 'all crowded into a small cottage in Virginia row', with their coloured nursemaids. 'A rather unique and picturesque feature of the place is a pretty little spring-wagon drawn by a pair of goats. These docile and well trained animals are the property of little Nannie (aged ten) and Phyllis Langhorne and can be seen trotting around the grounds with as many as six little girls aboard.' Nanaire 'remarkably bright and vivacious' was mentioned as having given a 'Violet lunch' – in which everything from the candles to the cake to the tablecloth, from the flowers to the ices were, as one might expect, coloured violet and wildly praised ('the candles hid their heads under violet bonnets . . .') in the *Richmond Times-Dispatch*. The 'irrepressible'

Chillie Langhorne had a stag party, which strangely included dancing as well as 'high jinks' and songs which 'kept everybody in that section of the place awake till dawn'.

But entrepreneurial money had changed The White. Harvard men were turning up; families from the North who brought a different, racier style. Lawyers and brokers came with the railroaders. And the Southern girls, pushed by their mothers, were using the system to escape the menace of genteel poverty. The top ones were making good marriages outside, mostly to Northerners, mostly to millionaires. The Southern invasion of New York had begun.

Irene was hurled into a regime that required immense stamina to survive. There was little opportunity for sleep. The balls ended at 3 a.m. Riding began at 7. There was 'Treadmilling' after breakfast — trooping around, four or five abreast, making dates for the 'Germans' (the cotillions) which were held in the morning from 11 to 1 and again in the evening. No refreshments were served at these dances and in the gaps there were 'watermelon struggles', bowling parties, 'candy stews' and photography sessions. The Germans, held in broad daylight in the middle of the morning in evening dress, were something new to a northern eye. One reporter wrote 'The effect produced by so many colours in perpetual motion beneath a strong light is very bewildering.'

Unlike May Handy, Irene had never been groomed for her part. She had simply emerged from Mr Langhorne's circus — no make-up, no attendant hairdresser — and was one day taken on to the dance floor at The White. She had been noticed by the New York papers while she was still a schoolgirl, to the annoyance of her father who threatened to go to New York to shoot the editor. 'She is tall and fair,' wrote the *New York Times* in the offending passage, 'and dances like a dream. Her carriage is queenly and her complexion perfect.' She was taller than her sisters, serene, upright, with a dimple on her chin and (fashionably) 'violet' eyes. She had the rounded hips and the forward-weighted bosom of the classic Belle, the bosom that ended at a twenty-inch waist, of which she would say, coyly, 'The beaux were supposed to be able to put their hands around it. But my Father never let them.' She had a luminous quality, 'she lit up' a room like May Handy's aureole, or according to Nancy Lancaster, like Lady Diana Cooper.

Lizzie disapproved of Irene's success, thinking it the height of vulgarity to be in the newspapers at all. And the crepe-veiled widows of Richmond were beginning to look down on Mr Langhorne for having broken ranks by collaborating with the Yankee occupation and getting rich. The social system of Richmond deliberately excluded money. Nancy Lancaster remembered the first woman to wear a suit from New York, as late as 1910, 'And we looked out of the window, fascinated. We called her the Southern Heiress.' Richmond was a town obsessed with mourning and commemoration, with unforgiving resistance to burying the hatchet, particularly on the part of the women. It was not so long ago, at The White, that Robert E. Lee had had to make his own symbolic gesture to end the war, by walking across the lawn to greet a shunned and ostracized family from Pennsylvania. When she was growing up with her mother Lizzie, Nancy Lancaster recalled how 'People in Virginia looked very down on the Astors and Vanderbilts. They were supposed to be fur traders and Mr Vanderbilt was meant to have ferried a boat. I remember my grandmother talking about them. Shocked and horrified. We looked down on the deep South. We looked down on the North . . . There was that terrific feeling that there was nothing better than a Virginian. You felt that was the passport.'

In 1893 Ward McAllister wrote to Irene, asking her to lead the grand march at the Patriarch's Ball in New York, which meant instant stardom. She would become one of America's four top Belles. Chillie Langhorne would have hated McAllister, who came from Savannah, Georgia, but had, like some irresistible plastic surgeon, achieved absolute control over the social life of New York and the satellite resorts. His aim, and that of his co-conspirator and patron Mrs William Astor (*the* Mrs Astor), was to keep the flashiest and most vulgar of the new age profiteers out of the New York ballrooms, especially out of Mrs Astor's ballroom which held 400 people. McAllister, who invented Mrs Astor's '400', wrote gloating descriptions, after he had been dismissed by Mrs Astor 'like a servant', of how mothers had come to plead with him, waving proof of lineage from Kings of England, and First Families of Virginia, desperate for their daughters to be included in his whimsical list. He was a prototype walker, Nancy Reagan's Jerry Zipkin. Louis Auchincloss described him as 'the kind of fashionable ass that is taken up by idle women and despised by their husbands'.

This was Yankee vulgarity in excess: looting statues from France for dinner parties; having their guests dig for jewels with silver spades in sand-pits on the table. The Patriarch's Ball was the great annual event of the Gilded Age, a moment of hysterical exclusivity. Chillie Langhorne was asked to escort Irene into the ballroom at Delmonico's, where almost everyone who marked her dance card would be a millionaire, and where McAllister would be dressed as an archduke. And he willingly accepted.

From there, Irene was asked to open the Philadelphia Assembly; to be a Queen of the Mardi Gras courts in New Orleans; to open every fête and dance on the national round. Chillie and Nanaire went with her. Nanaire, having become a stage mother, was glad to have these adventures with her débutante daughter, travelling from Maine to the Gulf of Mexico, spending money, and free from her domestic chores. When Chillie wasn't with Nanaire, chaperoning Irene to the ballrooms that she now 'adorned', he was out fixing the contracts on the New River, Bremo and Clinch Valley divisions of the C & O, all quite close to home, and along the Big Sandy River in Kentucky. Irene had undoubtedly been very good for business and all of them, now, were famous.

Nancy took pleasure in her early teens, while all this was going on, in making cut-out figures from the fashion plates and new illustrated black and white magazines, calling the male figures after Irene's beaux. She and Phyllis would construct houses and invent whole families to inhabit them. Nancy kept the score of Irene's proposals, which by the time of her marriage would reach sixty-two – the rising index was public knowledge in Richmond, a matter of civic pride. Mirador, in full swing by 1893, was full of suitors, bringing lavish presents. A rich banker, twenty years older than Irene, sent her a diamond bracelet, telling her to throw it in the mill pond if she wouldn't accept it. Nancy got out their swimsuits, but Chillie made Irene send the big presents back. Nancy wrote to Phyllis in 1912, recalling 'the excitement of Irene's presents & oh the joy when her beaux began to send us bribes! Yr big doll & my 3 bottles of perfume in a Colgates box. I remember I got quite giddy with excitement & stood dazed in the hall.' In her memoir notes Nancy wrote that many of the beaux were literary men 'and as Irene had no literary talent whatever, they often recited the poetry they had prepared for her, to me'.

Irene, now known as 'Queen Bee' in the family, was beyond reproach in her father's adoring eyes. She was tactful, never opposing him. But she was slower-witted than the others, already outmatched by Nancy's speed and aggressiveness, her feelings were easily hurt, and thus often provoked. Her supremacy went unquestioned but the sisters fell upon her in the truth games. One day when she came back from a ball, the papers full of her praise, Nancy told her, 'You may have looked beautiful at the party. But they should see the way you look now,' and Irene burst into tears.

Nancy was quite unlike Irene. She was small and trim with striking, boyish looks, fair hair and piercing blue eyes. She was restlessly energetic, sharp-tongued, always pushing herself to the centre. Phyllis was her taller, darker, moody opposite, mysterious and introverted. The 'vital influence' in her life, her twin soul, was the Mirador groom Charlie Jordan, an ex-jockey who, like Phyllis, was interested in music as well as horses. She would spend hours in her room polishing her bits and bridles, developing what she called a 'homesickness for solitude'. Unlike other Langhornes Phyllis didn't need constant company. For this reticence she was told that she wasn't a Langhorne at all but a foundling, or a child of the gypsies Nanaire always befriended. She was the sister all the others loved best.

Nancy and Phyllis had that strenuous, athletic quality that seemed so modern, unlike the older Southern girls who fanned themselves on the piazzas. They not only competed fiercely in the horse shows but played squash and tennis, shot quail and rode bicycles, wrapping themselves in sweaters when they took exercise, even in the heat. They were careful to look after their figures, their twenty-inch waists pulled in like Christmas crackers with belts tightened like girths – a vanity that was to cause Nancy grief in later years. They hid their complexions from the sun under wide Panama hats and went riding in kerchiefs like bank robbers, showing only their eyes, to keep out the red clay dust. They chewed dogwood stalks to whiten their teeth. Nancy had forgotten all this when she wrote in her memoir notes that they never considered their looks, and took their beauty for granted. They look extremely pretty in the photographs, in their long plain skirts, their big hats attached loosely with scarves, as they giggle at the camera.

Nancy and Phyllis were the closest allies within the family, always taking the same side in the nerve-testing quarrels that amazed visitors. Irene was the peace-maker, officially neutral. Lizzie depended on Nanaire, and interceded for Keene and Harry with their father, who would criticize them for not going off on their own while never allowing them their independence. In later life Nancy would mythologize her brothers in the Uncle Remus-type stories she told her children about her childhood. But in her correspondence with Phyllis, full of longings and reminiscences, they are hardly mentioned except as 'poor Keene' and 'poor Harry'.

Neither of them would ever conquer their addiction to drink in their short lives – any success would send Keene reaching for the bottle, unable to sustain what his father expected of him. He finally left his father's employment after managing to spend $5,000 of the company's money in a small railroad stop with one house, where with lavish catering supplies sent from Washington he entertained an entire travelling circus. Nancy wrote to her father in 1914, 'I am sorry to hear that Keene is off again. I really sh. put him in the Staunton Lunatic Asylum.' One of her nieces' earliest memories as a child was hearing Nanaire on the telephone saying, 'Oh God. Oh My God' as she listened to the bulletin of Keene's latest bender.

Both he and Harry married their wives on sprees, it was said, perhaps to explain that they were from lower-class origins. Keene married Sadie Reynolds from Kentucky, was bought a farm south of the James River, in a remote area and declared himself 'King of Buckingham County' because he was the only white man in the area. He dressed like his Irish antecedents, in well-cut, ill-matched tweeds, his hat cocked at an angle. He lived the life of an almost well-provided-for country gentleman, eventually doing his rounds in a battered model T Ford. Harry married Genevieve Peyton, daughter of the Charlottesville station master, who had ridden with John S. Mosby's irregulars in the war – a great distinction but not enough for Lizzie. After Buck married Edith Forsythe from quite a rich family, who did have a large manor nearby, she would say 'At least Buck married a lady.'

Born in 1874, five years before Nancy, Harry also had the misfortune to share at least some of the nursery years with Nancy and Phyllis, who teased him mercilessly. He was the cleverest boy but also the least popular. He was humourless, compared to the others, with a streak of violence. He was also shy and excessively prudish, and it was this that Nancy and Phyllis found irresistible. They would kick up their heels and show him their knees, at a time when even ankles were forbidden from view. It would drive him to paroxysms of rage. 'I have a real knack of infuriating people,' Nancy wrote to Phyllis much later, almost in surprise. 'Do you remember how poor Harry would grit his teeth and vow he would like to choke me? Waldorf (her second husband) must often feel the same way.' You could always tell when the sisters were fixing for a tease: they would begin by rattling their bracelets.

Lizzie must often have wanted to choke Nancy too as Nancy began to exert her power. As her siblings grew up Lizzie had made the mistake of trying to pull rank on them, believing she should be automatically deferred to and obeyed as the eldest. And when Nancy exploded at her, matching her will against hers, she was hurt and surprised. 'She had great sorrow in her sisters' treatment of her,' said her daughter Nancy Lancaster. 'It did not match up to what she felt it was their duty to feel.'

Lizzie was 'high tempered' and Nancy was merciless in attack; they were like 'two bearcats' together. Phyllis described a Mirador reunion for Chillie's birthday some years later, when nothing had improved between them: 'It was nip and tuck whether Nancy and Liz were "going into action" there and then. I was constantly kicking Nancy below the table, and above board giving her a look that said "not now, after the feast". I was relieved when they parted at 3 p.m. with no broken bones or black eyes and very few words. Nancy has less control of her tongue than me, but more control of her fists. I like using them when I get mad! and I think I should have one or two go's at Liz – poor Liz, we *are* brutes about her.'

Lizzie's image in Richmond was quite different from the way her sisters saw her. There she was an important and popular figure. Her house on Franklin Street was always full of people. She was considered a woman of taste, 'who looked rich on nothing', and was the soul of generosity. Even Nancy, in an unguarded moment, recognized that people thought Lizzie a 'wit'. After her sisters' success Lizzie told people that in future she should be properly addressed as 'Mrs Obscure Perkins'.

In Richmond, Nancy and Phyllis had a formidable schoolteacher called 'Miss' Jennie Ellett, who remained high in Nancy's pantheon all her life. A witty, bow-legged woman, who was also something of a feminist, and who had a 'secret lover at Harvard', she inspired at least two generations with her instruction, her love of history and literature. She taught little American history – which may account for some of Nancy's sweeping, ill-founded generalizations later in life. It was Virginian-Anglophile, based on the classics, on learning passages of Shakespeare and Edmund Burke by heart, on the dates of the English kings and queens – an early obsession with Nancy which never dimmed. 'Nancy has always liked Royalties,' Phyllis wrote to Bob Brand when the King visited Cliveden for tea in 1908. 'Say what she likes to the contrary, they thrilled her as a child to read about, and now they are giving her a ripple of joy to see now. Don't tell her I said so.' Nancy declared that Jennie Ellett instilled in her a 'passion for learning' — though in reality learning was never to be her strong point. John Grigg, in his biography of Nancy, identified this as the moment when she acquired, instead, a consuming reverence for learning itself and for her intellectual betters, which was to mould the course of her life. Jennie Ellett was deeply religious, as Nancy was now becoming too.

In the summer of her thirteenth year, Nancy formed a deep admiration for an Oxford-educated English preacher, the Venerable Archdeacon Neve, who had recently arrived in the district as a missionary working with poor white hill farmers stranded in the Blue Ridge and Ragged Mountains. Some were descendants of German mercenaries, Hessians, brought over by the British in the War of Independence, and some simply remnants of the failures of westward pioneering. Nancy was amazed and shocked to discover such destitute, illiterate people in the middle of her childhood world.

The Archdeacon, enormously tall, rugged looking, with a swivelling wall eye, rambled over the mountains on his horse in all weathers, tending the sick, baptizing children, and opening these communities to the outside world. Nancy rode along with him. Having been awed by learning, she now fell in love with goodness, in the person of the Archdeacon, and it never faded. 'He was a man of God. From the first I loved and respected him,' she wrote. She read the Bible from cover to cover. She took it literally, for the rest of her life, particularly Genesis and Proverbs, its contents never differentiated by further study or reflection. It became her constant companion. She used it like the southern preachers, black and white, to 'declare the truth'. Nancy discovered her own gifts for soapbox oratory, her gift for communicating through her wit at the Sheltering Arms, a home for the elderly and physically handicapped, where she was a great success. She discovered too, that 'all the people there had an inner life', and from that 'a lesson I have never forgotten: that happiness has nothing to do with possessions'. She wanted to be a missionary until the duality of her personality reasserted itself. To do anything in the world, to improve and crusade, you needed a little more power than

Nanaire. You needed the power of Chillie and a little of his wealthy authority.

One of the images Nancy was cutting out from *Life* magazine was that of the Gibson Girl, the new icon of American female beauty and style that older girls across the nation were imitating in minute detail. The fame of her creator, Charles Dana Gibson, was something quite extraordinary, certainly for a graphic artist. In that great age of black and white illustrators, who came into their own with the invention of photogravure press and nationwide magazines, Gibson was the most influential and perhaps the most brilliant. He came from an old but modest Boston family, and at nineteen he was taken up, as a young and unsuccessful artist, by *Life* magazine. Five years later, by 1891, his drawings with their sharp conception of the social theatre of New York in the Gilded Age, had caused something near to a social and sexual revolution. He had become the highest paid employee ever in national magazine publishing, receiving one annual contract of $100,000.

Gibson had an extraordinary talent for a dashing, stylish outline drawing in pen and ink, using vigorous cross-hatch shading, a style freed from the fussiness of woodcut or steel engraving and suited to the new half-tone reproduction. He was a highly trained artist; there was nothing he couldn't draw well. In America one of his teachers had been Thomas Eakins, but his main influences were the Australian illustrator Phil May and in England, George du Maurier of *Punch*. A brief stint in Paris at the Atelier Julien in 1889 – on loan from *Life* – honed his final distinctive style. It added a Gallic sharpness and buoyancy and precision to his drawing and an ability to create a sense of chiaroscuro and almost of colour on the page.

His satire on the New York scene was popular partly because it mocked the idea of money being synonymous with status. It would have gone down well in Richmond. He turned the Ward McAllisters into poodles, and portrayed rich hostesses sitting alone in their ballrooms, suddenly out of favour. Gibson moved easily in New York society – he was a charming, engaging man – and mocked it as much as he flattered it from a patrician, lightly moralistic Boston point of view. He believed in some romantic, aristocratic idealism, in which money played no part, in which 'Love Conquers All' – a typical caption to his drawings. The vogue of Anglophilia – of what he saw as young American heiresses giving in, from the misguided snobbery of their mothers, to the desperation of down-at-heel English aristocrats – was one butt of his satire. The shameful spectacle of social-climbing industrialists and their wives scrambling for status was another.

Then in 1890 he created the Gibson Girl. She was tall and straight, competent and strong, very sexy with her flowing straight skirts and waisted shirts and her imperious, steely gaze which fixed you from beneath half-closed eyelids. How much was disdain? How much adoration? It was clear that she wasn't so independent that romance and the prospect of love and marriage didn't occupy her thoughts constantly. But she married for love, not money – she couldn't be bought. It was another twist in the chivalric ideal that had sustained the spas of Virginia. But this time the Gibson Girl was the flowering of the all-American pioneer spirit, untouched by European imitation. She was a national treasure, a definition of style that taught an entire generation how to walk, talk and dress. The fact that all Gibson's models were New York society girls made the ideal even more exciting and unattainable.

The Gibson Girl was much more like the real Nancy and Phyllis than the Belle Irene. She was an outdoor creature who existed only in the summer, riding, bicycling, playing sports that were unheard of for women until now. Gibson had wanted her to be equal if not superior to men. He drew her in a football match set in the future between Harvard and Vassar, in which the Vassar girls were dressed as generals, perhaps displaying a certain level of sexual anxiety. His Gibson beau was a stunned, tongue-tied votary, brittle, incompetent, confused. He was often modelled physically on Gibson's handsome and equally famous friend, the journalist and adventurer Richard Harding Davis, whose books echoed the Boston romantic ideal. The phenomenon was a serial soap opera and a marketing bonanza – there was a huge trade in Gibson Girl ephemera – that lasted for almost twenty years, until the

1920s flapper pushed it aside. The art critic Robert Hughes once depicted the Gibson Girl as the American counterpart of 'La Belle Dame Sans Merci', the *femme fatale* who obsessed Huysmans and the Decadents. The Gibson Girl was the New World version – wholesome, full of innocence and promise.

Irene went back to New York with her parents in the summer of 1894 for the annual horse show. Irene was never much of a rider compared to Nancy and Phyllis but by this time she was required to do hardly more than hold the bridle to have yet another accomplishment attributed to her. One night a dinner was given in her honour at Delmonico's, the most fashionable restaurant in New York, and the scene of the Patriarch's Ball. At an adjoining table sat Richard Harding Davis, now the Greek god of New York café society. Beside him sat his friend Charles Dana Gibson.

Never one to pass up admiration, Irene made a detour, as she left, and rustled past their table. A third guest who was dining with them and knew Irene summoned her back and made the introduction. There was tea the following day and then, as Irene wrote to a friend, 'I visited his (Gibson's) studio, something unheard of in those days. I played and sang "Goodnight Beloved" and, well, I just sang him into it.'

Gibson was hooked and began his seduction by sending Irene a drawing of a Gibson Girl singing at the piano, eyes closed, mouth open, with a choir of disembodied cherubim crowding the background of the picture, also in full chant, their eyes bursting with effort. It was called 'Love Song'. It was an example of Gibson's most vulgar style, falling into a pastiche of Spanish devotional painting, in the cause of infatuation. It might have been Irene's autoportrait. It was either very like the way she liked to play the piano or certainly how she did so from now on. Irene, who had never read a book, disingenuously sent Gibson *In Ole Virginia* by Thomas Nelson Page, to show where she came from.

Chillie Langhorne hadn't taken in the fame of Charles Dana Gibson, despite his recent education in New York society. He gave him a rough ride when he arrived at Mirador in a buggy from the station, suggesting that he keep the buggy waiting for the next train. He couldn't see the point of what he called 'this damn charcoal artist', and 'yankee sign painter'. Having got this far, and now able to take her pick of any one of America's eligible young men, Irene was perversely settling for the equivalent of an impoverished Virginian. Chillie warned her that she would starve if anything happened to him: it was clear that he didn't own any railroad stock. But Nancy and Phyllis liked him. They had read about him and asked him to 'Tell us about Bohemia'. All Irene's suitors melted away in the following months and she never looked at anybody else. Chillie Langhorne was won round by Gibson's charm and a letter from the ever-useful Thomas Nelson Page. When they were, at first secretly, engaged, Irene wrote to a friend, 'He makes loads of money, or plenty anyhow and is the most determined soul you ever knew. In London we shall have a delicious time. He knows many people and his reputation has gone before him.'

Their wedding in Richmond in November 1895 was seen as a symbolic end of the Civil War. It was the end, too, of the Belle era. The event was as fascinating in the popular imagination as the wedding of Gertrude Vanderbilt and Harry Payne Whitney, a marriage that would link two families of enormous wealth, the following year. The Gibson wedding was described in the headline of the *Richmond Times-Dispatch*, which devoted its front page to the event, as the marriage of 'Beauty and Genius'. For Gibson's fans it must have been difficult to separate fantasy from reality: Irene really did seem to be the incarnation of their Girl, in which case it was also a day of mourning. In fact something strange had happened. The drawings that Dana Gibson did of Irene now bore no comparison to the photographs of her as a Belle. The flat, parted hair had been brushed up and back showing a long neck, the face had been thinned and streamlined. She seemed to have lost weight. The wide eyes had dimmed. The transition from Southern Belle to Gibson Girl was seamless, if cosmetic.

The ceremony took place at St Paul's Church, the church of Robert E. Lee and Jefferson Davis. Private railroad cars had brought more stars from New York: Richard Harding Davis, who was an usher; Stanford White, already famous for his Memorial Arch at Washington

Square and for Madison Square Garden; Dana Gibson's brother, Langdon, an Arctic explorer who had been on one of Peary's expeditions. Many of them stayed in the magnificent Jefferson Hotel, newly refurbished, with its staircase (later used in the film of *Gone with the Wind*) and its live alligators in the lobby. At Nanaire's house on Grace Street the guests were given, among other forgotten southern delicacies, 'Boucheese St. Jourdan', 'Charlotte Russe S. Honore', and 'Viennoise Panier Garni'.

The couple set off for Gibraltar, Spain, Naples, Rome, Florence, Monte Carlo, Paris and London. Here they installed themselves in Albany, the exclusive, barrack-like apartment building in Piccadilly, where, until Irene's arrival, no woman had been allowed to take up residence. At the first dinner party Irene gave — a disaster at which the food ran out almost immediately, and for which she was teased for weeks by her friends sending round food parcels — the guests included John Singer Sargent and Henry James, 'gravely wounded and abysmally depressed', suffering from years of neglect of his novels and currently at work on *The Awkward Age*.

4

Mr Shaw and Mr Brooks

Nancy and Phyllis were bridesmaids at Irene's wedding, 'two of Virginia's most charming little ladies', as they were described, 'fetchingly apparelled in exquisite French gowns of taffeta with long white gloves and large leghorn hats trimmed with white ostrich tips'. The ceremony affected them in different ways: Phyllis, aged fifteen, was overcome with tearful emotion; Nancy, dry-eyed, concentrated with delight on the thought that she could move into Irene's old room that night.

The newspapers had immediately granted Nancy rights of succession and elected her a Belle. Ambition dictated that she should also inherit Irene's fame and privileges. She imagined marking up proposals on her score card in the same way. Chillie's sons having failed, the burden of success – or so it seemed to Nancy – was transferred to his daughters. Furtherance depended entirely on men, however, and therefore on marriage. But Nancy seemed to treat men like boys and younger brothers rather than suitors: she would rather, quite literally, compete than flirt with them. Ingrained in the girlish memory of Mrs Beatty Moore is the way Nancy shocked the conventions of the Richmond horse show, by entering in a man's class. She remembered her 'in a white linen riding habit on a lovely horse and I remember the name of the horse to this day – it was Queen Bee. Bareheaded, nothing

on her head. She had lovely hair. And she was ruled out. She had no
business entering a man's class, of course, and she was furious and she
dismounted and threw her reins over the pommel and gave Queen Bee
a whack and stomped out of the ring and when she got to the fence
some man gave her a foot up and she came over the fence like she was
mounting a horse.'

Nevertheless Nancy still expected the beaux to behave in the tra-
ditional way – which meant to propose almost as soon as they paid
attention to you. If they hadn't actually fallen in love they were
expected to play the part. There existed no other variation or form of
courtship. She had some brittle confrontations: romance in her teens
seemed to consist of counting up the proposals she had rejected and
unfavourably comparing her score to that of Irene (by the time she was
married she counted only sixteen to Irene's sixty-two). Nor did the
beaux find Nancy as companionable as Phyllis, who genuinely enjoyed
their company. 'Nausea' was what Nancy felt when an admirer sent her
a stream of letters and poems. But love was a difficult subject for
Nancy, an abstract necessity to be conjured with. As in later life it was
the conquests that hadn't quite worked that preoccupied her – the
admirers who walked away without first being rejected. Phyllis would
later say that Nancy never understood love in her endless struggle to
separate the spiritual from the material, the spirit from the flesh
(although the flesh was never a fierce combatant). Nancy only seemed
to like men in some idealized form, like the figures she cut from the
magazines. Otherwise she was easily bored and irritated by them. It
was perhaps something to do with these conflicts of identity that caused
her, in her adolescence, to show signs of delicate health: melancholia,
nervous debility, unexplained neuralgias. Nanaire, considering her too
fragile to take part in her débutante season, forbade her late-night
balls.

Instead, while the rich Yankees were sending their daughters
south to learn manners, Chillie sent Nancy to a finishing school in
New York, Miss Brown's Academy for Young Ladies, to acquire polite
accomplishments. It was a grave mistake, an experience which taught

Nancy, if anything, precisely the opposite of the Miss Brown prospectus. Whatever Chillie and Nanaire thought was lacking in Nancy's upbringing is not clear. Miss Brown's seems to have been a social move but they underestimated the impact of the worldly North on the sensibilities of a girl who had hardly been out of Virginia. Nanaire had packed Nancy's entire wardrobe: one tailor-made and two home-made dresses. Nancy arrived to find that her room-mate had eleven suits and dresses and her jewellery scattered about the room, which caused Nancy particular anxiety. She complained to the teacher: 'What if they disappear?' The girls talked only of their wardrobes, of how much money their fathers made. But worse, according to Nancy, were the 'odd, and to me, quite revolting affairs going on between them and young men. I remember my shame and horror when one of my companions winked at a man in the street.' Nancy, feeling for the first time at a disadvantage with her contemporaries, reacted like a cornered cat to this sinful, unfamiliar Yankee world. She wrote later, 'I have never forgotten how it horrified me.'

She set out to shock her fellow pupils and the staff by transforming herself through vaudeville and mimicry into a Southern caricature, broadening her accent to fatuous elongations. She would put on a yellow blouse with a pink bow on one side and a green bow on the other; she told them that her father was a drunk and that her mother took in washing. She challenged the entire establishment, concealing her misery under war paint. They began to find her, as a result, exotic and exciting, rather than shocking, and then one day, to compound their confusion, when Irene Gibson arrived to take her riding on Long Island, Nancy claimed that she was her elder sister.

When Chillie and Nanaire came to visit she pleaded to be taken out of this misery. She was returned to Mirador, to riding and picnics, and the last summer of her childhood. By the spring of 1896 she was back in the North, staying at Newport with Irene and Dana, and it was there on the polo field that she met Robert Gould Shaw.

She saw him playing spectacularly from a one-eyed pony, taking falls, getting up unscathed. He came over to talk to Nancy's group and was introduced to her as 'Bob Shaw, son of an old and distinguished Boston family'. Shaw took one look at Nancy and decided immediately that he was going to marry her. Nancy was seventeen, Shaw in his mid-twenties, a good-looking playboy, who had been on the Harvard polo team in 1890, whose friends knew that he kept a mistress and whose father Quincy Adams Shaw was, by Boston standards, an extremely rich man.

The Shaws were later relegated, in both oral and written family history, to insignificance, even obscurity. Nancy had reason to suppress her past but otherwise this lack of curiosity about these aristocrats of the eastern seaboard, with whom she was traumatically entangled for six years, is curious. Bob Shaw was a nephew of the famous Robert G. Shaw, killed at Fort Wagner, South Carolina, leading the 54th Regiment of Negro soldiers in the Civil War, whose statue stands in Boston. His grandfather was Louis Agassiz, the greatest zoologist in the USA in the late nineteenth century who had come from Switzerland to teach at Harvard in 1848. He founded the Museum of Comparative Zoology at Harvard and revolutionized the teaching of science in America.

His daughter Pauline, from his second marriage, married Quincy Adams Shaw, Bob Shaw's father. 'Old Mr. Shaw', as Nancy later called her one-time father-in-law, had amassed Boston's, perhaps America's, greatest collection of Barbizon school paintings, including fifty-six works by Millet, whom he had befriended and commissioned in France in the 1870s. He was the younger son of a rich father who had speculated in real estate and traded with China. Quincy used his own inherited money to develop the purest seam of copper ever discovered in the New World, in the mid-West, and made his own fortune in the 1860s, all the while, from the 1850s onwards, visiting France and building his art collection. By 1900 he looked like an old, bearded patriarch. He died eight years later at the age of eighty-three, having bequeathed most of his collection to the Museum of Fine Arts in Boston. He must have been somewhat distanced by age from his son, Bob. He was no brash Yankee capitalist, but a man of impressive scholarship and achievements. One can understand why Nancy, with her reverence for learning and respect for her 'betters', always liked Mr Shaw.

When the rumours began of an engagement, it was thought there must be some mistake as Nancy was not officially 'out'. Bob Shaw seemed to have made an impulsive move; to have merely declared his rights over the new catch of the season. Nancy was flattered to have made what was considered a spectacular conquest and to be suddenly at the centre of the picture, where she had always yearned to be. She liked Bob Shaw – he was easy-going, charming. He was also a spoilt, wilful, sheltered boy, with a tendency towards drink: attributes that Nancy didn't seem to notice at the time. His family put his peccadilloes down to youthful ebullience, to the sowing of wild oats. They believed that marriage would settle him and perhaps even get him down to work.

In the wake of Irene Nancy never found herself in the limelight in the way she expected. She wrote with commendable frankness, 'The engagement of any Langhorne was a sensation, and mine was announced with the usual enthusiasm and excitement. I was supposed to be making a brilliant match, but I noticed that I was alluded to, still, as "the beautiful Irene Langhorne's sister".'

Nancy was never in love with Shaw, although for a time she forced herself to imagine otherwise. When her doubts made her break off the engagement, she came under enormous pressure, both from her own family and the Shaws, to go ahead. Mysteriously Nanaire failed to read the signals. 'Mother was amongst them,' Nancy wrote, 'and I had always listened to Mother and tried to do as she wished.' Because Nancy liked and admired Bob Shaw's parents, the pressure applied by his mother Pauline finally persuaded her to agree to be married. The fifteen months of the engagement gave Nancy pause for further doubts as she saw distressing warning signs of Bob's dissipation, which Chillie largely ignored. He did, however, feel it necessary to travel to Boston at one point for reassurance from the Shaws, which seemed to calm him. Nor did he come to hear of the strains of melancholia in Bob's maternal Agassiz family, to which his mother Pauline would eventually succumb: Bob's brother, Quincy A. Shaw was already beginning a lifetime of confinement for manic depression. But what was locked away was, evidently, of no consequence.

The ceremony took place in October 1897 in the drawing room at Mirador, and was remembered by Phyllis, Nancy's 'maid of honour', only for its 'gloom'. It was never quite clear what happened at the Homestead Hotel, Hot Springs, where the couple began their honeymoon. Nancy, aged eighteen, and Bob Shaw, twenty-four, knew so little about each other that their first taste of proximity shocked them both profoundly, and effectively ended the marriage quite literally before it had begun. But Nancy later, in a rare moment of candour, told her niece, Nancy Lancaster, that she had slept on her stomach for three nights before Bob took her back to Mirador. She claimed officially that it was extreme homesickness that made her beg her husband to take her back to her father's house. Apart from Miss Brown's Academy she had never been away. But there was the question of sex – a subject that Nancy later put very low on the scale of human activities. Hot Springs was either a disastrously failed initiation, which marked her deeply, or she naturally hated the idea of it.

It was Chillie who persuaded Nancy to go back to Boston and continue her marriage, and this must have required some courage on Nancy's part. She was determined not to admit her mistake publicly. Divorce was an unthinkable disgrace; separation equally damning.

Bob Shaw, meanwhile, was 'dismayed' by his wife's frigidity and her strong disapproval of drink. He resumed his affair with his mistress; and was consequently 'untruthful' – as Nancy complained. 'He started drinking again,' she wrote later, 'I was horrified and frightened . . . I learned that drink had been his trouble for a long time.' No doubt Shaw was also getting the sharp end of Nancy's teasing wit and seemed to have responded, on occasions, violently. Nancy was never to forget the connection between her sufferings and alcohol.

Despite fleeing the Shaw home several times, or obeying her husband's command to get out, three months after her marriage Nancy was pregnant. The only clues as to how this came about was Nancy later claiming that she woke up one night to find her husband in the bedroom with a chloroform-filled sponge. When she finally left Shaw, she justified it on the grounds that she could not 'risk having any more children by him'. Even more chilling than the suggestion of rape was the idea of the procreative male as a kind of incubus who comes in the night. Bobbie was born the following year, 1898.

Nancy turned her attentions to her son to take the edge off her misery, turning him into an ally, a bulwark against loneliness. It was the beginning of an intense emotional interdependence in Nancy's life which she was never to loosen. Everywhere Nancy was surrounded by optimistic advice. Bob Shaw could be 'got right'; 'marriage' would still do the trick. But in the summer of 1900 Nancy finally went to her father-in-law and told him that she couldn't go on. He was very kind, she said, and 'much distressed by the whole affair'. He told her to go back home for six months; that he would straighten out his son. But when Nancy came back the situation was unchanged: Bob was drinking heavily; the mistress still in place. A letter written by Nancy to Mr Shaw in 1906, refusing permission for her son Bobbie to visit his father, reveals more. Bob Shaw's mistress was Mary Converse, née Harrington, born in London. 'If you will remember before I left Bob,' Nancy wrote, 'you & I both warned him of this woman . . . she was his mistress at that time & did all she could to break up & ruin his & my home & life.' Mrs Converse was clearly in place during the whole period that Nancy was trying to restore her marriage – a fact she left out of her short memoir.

Also left out of Nancy's account is any speculation that Shaw had seriously fallen for her, found her fascinating and attractive and was tortured by unrequited love. Drink can't have been that much of an endemic problem. He later married quite happily and produced four sons. Nancy seems to have used drink as a smokescreen for the horrors of sexual and emotional incompatibility: of being locked up with someone who turned out to be a stranger. There is no doubt that they were extremely ill-matched: Shaw brash and arrogant, both determinedly wilful, 'like two pieces of steel swinging at each other'.

Nancy refused the advice of her family, even of the Archdeacon

Neve, to get a divorce. It was still something 'that decent people had nothing to do with' but most important it was something not countenanced by her Bible. She signed a deed of separation in 1901, at the age of twenty-three, which would have prevented her marrying again, 'cutting myself off from life completely', and returned with Bobbie to Mirador, 'unwanted, unsought, and part widowed for life' as she 'laughingly' told her father.

Phyllis had also been sent north to a finishing school, with more success. The Langhorne plan, it seems, was for her to meet exclusively northern friends and beaux from now on. She had visited Nancy several times in Boston, and watched her marriage foundering, while she herself was being fêted as New York's latest sensation in her débutante season. She had become the replacement Langhorne for 1900, effortlessly pushing aside the many other Southern beauties who had now invaded Northern society. Nanaire had many more cuttings to fill her 'Mark Twain's Scrapbook' — whose ready-glue stripes still shine and stick ninety-five years later. The coverage on Phyllis is phenomenal by the standards of those days. It is clear that she spent most of 1900 and 1901 in the North, ignoring the Richmond season, and even the hunting at Mirador, in favour of Newport, Long Island, Palm Beach, Boston, Philadelphia — the 'homesickness for solitude' temporarily allayed.

She hunted in the area around Hempstead, east of New York, now a commuter suburb, then the height of social fashion in the country. She went, in Scott Fitzgerald's phrase, '. . . wherever people played polo and were rich together'. She had many admirers among what her letters describe as 'spotin' gents'. Unlike Nancy, Phyllis's heroes in her youth had been chivalrous and daring figures. But it was at that same polo field at Newport where, despite Nancy's near banishment from Northern society, Phyllis found her own polo player in 1900.

It was Irene, Phyllis's chaperone, who arranged the meeting. His name was Reggie Brooks and he was, of course, very good-looking. His rich parents belonged to the inner circle of isolated Newport grandeur. His father, H. Mortimer Brooks, had a huge showpiece villa there, a blend of inflated Bavarian chalet and French Renaissance called

Rockhurst, where he lived most of the year round and gave some of the most elaborate Gilded Age parties. In the city they kept a permanent apartment in the Waldorf Astoria. The Brookses were very much part of the Astor and Vanderbilt set. H. Mortimer Brooks was one of the founders of the exclusive Spouting Rock Beach, a stockholder in the Casino, the Reading Room, the Country Club and the Newport Golf Club. The real wealth, many millions of dollars, came from his wife, Reggie's mother, Josephine Higgins, who had inherited from her father, a real estate operator. Reggie was her only male heir. Phyllis was being courted at the epicentre of the most concentrated group of millionaires on the eastern seaboard.

Reggie was not unlike Bob Shaw. He had been to Harvard; he was spoilt, idle, handsome. He played polo and drank steadily, in the style of most of his former classmates from the Porcellian club of Harvard of 1896, from whom he was inseparable. But to Phyllis he was the complete sporting gentleman, and she quickly fell in love with him that winter of 1900 in Aiken, South Carolina, the hunting ground of the Newport and New York rich, where the family had a large estate.

Reggie did nothing all year other than follow the seasonal migration of rich sportsmen. Aiken was the winter headquarters for hunting, and for quail shooting in April, then Boca Grande in Florida in May for 'Mr. Tarpon' as Reggie called it ('until you have killed one,' he wrote to Phyllis during their courtship, 'your sporting education is incomplete'). In Florida he shot alligators, duck, snipe. Early in the summer he went to Newport; in 1900 'to get my boat in commission [Reggie owned a 30ft yacht called *The Wawa*] also if possible to reserve my berth on the new [America's] Cup defender, which I believe is to be launched Saturday.' There was the polo at Newport, tennis tournaments, more social than sporting, in which Phyllis took part in 1901, and then back to Aiken. Between these fixtures there were bear hunts, deer hunts and moose hunts in Alaska, Canada — and many shooting parties. His parents had discouraged Reggie from working. They seemed proud that he remained with his old classmates, playing boys' games, even six years after he had left Harvard.

One reason that Reggie took to Phyllis was that she seemed to understand the natural need for all this, and took part in some of it herself. In this somewhat asexual world, which excluded women for most of the year, she seemed to be an exceptional catch. In one of the few jolly, excited letters of Reggie's that survive, written after their engagement in August 1901, he told Phyllis how pleased he was that one of his Porcellian friends had described her as 'the best girl he ever met,' adding, 'He also says that usually when a friend got engaged it means [sic] losing him to his sporting friend. My case he considers different as it is merely "the addition of a congenial spirit to the family circle" [family comprising those who hunt, race, shoot, polo etc].'

They planned to live permanently in Aiken, South Carolina, after their marriage. There was a quorum of classmates, a country club, hunting all winter. Reggie's letters are full of shopping lists — horses, saddles, bridles, stable staff. He was fastidiously attentive, sending her presents from Tiffany's, making sure her riding boots were properly dispatched from the menders, sending shoelaces ahead by mail. He had given up drink, he said, and taken to a milk diet. Otherwise he wrote of sporting achievements or defeats, like a little boy writing from boarding school: qualifying rounds, finals, cups, rivals, excuses. Soon he began to sign himself 'Rege Pege' — the name Phyllis gave him and he called her 'dear Old Pills', or simply 'old man'. He wrote to her, 'When I come to Greenwood you will probably say "poor old Rege Pege, how bored he looks, too bad it is so quiet down here and there is nothing for you to do." You old rascal if you attempt any of this line of talky talk I'll spank you.'

They were married on 14 November 1901, at the Brandon Hotel, Basic City, Virginia, now Waynesboro, a few miles from Mirador, within a month of Nancy's separation from Bob Shaw. Chillie took the whole hotel: the guests could check in straight off the train. Hitched to the Fast Flying Virginian Vestibule Limited from New York were two private railroad cars for the guests, 'one with ushers sports and dudes', as Reggie described it, 'and the other one for their females — wives, daughters, cousins.'

The *Richmond Gazette* reported it as a 'gathering of the "400" on Southern soil'. It also reported that after the lunch 'there was a summons that hushed all talk, while a voice of infinite melody and singular pathos to the soft accompaniment of an orchestra, began to sing the old song,

> I'm going home to Dixie,
> I'm going where the Orange blossoms grow.

It was, of course 'the incomparable Chillie Langhorne' doing his now-famous turn; the audience listening, apparently 'with some deep emotion to the simple, plaintive tones'. It was all a lot gayer than Nancy's wedding, four years earlier, when Chillie didn't sing. Phyllis had no doubts about her own wedding, believing, as she said later, that she had married 'a real gentleman and a sportsman'. Only Nancy, who hadn't liked Reggie Brooks from the moment she met him, thought that Phyllis had made a mistake.

5

Going Back in the Boats

In her own case Nancy was trapped. The North — Newport, Boston, Bar Harbor — was closed off to her. She was neither married nor unmarried. Mirador, where she had returned with Bobbie in 1903, was at least open all year round, now that Chillie had decided to retire from railroading. He had sold the house in Grace Street and retreated with Nanaire to the Blue Ridge, declaring (now that he had made a million dollars) that work was only suitable for Blacks and Yankees. Only Yankees, as he saw it, would go on working themselves into the ground to amass more money than they needed. He now wanted to enjoy himself. He was pleased that Nancy was back, despite their continual clash of wills. Part of him had resented his daughters leaving home, thinning out his family.

It was inevitable that, having burned her bridges in the North, Nancy would be looking across the water to England, to the Virginian's natural second home. The romance of kings and queens was only one factor. Irene and Dana had spent much time being fêted and praised in London since their marriage. Irene had been presented at Buckingham Palace, where Dana had been allowed to sketch the proceedings. She had made some major flirtatious alliances in high society. The amorous Prince Arthur of Connaught, Queen Victoria's son, had fallen in love with her. Lady Airlie and Lady Minto, two of the most powerful hostesses of the period, had become her intimate friends. Americans were fashionable in England on that high social level and were favoured by the Prince of Wales, who became King Edward VII in 1901. Dana had all but dropped what he called his 'sensitive patriotic chip' about the English and had swung round to being an ardent Anglophile.

Nancy took all this in as she 'knocked around in an old riding habit' with the horses at Mirador. It was almost a cliché that Virginians recorded, on their first trips to England, how they felt they had come home 'after a long absence'. The reverse was also true. Mirador was a centre for a group of young Englishmen from aristocratic or county families, 'making their way' in the apple business or the railroads, who had found their natural home in Virginia and had gravitated towards the Langhorne family. These were the same young second sons who might otherwise have gone to East Africa as pioneer farmers at the turn of the century. There was Ned and Algy Craven whose father was Master of the Pytchley Hunt; Angus McDonnell, a younger son of the Earl of Antrim, who worked for the railway at Manassas and who fell deeply into unrequited love with Nancy, which clearly gave her pleasure. Nancy and her sisters felt a much closer affinity with these young Englishmen than with the beaux from Boston or Philadelphia. They shared an idea of caste, of paternalism, of the horse-centred, mildly dilapidated pastoral life. But Nancy noticed that when visiting Englishmen came to Virginia they all seemed to have so much money. Their relations seemed to die frequently and leave them more. By contrast, there was no inherited wealth in Virginia. 'Nothing came to us free and we all had shoals of poor relations hanging on to us,' Nancy remembered. Some of these, 'down at heel, peculiar and untidy', as she described them, caused her embarrassment. She wanted to disown them – a lapse in her Christian attitudes – but Nanaire insisted on taking them in and helping them.

As the most ambitious of Chillie's children, Nancy had always outreached herself, tried for the spectacular, competed fiercely, secretly matched herself against Irene. Her present situation seemed insoluble, until a message came from Boston from old Mr Shaw. Bob Shaw had actually gone through some marriage ceremony with Mrs

Converse – while still married to Nancy – convincing her that he was now divorced. He faced various charges relating to bigamy, and almost certainly a prison sentence, unless the matter could be cleared up, and covered up, quickly.

Old Mr Shaw now 'begged' Nancy to change her mind and agree to a divorce. They wanted it done quickly and quietly on the grounds of incompatibility of temperament. Nancy refused. She stood by the Bible, agreeing only to grounds of adultery. Adultery made news and bad publicity, but Nancy was adamant. It took considerable bravery, at the age of twenty-four, to resist the pressure from the Shaws. There was a struggle and much bad feeling between the parties. Three years later, when Nancy's luck changed, on the eve of her second marriage, she wrote to Chillie, 'I shall never forget how you were when my troubles came & how you took me in yr arms & said as long as I had you I need never fear anyone doing me real harm & you wd shoot Bob & the whole Shaw family if you thought it necessary!' The divorce was put through speedily in a Charlottesville courtroom in the absence of either Bob or Nancy, on grounds of adultery and with a substantial settlement, in February 1903. Three days later Bob was 're-married' to Mrs Converse in New York with his mother Pauline as a witness.

Earlier that year Nancy went on her first trip to Europe with Nanaire, 'to pull herself together'. They went to Paris and then to England where Nancy predictably recorded 'the strange feeling of having come home'. Irene's social contacts were there to greet her. But more important for Nancy had been the meeting on the boat with the worldly, formidable, exotic-looking Ava Astor, estranged wife of John Jacob IV, the head of the American branch of the Astor clan, who later went down on the *Titanic*. Ava, born in Philadelphia, was ten years older than Nancy, and was considered, in society-obsessed America, the most beautiful woman in the public eye. Nancy had never met anyone like Ava, Boston notwithstanding. She had pure white hair, huge dark eyes and porcelain-like oriental looks; she dressed impeccably, never wore jewellery. Nature had designed Ava to be admired by men and this was her occupation. She was also magnificently selfish and spoiled, sharp-tongued, fearless in her pursuit of pleasure, furiously social and permanently dissatisfied. She was the antithesis of the improving, correcting, Bible-reading side of Nancy's nature. 'Nonchalante et froide' was how Robert de Montesquiou described her. Her son-in-law Serge Obolensky described her as 'one of the most courageously uncompromising females that ever lived'. What must have appealed to Nancy was her social power as a single woman – and the fearless sharp tongue – especially with men who bored her.

Ava took to Nancy and invited her to stay on in London for a month while Nanaire went home to look after Bobbie during this, the only recorded separation between mother and son. She took Nancy to a ball at Devonshire House, deeply impressing her with 'the glitter and atmosphere' on a scale grander than she had ever seen. It was Ava who showed Nancy the possibilities in England for an American divorcée shunned in Boston. The fashion for American wives – dollar princesses – was gaining height among the English aristocracy, beleaguered by agricultural depression and new taxes. The Duke of Marlborough married Consuelo Vanderbilt and $1m of railroad stock in 1893; the Earl of Essex, the Duke of Roxburghe, the Earl of Ancaster had all married heiresses from Newport or New York by 1905. The Duke of Manchester married another Consuelo millionairess from New York in 1876. They were all Yankees of course, and Mr Langhorne's dowry could never match theirs. But only the most hidebound Tories now looked down on American brides as over-determined and ruthlessly ambitious. They were popular, needed and welcomed in society.

When Nancy returned home to Mirador, Angus McDonnell, Lord Antrim's son, noticed not only that she had returned with a complete outfit of Louis Vuitton trunks and suitcases but that she now dressed up for her many visiting admirers in slim-fitting, sequinned dresses, looking very 'soignée'. It was clear that Mirador wouldn't hold her for long.

The only sister still at home when Nancy came back to Mirador in 1903 was Nora, aged fifteen. Buck, aged seventeen, was the only brother there and it began to dawn on the family that, as one of them put it, 'Chillie had eleven children but when it came to Buck and Nora there was something left out of them'. Buck was a cadet at the Virginia Military Institute, spending most of his time playing craps, riding horses, dating girls, and failing his first-year exams. He was growing up a country boy, full of 'yee-haw' humour and high spirits. When asked by a newspaperman if he was related to the Langhorne sisters he said, 'Hell, I'm one of 'em'. Irene wrote in a letter, 'Bless his heart he is a sweet boy but ssh shh! not really bright. His eyes are wide open and also his mouth & full of nigger stories.'

Whatever was 'left out' of Nora, however, was amply compensated for in other ways. Nora had a wistful, distant look about her, often with raised eyebrows which gave her an expression of innocence, or with heavy eyelids which made her look sad, and disguised at first sight her vivacity and her wild imagination. She could throw a ball overarm like a boy; she was a pitcher in the local children's baseball game. She was pretty if not beautiful, slight, but not small, with high cheek-bones and very fine, almost unmanageable, hair. She was already being criticized for a certain vagueness and a lack of concentration but her most obvious and disturbing fault was a pathological inability to tell the truth. 'It's not that Nora had no sense of right and wrong,' they would say, 'she's just got no proper sense at all.'

Nora's school career had come to an end that year, leaving a more or less clean slate, and an inability to spell. She had been to a great many schools. From each one she would cry her way home, and the now lenient Chillie would let her off. Nora was 'spoilt', in the opinion of the others. They noticed her tendency to gaze at herself in every mirror she could find; they noticed her impressionability and her extraordinary talent for mimicry. Later she told her daughter, the actress Joyce Grenfell, who inherited these talents, that the reason she did so badly at school was that all her concentration was taken up studying the mannerisms and idiosyncrasies of the teachers.

Her sisters couldn't fathom Nora, although her mythomania, which was inventive and got her into serious trouble, no doubt originated as a defence against their intruding, dominating ways, their truth games and their fighting. Her main interests, if one could pin them down, were dreaming and music. She learned to play the guitar and banjo, to tap dance better than the others, and to tell stories. Even when she was only fifteen younger children loved her, and found in her a special, way-ward magic. Letters between the sisters describe their concern: 'Nora's behaviour grows more and more utterly hopeless'; Nora needs a 'strong firm hand'; Nora is 'wrong in the head'; 'Nora knows only one God and that's Nora.' Nora had begun to show a keen interest in her sister Nancy's beaux who came and went from Mirador. But with Nora whatever remained of the beau system was about to spin out of control.

When Nancy's divorce was published in the newspaper, Lizzie drew down the blinds in her house on Franklin Street as if it were a funeral. Oral legend had it, wrongly, as 'the first divorce in Richmond' and she saw it as a disgrace. Despite ten years of publicity in the papers about the Langhornes, Lizzie still insisted it was vulgar to reproduce pho-tographs of them. Lizzie rang an editor of the *Richmond Times-Dispatch*, invoking the old convention, outraged that he should use the divorce story, and was told bluntly that they couldn't keep out what had already been in the national press.

Lizzie's world was falling apart. Her marriage was foundering and she was permanently in debt, which led to fights not only with Moncure but with Chillie too. Moncure had retreated prematurely from the rough and tumble of life, taking his stand in the Commonwealth Club in Richmond, 'drinking like a gentleman'. The club was conveniently situated a few steps from their house on Franklin Street, from where his children were occasionally sent to summon him home for meals, and the trouble that he wanted to avoid.

Poverty didn't matter so much in Richmond. Its gentry could all be poor together. But Chillie's wealth had undermined Lizzie's uni-verse, and her family relationships. Her daughter Alice said, 'It was like farmyard girls suddenly grew wings and they kept marrying rich people whereas my mother had a great feeling for family, felt that she was head of the family and she very much resented that all her family were very rich and having a wonderful time and she was pinned down.'

Nancy Lancaster recalled her parents' rows over money and thinking 'Oh God, could you stop them fighting?' But there was another, deeper root to this 'fussing'. 'Sex was a forbidden thing in those days,' said Nancy Lancaster. 'It was supposed to be perfectly terrible and ladies were not supposed to enjoy sex but mother must have been rather passionate. She was jealous of Father. She was madly in love with him and when he came in late she would say "Where have you been? I know you've been to see so-and-so." And he was a tease. He would just laugh at her. She couldn't fight Father and that annoyed Mother. It was like hitting a sponge bag.'

Extravagance was one way Lizzie kept her spirits up, a high level of spending which would oblige Chillie, from time to time, to bail her out. He had, after all, poured gifts in the direction of his favourite daughter Irene, even paying for the town house on East 73rd Street in New York, designed by Dana's close friend, Stanford White. But Lizzie was permanently in the doghouse about money. Gifts were not appropriate for such a backslider as she. Lizzie's passion was for clothes and hats, which she wore well, and antique furniture for which she had an original eye: Nancy Lancaster later attributed all her talents as a decorator to her mother's taste. When asked why she always went for the most expensive items, she replied, 'Because I'm bound to have them.' The problem was that Lizzie couldn't stop buying, couldn't keep out of the auction rooms. It was a major source of debt. She would explain that she was 'collecting for a house in the country', assuming that this, too, she was bound to have.

In October 1903, as Nanaire was getting out of a victoria outside the entrance to the Lynchburg horse show, where she had come to watch Nancy ride, she had a stroke. By the time she was brought back to a cousin's house where they were staying in the town, she was dead. There had been no warning; no preparation.

Her death, at the age of fifty-five, traumatized her family. Phyllis was to dream of her vividly every night for the next six months. But Nancy, aged twenty-four, was by far the worst affected. At first she wondered whether she had killed her. Nanaire always suffered watching Nancy jump the five-foot-gate fences and would say 'One of these days I shall die.' But it touched Nancy on some deeper psychic nerve, beyond natural grief, as if she had been cut off from Nanaire at a crucial moment in her development and left with an impossible standard. She suffered a depression that made her ill and wretched for months; she felt 'sorrow such as I had never known or imagined. The light went out of my life.' In some ways she never got over it. Fifty years later she still declared that it was 'a shadow' on her heart. The sister with the greatest nerve and independence, with the boldest ability to reinvent her life later on, was the one, as it turned out, most reliant on her mother.

For the next twenty years or so, Nancy would express – only to Phyllis and Irene – this deep, unhealable regret. In 1923, at the age of forty-four, when she had already been an MP for four years, she wrote to Irene: 'Mother Oh how I long to see that woman, mother, mother the one love of my life, no one will know how I miss her, she dwarfed all other love for me.'

Nancy associated Nanaire with a happiness that could never come again. She came to see their mother–daughter relationship as the only ideal of earthly love; invested her with near-divine qualities in her imagination, consigned her to a separate compartment from other mortals. 'I feel if anyone on earth or in heaven was getting near the truth, it's mother,' she wrote, 'mother, with her yearnings and longings & always for something higher.'

When Nancy tried to replace Nanaire and take charge of Mirador, she ran it, according to Angus McDonnell, like Chillie's 'Batalion Sergeant Major'. She tried to garden but she had never done it, and had a 'thorough' (and unVirginian) dislike of it. A housekeeper

Chillie hired to relieve her was ejected by Nancy in a short, furious battle. Irene, who took over Nanaire's peace-making role, was brought down to try to mediate in the crises that Nancy created. Lizzie was angry and hurt that the housekeeping job hadn't been naturally given to her: it would have solved her problems perfectly, and her battles with Nancy became worse than ever. McDonnell noticed that Nancy was always, unlike Mr Langhorne, setting herself tasks beyond her capacity, and seemed to be constantly fighting a 'civil war' within herself, between her generous, gentle side and an ambitious, abrasive super-ego, which would make her 'do and say dreadful things'. She clashed often with her father. She felt 'ill with misery' and depression. She also felt keenly her separation from Phyllis who now inherited the unqual-ified, uncritical love that she had previously reserved for Nanaire. Phyllis was her twin, her *alter ego*, her 'better half' who, in Nancy's eyes, had all the virtues to which she aspired.

Out in Long Island, soon after the birth of her son Peter in 1902, Phyllis was beginning to wonder about her own marriage. The house Reggie had planned to buy at Aiken had never materialized. Instead his parents had rented, but refused to buy them, a large house called Meadowbrook Park at Westbury, Long Island, twenty miles from New York, in a newly developed series of estates for the very rich designed for hunting. It had been a secluded community of Quaker farms, of wooded, rolling hills and meadows, which had been turned into huge self-contained private domains with polo fields, steeplechase courses, race-tracks, tennis courts, golf courses, swimming pools and formal gardens. Phyllis wrote, 'How sane people buy and build here I cannot imagine . . .' She was trying to persuade Reggie to buy a place further down the Island ('as long as I know I can never live in Virginia I get depressed when I think of the rest of my life being spent on this unin-teresting island with motors, jews and dagoes [the Virginian prejudice was not specific to any particular race, but applied generally to all 'immigrants']. Saturdays and Sunday are dreadful here with people dropping in all days. Westbury is just now very busy with polo, racing and so forth, but I am so sick of seeing people that I don't leave this place except to ride. I am sure I shall end my days a recluse, caused by an overdose of people').

Phyllis loved the polo and the riding, and she was still very fond of Reggie. But Reggie didn't like her leaving these otherwise demoralizing surroundings to make her occasional trips to Mirador, even when he was away on his hunting expeditions. Phyllis longed for company, especially that of her sister Nancy. 'I do so hate the idea of Newport,' she wrote to her. 'It will be dreadful this year judging from the people I hear are going there. Do you get blue? I hope not, but I do keep thinking that I might be with you and ain't but you know dear Sis it is where I would rather be than any place in the world.'

Occasionally Phyllis did manage to persuade Reggie to come to Mirador, but he was gone almost immediately. He wrote from Georgia, 'My mind is pretty well busied with Mr. Quail bird . . . I hope the little lady won't get gay in my absence and go to kicking her heels.'

That was prescient of Reggie. Chillie had already suggested that one way out of Nancy's gloom might be to go to England for the hunting season, to mix, under Irene's management, with some of English society. She would go with Phyllis in the winter of 1904–5 and they would take their children. Nancy was eager to get back to England and this was the best way: to have three months' hunting in Leicestershire. In fact, there were no similar options in America for her now. Chillie would stay at home and Nora, having recently lost her mother at the difficult age of fifteen, would do her best to look after him. He would join them for Christmas – his first trip to Europe. It took a long time for Chillie to persuade them to go: Nancy felt at first that she was forsaking her mother's duties; Nora's new role worried the other sisters, who realized that she wasn't up to any ordeal of this sort despite 'a grave talk on her new duties'. 'Now father you know Nora,' Nancy wrote before she sailed. 'You will know her well enough to know a few corrections are pretty necessary.'

6

Nancy and the Astors

To go foxhunting in Leicestershire was a deadly serious business, an activity considered superior to almost any other by the Edwardian upper classes and their graded subordinates. As a social ritual it was more protected and specialized than any other, with its rules and conventions and its stratified world of cliques and sets. It made the Deep Run Hunt of Richmond look like a rabble army by comparison. The area around Market Harborough provided the finest hunting in the world, its best coverts as venerated and talked over as the battlefields of Virginia. This was where the confident were immediately separated from the pretentious or the unsure. To be praised on the hunting field was the highest accolade which also absolved you of any other sin. It forgave idleness, the frequent offenders in marital infidelity, impecuniousness, and even drink. Hunting was often by invitation, by permission of the Master. To be banned, if only on the grounds that it occupied three days of your week, was far worse an exile than a banning from the Royal Enclosure.

Presentation at court was the ambition for most socially minded American women at this moment. But they could have found a surer and quicker way to social ascendancy by cutting a good figure at Market Harborough or Melton Mowbray. The combination of a well-groomed horse and the level of elegance of the clothes that made such demands on your tailor; the perfectly fitting Busvine riding habits, the handmade boots, the chamois leather worn next to the skin against the cold to avoid disfiguring layers of clothing, the tall hat tilted at an angle, the hair bound up in a certain way to show the nape of the neck, the veil that pressed on to the face, the liquid red on the lips – all of this mixed with the high-pressured excitement and the real physical danger on those crisp winter mornings created an atmosphere of erotic possibilities which had the cutting edge over the ballroom. Nancy put it differently, writing to her father after her first season, 'I do want to hunt some next winter – it beats society "all hollow" to be really slangy!'

The 'fast set' as Nancy discovered, were out in numbers – predatory males, women on the make, mixed in with the money, the titles, the ownership of great acres. All were at least agreed – as they still are today – that there was no greater physical thrill than chasing the fox at speed over high fences.

In 1904 Phyllis and Nancy installed themselves first in London, with their children, a nurse and a governess, at Flemings Hotel near Green Park, where the children could play. Nancy rented a small house, a 'hunting box' on the Bowden Road near Market Harborough, hired horses and equipment (in later seasons the two sisters would ship their own horses, linen and equipment across the Atlantic). And then they went out to try their luck in the robust world of Edwardian blood sports.

Phyllis did not stay long; Reggie demanded her return. Reminiscences of that time are all of Nancy. The beautiful Virginian divorcée was the object of fierce scrutiny among the hard riders of Leicestershire, and of fear among the wives. Why had she come so far? It must have been an intimidating ordeal to go out on that first day. She hired the biggest horse she had ever ridden, well over sixteen hands. As it jumped under a branch she fell off and landed in a ditch. The Master asked her 'Can you mount from the ground? Shall I get down and help you?' Nancy turned on him and snapped, 'Do you think I'd be such an ass as to come out hunting if I couldn't mount from the ground?' (In her own initiation later on Nancy Lancaster told me how she would act the helpless American. 'If someone said, "I think your curb chain is loose," I'd say "Does that mean ma braadle's comin' off?"')

Nancy's second recorded exchange was quickly circulated. Waiting together near a wood, Edith Cunard, wife of the industrialist Sir Gordon Cunard, expressed the consensus view, 'I suppose you've come over to England to take one of our husbands away from us.' 'If you knew what difficulty I had getting rid of my first one, you wouldn't say that,' Nancy replied. From that moment Edith Cunard and Nancy became friends and Edith provided Nancy with the protection that she needed.

She had to be careful with the gossipy fast track of the hunting set; she was fiercely concerned with preserving her reputation and her independence. She avoided getting on to Christian name terms with her new acquaintances. She never drank, she didn't play cards; she went to church regularly; she refused offers of horses, keeping to hirelings until Chillie bought her two of her own. She hunted her horses right through the season, 'until they were so tired their tails were dropping off', but, as she boasted proudly, she never once lamed them. According to Victor Cunard, Edith's son, who remembers the stories of her successes, Nancy was particularly scrupulous in observing the complicated conventions of the hunting field. What stood out, he said, apart from the 'painful lash of her ridicule', were her 'shining candour and almost Puritanical respectability', but also her wit; she was becoming a catch to liven up the dinner parties.

'I began to live again,' Nancy recalled, 'I had suitors and to spare, but with wisdom beyond my years I kept them all at bay and I had my own way of doing it.' Part of her defensive shield was her mental agility. Many men were afraid of her. To one rich sporting gentleman, 'not particularly desirable' to Nancy, who had told her that his family never married beneath them, she replied, 'I know they can't but I never knew they realized it.' She always had her maid pick her up from balls and parties, which drove one suitor with a reputation for marriage-breaking to say to her, 'Poor Mrs Shaw. Not much fun, a maid to see you home.' Nancy replied, 'If I had known who I was going to meet, I would have called a policeman.' Another suitor who had been paying her a lot of attention told her, at a ball, that he wanted her to kiss him but he was afraid she might tell his wife. 'I wouldn't tell her,' Nancy replied, 'I would tell the whole hunting field.' She remembered another hunting acquaintance 'who himself looked longingly at the house of Lords' saying to her: 'I think you should realize Mrs Shaw, that it is a very serious matter to refuse a peer.' But in general it was the courtesy that she remembers, the 'correctness' of most Englishmen in their attitude towards women, which she later thought women had sacrificed 'when they cut off their hair and their skirts'.

It was from the peerage that Nancy's 'Apollo', as she thought of him, appeared in late 1904, putting her into a state of flustered adoration that she had never known before and which was never to be repeated. His name was John Baring, Lord Revelstoke, forty-one years old, sixteen years her senior, chairman of his family's merchant bank, Baring Brothers. It would have been possible to fall into some kind of rapture even over the surfaces of Lord Revelstoke's life – the high varnish of his chocolate-brown carriages with their tailored coachmen, an unrivalled sight – or with the elegance of his house at Carlton House Terrace where he was a neighbour of Lord Curzon. Revelstoke had a fantastic, marbled smoothness about him: a spectacular handsomeness, despite his baldness; a long chiselled face; and an expression of pained superiority as if wincing with compassion for the world beneath him – a preciousness that disguised a hot business brain. He had taken over Baring Brothers from his father at the age of thirty-four, when it was on the verge of collapse and brought it back to prosperity in seven years, earning himself a reputation as one of the leading bankers of the country.

It seems that Nancy not only fell deeply in love, she also experienced something quite unfamiliar: a powerful physical attraction. And at first Revelstoke seemed similarly afflicted. 'For a time,' Nancy remembered, 'I was deliriously happy . . . so that when I look back on

those days, the sun always seems to have been shining.' In fact in
Revelstoke she had met the most pompous, evasive kind of
Englishman. Perhaps it was this very remoteness and apparent invul-
nerability which attracted her at first. He was utterly incapable of
expressing his emotions – to Nancy at least – except in a rather clumsy,
wordy, abstract fashion, and yet his vanity meant that he could be easily
wounded, as Nancy was to find out.

Revelstoke had strayed from a particularly rarefied and self-pro-
tecting coterie to court Nancy. Since 1891 he had been having an affair
of an indeterminate and changing sort, but certainly a sexual affair,
with Ettie Grenfell, later Lady Desborough. With her husband Willy
she was a founder of the Souls, a rather precious group whose men
were mostly prominent politicians, the women beautiful and intelligent, a circle considered scintillating for their wit and erudition, their
elaborate games, both intellectual and flirtatious, and what Ettie herself called, without irony, 'an extreme lightness of touch'. Ettie was
certainly clever and she was captivating to men. She was a woman
addicted to adoration, to the need for constant reassurance from her
lovers and admirers. From Taplow Court, her turreted house above the
Thames, she had also established herself as a powerful society hostess.
Revelstoke, despite his affair with Ettie Desborough, as she became in
1905, was not a Soul; he was perhaps too prosaic, even though he was
rich and decorative and his family were cosmopolitan and artistic. He
also had to share Ettie with other admirers and show no jealousy to
spoil the 'Ideal'. Revelstoke had had other flirtations and mistresses
since he met Ettie, but all kept secret in accordance with the rules. The
whole languid ethic, and talk too, of the Souls was unknown to Nancy.
(Revelstoke would write in code to Ettie in the third person, assuming
a female character for himself, expressing, for example '. . . such a
yearning that it may be a very short time before she has the precious
heaven of seeing her dear beloved again.') Nothing could be guessed by
outward appearances. But in Revelstoke, Nancy had picked a classic
romantic masochist, and in Ettie, when she discovered the connection,
a sophisticated rival. 'Mrs Grenfell is John's old love,' Nancy wrote to

Phyllis. 'She's most attractive – very clever & lovely figure but v Affected & talks a deal for effect.'

Beneath the lavishing of attention and gifts, and the droning tone of his letters, Nancy began to detect mixed signals from Revelstoke early on in their romance. He was unable to commit himself; he wouldn't immediately propose to her, which Nancy as always took as a mystifying rejection, even more so now that she had discovered romantic love. She confided in Phyllis, two years later, that she had found herself in a state of 'unrequited passion – the most painful of all ills'.

In fact Revelstoke was infatuated, but he was also scared. At the first sign of his doubts Nancy had gone on the attack. She had lectured him disapprovingly about the profession of banking and how she disliked the boredom of Revelstoke's world – the dinners and ceremonies, the 'Russian loans'. 'You hate them all, I know' he wrote to her. By the early spring the gossip began to reach Nancy. She was 'warned' against Revelstoke and his liaisons and she told him so. There was no shortage of advice from a group of women who were watching the affair closely. Revelstoke reminded her of his 'poor little advice given long long ago not to talk to your so called "women friends", some of whom, believe me, can only be the cause of much & deep unhappiness'.

They began to have difficult telephone conversations – usually the fault of the primitive lines. She accused him of being unpunctual when clearly he was a man of clockwork precision; of being 'sharp and cold'. Revelstoke's response to these attacks at first was passivity to the point of condescension. 'You have been so tolerant and golden and unselfish . . .' Finally, he used the tactic of self-deprecation as he backed away. He was too slow, his preoccupations too 'humble' for someone of Nancy's 'enormous vitality and quickness'. He was thinking only of her happiness.

Ettie Desborough had been away when their romance began and Nancy believed, as she wrote in her brief memoir, that on her return Ettie had 'put doubts in his mind'. But she could never broach the subject directly with Revelstoke, and the gossip built up around them. 'I believe John & I are discussed at every dinner party,' Nancy wrote to

Phyllis, ' — some say he's flirting, others he's jilted & so on! I think he's
as unhappy as I am — I never thought I sh ever fall in love! & I never
want to again & struggling to fall out.'

Nancy claimed later, to protect her pride, that the death blow to
the romance had been Revelstoke's question, 'Do you really think you
would fill the position that would be required of my wife? You would
have to meet Kings and Queens and entertain ambassadors. Do you
think you could do it?' Nancy replied that she was certain she never
could. She took it to mean she was an 'empty headed', unpolished,
country provincial from Virginia and it devastated her, although it also
gave her something concrete on which to focus her anger. She saw it
not only as a rejection of her personality, and confirmation that she was
unmarriageable, but as a cover-up on Revelstoke's part for unchival-
rous, unbeau-like behaviour. Neither of them could establish terms of
disengagement. Nancy wanted to get to the bottom of it, to understand why she had been rejected. Revelstoke went to enormous lengths
to pretend that he was doing it for Nancy's good and that 'fate' would
somehow work it all out.

Nancy wrote to Phyllis from Aldershot Park on 9 June 1905,
'This is a v private letter so please treat it as such! I have been & am still
going through tortures — you can't realise it — I never did before — All
is off between John & me — There are many reasons — which I can't
write I can only explain — but I have decided its best never to see him
again — so please absolutely deny our engagement. It is v awkward for
me as it was copied in the English papers — . . . I can't eat sleep or think
& weep as I am spoken to! A nice state of affairs.'

Nancy then wrote to her father at Mirador, telling him she would
be back home by mid-July. She added, 'John has not "popped" and he
doesn't mean to. That is back history and we never meet unless by
chance which isn't often. He has been v. nice. Our separation was
mutual — so don't think me jilted!' Chillie Langhorne, who had come
over for Christmas, had taken an instant dislike to Lord Revelstoke,
asking her 'Why do you want to marry that old Jew?' ('Jew' for Chillie
meant more or less anyone in the banking business.)

As she was leaving for Liverpool and home another admirer came running down the platform, jumped on to the train and proposed to Nancy. This was Sidney Herbert, the 16th Baron Elphinstone, whose family seat was Carberry Tower, Musselburgh in Scotland. Elphinstone, aged thirty-six, had been wandering around the world shooting tigers until this moment. He was a charming, down-to-earth character, without guile, the opposite of the worldly Revelstoke. He had also promised Nancy houses and hunting and eternal devotion. Nancy found him very good-looking and she didn't discourage him. She thought it necessary to tell Revelstoke of the incident, even though she had banned him writing letters to her.

Nancy had arrived home in a state of emotional confusion and hurt, still casting around for explanations. Revelstoke, beside himself with wounded vanity on account of Elphinstone, defied the ban and wrote to Mirador. Nancy couldn't resist replying with her own obviously highly critical letters of complaint, still trying to force the truth out of him, trying to ease her wounded pride.

Revelstoke wanted above all to save his reputation. His letters were supine, defensive, ponderous with self-justification. He wrote from Aix-les-Bains, where he had fallen ill, in August, 'You silly dear, you have been racking your dear brain for "mysteries" and "dreadful reasons".' He also wrote, 'Do not say again people warned you. It makes me so sad (I'm so sad here, so alone).' The explanation was simple and straightforward. It was only, he said, because of his high opinion of Nancy and what she deserved that he felt 'very diffident'. 'I meant so well . . .' he ended one letter, 'I want you to think well and justly of me more than anything else in the world. What a pathetic failure I have been.'

When Nancy came back to England with her father in December 1905, Elphinstone imagined that they would be married. His was the front-runner of five proposals she received that winter in England, and marriage was now an urgent concern for Nancy. He planned to meet her at Liverpool dock. But his and Revelstoke's dark, almost invisible rival when she arrived was Waldorf Astor, aged twenty-six, quiet, courteous, boyish-looking, Nancy's exact contemporary (to the day of their births) whose father, William Waldorf, head of the American Astor clan, was now settled in England.

Waldorf's frail health had kept him from the hunting field but he knew all about Nancy, and that he would fall in love with her at their first meeting. He had already made up his mind to marry her. His presence on the boat was portrayed as a coincidence, although in those days of competing steamships, the first-class passenger lists were available to any good travel agent. Waldorf had sent a message through a friend, asking to meet her. Nancy, who was seasick, had put him off for some days. Instead, Waldorf talked to Chillie. 'So Waldorf wooed Father,' wrote Nancy. 'He knew what he wanted. A clever man can always find more ways than one of getting what he wants. Waldorf knew all the ways. He was very good looking, and he had immense courtesy and very great charm. He soon had Father eating out of his hand.' But the courtship was so discreet, so confident from Waldorf's side, that for several weeks after their meeting Nancy didn't see him at all.

Wealth was unashamedly high on Nancy's list of demands, and she wrote home to Phyllis that Waldorf was in line to be the 'fourth richest man in the world'. Certainly his father, William Waldorf, was calculated as being the richest man in America. The Astor clan had managed to multiply the original fortune – the largest single American fortune when it was first made by John Jacob Astor in the early 1800s – across three generations. John Jacob had acquired it through the fur business, pioneering trade with China, importing tea and silk, investing the profits in large chunks of New York land and real estate, and dying in 1848 with an estimated fortune of $25 million, calculated as one fifteenth of all the personal wealth in America. Income from rents and property had withstood all the economic downturns; his son and grandsons made wise investments and large accumulations, until there was hardly a section of New York that the Astor estate didn't cover in some way. Running through the male heirs the fortune had been split for the first time only in the third generation, between John Jacob Astor III and his brother William Backhouse Astor, with the lion's

share going to John Jacob who was therefore the richest man in
America. William Waldorf, Waldorf's father, was John Jacob's only son
and had to share his inheritance with nobody.

By 1900 the income from Manhattan rents was $9 million a year
and the Astors were under general attack in their native press for being
unreforming landlords of the worst slum tenements in New York.
Most of the buildings were sub-let, which gave them no protection,
and in 1900 they began to sell the worst of them. But an unAmerican
idleness was also perceived in the business of collecting rents from
rises in Manhattan property values.

The Astors kept a high social profile in the Gilded Age, despite a
marked, endemic shyness and introversion among the males. And as
the commercial eagerness had worn off strains of remoteness, eccen-
tricity, arrogance, even quasi-royal pretensions, had begun to appear in
the fourth generation, offering further copy for a hostile press.

These qualities were marked particularly in William Waldorf
Astor, Waldorf's father, an only child whose 'sinister' and severe
upbringing, isolated from the world, had left him prone, increasingly as
he got older, to severe depressions and crippling shyness. He had taken
refuge in the romantic past, believing himself to have been elevated
mystically through wealth to the status of a Great Man; in his mind he
communed only with his equals, the Borgias, the Medici princes,
Napoleon. In such a spirit he offered himself to run for Congress,
despite his inhibitions, in 1880. He was humiliated by the American
press, an insult for which he never forgave his native land. He left
America for Rome, as American ambassador in 1882, when Waldorf
was three.

He was a highly intelligent man, as well as unstable, and a considerable scholar with a fine eye for art. In Rome he had begun to collect,
with a mania, Holbeins, Murillos, Roman marbles and statuary, as well
as an armoury of antique weapons: cross bows, halberds and medieval
armour. He bought the 200-yard-long terrace of the Villa Borghese,
which he later shipped to England in thousands of numbered pieces. The
world in which Waldorf grew up, with his sister Pauline and his younger

brother John, was filled with governesses, tutors, secretaries, quirky discipline and gloom. His father was unreachable on any known emotional level; his mother Mary was deeply unhappy in her exile, living under the rules of her almost insanely unsociable husband. In the early years in Rome the children had communicated with their father only by writing him letters in French and Italian, which Waldorf spoke fluently (he could also *speak* Latin). More than his other siblings, Waldorf broke the mould of his bizarre upbringing, against heavy odds. At the age of nine, when his parents returned to New York after the ambassadorship, Waldorf was sent to England, to an English prep school with its bleak discomforts and dangers for a foreigner. In that harsh and rigidly conforming society, he must have stuck out – the richest boy on earth.

But, contrary to expectation, Waldorf shone at boarding school. He was popular, athletic, highly intelligent. What had partly saved him, more so than Pauline, who suffered later from her own bouts of depression, was a good nanny and a governess called Madame Fleury, to whom he was devoted. He passed well into Eton where he won extraordinary honours, academic, athletic and social. Certainly no American had ever achieved such success. He carried it all with modesty, conscientiousness and reserve. In 1890 Waldorf's father, back in New York, inherited the effective leadership of the Astor family, and a fortune estimated at $170 million (from which he drew an income of $6 million a year). That year William Waldorf also turned his back on America and came to England, publicly insulting his fellow countrymen for their ignorance and vulgarity, declaring 'America is not a fit place for a gentleman to live.' When it was announced, later, that he had become a naturalized Englishman, a crowd paraded down Broadway with his effigy and a placard which read 'The Traitor'. He saw England as the refuge for a true aristocracy, and set about making himself eligible for its honours, bidding quite openly for a peerage, and for power. In 1892 – looking for political influence – he purchased the evening newspaper, the *Pall Mall Gazette*, turned it from a Liberal into a Conservative paper and employed Harry Cust, writer, poet and Soul as editor; its contributors included Rudyard Kipling, H. G. Wells and Sir

James Barrie. Cust turned it into the leading evening newspaper in the country. William Waldorf began, at the same time, to contribute cautiously to the favourite causes of the Tory party: he bought an artillery battery for $25,000 as one of several contributions to the Boer War.

He bought Cliveden in 1893 when Waldorf was fourteen. Waldorf's mother died the following year, in 1894, triggering his father's decline into permanent melancholy, and leaving Waldorf, Pauline and John effectively parentless. But William Waldorf saw Cliveden as the place where he could finally display the status due to him, despite Queen Victoria's remark when he bought it, 'It is grievous to think of it falling into these hands.' The Restoration baroque house, rebuilt by Charles Barry in 1850, had belonged to the Duke of Sutherland. It looked down from a high, wooded hill on to the Thames at Cliveden Reach – one of the most beautiful stretches of the river – across formal gardens of great elegance. Here, above these gardens, William Waldorf put up his balustrade from the Villa Borghese, with its statues. At the end of the long, wide gravel drive he erected a vast baroque fountain made of Sicilian marble, by the American sculptor Waldo Story, called 'The Fountain of Love', depicting a woman in a giant cockleshell wrestling with Cupid. Cliveden's interior – the mosaic, the dark bronze sculptures, the mahogany, the sarcophagi – acquired the unlit, unventilated grandeur of a corner of Siena cathedral.

Those guests William Waldorf received were subjected to rigid rules and timetables, which he saw merely as the proper conventions. He had a mania for punctuality, which kept his entourage in a permanent state of anxiety.

In 1903, he bought Hever Castle in Kent, which had belonged to Anne Boleyn, filled it with his Holbeins (one of Anne Boleyn and one of Henry VIII) and constructed a Tudor village, where the guests would stay separated from the main house, cut off and imprisoned at night by a moat: William Waldorf suffered from paranoia, especially from fear of physical attack; at Hever he slept with two loaded revolvers beside his bed. His remoteness from the world produced stories of chilling sadness: for the sombre coming-out party for his daughter Pauline, for example, he had written to the Bachelors Club, asking them to submit the names of fifty of their members as eligible guests.

At Oxford, released from all this quirky discipline and gloom, Waldorf succumbed for a brief moment of his life to a period of frivolity. He gave up working hard, fell in with the sporting set whose club was the Bullingdon, drank and rode horses, played polo, became the Master of the drag hounds (he took them home with him to Cliveden for the holidays) and began his lifelong passion for breeding bloodstock. He left with a fourth class degree, angina and incipient tuberculosis. After Oxford he led a life of gentlemanly idleness. He went shooting, he schooled and bred horses, he travelled; he began to plan a career in politics. He displayed qualities that he certainly didn't inherit from his father: intellectual independence, a sense of justice, a desire for public service; liberal, even radical opinions, all within that framework of the assumed responsibility of the ruling class, for which his wealth had prepared him.

His closest female friend in these years, although she was evidently not his lover, was the beautiful, theatrical Princess Marie of Rumania, granddaughter of Queen Victoria. She struck up a friendship with Waldorf and his sister Pauline in 1902 on a rare visit to England. They often visited her in turn in what she described as 'this quiet godforsaken little country of mine', into which she portrayed herself as having been kidnapped by arranged marriage to Crown Prince Ferdinand. She developed a strong, possessive love for Waldorf, one of her few contacts with the outside world. Nevertheless, she had much to do with the broking of the engagement of Waldorf and Nancy.

According to her contemporaries, Nancy was not in love with Waldorf, any more than with Lord Elphinstone (whatever her joyful letters said later in the excitement of the announcements), while Waldorf was beside himself with infatuation for Nancy. 'I sit and think here by the hour but I can't decide . . .' Nancy wrote to Phyllis, '. . . one has one thing I like best & the other has another. As soon as I have selected the unfortunate young man I will wire you! . . . Waldorf

sends flowers fruits vegetables potted food and everything imaginable
and Ld E the same! . . . I feel rather nervous entering the Astor family
after having seen Jack [Astor] as a spouse . . . [Waldorf] . . . seems a boy
and Lord E v quiet and v prim . . . I am longing to make up my mind
chiefly as it wd end much trouble and secondly it wd mean your
coming over to hunt. So prepare yourself to sail.'

Nancy and Waldorf were well suited to each other on paper if
only because they were temperamental opposites. Waldorf had never
met any woman like her, never encountered such audacity and surprise.
He was a man of saintly disposition, but no scintillation, no great joy.
He made little conversation; he had none of Nancy's wit. Nancy sensed
in his single-minded determination a rock-like indestructible force that
could contain her. And beneath this he had independent, highly
unorthodox views for his class and time and high ideals. He wanted to
make up for his father's lack of public spirit; and he took the view that
his millions would not belong to him, but be held in trust for the
improvement of the world about him. The fact that he was partly
American – and not rooted in the English ruling class – gave him an
independence that Nancy valued, and he was to turn out to be surprisingly radical for the Tory Party, to which he attached himself. Marie
of Rumania pleaded Waldorf's case but it was his wealth as well as his
'values' that persuaded Nancy not only that he was the best suited to
her, but also that he would be a good father for Bobbie.

'The gig's up & I am engaged to Waldorf,' she wrote to Phyllis in
early March, '– & better still I am v v happy & I know you will love
him – & he's prepared to adore you.' Nancy then wrote home on 8
March 1906: 'Dearest Father. It's Waldorf & I am v. happy. We are
coming home in July so please paint the dining room, bath rooms and
plant the garden. Please sir. Waldorf's like a lunatic and poor Lord E
desolate.'

Two obstacles remained. Would William Waldorf oppose his son
marrying an American divorcée, instead of making a marriage into his
adopted English upper class? Waldorf travelled to his villa in Sorrento
and met with no objection. When Nancy went to see him she found

him in a lonely pitiable condition. 'He's curious and not really human,' she wrote to her father, 'but I think a just man.' He confided in her his permanent state of depression and told her, 'If you're good enough for Waldorf, you're good enough for me.'

The other problem, about which Nancy cared deeply, was whether a divorcée would be able to marry in a church. She went to see the Bishop of London and despite the extraordinary marriage she was about to make, told him — standing again by her Bible — that if the Church wouldn't sanction it she would call it off and return to America. She explained the circumstances of her divorce and the Bishop gave his permission for a full Anglican service, provided that it was confined to the immediate family and that there should be no publicity.

Nancy and Waldorf went to Paris to celebrate their engagement and stayed at the Ritz from where Waldorf wrote to Phyllis, 'Nancy has spoken to me so much about you ever since we left New York on the same boat in December whereas I've only begun to really interest her during the past week or two . . . I do hope you will approve of her choice. Personally I'm so happy that I find myself smiling inanely at total strangers when alone and completely neglecting even old friends if she's anywhere near.'

The wedding took place on 3 May 1906 at All Souls' Church, Langham Place, in great secrecy. Even the close members of the two families hadn't been told the date until the last moment. 'The Astor diamonds are wonderful,' Nancy wrote home to her father. They included the great Sancy diamond, shaped like a pear and weighing fifty-five carats, which had arrived in Nancy's possession by way of Elizabeth I of England, James II and Louis XIV (it is now in the Louvre). It was an exhilarating foundation piece for Nancy's passionate and neverending acquisition of precious stones.

They left for their honeymoon in Cortina, in the Swiss Tyrol, both of them in delicate shape. They planned to go to Islesboro to visit Irene before descending on Mirador. Nancy wrote to her father, 'Please don't let Lizzie stop in my room. She threatened to stop in the

house but you know what that means – !' She added '. . . Bobbie is
delighted with Waldorf & it will be nice for us having a home, if a "po'
white" like me could call such an enormous place home.' William
Waldorf had given them Cliveden as a wedding present and there in
September 1906 Nancy's career as Mrs Astor began.

7

Nancy the Good

It was a fantastic inheritance, and at first overwhelming for Nancy and Waldorf. Nancy wrote to Phyllis on their return from America, 'My heart sinks at the thought of Cliveden and the strangeness of an English home everything so utterly different and children so young . . .' They were both only twenty-seven years old when they moved there, with Bobbie, aged eight. 'Here we are with no servants,' Nancy wrote to her father that autumn, 'They all went with Mr Astor except the butler who went mad!' Waldorf, suffering from angina attacks, was ordered to go as often as possible to the German spas at Baden and Marienbad or to the brisk cures at Folkestone. At one point, in the first year of their marriage, they were forced to sleep outside on the freezing balcony of a hotel in Scotland to prevent Waldorf's incipient tuberculosis. Not only did Nancy not object, she adopted ice-cold rooms, cold morning baths, swimming in the winter sea for the rest of her life. Nancy fretted about Waldorf in her letters to Phyllis and feared the separations that the medical journeys would entail.

Cliveden couldn't be abandoned in the early stages of their marriage. They had moved into the same spiritless and gloomy décor that had provided the background to Waldorf's childhood – the German armour, the mosaic floors, the ancient leather chairs. Waldorf's father had left them everything as a wedding present, including his art collection, and retreated to his fortress at Hever Castle, promising never to return.

Perhaps from shock at her sudden transformation Nancy, too, was mysteriously prostrated with ill-health. She spent most of the day, and often a whole week, in bed sick with unnamed neuralgias, condemned to the prescriptions and diagnoses of the period, including over-eating for 'underfed nerves'. Nancy suffered partly from chronic colitis (inflammation of the colon), a disease associated with stress and no easier to cure now than in 1906, and from other internal disorders, including 'organs out of place', to which the pulling in of waists to eighteen or twenty inches for many years had certainly contributed. But there were clear signs of psychological pressure, too. Her diaries of the period record paralysing exhaustion and also 'fear'. Most days she was only able to get up briefly for lunch: 'I am dog ill, so tired and frightened. Not able to move a hand or foot and it's my birthday. Twice I've tried to dress and twice failed. I am too weak.' She added prophetically, 'Don't put "rest" on my tombstone – when I die I hope to have a busy life and cease this eternal resting.'

Even so her letters describe a high level of activity when she was on her feet; the application of sheer will and effort to dominate her surroundings. They express excitement at her new possessions and at the work to be done. It was as if the Astors had wandered into a disused Camelot with an inexhaustible budget and an army of servants to engage in the venture of making it hum and glow again.

Such was the high organization and availability of domestic service at the time that in fact it took only two weeks to replenish the household and outside staff of over a hundred employees. Apart from the butler, groom of the chambers and three footmen there was also a valet, four people in the kitchen, including a chef, two in the stillroom, six housemaids, six laundry maids, Nancy's lady's maid, an 'odd-man', a house carpenter and an electrician. They hired one of the great gardeners of his time, Mr Camm, who worked with between forty and fifty men tending the 375 acres. There was also a coachman, a chauffeur, and twelve stable hands. A photograph of one of the early staff banquets in 1910 shows them crowding the indoor tennis court, shoulder to shoulder at trestle tables, the numbers – with wives, farm and estate workers – swelling to at least 300 people.

'Bobbie is the only person really settled,' Nancy reported to her father in November. 'He rides daily and milks his cow & has the coachman's daughter to play with. He has begun his weekly letter to you – He is so happy & says he thinks you will love Cliveden.'

The main building works were postponed until the following Easter of 1907. In the meantime they invited Chillie, Phyllis, Reggie, and Nora – a constant source of worry – for Christmas 1906. Nancy had written to Phyllis, 'Well your letter from home brought the picture up. Lizzie rocking, poor, poor Harry growing feebler, [Harry was dying and still drinking] Father economising & Nora. Nora! Oh Phyl that girl keeps me awake at night.' At the age of nineteen, Nora's now elaborate mythomania and her extraordinary ability to seek out and attract partners was causing alarm. It seemed only a matter of time before she caused some catastrophe and disgrace to the Langhornes. Nancy had not married Waldorf and crossed the Atlantic to lose control of her sisters. She was intensifying and consolidating her new pre-eminence from the aptly named Cliveden Reach. The power of the purse, the tongue and the letter were already taking effect. Nancy was still giving Chillie instructions for running Mirador, reminding him to re-paint the kitchen before her next visit. 'Now please Sir! Be a man and live up to your word.'

The Astors moved 120 workmen into the house in March, attempting through weight of numbers to complete the entire redecorating programme in two months, while they stayed at the Ritz in London, where John Singer Sargent began a portrait of Nancy. In April 1907, when they moved back to Cliveden, the work almost completed, Nancy was five months' pregnant. She wrote to Phyllis, almost every day, letters of intimacy and regret, in language she would never use with any other correspondent, sister, husband or admiring male, sharing the secrets of her boudoir. No one would ever be as close to her

as Phyllis. Only her sister ever knew of Nancy's uncertainty and distress
in the early years of her second marriage. In these early letters from
Cliveden the crowded illegible pages contain a mixture of elation at her
surroundings and acute homesickness for her sister. 'The woods are
like fairyland . . . Camm has small apple trees decorating the house and
strawberries twice a day v delicious ones. Oh Phyl if you could only be
here. Not one hour of the day passes that I don't think of you and long
for you and it's a cruel fate that keeps us 3000 miles apart.'

The most striking pictures of Nancy taken at this time show her
leaning back on pillows with a large bowl of roses at the foot of the
bed, violets and lilies of the valley in vases, a box of watercolours in her
hand. Despite her illness the expression is clear, sharp, strikingly beautiful. She described her complexion nevertheless as 'yellow as a
Chinese'. 'Sargent says I look like Ophelia,' she wrote to Phyllis, 'in
other words bats!!' The letters to Phyllis ('All my time is spent writing
to you . . .') were often impulsive streams of consciousness that darted
between topics and fragments, giving her writing an immediate, restless style. 'The river is delicious in a punt on weekdays – hardly a soul
on it. It is blowing a gale but I don't mind anything but the heat . . . [an
indication of Nancy's advancing pregnancy] How soon will you want
the grey gown like mine? . . . Nora wears dresses to her knees – I hope
you will put a stop to that – I dread to hear. Darling Phyl, write in
detail, write me everything, every thought, joy, sorrow etc. If only I cd
be much more "showy" in my love and affection, if only I didn't love
you so much.'

Nancy had chosen the room with the best light for her bedroom,
on the first floor with a large balcony extending along the east side of
the house. Its view was perhaps unsurpassed by any other English country house. It looked down on to the great arcaded upper terrace, below
that to the stone and red-brick balustrade taken from the Villa
Borghese, and across the parterre further below to three and a half
acres of formal garden and lawn with its French beds cut in geometri-
cal shapes, bordered with box, filled with senecio and santolina.
Beyond that the Cliveden beech woods dropped sharply down to the

Thames and stretched a mile along the river from Cookham to Taplow, hanging low over the water and obscuring the banks in summer like the upper reaches of the Hudson, or a domesticated Amazon. The Cliveden woods still give the garden its exceptional beauty, despite the ravages of hurricanes. From the parterre an arc of the river is just visible over the tops of the trees, far below the house, like Coleridge's sacred river, bordered, on the opposite bank, by a line of Lombardy poplars. The writer Freya Stark wrote to Stuart Perowne on a visit forty years later, 'This is the [drawing] room with the view you love, a still summer day, a little haze lying on the river, the trees as if cast in metal so warm and still. The most peaceful view in England.' Looking up from the river on Cliveden Reach, the house sits high on the skyline, square and grand. 'Solitude, precipice and prospect,' is how John Evelyn described the site of Cliveden in 1679.

For all his *folie de grandeur*, it was William Waldorf who had completed this masterpiece. He took his scholarship seriously. He had distributed the mixture of English Palladian and Roman cinquecento styles that gave the house its particular distinction — with some Renaissance added — around the 450 acres of garden and woodland with classical statues and fountains, temples and pavilions, stone vases and urns. He had cut out rides and walks and mown clearings with plantations of ilex and evergreen, often with only a shade of distinction between the wild and cultivated areas. He had made water gardens and rose gardens and put up a pagoda bought from the Château de Bagatelle. From the front, the house looked past twenty-foot-high yew hedges with Roman sarcophagi at their foot, down a wide avenue of gravel bordered by lime trees planted in the eighteenth century, towards the massive marble fountain. From there the drive turned off and weaved through valleys and high banks of rhododendrons towards the iron gates on the public road.

Despite her illness and pregnancy Nancy took control of the decoration inside the house, tearing up mosaics and replacing them with wood, removing stone urns, installing French furniture and comfortable sofas. Mr Astor's sepulchral entrance hall of dark carved oak with

its high sixteenth-century stone fireplace became the centre of entertainment and Nancy put a huge red sofa, large enough for someone to
lie flat in its depth, in front of the fire. She enlarged bedrooms,
installed bathrooms, built bookcases, put in chintz curtains and covers.
She did up the spectacular dining room with its Louis XV rococo *bois-
eries* and painted-over doors, taken, yet again, wholesale from the
Château d'Asnieres in Paris. And she filled the house with cut flowers
mixed together in large bowls in the Virginian style – an innovation
which quickly caught on in England, a prototype of the look of 'organised chaos', Virginian in origin, with which her niece Nancy Lancaster
was to make herself famous as a decorator in England.

The sheer scale of the production began to intimidate Nancy.
She couldn't get control of it, and this seemed to worsen her health.
She began to dread Waldorf's departure to Marienbad: 'I don't know
what I shall do without him. I shall be helpless here with a butler
groom of the chambers & 3 footmen all to manage!'

The English servants were specialists; the etiquette of the servants' hall, its social distinctions were far stricter and more rigid than
those on Nancy's side of the green baize door. The housekeeper, Mrs
Addison, who arrived around this time, was a celebrated figure in this
grand underworld, and would stay on for forty years, loyally resisting
attempts by rival houses – including the King's Household at
Windsor – to poach her. But at first Nancy couldn't understand the
exact functions of the staff, or decipher in which part of the house
some of them slept. The running mechanics were mysterious and subterranean: along the length of the basement was a railway track on
which vehicles resembling coal hods shuttled laundry and provisions.
Coal, a hundred tons a year of which was burned, was carried up and
down stairs, along great distances, by hand in frequent relays. Nancy
wrote to Phyllis of her astonishment that during one of her first weekends of hospitality sixteen breakfast trays had been carried upstairs for
the guests each morning. These came from the still room, a long journey up one storey from the west wing to the east wing where most of
the guest bedrooms were. For Ascot that year, despite her health, she

had twenty-eight guests. This meant that each of the six housemaids, who started work at 5 a.m. would have made around fifteen trips along these stairs and passageways by breakfast time. It was hard physical work, and the house was run with military precision.

Proximity to Nancy required special skills from a husband, and with Waldorf she was constantly astonished at her luck. Waldorf was 'a wonder as a man for all men are trying,' she told Phyllis. She saw him as a rare exception, an 'angelic' mutation of the gender. 'He's a man in 10,000,' she wrote, 'but he's got stone walls & I keep knocking into them & they bruise – still perhaps that's my fault – & I sh. just be on the look out for cracks & crevices – but some how am not built on the harem pattern. Every woman [should] be to make a perfect wife.'

There were several early battles in which she tested him – all reported back to Phyllis. Nancy was indignant that, after the birth of their first child, Waldorf had insisted on 'that lunatic Princess' Marie of Rumania, Waldorf's old friend – whose letters to Waldorf Nancy had already put a stop to – becoming the child's godmother. Nancy had made her own list; Waldorf held his ground. 'I hate it but I gave in to Waldorf,' she wrote, adding 'I hear her hair is v. yellow these days and her cheeks v pink.' But Waldorf had to get the measure of Nancy's starkly elemental nature in which reason and logic – Waldorf's cherished guiding principles – played no part. 'I've long ago contented myself with having little mind and no intelligence & find I am happier,' Nancy wrote to Phyllis. Restless, intuitive, relying on instinct, impatient with argument, Nancy expressed genuine disbelief when she was opposed. Resistance was an act of hostility or at least disloyalty. Waldorf's technique was never to engage Nancy head-on, except where his clear will was involved. 'It was like watching an animal trainer with a rather dangerous animal,' was how one of their friends saw it. 'How lucky I am,' Nancy wrote in her diary, 'Vice has no allurements for me. My greatest battle is with my tongue. It's far too sharp and inaccurate.' But it was a battle that she never really joined. In her moments of verbal shoot-to-kill, Waldorf, who considered arguing – as opposed to argument – bad taste, would nod his head rhythmically and gravely, the stone wall. 'I am always hateful to anyone except you and Bobbie,' Nancy once wrote to Phyllis.

It had been clear to Phyllis that Nancy was not in love with Waldorf when they were first engaged. Nancy didn't know what her feelings were, beyond a growing sense of safety from which her affections followed. 'Oh Wal how am I to get on without you?' she wrote in September 1907, when he had gone on a cure, 'Will you miss me? Please do . . . I can't write anything except I <u>ache</u> to be with you . . . You must <u>cherish</u> me and be v. tender as I feel I deserve that & emeralds & two yards of pearls and [unreadable] checks.' But Waldorf would never achieve the status of 'soul's companion' – the closeness reserved for Phyllis and, in a different way, for Bobbie. Nancy's letters to Phyllis often gave away her fixed order of affections. 'I think if anything happened to you, Bobbie or my family I should feel inclined to jump off the house top.'

Phyllis felt that Waldorf's austerity needed to be 'warmed up and cuddled a bit'. But Nancy found this difficult if not impossible. Her solution to the unpleasantness of sex was to 'eat an apple', she once confided to a niece. Nevertheless Waldorf was clearly not shy in pressing his attentions on his sexually unallured wife. 'One needs much prayer in matrimony,' Nancy wrote to her sister. 'I admire Waldorf's will but I feel I sh like to be able to resist sometimes BUT I won't,' and in another letter, 'I can't get used to sharing my bed with anyone and someday I shall be firm about that.' Waldorf, she said, was 'more jealous than Othello and with less cause'. At one society ball that spring, to meet the Prince and Princess of Wales, she had been asked to dance by one of his party but caught Waldorf's 'enraged eye' and had refused. Nancy in turn worried about Waldorf's attractiveness to other women, 'I hear St. Moritz is a v. dangerous place for husbands and I am feeling slightly nervous about Waldorf as he is looking verra handsome just now. In fact I think I am asking for trouble – but what can I do?'

Only to Phyllis could Nancy get down to the material details of Waldorf's astonishing generosity. He immediately gave her complete and uncritical access to his fortune, having declared that the great advantage of his wealth was that he never had to think about money. But Nancy thought about it constantly (and was confident enough very early on in their marriage, she admitted later, to charge jewellery to their hotel bill at St Moritz without asking him). It gave her great pleasure to have this unlimited wealth, but it never calmed her old fears about running out of money. Perhaps she realized that her appropriation of the Astor purse strings was an illusion of the financial independence she had always wanted. She was dependent on Waldorf remaining the perfect husband. Her famed generosity all her life, however commendable in spirit, or uncommendably to do with exercising power, was first and foremost Waldorf's generosity, not her own.

It was somehow classic in a situation like this, where the good fairy had suddenly opened a bottomless handbag, that in the first year or so Nancy portrayed Waldorf and herself as comparatively penniless young marrieds. Waldorf's money from his father had not come through and he was living on credit. Nancy consequently described him to Chillie as a 'pauper' when she asked him to pay their bills at Islesboro on their honeymoon. 'Waldorf is busted,' she wrote to Phyllis in November 1907. Waldorf had been given $100,000 for his birthday (a huge sum) from his father but this apparently didn't help their liquidity problems. It had to be put aside to buy a farm. Cliveden would be a model community, surrounded with progressive experiments, and indeed White Place Farm, set up by Waldorf, was to become an early model of ecological agriculture.

Nancy entered into the spirit of early-married thrift. 'Waldorf tempted me with a string of pearls for my party in August but I refused as he has no money to pay for them and as I'd rather have an Alms House for the aged of Cliveden.' When William Waldorf gave her £1,000 she declared that she would give this, too, to charity, but later relented, 'I am almost sorry I promised Mr. Astor's cheque away,' and finally bought Irene some dark sable furs for $400, 'as I am v. rich with Mr. Astor's cheque.'

There were two non-competing sides to Nancy's character:

'Nancy the Good' as she once signed a letter to Phyllis, who wanted to be a saint, who felt 'luxuries leave me cold', lived alongside Nancy the shopper, the lover and hoarder of jewellery, the wearer of fashionable clothes bought in large quantities. In 1915, when Waldorf was talking of selling Cliveden to put his fortune into the war effort, she told Irene, 'It has been a joy being rich and acting so but I fear them days are over.'

The contradictions appear together, strikingly, in a letter to Phyllis in 1908. She wrote 'I am getting a tea gown from Worth that will do me for a year. I am very economical and can't spend money on clothes, never could and don't think I ever will.' She then wrote a shopping list – Phyllis was going to Paris to visit the Gibsons: 3 pairs of bedroom slippers, 1 pink, 1 blue and one leather tan with blue trimmings; 2 blouses of chiffon or lace; 2 tea gowns 'if you see pretty models there for T not dinner'; bed jackets, dressing gowns 'with petticoat to match, so that on occasion I could wear it to breakfast'; 'alluring' country hats; a cloak, a cape, 'anything alluring for the neck'. She ended 'No more to get!' Her letters are full of fashion advice to her sister. 'Another thing is please confine yrself to soft white evening dresses & never wear those harsh colours – they make you look like a mangy old gypsy.' She was to amass, in her life, a vast collection of jewellery, 'an Ali Baba horde' as one of her sons described it, and to give much away.

Clearly Waldorf at one point did have some version of a liquidity problem. Or more likely the fact of borrowing even small amounts was so completely strange, it may have even felt somewhat immoral. There were tussles about money, mysterious transactions. 'You wd laugh if you cd hear Waldorf trying to make me pay for his birthday present to me!' Nancy wrote. 'Never lend money. Lent Waldorf $1000 and now it's like a present from him if he ever returns it. It's such a mistake.'

Nancy's real heartache, though, was her longing for Phyllis. She could never get over or accept separation from her sister. Not only did she love her intensely and possessively, she also worshipped her, often using the terms of romantic infatuation to express her feelings. The letters she wrote to Phyllis after her visits alternate in tone between that of a child abandoned at school and a lover suffering an enforced separation. In their lack of inhibition the letters reveal a passion that only Phyllis could awaken in Nancy. 'Not another thing have I got to say except my eternal longing for you,' she wrote, '. . . If you were here all would be well – I love you. More every day!' She thought of Phyllis, she said, 'every second'; wished for her 'soul companion' whenever she saw anything beautiful. Nora observed them together one day at Cliveden and wrote to their father: 'Waldorf has gone to Kingsclere to look at his horses and Nannie and Phyllis are having their dinner together downstairs. They are like lovers.'

It was a form of narcissistic love on Nancy's part – a reflection and embodiment of herself. She insisted that she and Phyllis were indivisible, their lives interchangeable and that their love excluded all others. Feeling lonely on Long Island Phyllis once wrote that she was jealous of Nancy's English friends. 'Never be jealous of anyone,' Nancy replied '. . . you are part of me and one can't be jealous of oneself! You stand alone in my affections. I can only say that I love you like mother, father, child, husband all in one and every night I thank God for having given me such a perfectly understanding sister.' With everyone except Phyllis – and Bobbie – Nancy's capacity for love went no deeper than a form of possession, a desire to come officially first in the affections of those close to her. And she would attempt to hold on to this position by various degrees of force.

Phyllis found Nancy's company 'one of the greatest joys of my life', but with Phyllis love and affection were also a vital emotional necessity. Nor did Phyllis share Nancy's downgrading view of men: that they could never be the source of happiness, that they were 'sad bringers or givers of pleasure'; that 'Men are such babies.' Hearing of romance between two people made Nancy feel 'tired'. 'To be free of one's evil passions is well worth fighting for,' she wrote, 'God has been kind to you and me & I feel we don't have many struggles in that line.' Apart from her lack of interest in it, Nancy wanted to banish sex because its domain was beyond her control. But Phyllis did not share that aversion of Nancy's. She still held out for the principle of romance and she had no shortage of admirers on the English hunting field where Reggie now refused to accompany her.

Their marriage was in trouble and this preoccupied Nancy – how to make Phyllis independent from a difficult husband, which meant of course financial independence, the old predicament. Nancy had always disliked Reggie, his idleness, and most of all the fact that he had married Phyllis. Reggie was made aware of this when he, reluctantly, accompanied Phyllis and five-year-old Peter to England for Christmas in 1906.

It had not been part of Reggie's vision of his marriage that Phyllis would need these life-giving weeks and then months in England – for hunting and communion with Nancy. Yankee women and Virginians got on well in England, but not, on the whole Yankee men, especially those like Reggie whose life was circumscribed by Newport ritual. Reggie's adoring attitude had changed soon after Phyllis's first trip to England in late 1904 when she turned the tables on his frequent absences. His forlorn letters reveal his dependence on her as soon as they were separated. But he changed into a tiresome partner as soon as they were together again, punishing her for her absences, demanding attention. He stubbornly refused to visit Mirador, let alone live there. And still the Brookses wouldn't buy the couple a house.

Over two years later, by 1906, Phyllis's true sportsman and gentleman, the doting, fun-loving Reggie, had turned into a coarsened, hard-drinking version of that same eternal boy, haunted now by boredom and idleness, plagued with a terrible restlessness, which could only be momentarily dampened down by whacking balls – and drinking whisky. Hunting had palled, and so had shooting. His complexion reddened and deepened. He spent, Phyllis noticed, many hours and many gallons of water on his morning and evening ablutions. In England he sulked, refused to act as Phyllis's hanger on, chucked invitations, went off alone. Nancy was 'ashamed' and 'embarrassed' by his behaviour and his endless complaints.

Nancy wrote to her father 'Don't let him fool you about his affection for Phyllis. He loves her when it suits him and not otherwise. I truly confess I have never known a more deceitful man, not even my late lamented.' Phyllis had by no means written off her marriage, despite Reggie's neglect and his heavy drinking. But Nancy monitored it with vengeful attention. She believed that Reggie could be brought round by force or sanctions but also that the marriage would have to continue. Adultery was the only grounds for divorce in Nancy's view.

Phyllis had taken a box at Oakham for the New Year's hunting in 1907 and stayed on in England, with Reggie and Peter, until April. They had been away from home for four months, which did seem reasonable grounds for complaint on Reggie's part, since he was so obviously miserable. Phyllis was not only restoring herself against the dread of a Newport summer, but she was also gradually attaching herself to Nancy's English life, as if she felt she had been left behind in the migration. When she finally went home, Nancy wrote, in one of her many departure letters, 'Dearest Phyl, Never was a lonelier creature left than one Nancy Astor when the motor whirled you away . . . If I felt you were happy I sh not mind you going to Arabia! But I think I know as no-one else in the world what your feelings are.' What was to be done about Reggie? 'Remember this,' Nancy offered, ' — it just happens that I have married one of the few men on earth who can & will always see that you are provided for . . .' She wanted Phyllis to be able to tell the Brooks family that she was no longer dependent on them — a start to Phyllis running her own life and living where she wanted to. 'If Waldorf had been a monster I sh. have willingly married him to help you,' wrote Nancy ' — so [he] being an angelic soul I feel doubly blessed.' This was built into the theme of sisterly love — the idea that Nancy had married Waldorf as much for Phyllis's benefit as her own. Weren't the sisters interchangeable? 'If only you had married Waldorf & I Reggie,' Nancy wrote, 'I love you so that honestly I think I wd. change.'

Phyllis had already created a mystique around herself in England. She was the dark sister, the soulful one, melancholy and reserved but still Langhorne-like in her ability to connect, her ease of manner. The fascination Phyllis had for men is elusive but its effect was almost universal. 'She had a quietness about her that none of the other sisters had, and Phyllis had heart,' said her niece Nancy Lancaster. 'She was a good listener. She could put herself in your place, rather than getting you to be an audience, like Nancy. Phyllis had real charm. The others had magnetism, but charm is a curious thing. People loved Phyllis, they really loved her.'

Between 1907 and 1908 John Singer Sargent drew Nancy, Phyllis and Nora: Nancy with piercing, alert eyes, Nora with wild, loose curls, looking vague. A mark of Sargent's talent was his ability to reveal his subject's character, especially the women, by painting them as they wished to appear to the world and to society. The portrait of Phyllis is not one of his best – it has a tightness and pertness about it that makes her look pleadingly sweet. But the mouth slightly curled at the corner, hinting at a smile, the long neck, the delicate clothes, give her the look of a fresh, classic beauty, at ease with herself. The melancholy is in the liquid rim of the eyes, the weight on the lids – a subtle touch of charcoal drawing. It is a portrait of the period, resembling those other Sargent sitters of the time, described by the Boston art critic Trevor Fairbrother as the 'intelligent, lovely, compassionate yet sad women that appear in Henry James's fiction'.

Nancy had promoted, and also partly created, the Phyllis mystique. That her sister was wonderful was set in stone for all to believe. And Nancy didn't discourage the admirers who were circling around her sister, even though she was against a divorce. It was public knowledge that Phyllis's six-year-old marriage was faltering. Nancy openly wrote the gossip to Phyllis. The drunken Lawrence McCreery, an old and doomed admirer of Nancy, kept her informed. One suitor was Reggie Wyndham, brother of Lord Leconfield. 'McCreery,' Nancy reported, 'says Reggie W is waiting for your Reggie to clear out, but that if he did the field would not be a narrow one.' Another was Geoffrey Robinson (later Dawson), future editor of *The Times*. Nancy knew all Phyllis's secrets, including the biggest of all. She first referred to it in November 1907: 'I saw your young man of Oakham. I forget his name. Capt? He asked tenderly after you.'

In the spring of 1907, when Phyllis returned to what she called 'the flat plains of Long Island', a depression came over her, a loneliness that made her feel that her soul was 'disintegrating'. She found it 'an ugly country' at the best of times. Reggie's coldness and antagonism towards her when they returned, had transformed it into a place of enforced exile. 'I can scarcely look out of the window I dislike the country so & also I simply cannot bear any tender demonstrations from Reggie! and his smell! Ugh! It's a clean smell but I prefer a dirty one now, I think I'm a little nutty really . . . I must say I can't help having depressed moments when I realise how thin the foundation of our future matrimonial life is. R seems perfectly oblivious to the fact that there has got to be something besides idle amusement all the time.' She talked only of the companionship of Peter, now aged five. She had come to dread the world of the Meadowbrook Club – which had dazzled her at first – and now despised the 'ultra rich vulgar of Newport' and the 'smugness of the Bostonians'.

Trying to steady her sister, Nancy reminded Phyllis not to forget how it might have been: 'Some times I am overcome by our luck in not having been born into the gypsy class or having drunken husbands & 8 children to support.' But when the warm weather came and the season at Newport began Reggie's mood momentarily improved as his friends reassembled. Phyllis longed for any sign of affection, for a change from the cold attrition. The result was that in July she was pregnant with her second child, Jackie, after a gap of seven years. But little, in fact, could please Reggie and certainly not this.

In August Nancy wrote a jittery letter to Phyllis while she waited for the birth of William Waldorf Jr, or more likely, she thought, her death. She described her moral confusion with comic brevity, 'I am too good for this world, so I am filled with the fear of death. In fact I feel death must be near, as I have more than I deserve.' She added that Phyllis should not stop Waldorf marrying again. Phyllis, if released, was the obvious choice for his next wife as 'I strangely mistrust his judgement in females. I feel that I was an accident.' Her real dread of death was separation from Bobbie, now a physical component of her anatomy. In her black and white judgements she had cast his father Robert Gould Shaw, the polo player from Boston, now remarried, as the earthly incarnation of the devil. 'To think he [Bobbie] shd ever have to see his Pa fills my soul with anguish . . . Oh Phyl if I die keep Bobbie from them. Move Heaven and Earth. It's my last will and testament. Don't bother about the baby but look after Bobbie. I can't provide for what I ain't seen.'

Let out of a nursing home only a few days earlier looking 'yellow and bilious' Nancy was pulled through the birth at Cliveden, with 'Dakin and Moore', the doctors in attendance, and with much chloroform. Fifty-six telegrams were written. A child with no chin or hair, a red and peeling face, was announced, his health drunk at a dinner for 200 servants and tenants. There were fireworks, a brass band, and a cricket match to keep Bobbie occupied. Too young to recognize his future role as the cuckoo in the nest, Bobbie was, according to Waldorf, 'clean off his head with excitement', regretting only 'that he didn't have an extra pair of flannel trousers to lend his brother to play against the Hedsor choir boys'.

Nancy made it clear to Phyllis, five days after his birth that Bill, as the infant William Waldorf Jr was to be known, had already been consigned to second ranking, as an 'Astor', after her beloved Bobbie. 'He's not so nice as Bobbie was,' she wrote, a conviction she was to hold, tragically for Bill, forever. Nor would he 'grow up as handsome'. Bobbie was 'beautiful' and 'really so much nicer than anyone except Pete'. She knew Phyllis was pregnant with her second child, due in March the following year, and imagined she would feel the same way about Peter when it arrived. 'We can never love any children like one's [sic] first borns, can we?' she wrote.

Nancy's diaries show how, over these years, she had clung to Bobbie. He was a companion of her heart, her ally all through the misery of her divorce years and she had suffocated him with adoration. 'I tell you truthfully, Father,' she wrote to Chillie, 'I am never happy with Bobbie away from me. He is like part of me.' It was clear from her letters that no new Astor child would ever come between them. Bobbie was taught to call Waldorf 'Papa' to help the process of forgetting his real father, and Nancy watched fearfully for any signs of instability in his character that he might have inherited from Bob Shaw, now relegated to the status of a monster. 'I wake up with a shiver when I think Bobbie is a Shaw and Bob's his father! Yet shuddering won't help. Nothing helps but to keep one's pecker up and look on one's blessings, above all to thank God that we aren't bedridden with dirty sheets.' (Many years later Bobbie went to the Ritz in London to meet his father for, as far as he was concerned, the first time. He found a small mild-mannered man sitting in the lobby. Bobbie said that he understood only then why he had needed chloroform to exercise his marital rights.)

Soon after Bill's birth Nancy had to send Bobbie to boarding school, aged nine, when he was quite unprepared to cope with such a sudden separation from his dependent mother. Nancy, for example, was writing in her diary one year later, when Bobbie was ten years old, 'B sleeps with me & is the greatest joy.' And predictably the banishment changed Bobbie – that unmistakable shift in the relationship when a child comes home after the first term. His school report showed lack of concentration, 'wool gathering' and the fact that he was bottom of his class. He had developed 'an insolent streak' and was trying his mother's patience; he was 'v. sassy and bad mannered of late disputing everything and really tiresome'. Nancy's response to this was an attack of conscience at the trouble she felt she must have caused Nanaire, 'I wd give anything on earth if only I had been good, for I see now how one's children can make one suffer.'

8

Conquering Society

Nora's two years as Chillie's housekeeper at Mirador since Nancy's departure had been a disaster. She complained that the task had 'nearly killed' her. The 'necessary corrections' that Nancy had urged Chillie to apply to Nora had been overlooked and she was merely developing all the faults of which she had always been accused. Depressed by the loss of the family and the cramping of old age, Chillie had become dotingly fond of Nora, yet fed up with her too. He had indulged her and defended her against her sisters. 'Don't you all be too hard on Nora,' he wrote to Nancy, 'She can't help the way she's built.' Nora, in turn, had closely attached herself to Chillie and had succumbed to late-adolescent father-worship.

By 1907, when Nora was eighteen, it was clear to Nancy and Phyllis that the only way to take her off Chillie's hands and to contain her was to find her a husband in England, however unprepared Nora might be for matrimony. The old Virginian and Langhorne imperative to make a good marriage was now applied to Nora. And it was better someone you could have a hand in choosing, as Nancy and Phyllis vainly thought, than someone to whom Nora got engaged after one conversation. A long and cynical campaign now began, given Nancy and Phyllis's experiences of their first marriages, to marry off the 'undeveloped' Nora. First she had to be introduced to the 'right sort of society', as Nancy put it to Chillie, trying to persuade him to give her up and face his loneliness.

'Settling on Nora's career' was a long-established variation on the truth game of the sisters' childhood, and one that caused particular turbulence. Writing to Phyllis, Nancy remembered, 'Your nerves could stand [playing] it with me but not alone . . .' But at the beginning of 1907 Nora began to take her career into her own hands. On her first visit to England at Christmas and Paris in the New Year of 1907 Nora, despite a chaperone, had left behind a trail of misbehaviour which Nancy was continuing to discover long after her departure. In order to catch up with her sisters she had blurred the difference between 'proposal' and 'engagement' and without a word to her family had apparently agreed to marry a man she had met on the trip over to England called Oliver Valpy. It was a mystery exactly where and how she had met him and no one would have known about it if Valpy himself hadn't crossed the Atlantic and turned up to claim his fiancée at Mirador. Valpy found the house empty and returned to England, determined to claim his bride-to-be.

Nancy set about removing him from Nora's life. She reported to Phyllis: 'Mr. Valpy – Nora will have to be called Mrs Vapid!! – came and I had the painful duty of telling him Father would like to shoot him and he had no right to make love to Nora etc.' Nancy warned Valpy of Nora's fecklessness; Valpy told Nancy that he believed he knew Nora better than she did and that he would wait for as long as necessary. 'He . . . looks like a consumptive,' wrote Nancy. 'Oliver Valpy! From somewhere in Devonshire.'

There came further news, after Nora's return to Mirador, of a string of fabrications that she had been disseminating among Nancy's society friends – including outlandish versions of Langhorne family life. 'Father please try to stop her telling lies to everyone she meets,' Nancy pleaded, 'There's nothing she won't tell & I tremble when I think about it. She will make you & us out monsters to suit her case!! She told Lady Grey she was misunderstood at home! Misunderstood!' There was more to come, this time from Paris where Nora had gone to

visit Irene and Dana in the New Year of 1907. Nancy wrote to Chillie:
'Phyllis has just come from Paris – She says Irene received a photograph
of Nora taken in men's clothes with her legs crossed, the most disgusting and revolting thing she has ever seen. She says Dana is
absolutely shocked by the way Nora lied to and deceived them. I
implore you not to let Nora go away from you as she's not to be trusted
& God only knows what she wdnt do . . . I gather she's considered
fast.'

Lying was Nora's only defensive shield against the rigid monitor-
ing and reproaches of her family. She desperately wanted to make her
own glamorous life, to have fun, just like her popular older sisters, each
of whom had been surrounded by pleading admirers and had married
quickly with their father's encouragement. Somehow events were
taking a slower turn for Nora and she needed to find a way to speed
things up.

A string of suitors came to Mirador in the summer of 1907.
Oliver Valpy had been quickly forgotten. Each of Nora's admirers
proposed and each one was accepted. Her niece Nancy Lancaster said,
eighty years later, 'If anybody said, "Will you marry me?" Nora said,
"Yes". She said yes to everything and the next moment she'd forgotten
she'd said it and grandfather had to keep breaking off these engagements and writing to these young men and saying "I'm afraid my
daughter doesn't know what she's doing."' Two brothers called
Whitney and their friend, Stuart Webb, all at Harvard, were on a train
one day on their way to a ball game. One of them said confidentially, 'I
must tell you boys that I'm engaged to Nora Langhorne.' 'So am I,' the
others replied. They sent Nora a telegram pledging devotion and
signed, 'Whitney, Webb, Whitney.'

At first Chillie Langhorne appreciated the company in his loneli-
ness, even though many of these young men were terrified of him.
Then he became enraged by Nora's absent-minded auctioning of her-
self. One of them only managed to pluck up courage to confront
Chillie from a position behind the door when he was in his bath: 'Mr
Langhorne I want to ask you for the hand of Nora Langhorne.' Chillie

shouted back, 'My God, you're the fiftieth man in a month who's asked me for Nora's hand. If Nora's still in love with you after three months you can *have her.*'

One of these suitors was a Spanish dandy called Sorriano, who had mysteriously slipped through the chaperone net while Nora was at the Palace Hotel in St Moritz earlier that year. Like Valpy he had followed her to Virginia, bringing a large collection of polished footwear. 'Why do you need so many damn shoes, Sorriano?,' Chillie asked him one day. 'Are you expecting to *walk* back to Spain?'

To add to Chillie's aggravations in the spring of 1907, Lizzie had imposed herself by moving back into Mirador and she looked like staying. Father and eldest daughter were getting on worse than ever, but there was nowhere else for Lizzie to go. Her marriage to Moncure had become unbearable; she couldn't cope with the drinking and the teasing, the endless squabbles about money. The previous year Moncure and Lizzie had separated, when their son Chillie was fifteen and their daughters Nancy and Alice were nine and four years old respectively. But all this meant, in effect, was that Moncure crossed the road and lived with his mother, Mrs Perkins, the houses close enough for Moncure to be able to talk to his wife across the balconies. Lizzie, the puller-down of blinds, thought it was undignified for a grown man to be living with his mother, and for this very visible separation to happen to someone – like herself – with a 'position'. Moncure would tease her mercilessly about that sense of convention, shouting across the street, 'Oh Lizzie? I'm comin' out on the paw-worch!', breaking the word into two sing-song syllables and then roaring with laughter. He would taunt her cruelly about her figure, now expanded through her love of eating Virginian 'hot breads'. But Moncure wasn't looking his best either, according to Phyllis's unsparing descriptions of him as 'bloated' and 'greasy . . . but of course very cheerful'.

Lizzie was glad to get out of the temporary indignities of her Richmond life to the safety of Mirador, but things soon started to go wrong between her and Chillie and he found it impossible to share the house with her. Phyllis came on a visit in the spring of 1907 and reported 'just the same thing, Lizzie rocking all day on the porch and wants to talk all the time. I can sympathise with Pa how she gets on his nerves. I am ashamed to think how she gets on mine . . . Oh my what an uncompanionable person she is. It's really sad – she's so pleased with herself and her ideas that you feel like shaking her sometimes.' Nancy wrote to Phyllis in June 1907 – 'I am really depressed about Lizzie but I agree it is hard on Father & far best that she shd go – only where is she to go? . . . Poor Liz she is certainly an unfortunate disposition for our family.' Lizzie hung on through July until Chillie was persuaded by Irene and Dana to go to Islesboro and decided to close down Mirador instead of leaving it for Lizzie to stay in.

Lizzie's few surviving letters, written in a spidery, nineteenth-century copybook hand, have a sad, stoic tone about them, as if it was only a matter of time before her family's sense of 'duty' to feel differently towards her would prevail. But they reveal that Mr Langhorne was able to say things to Lizzie he never would have said to any of his other daughters, least of all to Nancy and Irene. The imperious Lizzie grated terribly on all their nerves. In a letter to Phyllis, Lizzie described her showdown with Chillie just before he left Mirador and Lizzie returned to the heat of Richmond. Chillie's temper was clearly unleashed by the mint juleps he had been drinking most of the day. 'We had a big fuss,' wrote Lizzie, 'and I must say he hurt me more than I thought he could, his opinion was so high of me & he told me so many unpleasant things that he said were shared by all my family that somehow I feel as if I had someone dead about me. I was never so downed. He spent the day with Charley Moore & was hardly able to navigate & took it out on me.' She would have left, she added, but decided not to 'on account of inconveniencing him at the last moment'.

Lizzie's sense of hurt was compounded later that year after her brother Harry died, drinking to the end. ('He didn't want to die and just clung on. He suffered so and got so nervous,' wrote Nancy.) Chillie asked Genevieve, his widow, to keep house at Mirador, a job she did with great efficiency, ousting Lizzie from the position she wanted for herself. Lizzie had already failed to secure the job when Nanaire died and she despised Genevieve, to whom Chillie was considerably attracted, openly demonstrating her jealousy of her. Lizzie was losing everything: her life in Richmond was untenable; her love of luxury was thwarted by poverty. With Moncure defaulting, she depended on hand-outs from Chillie and, even worse, from Nancy.

Nancy and Waldorf became leading players in English society in a remarkably short space of time. At the time of her marriage, when she was showered with jewellery and gifts, Nancy wrote to her father that God was giving her more than she deserved '& I will try to lead a higher and better life in every way'. Instead, her instinct for power compelled Nancy, as a first priority, to get to the top of English society and conquer it. Her most obvious rival was her neighbour Lady Desborough at Taplow Court into whose coterie Lord Revelstoke had returned. At least in terms of houses, Cliveden was a bigger stage on which to play, and to offer hospitality on a grand scale. The visitors' book for 1908 shows their rapid and apparently effortless conquest of the Edwardian *beau monde* — a ruthlessly exclusive and formalized world, centred on the Court and the Royal set. It was Nancy who drove the programme, despite the bedridden days and her many visits to nursing homes.

At first the racing and shooting set, the landed aristocracy, includ-ing many dukes, dominated the guest list, some of them friends Nancy had made when she first came over to hunt: the Cecils, Cavendishes, Portlands, Roxburghes, Portmans. Nancy's early letters to Phyllis are full of excited news about Waldorf's racing. He already had the begin-nings of a highly successful bloodstock line, to which he applied himself studiously, his yearlings all bred from one mare he had bought at Oxford. But as she moved towards higher society and power Nancy gradually took against the unimproving society of the turf and the racing set were marginalized, 'Newmarket to me is ghastly,' she wrote to her sister, 'all racing people, a lot individually nice, but collectively tiresome, I think.' She never relented and later on would shock Phyllis by pointedly reading her Bible in the grandstands at Newmarket and Sandown when Waldorf's horses were running.

Nancy was motivated less by social conquest than by the excitement of being able to meet anybody she wanted. She was fearless and artful with the telephone and telegram. She wanted to rope in people who were cleverer than herself, her 'betters' as she called them, people she could admire and even idolize. She went straight for the big stars.

H. H. Asquith was already a friend before her marriage to Waldorf, mainly through his vivacious and socially glittering wife Margot, née Tennant, who had made Nancy her young protégée while she was looking for a husband. When Nancy first met him Asquith was already the acknowledged leader of the Liberal Party and in 1908 he became Prime Minister. The Asquiths dominated the inner circle of smart society. 'I wish I could make bon mots like Margot Asquith,' Nancy wrote to Phyllis, 'she seems to have met all the men of note for the past thirty years.' They had some similar traits: reckless audacity, courage, egotism – and a sharp, wounding tongue for those close about them. Margot once remarked, as Nancy might have done, 'I have a great longing to help those I love which leads me to intrepid personal criticism.'

Nancy went after Arthur Balfour, Asquith's friend, the last of the great and gifted aristocratic leaders who had been Prime Minister from 1902 until 1905. He was still at the height of his career, now as leader of the Tory opposition. When an early invitation failed, Nancy wrote to Phyllis, 'I sh. have liked having him and then my neighbour [Ettie Desborough] would have hated him coming.' But by October 1908 Balfour was a regular guest and golfing with Nancy (a game she played fervently all her life with uncharacteristic, plodding caution). Through Balfour and Margot Asquith, Nancy's house parties took on a strong 'Souls' flavour and a big intellectual leap. Margot and Ettie Desborough were founder members of the 'Souls' and Nancy was openly setting up Cliveden as a rival to Taplow Court.

In 1909, another key Soul, Lord Curzon, Chancellor of Oxford University and former Viceroy of India, became Nancy's flirtatious admirer. Edith Wharton, approaching the height of her literary reputation, came to stay in late 1908 and reported 'a large and very charming party'. Nancy also made friends with Winston Churchill, a rising star of Asquith's cabinet, although they were later to fall out. Phyllis evidently thought Nancy was straying into dangerous territory. She wrote to her in July 1909: 'I feel you enjoy at heart the company of the Souls! The samples I've seen are certainly amusing, but perhaps not too healthy! I look upon Waldorf as such a matchless husband, & I am so afraid you are going to "exasperate" him, please be careful.'

One of the great skills Nancy possessed was already in evidence — the ability to make and maintain friendships with older, cleverer, married men she admired, some of whose approaches were, at first, sexually predatory. She couldn't depend on the normal rules of courtship, of sexual flirtation, which her neighbour Ettie Desborough employed with such sophisticated skill. Nancy was entirely without that kind of vanity, even though she worried constantly about her appearance. Men would revert to a defensive, mock-romantic tone with her, as if the ritual couldn't be abandoned altogether. Nancy's power of seduction was a chaste Virginian form, a teasing, challenging directness, a mock bullying in which she paid her targets a great deal of attention and also made them laugh. It won over the womanizing Lord Curzon and the shy John Singer Sargent. She had an odd intuition about character. Those she admired she treated with great care, and quite differently from the rest. With Balfour she developed an intimacy like that of a child to a respected adult, never nagging or teasing, never taking a liberty.

But Nancy's letters are more preoccupied with the women against whom she measured herself — their beauty, their antics, their influence, their jewels — than with the men, whose power or wealth she seemed to take for granted. She had to try to pick her way through the complexities of Edwardian high life and the Royal mistresses with some degree of tact, although she confessed, 'I am like mother. Tact to me is

just a form of lunacy.' She was often out of her depth, and shocked by
the lax and wicked morals of the Edwardians. Her letters are full of
breathless gossip, mostly about the Court of Edward VII (with the
self-exonerating 'Don't breathe it to a soul' and 'I shudder to think of
the indiscretions I put to paper.'). She paid close, and scathing, attention to such society beauties as Lady Constance Stewart-Richardson, a
favourite of the Prince of Wales (the future George V), who danced in
the style of Isadora Duncan ('a sort of cake-walk . . . her clothes were
scant') and with whom she would later come to blows.

As the Astors moved into the Royal circle, Alice Keppel, the
King's favourite, came into Nancy's sights. 'She is the medium through
which one approaches the King,' Nancy reported knowingly. 'They
say she absolutely rules him. She rather snubs me! I mean she wd if she
got the chance. She is so bejewelled and airified. She reigns supreme
and is treated with all the dignity of a Pompadour. She told some one
I talked so much – I replied if she thought I talked much when she was
in the room she just ought to hear what I said when she left it. Only
don't repeat as you know how things get around.' She watched with
disdain the pushy 'titanesses' from Chicago trying to buy their way into
the inner circle. 'Its too disgusting just like the novels one reads, but
after all its just the scum of society. England is full of nice people and
if I can keep clear I hope never to go with these "loosers".'

But it was her Yankee compatriots – the 'dollar princesses' who
had married earls or dukes – who provoked Nancy's sharpest venom.
Consuelo Marlborough, who had recently left her husband, the Duke,
and Blenheim Palace, on the grounds of misery and boredom, suspected Nancy's sharp tongue wagging against her and would 'quail at
her mischievous appraisal'. She was right to do so. Nancy wrote to
Phyllis of a dinner with three of them, including Consuelo, 'It was an
appalling collection . . . they have the form, the taste, the desires of
every single one of those rich N.Y. soulless sort of women, May Rox
[burghe] the same, also Consuelo M. We are far more like English than
Yanks thank goodness. They are so cold and self contained.' She added
scathingly to her criticism of Consuelo, indicating the new direction of

Cliveden life, 'Her life has been spent with the smartest & fastest set in England,' she wrote to Phyllis, '& I don't believe she has a single friend who's worth "twopence" as a Thinker or Reformer.'

Nancy's rise was watched with 'amused' attention from neighbouring Taplow Court, where Lady Desborough was having, if anything, smarter weekends but with similar guests. Mrs Keppel had pronounced her the cleverest woman in England and she was much more closely surrounded by great men, some of whom were her lovers. Nancy, the parvenue in this world, was apprehensive that the cool Ettie Desborough might think that she was setting up in competition with her. 'She's a marvel for 40, looks about 30 & the slenderest waist you've ever seen,' Nancy wrote admiringly. 'She was v. pleasant but somehow she leaves me quite cold!'

Nancy still felt touchy about the frequent proximity of Lord Revelstoke, now 'v. fat' and 'a poisonous snob', who often visited Cliveden on his way to Taplow Court. 'John is lunching with Lady Desborough today,' Nancy told Phyllis. 'Pretty trying for me isn't it? He sent me a tiny old locket – v moderate.'

When the King came to visit Cliveden in July 1908, crowning Nancy's season, he came by way of Ettie Desborough. Nancy wrote to Phyllis, 'On Sunday a.m. Lady Desborough telephoned Waldorf that the King wished to come over so he came followed by 16 courtiers for tea and stopped 2 hours & went over the house and gardens & seemed v. pleased with it all. Of course Mrs Keppel came & John Revelstoke who went back and wrote me how wonderfully well I had received his Majesty. The nephews and nieces were furious at his coming as it broke up their tennis. He was v. pleasant and thought Cliveden the prettiest place in England. I don't think the Desboroughs enjoyed his visit but they behaved "nicely". Only I do think it slightly strong bringing 16 people, it made us 40 for tea.'

As a result, an influx of uninvited, freeloading Saxe-Coburgs and Battenbergs motored down to inspect the couple. Queen Alexandra had enjoyed it so much she came back unannounced, boating up to Cliveden Reach where she tried and failed to struggle up the steep hill for tea. 'I wish I had known,' Nancy wrote graciously, '& could have sent the motor or pony cart down.'

Looking at pictures of Nancy at this time — the frail, classic beauty propped up in her sickbed, or sitting upright with her children for the formal portraits, or standing modestly beside Waldorf, trimmed in sable stoles — it is hard to imagine the reckless lack of caution and irreverence with which she dealt with this world. It was this — Nancy's performance — that had such a 'volcanic' effect on the wooden conventions of English society of the time. She was disarming and direct to the point where she was branded 'vulgar' and 'preposterous'.

One of Nancy's comic routines, which shocked worthy guests, employed a set of large plastic teeth which she always kept to hand in a little bag with a gold chain. She would put them in suddenly, usually at meals, and become, in one impersonation, the loud hunting lady from the shires, saying 'Eton will make a white man of the boy'. Because Nancy managed to make her mouth so much larger and the teeth stick out a long way, it was a hilarious act. She imitated Margot Asquith talking about 'vulgar Americans', or the languid Ettie Desborough, cooing and wincing with appreciation in the Souls' style, using the word 'deevy' for divine, and pronouncing everything 'golden'.

An observer described Nancy at a Royal dinner: 'She went over to Hatfield to meet the King & Queen. She behaved in the true manner of a red-hot Virginian republican for 2 hours on end conversing with His Majesty, imitating Margot & Ettie & all the rest & treating the King as a human being & making all the courtiers off their heads with anguish & anxiety. She made Hugh Cecil sit down with her on a window seat & then turned round to the King & drew his attention to the terrible fact that Hugh C. was sitting down & so on. Anyhow she had a high old time & thoroughly enjoyed herself.' But Revelstoke was not amused. 'I hear he is furious with me,' Nancy wrote, 'says some day I will go too far! I feel I can bear his ill will with more calm than I bore his love!'

'She didn't care what anybody thought,' said the wife of a British ambassador, rather disapprovingly, remembering a visit to Cliveden.

'She was a Southern Prima Donna,' she added, waving her arms in the air for illustration. 'She would do *cartwheels* in the hall at Cliveden.'

Nancy seemed to relish the hordes of people that came through the doors at Cliveden. But one arrival, just as she was gearing up for the party season, gave her consternation. Lizzie had decided to escape from Richmond. She had wanted to come to Cliveden the previous year when Nancy was pregnant, but had been put off. 'I shd die of nervous prostration trying to keep her amused,' Nancy told Phyllis. But early in 1908 Lizzie announced that she would go to France (via Cliveden), taking her daughters, Alice and Nancy. Lizzie had always seen herself as a Francophile. She had no interest in her sisters' fantasies about England or English culture. She read the French classics, cooked French food, even assumed a little of the Gallic in her style. Once when Irene, visiting Lizzie in her home, had politely praised her chicken pie, Lizzie had replied curtly, 'Vol au vent, Irene dear.' France would now temporarily restore her self-respect. Her son Chillie Perkins, who was at boarding school, would be left with Moncure. The trip, encouraged by her father, would be financed by family hand-outs or unreliable cables of money from Moncure extracted by moral blackmail.

Lizzie arrived looking 'rather worn' and 'fat as a pig'. Writing to Phyllis, Nancy contradicted herself in almost consecutive sentences: 'I hope she will stop on at Cliveden as long as she likes' and 'personally I feel my nerves could not stand a long siege'. But Lizzie did leave, with $300 from Moncure 'to last as long as she could', topped up with $200 from Nancy for her birthday and the promise that she could have more if she needed it. Lizzie went to Paris with no idea of where to go or what to do, with few contacts, and for several weeks drifted between hotels.

The idea had been to cut off completely from the spiralling war with Moncure, the misery of her Richmond life, the endless affront to the conventions she lived by; to 'get some rest'. But as soon as she heard that Moncure had moved back into the family house with his sister, Bell Perkins, to look after him, Lizzie couldn't help writing from her hotel in Paris, telling him to get Bell Perkins out of her house, thus starting a war of correspondence between Richmond and European poste restantes from France to Switzerland. The first reply came from Chillie, not Moncure, 'a most cruel letter' that Lizzie forwarded to Nancy. Chillie had written that if Lizzie continued to treat Moncure so vindictively she need not depend on his (Chillie's) help.

Then Nancy went on to the attack in the slow-moving postal battle with its fortnightly delays. She kept Phyllis up to date: 'Poor Liz longs to go home but feels she should stick it out. Oh Phyl I am sorry for her. Moncure wept to father and he was taken in by him!' She wrote to Chillie, 'I should think you wd. know Moncure & his ways well enough to give Lizzie a chance. I thought you agreed that she sh. leave him for a while but I fear there's no chance of happiness or even peace in her life – unless you back her up. You sh. see Lizzie she is living in tiny rooms in a tiny hotel. She is as lonely as anyone well could be & longs to return to Moncure if only he will stop drinking. Remember father what a bad husband he has been all of these years . . . When you speak of Moncure's lips trembling I can't help from smiling. They trembled the whole time I was in Richmond but it was from drink not emotion . . . I think Moncure deserves never to see his children . . . Imagine any man treating Irene that way.' It had the desired effect. In a crisis of conscience, Chillie invited Lizzie to return to Mirador. But Lizzie wisely refused, demanding money instead. She made a list of her needs: a basic $350 a month (the equivalent of $6,000 today) '& besides I have gotten some things myself & will have to have dress money.' Clothes were the essential item, as well as a general letter of credit, 'for I think a loan [sic] woman is so unsafe without a bank to look after her faraway.'

The news from the Langhornes' Richmond lawyer was that Moncure would die 'quite soon' if he didn't stop drinking and that he had 'lost all his money'. In July 1908 Lizzie reported that she was enjoying herself and was loath to return to Virginia, whatever Moncure's state of health. 'Who wouldn't be when you think what she left?', as Nancy put it, although warning Phyllis again not to give her any money. 'I believe it's the worst thing one can do for her. In time I've no doubt I shall have to support her & I shan't mind. But I hope she will learn some sense.' Nancy was wrong not to fear having Lizzie on her purse strings, without help from her father or Moncure.

Lizzie's spending was soon truly out of control, which explained her lifting mood. Either out of revenge, pride, or the insatiable need for treats, she was getting through, on her foreign trip, the equivalent of $6000 a month while writing to Chillie plaintively, 'I try to be as economical as I can.' 'She's certainly doing herself well,' wrote Nancy, 'I wrote and implored her not to be extravagant as I know Moncure would talk.' But that was the point. Abroad, she had them all over a barrel. No one wanted the potential embarrassment of Lizzie being discovered living in penury and shaming her relations. When she over-spent money had to be sent. By the end of her trip she had spent close to $45,000. The old idea of accepting genteel poverty with all this money around was impossible for Lizzie.

But she was almost pointedly ungrateful for the hand-outs. Part of the irritation she generated in her family was that she took their sub-sidies for granted. Lizzie had confronted, rather than beguiled, the family with so many demands for money that she didn't have a single ally left, except ironically, Nancy. But Lizzie didn't respond to Nancy's ideas of charity, which required some satisfying result, some evidence of being 'raised up'. She thought of her only as a younger sister and a brat who had married an Astor. Nancy decided that Lizzie had to be adequately supported otherwise there would be nothing but protracted guerrilla war. Chillie had forbidden Nancy to hand out further 'promis-cuous' presents to Lizzie to spend on 'furs and furbelows'. Trying to force him to make some arrangement Nancy wrote to him: 'If you don't want to give her anything please sir, write to me. If you don't mean to we must give her more as she can't live on what we give her. I know father how hard it is for you — for there's nothing on earth so killing as unappreciativeness.'

By the end of 1908, however, Chillie was pushing the Lizzie prob-lem on to Nancy and it heralded disaster. It was as if Nancy and Lizzie

had both agreed to fight a deciding duel. And when Lizzie returned to
Mirador that September, her father cold-shouldered her after all those
months abroad, refusing to meet her at the station or to 'walk' her up
to the house. Lizzie found this 'naughty and haughty' of him – a phrase
she might have used of herself. She told Nancy that she'd 'dare not
stop' at Mirador for fear of a row with him.

Phyllis's second child Jackie was born in March 1908 when Peter was
six. That summer she refused to go to Newport, unable to face her
parents-in-law and the long meals at their great villa, Rockhurst.
Reggie was now pointedly neglecting her. ('Poor Phyl I fear Reggie
goes his own way as ever – no one knows how Phyl suffers,' Nancy
wrote to her father.) Phyllis found pleasure only in Peter and Jackie,
in whom Reggie took little interest. Yet although Phyllis wrote to
Waldorf that she didn't like to leave Jackie, now six months old, she
also planned to send him with Peter to Newport when it got too hot
in Westbury, in August. 'I shall go up now and again to see how they
are.'

    She was there only by chance when Jackie contracted an obstruc-
tion of the intestines later that month. She cabled Nancy, who was
pregnant with her daughter Wissie, on a Saturday night at Loch
Luichart in Scotland, where Waldorf was stalking, to say the child was
very ill. Nancy 'prayed all night that God would give me a miscarriage
& much suffering and spare you this sorrow'.

    On Sunday they managed to have the post office opened up,
where a cable had arrived saying that Jackie was dead.

    Phyllis had sat by his bed for two days. She wrote of 'the hopeless
agony of seeing your baby taken from you forever'; how '. . . he had
hiccups and then suddenly cried out in pain and fainted away. Oh
Nannie to have to sit by helplessly and see your baby die and hear his
poor little whimper just tears your heart out . . .'

    Nancy, suffering like the identical twin she imagined herself to
be, poured out her own agony in her letters. She wanted to set sail but

the doctor ordered against it. 'I sit here & weep weep weep,' she wrote, 'I can see yr dear face & hear yr sobs I can't stand it – its worse than seeing it in life – this awful mental picture that I make of you. Yr mind must be taken off of yr sorrow for I know how morbid you get.' Her almost immediate response was to order a piece of jewellery, a bracelet with a locket in which Phyllis could carry a lock of Jackie's hair.

When Bobbie left again for boarding school a few days later, Nancy offered an angle of commiseration. 'He wept and clung to me and vowed he would die and I wept and clung to him,' she wrote. 'Oh the pain of it and Phyl I thought then far better to lose a baby than a boy who is older for they do enter into one's life and are such companions. Imagine life without Peter.'

Phyllis took to her bed, paralysed with a depression that seemed to have no reason to lift. She felt 'caught up in fear' as she described it, 'believing that sorrow followed joy so quickly'. She felt guilty for Jackie's death, convinced that she was 'wicked', that she shouldn't have abandoned him and that God had decided to punish her. 'God only means to try your faith,' Nancy told her. 'You have never done anything wrong in your life. I can't tell you what I think of your character and goodness only I pray every night that I will be as good.'

Three weeks later Phyllis went to Mirador to stay with her father, then in mid-October 1908 returned to her house in Westbury, writing to Chillie that 'now it seems to me a perfect wilderness'. Jackie's death had distressed Reggie and momentarily scared him. He even confessed, in a letter to Nancy, that he had neglected Phyllis. There was a moment of respite and tenderness that gave Phyllis hope, but alarmed the watchful Nancy in case Phyllis became pregnant again. But Reggie couldn't sustain the mood. Although there is barely a mention in the surviving correspondence of Reggie's drinking it was certainly steady and heavy and his later behaviour suggests that it made him cold and uncommunicative, when he wasn't being 'querulous'. He showed few of the outward signs that might have alarmed Phyllis, who never drank. The conventional view was that it was permissible to 'drink like a gentleman' which meant no idiocy or falling over. Given Nancy's terror of it – and her memories of Bob Shaw's habits which she told Phyllis still made her weep – Reggie was disguising it well, confusing Phyllis's understanding of what was wrong between them. It may explain, too, why Reggie could never spend more than two days at a time at Cliveden and kept refusing weekend invitations and disappearing.

He soon reverted to alternating between silence and complaint. 'I shall go on wanting certain considerations from Reggie but I shall not expect them,' Phyllis wrote, '. . . a man that has been self absorbed for 34 years <u>cannot know</u> that part of his nature has long since died and one must appeal to him in a roundabout way, first his vanity, then his comfort.' 'I knew Reggie wd be the same in a week,' wrote Nancy. 'Men – what ostriches they mostly are – they take us for idiots.' Nancy insisted that Phyllis should come to England for hunting that winter for her 'sanity': 'Don't shut yourself up Phyl & think yr brain can stand it. No-one's could. I am hoping to get a cable in a few days saying you will sail soon.' But Phyllis couldn't bring the subject up with Reggie, knowing that it would provoke a fight or a deeper cycle of hostility – now an annual event as the English hunting season approached – even though Reggie always gave in and came along in the end. Reggie could never agree to let Phyllis go alone to see Nancy.

It became a matter of urgency now that Phyllis be sprung from her misery, 'neglected in sorrow', as Nancy put it, without divorcing Reggie (there was no evidence of adultery) and Nancy proposed a plan. She had written to the Brookses, urging them to give Phyllis 'a house and garden of her own', but they hadn't responded. So now Phyllis would get her financial independence from them – paid for by the Astors. 'You never need bother about money,' Nancy wrote to her. 'I know how one is tied down without it & I long for you to have an independent income & any moment you want it it's here. Waldorf has arranged that.' Waldorf had already arranged that if Nancy died (as she always expected to die in childbirth) Phyllis would receive a good income. 'Think Phyl how rich Waldorf may be some day [Nancy still portrayed Waldorf as struggling with his creditors: 'Waldorf is badly in debt. Please don't mention it. He will pay it back next year.'] & think of the joy of knowing you are absolutely independent! It is comforting – I sh have married an ogre for that!' Phyllis was to use some of the money to buy a small house near Smithtown, Long Island, and the Astors would furnish it.

As for Reggie, he could either come and live with her or stay where he was. Phyllis, Nancy ordered, must never depend on his affections for her happiness – that was always her naive mistake. 'My dear, don't complain of Reggie's lack of attention it makes you much freer . . .' She should revise her romantic idea of husbands and marriage, of physical proximity. 'You keep on dreaming, and longing for something to happen that will make him like you. Don't try to make a silk purse out of a sow's ear!' Nancy was also proposing something that perhaps only Nancy herself could have managed. Phyllis was expected suddenly to guillotine her feelings of neglect and sadness and make a success of an affectionless relationship – something deeply alien to her nature.

And Nancy couldn't help poking up Reggie directly. 'I am very patient but some days I can't stand it and today is one of those days. I shall write Reggie – why sh I never speak to him of what I feel?' It was, of course, a bad move. She described the letter to Phyllis as a 'heart to heart', containing some 'kindly truths' on the certain grounds that Phyllis's business was hers as well. In fact what she told Reggie, baldly, was that if he disliked her so much, she would be prepared not to demand that Phyllis came to England, but only as long as Reggie made her happier. Otherwise Phyllis would have to come 'as you were too good to be neglected by him'. Furthermore, if Reggie couldn't come 'cheerfully' with Phyllis, he had better not come. 'I wonder if he will be cross with me,' Nancy mused. When his infuriated response to his sister-in-law's letter duly came Nancy wrote to Phyllis, 'Heaven knows I did it for the best which I see now as "worst".' Reggie soon caved in to this peculiar ultimatum, agreeing to come across the Atlantic 'for two days'.

In the spring of 1909 Nancy gave birth to her second Astor child and only daughter Phyllis, nicknamed Wissie, which was her sister Phyllis's nickname among Nancy's children.

For some time now Chillie Langhorne had been lonely and unhappy at Mirador. Nora was often away, staying with Irene or on débutante trips. He would go on occasional 'gadding' expeditions into Richmond or Charlottesville, and would even hail strangers from the road to come and drink with him – not an uncommon procedure in Virginia – and he drank quite a bit these days. He complained about his family, and made trouble where he could, but there was little grist to his mill.

He had been threatening to abandon Mirador altogether, since clearly nobody needed it, or himself, any more, and move into a smaller house, with Genevieve, Harry's widow, as his housekeeper. Now, with some persuasion from Nancy and Irene, Chillie decided to rescue Phyllis in her crisis after the death of Jackie. He would move and give her Mirador and 500 acres as part of her inheritance, instead of the Astors buying her a house on Long Island. The idea was that Reggie would finally settle down, and take to 'farming' or at least take to living in the country. Phyllis would have her independence and the upper hand in her marriage.

Chillie bought a small, ugly house across the road which he called Misfit and planned to move the following spring of 1910. 'He called it "Misfit"' said Nancy Lancaster, 'because he said it was a damn misfit for him and he was a misfit for the neighbourhood because there was nothing but a lot of Yankees and Westerners moving in, and he was the only Virginian there.' There was one problem with the plan: what to do with Nora.

9

The Marriage of Nora

It had been assumed for two years that Nora would soon be married, but the plans had gone badly out of her sisters' control. Nancy still believed she could fix it if only Nora would come to England. She had been pleading with Chillie to send her over for almost a year. But Chillie alternated between saying 'For God's sake see that she marries some nice young man', because he was 'fed up' with her, and saying he wanted to hold on to her because she wasn't ready for marriage. The last was partly a ploy to resist Nancy and feel his waning power. Nora, too, resisted going to England to be bullied out of her wayward disorganization by Nancy. She was cosy with her spoiling father, now that she was relieved of her duties. 'I know Father you hate giving her up,' wrote Nancy, 'but don't you think it's only fair to Nora to give her the chance of having such a good time?' But Cliveden, Nora knew, would be like boot camp: constant surveillance, nagging, chiding, taking orders. Nora's tactic with Nancy, aided by Chillie, was to promise to visit and then cancel for various reasons, finally refusing to come at all. By September 1908, Mr Langhorne's new ploy to keep Nora with him was to say that she was better suited to the 'simple life'.

Then Nora fell helplessly in love with a man called Baldwin Myers from Norfolk, Virginia, and declared that all past bets were off and Baldwin was the man she intended to marry. Mr Langhorne seemed to think that Baldwin was as good as anybody and gave his approval. At least Nora had made up her mind. Not so Nancy, who wrote in September, switching tactics shamelessly, that Nora was too young to marry anyway. 'I can't tell you how unhappy I am,' she wrote, 'as I know Nora's fickleness & I am so afraid she is just marrying to marry. Please write me about him. Where does he live & did I know him as a boy? Is he a cousin of Lilburn? Please sir write me all.'

By October there was still no news, so Nancy wrote again to her father. Baldwin Myers, she had learned, was 'a mere youth with padded shoulders and a pipe in the corner of his mouth & if he has no money what will Nora do? End in prison for debt I foresee . . . tell her I am going to have all sorts of charmers to meet her & if she stands the test we shall know she's in love.'

Chillie relented. It fitted in with his house-moving plans and he couldn't face the responsibility of Nora making what might be a bad marriage. A corrective voyage was required; Baldwin Myers had to be erased from Nora's mind. A husband had to be found in England – that reservoir of suitable young men.

Nora was devastated at leaving her father, but mostly at leaving Baldwin Myers. She wrote pathetically and ungrammatically from the Waldorf Astoria, on her way to England, complaining that for the first time in her life her father was not there 'to care for me and tie my things before leaving'. 'I suppose I am a disappointment but you have always loved me as a disappointment and please do now,' she wrote, 'I have missed you so much today, not having our rooms together [on their visits to the Waldorf Astoria in New York] and going in to the dining room with you and all the little things we have done so often together. I do love you and God knows I do. For my sake don't leave me. I have got some good in me, every body has some and I love you with it all. God Bless you. Nora. We only live once.'

She wrote again to her father when the *Mauretania* put in at Queenstown (renamed Cobh, in Cork Harbour) in Ireland on 5 November. 'I have never felt so alone in my life as I have lately and I know I've brought it all on myself, and have got to pay for it, and I am doing that already. If I had only been steady all my life, now I would be the happiest person in the world for I could convince people that really loved and knew my mind. But I don't blame you, that's what I deserve. How I love home you don't know. God bless you my dearest Father and come soon. God bless you Nora.' Chillie ignored the messages of distress. He complained, merely, that Nora's letters lacked content and were emotionally repetitive.

Nora knew that she had said goodbye to her freedom. Her worst fears of imprisonment and servitude to Nancy were confirmed as soon as she arrived. Nancy was shocked by her appearance when she turned up 'in rags' on her doorstep, 'so washed out & pale & red eyed'. She had employed 'a nice old maid who looks after her like a nurse', she proudly told Chillie. 'I shall soon have her straightened out.' Nora wrote home, describing Cliveden as 'the lonesomest place in the world – but lovely and luxurious'. When Nancy went off to Plymouth for a few days she placed Nora in the care of someone called Elsie Peabody at Market Harborough, who knew 'all of Nora's tricks & manners'. The idea was to surround Nora with men, force her towards marriage – a strategy that Nora was happy to fall in with, as long as she could get Nancy off her back. And yet she longed for the forbidden Baldwin from Norfolk, Virginia.

'I am being v. tactful with her,' Nancy reported to Mirador, 'and telling her to of course marry B. Myers if she can face poverty and a poky life in Norfolk . . . She is so surprised that I am not opposing her that she almost thinks my way! I don't think she will remember Baldwin in a months time. I am sorry for you Father, as I know how she has tried you – but remember she may improve & think how wonderful the rest of us are!'

By Christmas time Phyllis had arrived, with Reggie, and was on hand to help push Nora into an English marriage. Lord Elphinstone, always on the loose and 'in love with the Langhornes', was duly asked to join the Astors and Nora at St Moritz early in 1909. 'I think she has her eye on him,' Nancy wrote to her father, 'I hope he will "pop" but I doubt it.' Here Nora played a trick on her sisters that gave her, at least, some breathing space. She persuaded them that after a few days of skating and tobogganing Lord Elphinstone had popped the question. Nora told them that Elphinstone had asked her 'as a favour' not to talk of it. Phyllis and Nancy were taken in. They believed in their power of persuasion over the feckless Nora — above all to persuade her to be faithless to Baldwin Myers. Phyllis wrote to her father to 'divulge a great secret' ('I implore you not to tell.'). 'Lord E. is certainly a nice man and she will never get a nicer or a better offer, but Nannie & I are not trying to persuade her one way or the other.' Nancy echoed this by telling Chillie, 'I think she should decide the question for herself.'

Having sworn her sisters to secrecy, Nora then told everyone else she knew of this fantasy proposal including, according to Nancy, 'Angus McDonnell and Paul Phipps [a young admirer who had been hanging about at Cliveden] & Heaven knows who else'. Nora went even further, moving the scene of the proposal from St Moritz and placing poor Lord Elphinstone on his knees in the conservatory at Cliveden, among the potted palms. This, she claimed, made it impossible for her to take him seriously.

At the end of February 1909, Nora was homesick and miserable. She longed to return to Mirador, to her father and Baldwin Myers. She had never been more faithful to any other beau, but Nancy wouldn't have it. Nora was to stay on and have a London season in the spring, where she would have 'a glorious time'. But Nora wrote to Chillie, threatening a breakdown under all this pressure: 'I don't really believe I could stand a London season in the first place and I would hate to be sick. So I do think I had better come back with Phyllis.' Nora was also angry that Phyllis had supplanted her at Mirador. 'I thought Mirador was going to be mine always but now my only chance is to come and stay there while I can. You may think the others love it but you will never know how I feel.' She had the chance to live in Lord Elphinstone's castle in Scotland, she said, but had 'taken Virginia' as her choice. 'I bet you Phyllis would take the other like a shot.'

'I think she's crazy,' wrote Nancy to Chillie. 'She lies like a trooper so I never know what she really feels or thinks. I think she thinks a good deal and feels nothing.' But with Nora it was always the other way round.

Then a bigger issue came along which put Chillie back in play and restored his sense of rampageousness. Nancy reported that Nora, a week after planning to return to Baldwin Myers, had suddenly decided to stay in England all spring. 'Between you and me she rather likes Paul Phipps, but so far it only seems friendship,' Nancy reported but added, 'I think it would be fatal for her to marry anyone yet as she's in love with no-one & she's so young and changeable.' Nancy was to regret these words, spoken so soon after Chillie's hopes for Lord Elphinstone had been raised, and on such slender evidence; she had also misjudged Nora's change of mood. Nora's roulette wheel had suddenly slowed and stopped and she had put her mark on the 'ticklist' as Chillie called it ('It's a ticklist question who Nora marries') at Paul Phipps. He had stayed many weekends at Cliveden and watched the Elphinstone episode at close hand, but Nora barely seemed to have noticed him until the beginning of March 1909. Nora was 'pale' again but this time with love, and not homesickness.

Paul Phipps was a struggling young architect who had been a contemporary of Waldorf's at Eton and Balliol, Oxford, where, according to his daughter Joyce, he had been 'awarded a gold watch for his fine handwriting'. His father was English and his mother American. He had big flat ears, a long broad face and a 'lantern' jaw. There was an air of elegance, even dandyishness about him; he wore bow ties and was unable to pronounce the letter 'r'. He was popular, 'witty and urbane', considered to have 'the charming manners of a true gentleman', and he was 'the best dancer in London'. Indeed, in her book *Remember and Be Glad* (1952) Cynthia Asquith recalled that no girl was truly 'out' until Paul Phipps had danced with her. H. H. Asquith's daughter Violet, later Bonham Carter, had sat next to him after dinner and recorded in her journal, 'He is very easy — almost too easy. Rigid impartiality to all subjects is a little discouraging.' He had been articled for a time to Sir Edwin Lutyens and was just starting out on his own career. He was a major catch, definitely suitable.

There was nothing new about Nora getting engaged, but this time she had acted with speed and conviction. She decided on it with Paul on a Sunday night at Cliveden; told Nancy the following noon and sent a cable to her father, asking for his consent. If Nancy had seriously opposed it, none of this would have happened.

In fact Nancy and Phyllis seized on Paul Phipps and were propelling the project along, hoping to catch Nora in mid-delirium. Paul Phipps was suddenly the best bet, or at least 'the best Nora could expect' and this time Nora was not going to be allowed to get out of it. The timing fitted so well with everyone's plans, particularly Phyllis's plans for Mirador. Nancy had once again swiftly turned about in her view of Nora's suitability for marriage and the two sisters mounted a campaign to get Chillie's approval. The letters they wrote to him show how awed they still were by his authority and how cynical they could be when it came to their sister and the life-binding vows of matrimony.

In their first letters, written in the hours before Chillie's cabled reply arrived, they had to backpedal hard on Lord Elphinstone whom they had overpromoted, in case Chillie thought that Nora was up to her usual double-dealing or, perhaps, in case he smelled a rat with all this sudden haste. 'Nora isn't a bit in love with Lord E. nor he with her — they seem to be just friends,' wrote Nancy. Phyllis conceded in turn that Nora 'does not in the least like Lord Elphinstone & was quite bored when he was about'. Paul Phipps, according to Nancy, was 'one of the nicest men I know. Clean-minded, high-minded, clever and charming. I don't think she could have got a nicer man. The tragedy is his!' Phyllis wrote that he was 'a great gentleman', and 'very intelligent', adding with hindsight, 'Nannie & I thought she had her eye on him some time ago.'

But the transatlantic exchanges fell into slapstick and confusion. In her first cable to Chillie Nora forgot to include the name of her fiancé and Nancy, thinking Chillie would only respond to a visual description, had referred to Phipps in her cable only as 'the lantern jaw boy'. When Nora received Chillie's cable of consent and congratulation the following day, she was overjoyed, not realizing that Chillie's blessing was for Lord Elphinstone and his Scottish castle. No names except 'the lantern jaw boy' had so far been mentioned in the exchanges.

Unaware of this misunderstanding, Nancy and Phyllis's letters, extolling the virtues of Paul Phipps – assuming that the marriage was a *fait accompli* – began to reach Chillie more than a week after he had sent his cable of consent. Relaxing her guard, Nancy added at the end of one letter, 'Only one drawback – No money.' But this was no longer the urgent requirement, at least in the opinion of her sisters. A visitor to Islesboro that summer remembered Irene looking out over the water through binoculars at a large yacht sailing up the coast of Maine and saying to Dana, 'There goes the man we thought wasn't rich enough to marry Nora.'

Still certain of Chillie's approval for Paul Phipps, Nancy and Phyllis began to rehearse the usual criticisms of Nora's character to cover themselves against what they really believed: that any marriage undertaken by Nora was a foregone disaster. 'Now the only question is whether Nora will make him happy,' Phyllis wrote. 'Personally I don't see how its possible as she hasn't a taste in common with his . . . They are a rather literary lot & so is the young man, which does seem something of a joke for Nora & I think if he ever discovered that she told stories that it would finish him.' Charm wasn't everything, Phyllis continued, 'and I think this young man is going to be deeply disappointed at finding nothing else'. There was even now some regret for poor Baldwin Myers who had disappeared from the horizon 'like a shooting star'. 'I feel very sorry for him,' wrote Phyllis '& I don't see how Nora's got the heart to do it.'

When Paul Phipps returned to Cliveden, to put his case and apologize for being penniless, he was warned of Nora's 'virtues and vices' by Nancy and told not to expect too much of her. She told him that Nora was 'undeveloped' and extravagant although she was 'praying' to mend her ways. Nancy then took Nora aside and told her of the sacrifices she would have to make and how marvellous they would be for her character. 'Nora says nothing on earth wd stop her,' she wrote to Chillie, 'I've told her how dreary a thing being poor in England is. Its a cheap place for working people to live but not our class. I think it more expensive than any place and knowing Nora's love of amusement and thriftlessness it makes me nervous. Then, too, men hardly ever seem to make money in England no matter how clever they are.' Paul Phipps was poor, but unlike Baldwin Myers, whose poverty had been the major obstacle, he was 'such a thorough man and a gentleman'. 'Then what of her trousseaux about how much shall she spend on it?' Nancy asked Chillie. 'I should think 4000 dollars shdn't you as she will want linen to last her many a long day?' And Nora should have an annual settlement 'as I think that running to your husband for every single cent is the origin of much unhappiness'. Only Chillie could settle this; and only then could they be married. Nancy begged him to come to England immediately to do so. She added, 'Paul has a splendid influence on Nora . . . she is a changed creature & except for money I think it is an ideal match for her.'

Around 9 March Chillie's first letter, written straight after sending his cable of congratulations, and assuming that the marriage was to Lord Elphinstone, arrived at Cliveden. Nora replied in desperation, 'I am so sorry you have made a mistake. It isn't Elphinstone. It is Paul Phipps,' but went on, as if nothing had happened, 'I want to be so different. I will do right by him or die.' She pleaded, 'I know all of my weak points and that's a help. I have got that to begin on.' Each letter Chillie received from Nancy and Phyllis, overpraising Paul Phipps, criticizing Nora and demanding money for her dowry, had caused him mounting irritation. On 12 March, Nancy wrote timidly, 'I am so sorry you mistook the "Lantern Jaw Boy" for Ld Elphinstone. I had no idea you wd as I knew that's what you called Paul Phipps. I cabled you yesterday to please come over.' She added, and with good reason, 'I never quite understood Nora and Lord Elphinstone . . . Anyhow she wd never have married him . . .'

Chillie then sent a cable to Nora cancelling any consent. Rankled by his own confusion, Chillie was genuinely amazed that Nora should have plumped for Phipps so soon after his expectation of another good marriage. Chillie had, after all, met Lord Elphinstone and knew what he was consenting to. He felt he had been treated casually. Why suddenly choose this penniless young architect when Nora could have anyone she wanted? How could Nancy persuade Nora to do this? Didn't she know that Nora was changeable and probably wouldn't feel the same in a week's time? Didn't she remember how badly she had treated Baldwin Myers? Had Nancy told Paul Phipps of Nora's character, her weaknesses, the extravagance, the fibs? Why was Paul Phipps better than Baldwin Myers anyway? What was there to choose between them? He directly accused Nancy of a conspiracy to push Nora into marriage when (always with the exception of Lord Elphinstone) she wasn't ready to marry anyone. He didn't trust their judgement. He would wash his hands of it. Nora could marry in England and he would stay in America. He would not come to settle the affair.

Astonished by this reversal, Nancy went on to the attack. Not only had she had nothing to do with the engagement, she had tried to persuade Nora out of it, she said. It had come as a great shock: 'You ask why Waldorf & I did not tell Paul more about Nora . . . would you have had me tell him what I thought? . . . I do think Father knowing us – you go a little far in writing you feel we rushed and persuaded her into matrimony. We can't help smiling. You took a very different tone when you thought it was Lord Elphinstone. Perhaps you've forgot the letter you wrote her telling her to "consult her heart" – not to be persuaded by wealth or rank & no matter what she did you wd always stick to her & understand . . . You never mentioned how badly she had treated Baldwin when you thought it was Lord E. I think considering the way you have spoilt her – its pretty hard for you to now turn against her. You brought her up. You are more responsible for her ways than any one. So you can't turn her over to me here. Its too late.'

In the end Paul and Nora went to America to get Mr Langhorne's blessing. Paul had written many letters in advance full of apologies for Nora being a poor man's wife, saying how much he loved her, and how aware he was of what Nora was giving up in terms of Virginia. Somehow this display of fealty did the trick. They were married at the end of April in New York and returned to England, to Cliveden, for their honeymoon. Nancy wrote to her father the day after the wedding, allying herself with him once again: 'Nora never wrote me one line after she left here except a short letter from the boat. Now that she is married I am done. I will not be treated so casually & I know you feel the same way. We are all right but Paul has my sympathy!! Goodbye dearest Pa. give my love to all & I don't think you sh. pine over Nora. Remember what trouble she was.'

Nancy also indicated that she would now support Nora and Paul, fix them up in a house and give Nora an allowance to help pay the rent. Nora and Paul were thus on the payroll too. 'I can't help smiling when I think that you thought I persuaded Nora into this match,' Nancy wrote, 'you see I shall have her on my hands & mind always now – but I am glad she's near & I will do all I can for her for your and mother's sake.'

Chillie put in one final Nancy-baiting twist to the story. He gave Nora all Nancy's letters about her over the past few weeks – with lines such as 'the tragedy is his', and how Nora could never make any man happy. 'I shall never now feel that I can write you any thing in confidence,' Nancy wrote to her father in July of 1909. 'She showed them to Paul – who has almost ceased to speak to me. I can't understand how you dared send letters written to you in confidence. Nora is furious with me also Paul. You have succeeded in absolutely making them both hate me.'

The couple moved into a house, rented for them by Nancy in Montpelier Square, off the Brompton Road. Paul Phipps wrote to Mr Langhorne, who could hardly have believed what he read. 'Nora is very well & looks better and stronger than I have ever seen her. She takes a tremendous interest in everything to do with the house & is a most excellent and economical housekeeper. She goes about in omnibuses all the time & says it really is pathetic to think of anyone who thought as much about pretty clothes as she did trying how many ways she can do over a last winter's hat so as not to have to buy a new one & so be able to spend more on the house. She is excellent with the servants too & so dignified! We really are most awfully happy & hope you will soon come over & see us & our home.' Nora appeared, under Paul Phipps's influence, miraculously to have mended her ways.

By returning to Mirador as its new owner, Phyllis thought that she could reclaim her life. She was the one member of her family who still deeply loved the place. It transformed her mood that February of 1909, as she prepared to return from hunting at Melton Mowbray. 'I think of it all day and my head fairly buzzes at night with plans,' she wrote to Chillie. 'It has made coming home a different thing. We will have lots to do there you and me!!'

From England she ordered roses and box hedges and instructed the gardener to put in plots of mulch earth. She believed that she could 'get up Reggie's enthusiasm' once she got him there. Mrs Brooks had offered to pay for improvements, including a new tennis court and a swimming pool, to make Reggie more comfortable, finally conceding that his marriage depended on it. Wells were dug, cast iron pipes laid, 'as Reggie is set on having a fine flow of clear spring water – the one thing he seems to want is the water arrangements perfect'.

Still Chillie couldn't resist the opportunity to reverse all the plans – the old prerogative of his power. He declared that he was being made homeless and held up the building work on his new house. He had been having weeping spells – 'Poor father,' wrote Nancy, 'I know how he feels. Its very sad for him with once so large a family & complete Boss, to be left now.' Phyllis wrote to him, 'If I didn't have the prospects of Mirador, I don't know what I shd do, but even now if you feel you would rather keep Mirador, do it . . . I know how hard it is on you to give up yr. home but please sir, don't feel homeless now for you know wherever my home is, yours is too and I am sure you will be pleased to see one of your children taking a real interest in it.'

The reality of reclaiming her life was that Mirador was invaded by her relations as soon as Phyllis arrived that spring. Lizzie was over immediately. 'She's like a vulture,' Phyllis wrote to Nancy, '& hangs around the room asking how much everything cost . . . I have faltered several times today & thought am I wise in coming here in a nest of family to live. It has its drawbacks!' A month later she wrote, 'I am so tired of poor relations I could scream . . . When you get annoyed with Nora being there [at Cliveden] just thank yr stars you ain't sitting in the midst of a strolling company of relations. I feel like tying a tin can to all their tails when I see them strolling up the front walk.'

Chillie did, of course, move to his uncompleted house. But by July he was at war with Phyllis. She had to direct some of the work at Mirador, including the building of a library for Reggie to drink in, from Long Island and Chillie, watching from Misfit, interfered, criti- cized every move and shamelessly played the martyr thrown out of his own home. His relationship with Phyllis held deep-seated animosi- ties – and no amount of tact on Phyllis's part could keep Chillie from making her installation difficult. He had given her 500 acres of land but wouldn't give up advising her on how to farm it, as Phyllis set about making improvements.

To keep things lively, claiming that his conscience had suddenly pricked him, Chillie announced a plan to buy Lizzie a house not far from Mirador, and settle an allowance on her. Nancy's reaction was shocking proof of just how much of a pariah Lizzie had become in the family – particularly Nancy's confidence that her father would go along with her sentiments. 'Poor Phyl has been so "upsot" [sic] ever since she heard of it,' she wrote to him, 'I know you want to give Phyl the happiest home you can, & she says to have Lizzie so close wd. absolutely spoil the joy of Mirador – and I know you will agree and not think me meddlesome. Phyl is so looking forward to Mirador it seems to be the one thing she has to cheer her up & she needs a lot of cheering.'

But Chillie let matters take their course and Phyllis wrote in August, 'Well, the worst has come. Lizzie has bought the Rhodes place. I could weep . . . but I ask you ain't it my luck!! Liz is all aglow & talks very rich – She sounds a mental case to me, but I am glad she's so pleased . . . Woe is the day that I took Mirador. I imagined that place would be a peaceful abode . . . but with Pa on one side & Liz on the other I will just about catch it from both sides.'

'Have no fear,' Nancy had written some weeks earlier, 'Liz will never live near you on my money & she can't live v. well without it, so you need not worry about it.' In September Phyllis wrote to Nancy, acknowledging her victory: 'Thanks to you she has given up the Rhodes place & it is only because you said you would stop her allowance that she did it . . .'

Nancy managed to persuade Chillie to come to Cliveden that summer and reported to Phyllis on his state of mind, a description which gives some idea of the patience Nanaire had needed in their marriage. 'Of course he thinks you ignored him when you were doing over Mirador,' Nancy told Phyllis. 'He says he longed to help but you never suggested it. Also he could have saved you $10,000. I told him it was not fair on either of you. He says I only take your side. My heart aches for him but I don't see how it's possible for him to live at peace with any one of his children. He gets what he wants by quarrelling and discussion.'

Mr Langhorne returned to America and wrote to Nora, complaining about the way he had been treated at Cliveden and how much he had disliked his fellow guests. To have confided this to Nora guaranteed the letter wide circulation. She sent it first to Nancy, who wrote to her father: 'I have just seen yr letter to Nora – I am very sorry that you find the people you meet in our house so very distasteful to you. If you will only let me know in time enough before you come I will see that there is no one there.'

In the meantime Phyllis was suffering an overwhelming desire to have another baby to replace Jackie, writing to Nancy in July, 'Surely, surely I am not a baroness!' and suggesting that 'unless I get this way [pregnant] soon I vow you will have to have one for me, as I simply can't wait much longer and of course I should feel about it just as if I had had it, so consider my poor disappointed heart and engage Waldorf's services for me about Sept . . . I now realise how women can have hysterics when their hopes are blighted each month.' She had complained about Reggie's 'appalling idleness', believing he might 'just simply croak with ennui! . . . he really tries I believe to see how bored he can be . . .'

Nevertheless Phyllis took her chance, once again, with the seasonal mood change in Reggie – or perhaps she had taken the advice Nancy had sent her: 'I wish you cd drink a love potion like the woman in Midsummer Night's Dream – I sh like to see you entwining Reggie's head with garlands of Roses – & stroking his ears tho of course he's not an ass! & wd hardly like this simile.' Whatever the reason, in August 1909 Phyllis, now finally installed at Mirador, discovered herself to be pregnant with her third son.

10

The Returning Pilgrim

Nancy's prostrating illnesses couldn't be explained; they came in combinations and lasted for weeks. Phyllis, who knew her best, was mystified by the paradox of her prodigious vitality, her strength 'like a sturdy pony', compared to these collapses that immobilized her, even though they had first been evident when Nancy was a teenager. Her doctors had no specific cures for the colitis, headaches, rheumatism, rashes and the extreme fatigue that assailed her. They could never get beyond their diagnosis of 'nervous exhaustion' or their prescription of bed or the nursing home.

A typical diary entry described these afflictions: 'Tuesday I wd have been in this blessed bed one month. I have catarrh of the stomach and have just escaped jaundice – I have a nasty itchy rash all on my face & I am as yellow as a Chinese.' No one, including Waldorf, could easily have divined the underlying cause, since she kept it carefully concealed behind the liveliness and showmanship. But there are clues in her letters to Phyllis. Only she knew of Nancy's bouts of depression and loneliness, of the feeling that she had strayed into a place in which she didn't belong. 'I know its sinful to care as much as I do,' she wrote to Phyllis, 'but when you go it's like being left in a strange land without one scrap of youth or one familiar face.'

Never having read these letters, her fourth son Michael suggested in his memoir *Tribal Feeling* that Nancy was suffering from a kind of 'vertigo'; that she had outpaced herself. The rapid transformation from thinking her life was ruined by her divorce to her rise to the edge of power and the pinnacle of social success, to wealth and possessions on such an unimaginable scale, had left her fearful and conscience-stricken. 'Psychologically, intellectually . . . she had swallowed more than she could digest,' he wrote. 'She was ill and tired and for the first time in her life thoroughly unsure of herself.'

The roots of Nancy's crisis, which lasted for at least five years, could be traced back to Archdeacon Neve's mission, where she had acquired the simple moral certainties and Bible preaching that had answered her teenage confusion and which she hung on to all her life. There was black and white – 'the simple life and the sinful one'. Wealth, possessions and society were dangerously close to worldly wickedness, and far from God and the inner life. Nancy needed to square her missionary zeal, her 'furious' desire to do good, with her new worldly exercise of power; to impose her values on Babylon. She had no means of resolving the conflict and it left her feeling guilty and vulnerable. 'I feel unless I am careful I shall be going backwards instead of forward,' she wrote to Phyllis. 'God has been so good to me and I don't do half enough. I sh try to make myself a sort of fashionable saint!'

Her confidences to Phyllis were expressed in the form of childish longings and acute homesickness. In a letter from Scotland in the summer of 1908 – the summer of Jackie's death – she wrote, 'Phyl I had a dreadful day yesterday. It was just as tho Mother had just died. I wept – wept, wept. It comes over me sometimes like a flood and there's nothing to do but weep. It makes me ill for days.'

It was the autumn season that brought on Nancy's worst depressions. 'There is not one piece of news to write you,' she wrote that autumn of 1908, 'except my feelings and alas they are not new but as old as the hills, homesickness and lonesomeness and yet I am so grateful for every sort of blessing that I haven't the cheek to indulge in my feelings. Every time that I do my conscience hurts me.' On one day of autumn longing, Nancy described how she'd wandered through the Cliveden woods humming 'I'm going back to Dixie . . . That's as far as I get. Naturally I can't tell Waldorf but Phyl I feel I simply must go home . . . Oh Phyl I sh like to just be at home for a month, this autumn. The autumn always reminds me of mother and our new dresses and chestnuts, apples woodfires and a general cosiness that I can't find anywhere else . . . Oh Phyl if only it was just a bad dream and one could wake up and find mother. I think I miss her more as I grow older. The glamour of youth covers a lot of sorrow that creeps out in middle age.'

In October she wrote again, 'I lie here and try to go back to our days of Duchess and riding Algie's Texas. I can smell the first pantry at Mirador where the ginger snaps were kept – can't you? One thing looms up so gloomy and that's Sunday afternoons in Richmond. Do you remember how we used to return from our long walk and the house was always half dark. I shall never forget how gloomy it seemed to me, yet I sh like to slip back to that gloom.'

In these early shaky days of her marriage, when she was searching for an identity, Nancy would write from Cliveden as if, like Marie of Rumania, she had been kidnapped into some dynastic marriage. She felt, in the Astors, as if she had joined something stronger than herself, a foreign (and Yankee) tribe that she wanted to reform and control. She would talk them down, half mockingly ('those skunk skinnin' Astors') as if she didn't belong to them. These were days when she clung instead to Bobbie and Phyllis. In 1910, four years after her marriage, she wrote in her diary after another of Phyllis's departures: 'I wept and shall continue to until she returns.'

When Nancy professed selfless love – her highest ideal – she could only apply it to Phyllis. She wanted their love to be perfect and almost claimed it to be so. With others close to her she could only express a competitive desire to be loved better, and exclusively, as if she had never really felt or understood the nature of love. Among her sisters she was constantly on the look-out for greater affection being shown to anyone but herself, attacking her father, for example, for having made the 'mistake' of loving Irene better than her. 'Go to Irene for "Hot Air",' she advised him, 'and come to me for thoughtfulness.'

Nor, it seems, was Nancy able to establish any genuine, confessional intimacy with Waldorf: 'I long to be in Virginia with you, just long to. I get so desperately lonely with no-one to talk to,' she told Phyllis. Phyllis could see the danger, warning Nancy in 1908 to give Waldorf 'some attention': 'He yearns for it.' Nevertheless both Nancy and Waldorf knew what they wanted from each other. Waldorf was too intelligent not to have understood the challenge of managing Nancy, the impossibility of calming down her firecracker instincts, and the unlikeliness of real intimacy. This fitted well with his controlled, austere nature – there is never a hint from his side, in these early years, of anything but happiness. There were no doubts or second thoughts. And yet, towards the end of 1908, Nancy was concerned and wondering what to do with Waldorf. 'He wasn't doing anything,' she recalled in her memoir. He was wasting what she considered 'so much brilliance and capability'. Illness had now prevented him from riding and polo; he was 'frustrated and annoyed' by his immobility. She decided that she couldn't face the prospect of permanent, dual invalidism with him and went for advice to her friends Arthur Balfour and Lord Curzon. They suggested that Waldorf, a popular figure since his days at Eton and Oxford, should stand as an MP. For them he would be a useful, well-financed asset in the Tory ranks, and influential as the son of a newspaper owner. Later Nancy told a friend how she had forced Waldorf on to the political stage, taking a risk with his health: Waldorf had been told that even working on the *Pall Mall Gazette* would be too strenuous. Politics was already his great interest but he had planned a quiet life on the sidelines, using his influence and offering his services, until Nancy forced his hand. Clearly neither he nor Nancy had much idea what canvassing and elections entailed in terms of sheer physical stress.

These were days of great turbulence in British politics, of radicalism, militancy, of sharp divisions in the country and real political crisis of a kind that hadn't been seen since the Reform Act of 1832. The bitter argument between the tariff reformers and the free traders, which had dominated the 1906 election, was as clearly drawn, as culturally deep, as the old, almost evangelical philosophies of Adam Smith and the freedom of the individual from the state versus the idea of the corporate state. More topically it was an argument of liberal imperialists versus Little Englanders. It had divided the Unionist Party under Balfour, who was nervous of protection and the votes it would cost, due to the popular belief that it would raise prices for food. Abandoning free trade lost the Tories the election, giving the Liberals under Henry Campbell-Bannerman, Asquith and Lloyd George a landslide majority in the House of Commons.

With this the Liberals set about a programme of radical reform which the die-hard Tories saw as something near to revolution. The legislation addressed unemployment, sweated industries, bad housing, the provision for manual workers in sickness and old age. Trade union funds were put above the law of damages. The working day in coal mines was restricted to eight hours. The Lords, with their veto, blocked other Liberal measures of land reform, education and temperance. But it was their blocking of Lloyd George's radical 1909 budget that set up a major constitutional struggle between the upper house and the government and which dominated the coming elections of 1910.

Waldorf had taken up passionate liberal beliefs with crusading conviction. Nancy would later say that he was the braver of the two of them when it came to taking radical stands against the party line. His hero was the great reformer and parliamentarian, Lord Shaftesbury, leader of the Evangelical movement of the mid-nineteenth century, a fighter for humane conditions and workers' rights, whose concerns had been similar to those of the new Liberal government. Waldorf had a touch of the Methodist about him, or of Toynbee Hall, the nineteenth-century Oxford-based movement for slum improvement. He was a stern moralist on these matters; an extremist. It was not a pose and he never wavered from it. In the process of finding his own identity

Waldorf had swung as far to the left as his father had been to the mystical right, but it would have been eccentric for him to have joined the Liberals. Waldorf was a Conservative by loyalty. Most of his friends were Unionists of the old, moneyed ruling class. And for her part Nancy was a Conservative by instinct, with a romantic, Virginian view of the English aristocracy and its institutions, and these same people had taken her in when she had first come to England. She wrote in her memoir that one of her reasons for supporting the Unionists was that, but for them, 'England would not have had a Navy' and Britannia would no longer have ruled the waves.

When he was learning about racing bloodstock, Waldorf had apprenticed himself to a vet. Now he went, with equal conscientiousness, to Tory central office to learn the ropes. He had been offered a safe seat, but that was against his principles. He preferred to learn through adversity. In November 1908 he was adopted as Conservative candidate for the Sutton division of Plymouth, a largely working-class constituency where the Liberals had a large majority.

Nancy had the familiar 'strange feeling' that she had come home when she first visited Plymouth. She had a romantic notion of herself as the pilgrim returning to the place from which Drake had set off to reach Virginia. She even felt there might be divine inspiration at work in the choice of constituency. She was moved by the 'missionary' possibilities of the Barbican, whose maze of alleyways near the fish quays of Plymouth represented the third worst area of deprivation in Britain — a national disgrace, worse than anything Nancy had seen among the poor whites across the Blue Ridge Mountains in Virginia, or the black communities in the South. There was almost no sanitation; families were overcrowded into dangerous tenements built indiscriminately over back gardens, over roofs of old sea captains' houses, anywhere you could fit a human container. It was a place of violence, extreme drunkenness and abject poverty, a Calcutta-like inferno of human misery on the coast of Devon. Such a constituency offered, of course, great scope to a politician with Waldorf Astor's wealth and sense of social justice and he was prepared to spend or acquire millions

for the welfare of its inhabitants. The only welfare net provided by the
state was the workhouse and poor relief – a brutal Victorian last resort,
for which the recipient had first to sell all his remaining possessions.
Private charity and voluntary organizations provided what little there
was of the rest.

'Politics are discouraging,' Nancy wrote to Phyllis as the Astors
began their seduction of the town, 'as a man has to be so frightfully
pushing to get along in them & Waldorf never was a "thruster", but I
hope he will become one now.'

On the other hand, Nancy seemed to have found her *métier* for
the first time since her days in the Ragged Mountains with Archdeacon
Neve. She had an outlet for what she called her 'vitality and immense
energy'. 'I had a feeling my life had really begun,' she recalled later. 'I
had never really known before what I wanted to do, or could do.'
Plymouth offered her the chance to combine two of the driving forces
of her personality: the instinct for power and the religious desire to
help 'every single soul'. She threw herself into constituency work,
canvassing from door to door, and 'loved every minute of it'. For five
months from August 1909 they lived in hotels and rented houses,
returning to Cliveden for only two weeks. Nancy immediately became
a novelty. MPs' or candidates' wives had never pounded the streets, or
talked to people in anything other than the most formal language.
Nancy had already discovered 'this power to talk to people easily and
make them talk to me' when, crossing the Atlantic with Waldorf soon
after her marriage, she had started an impromptu meeting of the stok-
ers on the deck of their ship. She felt she had an advantage. The trouble
with English people, she said later, was that they could never be quite
natural with each other. She genuinely believed that there were no
class distinctions in Virginia, whereas the English couldn't help 'form-
ing little cast iron cliques everywhere'.

But more than that, she was genuinely moved by the conditions
she saw around her, reacting in a way that was unusual for a prospective
Tory wife. 'I visited all this a.m.,' she wrote to Phyllis, 'I only visit the
poor & Oh Phyl, they are poor. I match them against our mountain

poor.' In another letter, 'I have no news – only a heavy heart at all the poverty I saw in Plymouth. Yesterday a tea for street waifs. One poor little consumptive cripple and his father gets 7/- a week & had 6 children! It makes one think – there must be something v wrong with civilisation which allows such things. Of course a lot of the poverty is through drink and illness & I am a stronger teetotaller than ever. I just long for you at Plymouth, there are so many things that we can do together. Tomorrow I entertain 26 girls from the East end – poor workers. I am greatly looking forward to it.'

Waldorf first stood in the crisis election of January 1910, in the wake of Lloyd George's 'People's Budget' of 1909 – the most radical ever introduced in Britain. It declared war on poverty, proposing a supertax on large incomes, tax on unearned incomes for the first time, tax on gains in land values. These taxes were designed to provide funds for rearmament, old age pensions and social services, also for the improvement of transport, for agriculture, for research, all of which were areas close to Waldorf's heart – except for the punitive tax itself. Balfour, his party leader, had called it 'robbery' in the Commons. The House of Lords had angrily thrown it out.

There were two rough and raucous elections in 1910, with public meetings often teetering on the edge of violence. The January election was fought over the budget against a background of the rising militancy of women demanding the vote, demonstrations and clashes with the police, strikes, lock-outs and the old question of Irish home rule, which was to bring the country to the brink of civil war in early 1914.

Elections were also a rare opportunity for mass public entertainment, with packed constituency meetings – and it was the theatrical nature of political life that suited Nancy so well. She, and the people of Plymouth, soon discovered that she had a real talent for knockabout politics, a talent reaching far beyond the Langhorne sisters' 'common touch'. She was fearless, fast on her feet, as quick-tongued as any stand-up comic. Never well-tuned to psychological complexities in individuals – thinking them mostly good or bad, right or wrong – driven by emotion and instinct, Nancy completely understood the psychology of crowds. 'Addressed a collection of workmen,' she wrote in her diary. 'I am becoming a mob orator. A female Lloyd George – God forbid.' In all the meetings she was dressed, deliberately, in her smartest clothes, standing out like a film star. She wrote to Phyllis, 'I know nothing of interest but politics. Soon I shall become a sort of Suffragette but for Waldorf's rights, not mine. Nora tells me that all my friends think I'm a political bore!'

Nancy was fascinated by Lloyd George, and jealous of his brilliance with crowds, his power, his convictions and the fact that, whatever Nancy thought about the Liberals, the ground he was claiming was very similar to Waldorf's crusading concerns. On the hustings Lloyd George declared that his budget 'will drive hunger forever from the hearths of the poor' – which was certainly one of Nancy's ambitions but she would have preferred to have done it with Waldorf's money and her own proselytizing. She was deeply contemptuous of a tax-raising state as a competitor in good works. 'You see the Liberals are telling the Poor [Nancy used a capital] that Tariff Reform means dearer bread but of course it doesn't,' she wrote to Phyllis '& they also say they will tax only the rich. I simply loathe them & don't see how I can ever bring myself to speak to one again.' She affected to despise Lloyd George for his private morals. In her diary she wrote, 'My prayer book says "Love one another", How oh how can I love Lloyd George? Perhaps his soul but not his mean and ignoble ways.'

Politics had released Nancy's energies but hadn't cured her health. Each day required a huge effort of willpower to crank herself up to get to the meetings and to go canvassing. Her diaries tell on successive days, 'Could not move with fatigue', and 'I fear I shall die of fatigue.' To compound her other problems, she also suffered from insomnia and even at the height of the campaign she would often have to sleep until lunch, once until four in the afternoon, and often for most of the evening.

Waldorf had to stop campaigning for the January election after a sudden attack of heart trouble. Nevertheless, the Tories gained 100 seats and tied with the Liberals, who now depended in Parliament on the support of the emerging Labour Party and the Irish nationalists. Waldorf lost, but it still seemed to Nancy like a victory. 'Never have I seen such enthusiasm,' she wrote to Phyllis, 'They dragged our carriage home, about 1000 men and women; sang and shouted themselves hoarse. It was all very personal and delicious and I shall <u>never</u> forget them.'

Despite their infirmities, and as if to announce that Waldorf's eventual election was a foregone conclusion, he bought one of the grandest houses in Plymouth at 3 Elliott Terrace, looking over the sea and the Hoe from where Drake sailed to meet the Armada 'to show that we have come to stay'. The Astors would stubbornly lay siege to the constituency until Waldorf was elected.

Not long afterwards Nancy was writing to Phyllis, 'Oh! Phyl, I am torn to pieces. The Dr. says Waldorf has certainly got consumption and must go at once to St. Moritz until the snow melts . . . he says he will be absolutely cured if he's careful.' They went there in February, for days of inactivity at the Suvretta House Hotel.

In 1910 Lizzie staged another dramatic flight from Richmond, taking Nancy aged thirteen and Alice aged eight to Paris. They spent Christmas in the Hotel de Calais in the Rue Cambon. She had finally decided to leave Moncure for good, and had planned to go into exile in Europe for two years to make the break. Nancy Lancaster remembered being 'delighted that they had separated because I couldn't bear the rows'. Moncure, defying the dire prognosis on his health, had clearly reverted to his old cheerful form. 'My father would say,' said Nancy Lancaster, 'I ran into your mother on the street and her eyes looked like little raisins. She's got as fat as a little pig.' He roared with laughter about it. Poor mother was absolutely desperate. She would say 'Now children, if you all want me to I'll take your father back for your sake.' And I remember saying 'Oh for God's sake don't, we've had peace for all this time.'

Chillie had turned the Lizzie problem over to Nancy, and Lizzie was now mostly dependent on Nancy's allowance. Trying to explain further extravagances to Chillie, Lizzie wrote to him, 'I always hope for Xmas but alas I got a diamond pin [from Nancy] instead of money.' As part of the deal Nancy had demanded that Lizzie keep an account of her spending, which to Lizzie seemed an outrageous insult. 'An indignant letter from Lizzie,' wrote Nancy to Phyllis ' — saying my letters were impertinent & cruel & Lord only knows what. I beg you to explain how I feel — that I want to help her to live but not to buy French frocks. Poor Liz I suppose I am a brute.' Lizzie defiantly stayed in the Suvretta House Hotel in St Moritz that February instead of cheaper pensions, writing to say her money was 'going fast' but evading Nancy's questions. 'I shall give up and she can do as she likes,' Nancy wrote to Phyllis. 'I fear she has little delicacy, poor Liz.'

In May Lizzie finally turned up at Cliveden. 'I know why she came,' Nancy wrote to Phyllis. 'She said it was homesickness but I fear she was busted. Poor Liz, poor us.' She stayed for a month, severely straining Nancy's patience by spending lavishly at the most expensive London stores. Just before she left, Nancy reported to Phyllis, there was a 'big fuss'. 'Lizzie began about her independence and upbraided me etc. And I told her I thought so long as she took Pa's money she might take his advice and mine too as for that. She never sews a stitch and spends her days playing bridge if she finds other Idle Rich.' Lizzie waited until an hour before her train went to make another financial request. 'She said, "I suppose you'll be furious but I've only got seventy dollars in the world and that's in French money,"' wrote Nancy. 'I had to give her seventy-five dollars then and there and gave her five hundred dollars after, I asked why then she had bought the children so many clothes and herself. Her reply is as ever, "because I am bound to have them."'

Lizzie headed for the shore of Lake Geneva with her daughters, to Vevey, and then to a small town near Montreux. She moved to Tours in France where she stayed for a year, sending the children to the local *lycée*. Her daughters remember her loneliness, her lack of friends, her

longing for home and Moncure. She would spend the evenings reading
French history to them in the hotels and pensions by Lake Geneva or in
rooms overlooking the rue National in Tours. Above all they remembered her warmth and affection towards them. She presented their
odyssey positively as a kind of finishing school, even though the children
were so young. The choice of Tours, according to Alice, was that it
was 'the best place for French' and that she was determined that her
daughters should 'speak the most wonderful French and marry diplo-
mats'. In 1911 Lizzie came to England for King George V's coronation,
and then returned to Richmond where Moncure had taken up residence
in the Jefferson Hotel and where, according to Alice, he 'spent most of
his time in bed reading Balzac and the Saturday *Evening Post*, always
cheerful and uncomplaining'.

Lizzie's distress, on the other hand, at being forced to itemize
accounts for Nancy, was ingrained on the memory of her teenage daughter Nancy. 'Every Monday morning the letter came from Nancy to my
mother to Richmond and I saw mother absolutely made miserable.
Every time I saw that blue envelope come she would say, "How can she
do this to me?" and I remember saying to Nannie later, "Aunt Nancy
I'm never going to like you or forgive you. You absolutely ruined my
life. I saw my mother weep and I'll never forget it." And Nannie was
very big and said "I'm ashamed. I was wrong to do that. I'm older now"
and then I became very intimate with her because she was big enough
to admit her faults.' It was a rare admission and indeed Nancy had
been unrelenting, 'hard and obstinate', as she described herself, berating Lizzie for her luxuries and reporting it all to Phyllis and Irene: 'Liz
writes she's hardly enough to live on. Then why keep 3 servants for 5
people when she's never had but 2 before. It's rot!' 'No Phyl,' she
wrote, 'I've no pity for her. I sh. pity most but not Liz. She has her
pride and takes things more for granted than anyone I ever met. She
promised me she wd. keep some sort of account but she won't do it
and I can't make her. Unless she puts the children in school I shall just
take the schooling money away, but I hope its only for a time. She will
be upset.'

The insult to Lizzie was compounded by the way she saw Nancy press money and gifts on to Phyllis — who received emeralds, pearls and furs — and on to Irene and Nora too. Chillie had already bought Irene a house in New York, and when Dana lost money in the Wall Street crash of 1907 Nancy provided Irene with more than just an allowance. 'Please don't stint yourself,' she wrote to her, 'otherwise next year I will cut you off.' She sent her sables to match her gift to Phyllis and there were many other forms of gifts. If Phyllis ordered something expensive through her Nancy would tear up the cheque, writing 'It really hurts me to have a larger bank account than yours.' As often with families it seemed easier and more natural to give money to the ones who already had it, restricting the needy ones so as not to 'encourage' bad character and dependency. By 1912 Nancy had all the sisters on her payroll but only held the eldest, Lizzie, to account.

In the second election of 1910, in December, Waldorf was elected to Parliament and thirty-five years of the Astors' munificent, attentive devotion to the city of Plymouth began. Waldorf had set out to be, as he put it later 'co-operative, progressive, independent, broad minded', and he immediately put his ideals into practice. Early in the Parliament he voted against his party — a courageous act — and with the Liberal Government on Lloyd George's Health and Unemployment Insurance Bill (from the conviction, he said, that this was in the interests of his constituents). It made the headlines and scandalized members of the Tory Party, but it initiated a friendship with Lloyd George, whose name, despite Nancy's fervent aversion to him, soon began to appear in the Cliveden visitors' book. It also led Lloyd George to appoint Waldorf as chairman of the state Medical Research Committee. Waldorf was now one of the two most radical members of the Unionist Social Reform Committee, a parliamentary group led by F. E. Smith (later Lord Birkenhead) which opposed the right wing of the party, the Tory diehards, and the defenders of the Lords.

Waldorf made another move towards power that year when he persuaded his father to buy the *Observer* newspaper from Lord Northcliffe. It was bought partly to acquire the services of the brilliant and influential J. L. Garvin, its editor, who had had a spectacular success putting the ailing *Observer* back in business. Garvin would simultaneously edit the Astors' *Pall Mall Gazette*, whose fortunes had also been slipping.

In the next three years, as Waldorf and Nancy gathered power, they also gathered houses. They built Rest Harrow in Sandwich Bay, Kent, which Nancy described as a 'cottage' in the Newport way of describing a large seaside house. Paul Phipps, whose business was not thriving, was employed as the architect and did a remarkably good job. It was a place designed for intimate friends, and for golf – it was next to three championship courses. No expense was spared in the thoroughness of its detail: the brass hydraulic hinges that kept the doors from slamming in the wind are still in working order, the wooden balconies hardly affected by eighty years of Kent coast weather. The design was modest and plain: large stone fireplaces, dark blue and white ceramic fires in the bedrooms, light brown runner carpets edged in red on the stairs, painted floorboards. The bell signal outside the pantry still shows the status of its occupants, announcing 'Master R. Shaw's bedroom'. And, as usual with Nancy, it was extremely comfortable: there were as many rooms for the servants as for the guests. It was, in some ways, the most delightful of her houses, sitting in its featureless landscape on the Kent coast, resembling those parts of Long Island, the beaches of the Hamptons, for example, with their banks of reeds and grasses and low dunes and their houses a few steps from the sea.

As their power base in London the Astors leased, at first, an eighteenth-century palace in the corner of St James's Square, which stretched from there to Regent Street and was almost as large, in terms of its public rooms and its scope for entertaining, as Cliveden.

To make everything a little rosier, they had received an unexpected boost to their income. Nancy, once so worried about Waldorf's debts, wrote to Phyllis, 'My dear what do you think Mr. Astor has done. Don't breathe it even to Reggie or a soul. He has given Waldorf the Waldorf Astoria Hotel for a birthday present! It sounds like a joke, but it's a jolly good one – about 40,000 pounds more a year. Did you ever hear such a thing in yr. life!' Yet Nancy still felt she had to keep Waldorf up to scratch, writing from the rented St James's Square, 'I am pleased but fear Waldorf may turn into a screw as he refuses to buy this house.'

11

Phyllis and the Captain

Since early in 1907 Phyllis had been conducting a secret friendship with a young Grenadier Guards officer, Captain The Hon. Henry Douglas Pennant – her 'young man of Oakham'. They had met riding home from hunting at Melton Mowbray one afternoon that winter during one of Reggie's sulky disappearances. Oakham was where the Captain kept his horses.

The story of the affair between Phyllis and the Captain has always been sealed away in secrecy, dealt with in only two or three lines in family memoirs. And yet Phyllis described it as the first great love of her life – having revised her early memories of Reggie – and it lasted for six years. The real story lay hidden in Bob Brand's black ocean trunk. In loyalty to Phyllis's memory he had kept Douglas Pennant's entire correspondence with her, and most of hers written towards the end of the affair. They describe an extraordinary character who seemed to have emerged from nineteenth-century fiction, a classic soldier-adventurer, an outsider, a romantic misfit. In Phyllis's case, the letters show a remarkable ability to project her fantasy on to her own life, and to sustain it up until the moment it turned, predictably, to disaster.

The Captain was very different from the rich Boston sportsmen of Nancy and Phyllis's first conquests. He was a reversion to Phyllis's childhood ideal of knightly romance: stiffly handsome, courageous, 'a very good soldier and a very good horseman'. He had a neat moustache; his speech was clipped and perfunctory and he laughed in short, explosive bursts. There was a gallantry and beau-like attentiveness about his behaviour. 'She adored him,' said Nancy Lancaster, 'she said he always put a cushion behind her back when she sat down' – a small detail of male chivalry held in her niece's memory for seventy years. He was the second son, by the second marriage of Baron Penrhyn of Penrhyn Castle in north Wales, disinherited by primogeniture from his father's vast wealth and estates. He had fought with distinction with the Grenadier Guards in the Boer War in his early twenties. When Phyllis met him, at the age of thirty-one, he was on hunting leave from his regiment and about to leave the army for the reserve list. He was as passionate about hunting as Phyllis, and as good a rider, billeting himself at Oakham like a soldier, 'in cold and draughty lodgings and pubs'. At first it was a chaste, discreet attachment with nothing declared on either side. But Nancy picked up Phyllis's attraction for 'The Capt.', as Phyllis called him, and in February and March 1908 she invited him to stay at Cliveden with Phyllis and Reggie.

The Captain added to his attraction in Phyllis's eyes by taking up, after he left the army, the dangerous and exotic job of hunting game, collecting rare and fine specimens for the Natural History Museum in South Kensington. The commission would take him to the bleakest, remotest parts of the earth – Central Asia, Mongolia, Siberia – for long stretches, and increase the time and distance between them. It was the profession of someone who sought out solitude and hardship; of a Rider Haggard hero (whose books had inspired this generation of gentlemen adventurers). Phyllis appreciated that this self-imposed banishment suited the Captain's love of the 'natural' existence – a fashionable topic – and his dislike of the affectations of metropolitan life. 'The sedentary life,' he warned her, in his clipped way, 'is a terrible trial for a man of my habits.' For Phyllis, the physical distance that separated them ensured the secrecy which was important to both of them, and kept alive a notion of romantic friendship between two people who could rarely spend time together.

The Captain's earliest letters to Mirador in 1909 were written from the relative comfort of his first assignment in British East Africa, later Kenya, where he had gone to shoot lion and elephant. East Africa was overrun at this moment with shooters: ex-officers, remittance men, trophy hunters, millionaires, British peers, royalty, and ex-President Teddy Roosevelt. It was the beginning of the boom in the early, luxurious safaris, of the tented campaigns with their armies of porters and supply trains; the time of the Kenya hunter-pioneers: Delamere, Grogan, Berkeley Cole, Percival, the murderous Richard Meinhertzhagen.

The Captain worried about the status of his profession in Phyllis's eyes; he wrote with self-mockery in his awkward letters that it was 'the only thing that raises me above the level of a bum'. There had been few openings after the army. His family had offered him the job of training their racehorses, but he had an aversion to the smart racing society of Newmarket. Now he found he had much in common with this officer tribe on the equator, refugees from Edwardian society, many of whom were sons of the aristocracy. 'This is a top hole climate,' he wrote to Phyllis in his first letter. 'Have met such heaps of friends of other days out here leading happy pastoral lives.'

After only four months Douglas Pennant had the all-time East African record for shooting lions singlehandedly. He shot eleven of them in a month — like leopards they were classed by the settlers as vermin, requiring no licence. 'Pardon my bucking!' he wrote to Phyllis '. . . Count Brickart a Belgian had ten in January — but all the other shootists have been in a party.' Now he admitted modestly that he had become a 'celebrated' big game hunter, almost overnight; the new boy put to the top of the class. And clearly he was a brilliant shot, able to bring down buck from a galloping horse, inventive enough to hunt on a bicycle — 'the best way to travel down the native paths', his rifle slung from his shoulder. How exhilarating the Captain's letters from Nyeri, Marsabit, Meru, Naivasha must have been to Phyllis living at Mirador with the moody Reggie. 'I got such a capital lion today but he made rather a mess of one of my horses before being finished,' he wrote in his neat miniature handwriting. He addressed her as 'Dear Mrs Brooks' or occasionally 'Dearest Friend', straining to declare his love without being able to do so, risking the odd phrase: 'How are you? Please be careful of yourself. It is hot here now. Next to seeing you the thing I should like best of all just now would be a dozen oysters and a pint of pop. Yrs sincerely G. H. D. Pennant. Please excuse this dreadful scribble.' And later, 'I feel so much that I want to see you and talk to you that I am compelled to ease my feelings by writing to you. Please do not be angry.'

Phyllis couldn't have avoided picking up on the Captain's infatuation. He had fallen in love early on in their friendship, and now he was mesmerized by her in his solitude. Quite apart from the qualities that made men fall for Phyllis, she provided something for the Captain that he had never experienced in a woman, inside or outside his family. She was sympathetic, she offered friendship, she seemed to appreciate him for his abilities. It was balm of Gilead for the Captain. When her letters came to him – delayed by weeks – he confessed later that they had 'sent a thrill of joy through all my mind – and body'.

The fledgling romance nearly ended in the Rift Valley, Kenya in September that year when, as the Captain described it, 'I was misguided, or I am afraid I must say FOOLISH enough to chase a wounded leopard in ground very much in favour of the leopard with somewhat disastrous results . . .' The leopard, who had 'sunk his teeth in the side of my face and skull', had done enormous damage to the Captain before one of his bearers managed to shoot it. He had been forced to travel 130 miles on an improvised litter, swimming oxen across flooded rivers, with a huge wound which exposed his vertebrae, to the nearest railroad point at Kijabe and the nearest morphine – a terrible ordeal that deprived him of sleep for four days. Nevertheless he managed to record in his journal, without surprise or comment, 'Reach Kijabe station in the afternoon, having met not long before Harley, formerly my fag at Eton, who with his wife was camped close by.' The Captain was only out of danger after spending a month in hospital in Nairobi; and his wounds were still being cauterized on the boat going home. It took

him a year to recover fully. The leopard mauling did the trick with
Phyllis. Having described the liaison to Nancy in 1909 as 'a little
harmless fling' with the Captain, confessing to 'a strange attraction for
him' though 'not as yet very deep', she admitted later that it was at
this moment she realized how much she had been thinking about him,
imagining his movements each day, waiting with excitement for his
letters, worrying about his safety.

The relationship changed gear late in 1910. The Captain managed
to visit Mirador on his way to Canada to shoot; their first meeting, as
he records in his diary, for eighteen months. And there, finally, he was
able to declare his love. David 'Winkie' Brooks, born in May 1910, was
six months old, and Reggie was absent on a hunting trip with friends.
Clearly, Phyllis didn't discourage him. The Captain's letters on his
departure became open and confident, full of memories of the months
of waiting. 'My only solace when I couldn't write was to think of you
which I used to do at all hours of the day and night,' adding, 'though we
may not meet again for years my love will not grow colder with age.'

Soon after that visit to Mirador the Captain made Phyllis the ben-
eficiary of his will, leaving her a small income – a gesture that showed
how little he regarded his own family. 'It is only a paltry thanks offering for your friendship,' he wrote, 'and for the strange feeling that
often soothes the pain my rather selfish nature gives me – that after all
there is one woman in the world for whom I could have lived, and
loved more dearly than my life – darling friend.' On leave in London he
put one of his clocks back five hours to imagine her 'doings and occupation', noting the moments when they could both see the sun and the
same stars, and claimed that he could plainly hear her voice. Phyllis had
fallen for the Captain but as a romantic fantasy kept apart from the
everyday reality of her life at Mirador. It hadn't lightened her state of
turmoil and despair about her marriage, the feeling that 'I almost
wished my life was over.' Still there was no move towards divorce or
separation. Extracting herself was fraught with legal difficulties. Reggie
would never make a move himself. Furthermore, any suggestion of
divorce would have to be negotiated with his parents. It would involve

the settlement of money, and that meant opening up a battle against a rich family, surrounded by lawyers who made every decision about the Brookses' lives and finances.

Phyllis missed the hunting season in England, although the Captain stayed several times at Cliveden as Nancy's guest. He saw Phyllis only twice in 1911 at Mirador – hurried visits, surrounded with caution. Chillie was watching for trouble and gentlemen visitors from across the road at Misfit. On one of his flying visits Phyllis and the Captain were forced to meet in a Washington railway station, Phyllis telling her father that she was visiting the dentist. Even so, the Captain told her that Mirador, where they had ridden together, was 'more like a home to me than any other place since my father died'.

By 1911, the experiment of Reggie living at Mirador had failed, despite the flowing tap water from the newly dug wells. Reggie had built a swimming pool and a new tennis court but in the words of Nancy Lancaster, 'He got bored to death because there was no one for him to play golf or tennis with in Virginia so he just sat there in the library and drank all the time. He couldn't bear it. He wanted to go to Palm Beach and Aiken.' Phyllis was very sad. She 'would wrap her head in veils and sit at the piano making musical faces and singing "Farewell Manchester".' Reggie was frequently absent from Mirador. When he was there he refused to meet anybody, sneered at Phyllis's efforts with the church and the poor and criticized the way she ran the house and the farm. As his drinking got steadily worse, he told her frequently that he no longer loved her and that he would be glad if she left him – unable, apparently, to take this action himself. Most of his time was spent alone.

Eventually it was Nancy and Waldorf who persuaded Phyllis to take action. There had been another Christmas in England with Phyllis looking 'thin and nervous', and hunting while Reggie disappeared. After they left in March 1912, Nancy wrote to Phyllis, 'your days of Reggie are numbered & you won't have many more to stand – I can promise you that & I warn you it will be very easy to do.' Nancy had to make another exception in her moral stand against divorce, to include her sister now as well as herself. In Phyllis's case the grounds were clinical: 'I am convinced that you could never do anything but ruin your health and your disposition – & I think that your first duty is to your children.' It would have to be, of course, on the grounds of adultery – the Bible sanctioned nothing else. Nancy went to work. 'Nanny behaved very badly,' Nancy Lancaster remembered and laughed, 'She didn't like Reggie and she wanted Phyllis to marry over here and she put a detective on him.' She hoped to catch Reggie in the *maisons de passe* that he now frequented in Mayfair on his hated trips to England.

But Phyllis wouldn't divorce on grounds of adultery. She thought it was shaming to her children to bring such a case and have it contested with underhand information. She hoped for grounds of incompatibility but Reggie, sensing disaster, had given up drinking for a while which seemed to snag the plans. Nancy wrote, 'Dearest Phyl, Irene seems to think if Reggie is not drinking you wd be unwise to leave him this winter & only get greatly criticised.' Instead, before Reggie fell off the wagon again, she got him to agree to a separation which took effect in the summer of 1912, the terms still to be negotiated. It was a bad decision that boxed Phyllis into a corner. By her marriage she had become a resident of New York, whose laws required a three-year delay between separation and divorce if it was to be settled on grounds of incompatibility. It also barred her – such was the law – from producing Nancy's adultery evidence against him in any future divorce case. Phyllis believed that after a year or two of separation, Reggie would come to her and ask for divorce himself, admitting adultery. It would be quiet and uncontested, like Nancy's divorce from Robert Shaw.

With the separation there was an even greater need for secrecy between the Captain and Phyllis. Being named as the guilty party in a divorce case, or even publicly consorting with a married woman, was severely looked down upon, a potential disgrace to the Captain's family. 'Keeping away from the King's Proctor', was how a nephew described it succinctly eighty years later: 'Tiger shooting for a broken heart. Common practice.' For the next eighteen months their love affair depended on unreliable postal services through which Phyllis received extraordinary descriptions of the Captain's nomadic life. He wrote of struggling with overturning carriages in the mountains near the Mongolian border; gulping down soup and fresh caviare 'with delicious chopped spring onions' at a Russian railway station on his way to the south-west corner of the Caspian sea; eating a Christmas dinner of wild duck and pickled cucumber huddled by a fire in his fur-lined coat; haggling for horses in central Asia; hunting with Kalmucks and Turcomans; 'cadging' food and shelter from Russian peasants. The Captain was stoic and brave, and physically extremely tough. Only occasionally did he let out an understated complaint about the frequently terrible conditions in which he lived – climbing dangerous rock faces in pursuit of ibex, hacking his way across sheet ice. Of Mongolia, where the Captain 'did not see a tree or shrub for nineteen days', he wrote, 'I did not feel quite myself in that dreadful cold and bleak country', but put this down merely to having got used to the sultry climate of Africa. All the bluff and self-consciousness is dropped when the Captain describes the earth around him. He writes well about the landscape – and one can see how the loneliness sustained him. He wrote from the mountains of Tien Shan in Central Asia, 'The colours are too lovely – all sorts of pinks and light and dark greens. It is the burning of the mountain ash that gives the best sort of shades – bright blue skies most days and glittering snow on the hills – can you wonder that I prefer it to an artificial existence of snobbery and lick-spittle, in spite sometimes of its discomforts & solitude.'

It emerged from his letters to Phyllis, but only after two years of correspondence, that the Captain was in a state of wounded rebellion against his background, as great perhaps as someone from his class and his position as an army officer was able to be. He had taken a stance, in this period of pitched battles between capital and labour, that amounted almost to class betrayal. The fairyland from which he was exiled was the great fortress of Penrhyn Castle, a building of stupendous proportions set in a park that sloped down to the edge of the Menai Straits in north Wales. It had been built in the 1820s and 1830s on a scale that dwarfed almost any private project of nineteenth-century wealth – even in Newport, Rhode Island. It was a colossal exercise, one that took seventeen years to complete, and was designed in the 'pseudo-Norman' style, a brief fashion after the Gothic revival, 'with doors so massive', the Captain wrote to Phyllis in an early letter about his background, 'you could hardly open them'. It was the size of Windsor Castle but almost certainly heavier, 'too massive and huge to be vulgar', as the Captain observed.

The Douglas Pennants' enormous wealth had come from their slate mines, great cliffs of open-cast quarry near to Penrhyn Castle, up whose ledges and galleries, in the depictions of the Victorian Romantic painters, the Welsh slate workers scrambled like eager mountaineers. It was, and is, the biggest slate quarry in the world, bought in the late eighteenth century with the profits from the family's Jamaican sugar estates. When Henry was growing up there the estate, much of it grouse moor, occupied the entire heart of north Wales around Snowdon, land accumulated by the Captain's grandfather in the twenty years before 1890. It amounted to almost a third of the whole district of Gwynedd in Caernarvonshire, a truly enormous amount of land for one man to own.

Henry's elder half brother, the heir to the estates, was twelve years older; his own younger brother a year his junior. He had twelve sisters from his father's two marriages. Deferring to an older half brother would not in itself have caused him bitterness; he would have been prepared for it in childhood. But the family was divided and unhappy. The children of Lord Penrhyn's second marriage, including Henry, were treated as interlopers at Penrhyn by the elder branch. As well as a general lack of love and a nanny who, according to a nephew, 'stuck pins in his tongue', Henry's sisters had dominated his life, treating him as a figure of fun and teasing him for his stiff soldierly ways. He had grown up at Penrhyn, feeling 'second echelon' and inferior. His only ally in childhood had been his father.

By the time he was writing to Phyllis, early memories of hunting with his father, and the landscape itself, were all that attached him to Penrhyn. His father, George Sholto, 2nd Baron of Penrhyn, was an arch

Tory, a man of 'robust' views who, for many years, had been Member
of Parliament for Caernarvon. In 1900, while Henry was fighting the
Boers, he embarked on what still remains the longest, if not the bitterest, industrial dispute in Welsh history when the slate workers went
on strike and Lord Penrhyn dug in his heels and locked them out. The
battle endured for three years. Lord Penrhyn at first had the backing of
his class – the Prince of Wales sent telegrams from Biarritz – who saw
it as a front line against the menace of syndicalism. But finally even *The
Times* was forced to complain about his obduracy as the Denbighshire
Yeomanry were sent to occupy the villages to keep the peace. There
was no winner; an entire community was destroyed in the process and
with it Lord Penrhyn's profits – and his relationship with his son.

His family had engendered in the Captain a fierce dislike for the
attitudes of his class and their 'snobbery'. A letter was leaked to his
father by the family doctor, in which Henry warned that he would
become a Liberal MP – the equivalent, in Lord Penrhyn's eyes, of
joining the Bolsheviks or siding with the miners – Lloyd George had
supported the strike. His father 'took it very hard indeed', according
to his family, that Henry had become 'anti-Tory and anti-establish-
ment' and they hardly spoke in the years before he died. The rawness
of feeling left by the dispute in an already divided family meant that the
Captain thought it wise to keep his views secret after his father's death
in 1907, the year he met Phyllis. He wrote to her in 1912, 'As a
matter of fact my leanings – but this please only between us two – are
very strongly on the Radical side. That is the side I feel for and admire,
though of course, family connections and the repose that dead men
seek restrain me to the others.' He had been influenced in recent
years, he said, by 'the poorer demanding classes' rather than the
'richer holding ones'.

Phyllis smiled on these radical sentiments: they went with the
Captain and his attraction. She thought she had some of them herself,
mostly directed at 'the idle rich of New York' and the Brooks family,
but without understanding their context. Perhaps, in reality, if they had
spent any time with each other, they would have found flaws in their

mirror romantic images. The influence of his twelve dominating sisters had turned the Captain into a misogynist, judging by his letters. He was passionately opposed to women's suffrage, whereas Phyllis, Nancy and Waldorf were ardently for it. English women, the Captain claimed, 'without the slightest doubt' were 'as a class . . . when urgent questions arise, ill-balanced and prone to enthusiasm to the very verge of craziness'. He considered it a mistake to give the vote to a 'preponderant element of different reasoning people'.

There was a sadness, too, about the Captain, which made Phyllis feel sympathetic and protective towards him. She described him as 'straight and white' (loyal, honest, pure in heart). He confessed to her that he was 'outwardly ungracious', cranky, awkward in company, and he worried that this would make Phyllis wonder about his affections when they met. And indeed many people who met him found him almost unapproachable with his brittleness and disguised shyness. He was grateful to her for 'humanizing' him, he said, despite his suffering from the 'irregularity of our attachment'.

For Phyllis there was undoubtedly a strong erotic attraction to the Captain that had long ago displaced the image of the sexless ballroom beau. It was a flattering conquest to have the devotion of a man who had turned his back on women and on society; who preferred to live in tents; who was rough, like Esau, driven and difficult, not smooth and charming like Paul Phipps. Phyllis fancied that she could tame the Captain, civilize him and lead him out of the darkness. He confessed to her, 'Till well over 30 I am nothing better than a dunce, ignorant of any sort of literature or useful knowledge save the elements one learnt at school and as speedily forgot – with no experience then of how to apply anything to present day uses.' The Captain's reading matter was limited to copies of *The Times* sent in weekly batches along the Trans-Siberian Railway. Part of Phyllis's humanizing influence was to have introduced him to books; she provided the reading lists for his travels – something alien to the world of Penrhyn Castle. Not all her selections were a success. 'I see I shall have to fall back on Anna Karenina,' he wrote from Siberia, 'I hate novels.' But he persisted, and wrote a few weeks later, 'I think the best part of the work is your having read it. Thank goodness Mrs AK threw herself under the railway carriage last night — so I am nearly through — after that my stand by will be my two vols of history.'

Before an operation on her kidneys that year, Phyllis had sent a list of her last wishes to Nancy. She would leave her Sargent portrait to Henry Douglas Pennant, 'whom I loved very dearly and who was the best friend I ever had'. Already jealously referring to the Captain as a 'half-wit . . . Oh that C. I hate him,' Nancy responded, 'I am really discouraged by your feelings for the C. My goodness, don't you want a mental superior? It's rot saying someone is clean and well bred . . . No Phyl that aff. will never have my blessings I warn you so don't expect it.' The Captain was an anathema to Nancy. 'She never understood about love,' according to Phyllis, but Nancy genuinely couldn't see the point of Phyllis replacing one brainless 'spo'tin' gent with another, especially as she was now busy collecting more 'mental superiors' around her at Cliveden. 'Next year,' she wrote to Phyllis in 1911, 'I shall have young and charming intellectuals for you to meet.' She was about to acquire a package deal, a ready-made think-tank of young men whose arrival, she said later without exaggeration, 'changed all our lives'. Douglas Pennant had no place in these improving plans, in this crusade of self-enlightenment. Nancy hadn't understood the Captain, or measured his strength as an adversary. But he had understood Nancy, and for once the contestants were evenly matched.

12

Brain Fag

The 'charming intellectuals' that Nancy had promised to collect for Phyllis's entertainment belonged to a group of young men known as 'Lord Milner's Kindergarten' or simply 'The Bright Young Men' and they were certainly the brightest and the best to be had. They were surrounded at this moment by fame and praise, and much talk, for having seemed to have conjured the Union of South Africa out of the unhealable antagonisms between its two white races. They had returned to England in 1909 with the distinction, in the words of one newspaper, of having 'transformed the Empire's most sordid war [between the British and the two Boer Republics, the Orange Free State and the Transvaal] into the world's most enlightened peace settlement'. They had saved South Africa for the Empire, as a self-governing Dominion, and almost certainly from a further civil war, with the willing acquiescence of the Boers.

The name 'Kindergarten' had originated as a jibe from their enemies in South Africa, because of their tender ages and the more or less unaccountable political power they wielded over them. They had been recruited, in many cases almost fresh from their Oxford classrooms, by Alfred Milner, the colonial governor, himself a Balliol prodigy, to help him remake a country destroyed by war. The name stuck to them for the rest of their lives and for posterity. They adopted it, with a capital 'K', as a mark of honour higher, in their estimations, than anything they were to achieve in their later, and in all cases, distinguished careers. What made them famous was the combination of their youth – most of them were barely thirty when they returned to England after eight or nine years – and their collective influence, so it seemed, not only on British imperial policy but on the Anglophobic Boer leadership. They were operating, too, many thousands of miles away from Westminster and Whitehall.

Of this group of young men, it was Philip Kerr, grandson of the Duke of Norfolk, and Bob Brand, son of Viscount Hampden, both from New College, Oxford, and considered the ablest pair of the group, who were to have such a profound, transforming effect on the lives of Nancy and Phyllis. But it took Nancy two years to get to know this new breed of intellectual, and then to annex the group to Cliveden.

At first it was straightforward celebrity-gathering on Nancy's part that brought them into her orbit. She had been collecting fresh blood from the world of letters. Nobody, it seems, refused Nancy's summons: Rudyard Kipling, Hilaire Belloc, G. K. Chesterton, Henry James, J. M. Barrie were now regulars at St James's Square or weekenders at Cliveden. (On a visit to Cliveden in July 1912, Henry James had concluded that Nancy was 'full of possibilities and fine material – though but a reclaimed barbarian, with all her bounty, spontaneity and charm, too'.) The Kindergarten were 'thinkers and reformers', in Nancy's phrase, which meant political action, superior in her book to the writer-entertainers, whatever their subject. And these liberal reformers had brought off a *coup* that was the wonder of British and imperial politics. Their success had its roots in the Boer War which everyone in Britain had been keen, until now at its brilliant resolution, to forget.

Lord Milner, their mentor, had been sent out as an 'emergency man' as he called it, before the Boer War began, to try and save South Africa for the Empire, to restore British prestige. Milner was an administrator of genius; the greatest public servant of his time, whose brilliance had been seen in the Egyptian Ministry of Finance in the early 1890s and then as chairman of the Inland Revenue in Britain. As governor, first of Cape Colony, he had forced the war on the Boers, judging it inevitable. British settlers were being pushed around and denied political rights in the Transvaal, the autonomous Boer republic and the biggest source of gold in the world, but beyond direct British control. The two British colonies, Natal and Cape Colony, and the two Boer republics, were increasingly at each other's throats, warring over tariffs, locked in debilitating rivalries that were attracting hostile foreign interest. The deeper struggle was for control of the whole country, but more important to Milner was the fate of the British Empire. In 1900 it encompassed one fifth of the globe, but its ties were being loosened by nationalism in Canada, Australia and India. The Empire was held together now only by sentiment, it had no common defence strategy and was being menaced by the rise of Germany which had been shipping arms to the Boers. To Milner the future of South Africa was vital to the future of the Empire and therefore, in his view, to the British race.

When the war was over, Milner annexed the two Boer states to the Crown and embarked on a massive and, for the Empire, unprecedented programme of reconstruction and social engineering, centred on the Transvaal and Johannesburg. It was for this project that he sent for the young civil servants and graduates. He wanted men so far untainted by politics and prejudice, with 'the best brains and the greatest possible energy', who wanted to work for the public good – and they clamoured for the job. Milner didn't recruit them directly: they appointed each other, haphazardly, through the Oxford Common Room network, by word of mouth.

Milner's aim was to create a new prosperity which would attract a wave of British immigrants to overwhelm the Boer population; to reform the entire country along British lines and eventually, when British ascendancy was assured, to grant independence. It was a long-term plan and behind it was Milner's Great Idea, his doctrine of the 'New Imperialism', whose missionary purpose had so attracted this generation of idealistic young men. The idea was not exclusive to Milner although he was its greatest advocate: to bind the Empire together in an 'organic union' of equal nations, with a single foreign policy removed from Westminster. It would create the strongest power in the world and give a new lease to Pax Britannica which had kept the peace since 1815. This version was not for commercial conquest and domination, it was an instrument of social reform and prosperity, a stabilizing force for global peace. Milner had an almost Messianic belief in the Empire and the British race, in whose ideals, he saw 'the principal hope for the future of mankind'. Unless it was bound together, he preached, Britain would sink into oblivion.

If the reconstruction of the Transvaal had been the Kindergarten's only achievement they might still have been celebrities. They transformed its infrastructure and economy in three years of grinding hard work: amalgamating railways, resettling the farms, reviving the mines, the ports, the schools, creating model municipalities, laying communications. By 1905, when Milner went home on grounds of overstrain and ill-health, and handed the High Commission to Lord Selborne, the task was almost completed.

But the settlers never came. In fact they left in large numbers after a two-year drought. Back in England in 1906 the Liberals won their landslide victory, largely on the anti-Tariff ticket, but also skilfully using Milner as the scapegoat for what was now seen as a shameful war, casting him as arch-imperialist and bully. Out of guilt and political fashion, a mood as visceral as the jingoism it claimed to replace, the Liberals immediately gave back to the Boers their independence in the two Boer republics. In elections in 1907 Boer parties won majorities in three out of the four South African states, ensuring a Boer domination in any future union. The verdict of the war seemed to have been reversed; its costs and sacrifices wasted.

The Kindergarten were bent on saving something of Milner's plan in the cause of idealism and love of Empire. For four years after Milner left, having in the mean time found themselves other jobs, they mounted a campaign of persuasion, propaganda and fact-gathering to convince British and Boers that they must unite in their mutual interest or disintegrate together. They amassed all the information on which such a settlement could be based, even drafted a constitution. In 1908, Boer opinion suddenly moved in their direction.

In a matter of months, a constitution for a self-governing Dominion, drafted by the Kindergarten, was signed and the Union created in September 1909 on terms that pleased both sides, restoring settlers' rights, amalgamating the warring provinces, merging their identities and setting up a balanced franchise. And it was brokered between parties recently locked in deep mutual hatred and after a war of exceptional cruelty. A present-day equivalent – as it was seen at home by all parties – might be the solving of the 300-year-old Ulster crisis by a group of Oxford graduates with no previous political experience, obtaining a lasting settlement of a united Ireland of which all sides approved.

Balfour, by then leader of the Conservative opposition, called it 'a work without parallel in history'. What he meant, in part, was that the Kindergarten had devised a decolonizing constitution that was superior to that of the United States, and the Canadian and Australian imitations of it. Instead of those federal systems, which caused weakness for government, they passed a unitary constitution. Its fundamental principle was the supremacy of Parliament over each of the colonies, the constituent governments having only limited powers. The young Alexander Hamilton had wanted such a system for the United States but had acquiesced to the federal version because no other means of union was possible. A current biography of Hamilton, by F. S. Oliver, had indeed been the inspiration of the Kindergarten. They had seen themselves as the young federalists of America who had been told that their plan was 'fantastic and unworkable, that it was but the wild experiment of "visionary young men"'. It was a blueprint of how young men could influence history.

Milner's most fanatical disciple, who had more or less forced his way on to his staff, was Lionel Curtis, who had first come out to South Africa in the Boer War to fight with the City Imperial Volunteers. Curtis was their driving force. Milner called him 'a man of energy and power of work almost amounting to genius'. It was he, as Town Clerk, who had turned Johannesburg, an anarchic mining camp, into a working municipality. He was given, however, to utopian excesses and wild theoretical abstractions, often maddening to his colleagues. The work of the Kindergarten, for Curtis, was instructed directly by God. He was nicknamed the Prophet because of his likeness to Isaiah and his air of absolute certainty on all matters. The historian Philip Ziegler was to say of him in 1997 that if one man 'singlehandedly encapsulated the history of the British Empire and Commonwealth from 19th century to the present day', it was Lionel Curtis.

But it was the modest and retiring Bob Brand who had perhaps collected the laurels in South Africa. He arrived, aged twenty-four, with a Modern History first from New College, and as a Fellow of All Souls, that unique Oxford institution described as 'an unofficial committee for running . . . the destinies of the British Empire'. Milner had picked him out early on as 'a fellow of real ability', praising his grasp of the issues and his lucidity of exposition and putting him in charge, at the age of twenty-six, of amalgamating the railways – the source of all strife between the colonies – along with a £35 million budget. Brand sent for Philip Kerr, whom he remembered from Oxford and who was working in Government House, Pretoria, to join him. Four years later, Brand had drafted the complex constitution for the Union and put together the final nuts and bolts, working in partnership with Jan Smuts in the Transvaal delegation. His nickname, 'the wisest man in the Empire', was coined by a newspaper correspondent in South Africa around this time and endured to make the headlines of his obituaries fifty years later. Smuts called him 'the outstanding member of a very able team'.

Bob Brand had been known since he was a schoolboy for his air of sagacity. Since then, the premature baldness, the narrow eyes behind rimless spectacles, his mild and calm expression, had all added to the image (he was later described as 'a Chinaman from Hertfordshire'). He was tall, almost gangling, with a narrow face, a slightly protruding lower lip balanced by a moustache. Although there was a vein of steel in his make-up – a rigorous independence in his thinking, a dislike of abstractions – he had charm, too, a sweetness of nature, a fascinated curiosity about human behaviour and an ironic sense of humour.

Philip Kerr not only had a first-class brain – he too had obtained a first at New College, but had failed the All Souls exam – he had the looks of Adonis and the air of easy superiority at all things, more famously claimed by Balliol for its graduates. He was an athlete, a good tennis player and a gifted natural golfer. His face was long and beautiful, sensitive-looking, with 'bright intelligent eyes', matched with a certain careless untidiness in his appearance. He had the habit of running his fingers through his disordered hair while 'his hands and arms, in and out of his trouser pockets, kept time with his fluent sentences'. He had, by common consent, exceptional charm, although he was aloof and elusive, self-contained.

His mother, Lady Anne Kerr, was the daughter of the Duke of Norfolk, lay head of the Catholic Church. Philip was in line to inherit the Marquisate of Lothian along with four of the most beautiful and ancient houses in England and Scotland: Blickling, a classic Elizabethan house; Monteviot, an estate in the Border country; Newbattle Abbey near Edinburgh; and Ferniehirst Castle, a Border stronghold, the most ancient of them all. The dominating force in Philip Kerr's life had been his Catholic education, monitored with 'deep earnestness' by his parents, their attendant priests and his schoolmasters throughout his childhood. Nothing was more important to his mother than Philip's religious education. The faith, sewn so tightly around him at his schools, had begun to unravel at Oxford, with disturbing side effects and dismaying doubts. There were signs of the onset of depression, which only the relentless hard work in South Africa and the unmixed male camaraderie had temporarily held in abeyance.

Brand and Kerr quickly became friends, Brand observing that Kerr 'really had no prejudices at all, certainly none of the ordinary English upper class prejudices'. But, perhaps as a result of such open-mindedness and sympathy, Brand found one quality in Philip Kerr 'disconcerting': he had a chameleon-like ability for 'taking colour at once from his surroundings . . . swinging impressionably between extremes of argument'.

The Kindergarten — eleven of them — governed the Transvaal, the hub of the South African economy, by edict for a number of years, 'no doubt much to the disgust of both of the British and the Boers', Bob

Brand wrote later. The native reserves of Bechuanaland – now the entire country of Botswana – were run by a twenty-six-year-old graduate from Magdalen College, Oxford. The *Transvaal Critic* wrote indignantly of 'giving youngsters our public undertakings as toys to play with'.

In the photographs, the *Kinder* are always elegantly dressed in a slightly rough way, in thick tailoring despite the heat, with stiff collars, their trouser-ends always short above black lace-up boots. This last generation of servants of the Empire, of the race that George Santayana called 'the schoolboy masters of the world', were photographed standing in the reflected light of a Cape Dutch building, in surroundings that illustrated their effortless transition from Oxford quadrangles to this raw, potholed mining camp in Africa.

The Fellows of All Souls observed their rituals from afar. One 'joyous' evening '*super flumina Babylonis*' ended with a pair of them 'standing on the seat of the Cape cart and chanting Homer' in the moonlight. They would dine in evening dress in the sanctuary of the Rand Club. They would play billiards. Their parties were 'bachelor parties' – female companionship was sporadic. But mainly they talked, endlessly and obsessively into the night – grave and deep debates. 'We live in a state of perpetual intellectual excitement,' Bob Brand wrote to his mother, telling her that there were definite advantages to the bachelor life, living here 'among first class brains'. Brand and Kerr particularly would get into interminable dualogues, 'We literally go on for hours,' Brand wrote home, 'until we have reached the most extraordinary conclusions and opinions'. They called themselves 'The Moot' because of their endless discussions – the name derived from the Anglo-Saxon assemblies – and most of them lived together in a specially built dwelling called Moot House.

The landscape had a potent effect in this highly charged moment in their lives. Kerr and Brand would make treks across the veld with the railway committee, visiting distant lines. On holiday they made a momentous journey into the high veld in Bechuanaland with a full span of sixteen oxen, moving at night, shooting in the day, riding down buck on horses, crossing country where only the most accurate navigation and strategy of their guides would keep them in touch with water. They bartered with sixpenny knives and tobacco. They shot red-headed pheasants and partridge, korhaan and guinea fowl, steenbok and duiker. Their companion on this trip was the novelist and politician John Buchan, author of *The Thirty-Nine Steps*. *Prester John*, his bestseller published in 1910, vividly portrayed this landscape, as well as Milnerite ideals of white civilization, even of a new 'white ethnicity'.

Returning colonial civil servants might naturally have drifted apart, but the members of the Kindergarten never did. As a kind of 'intellectual commando' they were a unique phenomenon in the history of the Empire. Oxford ties, the forcing house of Milner, the Great Idea, the landscape – it was the first time many of them had been abroad – had forged such a powerful clan loyalty that they remained, whatever else they were doing, a cohesive brotherhood, a network bent on influencing international politics behind the scenes, and often in practice, for the rest of their lives. These were bonds that even major disagreements, especially in the late 1930s, could never break. And they were some of the ablest men of their generation.

I recall some of them in Bob Brand's, my grandfather's, house in the 1950s, old men still talking gravely and interminably together, all members of the continuing London 'Moot' of the Round Table. Their names, when I was aged fifteen, had become familiar from repetition, like unknown relations or dead prime ministers: Lionel Curtis, Percy Horsfall, 'Dougie' Malcolm. Some of the names were more memorable because my grandfather would often have to shout them – still addressing some of his closest surviving colleagues by their surnames after fifty years – into the telephone, trying to make contact, the lines from the Byfield exchange often bad, and the party at the other end sometimes deaf. 'Hailey' always presented a problem. Sir William Hailey had been Governor of the Punjab in the mid 1920s.

They were unique, too, in their own brand of high-mindedness – a term now vanished from politics – in their disinterestedness and sense of duty. It was as if they had been instructed to worry on behalf of all mankind. And they went on, despite their differences, until the grave, arguing, debating, wading into the most difficult problems, verbally and in print, ambitious to make sense of the world. No government or party was behind them, no university, nobody asked them to do it and mostly they did it for nothing. Their concern – the familiar phrase amongst them was 'world order' – was how to use the power of the past, the power they still considered they had, to get a global strategy for peace and against chaos. Who will rule the world, hold back nationalism and the arms race? Such concern seems now to have a poignancy, even a quaintness about it, given the catastrophes that swept away these high ideas. But it was catastrophe that they were struggling to prevent – at least before the First World War they could see it coming. This was no dreamy imperialism, but the first seeds of a way of thinking that was to produce the League of Nations, NATO, and the United Nations. This has now become the urgent concern of the millennium. Yelena Bonner, the widow of Andrei Sakharov, writing in the 1990s against Russia's use of force against minorities demanding self-determination, was echoing Milner when she wrote that the whole world has to 'accommodate the demand for self-determination through new forms of confederation or Commonwealth'. Failure to work out these new patterns, she wrote, would reduce the world to 'one huge battlefield'.

Lionel Curtis was the most tireless talker of them all. Towards the end of his life the utopian vision of a federated Commonwealth, as a model for world government, had become 'an almost psychotic obsession', and he would bore all comers on the subject. His colleagues had split off early on from Lionel's crusade for the moral conversion of mankind but never from him. They recognized that he had kept them together. Yet he remained an extraordinarily successful lobbyist for them.

Milner's spell, his Great Idea, would stay with them in some form all their lives. His public image was of a gaunt, remote authoritarian, with the drooping moustache and angular features of a frontier US marshall. Alert, tight-jawed, narrow-eyed, declaiming with a small, reedy voice, he was a man utterly without the popular political touch, easy for his enemies to caricature. Ruthless, practical, possessing a

mnemonic brain power, he was a dynamo of action, who despised
Westminster politics ('the whims of men who have been elected for
their competence in dealing with Metropolitan tramways or country
pubs'). In private he had considerable charm, and he was encouraging
and inspiring to his young employees who saw him as the greatest
statesman of the Empire, the Socrates of their time.

Bob Brand described his returning band of brothers as 'earnest, unso-
phisticated young men', into whose lives Nancy entered 'like a bolt
from the blue'. 'We had never met anyone like her,' he remembered.
'She was quite unlike our sisters, cousins, or the female friends we
were accustomed to in England.' He listed her 'startling combination' of
beauty, energy, 'dashing initiative' and wit. But it was also her frankness
and friendliness, her ability to connect immediately that was so utterly
foreign, a direct import from the South, and which broke all known
rules of engagement. In addition, the *Kinder* weren't used to female
company at all. Only one of its members, Peter Perry, a Fellow of all
Souls, had broken ranks and got married – a ceremony deplored by
Lionel Curtis, who described the couple driving off 'in a cloud of rice
and vulgarity'.

    'Nancy's charm was such that we all fell easy victims,' wrote Bob
Brand. 'She liked our society because she was full of desire to do
things in the world, to help things forward, to do good, and she
thought our aims were the same.' Nancy first met Philip Kerr at
Hatfield where Lord Selborne had taken him to stay with his brother-
in-law Lord Salisbury some time in 1910. But he and Lionel Curtis
don't appear in the Cliveden visitors' book until the summer of 1911.
Bob Brand wasn't invited to Cliveden until the following summer of
1912, with Lionel Curtis and J. L. Garvin, editor of the *Observer*, and
soon afterwards to a weekend alone with Nancy at Sandwich. Nancy
was, at this point, pregnant with her third son, David, who was born
that year.

    Nancy asked him his opinion of a letter she was writing to Lizzie,
'lambasting' her for spending Nancy's hand-outs on hats. He told her,

and remembered that the advice was ignored, that if she ever wanted Lizzie to speak to her again, he would advise not sending it. When his own mail came one morning she asked him: 'Are you an Honourable? I see a letter addressed to you like that.' 'Yes,' he replied. 'I'm astounded,' said Nancy. 'I thought you were absolutely middle class.' Nancy had put him automatically in a different category from her landed guests. She would have found, had she looked him up, that his mother, Susan Henrietta, was the daughter of Lord George Cavendish, brother of the 7th Duke of Devonshire and the granddaughter of the Earl of Harewood. His father Lord Hampden, who died in 1906, was the 24th Baron Dacre, a title created in 1321. His grandfather, 'Speaker Brand', had been Speaker in the House of Commons.

Bob Brand's Victorian upbringing was unlike anything resembling the Langhorne way of life in Virginia, although there were superficial similarities. At the great house, The Hoo, at Welwyn in Hertfordshire — a county the Dacres had represented in Parliament for the Liberals for three generations — there was land on which to shoot and ride, gravel and cedars, great lawns, many servants. But the image concealed a declining fortune. It was managed at a pinch and Bob Brand never lost the habit of the parsimony of his upbringing. His early years, as the youngest-but-one of seven children, and the third brother down, had been comfortless and spare of affection. He was sent to Marlborough, the hardest and grimmest of the public schools of the time. Whatever scant emotional support there was came from his brothers and sisters, but to them his signs of cleverness were always considered an oddity, 'different' even 'deranged'. They were 'disgusted' that he wanted, in his youth, to become a schoolmaster. He never spoke of his mother, who died the year he came back from South Africa in 1909. He remembered his father, Lord Hampden, visiting the nursery floor only once in his early childhood, and merely commented in an interview when he was over eighty: 'He was a Victorian father. These were Victorian times.' His letters to his son were signed 'Hampden' and Bob's in reply, 'Yours sincerely, R. H. Brand'.

Nanaire Langhorne

Chillie Langhorne

Lizzie Langhorne

Irene Langhorne

Nancy (left) *and Phyllis Langhorne*

Nancy Langhorne

Nora Langhorne

Irene Langhorne

Phyllis and Chillie Langhorne

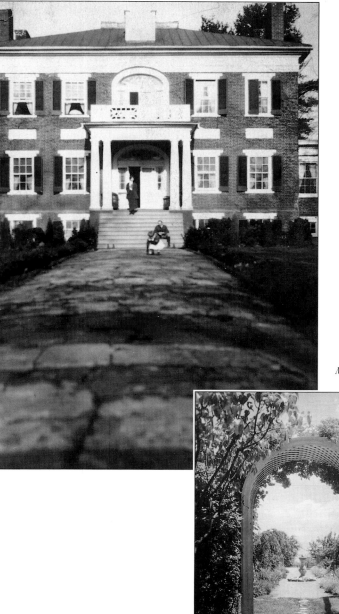

Mirador

The garden at Mirador

Phyllis Langhorne

Nancy Langhorne

Phyllis and Nancy Langhorne

Chillie Langhorne, Nancy and Bobbie Shaw at Mirador

Nora Langhorne

Centre back row: *Chillie and Phyllis Brooks*; front row: *Nora Langhorne and Sorriano at Mirador*

Keene Langhorne

Buck Langhorne

Reggie Brooks

Moncure Perkins

Nancy Astor

Waldorf Astor

Cliveden

Nancy and Waldorf Astor

Nancy Astor

Philip Kerr and Nancy Astor

Phyllis Brooks

Lord Milner's Kindergarten – rear left, *Bob Brand*; front row centre, *Philip Kerr*

Paul Phipps

Philip Kerr and Bob Brand in Johannesburg

Nancy Astor

Returning one day to his rooms at New College in 1900, Bob found a note left on the bed. 'My dear Bob,' it read, with unusual familiarity, 'I'm afraid I shall not be able to leave you very much when I die. Please therefore immediately learn shorthand and bookkeeping. Your affectionate Father.' It was the brevity of the note that Bob always remembered. Economy of expression was even more marked in his maternal family, the Cavendishes, whose males at least, and their houses too, were famed for a silence broken only by the most rudimentary exchanges.

Lord Hampden had been keen to get his sons quickly employed. Bob's brother Bertie was bribed with half a crown to join the navy at the age of twelve. By 1916 he was Chief of Staff of the British Navy under Lord Beatty, commander of the British Battle Cruiser Fleet at the Battle of Jutland, and every schoolboy's hero. Bob speculated later that his father had lost much of his money with a shadowy investment syndicate in South America which seemed to coincide with his appointment as Governor and Commander in Chief of New South Wales, Australia, in 1895. His qualifications barely stood up to examination: he had been an unremarkable Liberal MP, and was listed otherwise, in the *Complete Peerage*, as 'sometime Capt. in the Coldstream Guards'. The circumstance of his appointment was uncannily echoed in Hilaire Belloc's famous 'Cautionary Tale of Lord Lundy', in which his exasperated grandfather, the Duke, tells him 'But as it is my language fails. / Go out and govern New South Wales.' It was published in 1907 shortly after Lord Hampden's tenure. Bob had been sent to Marlborough, a 'plebeian' school, as he liked to joke to his Etonian grandsons, because his father was making economies. The lower fees included a starvation diet. When Bob Brand's health broke down during his first term at New College, Oxford, it was as a direct result of malnutrition at Marlborough when he was growing rapidly to over six feet. He was sent away for a year to recuperate at Government House in Sydney. His Oxford tutor was the great historian H. A. L. Fisher, who was surprised that Bob Brand got a First in the Schools in 1901, because of this missing year, and who discouraged him from

taking the All Souls examination. Happily he ignored this advice: it was
the passing of that examination, Bob Brand said later, 'from which all
my good fortune came'.

The Kindergarten were fired up with ambition when they returned to
extend their skills to the world stage, to work for an organic union of
the Empire. They had been locked in grave meetings, with Milner in
the chair, planning the launch of a new magazine, a quarterly journal of
imperial affairs, called, in homage to their cause, *The Round Table*. Kerr
would be the editor. It would pool information from around the globe,
have the best information in the world for discussion of international
affairs and raise the level of debate where in fact almost none existed.
Kerr and Curtis, the two idealists, were given the leadership and the
only full-time employment.

'Working for a great idea in the sunshine of the Southern
Hemisphere,' as one newspaper put it, had particularly affected the
health of Bob Brand and Philip Kerr. 'I never really stopped working 8
or 9 hours a day since August 1905 when Brand went on leave,' Kerr
wrote to his mother in 1909, 'I suppose I've got a touch of brain fag.'
'Brain fag' was their particular *Kinderkrankheit*, contracted from years of
cerebral overload at the altitude of Johannesburg. It was a form of anti-
climactic stress which attacked mental concentration, causing
restlessness and engendering 'bad nerves'. Bob Brand's doctor, in the
meantime, suspected heart trouble, also caused by the altitude, and had
sent him on a series of cures to the clinics of the Black Forest, to the
fashionable 'Dr Dapper' at Bad Kissingen with his eating cures and
enforced rest without reading.

But Philip Kerr's problems were deeper than his friends at first
realized. He was under severe psychological strain, tortured by religious doubts, hovering back and forth on the edge of a breakdown. He
wrote to Bob from Ottawa of his 'partial collapse'. Astonishingly, he
managed a huge amount of work on his trip and travelled great distances, although his 'craving for movement' was considered a further
symptom of his malaise. For three years after his return from South

Africa Philip Kerr had been unable to escape these hounding depressions and attacks of nerves. He caused great consternation among his friends, although the cause of his problems was obscure. Only later did they realize that the troubles were connected with a crisis of apostasy from the Catholic Church.

Kerr had gone to Oxford after eight years of instruction in the purest Catholic faith at the Oratory School in Birmingham. (Bob Brand remarked that Kerr never once referred to the years he spent there, or any boy he had met.) To then meet people, at Oxford, who were able to think and say what they liked; to read what he himself chose to — Kerr cited particularly his traumatic discovery of Bernard Shaw — had had a devastating effect on him. His faith was shattered; Oxford robbed him of his certainties yet at the same time left him with the greater need of them.

Brand and Kerr were devoted to each other, sharing the same houses for fifteen years, but they were utterly different in temperament and outlook. Bob Brand fiercely protected his freedom to think for himself and reject doctrine. He remembered at the age of ten, lying on the grass on Reigate Common with a friend of his at private school, looking up at the sky and expressing the firm opinion that eternal punishment was 'absurd'. Philip Kerr felt that convictions were always better than freedom, that doubt was the worst thing of all, although to have such certainty meant that there were many things into which one could not freely inquire. Harold Nicolson later described Kerr as having a 'magnificent and impressive intellect'. Bob Brand thought Kerr had 'a touch of genius'; he thought him extraordinarily critical and acute until he came up against something from his early teaching and then his mind, Brand discovered, was quite closed.

There was an early example of their differences in the domain of love. Emotional turmoil was taking place in the lives of both men at the Moot at 14 Wyndham Place, London, where they had set themselves up. After all those celibate years in South Africa, and both undoubtedly virgins when they returned to England, they had both fallen into romantic entanglements of dismaying difficulties. (In Lionel Curtis's case there is an entry under his name in Deborah Lavin's biography which says simply 'discovers women'.) Kerr, the protected Catholic, had fallen not only for a Protestant but for Lady Beatrice Cecil, 'Mima' (pronounced Myma), the daughter of Lord Salisbury, who was titular head of the Anglican Church. Brand, the agnostic, had fallen for Kerr's sister, Margaret, whose uncle, the Duke of Norfolk, was the lay head of the Catholic Church. For each family the match, at first sight, would have been a calamity beyond any possible repair. The plot, therefore, even without this complication of the protagonists' religious faiths, was a four-handed *Romeo and Juliet*. In the case of Bob Brand, at least, it was made clear by Margaret Kerr that he would first have to be accepted into the Catholic faith. The case of Philip Kerr was greatly more complicated by his crisis of faith, which he had to keep to himself, even from his closest friends.

It would have been enough of a blow to Kerr's family if he had left the Church – a trauma, almost like a death in the family – but to combine this with marrying a Protestant who was standing her ground, and a Cecil too, was unimaginable. Yet Kerr believed, as he wrote in a letter to Nancy Astor, who became his confessor on the subject around this time, that if he could get a response to his love, 'then the religious difficulty would vanish away'. And he believed he had 'touched her soul'.

Meanwhile Philip had confided to Bob that when it came to the female sex he had been frightened from an early age that he would be 'pursued', and therefore looked on women as a permanent source of danger. He believed that no one who had not really grasped the monkish ideal, the true meaning of the ascetic life, could have a real understanding of the world and of human life. He described love as an absurd, irrational fever, a sort of 'microbe', which made one for the time being foolish and irresponsible and which must be resisted at all costs. Philip Kerr had set himself up as the captain of his soul, and it was taking painful revenge. He later wrote to Bob of this period of lovesickness that 'troubles of the heart and soul nearly destroyed my body'.

Bob Brand's response to the obstructions put in his way was to make a genuine attempt to embrace the Catholic faith, starting from the position of a thoughtful Anglican sceptic. He was sufficiently struck with Margaret Kerr to spend a year wrangling on All Souls' writing paper with a senior figure of the Catholic establishment, Baron von Hugel. Bob Brand went to extraordinary lengths, in many carefully thought-out letters, to get answers to what was, in the end, unanswerable for him. The letters to the Baron begin searchingly and benignly. He believed in God, he said, mostly because he believed 'that the things of the spirit are the only things of real value'. And for him it was necessary to look no further than the New Testament for the deepest spiritual truths. 'The Christian religion of love,' he wrote, 'seems to me to fulfil all man's spiritual wants. That is where those who talk of the ultimate perfection of man seem to me to go so hopelessly wrong.'

It was clear that something quite cosmetic could be arranged to satisfy the doctrinal and family requirements, but Bob Brand couldn't square this with his conscience. It was impossible to get the supernatural assurance that men had in the past, he wrote. 'All the dogmas of the Trinity are useless to me spiritually. Theologians' metaphysical accounts of God strike me as dead language. I find the whole universe much more incomprehensible than orthodox Christians.' The Baron would return his letters with these passages of scepticism coolly underlined.

Towards the end of the correspondence Bob began to raise the tone of his letters, as he found the brick wall of orthodoxy in his way, and began to doubt whether Margaret Kerr's views were really her own. 'In order to protect the kernel of religion is the whole husk of miracles and medievalism really necessary?' he asked. ' . . . Notwithstanding my feeling of the immense spiritual value of the Catholic tradition, I sd still consider it a catastrophe were the Catholic Church to rule the world. Can she never learn to confine her claims to the kingdom of the spirit? The rule of any priesthood in the world wd simply lead to obscurantism & it is in despite of the Catholic church that the human spirit & mind has asserted its freedom.' And Brand confided to a friend, 'The moment I get in the atmosphere of priests etc I feel as if I were going to suffocate.' One surviving sentence from Margaret Kerr's letters gives some idea of the hopelessness of her task: 'I wish you would not speak of miracles as an interference with the course of nature . . .'

After a year of unhappiness, Bob Brand formally ended the courtship. He criticized himself for his naivety and blamed himself for proposing to Margaret Kerr, confessing to a friend, 'I hadn't the slightest idea what I was up against. I was a pagan & hadn't any idea that you could use religion to erect barriers between yourself and other people.' But he had strayed into a sect for whom the Reformation was a calamity hardly less recent than the Boer War.

Bob Brand had been on the point of returning to South Africa at the end of 1910, believing there was no future for him in England. He had accepted bachelorhood on the basis, apparently, of a few fruitless weekends touring country houses, meeting only spinster cousins. He described to a friend his predicament, staying at Hatfield with Lord and Lady Salisbury, 'I am staying with three female cousins of mature age here, called Egerton. [They were nieces of the 8th Duke of Devonshire, their mother being Lady Louisa Cavendish.] Altogether I have 8 female Egerton cousins all unmarried. It's a great pity, as they are all thoroughly good fellows & wd. make extraordinarily good strong sound stock. But I suppose the possession, even in a larger degree than with me of the Cavendish lip [a floppy lower lip, pronounced since the 8th Duke's generation, exacerbated by marriage in that of the 9th] has done for them.' Then he fell ill just before the boat sailed. Before the next one left he heard through a chance conversation that Robert Kindersley had joined the merchant banking firm of Lazard Brothers and was looking for a partner. He offered Brand a job and a partnership that was to last fifty years.

In the meantime Bob Brand had been writing up the Kindergarten experience in his book *The Union of South Africa*. It contained a prescient warning for future generations. By giving autonomy to the Boers, the Liberal Government had dumped what was called 'the native question'. It was hardly dealt with in the struggle to form a Union. Bob Brand wrote, 'The man in the street and the man on the veld seldom realise even the elements of the stupendous problem with which they are faced . . . The policy that attracts them is often one of simple repression. Take away from the native the lands which he possesses, and there will be more compulsion upon him to work for the white man. Do not educate him, or else he will become too independent. Keep him in his place. That is the simple creed of the average white man. He fails to see that in his own interests it is fatal. For, if the black man sinks, he will inevitably drag the white man with him. The Kaffirs too now number six millions. They will soon number ten and twenty millions. By raising in their breasts a sense of wrong the white man will surely be digging his own grave.'

Philip Kerr, confused about religion and doubtful about marriage, did not propose to Mima. He couldn't decide on anything except to postpone a decision and hope she wouldn't go away. It was obvious to those around him that he would never make up his mind. In fact the whole performance appeared to be an elaborate, if subconscious avoidance of entrapment, a Temptation in the Garden. Nevertheless he was now 'perfectly contented' that he had done the right thing by deciding on nothing except to disappear and 'keep silence'.

Perceiving that he was about to collapse with a nervous breakdown his friends had taken the odd decision to send him on a further exhausting trip around the world in November 1911, while Brand and Curtis would look after the Round Table. He wrote from Egypt that month, 'Here I am in a complete state of mental coma . . .'

Nancy was now playing mother hen to the entire Round Table, instructing Lionel Curtis not to marry a young woman for whom he had nursed a 'hopeless passion' since adolescence, adding, 'These are strict orders. Remember even a Round Tabler is not perfect – though of course you are all wonderfully wise and brilliant and Beautiful Specimens – + in spite of this I love you all.' She had also pursued Kerr on his journey with worried letters.

The months of travel, meanwhile, had brought Kerr no nearer a decision. Towards the end of 1912, when he had been back for some months, the decision was made for him by Mima and her mother Lady Salisbury. 'It's all over,' Philip Kerr wrote to Nancy in December. 'I had

a talk with M. today &, as I feared, religion was a bar to further meetings . . . The world seems very empty & cold . . . Thank you so much
for all you have done. There is nothing more to be said – a years dream
has come to an end.' In fact his feelings may have cooled towards Mima
during his travels, although he was unable to face up to that either. He
hinted as much to Bob Brand: 'if you feel attracted by someone and are
going on a long journey,' he wrote, 'don't take any photographs. You
get tired of them.'

Nancy was moved by his condition and his troubled conscience,
writing to Bob Brand before Christmas 1912, 'I am miserable about
Mr. Philip – He's too good. I am getting to feel about him like you do –
& I feel he would break our wicked hearts.'

Remarkably, given these vicissitudes, the *Round Table*, by the
end of 1912 under Kerr's intermittent editorship and with many of
the contributions written by him, had become a journal of real influence. Kerr developed the major creed of the Round Table movement
in these articles, with an eye on the menacing rise of German nationalism: pacifism by itself was a lost cause as a means of avoiding war.
Nor would you get peace by passing international resolutions and
extracting promises. The only way to apply any peacekeeping rule of
international law was through the threat of one superior, organized
force applying it with a single foreign policy. Otherwise nationalism
and state sovereignty would inevitably lead to war and more war.
Since most of them had accepted that an imperial federation was
impossible, that the Dominions didn't want it, they realized that any
wide federation of the democracies for this purpose would have to be
built around the United States. But the *Round Table* covered the whole
spectrum of contemporary political issues, not just imperial ones.
Walter H. Page, the American Ambassador, and an editor himself,
spoke of the Kindergarten as 'perhaps the best group of men here
for the real study and free discussion of large political subjects.
Their quarterly, *The Round Table*, is the best review, I dare say, in the
world.'

By the end of 1912, with some help from Nancy and Waldorf, the

Round Table had moved closer to the national power structure. The Cliveden visitors' book was full of *Kinder*; that summer there was hardly a weekend without them. Geoffrey Robinson's (hereinafter referred to as Dawson although he didn't change his name until 1917) diary records 'sitting obedient to Lionel Curtis in Committees and summer houses all morning', discussing the future of India. Dawson became the editor of *The Times* that year; Edward Grigg (later 1st Baron Altrincham) was its imperial affairs editor and joint editor of the *Round Table*.

A key figure (although not a member of the group) from this point on was Waldorf Astor, who had been a friend of Bob Brand at Oxford, and who was now moving into a position of real influence on the liberal side of the Tory Party. The Astors in addition owned an influential newspaper in the *Observer*, of which Waldorf was the proprietor, collaborating closely with its editor J. L. Garvin. At Cliveden the Kindergarten could now rub shoulders on any given weekend with Curzon, Kitchener, F. E. Smith, Balfour, Asquith, J. L. Garvin, Austen Chamberlain, Lord Cromer, with Cecils, Rutlands, Roxburghes, Portlands, as well as the literary guests. They were convenient gatherings for Kerr's ambition for the Round Table 'to influence the best people', or, as Curtis described these new friends, 'powerful levers to work things in the direction we want'.

The Round Table were, in fact, developing as the perfect microcosm of establishment networking, the prototype of later models. Family links, Oxford – particularly All Souls – money, no political accountability, a desire to work behind the scenes, continuity of access to power were all the basic requirements. The Astor connection had given a huge boost to their movement and had enabled them to become a working institution. This indirect approach became the ethic of the Kindergarten – to govern without accountability in the pursuit of the shining idea – and later they would be criticized, even to their surprise disliked for it, as a shadowy cabal of dreamy imperialists.

'I have an incurably cross bench mind,' Philip Kerr told Ramsay MacDonald, 'and one of the advantages of being out of active politics is that one has not got to mix up with the necessities of partisan polemics.' They straddled the centre ground of politics. Philip Kerr was soon to become Lloyd George's private secretary; Milner his war supremo.

Nancy bound the Kindergarteners closely around her. She wrote jealously to Lionel Curtis when they went elsewhere for their grave councils. Curtis replied, somewhat overstating his loyalty: 'My Dear Nancy, If you think we come to Cliveden to eat your magnificent food & drink your wine & look at your pictures you are vastly mistaken. I was there once when you chucked us all & it was dull as ditch-water & we all gave a sigh of relief when it came to an end. You know perfectly well that we just come to see you & Waldorf & would come from the ends of the earth to see you if you lived in a kennel.'

After one of their communal visits Nancy wrote to Bob Brand, 'I can quite truthfully say that I never enjoyed a Sunday more. I am beginning to get quite a romantic friendship with your Round Tablers. Will it break up my Home Life? I hope not.' And she wrote to Phyllis, 'Bob Brand has just been in and handed me a pamphlet on Labour. These interesting people are a drug for me. They give me to read and discuss deep subjects daily. I only understand half and in the meantime they have killed my taste for shallowness.'

Although Bob Brand now came as often to Cliveden as any of his friends his opinions carried much less weight with Nancy and Waldorf than those of the two idealist-publicists, Philip Kerr and Lionel Curtis. When Bob was seen to be out of sympathy with their views, his own tended to be discounted as 'materialistic', especially now that he was a merchant banker and lacking in spiritual flight.

Given the materialism tag, Bob Brand recognized that Nancy had paid him a great compliment when, on the eve of a business trip to America in 1912, she gave him a letter of introduction to her much praised sister Phyllis. 'I had heard so much about her from Nancy, who adored her more than any other human being in her life, that I was interested in seeing her.' He expected someone other-worldly, from the descriptions, someone more beautiful than Nancy. But the woman he encountered one day in New York was beyond anything he was prepared for.

He wrote to Phyllis as soon as he arrived in America. Phyllis wrote back: 'Until your note came to-day I was beginning to think you were a myth.' She asked him to come the following Sunday, with instructions to 'change in Washington onto the Chesapeake and Ohio R.R. leaving there at 3.15 p.m.'

They first met at a dinner given by Irene at her house on East 73rd Street in New York, where Phyllis was meeting lawyers, sorting out her separation proceedings with Reggie. Bob Brand described his first sight of Phyllis many years later: 'She had come up by train from Mirador and arrived laden with different gifts for Irene and Dana, including a ham. As she shook hands with me in that sort of way she had, using her whole arm, she looked away and talked to someone else.' He managed to tell her that he was going to Washington with Peter Perry, a member of the Kindergarten, and could come on to Mirador from there. Bob was 'knocked over' by this first meeting. There was a certain 'angelic look', a loveliness, an inner calm, that he first saw that evening and never forgot.

When he got to Washington Brand found a note from Phyllis saying that it would be better if he didn't come. Mr Langhorne, across the way at Misfit, had been 'raising hell', sensitive about the separation proceedings, not wanting unattached men to come visiting. But Bob was now determined to get there, to see Phyllis once more. He took his bags to the station and found her carriage. He remembered her saying 'Oh come along down then.' Phyllis carefully arranged all her belongings so that Bob had to sit on the other side of the aisle in the Pullman. She wore, he remembered, a large black picture hat. Bob was astonished by the buggy ride from Greenwood station to Mirador – he couldn't believe that he would find such a beautifully furnished house in what he thought was the back country. But he was without his luggage, which had mistakenly been shipped to Florida, leaving Bob with only his 'Wall Street suit' to wear for this special expedition of twenty-four hours. That night, breaking his South African rule of always sleeping naked, he slept in Phyllis's pink silk nightgown.

He was put, next morning, on Castleman, Phyllis's oldest and favourite horse, the one on which she had made her name. Bob Brand, dressed in his 'slippery' city trousers, and not having ridden for months, fell off at a fence. Castleman had thrown up his head and hit him on the nose, causing a nosebleed; the rimless spectacles disappeared into the grass. Phyllis was 'kind enough not to laugh'. After lunch that same day Bob took the train for New York to catch the boat for England. 'As I left Mirador,' he wrote, 'I have a picture of Phyllis in my mind, standing on the porch waving goodbye, with a basket on her arm, gloves, and a pair of scissors going to cut dead heads off the roses. I left knowing that I had fallen in love at first sight.'

He knew about Phyllis and Henry Douglas Pennant, although he had no idea of the extent of her affections for him, or of the volumes of their correspondence. And there were others: Reggie Wyndham, Geoffrey Dawson — who had also begun a correspondence with her. There were the American beaux who had never given up: Johnny Saltonstall, from Boston, a childhood flame with whom Phyllis had been, perhaps still was, in love; there was Jimmy Appleton. She was corresponding with them all. Bob Brand had no idea how to keep in touch with Phyllis. It was compromising, the height of bad manners, to write more than a thank-you letter, unless a correspondence was encouraged. He had promised to send her, nevertheless, a copy of the *Round Table*. Phyllis, too, was bent on reform, he discovered, as she dipped into the 'progressivism' that was now fashionable in intellectual circles in America.

In the end it was Phyllis who wrote first.

Dear Mr. Brand,

How you must have cursed Mirador, Virginia, Castleman and everything south of Washington when you discovered the loss of your luggage . . . I was so glad that

you did come to Mirador and it was most awfully good of
you to have taken so much trouble for those very few
hours. The next time you must make it longer and get
your innings back on Castleman. It was very thoughtless
of me to have insisted on jumping fences when you hadn't
done it for so long. I should hate any lady that played me
such a trick, but I hope your nature is not so small as
mine.

Hidden from Chillie Langhorne in Virginia, Bob Brand met him
at Cliveden that Christmas of 1912. It was not a successful visit. Mr
Langhorne had come, it seemed, intent on plunder and rampage. He
was becoming ever more difficult, angry at being abandoned, as he
interpreted it, at Misfit; irritated at having nothing to do. He had
warned of his mood ahead of his arrival. Nancy wrote to Phyllis, 'Yr.
Pa wrote me a sarcastic note about not putting off the nobility for
him – if he came he would not mind being left alone etc! Really it's not
surprising Irene won't grow up when she's by a "Child Pa".'

By mid-Christmas, Nancy reported to Phyllis, 'Well now to Pa –
poor soul his restlessness is a curse. He gets so excited & odd when he
talks over things. I am sorry for him, but Phyl its awful . . . You know
how father is – He likes to sit around & talk all day & method drives
him wild. He says some day we shall be surprised he will cut loose & go
off where no one can interfere or criticize him!'

But Chillie found ways to entertain himself. To Nancy's fury he
managed to get many of the guests drunk on his special egg nog. (It is
a common misconception that Nancy and Waldorf, teetotallers and
later legislators to raise the drinking age in pubs, forbade drink at
Cliveden. The guests were invariably offered wine, port and brandy at
meals, although cocktails beforehand were a matter of negotiation with
the butler. The staff, too, had their own licensed club.) Chillie had
brought two mules with him as a present to his grandson Bobbie. To
please the child, and to the amazement of the staff, he led them
through the front door and into the hall. He was found, one morning,

frying his own cut of bacon on a skillet in the fireplace in the hall, underneath the Salamander emblem of François V, complaining that the English didn't know how to cook it properly. He would go off on unscheduled shooting trips into the park with the gamekeeper Mr Cooper who would later tell how Mr Langhorne, like any eighteenth-century squire, never shot more than a couple of pheasants, horrified by the modern idea of driving birds and shooting hundreds at a time. 'What's the point of that?' he told Cooper, 'You lose all your sport in one day. You want to spread it right through the season.' A cuspidor had been placed in the hall for Mr Langhorne. Nancy was asked by a guest whether he was a good shot. 'He never misses the fireplace,' she replied.

13

Fly Sickness

St Moritz was one of the standard cures for weariness prescribed for the rich and Philip Kerr was ordered there for yet another 'long rest' early in 1913. Nancy, suffering another of her recurring bouts of 'nervous debility', was staying at the Palace Hotel with Waldorf and invited Philip Kerr to join them. And here, on the ice rink, in the ballroom, in the alpine air, an adventure, a mutual fascination began.

It was to Phyllis that Nancy innocently confided her new preoccupation, writing on 30 January: 'I am becoming a better woman since seeing so much of Philip Kerr. I fear he will eventually become a priest. He certainly has the true spirit of a Christian, such sympathy, such understanding. You wd. like him.' And a day or two later, 'You will read a lot of Philip Kerr in my letters . . . He is really a most unusual creature.' Philip Kerr, in turn, wrote excitedly to his mother: 'The bracing air, and the still more bracing company, has entirely removed the depression which has weighed on me for a long time past . . .', adding somewhat selfishly, 'I no longer sympathise with suicides. It is a real work of mercy on N.A.'s part to bring me here. You must go and see her as soon as she returns – Feb 1st – and thank her for rescuing me from a depression which was worse for my nerves than anything else. Write and tell me about your interview with Mrs A. She's not quite like anybody you've ever met before.'

In the mornings they skated around the hotel ice rink, working at their inside edges, hands behind the back. Nancy worried that she was 'too old and too timid to become a swallow on ice'. Philip, of course, was as charmingly good at skating as he was at everything else, in Nancy's eyes. There were many dances at the hotel, for which Nancy made a special effort with her appearance, despite her physical state. She wrote, 'My headgear hasn't come for the fancy dress ball. I shall go as Night in black velvet with a star in my hair. What a boring thing it is to try to look pretty. I never tried for so long a time before.'

She sent health bulletins on Philip to Bob, thrilled at the thera-peutic effect she was having on this chronic invalid. 'You would rejoice to see how much more cheerful Philip is,' and added, encouragingly, 'Phyllis says "if Mr. Brand liked me he is certainly a marvel at disguis-ing his feelings."'

Bob had confided only to Philip and in great secrecy that he had fallen in love. Meanwhile his only excuse for writing to Phyllis was to accompany the copies of the *Round Table* she had asked for. He even sent her the first portion of Lionel Curtis's massive 'Egg' – his blueprint for unifying the Empire – telling her that he disagreed with most of it and that Curtis had asked him to refrain from further comments.

Bob also told Phyllis that Nancy had invited Philip and himself to Biarritz in March for a drive through Languedoc and Provence, but that he would be too busy to accept. When he discovered that Phyllis had been invited too he cancelled his work and joined the party only to find that Phyllis's divorce proceedings had forced her to stay at home, bit-terly disappointing Nancy too who declared herself 'weepy on the subject'.

Bob wrote to Phyllis from the Villa Notre Dame rented by the Astors: 'The most morose individual cd. hardly help being cheerful & happy, when your sister is about. She has a genius for making other people feel happy. A great deal of conversation & prattling goes on all day about all things in Heaven and earth. Philip Kerr & I are both rather unused to female society, especially of the standard your sister supplies. Instead of the solemn boring discussions about the Empire &

other stupid subjects we have all day long at other times, we are enjoying something much more amusing & personal. Nancy has done wonders for Philip Kerr & kept him very cheerful for 2 months. He is now your sister's devoted slave – & I am afraid will be very depressed, when the journey comes to an end.'

Phyllis received a flow of letters from Nancy praising Philip: 'I can't tell you what [he] is . . . so brilliant, so understanding . . . He & Bob Brand are like you & me.' Not only was he 'nearer a saint on earth than anything that I've ever seen', but at golf he was scratch; and 'you sh hear [him] strumming the piano . . . Mima Cecil was an ass – poor soul she has given up a life in the stars!' (In fact Philip Kerr had been too preoccupied with his own sufferings to notice that Mima had married William Ormsby Gore, later Lord Harlech, who was soon to become Milner's parliamentary private secretary, only a few weeks after Kerr's final parting from her.) Nancy added 'R. Brand asks hectically after you. I must say that was quite speedy work on your part.' Here was the first confirmation Phyllis received that Bob had fallen for her.

Nancy took the newfound saint and Bob Brand to Cartier in Paris on their way home and bought them gifts. Bob remembered his own as a 'consolation prize' – a set of gold buttons for a white waistcoat. He still had them fifty years later. The following morning he left early for England. He went into Nancy's room at the Ritz to say goodbye and found her writing a letter. 'And then a sudden thought seemed to strike her,' he recalled. 'She got up and came to me as I was standing by the mantelpiece and said "Are you in love with me?" and I said "Yes" and then said goodbye.' It was the complete absence of any real sexual flirtatiousness which allowed Bob to give what was, in fact, the only possible response. He knew that she only wanted to collect 'another, even if unwanted scalp'.

'Is Philip Kerr in love with Nancy too?' Phyllis asked Bob Brand in April. 'Answer me truthfully. I shall see myself as soon as I see them together, so you might save me perhaps a month or so's curiosity!!' She added, 'Please do not think you have to have an excuse for writing to me, let the mere fact of my liking to get your letters be enough – please.'

Was Philip in love with Nancy? An intimate question which Bob Brand replied to at length. He concluded, 'Yes, on thinking it over I wd. certainly say he was in love with her, tho' it doesn't yet take away his appetite, his sleep, or his placidity of temper, or make him depressed & morose.' He declared himself a bad judge but revealed, at least, 'Nancy told me Philip had a great idea of platonic friendship & that so had she, & that I cdn't understand this. She then told him & me that she had been so cocksure of herself for 6 years & now she was beginning not to be so cocksure. I told her that surprised me as I always thought that the great thing about platonic friendship was that it was so safe & cocksure.'

This letter advanced Bob's intimacy with Phyllis but it showed, too, his closeness to Nancy. Bob, secretly in love with Phyllis, Nancy, bowled over by Philip, needed each other. On her side she needed information – of a kind she had never bothered about since her days as a débutante Belle in Richmond. 'Tell me what you think Philip thought of me,' she had written, after their trip, 'Tell me the Truth.' Bob was taken into the inner circle, commissioned to stock her new library at Cliveden, told to purchase 'French classics and enjoyable reads'. As a sign of her affection she began to tease him in her bullying way, with her nerve-hitting attacks – to subject him to Langhorne truth game techniques, accusing him randomly of 'selfishness' and 'incompetence'. At first Bob fell into the trap and wrote a pained letter, asking whether this meant that their friendship was over. Nancy wrote back, without any apology, 'You are nice but you are cracked. It's a lunatic asylum you need, not a rest cure. Really you are an old silly. I was only chaffing you. All men are selfish or they wouldn't be men and loved by women. The most unselfish man I ever met was despised by women. Please don't take my light words to heart – you like us all have faults but I find you a charming companion and a most true and loving if incompetent friend.' Bob learned fast and was soon writing to Phyllis, 'If everyone took notice of her insults we sd. be having trouble all day long.'

He finally confided to Nancy his love for Phyllis, just before
Phyllis came over for the summer of 1913, bringing Peter and Winkie.
She would travel, via Cliveden, to the Astors' rented house at Glendoe,
overlooking Loch Ness. Nancy, for once, didn't put herself between
Phyllis and a male admirer. She partly saw Bob as a good way to divert
Phyllis from the hated Captain who was away on a long expedition that
summer. Her campaign of abuse against the Captain had never let up,
in his absence. After a letter from Phyllis, giving some innocent news
of his whereabouts, Nancy had replied, 'My dear you can't rouse my
interest in the C . . . Surely you realise how stupid he is. It's not possible that you don't. I don't believe anyone whose mind & soul are alive
can ever be happy with a stupid mate <u>no</u> matter what fine qualities they
possess.' Although she did not believe that Bob stood a chance with
Phyllis's affections, she decided to promote his cause. 'You can come to
Scotland,' she wrote, 'so don't fret – only you are not to be trusted. I
long to see you and want you to come down [to Cliveden] if you can.
I have a plan. 'Tis deep and dark.'

He met Phyllis in the hall at Cliveden, eight months after his
visit to Mirador, and was struck again by her beauty, soulfulness, gaiety
and charm. The quality that particularly affected Bob was what he
called her ability to 'feel happiness as well as sorrow intensely'. His
infatuation was re-primed. Punctilious and controlled, unable to
declare himself, Bob invited her to Oxford, a visit she cancelled. They
went once to the theatre and he sent her books – more poetry. She
thanked him by letter. 'You are very good to want to "entertain" me,
but you must not have me on your mind,' she wrote warily. Bob waited
for his invitation to Scotland, ready to leave work at a moment's notice.
But there were delays. Nancy had overbooked the house with guests,
health practitioners and do-gooders.

What Phyllis loved in the Captain was his beau-like attentiveness; his friendship and physical attractiveness. At the same time he
needed managing and reassuring with his self-confessed 'lack of understanding and bitterness'. After the Captain had visited Phyllis at
Mirador in secret in February 1913 she wrote to Nancy, 'I do find his

absolute devotion ['servility' was another word she used] very comforting and I do love him very much for that but he knows the situation
I am in and if I were free tomorrow I told him I should not think of
marrying <u>anyone</u> until I had gone about for several years. He has it
pretty badly & I can't say I'm untouched!'

In Bob, whose attentiveness and 'understanding' company she
greatly appreciated, she had acquired a flattering friendship. Soon after
his visit to Mirador she had described him to Nancy as 'the most livable
sort of creature, like a cosy livable room and as you say a clever being . . .
but of course not so clever or farseeing as the C!!!' Nevertheless she now
saw Bob as a valued teacher in the self-improvement crusade.

Like Nancy, she had discovered in the intellectual aura of the
Round Table an exotic 'drug'. And soon, instead of being wary, she
encouraged him, sending almost flirtatious news bulletins from
Glendoe. 'You would have been amused to see a Cliveden footman on
the train in livery,' she wrote, 'with his arms full of Cliveden sheets and
pillow cases for us to use – all the railway blankets ripped off the beds
and Cliveden rugs put on instead – maids and servants falling over
each other, Kyte (the butler) scraping and bowing and saying
"Thankyou, Madam" whenever asked to do you a favour.' In this first
letter she asked him whether, with all the outdoor activity he was in
for, it would embarrass him among his city friends to return with 'pink
cheeks'.

The Astors travelled on the train with their own cow for the
children's milk, but also for the cream on which the chef based the rich
sauces he served with almost every dish, causing Phyllis to see 'black
patches in the atmosphere'. She found Nancy in the grip of a health
adviser, talking incessantly about 'nerves' – 'If I hear the word nerves
again,' she wrote, 'I shall fly out of the window.' Nancy still spent
much of the day in bed, suffering from exhaustion, rheumatism, colitis, getting up for the rich sauces, and being forbidden from taking
exercise.

'Yesterday,' Phyllis related to Bob, 'feeling perfectly well and
strong, I started out for a stroll (not even a walk). I was called back by

both Nancy and Mrs. Williams and told I would wreck my nerves too
if I overexercised! I was made to loll in an easy chair instead! I have a
headache in consequence this a.m. – for not having taken an innocent
little stroll.'

Phyllis felt she already knew Philip Kerr, 'the soul's companion',
intimately. When he arrived she reported her mixed impressions to
Bob Brand. She was put off by the way he plunged headlong into the
nerves and health seminar; he and Nancy spending a great deal of time
together, comparing ailments and applying theories, until it seemed to
Phyllis that she had joined a convention of hypochondriacs. In all this
there was little mention of Waldorf, who spent much of the time fishing
and stalking – taking exercise, nerves or not – with the children.

Finally, in late August, Bob Brand arrived at Glendoe. For his own
ailment – undeclared love – there seemed no solution as the days
passed. But then, on a Sunday afternoon, at the very end of his stay, he
made a clearly 'incompetent' move that ended in a muddle of embarrassment and misunderstanding, crushing all the careful months of
preparation and hope into a blank panic of retreat and apology.

It is impossible to tell from the agonized letter, written on Bob's
way home, precisely what happened. It is written in the code of a different era – the correspondence provides a textual puzzle as well as a
piece of social history. It seems that Bob Brand had declared his love,
totally misreading the circumstances and the response and pressed his
luck further, perhaps attempting an embrace, or worse, demanding
one. It is clear that Phyllis said something reserved for all beaux, something flippant and encouraging in the Virginian style. She certainly
gave a very mixed signal at a moment when Bob's state of tension had
been at a pitch for many days. 'A man feeling as I did then ceases to be
able to judge things and clutches at any straw,' he wrote to her. To spare
him pain, he said, she had been 'kinder to me than you ought to have
been . . . You didn't know what an effect your kindness was having on
me. Overcome with joy . . . I said what I would give anything not to
have said . . . I quite realise I ought never to have done what I did, but
it was innocently meant. I felt I wanted in some way to seal a contract.'

Bob knew that Phyllis was, in her phrase, 'willingly bound' to the Captain, and it must have seemed to her that he had wilfully ignored this situation, appearing to her 'in a bare light'. 'You told me you wd. forget & forgive & I am sure you will,' he wrote two days later, 'but I cannot & shall not for many a long day forget or forgive myself . . . The love that I have for you is not an unworthy one. You are my ideal & tho' you say that is foolish, I can't help it. The very thought that I shd. have done anything which mt. be construed as wanting in respect to you, when I revere every hair of your head, tortures me.' He ended his letter: 'I do not think I can cut myself off wholly from your friendship. I can undertake, as I did on Sunday that we shd. act as friends. I know now how matters stand & shall not misinterpret you again.'

In reply Phyllis wrote:

Dear dear Mr. B. Brand,

How can I not answer your letter? The thought that you should be suffering through fear of my not understanding anything you might have said or done tortures me also. I do, honestly, realize and understand so perfectly how you meant what you said to me, and anything further from my mind than thinking the less of you for it, could not be. How can I make you believe this? I wish I knew.

You say that you understand the feelings that prompted me to give you unconsciously more encouragement than I intended. I should not have done this for ANYTHING in the world if I had known what it meant to you. It was a stupid way on my part of trying not to throw back into your face the love which you wanted to give me. I cannot say that I do not value your love, for I do, indeed, very much, and while I want to keep the real and true affection of it I cannot accept what men call love, but I will accept 'the love that the heart lifts above and the heavens reject not'. May I do this which means a friendship that years

and distances and silences cannot disturb. I am so glad I
have had it, it has certainly been one of the pleasantest I
have ever had in my life.

It was odd to describe their new friendship as one of the pleasantest she had ever had. Apart from the letters its history could be
counted in mere hours. But having conquered Mr Brand, Phyllis was
not going to let him go. She wanted to see if he valued 'the better side
of her nature' enough for friendship, unaffected by infatuation, by
looks, by Eros, even though, as Bob's relieved reply revealed, she had
coolly and conceitedly warned him of the danger. 'My love may be
doomed to be, as you say, "the desire of the moth for the stars" but, if
I get my wings singed by seeing you every now & then & writing to you
sometimes that is my own look-out.' He would accept a deal of friendship, he said; he greatly appreciated this, 'but I can't help going on
loving you so it is useless to pretend that I don't . . . I don't love like a
boy of 18'.

'You know, Mr. B. Brand,' Phyllis replied, 'I have not had in my
life many companions like you. They have all, more or less been a
peculiarly nice, kind, thoughtless lot of human beings, but I can't say
they have been very understanding. Nancy and a few women that I
know have that understanding, but very few men, therefore, you see,
I value it in you as a friend very much . . . Should you have nothing to
do on Monday night, you might take me to see Barrie's new play. I
should love that, but of course if you have any other engagement don't
hesitate to say so.' Phyllis had already told Bob Brand that she didn't
think platonic love – of the kind that Nancy and Philip professed – was
anything more than playing with fire, and now, almost coquettishly, she
was promoting it.

Phyllis had made the classic mistake of suggesting that further
meetings – in the time she had left in London after her return from
Glendoe – would help to blunt the edges of Bob Brand's infatuation and
keep the friendship alive. There was always a touch of the *allumeuse* in
Phyllis: 'If I have given you pain,' she wrote, 'I do most earnestly regret

it. If I have given you even a little bit of happiness, I am thankful.' She
sent Bob Brand a book of prayers with a sprig of white heather in its
leaves to remind him of their moment in Scotland. Nancy saw it all
clearly: 'Oh that Bob Brand I pity him', she wrote to Phyllis, 'only I
would have more pity if he would have more competence. He writes
that he can't give up hope but he really must – so don't encourage him
and have that on your conscience. I see he means to bombard me with
letters trying to get me to encourage him.' For someone who, as Phyllis
said, 'didn't understand about love' Nancy's postcard to Bob Brand
showed a rare compassion: 'I hope you are not blue and troubled. I am
sorry you have set your affections on such strange and difficult ladies.
But you like overcoming obstacles so perhaps had you loved the vicar's
daughter you wd have been miserable. Nancy.'

Phyllis booked her return passage to America in mid-September
1913: Peter had to go back to school. Nancy, still in Scotland, was
almost as distressed as Bob, writing to Phyllis, 'You see when you go
you leave such a tremendous gap that even 4 houses 4 children one husband & 86 intimate friends don't even cover the bottom of that gap.
Still I am happy about you now & I don't mind anything so long as I feel
that you are happy – G[od] . . . what a dull dog the C [Captain] is – I
wd be happy to see you married to a blacksmith provided he made the
best in you happy. I only want yr well being NOT my own – I can honestly say my love for you is as selfless as it is possible for a human love
to be. Now enough of my NOBLE selfless feelings . . .' She advised
Phyllis to go on stuffing herself with three 'square nourishing meals a
day' and above all never to exercise.

On the eve of her departure Bob wrote to Phyllis, enclosing a
book of Matthew Arnold's poems, marked with his selections. Try as
he might, he told her, he couldn't accept a deal of friendship although
he would abide by the rules. 'I suppose happiness & pain are generally
very near together,' he wrote. 'Forgive me . . . I promised to behave in
future simply as a friend & I have tried my hardest this time in London
to do so, & I will in the future. But I don't think I can forget. You
cannot prevent me loving you & I am ready to take the consequences.'

Phyllis replied, alarmed now, as the RMS *Baltic* was leaving. 'I simply cannot take it in that I could mean to anyone's life what you say I do to yours . . . I do hate to think I have caused you a moment's suffering. I am so DREADFULLY sorry for that and wish I could undo any damage I have done . . .' She sent him a further plaintive telegram – and not one designed to dampen thoughts of romance – from Queenstown, Ireland: 'GOODBYE HOPE THE SKIES ARE NOT AS LEADEN AS MY SPIRITS.'

Love letters from the Captain dating back to July were waiting at Mirador. They were postmarked from the railhead at Biysk, in Russia, 200 hundred miles north of the Chinese and Mongolian borders. By August the Captain had travelled several hundred miles further south to the remote valley of the Tekes River in foothills of the mountains of Tien Shan. He was preparing another hunting expedition that would take him across the mountains into Chinese Turkestan and Sinkiang – his most ambitious journey so far, one that would occupy him until November that year, 1913. His hair was cut 'as short as clippers can make it', giving him the look of a 'speckled ostrich'; his valuables strung around his neck with fishing line as he swam his horses across rivers with his Kalmuck and Turcoman companions.

He and Phyllis had last met at Mirador in April that year, an intense moment between them given the months of separation ahead. He had written from the departing train, 'I watched your carriage as it walked away . . . I felt that all your best was coming along with me, and you can be so absolutely sure I will so guard and cherish what is of priceless value. Dearest, dearest, you have me now and for always and I will think and feel the same of you.' He had given her, as a parting present, a set of pearls valued then at £1500.

The Captain wrote with a new intimacy from this moment even though their affair, it seems, was not yet consummated. He wrote, describing a poem she had sent as 'warming and caressing'. 'It makes one think in parts of things that perhaps one didn't ought to (yet). How long has that got to be?' He had, he said, 'derived more comfort from looking at yr stocking! which I keep in my writing case along with other relics. It reminds me of some pleasant moments, aren't they ever going to come to LAST? DO hurry up. What long legs you have. It reaches nearly to the top of mine.' Phyllis dabbed scent on her envelopes, at his request.

The Captain knew about Phyllis's new interest in 'yr clever young men' as he called them and that Bob Brand had been corresponding with Phyllis but that, until now, was all. He had imagined this first love of his, with its pacts and secrets, to exclude the world but now he began to sense an intrusive rivalry. He was touchy about these fashionable intellectuals who, with Nancy's encouragement, surrounded Phyllis while he was away. Phyllis had persuaded him to take several copies of the *Round Table*, her new source of wisdom. The Captain thought much of their content 'savours of the backstairs and the boudoir' and sent letters back written on their torn-out fly leaves. Phyllis also wrote so much news about the group. He saw unfavourable comparisons with himself. 'Thank goodness my education in the way of meeting people has been a wide one,' he wrote to Phyllis, ' – I do not refer to the very distinguished company that gather at times under yr sisters roof; they are not the sort that count . . .'

Douglas Pennant had ample cause for paranoia – although he had acted, up until now, with soldierly control. Nancy had attacked him from the first moment he appeared and had made no secret of her disapproval. 'I cannot forget the glad light that filled your sisters eyes when I announced my plans of being away for the summer,' he wrote. Nancy followed him to Sinkiang with letters, addressing him as 'Dear Capt.', containing phrases such as 'Do you ever think of anything else, in your solitude, except love?' He drafted and redrafted letters of indignation but for the moment didn't send them. He took the view that Nancy was dangerous but a little crazy, the sort of woman who needed 'a firm hand', and whose craving for public attention was 'an incurable disease'.

Only marriage to Phyllis would finally stop Nancy, but now there was a shadow over its prospect and he believed Nancy had something to do with it. The timing of Phyllis's divorce depended on Reggie, but contrary to Phyllis's certain predictions, Reggie did not seem to be coming forward, demanding his freedom. She was therefore at the mercy of Reggie's mother, who was playing out the process, fearful of her son's reputation and trying to avoid a financial settlement. If Reggie refused to set a divorce in motion Phyllis would have to wait two years until late 1915, when she had the right to automatic divorce. All this was depressing to Phyllis, and irritating to Pennant, who had advised her originally to get a divorce on grounds of adultery.

There were other, longer term worries on his mind, communicated to Phyllis by relays of runners slogging back to the post station at Kuldja or Biysk. They had often talked about 'playing the game' and becoming man and wife but never, it seems, of the practicalities of marriage. Where would they live? Would Phyllis give up Mirador when Peter and Winkie's schooling, under the separation agreement, perhaps under the divorce, would be in America? How could he provide on his soldier's half pay, or afford to hunt with Phyllis in England? He began to express the exiled soldier's fear of civilian life, of the contradictions he had left behind in England.

Phyllis had assumed that he would give up the dangerous life of hunting that took him away for so long. However glamorous, she didn't rate it as a serious profession. She assumed that he would drift into politics, become a gentleman MP, and took it for granted, ignoring his radical Liberal sympathies, that he could get a safe Tory seat with the combined contacts at their disposal. But now, in a veiled attack against the Round Table, Cliveden and Phyllis's new circle of admirers, the Captain wrote, 'If it's public characters and the like that you prefer there is no chance of your finding them in the likes of me.'

The Irish Home Rule Bill, which the Captain passionately supported, and was due to be enacted the following year, would be violently opposed by the Tories who mostly supported the Ulster Protestants. There was a major crisis ahead, a test of loyalties, possibly rebellion and civil war. 'I rather doubt the policy of chucking ones friends by appearing as a Radical lobby trotter,' the Captain now told Phyllis, 'but that is the only one I could go through now. Heavens.

Fancy one of the family a Home Ruler, yet so I am but don't tell anyone please . . . I wish I could look at things from a conservative standpoint but altogether cannot. In fact I would not voice their opinions for anything that could be offered me. I look upon its devotees as strange relics of a bygone age as only indeed fit for a museum like my faunal specimens.'

There was something callous – even provocative – about the way Phyllis began to give unnecessary information to each of the two rivals about each other. She told the Captain of Bob's frustrated courtship – information no doubt magnified in the Captain's imagination as he lay in his tent in Mongolia, suffering from 'fly sickness'. He had written in October that year, 'I think BB must be a nice man. I could not behave like that I am afraid at least I don't think so. I think people who can are happier but I think with me I should keep away from what I wanted and could not have.'

The Captain saw his happiness slipping away. His tone began to change. He wrote defensively about marriage – a new tack for the Captain, but a ploy to punish Phyllis, to vent his frustrations at the legal hold-ups and to counter the suspicion that Phyllis was vacillating under the constant pressure of Nancy. Perhaps it was better after all that he continued, at least for part of the year, to wander the earth. Marriage now was 'all so uncertain it sometimes seems quite silly to seriously think of it. The more time goes on the more I feel my hunting is part of one's nature [sic] and that one's nature would be the worse if altogether shut off from it.' He predicted that it would threaten their happiness if he were hemmed in. 'This is just to say could I go off with my rifle for, say, 3 or 4 months while you did ditto with yr stud of hunters? But all this is looking far ahead I fear – perhaps too far.' He added somewhat harshly that she would probably be 'middle aged' before any change between them could take place, close on fifty when Winkie left school, 'a time of life when none but very tough old stir-about sort of ladies care about going far from home.' He wrote, 'I am deeply grateful for your affection but shilly shally is repugnant to ones nature, and unnatural positions . . . never can go on for ever.' The warning messages were mixed with others of longing and love: 'yr love for me is the opium and agent and the most precious of all that I possess in this world'.

He might have further doubted his unwritten contract with Phyllis if he had read her letter to Bob written around this time: 'I can't believe I was meant to live as I have done these last ten years; I feel there must be something better waiting for me somewhere. Hope has never failed me yet, it came very near it once.' These were not the words of someone who saw her future clearly mapped out with the Captain. He would have been incensed, too, if he had discovered that Phyllis, seeing a crisis coming, had idly asked Bob Brand to think up some job the Captain might usefully do. What to do with the Captain? Bob replied wearily, and with almost superhuman patience, like a housemaster abstractedly writing off one of his dimmer old boys: 'There are very few jobs he wd. like or countries he cd. stand, I sd. think . . . I wonder if he has any job in his mind.'

14

Outbreak of War

Melancholy came over Phyllis when she returned to Mirador in the autumn of 1913, homesick for Nancy and England. 'I simply dread our partings,' she told Bob of her sister. 'They seem to shake everything up just wrong.' Mirador had little charm now as a place of winter solitude, and she found the evenings especially 'sometimes very long'. The old crab of her on-and-off depressions, which Bob Brand romanticized as 'a capacity for sorrow and suffering' had some real cause in her sur- roundings. She confided in Bob, needing his letters and attention. The embargo broken, they wrote to each other at least once a week.

Winkie aged three and Peter aged eleven were her only perma- nent companions apart from Aunt Ann, the old cook. Phyllis had to cope with her un-Virginian dislike of her relations, who 'bore me to death', and the neighbours with their 'apple talk'. 'I am not unsociable really,' she wrote, 'but you know that sort of disintegration of the soul one feels when continually surrounded by uncongenial people.' Her carping father, across the road, was a menace, too. She wouldn't see the Captain for many months and meanwhile her divorce proceedings, the hours of legal talk, were weighing on her. She longed to go off, she said, 'to foreign parts where new faces and new languages and new breezes will help to blow the old remembrances all away. They some- how always lurk around here.'

That autumn she sent Peter away to boarding school, the Fay School in Southboro, Massachusetts, at the worst possible moment. He was already showing signs of anxiety after this first summer of shuttling between his father and mother and on the day of his departure 'we clung desperately to each other when the parting hour came'. When Peter's first letters arrived from the Fay School they were heavy with homesickness and yearning for his mother: 'It is half after eight o'clock and I am just wondering how you are and what you are doing. I feel very dreary and lonely. Goodnight my dear Mother. Goodbye from your one son, Peter Brooks.'

However, the fame of the Langhornes kept Phyllis supplied with a surprising range of visitors to keep her company. There is a letter in the Richmond archive, written in a shaky hand by John Singleton Mosby, the most glamorous officer of the Confederacy, the feared guerrilla tactician who had grown up in Charlottesville. 'I am anxious to see Chillie Langhorne,' he wrote to a friend. 'His daughters Mrs Astor & Mrs Brooks are my friends.' As if directly to rival Nancy's Round Table, Phyllis also managed to bring the cream of Washington's young intellectuals to her doorstep, notably Herbert Croly, whose book *The Promise of American Life*, published in 1909, was a landmark in the history of ideas and now considered a foundation stone of American liberalism. He was in the process of founding the *New Republic* with Walter Lippmann, who at twenty-six was already on his way to becoming the most powerful and influential American journalist of the century.

'I have just been entertaining The New Republic here, Mr. Croly and Mr. Lippmann,' Phyllis wrote proudly to Bob Brand some weeks later. 'They came for a few days and I enjoyed their intellectual conversation, at least as much of it as I could understand. They are making headway they say with their Anglo American Alliance . . . Mr. Croly arrived looking pale and anaemic, but left after 4 days with rosy sunburnt cheeks and a double chin. He is quite a good tennis player.'

The Progressive era was at its peak in 1912, a reforming force as strong in the Democrat as in the Republican Party and Phyllis had caught the mood. She had voted for the ex-President Teddy Roosevelt – the most radical of the main candidates in the election that year, which he lost to Woodrow Wilson – even though she had a soft spot for Wilson, the man who went to church on foot.

Roosevelt's new breakaway Progressive Party, the 'Bull Moose' party, had stood on a platform not dissimilar to that of Lloyd George, of comprehensive reform. The New Nationalism that he proclaimed promised to enforce the commandment 'Thou shalt not steal' and denounced the unholy alliance between corrupt business and corrupt politics. It was pro-labour, up to a point, in favour of votes for women, for restrictions on working hours, for government intervention and urban renewal. But it was also conservative, partly motivated by a defensive fear of syndicalism and revolutionary socialism: Roosevelt's campaign had received funding from J. P. Morgan, the powerful American banker and financier.

Bob Brand had teased her: 'I thought you were a Socialist but you still seem pretty keen on private property and running your own little show at Mirador.' Phyllis indeed liked to see herself as passionately committed to high-mindedness and social reform. But progressivism for Phyllis didn't mean a change in the *status quo*. The idea was Christian based, as she saw it; exercising righteousness, being fairer to the poor, but without necessarily enfranchising them. Phyllis kept to a particular and paternalistic view of politics in Virginia, for example. She wrote to Bob from the Greenwood train, 'I am on my way to Richmond. The colored porter, Ben, and I have just been chatting, also the conductor who tells me he brought the party up from Richmond when I was married 10 years ago and "your father invited me to the luncheon, but I couldn't git off and I've been regretting it ever since"! he said. Virginia is really the only true democracy that I know of – it's a delicious place.' There were those around, of course, who hadn't grasped the principles of the new enlightenment. There was always Ava Astor, Nancy's original social pilot in England, who was a handy marker against which a Langhorne sister could measure personal improvement; a luminous figure on the path of true selfishness. 'I was walking in Fifth Avenue one very hot day,' Phyllis wrote to Bob Brand, 'when just ahead of me I saw a lady in a long velvet coat with a huge fur collar, very thin stockings and high heel slippers, and little dashes of crepe worn here and there about her person. It turned out to be none other than Ava. She heaved a sigh or two and then began a tale of woe, chiefly about having to spend a week or two in Philadelphia, her old home, with her sister, to settle up her brother's estate, who has just died. I forgot to add she had a low neck dress, which would have put me to the blush to wear in the evening, much less on the street. I can't say that she gives me a sense of peace and calm. I've got no worldly courage perhaps! . . . It would be like having to eat delicious looking ice in the evening, all frozen and pink and white, then having to eat it again for breakfast, all melted and sweet and sloppy. That is an unchristian criticism but at the moment she has excited my wrath.'

Phyllis was eager to fill the gaps left by her years surrounded by sporting gentlemen. Bob Brand represented, as she thought, 'the intellect'. To keep him 'up to scratch', to give purpose to their correspondence, she now ordered him to take care of her education. The reading lists were already under way, some of them recycled to Douglas Pennant for *his* education, under Phyllis's second-hand direction.

'That's a pretty difficult job,' Bob Brand wrote. What did she have in mind? 'Do you want to learn history, philosophy, chemistry or what? I used to be frightfully keen, and am still, on the pursuit of knowledge & truth for their own sakes, as I thought that they wd. solve the riddle of existence & make the universe plain. But you realise after a time that the enigma will never be solved & that all the knowledge you can ever get is an infinitesimal fraction of the whole.' It would certainly make life more interesting; she could appreciate more sides of it, he wrote, but 'the soul is the important point & not the brain even in education so I don't see I have anything to teach you'. There were two sources for this new attitude of Bob Brand's: the impact of the Langhornes on his Englishness and the impact of romantic love. It was especially the 'capacity for feeling and emotion' in the Langhorne family that gave them 'their exceptional fascination and charm' in his eyes and which he now believed was 'a more fundamental quality in a human being than even reason and intellect'.

But he sent Phyllis the All Souls Fellowship Examination paper for 1913, which included the question 'Compare the achievements of Germans and Greeks in the task of civilising the Slavonic peoples.' 'Dear Mr. Brand, Heavens!' she replied, 'What a stultifying effect on my brain the mere sight of that examination paper from Oxford had upon me. Were you ever really able to answer all of those questions? Surely you never reach those heights and then fall so low as to choose the profession of money lending?'

Bob sent her a flow of books. The likeliest combination for success – with Nancy too – were works of strong religious feeling, mixed with pastoral imagery and symbolism and a touch of the Psalms. Bob had an early success with Tagore's *Gitanjali*. He took a risk sending *Thaïs* by Anatole France, a sceptical moral parable of an early Christian monk who tried to convert an Alexandrian courtesan and ended up being seduced by her. He compared the monk to Philip Kerr, deluded that his love was platonic and heavenly. 'I feel very much for the people who get caught by Circe on her island,' Bob wrote. 'By the way did you read Manon Lescaut?' – another tale of sexual moths and flames.

Bob Brand's finest success was with an extraordinary work called *The Roadmender* by Michael Fairless (the author's real name was Margaret, although she preferred 'Bill' in real life). It was a bestseller for twenty years – a book, to a modern reader, so cluttered with whimsy, fake poetic effect and affected sentiments that it is difficult to extract its meaning. But it certainly promoted the peace of God through humble physical labour, lamented the rural exodus and extolled the virtues of rose-covered cottages.

Phyllis did not enjoy Milton's *Paradise Lost*. 'Think how much more amusing the knowing Eve could have been about men,' she wrote, '– but perhaps Sylvia Pankhurst is getting off her chest all the things Eve would like to have said.' That November Nancy had sent the suffragette leader to Mirador. Brand wrote, 'I am sure Mirador must be the home of everything new just now, New Art, New Thought & new women – This present age is a strange one & cd. hardly be more interesting. Everyone is getting loose from the old moorings in religion, social life, morality, art, politics & everything is floating off into an uncharted sea. It leads to great trouble but it's far better than stagnation . . .'

In his competitive jealousy of the Captain, Bob could not avoid slipping items of self-advertisement into his letters: 'I spent most of the week in Newcastle. I've become a director of an electric power company, much the biggest in the world.' 'Dear Little Bright Eyes,' Phyllis responded. He described playing golf with Winston Churchill, First Lord of the Admiralty and already a central political star, and being taken on consultative trips on the Admiralty launch. Bob had a go at Herbert Croly, too, stung by a rival think-tank across the water. 'I really do think we are now getting an influence, & I believe we shall have more,' he wrote. 'It will be a "great adventure" in the next few years uniting the British Empire & reconstructing England. There is such a terrible lot to do . . . The advantage of the R.T. group over most other people is that they have sufficient experience to be constructive. . . . I think they have some advantage over your friend of the New Republic.'

For the chronic illnesses – the nerves, the anxiety, the brain fag – shared by the Astors and most of the Round Table, the presiding doctor was Sir Bertrand Dawson, doctor to the King, the landed, the famous, and the titled. His highly expensive 'cures' – they obeyed his every order, however extravagant or clearly absurd – were prescribed according to the patient's means. He would have done well as a travel agent, which perhaps he was. Thus Bob Brand, a salaried banker, never got further than the Black Forest spas. Philip Kerr, heir to a Marquisate, was sent for some therapeutic tiger-shooting in India in mid-1913. Sir Bertrand prescribed marriage as an energizing, anti-stress cure for the Round Table, the prospect of which, in Philip Kerr's case, had almost deprived him of his sanity. Brand was ordered to St Moritz to meet more women. At first it was only Phyllis who saw through Dawson, foremost as a snob and worse as a poor diagnostician. Despite the fact that he was highly regarded by his own profession, who considered him a particularly talented diagnostician, Dawson's public reputation – after he was elevated to the peerage – was commemorated in the jingle 'Lord Dawson of Penn/Has killed many men.'

'You are right about D. being a snob, I'm sure,' Bob Brand wrote to Phyllis. 'He pays gt. attention to Philip as P. has a chance of being a Marquis, very little to J. Dove & not much more to me, only I have the merit of being a friend of the rich, having been found at Glendoe.' By pure chance Sir Bertrand made an inspired suggestion to Bob Brand, to go back to the Black Forest, to Freiburg, to the care of a certain Dr Martin. As well as being a physician Dr Martin was an analytical psychologist, who followed the school of Carl Jung – whose break with Freud had occurred that year, 1913. It was the first time Bob Brand, or anyone in his circle had encountered these theories about the irrational side of human nature, of the conscious and the unconscious and the interpretation of dreams, or had heard the word 'complex' mentioned in terms of psychology. It had a profound effect on him and he wrote exhilarated pages to Phyllis from his clinic, thrilled with his discoveries and the newfound jargon. He was not suffering from a bad heart, which he had believed for sixteen years, but from a 'sympathetic nervous system' that was exceedingly sensitive to pain, pleasure, beauty etc., which caused his pulse to race. All geniuses had suffered similar symptoms, Martin had told him.

'I am sure my sub-conscious self – which has really come up to scratch in my dreams since I've been here – is much cleverer & more amusing certainly more imaginative than anything which appears in the daytime as my conscious self,' he reflected. 'It's only when the two begin to come into serious conflict that there may be trouble.' 'I wonder if you have any complexes,' those mechanisms caused by painful events in early life, he asked Phyllis. But any revealing answer was cut short: Phyllis had sent a letter asking him to accompany her on a six-week trip to Paris, to perfect her French, as if their platonic friendship was a *fait accompli*, and the Captain an absent beau whose feelings and situation she felt at liberty to ignore entirely. Bob Brand replied hotly in the new vernacular:

Dear Mrs Brooks,

I am told by Dr Martin that one ought to avoid internal conflicts between one's conscious & sub-conscious self. The very idea you suggest almost produces a storm between the intense wishes of the one & the repression of the other, between the ideas of what might under ideal conditions be & what can't be. It's only saints apparently who finally effect a complete reconciliation between their two selves & I am far from that consummation.

The idea of Phyllis travelling to France with Bob Brand would have caused no less amazement to Douglas Pennant, particularly since the trip would have coincided with his English leave between expeditions to Persia and Kashmir.

Then, before Christmas 1913, their letters crossed. Phyllis wrote to Bob on 8 December to say that Douglas Pennant, 'fresh from the wilds of Mongolia', had, like Bob, fallen off his horse on a recent Mirador visit, adding, 'It was very nice seeing him again, but no sooner do I begin to enjoy his society than he is off again. He left last week for Persia on another shooting trip, but not such a long one this time. I begin to suspect that this hunting life is beginning to pall upon him, I should be disappointed to think he could go on at it much longer.'

A letter from Bob was on its way telling Phyllis that he knew from Nancy all about the Captain's visit: 'I suppose after all that has happened such a piece of intelligence oughtn't to touch my feelings or interest me — But I can't help it. It does . . . I don't know what the present position is, or whether you will or will not be free to marry again — But if you will be or if you have FINALLY made up your mind, you can let me know.'

Phyllis spent Christmas night with her two sons on either side of her bed. 'It is wonderful to see children's faces on Christmas morning, I wish I had ten to sleep with me,' she wrote to Bob.

In late January 1914 she sent Peter back to boarding school and came to England with the four-year-old Winkie. She planned to hunt and to see the Captain who was on leave – the French trip abandoned. The Captain was invited for four weekends to Cliveden in February and March. A third suitor was Geoffrey Dawson, now editor of *The Times*, with whom, as Bob said later, he 'changed guard' at St James's Square in their pursuit of Phyllis. Bob and the Captain shared one weekend at Cliveden – with Winston Churchill: that at least gave Bob rights of attendance. They skirted around each other. Phyllis would send Bob notes of warning that would surely have ended the Captain's courtship if he had discovered them: 'Come in if you can before lunch about 12. I can't say stop for luncheon – I will explain why later,' and 'I am afraid Sunday here will not be much use as Henry Pennant is coming also Foxie McDonald and Fido, and I think it would be best if you didn't. You don't mind my being quite frank and telling you this, do you? But I am sure you will understand.'

In the face of this irritating competition, Douglas Pennant, hunting in Stony Stratford, changed tack again, this time to a lofty patience and understanding in which – as he hardly needed to say but did so nevertheless – he put his trust in Phyllis as 'a high class well bred woman who has a sense of what honour means' not to waver from their contract; and not to be unfaithful in her heart. The Captain left in March for Kashmir, planning to return sometime in the summer of 1914.

Philip Kerr was also exiled, but for reasons of health. Tortured by insomnia, incapable now of work, he had been sent under doctors' orders to India, to Lucknow and to Delhi where he stayed with Lord Hardinge, the Viceroy. In his earnest and much discussed search for his soul, for some certainty or even some leader he could follow, Kerr investigated Buddhism; he became fascinated with Gandhi – whom he met – and with the politics of Gandhism. But there was nothing he could convincingly latch on to. He sent frequent bulletins back to Nancy. He read *The Brothers Karamazov* and found that it coincided 'wonderfully with my present view of the universe and where truth in it resides' in its portrayal of the evil passions and mystic ideals which combined in the human heart. He wrote to Nancy: '. . . I sometimes think that Hell is this world with love left out, only efficiency and progress and passion and wealth left in.'

In February 1914, while he was on his way home and Phyllis was travelling between Cliveden and hunting in Market Harborough, Nancy became seriously ill. She had developed what even Sir Bertrand managed to diagnose as an internal abscess. He ordered an immediate operation, warning of a second one. The after-effects of the first were acutely painful: Nancy recalled many years later that she had never suffered such agonies or been so miserable. She was taken to Rest Harrow, Sandwich, to convalesce with a nurse in attendance. 'I had a nurse to look after me and I lay in the sunshine on the balcony that looks out over the sea,' Nancy recalled fifty years later. 'The world was so lovely and so peaceful I began to argue with myself as I lay there. This I thought is not what God wants. It is not what he meant to happen . . .'

Ironically it was Phyllis who had first mentioned Christian Science, the religion of Mary Baker Eddy of Boston, Massachusetts, who had died four years earlier. 'She told me,' wrote Nancy, 'that there were people in America who believed, as I did, that God never meant there to be sickness and suffering, and who could be cured by prayer.' Phyllis had also sent her a copy of Mrs Eddy's *Science and Health* and Nancy had sent a copy to Philip Kerr, but neither of them seemed to have read it at this point. When Nancy returned to Cliveden after her convalescence, as she wrote later, 'a wonderful thing happened. Whenever a soul is ready for enlightenment, and awaits it humbly I believe that the answer is somewhere to hand: the teacher comes.' The 'teacher' was the unlikely figure of Mrs Maud Bull, a Christian Scientist who knew many of Nancy's friends in America and had been invited, by chance, to Cliveden.

Bob Brand was staying that weekend and wrote later, 'My rec-
ollection is that Nancy went up with her to have a talk one night
before going to bed and came down a Christian Scientist, a case of
sudden conversion.' Nancy herself wrote in her memoir, 'It was just
like the conversion of St. Paul. Here I found the answer to all my
questions, and all I had been looking for. If I was spiritual I would not
have to suffer in the flesh, I learned. My life was really made over.
Fear went out of it. I was no longer frightened of anything. From
Cliveden Phyllis described the phenomenon to Bob Brand a few days
later: 'I found Nancy playing in the nursery with the children, transformed by her Christian Scientist friends into a perfectly well
woman – she had been up most of the day and looked VERY well – I
feel as if a miracle had happened, and a very "spooky" atmosphere
pervades!'

Nancy had tumbled into the most successful of all the American
mind-over-matter, self-reliance, self-healing cults ever devised and it
fitted her perfectly. Mary Baker Eddy had cannily pulled together many
strands of various nineteenth-century movements and medicine
shows – she had taken much from Emile Coué's popular New Thought,
although she denied it – and labelled it 'Science'. It was the key word
that attracted so many of her, at first, uneducated followers, with its
prototype psychological jargon and kitchen philosophy.

The 'divine metaphysics' of Christian Science, conceived by
Baker Eddy, and of which Nancy was to become a famous convert,
made some breathtaking speculations on the nature of God. They
explained away why, to most mortal men except Christian Scientists,
God seemed so unpredictable and unreliable. Born out of her own ill-
health, from which she also believed herself miraculously cured, it
centred on the idea that since he is made 'in the image and likeness of
God' man is a spiritual, not a material, being. What God has made
cannot be evil, Baker Eddy preached, *only* good and harmonious.
Therefore sin, sickness and death are illusions, shadows of reality.
Every form of 'error' or evil can be overcome, therefore, on the basis
of its unreality. Death, the 'King of Terrors' is a mortal illusion: 'For

the real man and the real universe there is no death process.' 'I deny disease as a truth,' said Mary Baker Eddy, 'but I admit it as a deception.' It was, quite simply, a denial of the physical world.

The 'insight' given exclusively to the Christian Scientist ('Knowing the Truth') could itself only come from a close and repeated reading of *Science and Health with a Key to the Scriptures* by Mary Baker Eddy – one of the most phenomenally successful books of all time. Nancy identified with Mary Baker Eddy; she probably never knew of her megalomaniac and paranoid tendencies. They had suffered from the same classic nineteenth-century psychosomatic ailments, above all 'nervous prostration' and colic, which had kept them bedridden. A part of the cure was the religious euphoria produced by repetition – excluding everything else from the mind – of Eddy's texts and certainties. This served as a wholesale distraction of Nancy's attention which cleared away all doubts and fears.

Her new religion enabled Nancy quite simply to leap, in her mind, from the material to the spiritual world and to pitch camp there permanently, on the high ground, armed with a dogma that, intellectually, it was useless to argue with. The proof of its efficacy for her was that she had hardly a day's illness for the rest of her life.

Nancy never wavered from the faith nor from her daily catechism, 'The Scientific Statement of Being', which begins unscientifically: 'There is no life, truth, intelligence or substance in matter . . .' and asserts, 'Spirit is the real and eternal; matter is the unreal and temporal. Spirit is God and man is his image and likeness. Therefore man is not material – he is spiritual.' This was the mantra that her children would be brought up to chant later on when something went wrong, when they felt pain, fell off their bicycles on to the gravel, suffered reversals in the illusory material world. This was perhaps their only hope for recovery, since Nancy turned absolutely, like all Christian Scientists, against medical science from this moment.

More telling, perhaps, than Nancy's joining the Church of Christ Scientist was the way she hijacked its doctrine for her own purposes with all its assumptions and simplicities. Her yearning for goodness,

and the struggle between good and evil, were simplified at a stroke by
the notion that evil was an illusion, a mere shadow. Nancy could now
use her textbooks to reduce everything to right and wrong: no more
complexities of human nature. The key, perhaps, was her discovery that
'If I was spiritual I would not have to suffer in the flesh.' Nancy had
always wanted to embark on the road to sainthood – a fantasy from
childhood – and now she saw the path to be a healer too, like Jesus
Christ or Mary Baker Eddy or the Archdeacon Neve. Many burdens
were lifted; all those worldly problems like sex and romance were
now fallacies (although she had temporarily deviated by getting married) and illusions, to be authoritatively talked down. Her conversion
relieved her deepest conflict, that between her bible-punching conscience and her Langhorne sister worldliness, although to the outside
world it accentuated these two aspects: the missionary on the one
hand, and the bigot on the other. Her life was simplified and energy
was released. Instead of making her solemn her new religion added a
few degrees to her sense of gaiety.

The Captain, naturally, treated the whole episode with scathing
contempt, when the news reached him. 'If anyone tells me that
Christian Science has done so and so much good,' he wrote, ' – well I
know then for a fact that so & so's complaint was almost entirely one of
the imagination. I can't take a better example than your sister.'

Phyllis had now been in England for two months and Bob was running
out of patience with this polite platonic friendship. Two or three days
before her departure to America he proposed marriage again. When
he was turned down, he declared a moratorium on the whole affair.
They must break off any meetings, he said, and end their correspondence. After this apparently final meeting on 2 March, Phyllis
returned to St James's Square and wrote to him: 'One seems always to
be hurting the people one least wants to hurt . . . I have tried very
hard, in my feeble way perhaps, not to encourage you with any hopes
of my changing my mind as to my affections, but I see now that one
has to be as careful with one's words, looks and actions as a painter is

with his brush, for fear one wrong stroke will change the whole look of his picture . . . If I should never hear from you or see you again, I should quite understand, but I hope with all my heart this will not be the case.'

She followed it with another message, asking to see him in person, adding 'I would like to say good-bye to you in less incongruous surroundings . . . so come to St. James's Square if you can – I will quite understand if you don't.' But Bob refused this melodramatic gesture. Instead he sent her a cable to the RMS *Olympic*, docked at Queenstown, and she sent a letter thanking him, adding the words, 'My heart feels heavy, and my eyelids burn with a longing to cry,' and ending, 'Remember your philanthropic work.'

The excuse, on both sides, for breaking the embargo a month later, was the death of Moncure Perkins, followed, less than two weeks later, by that of Lizzie. Moncure's death had long been expected, but that of Lizzie, who was forty-seven years old, was a severe shock, especially to her children, Nancy who was seventeen and Alice, aged twelve. Moncure was laid out in the front parlour of Lizzie's house for the Virginian all-night vigil by his four closest friends. Then an over-wrought Lizzie buried him at All Saints Church, putting on her deep black veil with, after some debate, a white organdie collar and cuffs. Then, as Nancy Lancaster described it, 'She went up to aunt Irene in New York, a week after the funeral. She borrowed a little hat from me – she didn't want to wear a long crepe veil – and they said that she'd never looked so well and her friend was coming for her and they went to the dressmaker to take these feathers that she'd brought up to put on a hat. And she dropped dead. And I was with Grandfather at Greenwood and we got the message and we drove across the mountains (to Richmond) and he was very sad and he said "'I can't remember a time when Lizzie wasn't there.'"

Lizzie, according to Phyllis 'died exactly the same way as mother – a stroke and never spoke', similarly induced by 'worry and nerve strain'. 'I think she felt father's treatment very keenly,' she wrote to Nancy, '& said to me just a few days before she died with her lip quivering how he tried all that winter to hurt and embarrass her.' Back went the family to the parlour in Richmond and into the black crepe veils to bury Lizzie Perkins. Phyllis described the three children 'sobbing and begging for Lizzie to come back once more. They were truly fond of their mother & Lizzie certainly adored them and did the best she knew for them.'

Nancy didn't seem to apply Christian Science when it came to Lizzie's death. She acknowledged to Phyllis how 'wretched' Lizzie had been, and how her attempts to help her had only made her 'more restless and miserable'. 'I look back on her life and always it seems to have been agitated & unhappy with only lots of social moments and no real peace or happiness . . . Poor poor Liz I hope and pray she will find comfort and peace in the next life.' To Bob Brand she wrote, 'Lizzie's death came as a great shock, you see we are such an intimate family.' Phyllis wrote to him, 'I feel as if I had suddenly been pulled down to earth from out of the skies somewhere, and I cannot yet believe it can be true . . . Although my sister was years older than me and I had not seen her a great deal lately, yet now she has gone I feel the strongest link to our childhood has gone too as she always seemed a sort of second mother.' Phyllis offered to care for Lizzie's youngest child, twelve-year-old Alice.

Weeks later came the Captain's own peculiar condolences from Kashmir: 'Very sorry to learn how upset you all have been about your sister. It is refreshing to find a family so fond of each other; the death of certain members of mine will not be mourned by those who are left . . .'

Putting her grief aside, Phyllis demanded that Bob urgently report to her on Philip Kerr, who had just returned from India. Bob took up his pen again and reported that Philip had visited Nancy at St James's Square within two hours of his arrival and had then gone immediately to Sandwich, on Sir Bertrand Dawson's instructions, to get some 'East Coast air'. His trip had done nothing to alleviate his nervous depression. Phyllis had predicted that Nancy would convert him to Christian Science on his return but Bob wrote, 'She won't succeed in that.'

To his amazement, the wisest man was wrong about the person he thought he knew best in the world. Within a matter of days, after years of intensely researched studies of Catholicism, Buddhism, Gandhism, Hinduism, Zoroastrianism, Islam and so on, the cleverest member of the Round Table group was converted to Mary Baker Eddy. Now Phyllis wrote to Bob, 'Didn't I tell you she would get P.K. into her way of thinking about C.S.? . . . I have come to the conclusion that he is ruled far more by his heart than his head, and that it is his subconscious self which is going stronger than his conscious self . . . I should think his family would very likely feel inclined to murder N. if he really took up C.S. . . . but I believe by now he must know that his affection for Nancy is a FACT.'

Almost immediately Philip Kerr came down with acute appendicitis, complicated by Sir Bertrand's misdiagnosis: it was 'poison caught in India' he said and 'would soon go off'. Philip Kerr was not advanced enough as a convert to see appendicitis as material error, so he, too, went under the knife and was out of danger in a few days. His mother, Lady Anne Kerr, and his sisters – the sentinels of his soul – gathered around his convalescent bed at Sandwich.

His family knew Philip Kerr was experimenting with Christian Science but they didn't know how far down the road he had gone. His deliverance from death, at first with Nancy by his bedside, had heightened the sense of 'vision' and revelation between them. Nancy had left to join Waldorf at Plymouth, but subsequently she and Philip Kerr wrote to each other every day. 'Sin and pain are lies,' Philip Kerr announced to her from his convalescent bed. 'They cease to affect you directly you know they are lies. Only it's difficult to be <u>sure</u> in my heart at first that they are lies . . .'

The feel of the letters between Philip Kerr and Nancy, although only Philip Kerr's survive, is one of euphoria and excitement, very similar to the exchanges between two people who have discovered an intense love for each other, but also of two people who have found an

'ecstatic connection with God', a vision on the road to Damascus. They
express fears that the love will disappear — although this, too, is
expressed only in the process of discussing their shared new faith. Philip's
conversion, which Nancy saw as a second divine intervention, was clearly
connected very closely with his love for Nancy, and hers for him.

He wrote on 13 April 1914, 'Dear Nancy, I'm going on flourishing.
Only it makes the day much longer not having you to talk to and see. I'm
only just beginning to realise how much you've helped me — that
morning before the operation and every hour since . . . I don't miss you —
only as I should miss a great pleasure — no aching or real loneliness — that's
the wonder of it. We shall never be alone again . . . Philip.'

Bob remembered Nancy giving Philip a book around this time
and writing in the flyleaf:

> You and I have found the secret way,
> None shall hinder us nor say us nay.
> All the world may stare and never know
> You and I are twined together so.

'I think really she is wonderful about you,' Philip Kerr wrote of his
mother. 'Just think what you would feel about Bobbie if a siren got hold
of him as you've got hold of me . . .' And yet there was, almost certainly, never a kiss, barely a holding of hands in all the years their
intense affinity lasted. Phyllis was right to be sceptical. 'Nancy was
furious with me for asking you if PK was in love with her,' she wrote to
Bob from Mirador, 'but she kept saying it was nonsense, yet I felt in my
bones it must be so — in fact just the expression on Nancy's face in those
Kodaks you sent me of her made me suspect.'

'Platonic friendship is such a reasonable and easy thing in theory,'
Phyllis revealed, 'but I have seldom seen it worked out successfully in
actual practice, but I will say for Nancy, she is one of the few women I
know that could have tremendous friendships on that basis — I call it
tempting providence!' The irony of this must have struck the lovelorn
Bob, but Phyllis hadn't accounted for the exceptional combination of

the characters of Nancy and Philip. The sublimation of their feelings for
each other into religious energy was genuine. 'There isn't any question
that they were in love, and also that it was never consummated in any
way,' was the belief of one of her sons. Nancy said later that without
Christian Science she would have lost Philip instantly. And she told
Nancy Lancaster that she would have lost him, too, had there been any
hint of sex. Not that Nancy would have welcomed the sexual aspect of
any affair. But Philip Kerr was too full of deep psychological inhibitions
when it came to the opposite sex, unwilling to enter into any conventional relationships with women. And he was never to get closer to any
woman than he became with Nancy. He was happier pursuing the
monkish ideal.

Their religion gave them many of the benefits of a close love
affair: the freedom to share their intimate feelings; reasons and excuses
to talk at great length, but always with the brakes on. They had the
advantage of spending a great deal of time together on the golf course,
a game they both played well, and in which none of their other friends
or relations had any interest.

Nancy thus acquired a spiritual guide, a replacement for the
Archdeacon Neve, and from now on she treated Philip Kerr as a saint,
as well as the most privileged person in her life, a privilege that
included the unique right to contradict her. In all the correspondence
between Nancy and Phyllis and Bob there was hardly a mention of
Waldorf, the provider, the self-contained, restrained, immensely hard-
working figure. His hours were consumed by work for his
constituency, parliamentary reform committees, the *Observer*, or his
racing stud. Phyllis described him only once in a letter to Bob when
Nancy was staying with her at Mirador: 'Waldorf writes her long long
letters of social reform news, and schemes of how much work he puts
into the 24 hours and etc. I am afraid that young man has not much
capacity for enjoying life . . . His letters to me sound very detached
from human beings, and as if he were working with and through
machines only. I do admire his desire to serve, though. When one
thinks of old Mr. A. it is quite remarkable.'

But Waldorf, who might have been, and perhaps at first was, threatened by Nancy's relationship with Philip, behaved with a cleverness, tact and intelligence that seems extraordinary in any devoted husband, however confident. There was clearly an intimacy, a kind of joy, between Philip Kerr and Nancy that he didn't share. Not only did he endure it, seeing it for what it was, but he also kept Philip Kerr as his close and valued friend and political collaborator. He trusted him completely and never showed a hint of embarrassment. Nancy wrote to Phyllis, perhaps defensively, 'I must say Philip comes nearer making Waldorf talk than anyone I have ever known. That is a Godsend.'

It was made easier for Waldorf by the fact that Nancy and Philip never showed, or apparently felt, a trace of guilt, and therefore concealed nothing. Bob Brand described to Phyllis, for example, the arrival of members of the Round Table to Cliveden on 30 May 1914. 'Nancy & Philip arrived by motor later & N said she was very sick to see us, as she thought she was going to have a tete a tete with Philip, which she was longing to have. However we had to meet to discuss an article. So we cdn't help it. Nancy says she doesn't care a hang for any of us. We mean nothing to her in comparison with Philip's pure love. Besides as she says he's so very good-looking.'

Bob Brand remained sceptical: 'I sd. like to change Nancy so that she suddenly became 20 stone in weight & infernally ugly too & see what happened. It is no good the handsome & beautiful people saying that their beauty & handsomeness only reflect an interior spiritual beauty . . . I believe he still thinks too that his affection for Nancy is quite different to other men's love for creatures of the other sex & that there is no "mortal dross" at all about it. But it isn't really so very different.'

Bob was still deeply puzzled by his friend's adoption of this religion. But explanation was close to hand. Bob eventually realized that it was Philip Kerr's only means of continuing his close relationship with Nancy. 'I am sure Philip has great need of her,' he wrote to Phyllis. 'Don't think I don't really know what their affection means. I hope Philip will get clear about all these religious things. It will be hard because of his family. But he isn't really altogether to be pitied, is he,' he added pointedly, 'since he is loved by the woman he loves?' In later years Nancy's close family were never in doubt about this. Christian Science was the *sine qua non* of their relationship and Philip Kerr had no choice. It was a sublime example of the human ability to believe with absolute sincerity what, for other reasons, it is expedient to do.

In the early days of 1914 the novelty of Christian Science generated as much comedy as mystification in Nancy and Philip's entourage. Bob Brand, whom Nancy was at pains to convert, referring to him in the meantime as 'Anti Christ' because of his 'pernicious' influence over Phyllis, remained a protagonist, if an ironic observer, although Nancy did manage to get him to a Christian Science church one evening. He described the dinner beforehand to Phyllis. 'Nancy had the very newest kind of dress on . . . very tight underneath, anyhow round the feet rather like a Turkish woman's trousers & with a flowing garment above it, rather like what I think Circassians wear.' Dinner, he reported, was interrupted by a flow of telephone calls and social visitors. 'Then it was announced that someone from Mr. Cartier was outside. So a bowing & scraping familiar gentleman was shown in, who said M. Cartier was sending over from Paris two gentlemen with some wonderful jewels that had belonged to the Royal family of France. Nancy said she was sure they were rotten anyhow; she no longer cared about those sort of things. It was no good their coming. Besides Waldorf wd. never buy the things. However it was finally arranged that, while it was all useless, they sd. call at 10 the next morning & I gathered afterwards it was on the cards that altho' Nancy absolutely despised jewels now, Waldorf mt. make a mistake about her wishes & give her something.'

Bob related a typical discussion at Cliveden, between himself, Hugh Cecil, brother of the Marquess of Salisbury, and Nancy on the new religion. 'I asked Nancy whether as a good C.S. & since she hadn't a body she wd lie down in front of a steam roller & let it pass over her soul. Nancy was doubtful, but said with the real believers it wd be all right. Hugh Cecil then became philosophical & was very good, I thought, but philosophy didn't appeal to Nancy. He said that everything no doubt was only an idea. That Nancy's idea of a steam roller wd pass over Nancy's idea of her body & tho it was quite possible neither existed in real matter yet Nancy's idea of what happened when her idea of a steam roller passed over her idea of herself wd be what other people wd call being squashed. For practical purposes the result wd be the same.'

That spring and early summer of 1914 Bob Brand's letters to Phyllis were charged with new excitement. He was able to report in great confidentiality ('I will tell you our secrets, as I know you won't tell a soul') that the Round Table was trying to broker a deal with all political parties to solve the Ulster crisis, which in April and May 1914 threatened to explode into full-scale civil war in Ireland. This was the classic role the Round Table had sought for itself: influence behind the scenes, the idea of 'intimate and private exchanges between leading statesmen' and what Bob Brand described as 'inciting editors'.

Winston Churchill, who had put the Navy on stand-by off the coast of Ulster – for which he had been bitterly attacked by Tories, including Waldorf Astor – asked Lionel Curtis, Edward Grigg and Bob Brand aboard the Admiralty yacht, *The Enchantress*, steaming around the coast of England, to discuss the Irish question for three days. 'It's no good being a sort of professional mugwump,' wrote Bob Brand grandly, 'unless at a crisis like this you are prepared to do whatever you can to help . . . Nancy is very angry with us for staying with Winston.' After three days of 'incessant talking' the Round Table came up with a scheme. 'Winston was very pleased with it, & so were other high Liberal authorities,' Bob Brand wrote some days later. 'None of the politicians know what they are talking about when they discuss it, so we are going to tell them. We want the R.T. to be in at the death.'

Despite its sensitivity Bob even revealed the details of the scheme to Phyllis: 'What we suggested – in its main outlines – was pass the Bill, [for Home Rule] leave Ulster out, call an Irish convention elected throughout all Ireland to discuss whether there were any terms on which Ireland cd come in as a single unit into a federal or devolutionary scheme, or in the alternative whether any amendments were possible to the HR Bill, which wd satisfy Ulster, ie leave Ireland to discuss the Irish problem by herself outside the English party game.' It was a sensible, feasible plan, not wholly unlike the proposals made after the IRA cease-fire of 1994, but it had less influence than the Round Table imagined. Needless to say, this and other such plans failed. Back-bench anger reached a level where concessions between the leaders became impossible.

Phyllis passed on much of the political intrigue, except the secrets, to Douglas Pennant – the news reached him surprisingly quickly with his network of runners. Perhaps she felt that this was all cheerfully to be shared between friends. But in her subconscious mind, as she would say about Philip Kerr, she seemed to be trying to cause a rift between herself and the Captain. This, certainly, was the effect of her news bulletins about the goings-on of the Round Table. The Captain's mood switched now from patience to anger and sarcasm. At first, on 22 June, he wrote from Persia, 'I am glad your Brand is writing you again – he is a cultured young man and I can quite understand your missing his letters. It means however that he will return to the charge again – you can be sure of that.'

One day, after three nights on a mountain unsuccessfully chasing a she-bear, the Captain suddenly let loose with his pen, in a torrent of hot temper, against the whole caboodle. The message was clear. Phyllis's friends were almost beneath his contempt. Would she read *nothing* that came from the Liberal side?

The Captain knew, because he had met him, how J. L. Garvin, the Astors' *Observer* editor, dominated the political scene at Cliveden, and knew, like everyone else, how powerful he was as the Tories' mouthpiece and policy-maker. Ironically Nancy never quite took to Garvin – he was too powerful, too much the centre of attention when he came to Cliveden. But Ulster exercised the Captain like nothing else. He saw the Tories as betraying the Empire through their anti-Home Rule policy. 'It is really difficult to see the depths to which the party of snobbery must now descend with their ill conditioned jungle man

Bonar Law and their flighty, ill balanced & irresponsible oracle Mr Garvin,' he wrote to Phyllis. 'I was glad I caught a glimpse of him at Cliveden; it fully confirmed the opinion I had formed as to his unsoundness . . .' He was 'disgusted' by the 'rabid partisanship' of *The Times* over the Ulster question. 'I can only conclude that G. Robinson (Dawson, the editor and Round Tabler) is after a peerage and Northcliffe an earldom.'

To their lasting shame, he said the Tories had 'seized on the benighted prejudices of the most narrow minded set of people of all the Anglo Saxon race — a people that has got no further in its notions than the Battle of the Boyne and the Siege of Derry — to endeavour to bring themselves once again to power at the expense of all that is vital to our imperial welfare.'

Phyllis must have been alarmed by his passionate outburst on behalf of Liberals, the Labour Party and the Irish nationalists, and the attack against the unassailably correct-thinking Round Table: she may have been a Progressivist, but she was also an honorary Tory. The Captain was straying from his role as the silent sportsman, so attentive and dependable. Evidently she sent a mild corrective, and the Captain replied: 'Please do not think I am prejudiced against Round Tablers, why should I be? I despise people who are prejudiced; toleration to all sections is my creed . . . I will say this tho, that I just cant abide PRIGS at any price and let those whom the cap fits wear it!'

Perhaps the one thing the Captain didn't know — since Phyllis seemed to tell him everything else — was that she had turned to Bob Brand and not Nancy for advice on her marriage problems, swearing him to secrecy. Phyllis was contemplating becoming a resident in France, briefly, which would enable her to get a divorce on some grounds of incompatibility. Yet incompatibility was not recognized by the Church, which was important to Phyllis. She was in a moral dilemma. If she waited she could possibly get the divorce on grounds of adultery at the end of the separation period. This put Bob Brand, potentially, under further pressure: should he give her advice that would hasten her divorce and re-marriage, perhaps to Douglas Pennant; or would this, by making Phyllis free, raise his own chances?

Or since the decisions Phyllis had to make were morally almost evenly balanced, should he counsel delay, believing that Phyllis would come to her senses about the Captain?

Bob advised holding on to obtain the divorce on grounds of adultery by any means, that incompatibility was no real grounds for divorce, and she must take into account 'her old moorings' — the Church, particularly, and other people's opinion, since it would 'make everyone treat you in a wrong manner'. Phyllis replied, 'You are good to write as you do, but I am afraid, Bob, I am leading you into paths of thoughts that I don't want to lead you into. Please be an angel and think of me only as your very grateful friend. I need an unbiased friend so badly now. I can almost hear you say "that is impossible", but try to be, anyhow for the present.'

What did she mean '*for the present?*' 'Do you mean until you are free and then we will have to part?' Bob questioned. And it was not Phyllis who led him down these paths, he said, but he himself. How could they be friends as they were now if she was married to someone else, and living in England? 'Nancy and Philip may manage it in the very exceptional circumstances of both their lives. But I hardly think you cd. I know I couldn't . . . I cannot give you only my friendship and if you want that you must take love too.'

Bob now turned up the campaign a few degrees and took it into the enemy camp. He suggested that he understood Phyllis better than she did herself; he could see the situation more clearly. She was, in fact, deluding herself, he said, about her feelings for the Captain. 'You told me that you were in love but I don't believe you are and refuse to believe it . . . I don't and won't believe your future is already decided. That's my ultimatum.'

In late June a batch of delayed letters arrived from the Captain, reacting to the latest news of the slowness of the divorce. They were full of spite and jealousy. Ironically he seemed to agree with Bob Brand about Phyllis's future. 'Meanwhile,' he ended one of these messages, 'I am and always will be more than grateful for yr interest in my most unworthy self — but at the same time the confirmation of what I had expected compels me to review my peculiar relationship with the lady I have so longed to marry. I see most of what has passed dissolving into cloudy space, still pleasant enough to look upon but leaving only a cold and foggy platonic present, but little indeed in sympathy with a nature unfortunate enough to be inflammable.'

Phyllis had inflamed him again by mentioning gentlemen admirers that she had obviously found pleasant and charming, both at Cliveden and on the boat coming over. She may have mentioned them only to mock them for their futile advances and to reassure him but he reacted badly. The names the Captain gave them: 'the gentleman from Sydney', 'HPW', 'the looker', are – apart from 'the brand' – not identifiable. Perhaps Phyllis had, finally, read the copy of *Manon Lescaut* that Bob had sent her. She was showing the same toying indifference to the Captain's love and suffering as the heroine of Abbé Prévost's tale. Her doubts about the Captain were certainly growing and now it seemed, unable to make up her mind, she was manipulating her two admirers into a battle of wills whose outcome would make the decision for her.

'I am glad you found time for another conquest, that was a pretty rapid one,' the Captain wrote, 'I suppose you are getting to know more of the tricks as you get older. I suppose next time I come to Mirador I may have perhaps the pleasure of meeting the looker as well as the brand – about the latter don't fret yourself about him not rolling up with his letters – it takes more than that to extinguish the particular fire-brand, and you will find passion as deep seated in a buttered bun as in people on whose faces you can see their temperaments more plainly written – He will be in correspondence with you again, principally because you wish him to . . .'

And then, unforgivably – but apparently deranged with jealousy and frustration – the Captain began to tease Phyllis with his own female admirers: 'I have by this mail 13 pages from my acquaintance in Paris, mostly saying how nice & charming I am! and how she would value my friendship if she cant have anything else! Why am I served like this? Women really are impossible once they decline to remain as acquaintances, anyhow for me . . . You don't seem to have done much with HPW aboard the packet, perhaps that was because of the looker! I don't suppose you are old enough yet to want any old thing hanging around! I certainly am not, so perhaps I may be able to pair off the gent from Sydney with the person from Paris!' He ended this apparently fatal letter, which would have shocked and enraged Phyllis, despite her callous behaviour, 'Do you love me still??'

On 28 June 1914 the Austrian Archduke Ferdinand was murdered at Sarajevo. On 4 August Germany declared war against France. England entered the war the same day. Bob wrote to Phyllis: 'As you know, Armageddon is upon us. All Europe except Italy & ourselves is at war & I think we shall be within 48 hours. It is impossible to tell what will happen. It is an appalling catastrophe, & if one measures the loss in economic wealth, almost immeasurable – I believe that war will bring with it enormous changes not only in the balance of power, but in social & political affairs as well . . . We shall have social revolutions in a great part of Europe, I expect. Pray God we beat the Germans at sea. If we don't, it will be hell, & a fateful hour for the British Empire. If we do, we shall be fairly comfortable, tho it will be disastrous in any case. I have this moment heard we have given Germany a few hours to reply about Belgium, so we are practically at war. Well, we must go right ahead & see it through now & win – We live in tremendous times.'

Douglas Pennant was already on his way back from India, to rejoin the Grenadier Guards. He had written sombrely to Phyllis on 15 August: 'It is an appalling thing to think that all our speeches and writings and institution of societies, and even boastfulness of natures working together for peace and the advancement of all that goes with modern civilisation, should now be boiled down to the most bloody mess the world has ever seen.'

The British Expeditionary Force landed in France on 17 August. At Cliveden, on those hot, bright weekends, they waited for news to see if the German Navy would come out and fight. Within two weeks came the first news of the bloodbath, the fierce initial slaughter and the British retreat at Mons.

Typically of the home-based letters of the time, Bob Brand described the unreality of the glorious, still weather, the 'lovely evenings' at the end of August. He wrote to Phyllis from Cliveden again, 'Everything is quiet & one can hardly believe that a few miles off men are being slaughtered in tens of thousands. It makes one feel ashamed somehow of enjoying oneself, playing tennis & so on – I suppose it is good for all of us to feel we must be willing to die for the state immediately the call comes.' The consensus of the Round Table at first was that 'the only respectable thing to do is to go at once to France & at any rate kill one German'. That gave way to the more sensible plan to go about their respective business, for the time being. Except for Philip Kerr all the Round Table members were above the recruiting age.

Contrite now that selfish questions of romance had so occupied him when the world was blowing up, Bob wrote to Phyllis: 'I have been thinking too over what I wrote you last week. In these times one tries to fathom what life really means & what it should mean. As I have pondered over things, I have felt I was selfish in what I wrote you & that in my love for you I merely looked at my own wishes & what wd make me happy. Therefore I want to write & tell you that you have, because you have asked for it, my friendship, all of it that I have to give, without any conditions on my part . . .'

Phyllis, her spirits low and depressed, thanked him in reply and ended melodramatically, 'Good-bye, make your countrymen stick to the Germans until they have crushed and made this spirit of militarism an impossible thing for them to ever again indulge in. Bless you all – I have to think what tragedies you will all have to see and feel and hear.'

15

Trenches

A day or two after war broke out Nora, who was living in New York, bolted from her husband Paul and their two children, taking off with a famous football player into the Mid-West. The war in Europe was still little more than a curiosity to most Americans, so it wasn't as if Nora had chosen this fateful moment for camouflage. She remained out of sight and contact for many days, each one piling up the weight of potential family disgrace. When the posse reached her they found her 'singing for her supper', performing her Langhorne sister close harmonies with her lover, in public and for money.

There was no doubt that her marriage to Paul Phipps in 1909, into which she was so gratefully and hastily pushed by her sisters, had quickly run into trouble. She had been in love with Paul then, although she later denied it in a rash of fibs about being unhappy at home and wanting to escape. She had pleaded with them to let her marry Paul and the sisters had let her 'rush off'. Later when Chillie wanted to warn his nieces against missing the right husband, by which he meant a rich one, he would say 'Don't just rush off like Nora.' Paul had been described as 'fascinating' and talented, but also, as Nancy had said, 'the best we can expect for Nora'. This, too, meant money. Nora, like Lizzie but not her other sisters, lacked all worldliness when it came to money and was genuinely not interested in the idea of a 'good marriage'. Nora went for what she liked. She had turned down more than one rich earl; she could have married Waldorf's brother John Astor, later Lord Astor of Hever, who was even richer than Waldorf, and who didn't marry until 1916. She flirted with him but never contemplated tying herself up to a life she couldn't lead. Nora wanted romance, excitement; she wanted a crowd around her to entertain and she wanted to have fun. 'Brighten up the corner where you are,' was Nora's hymn, and guiding principle.

None of these demands was answered in her first five years of marriage. Despite his talent, Paul Phipps was somehow never able to get steady work beyond the odd family commissions, like the 'cottage' at Sandwich Bay. Their daughter Joyce (later Joyce Grenfell) was born in London in 1910 and in that same year Paul had taken his new family across the Atlantic to get work in Vancouver. There had been talk of frontiers and challenges, and even new starts: Paul was now thirty years old.

That first winter in Canada nearly ended the marriage. They found themselves isolated, friendless and, despite Nancy's allowance, broke, with a small child in a small apartment. The 'frontier' didn't really suit them. There was no scope for Nora's talents. But the real ordeal facing Nora was that she had fallen out of love with her husband. Paul wrote deadening letters to England, full of boredom and complaint. It seemed that this young man who was such a delight to male contemporaries like Waldorf for his charm and his sweet nature was turning, under this pressure, into something of a domestic tyrant.

A year after their arrival in Canada he wrote a letter to Phyllis, telling of the 'fearful exile' for Nora. 'I have made up my mind that she must get away (with Joyce) for part of the winter and so she will anyhow go East. This is no place to stay in for too long at a time (either for body or mind) . . . she is almost literally alone & has not one single friend – for they don't exist. This Pacific Coast is going to be a fine place for our grandchildren to live in, but for us, strangers from a strange land it is powerful lonely at times.' By 1913, the year their son Tommy was born, Paul had moved to New York, without a job.

New York raised Nora's spirits, made things manageable, and put her back in touch with the family. She often took the children to Mirador to stay with Phyllis. But in the summer of 1914, on one of her trips to Mirador without Paul, Nora, taking literally the idea of the 'fresh start', reverted to one of her favourite pastimes and got engaged again, in Richmond. Lizzie's daughter, Nancy Lancaster, who was seventeen at the time, recalled: 'Grandfather [Chillie] was very ill and living in Richmond [he had moved out of Misfit and into a flat in Monroe Terrace] . . . and Nora spent some time there. She had fallen in love with a man whose father was parson of Grace Street Church, a very good looking man. I was living there with grandfather, and this man came and said he'd come to see Nora, that he was engaged to her. Paul had to come down and break off the engagement of his wife. Nora always became engaged to everybody . . . I mean Nora couldn't have a man in the room with her without that man falling in love with her.' Paul put this incident down to the extreme stress of their time in Canada and forgave Nora, out of guilt and remorse.

Nora's 'heart like a hotel', closed for some seasons on account of her marriage and children, was now open again, blazing with light and welcome. The war persuaded Paul to return to England to offer his services, even though he was well above enlistment age. He seemed to be tempting fate: it was not only the worst moment to leave Nora, but unnecessary since the army didn't want him.

Making up for her years of exile, Nora rapidly immersed herself in New York social life. She became popular at parties for her guitar and ukelele playing and her lovely voice; for her 'Yellow Rose of Texas', and the Virginian Negro songs. Long before the days of Edith Piaf, Nora's throaty Piaf-like turn was full of tragic exaggeration, imitating Irene's singing teacher in Paris, which would have everybody on the floor in stitches. 'If you think Joyce Grenfell was talented, which of course she was,' said Nancy Lancaster, 'Nora was a genius; she could mimic, she was brilliantly inventive, she sang better than anyone, but she could never finish the song.'

On one of these evenings, very soon after Paul had left for

England, Nora fell into some extempore close harmonies – to the enthralment of the guests – with a former Yale football hero called 'Lefty' Flynn. Nora invited Lefty the following weekend to the seaside cottage that Paul had rented for his family, and the following Monday she ran off with him, abandoning her children and leaving no indication of where she was going.

Lefty's full name was Maurice Bennet Flynn. He was a very tall Irish American with blue eyes who had been the star full-back on the 1912 Yale football team. His nickname was derived from his prodigious left-footed goal-kicking. He had set unreachable records at Yale in track events and in the high jump and was destined to be one of the most famous Yale athletes of all time. He had the reputation for being a very funny man – a prankster, or an inspired sporting buffoon – who also had a beautiful deep singing voice with Paul Robeson resonance. The Yale Glee club of college alumni, with which Lefty went on tour, was also a boys' drinking club, and Lefty drank quite heavily. In the year of his college stardom, 1912, he had eloped with a chorus girl called Irene Leary, married her in a haze of cocktails and jokes, and fled to Italy. Despite the efforts of his good-time friends, Lefty was not allowed back to Yale and he divorced Irene Leary in 1914, the year he met Nora.

Chillie Langhorne came rampaging to New York to direct operations. Paul was informed by telegram. Chillie instructed Dana Gibson to 'bring Nora back' and to bring Lefty back as well so that he could shoot him. Nora and Lefty had set off across the country, 'singing and playing ukeleles in the moonlight and behaving like teenagers'. It was by sheer accident that someone recognized Nora, after three or four days, and sent word back. 'So poor Uncle Dana had to go out,' said his niece Alice Winn, Lizzie's younger daughter, 'and he found them in a hotel where they were singing for their supper. They had no money at all. And Uncle Dana went in and said to Nora, "Hurry up, hurry up, the police are after you for bigamy." Well she hadn't got married to Lefty or anything but being rather stupid Nora didn't know what bigamy was. She thought it was something dreadful so she put on her clothes and left Lefty and came back with Uncle Dana.' 'It was terrible,' said Nancy Lancaster, imagining terminal shame on the family, 'I thought nobody would marry me after that.'

No one really bothered to speculate on the roots of Nora's problems: the total absence of any idea of cause and effect, the amorality, mythomania and the near desperate desire for attention and affection. But you didn't have to look far. Nora had been only fifteen when Nanaire, her last anchor to any trusting, restraining relationship, died and as Nancy Lancaster said, Nora 'just had to go with the wind after that'. She had been bossed around by her powerful sisters, especially Nancy, and been given a great many often conflicting instructions. She had been bullied in the truth games, told that there was something missing in the Langhorne genes when it came to her. And now she was fulfilling the role in which she had been cast, with the important added ingredient that she was irresistible to men.

Nora was sent back to England in disgrace. Her first 'slip' had been forgiven, but not this one. She did write to her father from the *Mauretania*, 'God Bless You Dearest father I can say nothing except please forgive me. Nora.' But Nora was infuriated that Paul came to Liverpool to meet the boat, behaving as if nothing had happened, as if he was another forgiving parent. There was no shotgun, no rampage, and Nora never forgave him for his indifference.

In the first four days of the war Waldorf offered Cliveden as a hospital for the Canadian Red Cross, the War Office having turned the project down. He gave £250,000 to the Red Cross and the Relief Fund – a figure which nowadays multiplies into many millions. Sandwich had been commandeered as an officers' billet; he had loaned St James's Square to stranded American teachers. Waldorf would pay the Canadian authorities for everything they needed to make a model hospital at Cliveden. Preparation began in September for the indoor tennis court, where the servants' balls had been held, and other outbuildings and grounds to be converted and equipped; for operating theatres to be installed. The house would be partly dismantled for a convalescent wing. When the hospital plans were laid that September Nancy wrote to Phyllis, 'I warn you we shall be broke & may not be able to live here for some time. It will be so expensive, but who cares?' They judged, even as early as September, that the war would last two years at least.

One of the Cliveden staff was a part-time special constable who acted as recruiting sergeant, rounding up the young and the not-so-young men on the estate. By the middle of August 1914, Nancy reported to Phyllis, 'Every one of our men from here have gone & all of the footmen, odd men, school room Samuel & the lot all but Edward who is here & George but they may go this week, I am really v proud of them. We shall get maids when they go.' Gardeners, stablemen, electricians, night watchmen went off, and very few of them came back. The Americans, said Nancy, were 'barbarians' not to come into the war – a big point of contention with the isolationist Irene and Dana. Instead, Nancy exhorted Phyllis dramatically, as if it was still a separate dominion: 'Raise a troop in Virginia to come & help England. I will help to get them over.'

Henry Douglas Pennant arrived back from Kashmir in August and rejoined his old regiment, the Grenadier Guards. For two months he waited in barracks in London, to be shipped to France. As soon as Peter was back at boarding school Phyllis sailed to England to see him, bringing Winkie and staying less than four weeks. Officially she came to help Nancy set up the Cliveden hospital and it was there that she spent most of her time. Cliveden was, in fact, the only place where she could meet the Captain safely and, whatever her feelings towards him, Nancy could not ban him without losing Phyllis too. Phyllis's divorce had now been agreed for September 1915 and she told Nancy that she intended to marry the Captain the day it came through.

The Round Table were guests at Cliveden, in different combinations, almost every weekend in the summer of 1914. Initially Nancy didn't know what to advise Bob; whether he should stay at Cliveden when Phyllis was there or whether he should back off. It was a delicate moment with the Captain leaving for the trenches. Given the casualty figures he would be exceptionally lucky to survive until the following September but in a panic that Phyllis was making a mistake again she wrote to Bob, openly supporting his suit: 'To save my soul I can't see her happy or even useful with that poor man. I am sorry for him. I don't know what to tell you – as far as I am concerned I long for you to see her . . . Why not try again?'

Shortly before Phyllis was to leave again for America, Nancy cancelled her weekend party and invited the Captain as the solitary guest at Cliveden, with Phyllis. At the end of October, on the day of her return to America, Nancy and the Captain went together to put Phyllis on the boat train to Liverpool. As the train was moving, the Captain jumped aboard. Nancy began shouting, then screaming at him, running alongside the train, shaking her fist. The Captain recorded in his engagement book, 'Nancy kicks up a great row.' That action was an open declaration of war between the two combatants.

Phyllis sent a placating letter to Nancy from the stopover at Queenstown: 'When we parted at Liverpool it was a bitter hour for me for I honestly love the C with deep deep affection & can't imagine ever loving any man in the same way . . . If it is my happiness you want then remember without him I should never be really happy again . . . I know it is uncertainty and a little jealousy that makes you say things I've forgotten . . .'

Letters from Nancy and the Captain, raging against each other, followed her across the Atlantic. As soon as she was gone Nancy pursued the Captain by telephone and asked to see him. She was furious that Phyllis had sent a departing telegram to the Captain but not to her. But the Captain refused.

The battle with the Captain showed just how passionate, possessive and deadly serious her love for Phyllis was. She had openly declared a monopoly over her sister's affections. The Captain now managed to hit Nancy on the deepest nerve, to show her that she had met her match. It was one of the few moments in Nancy's life when she was truly on the defensive. His advantage was that he saw clearly the nature of this force unleashed so violently against him. In his view it was pure jealousy of a shameless kind, without a trace of self-consciousness, the reaction of someone slightly deranged. 'To resent our love for each other, and to expect that she has the right to steer its current and divert it to herself! She must be veritably crazy!' he wrote to Phyllis.

The Captain, still on guard duty in London, had called Nora, at Phyllis's request, and Nora had invited him round. Nora then stirred up the conflict by telling the Captain that it was best if he stayed away from Cliveden because Nancy disliked him intensely and it was Waldorf who kept her 'up to the mark'. She told him that Nancy thought that the dislike was mutual. For once Nora was telling the truth. Pride was the Captain's only real defence against the sisters, and now against Waldorf, as he made clear when he angrily reported all this to Phyllis: 'I will back myself apart from LSD [pounds, shillings and pence] to be worth as much as all that he and his associates can bring to bear.'

In late October the Captain learned that his two nephews Alan Douglas Pennant and Vere Boscawen, son of Viscount Falmouth, had been killed at La Bassée. His younger brother Charles was killed a few weeks later. Earlier that month, Philip Kerr's younger brother David, who had joined the Royal Scots from Oxford, was killed in his first twenty-four hours in action. In early November the Captain wrote to Phyllis that most of the regular officers in the two Guards regiments — the Grenadiers and the Scots — had been slaughtered. 'I have lost pal after pal, people with whom I was intimate, many of them long before I met you,' he wrote. They were Eton contemporaries, hunting companions from Leicestershire and North Wales.

By the time the Captain finally sailed for France in mid-November, the original British Army had been wiped out and both sides were settling into the stalemate that was to last until 1918. The Captain wrote that it would be a relief to get across the water, and join the fighting rather than be 'stuck in a false position' at home. He sent a departing, defining broadside to Cliveden: 'I am off today. I should not like to go away without making one or two things plain. Heaven forbid that you should think I dislike you. I meet you as I find you that is all and I know you are at times very jealous of my having intervened between yr affections and Phyllis. But its no use being like that, you will only lose over it and give Phyllis no happiness. Whether you like it or not she will love me alive or dead better than anything else, it is natural for woman to love man more intensely than for woman to love woman. Not even you can prevent that. I am not looking at it from a personal point of view, but it is just a plain fact. I did not come to see you because I felt you would perhaps have tried to spoil the delightful memories I have of Phyllis and her visit, but you know I am grateful to you for many kindnesses.'

Nancy scrawled above the first page, 'I like his loving generous understanding spirit!' and sent it to Phyllis. Nancy's reply to 'My dear Captain,' was strikingly disingenuous. 'I wrote you several letters but tore them up. If you think me so small as to let my feelings stand in the way of Phyllis or yr happiness then I feel you are indeed wanting in understanding & its just that quality in you that makes me feel that Phyllis' happiness is not as certain as you seem to think it. I know that she loves you & that you love her but I also know that love without other things is not what makes for happiness. However it is no time to argue. I do hope & pray that you will keep well & come back safe & I hope some day to make you see a little further than you see now! . . . Write me some times & let me know if I can send you anything.'

The real truth she wrote in an accompanying letter to Phyllis. Nancy now had the authority of the Christian Scientist to call love an 'error'. She had expressed her medieval belief in the link between carnality and sin in a letter to Irene, 'Never make me believe that carnal love is anything but lust and that's Christ's whole teachings.' 'Here is a note I've just had from HDP,' she wrote to Phyllis. 'I really am amazed – you see he really thinks that I am personally jealous of him. He thinks I am so small as to stand or try to in the way of yr happiness & you too seem to think that it's jealousy on my part . . . Have I not always longed & striven for yr happiness? Has my affection for you been selfish? . . . You see this letter, you see the man in it, he just breathes out his feelings & God knows they are small enough. I know you love him & I know that he loves you but I know that as he is now you could & wd never be happy . . .' She added what might have been a sentence to end their relationship – as patronizing as it was insulting to Phyllis: 'I feel until he gets more knowledge of real things he will always be lonely & pitiful, but the kind thing is to show him better things & not just give in to his human cravings.' She followed up with an undisguised threat: 'Never, after his performance at yr departure & since, imagine for one second that if you marry the C that you can be with me what you were . . . It will be a great wall between us and the wall don't be of my building.'

Phyllis replied, 'There is no good of our writing about the Capt & I beg of you not to continue your lamentations about him . . . & I honestly don't think you could very well blame him if he didn't come and see you or write to you in a more friendly way. Do you realise that you not once but more than once practically told him you wd rather see me dead than married to him as he is now. You say you are hurt that I shd think you jealous on big things. I don't think you are a bit but on little things between me and the Capt you are – you confessed at Cliveden that night that you were & could not help it. If my saying that hurt you what do you think you have done to my feelings by yr letters since I got back? They have hurt me more than I could ever tell you for those weeks have been about as hard ones as I've ever had & you who I have needed to help me more than anyone else in the world . . . have kept hurting and hurting in every word you said against the Capt. It really seems to me as if you were just trying to build up that wall between us. Please please don't go on like this for it makes me more miserable than I can tell you –'

When Phyllis wrote that she 'longed to come back' to England Nancy saw further danger. 'I know why you long to get back,' she wrote relentlessly, 'and I have lost all faith in yr discretion & if the C does come back wounded I hope to goodness you wont come back. You loose [sic] yr head to such an alarming degree that I don't know what compromising thing you wdn't do in that case! I do pray & hope he will come back safe & sound but I pray also that you will never marry him as he is, that I pray with my whole heart.'

Soon after he crossed to France, the Captain wrote to his mother. The letter, now in the Bangor University Library, brings home in one startling detail the extent to which the Captain was estranged from his family – especially his half sisters. It describes three of them, Hilda, Violet and Ina, turning up at Victoria station to see him off. He saw them walk in ahead of him and presumed they were off on a trip to Paris, or some resort. 'It never occurred to me at first,' he wrote, 'what their kind intention was.'

For a day or two the Captain was pleased to be in the war zone. He was given command of the King's Company of the 1st Battalion of the Grenadier Guards, whose duty was to look after 500 yards of the front line, somewhere near Neuve-Chapelle. He felt it very odd, after all these years out of the army, to have to ask leave to go to Rouen for 'a good dejeuner', like a schoolboy. Soon after he arrived in the trenches on 12 December he was describing his surroundings as 'purgatory', and feeling, after only a few days, that he had been there a lifetime: 'the weather is too horrible and I don't think I have ever been so uncomfortable or having to live in such a state of piggery in my life. However we are all in the same boat, at least officers with men under them so that makes it easier. You could scarcely imagine the conditions of trench life.' The routine was four days in the trenches, standing in freezing water above the knees, and four days in billets behind the lines.

He was astonished by the noise, the 'pandemonium' of the artillery, the continuous crackle and whistle of sniper fire, and the stench of chloride and lime and rotten flesh, a smell so penetrating and poisonous that it could not easily be shaken off in the billets. He described the dead and the living too – the wounded and the unwounded – buried in the trenches by the shellfire and the mud, so that it was impossible to identify them. The men, he said, rarely knew their officers' names. He was shaken soon after his arrival when a soldier in his company, shot in the brain, couldn't be evacuated for seven hours from his dugout. 'It was depressing to have that poor fellow with the ghastly wound moaning in the cramped space here. I carry enough morphia to send most of my company asleep and was glad when it acted in him. One cannot use a syringe very well so put the stuff under his tongue.'

He reported the unrelieved exhaustion, Wilfred Owen's 'many days of work and waiting'. Between the routine stand-to's at dusk and dawn when the two sides peered at each other's earthworks, the night was spent keeping back the water, pumping, bailing, digging, repairing, fighting the mud. The trenches had been dug in an area which had the highest rainfall and the highest water table in France. 'The men have the greatest difficulty in keeping their rifles in workable order – one gets mud somehow even onto most parts of one's person below.' The mud almost brought the war to a standstill in those first months. The Captain described – and it must have missed the censor – the bizarre negotiations between the front-line officers of both sides to survive it, so that they could get on with the proper business of slaughtering each other across a battlefield the length of a football field: 'Just in this sector there is an understanding that the infantry of ourselves and Germans cease to molest each other by sniping fire – so that both can somehow "keep their heads above!"' And he added, 'We meet each other from time to time ½ way between the lines & arrange to carry on or not . . . but I don't suppose this will go on for much longer and that we shall be at it again before long.' That was the Christmas of the unofficial cease-fire, when all the troops met in no man's land, shook hands and exchanged cigarettes.

The envelopes I look at now, eighty years on, are often smeared with mud and water stains, written with a blue crayon which was waxy enough to penetrate the humidity and make an impression on the grey lightweight paper he used. Phyllis's letters, which reached the trenches within two or three days, were kept in a pocket of his khaki jacket; in another was 'the little box you gave me and the little photo of yourself in yr riding habit and black and white ribboned straw hat smiling away on the lawn at Mirador'. Phyllis sent him bacon from

Fortnum and Mason, crème de menthe pastilles, caramels. The postal
system to the front – the 'Field Service' – worked so efficiently she
was able to send fresh roast pheasant and chicken almost to his trench.
He further requested 'York pie', Oxford marmalade and caviare,
port, sloe gin and Grand Marnier. On one visit to Fortnum's Phyllis
discovered from a salesman that Douglas Pennant, in the middle of all
this carnage, had returned a piece of bacon complaining that it was
undercooked. The front was a place of the strangest incongruities
and contrasts. The Captain reported that because there was such a
shortage of officers he had a room to himself in the billets, 'nicely
carpeted with a cheerful fire and spick and span fittings and everything
cosy and nice. I sometimes fancy I can hear the clock striking on the
staircase.'

But by the middle of January 1915 the flooded state of the country was so bad that neither side could advance or attack. Trenches
couldn't be dug because the treacly mud stuck to the spades, and sand-
bagged earthworks, useless against artillery, were put up instead. The
Captain had long ago abandoned any impatience to get on with the
business of defeating the enemy, 'crossing the corpses of one's foes'.
Now he said the sheer numerical losses must surely bring all sides to
their senses. He thought that the war would just 'finish here . . . it has
been stalemate for so long'. Some of the losses were caused, he said, by
soldiers having a 'senseless sort of go', out of sheer monotony and a
desire to get out of the subterranean world of the mud.

He was due for leave towards the end of January when Phyllis had
promised to sail again from America, taking Winkie and leaving Peter
at boarding school. He asked her to rent rooms in London, 'I don't
want any roughing up with Nancy or even to see her,' he wrote. 'Could
you perhaps make arrangements where we could stay, surely we could
be together now!' He suggested that they get married on this hurried
trip – 'wave all sorts of silly conventions away. You could get the necessary licences ready and we could start honeymooning the day after I
arrived.' Phyllis found a flat in King Street, near St James's Square in
London. They had five days together before the Captain returned. It is

almost inconceivable they didn't live together in these few days as man and wife. Phyllis wrote, moments after the Captain had left in his taxi: 'Capt my dearest this last week must make us both feel that our affections are more sacred than ever before. I cannot describe to you what emotions of joy & tenderness come over me when I think of all the best in you must now be mine to march forward with in this game of life.'

She wrote again that night from St James's Square, 'I will join the ranks now of anxious females left behind & am quite ready to face the best or worst things that may befall, but I feel in my soul that God is on our side & a happy issue out of all this affliction will come — yr. affection, thoughtfulness & generosity — & even your crankiness have woven a deep web in my heart that nothing can obliterate. God Bless & keep you my own precious — the last few days have made it all more real and true.' When Phyllis didn't hear from him for four days she wrote to ask, without thinking, whether he had 'arrived safely' in his trenches.

The flooding was even worse by mid-February — it was widely believed that the gunfire had brought about the torrential rain — but the Captain had now come equipped with waders, 'unused since salmon fishing with my Father on the Dee', having failed to find boots that would let the water out. His letters contain much sympathy for the men under his command. He had an ear for the mordant wit that came out of the trenches, the irony and irreverence that was to change popular culture from now on. One letter, covered as usual with streaks of mud, contains the remains of a snowdrop, desiccated and stained dark brown, an astonishing and haunting relic from the Somme to find between the pages eight decades later. It came, he said, 'from a ludicrous patch of "garden" outside my dugout which is labelled "Guards Club". The garden was made by a light hearted Scots Guards sergeant. I'm afraid the flower is a little muddy. I have some flowerpots on the window sill outside also with snowdrops! My predecessor in this company was a little afflicted by nerves and told this sergeant to make the dugout bomb-proof so he proceeded to fit it with windows and flower pots.'

Once again, but this time at a moment when their love appeared to be on an intense, elevated plane, Phyllis reverted to her compulsion to tell the Captain about Bob Brand's presence, his courtship, his visits, even their outings together. If this wasn't cruelty, it was certainly a strange selfishness — as if her state of mind and her own confusion claimed attention above the appalling situation the Captain was in. He never once asked for news of Bob Brand or the Round Table — who now visited Cliveden almost every weekend — and it made him angry and anxious when he received it, leaving him mystified as to why Bob Brand didn't retire into the background at this moment when he was under fire and expecting any day to 'go up'.

Still he had to read in successive letters from Phyllis of what a 'trying ordeal' it had been for Bob Brand to be at Cliveden with her; how 'he looked not very happy but was very nice . . . I don't know what unrequited love is but I fancy it is about as uncomfortable as anything can be.' She had dreaded his visit, she said, 'but it's no good being unnatural about it. That only fans the flames for him really.' She said what a 'very decent man' Bob Brand was because he had told Nancy he had hesitated about coming 'as he didn't want you to think he was trying to take advantage of your being away'. But as the Captain read in the next letter, 'BB' had soon overcome his hesitation and was there the following weekend as well. 'Have no fears about me in that line, it is quite safe,' wrote Phyllis. Did the Captain need such reassurance? Perhaps he did because a few days later Phyllis reported that she had met Bob at a dinner party and they had gone on to a variety theatre together. 'BB sat next me at the play & if he had just met me for the first time in his life his conversation could not have been more formal — I almost felt inclined to roar out loud, or give him a punch or something. You should see the way the R.T.'s look at me as if I really had a screw loose for not accepting the proffered hand of BB. Its very amusing and I fear they have no respect for my intelligence. I believe several of their sage suggestions have been adopted by the government.'

Bob Brand's unstoppable pursuit of Phyllis, his passion as well as his patience, was indeed remarkable, especially in the face of the 'downward glances' that greeted the Round Table, according to Phyllis, for their not being in uniform. But when Phyllis wrote to the Captain how much she admired their courage in doing what they thought was best ('They must write not fight' – Nancy had ordained) he exploded: 'In war its a convention that males who can't do the fighting shd do the fatigues in back. So turn on yr Round Tablers onto this and make some use of the gang, put them on to digging refuse pits and filling them with the slops and if they do it properly and seem to take a pride in their work they will go up in everyone's estimation. I think you better tell them that even the "Vie Parisienne" put its shutters up and turned out to help its country in practical fashion. This isn't a time for prigs to flourish!' (In fact Edward Grigg, Round Tabler and later Governor of Kenya, had joined up at the age of thirty-five, fought throughout the war and was awarded the DSO and MC.)

Bob Brand felt an acute sense of guilt at not being in the firing line, even a little jealousy. 'It makes one simply hate oneself not to be there,' he wrote. He momentarily projected his family as a clan of warriors, writing to Phyllis of his own prospects on the battlefield: 'I'm sure no Brand would lack courage in a tight place.' Philip Kerr, too, was pricked by his conscience for not being at the front, although he had difficulty getting a Christian Scientist ruling on the question of bearing arms. The Moot needed Kerr to produce the Round Table, and his feelings of guilt were assuaged by marching and drilling with the London Volunteer Rifles.

At the end of February the Captain warned Phyllis that he was being moved to a more dangerous part of the line. Under censorship he couldn't explain, but he intimated that he faced almost certain death. Given the variety of ways you could be killed – mines, snipers, shrapnel, suffocation by mud – he said he found it 'really odd' to look about and see so many of his compatriots still on their feet. 'This is a funny life,' he wrote. 'It feels really as if one had finished up one's earthly career and was just going through a sort of other existence in the ante-room of what lies beyond, as if one is passing through some purgatorial sort of state. Who knows. Perhaps that is so. Anyway one cannot last out this life for ever from one cause or another.'

What he was unable to describe were the preparations for the first of the massive British offensives against the Germans, mounted in the area of Neuve-Chapelle. The intention was to break through a narrow part of the line using waves of assaulting troops, backed with an unprecedented artillery assault. The King's company, which the Captain commanded, would be deployed in its early stages. He wrote to Phyllis, asking if she would come out if he was wounded, 'and bring an aural set (for the ear!) that John Bell and Croydon of Wigmore Street (chemists) make up for me — 2 sorts of forceps and a rubber syringe in case mine should get mislaid on the way down should I not know what's going on but I hope that won't be!' He became superstitious, wondering if God would take pity on him, filled with fear of the unknown, speculating on their spiritual communion after death. He began to take morphine to sleep.

When there was a gap in his letters Phyllis felt 'Oh! The sinking feeling.' She wrote on 2 March 'My precious Capt, When I just looked into the post this a.m. I did not see a letter from you — I was on my way to breakfast & it suddenly took my appetite away, for I had been dream-ing of you all night, a mixed up dream of trench & taxi cab, & I woke up feeling not very happy.' Now that he was on the move she wrote, 'I shall move along with you & if I am a comfort my darling Capt then I shall feel 1000 times repaid for leaving Mirador & my possessions on the other side!' Peter, one of these possessions, had not seen his mother now since Christmas.

At this precise moment, on 1 March, the Captain received a letter, offering him a senior staff job in the Welsh Guards — a new reg-iment in the process of being set up. If he accepted he would leave the trenches immediately. It would mean a career in soldiering after the war — a job for ten years. He had written back that he would accept, provided he had the rank of Major and a battalion to command. 'You often said,' he wrote to Phyllis, 'that you didn't mind what sort of a job I got as long as I got something . . . so don't go off to the USA and I live in hopes of seeing you.' He added, 'Things are beginning to hum a bit.'

Phyllis's reaction to this news — which meant that he would honourably survive the war and that their plans for the future would become a reality — was astonishing. She expressed, in a series of letters written as the Captain was about to go into the attack, her profound disillusionment that she might become a soldier's wife. The letters make no disguise of the fact that this would make her unhappy; they apply barely veiled moral pressure to make him change his mind, or at least — and it would have been equally dangerous — to delay the decision.

The line she adopted was that of 'you know best': she was glad he could look forward to a definite job, 'but I must confess I never dreamt that this, for years to come would be soldiering! You always said you wd hate it after the war is over, however now that you have got back among soldiers I suppose you see it all from a different point of view.' She did add that she 'rejoiced' to think that this might mean seeing him soon, but then wrote, 'Whatever happens this whole new picture of the future has quite made me sit up & think — I suppose if this comes off it means politics gone to blazes, which I can't help heaving a little sigh over as my leaning has always been to politics more than the army, however when one gives one's best efforts in either direction it is not a bad thing.'

Phyllis's letters give the bizarre impression that she hadn't taken in the fact that the Captain was going to die. And perhaps they are the key to the real nature of her relationship with the Captain: her romanticized vision of the action man, the tiger shooter, the hero. They suggest that hers was a predominantly sexual attraction, that had been on the wane, with the help of peer pressure, until the war and the trenches revived its intensity. She could never have taken the Captain to live in Virginia where, like Reggie, he would have been lost. She might have given up Mirador eventually, but not for the Captain. Any other side of him — the safe husband, plodding away as a major on £400 a year and an army pension — held no real interest for her, although she said, 'Of course my darling I shall do all that I can to help you & you must do the same *for me*.' [my italics.] Was this the way Phyllis dealt with reality? To press him to make a decision that would keep him in the trenches? An 'anxious female' who loved the Captain would have been overcome with relief at this extraordinary intervention of fortune.

The Captain hadn't received this ambivalent letter when he wrote on 8 March that he might soon be out of 'regular' communication. His was another jittery letter from the ante room. 'Now darling you are not to get anxious over me. When I think of how many of my best pals have already shown me the way . . .' And still, in the mud and the cold, the vision of the courting Bob Brand nagged him with jealousy, primed by Phyllis's reports. 'What an uncontrollable passion he seems to have,' he wrote, 'I can see very well he is starting out on the road which has ended before in burning his fingers. I have no doubt he will ask you for a kiss again before many days are out — you see — I am sure he won't get one though!'

The three-day delay put these strange communications out of sequence. Phyllis was still preoccupied on 9 March, the day before the Captain went into battle, with the Welsh Guards and what a shock this was to her vision of their future. 'The possibility of it quite changes ones trend of thought,' she wrote, '& makes one try to look at things from quite a different point of view than heretofore.' Unless he had a chance of commanding a battalion, it would be 'a pity to leave the Grenadiers', and 'you wd. just waste so many good years of yr life'.

'I have somehow been picturing you in the back of my mind launching out as a politician,' she went on like some unlistening parent, 'and in some ways I am sorry if that has fallen through . . .' And yet the Captain had already told her that he couldn't face politics, and the turning against his family. He would have been a failure in that profession — this was obvious at least to Bob Brand and his friends. Inflexibly unsociable, he was clearly not cut out for political life, but this was still the only 'gentlemanly' work contemplated for him by Phyllis, the one woman whom he believed had ever understood him. But no one had yet heard of the Welsh Guards and Phyllis was now being asked to contemplate a life in Aldershot and Windsor. The contract needed some adjustment.

'Goodbye my old Sweet,' Phyllis would typically sign her letters, and now she wrote ironically, 'God bless you and keep you safe and happy . . . How I shall rejoice to see you again, it makes something sort of flutter at the very thought!' She presumed that despite her letters he was out of the trenches and 'fairly safe from bullets etc' and now asked him if he could take some photographs – she would send him a little Kodak. 'They wd be so interesting for us later & when our grandchildren are gathered about yr knees & you with a shaking hand & wavering voice will tell them tales of the great war of 1915!!'

When, a day or so later, Phyllis got his letter of 8 March, with its morbid projections, she replied that 'it rather made me stiffen my backbone to be prepared for any kind of news'. She would fly to him in France if he was wounded, despite the commotion it would cause. 'These are real times,' she wrote stoically, '& must be lived in real ways.' She then added, apparently contradicting herself, 'Don't think me a timid, weak-kneed sort of person when I write you that I wd like to see you safely back with the W. Gds. I shd. of course like it but not if it meant you came because you thought it safer. Thank heavens you are not built that way. It is one of the many things I like about you my old darling.' But the Captain was clearly not thinking of his present safety – but of how to support himself after the war. Phyllis now introduced this idea: that the decision was unheroic, or worse, a decision tainted with 'selfishness' as opposed to honour, possibly even with cowardice. And yet the selfishness is unmistakably on Phyllis's side, despite her declarations that she would support him in whatever he decided. She had effectively made the decision for him.

By 10 March the Captain had received her first letter about the Guards promotion. His reply, written that day, is heartbreaking to read. 'I realise that a possible future for you in the soldiering line is distasteful,' he wrote. 'I quite understand it may be a surprise for you.' He apologized for having suggested it at all. And now he 'begged and prayed' her to send two telegrams to the army to say that 'owing to private affairs' he could not accept the commission. 'That will end the matter.' He added, 'Remember there will be a lot of unemployed gentry after the war and I am a poor man. No doubt I could scrimmage for a place in politics. There will be many more able than myself doing that. I am not likely to rise to eminence as a soldier . . . A woman's first thoughts are the best so act as you thought at first . . . We will be in the thick of it tomorrow and it may be my lot to "go up."'

On Saturday 13 March, not having received this letter, Phyllis wrote routinely that Sylvia Pankhurst (suffragette and daughter of Emmeline Pankhurst) was coming for the weekend and that Bob Brand had also invited himself. 'I really think he is silly to come. I know I only hurt his feelings when I fly to my room whenever I find myself going to be left alone with him, but he is equally anxious to fly then too.' She asked again about the Welsh Guards: 'I shall sit quite still until I hear.' She wanted to know partly, she said, so that she could arrange a date to go back to Virginia – she would have to do this almost immediately he returned.

Phyllis posted the letter that Saturday morning. At 3 o'clock that afternoon the text of a cable was relayed to Cliveden from St James's Square, which read, 'Henry is killed but died quite painlessly. Gertrude Penrhyn.' The cable is preserved in the pile of letters kept by Phyllis – folded and folded again into a tiny square. Nancy later said she would never forget the pitch of the scream that Phyllis let out when she was told the news. The Captain had been killed early in the morning of 11 March. All Phyllis's letters since 6 March, the first in which she opposed the Welsh Guards scheme, were returned, unopened, over the next few days, marked 'Killed in Action' on the envelope. There was one more still to come from the Captain.

In his classic book *The Great War and Modern Memory*, Paul Fussell described the exact offensive in which the Captain was killed. 'The attack . . . died for lack of reserves and because the narrow frontage invited too much retributive German artillery. It was the kind of abortive assaulting, whose folly had still not sunk in by 1917, at Passchendaele.'

Letters to Phyllis from fellow officers described the Captain's last two days. One of them described waiting alongside him to advance on 10 March 'and he told me you did not want him to go into the Welsh Guards and I think he was writing to you on his knees in the field we were waiting in and he got a chaplain to post it'. He added, 'I saw Henry lead his company out of the trench and go forward with them and I saw shells bursting over them and I think he must have been hit very soon afterwards as I think he was brought in at 7.10am.' The Captain was hit through the lung by shrapnel, and was dead on arrival at the first-aid station. He was buried that night in a grass field on the west side of the Estaires–La Bassée road – the grave surrounded with wire 'to protect it from guns brought into the field'. 'He was buried exactly as he went into action,' the officer wrote, 'and your locket must have been on him as his collar and tie were just as he had put them on and an envelope of one of your letters was pinned on his blanket'.

The last letter, written on his knee, told Phyllis that he had himself cabled the General saying he would not take the job: 'I know you well enough to see on reading and thinking over your letter that you do not like my soldiering project. So the show is off and leave it to me. It was not quite fair of me to give you such a fright and I'm sorry my darling I did so! . . . So you can look at life under a pleasanter aspect than as a Major's wife. I cannot write you more now, all my love is with you and I feel a lot happier now I have given up that other place. It would have tied one down too much and too much routine to please either of us . . . All my love is with you as always, your most devoted x.'

If Nancy didn't know about love, Phyllis, who thought that she did, had certainly separated herself from reality in her relationship with the Captain. It even occurred to me, reading these letters, that she expected the Captain to die as the hero of her imagination – that there was no other solution in these 'real times . . . lived in real ways'. There is no trace of guilt in her later correspondence – and no oral history makes an issue of it. Technically, she had no reason for guilt. No orders had reached the Captain. But in a day or two, the Captain's cable refusing the commission would have kept him in the trenches and he would then almost certainly have died within a few days or weeks in the suicidal assaults that continued. And for that she would have been partly responsible. She suffered terrible grief, as will be seen, but saw it as 'a door slammed in my face', by God or fate.

Two months after his death her descriptions of the Captain reveal how his enshrinement was taking shape. She remembered the tear in the Captain's eye, 'the first I ever saw there', when he was saying goodbye in her cabin at Liverpool after the incident with Nancy. 'I believe way down in his soul he knew he was not to have the happiness he wanted & I poor soul never dreamed that it would not come.' It was the perfect attention, as ever, she remembered and still yearned for: '. . . gracious! how I love to think of his loving care of me, it was like a great valve after those miserable years I had had before'. She still felt as close after his death, so it seemed from her letter, as she had done during the six years of his absentee courtship when she so often saw him as an ideal beau, almost a fantasy figure. 'I can't help at times feeling I would give my life to see him again for an hour or a day but thank God I can feel he is with me just the same.'

Even after he was dead Nancy couldn't help turning her com-miseration into a lecture, suggesting that the Captain would have made a poor partner, and that Phyllis's sadness and loneliness were, in Christian Science jargon, merely 'error'. Ignoring this and forgetting, apparently, how Nancy had done everything in her power to destroy the relationship despite its importance to her, Phyllis tried to patch it up with her sister, insisting that in the end their sibling love was stronger than her romantic love with the Captain; that there had been no breach. 'I am glad we had it out but don't let us waste anymore of our time on fearing that anything on earth could make us love each other the less . . . No darling Sis we are like a tree with the same root. One branch might be in the sun the other in the shade thereby chang-ing the color but the same sap feeds both and can't change . . . but in all the love I had for him it did not in one jot shake my love for you, and this I believe in your heart you know . . . If I had ever thought the Capt had wilfully tried to come between us I could never have loved him . . .'

Phyllis inherited the income of the Captain's modest estate for her lifetime and wrote to his mother: 'His wishes therefore must be to me now very sacred and I could not be happy in doing otherwise than as he wishes, although I know I shall be subjected to criticisms of all sorts.' She also inherited his military kit, which was sent to Mirador.

One Sunday in the 1930s, when Nancy Lancaster was in charge of Mirador, Irene Gibson visited the 'coloured' church at Hillsboro with one of the Mirador staff – something the sisters often did. She saw Stuart Wood, Nancy Lancaster's butler, sitting in the pews dressed in the uniform of a Captain in the Grenadier Guards, medals and all. 'And she was simply amazed to find Stuart dressed up in the Grenadiers,' said Nancy Lancaster, 'and she was horrified and she made him take them off.'

16

Dear Mr Brand

The Cliveden hospital took the sharpest edge off Phyllis's grief. Three weeks after the Captain died its first patients were unloaded at Taplow station, directly from the battlefields at Mons and Ypres, the first of 24,000 to be admitted. Neither Phyllis nor Nancy had yet seen the horror close-up. Now Phyllis described to her father 'the startling idea of war', her disbelief at going into the wards for the first time and seeing 'fifty men lying there minus legs, arms, eyes' and finding the 'the worst of all', in the distress of the first gas victims who had had no protection from masks. Later, in August, the eighteen- and nineteen-year-olds arrived from the Dardanelles and the slaughter at Gallipoli. Phyllis wrote to Chillie, 'One of them had been in that fierce fighting when they made a landing at Suvla Bay. He was quite a young boy in the Manchester Regiment & was quite pathetic when he said quite calmly, "All our lads were killed early that day."' He was 'stone blind' but 'so good and so patient', wrote Phyllis, astonished at this soldier's courage expressed in meek good manners.

Nancy ran the hospital in partnership with a gangling, moustached Canadian surgeon from Yorkshire, Colonel Newbourne, a tireless, dedicated doctor in the old military-medical tradition and in Nancy's eyes an heroic figure whom she elected to her pantheon alongside Archdeacon Neve. The hospital brought out Nancy's comic talent which she used to raise the spirits of traumatized, maimed young men, pulling them back from the abyss when Colonel Newbourne could do nothing more for them, challenging, cajoling, even bribing them back to life. She used every technique. She worked these gloomy wards, transforming the mood, the surroundings, laying on, as one of them observed, a permanent weekend party. She organized visiting acts, kept the wards filled with flowers. She sat all night if necessary beside the beds of terminal patients. They loved her and they were fascinated, once they had understood the switches from tenderness to bullying. Nancy bet a Canadian soldier her Cartier watch that he would be dead the following day; that he had no guts, unlike a Cockney or a Scotsman. Few people could have got away with kicking around a dying soldier, but he attributed his survival to it, and took the watch home.

The journalist and critic Alastair Forbes remembers the same technique applied in the next war when Cliveden was back in service as a Canadian Army hospital and Nancy was even more fervent a Christian Scientist. 'Sometimes . . . her cheeriness was a bit on the kinky side,' he wrote. '"You're frightened of dying aren't you?" she insisted on repeating into my ear as she accompanied my stretcher while it was being wheeled into the operating theatre. Luckily, I wasn't, on that day at any rate.'

Bob Brand wanted to communicate with Phyllis, but felt he could say nothing. He was certain that she would marry him now the Captain was dead; it was just a matter of time, and of tact. He didn't know that Geoffrey Dawson, his Round Table colleague and editor of The Times, held the same conviction. He had not only been visiting St James's Square, but like Bob and the Captain, had been corresponding with Phyllis, at some length and frequency.

If the Captain had been transferred out of the trenches and promoted to the Welsh Guards, Phyllis would have returned to Mirador within a few days, as she had told him in her letter. She had already been away from Peter and from her neglected estate for three months. Now she delayed a further two months until May 1915. There were plenty of excuses: submarines, helping Nancy in the hospital. The

more likely explanation, however, was that Phyllis was simply immobilized by grief, and once again 'caught up in fear' – her apt description
of depression. To return to Mirador this time was to face real loneliness. Though there were moments when she revelled in the solitude,
there were also days of struggle, against 'dreariness' and black moods.
Mirador's real point, compared to the other *ante bellum* houses on the
James River, was that it had produced the Langhorne sisters, their
childhood, their fame, the family dynamics. This was now so far vanished that it seemed to belong to another century. It had been given to
Phyllis as a consolation for her unhappiness when her marriage was
over, but it had now become a place of provincial isolation.

    She might have returned sooner if she had had any real under-
standing of the needs of the thirteen-year-old Peter. His adoration of
his mother had been frustrated by a combination of boarding school,
where he had been sent the moment things began to go wrong in his
life, and her increasingly long absences. He had last seen her for
Christmas in 1914. He wanted to resume his childhood with her, have
his rights of ownership restored. He had been told to blame the hiatus
on the war. Phyllis's relationship with the Captain, which had dominated much of her life since the war started, had never been explained
to him. He must have wondered why the war in Europe meant that she
had to spend so much time in England. There was a difference between
being in boarding school while his mother was at home at Mirador, and
being in England, out of possible reach or visiting distance. 'Please
come and visit soon,' he would write continually while she was in the
USA. England had become a threat and a rival and he had begun to hate
it and everything about it. As his mother became more and more of an
Anglophile, he became a junior Anglophobe, despite his desire to join
her. And yet Phyllis's sense of the danger to Peter only surfaces in
occasional abstract worries in her letters.

    By contrast Peter's repetitive pleadings in his letters from his
new school, The Hill School in Pottstown, Pennsylvania, are pitiful to
read. 'I have been feeling very homesick lately also dreary and I miss
you extremely. Please come over soon. I just cannot wait to see you

and Winks.' Or 'Please please please please take me over to England.'
Phyllis must have written to him that she would come over and bring
him back to England in June, at the start of the summer holidays in
1915. 'Everything is just a mental [sic] whirl,' he responded,
'Whenever I see your picture I just jump and squeak a little.' But there
were delays, mixed signals and Peter switched to extreme politeness,
as if his childish eagerness might put her off or as if he was now an
obligation and 'being a bore'. 'In your next letter if no trouble,' he
wrote, 'I wish you would tell me about when you will come back
from England and if you don't come ("If" I said) what will happen and
who and how and by what authority will I get over there? Please send
me a little picture of you to fit in my little frame also one of Winks. If
it is any trouble do not by any means bother.'

Winkie was young enough to be kept close to his mother, before
his own dispatch to boarding school. But even at the age of almost six
it was clear that Winkie was the blessed child, born with gifts, with
looks and talents, 'the most alluring and attractive boy', as his mother
described him. Phyllis's descriptions of them both eventually give away
the tragic division, that of Cain and Abel. They describe the 'deli-
ciousness' of Winkie's presence, his laughter that she imagines hearing
in the house when he's away; her need to soak up precious moments of
his childhood. Phyllis insists on her affection for Peter, again and again,
as if to prove it to herself, but she is mystified by his 'oddity' and his
outsider tendencies, describing him as 'a funny boy'. When she looks
for the best in him she writes, 'He is a nice boy and I am always struck
by his thoughtful ways.' Lacking Langhorne spontaneity this was his
tag — 'thoughtful'. He was trying to please, but couldn't succeed in
charming like Winkie, with his 'pretty ways'.

Some of this could be discounted by the onset of adolescence,
which Phyllis called 'the boy problem'. She had watched, with growing alarm, its effect on Bobbie, Nancy's first-born and Waldorf's
stepchild, particularly his rudeness to his mother. It had taken Peter in
the classic way: feelings of inadequacy, shock at his own changing
looks, a belief that he was ugly, even repellent compared to others.

And compared to Winkie, an Adonis in the making, Peter was small in height, his large round head out of proportion with his body. He felt his arms were too long, his grin too wide and ready, 'like a Halloween pumpkin'. He signed one of his letters to Phyllis: 'from your first son with a peculiar face'. He sensed he was a disappointment to his mother and, of course, he was. He reminded her more of a Brooks than a Langhorne.

This was something that greatly worried Phyllis. She was under the impression that after her divorce she could turn her back on the now despised Brooks family and gradually shed her children of their influence. This presumed that her children would follow the Langhorne path, 'see things the right way' and close the chapter on their father. She couldn't bear the idea that she had ever been married to Reggie Brooks.

The separation agreement, which would apply in the divorce, laid down that Reggie would see his sons in the holidays and that they would be educated in America, including college. Phyllis believed that Reggie wouldn't care much after a while or would be too intoxicated to insist. 'The present situation is hard on everyone,' Phyllis had written back in 1914, 'especially the children who begin to look a little bewildered about things, and they think me very hard and unnatural when I reprove them after they have been running riot in Southampton.' She dreaded to see them go, she said, more so as they got older, 'for Peter is getting to the age now when I shall have to explain some unpleasant truths to him. He is such a nice boy that I'm sure it won't be difficult.' Peter, of course, knew all about his father's drinking, but there was something much more fundamental to get across – the general shallowness of the Brooks family and their certain kind of wealth.

Phyllis had developed an austere and superior attitude to the Newport and Southampton money that had once provided her with a good marriage and removed her from Richmond. The Brookses' wealth, their *values*, came from the Gilded Age – the days of the 'scandalously' rich, the monopolists and robber barons now so discredited in the new social gospel of national progressivism (of which Teddy Roosevelt was the chief spokesman). They were the idle, the unimprovable rich. The Brookses were 'a bad influence'. Phyllis had a *moral* purpose to keep her sons away from them.

Phyllis also believed in putting hurdles and obstacles in the way of children as they grew up, as if borrowing techniques from the training of horses. 'Human beings are like gold mines,' she declared. 'They have to be beaten and crushed to find out the gold from the dross.' Continual luxuries were 'dulling to peoples imaginations': 'Everyone needs strong discipline, nations as well as children. The USA needs more than any other and gets less.' She worried about the effect of Waldorf's wealth on Nancy's children. 'It's a pity those children don't have to rough it a bit now and again, they really are too comfortable always.'

When Peter came home Phyllis would create a deliberate contrast to Southampton luxury. He would be subjected to a few days of decon- tamination, salutary correctives, tedious long hours of weeding in the garden for pocket money which would then 'somehow', as Peter observed, be directed to the collection plate in church. Phyllis com- plained that Peter seemed 'disturbed in his mind' when he came back from these visits to his father; 'funny, stiff and reserved'. But it was Phyllis who ensured that the burden of coming and going was onerous and confusing. Peter was made to feel it was wrong to enjoy his father's company. Phyllis believed that any affection he might feel was based entirely on material enticements. He was expected to declare his loy- alty to his mother, to the Langhornes and to reject any such claim from the Brookses, who quite obviously didn't deserve it.

It was mid-May before Phyllis left for America. The reasons that she gave to Bob Brand for her departure made no mention of Peter: 'I am going away to see if I cannot find just that peace within that you speak of. It is difficult to do this at Cliveden, where one must neces- sarily be with and see so many more people than one wants to, and I can't help feeling now that they are intrusions, only keeping me from the only comfort that I have now – my own thoughts.'

This time Phyllis left Winkie behind, with Jennie White, a trained nurse from Bellevue Hospital, who had come to look after him when he was ill at Mirador and who would stay for forty years. She was clearly a woman of great sweetness of nature and she loved the young Winkie. This was Winkie's first separation. Phyllis thought she would be back in June at the beginning of Peter's school holidays although, in fact, she wasn't to return until August. Winkie was greatly disturbed by the sinking of the American liner *Lusitania* off the Irish coast while Phyllis was mid-Atlantic. The papers were full of pictures of the survivors. Jennie White wrote, 'Winkie asks every a.m. "If Mummie has landed and if the Germans will get the St. Louis."' 'I miss you every day,' dictated Winkie, 'and I don't want you to come back while the Germans are blowing up ships. Give my love to Grandpa. Do you ride Tom Brown and Castleman? Do you have any colts?'

Thirty years later, with another war over, I found myself in the same position as Winkie, left at Cliveden with a nurse while my mother went to America for four months to try and sort out her own troubled marriage, travelling on an ocean liner. I remember the acres of empty gravel, the chiming clock, the vast spaces, the giant yew hedges: although there was much more activity in Winkie's time, the landscape hadn't changed.

When Phyllis did come back she only saw Bob Brand once, towards the end of her visit, in September 1915. During her time of grief he had kept away. He needed to reopen the dialogue. He had to broach the subject of the Captain first but it was something they couldn't mention face to face. As she was leaving again for America he sent a letter to her ship. It was very carefully worded. He couldn't pretend, in this letter, that he missed the Captain, or even that he had liked him, but he must give credit to Phyllis for her deep feelings for this man, his rival, whom he saw as a cardboard romantic soldier. 'I should not like you to think I did not see his great qualities,' he wrote, 'There was nothing small or mean about him & he certainly had in a wonderful degree courage & steadfastness . . . His character was so marked that I think a woman wd either not like him at all or, if she loved him,

wd love him very much. There was no halfway house with him.' This
was an honest letter. 'All the Pennants I know are strange & he was no
exception . . .' he continued, and then, without knowing of the last
correspondence about the Welsh Guards, he managed to suggest again
that things might not have worked out for Phyllis: 'I don't think he wd
have been flexible enough for politics; that was a defect of his qualities
& in war you want strength & courage & not flexibility.'

But the letter was gratefully received and Phyllis wrote back to
say yes, everything he had said was true 'and the Captain had become
such an essential part of my life that it is hard to see how I can get along
without him'. If explanation was needed for this – Phyllis had spent
very few days of her life with the Captain – she provided it. It was his
attentiveness that she liked so much, the antidote to Reggie's disregard:
'You see he was the only person in the world that had never failed me
in anything and had always given me the very best that he had to give,
at a time when I appreciated these qualities very keenly.' When he
went to the front, she wrote, 'I went along quite cheerfully, believing
that God would not make me suffer again . . .'

That September meeting was the last Bob thought he would
see of Phyllis until the war was over. Taking children across the
Atlantic with the submarine attacks was becoming increasingly risky
and Phyllis needed to establish a solid presence in America now
because of the lawyers. She had also run out of reasons to come to
England so frequently. Then, timing being the handmaid of romance,
Bob and another Round Tabler, Lionel Hichens, were appointed by
Lloyd George, now Minister of Munitions – a skilful deployer of
bright young men who would never vote for him – to sort out the
crisis in the supply of allied artillery shells. They were sent to Canada
where the munitions were made: Bob Brand on loan from Lazard
Brothers. Production depended partly on American finance and the
arrangements were constantly on the point of collapse. Brand and
Hichens, after great difficulty, formed the Imperial Munitions Board
in Ottawa to get production flowing again. Bob Brand had found his
way of contributing to the war effort on a grand scale, applying his

'beautifully lucid brain', to the complexities of financing weapons production.

By December he was at Mirador, riding Castleman, playing squash with Phyllis, listening to her play 'Farewell to Manchester' on the piano. It was a hurried trip from Washington. But on this last evening, when he was dining alone with Phyllis, about to ask her again to marry him, two neighbours came to visit. Phyllis knew what was on Bob Brand's mind and she kept the neighbours talking for two hours, to his despair, until he had to leave for New York. He wrote from Mirador to Nancy that Phyllis complained of depression and loneliness. It was a year before he saw her again.

'Why have you stopped writing to me?' Nancy wrote to Phyllis in the summer of 1916. 'I am really hurt.' In fact Nancy hadn't written either. Her letters were 'shorter and fewer' by each post, Phyllis confided to Bob. The sisters' correspondence had been dwindling for some time and they – the closest alliance in the Langhorne family – were drifting apart. Nancy's interference with the Captain had taken its toll and she had missed the anniversary of the Captain's death. 'You must think me so heartless & cruel not writing you a line & I have thought so much about it . . .' she wrote, 'I know how dreadfully you miss the Capt . . . He loved you in an odd way far more than you ever loved him . . .'

On her trips to Cliveden Phyllis had found Nancy increasingly taken up with 'that continual inrush and outrush of people'. She couldn't understand her entertaining of streams of strangers, banging together social workers, racing peers, Christian Scientists and cabinet ministers as if she was casting a new opera each day. Nancy was becoming a public character; she had forgotten the art of companionship. Christian Science, which Nancy now carried everywhere, and was trying to force on to everybody, including Phyllis, was doing further damage. Nancy had already converted Nora and Paul Phipps, or at least ordered them into it. Phyllis found the whole bandwagon and Nancy's new entourage exasperating, with their obsession with their own souls and bodies and their idea that suffering didn't 'exist'. She found Nancy's CS language oppressive and irritating too, a further barrier to communication. Phyllis's own understanding of God, she said, had made her able to stand up under some hard blows without leaving any bitterness in her heart. She didn't want to be told now that everything she had been through was 'untrue'.

In 1918 Philip Kerr finally broke the news to his family that he was officially a Christian Scientist and no longer a Roman Catholic, which his mother, the kindly and saintly Lady Anne, treated as a greater tragedy than the death of his younger brother in the trenches in October 1914. Philip's soul was damned by this action – there was no salvation outside the Church. His mother prayed every day for him until her death in 1934. Philip Kerr said later that this was the most traumatic event of his life and that afterwards, as a result, he had avoided conflict of any kind in his personal relationships, or his political life. It partly explained why, until the very end of his career, he remained in the shadows as a powerful *éminence grise*, but never – and it was always the accusation against the Round Table – taking political responsibility, or even political sides.

Phyllis found it 'very dreary' to return to Mirador. She had 'wandered about aimlessly for a bit until I became adjusted'. She noticed it took longer each time to settle into the routine. She had been welcomed home by the parson, in the absence of friends or sisters. She could give no comfort to her father who kept telling her how he longed to see Nancy and Nora and Irene. Only Winkie – whom Chillie adored – kept the channels open 'with his diplomatic work between Mirador and Misfit'.

Phyllis was particularly bored by all the 'bossing' she had to do as chatelaine of Mirador. The romantically imagined symbiosis with the black Virginian staff, still the old childhood hands, was less charmed in practice. What really wearied her was making decisions alone, without a 'male protector', constantly settling something with the house, the church, the school, the farm, or, when people did come, having to deal 'with the most tiresome of all jobs – arranging food for people'. Phyllis had notoriously bad food compared to the excellence of that of her sisters: Nancy, Nora and Irene (who gave her name to Mrs Gibson's Egg Dish, still a classic of its kind). She was lonely but as soon as people came she wanted to be alone again. She would look back on her mood in this state of manlessness as 'a hungering heart for that essential thing'.

Early one morning there came a violent break with the old days. Three of her ageing horses, including Castleman, had to be put down, the pistol shots startling Phyllis as she lay in bed; the realization of what had happened making her 'sort of sea-sick'. 'I feel as if three human beings, especially Castleman, had been killed. Most of the fun of my life has been on his back . . . I wish they had not shot him so early this a.m. – 6.30 is a gloomy hour anyhow.'

When the summer came she made expeditions: to the Shenandoah valley with Peter and Winkie; to North Carolina for quail shooting, which meant more dreary evenings trying to make conversation with 'very' remote cousins. The English post was now the main event of Phyllis's week. She wanted to come back and work in the hospital at Cliveden: 'in spite of my unsociable nature I like the company I get there. They are far more like Virginians than the Yankees.' The Captain, the war, the Cliveden vortex had turned her into a committed Virginian Anglophile, emotionally and politically. But with Phyllis this was mixed with the twin fears of rural entrapment and the horror of the northern cities and Yankee culture. Staying at Islesboro that summer she clashed irritably with Irene and Dana Gibson who were pro Woodrow Wilson and his policy of neutrality and isolationism which would keep America out of the war until 1917. Irene had been chairman of the New York Democratic Committee supporting Wilson's election in 1912 – such was her enduring, vote-pulling fame – and in 1916 was chairman of what Phyllis thought was called 'Wilson's Women's League'. Phyllis feared she might come to blows with Irene 'who talks like a loony' about 'that slippery Wilson'.

She and Nancy blamed Irene's views on Dana Gibson, who turned his wife 'like a chicken on a spit'. Nor had Dana Gibson any right to speak on these matters. 'How could he know leading the life he does? He is a visionary and artist.' Both Phyllis and Nancy took a philistine attitude to Dana as a working artist, charting his movements to and from his studio when they stayed at Islesboro, and counting his afternoon naps; it wasn't what you call work. However, it was agreed that to avoid 'heated discussions' Wilson's name would never be mentioned between them.

Nancy had been pestering Phyllis to come over to England, warning her 'don't settle down too much if you ever mean to change your virgin state. Your young <u>old</u> men are getting v. restive.' Geoffrey Dawson was still 'true' and, wrote Nancy, 'I never met a better [one] so don't throw him over lightly.' Unsociable was the word now levelled against Phyllis. She received lectures on it from Nancy and even from the frustrated Bob, who accused her of a cult of solitude and, more provocatively, 'selfishness'. This was an outrageous accusation; one of the rudest words in their vocabulary. He got a shocked reaction. 'Your letter is full of sauce! and a very wrong assessment of my character.' Nevertheless, this trapped Phyllis into declaring herself: 'You ask me if I do not think it possible for one to get great comfort and relief in a true companionship with another person, sharing their whole life, deepest feelings and thoughts etc. Goodness heavens of course I do . . . and yet my reserve often keeps me from having it. Perhaps as I get older, and feel the need of companionship more, that reserve instinct will fade away.'

But Phyllis couldn't come over: 'I should leave in a moment if there were no children to consider . . .' This had not been a consideration when the Captain was alive, but now the U-boat threat was worse and it would be 'madness' to cross the Atlantic at this juncture. The consideration, of course, was not about abandoning Peter, which could still be done apparently, but about depriving him of a mother altogether.

By staying at Mirador Phyllis avoided a period of turmoil at Cliveden. The year 1916 was one of feuds and of terminal uproar between Hever

Castle and Cliveden: Astor against Astor, Waldorf against his father. It was also the year that Nancy's fourth son, Michael, was born.

Waldorf had discovered, having received a telephone call from a newspaper on New Year's Eve, that his father had accepted a barony from the Government in return for his years of contributing large sums of cash to Unionist funds, and also running two newspapers that supported the cause. When William Waldorf died, Waldorf would automatically inherit the title and his career in Parliament would be over, along with his political power base in Plymouth. Waldorf was a rising star, heading for ministerial office. His father had not indicated that this might happen, and there had been no consultation.

Although less radical and idealistic than Waldorf, Nancy was more outraged and embarrassed by what she saw almost as a social slight. 'We are so knocked out by Mr Astor's taking a peerage that you wd not know us,' she wrote. 'It has really made me ill, we never had a hint of it until the evening of New Years Eve . . . Mr A sent for Waldorf New Years day & I fear he got a shock when he saw Waldorf who was too hurt, disgusted & annoyed to even attempt hiding it,' Nancy wrote to Phyllis. 'Mr A asked him wd he like it to be Lord Astor of Cliveden & Waldorf said he felt too strongly about it to have anything to do with it at all. Never in my life have I heard of a straight man doing so shabby a trick, you can't think how dreadful it is, Sis I believe you can, you know my love of Plymouth & my disgust at most American Peeresses & now this.'

William Waldorf must have had some difficulty understanding his son. It was not inverted snobbery that made Waldorf protest but pride in the Astor family name, or, as Nancy told Phyllis, '. . . . the Astor family started with plain John Jacob & to think it has come to this'. According to their son David, 'Everyone knew it was a cash exchange. My mother always used to say it was "bought and paid for". She said "What does 'Lord Astor' mean? Everybody knows that the Astors come from New York. To be Mr. Astor of New York means a great deal. To suddenly call yourself Lord Astor is quite absurd. It makes one look ridiculous."'

Waldorf's career had indeed been partly fired by what Nancy called 'living his father down'. It was, ironically, under Lloyd George's patronage that he had succeeded so brightly. He had managed to take control of the *Observer* from his father in 1915, moments before he tried to sell it, again without consulting his son, who had been its *de facto* editor. And now Waldorf was using it, with his editor J. L. Garvin to espouse the radical Unionist cause. Waldorf was a Unionist in name only – in reality he was not far from a full-blown socialist, prepared even to outflank Lloyd George in radicalism. He believed that the state had the obligation to stem 'the tide of disease and sorrow', poverty and sickness – but this would be a reformed, model state with model institutions. Through the *Observer* Waldorf became entrenched in political intrigue, although he despised the obstructions of party politics. This was one trait he had inherited from his father. Waldorf wanted to work through a radical consensus, through publicizing the glaring truths, cutting red tape and overturning vested interests. In 1913 Lloyd George had made him chairman of the state Medical Research Committee, to pull together all the various strands of research and practice, which led eventually, also under Waldorf's guidance, to the formation of the first Ministry of Health in 1919. Undoubtedly Lloyd George was planning to make him Minister of Health in the coalition government. Waldorf sat on committee after committee – for foreign affairs as well as all forms of public welfare and social reform, agriculture and housing. In addition, he had been given the gruelling job of Inspector of Ordnance, with the rank of Major, by Lloyd George.

Waldorf vented his spleen against his father. Yet what he saw as a 'decadence' his father saw as a distinction. He explained defensively to Nancy, 'The late Lord Salisbury wished to give me a peerage in 1902' (after William Waldorf had contributed some artillery materiel to the Boer War), 'but the late King Edward, who hated me, forbade it . . . from that time I have never relinquished the purpose to attain what Edward's spite had withheld.' Nancy relished Rudyard Kipling's quip that William Waldorf should be called 'Lord Dis Astor', 'only don't quote,' she warned Phyllis, 'as if Mr. A – pardon Lord – A should hear it he will leave us penniless Barons! Oh the shame of it.'

At their meeting on New Year's day 1916, Waldorf told his father that he would try and get the law changed so that he could drop his title. His father, disappointed and furious, demoted him from the head of the family by inheritance, reorganizing the trusts so that the bulk of his wealth skipped a generation to his grandsons, and they never met again.

Waldorf, meanwhile, immersed himself in political intrigue, joining, later that year, in the plot to remove Nancy's old friend, H. H. Asquith, from power. Asquith's prosecution of the war – the 'Wait and See' policy – was leading to disaster and military defeat as the slaughter in the trenches rose to unimagined levels. The Empire was now under threat and the Moot wanted a new leader to win the war. Some small part of the conspiracy took place at Cliveden and St James's Square, where every Monday night a 'Ginger Group' met to lay plans. Its core was the Round Table, led by Alfred Milner, Leo Amery, Geoffrey Dawson, Waldorf, Philip Kerr, with Sir Edward Carson, the Ulster MP and J. L. Garvin. Neither Asquith nor evidently Margot had any idea of the forces collecting against them, even after a hint from Nancy who, declining an invitation to dinner wrote: 'Anyhow you would find us disagreeable company these days. The Wait and See Policy has turned me into a fighting woman.' Nancy had changed her tune since the days when she, like many other Tories, saw Lloyd George as a dangerous demon and radical, intent on scorching the capitalist class. He had charmed her, as he charmed almost everyone.

It was Waldorf who first put it to Lloyd George outright that he should make a move. His response was that he still didn't want Asquith to go. But by 4 December 1916, when some particularly bad news had come from the front, he finally agreed. Dawson put out an editorial, written at Cliveden, with the headline 'Weak Methods and Weak Men'. Asquith wrongly thought it the work of Lloyd George, who resigned on 5 December, triggering a crisis and Asquith's own resignation on the same day. He was succeeded as prime minister by Lloyd

George two days later. Curzon and Balfour, who Asquith thought of as his closest friends, were among the Tories to support Lloyd George and join his Cabinet. Most of the Moot now got jobs. Milner was given a place in the Cabinet, and in turn suggested Philip Kerr, who was appointed Lloyd George's principal private secretary, where he remained, as Lloyd George's closest assistant, for the rest of his prime ministership. Waldorf, who had worked with Lloyd George on the Insurance Bill, was rewarded too, and made his parliamentary private secretary. It was a satisfactory business all round. They were known collectively as the Cabinet Intelligence Branch, or the 'Garden Suburb', after the offices Lloyd George had erected for them in the garden of 10 Downing Street. Lloyd George's birthday party in January 1917 was held at St James's Square.

In the middle of these high politics there was a little local difficulty with Nora, who had been working contritely with Nancy at Plymouth with the wounded soldiers, and then in the hospital at Cliveden for most of the war. By 1916 Paul Phipps, who had been a musketry instructor in a remote depot, was declared unfit for soldiering due to a persistent disability in his knee, and took a part-time job at the Admiralty in London. But most of the time he was at Cliveden, where he refused to help with the hospital and began to resent Nora's long hours of work there. Apart from the Langhorne trust, which gave Nora $5,000 a year at roughly $4 to the pound, he and Nora were totally dependent on Nancy for money. He evidently believed that this was why Nora had to work so hard. 'Paul like everyone who accepts feels a certain grievance against us,' wrote Nancy. 'He is nearly driving Nora crazy always around and always complaining.' Nancy banned him from Cliveden during the week. 'He's certainly the weak end of the alliance,' she wrote to Phyllis, adding defensively, 'Nora is devoted to him . . . I really think they suit each other wonderfully.' And in her Christian Science voice, she said, 'I never saw anyone so improved.'

But Nancy was deceived. In Paul's absences Nora had taken up with more than one of the Guards officers who came and went from Cliveden. Her niece, Nancy Lancaster, put it more succinctly: 'Nora went through the Guards like a knife through butter.' Nancy Astor only saw the surface evidence. 'Poor Nora through kindheartedness has evidently got into great trouble at the hospital. She is too free and easy with everyone and I've warned her. I shall try to send her away for a week or so. I believe it would do great good but she really has v few friends. She has let people down so dreadfully . . . I'm trying to hold the right thought. It is the only thing that can help.'

Nora's new ally was Nancy's son Bobbie Shaw, who was eighteen in 1916. He had grown up to be extraordinarily good-looking, verbally sharp and funny, but Nancy's doting possessiveness of him had never loosened as he grew into manhood and he was showing signs of trouble. His schoolboy 'sassiness' had developed into a rebellious and difficult relationship with his mother, an ability to penetrate her defences like nobody else, to be, uniquely, her equal in verbal attack. In 1917 he joined the Royal Horse Guards as a subaltern. He never saw action but he discovered his *métier* in this mounted regiment. He had the right attributes; physical courage, excellence as a horseman and popularity. But Bobbie had also developed a wicked streak and a love of danger. In his new alliance with Nora, he acted as her 'chaperone' and alibi; it amused him to watch Nora betraying her husband.

Phyllis crossed the Atlantic in January 1917, risks and all, bringing Winkie. Of Peter, left at school, she wrote, 'I don't like putting the ocean between us.' She had written ahead to Bob Brand, who was back in England working for the Ministry of Munitions, asking if they could 'meet quite naturally and without constraint. My visit to England will be greatly marred if we could not do that.' She knew this was almost impossible for Bob; that he would propose again; that she would refuse and then apologize, and that despite this they would not break off relations. In this she was applying the Langhorne rule, first laid down by Irene, never to let a beau off the hook. What's more she had come over to England to get married. 'I do value your friendship very much and should hate to have it step out of my life,' she wrote. 'You see reserved people are usually lonely and need friends that understand them, as I think you do understand me.'

They met and he proposed. She said the difficulties were too great. This time Bob said they should never meet again. Phyllis wrote in the middle of February, 'I shan't write to you again, but just let me say now how deeply it hurts me to give you pain, I only wish I could say all the things you would like to have me say. I know you would not want to hear them unless they were absolutely sincere.' She said she would quite understand if he would rather not see her, but then they went to a concert and on a few more outings. And one night during a weekend at Cliveden towards the end of March 1917, as everyone was about to go to bed, Phyllis told Bob to come to her bedroom and, standing by the fireplace, she said she would marry him if he still wanted it. Bob thought his imagination was deceiving him. But she came to his office at the Ministry of Munitions the following Monday with her mind unchanged. 'I knew then as I had always known,' he wrote later to his children, 'that she had given me the greatest gift a man could have.'

There had been no preliminaries except for the fact that they had spent a great deal of time in each other's company. Phyllis had decided, prompted by Nancy, that she couldn't go back to Mirador and live alone again, that a deadline had come. Bob rightly surmised that Phyllis wasn't in love with him and wasn't certain of her happiness; that this was a tortured decision. All the unhappiness of the past years, she told him, had made her 'gun shy'. 'You ask if I can love you with all my heart and soul,' she wrote. 'If I did not feel sure I could do that I shouldn't for a moment contemplate marrying you. I believe it is best to have it come slowly but surely and percolate into one's system – which is the way it seems to be doing with me.' She ended, 'Bless you my darling.' She told Nancy that Bob Brand was 'like a child in his gratefulness'.

Perhaps one of the 'difficulties' that had held Phyllis back was Geoffrey Dawson who, it seems, took the news badly and ungraciously.

But somehow the main difficulty had been disregarded by Phyllis. Where would the new Brand family live if the children had to be educated in America? Phyllis had not consulted Reggie, nor crucially, the England-shy Peter. Perhaps she calculated that Reggie would be nice about everything now that the divorce was over. But Phyllis had underestimated the contest of pride that the Brookses, especially Reggie's mother with her army of doctors and lawyers, were prepared to enter into, rallying their friends against the Langhornes. It was Nancy who tried to force Phyllis to go over and see Peter before she married, to get his approval and to secure his alliance. He was, she said, 'at a curious and critical age'. It was a rare, possibly a unique example of Nancy's sensitivity when it came to children and their feelings. Perhaps she had learned something from the effect of her marriage to Waldorf on Bobbie, who had begun to refer to himself as 'the foster', turning his wit against himself to conceal his hurt at being displaced by his Astor siblings. But Bob did not agree that Phyllis should go over. From his point of view it might reverse her decision. Peter had been written to and they would wait, instead, for his reply.

The draft of Phyllis's letter to Reggie remains: 'Just before I left New York you rang me up on the phone & spoke to me & I was touched when you said "if ever I can do anything for you let me know."' There was something now that would make her life 'far happier'. She intended to get married; she wanted the boys to be schooled in England. She had no desire to turn Winkie and Peter into Englishmen – 'I have never liked expatriate Americans.' She also said that she would never give up Mirador and 'hope to spend much time there in future'. (How this would tie in with settling with Bob Brand in England, she didn't explain.) She couldn't get married, she wrote, unless he agreed to this – otherwise it would mean constant journeys across the Atlantic. Her future happiness was in his hands.

Three weeks passed. Bob was sent by the Ministry of Munitions on a tour of the French battlefields. Phyllis wrote that she had heard nothing from Reggie, 'but I do want Peter's letter most of all'. It arrived on 17 April. Peter had written:

When I received your letter about Mr. Brand I was very
much surprised so much that I read your letter over about
4 times in the mean time I missed a recitation and got 15
demerits.

I am so glad you wrote to me first of all. Still further I
am glad you are engaged to Mr. Brand above all people,
for I think he is a very nice man and I consent without
hesitation. You mentioned that I may not have realised Mr.
Brand's enthusiasm but there I beg to differ.

I am so glad that you will be happy at last after these 6
years of lonesomeness.

At first I must admit it kind o' hit me hard! It was a
large thing to realize.

I think Mr. Bob Brand is a very lucky man to have you.

When is the wedding coming off I wish I could see it
though I know I would weep. Who is going to give you
away? I can't bare [sic] to think I shan't see my little
Mother married away. It is most bewildering though I am
so glad you are going to have Mr. Brand and that you will
be happy once and for all. It will be nice to once more
have a partner who will share your woes. Please write me
your plans. Lots of love from Pete.

How are you going to explain to Winks?
I _am_ sad but _so_ happy please write.

In her relief Phyllis would have overlooked the ambiguities in the
letter, focusing on his touching attempt to please her with adult, statesmanlike words. She wrote to Bob in France. '. . . I am as secure as a
lock and very happy to see the way clearing for peace and happiness
with you. The very thought makes the world seem the right place
again . . . Goodnight my darling Bob, I shall miss you and think of you
very often this week – God has been very good in making you love
me.'

News from Reggie finally came at the end of May, six weeks after Peter's reply, via Irene. He refused out of hand. Irene had spoken to him by telephone. 'He was adamant,' wrote Irene, 'and as I said he would do, had talked to his friends and they all agreed he was right.' Irene added, 'Poor Phyl, I am afraid this will alter all your plans, for of course I am afraid if you are separated from the children it will add zest to the B's [Brookses] and they will become very attentive to the children and feel as if they owned them.'

Bob remembered walking over from Cliveden, on his return, to Greenwood cottage where Phyllis was living with Winkie, to find her in tears as she tried to tell him that, owing to the children, until she was 'right in her conscience' she knew he wouldn't want her to marry him. But Bob wasn't going to lose her now. America had just entered the war and he had been called to Washington as Deputy Chairman of the British Mission to look after the munitions for the British government. The questions about Peter and schooling could be postponed.

They were married ten days later at the Chapel Royal, Savoy, in June 1917. A letter came from Peter just before the ceremony. Clearly he hadn't been told that the marriage was to take place so suddenly: 'I can't tell you how lonesome I am. I wish this war would stop soon,' he wrote. 'Hang it all it gives me a pain. I'll die if I don't see you soon. I honestly feel so lonely I don't know what to do. Please let me know something about the matrimonial plans.'

Peter didn't have long to wait, although the submarines delayed the Brands' departure for a week. Winkie, aged seven, and soon to go to boarding school, was left once more at Cliveden, not knowing when he would see his mother again. She thought she would be away six months. In the event it was ten months before she returned. The Brands spent their submarine-enforced honeymoon in the Adelphi Hotel, Liverpool, waiting for clearance – a hotel, then, of great elegance. The delay provided a crucial opportunity for privacy and intimacy 'when all the barriers that stood between us were being broken down', as Bob reminded Phyllis a year later. Given the work ahead they would never have been alone otherwise, except in a cramped cabin on a fraught Atlantic crossing. Instead they played golf at Hoylake every day, went to Southport beach, and read H. G. Wells's new novel. Phyllis wrote to Nancy, 'Bob is a darling thing & we laugh and chat together until the days seem to have flown by.' Bob Brand wrote in turn: 'Phyllis tells me she is VERY happy & that you wd be jealous to see her so happy . . .' He added rapturous descriptions of Phyllis's qualities, predictions of their future bliss, and enclosed a souvenir of Southport beach.

In April 1917, the month America entered the war, German submarines had sunk 196 vessels in the British war zone and on the Atlantic route. Boats left Liverpool accompanied now by destroyers. Passenger ships had guns mounted on their decks, firing continuously for the first thirty-six hours of sailing at suspected submarines. The few passengers on these boats were issued with waterproof suits and helmets which would enable them to float head up and feet down if they landed in the water.

Nancy had sent deck-chairs ahead to the boat for the Brands' comfort but they had little chance to use them: it was to be an alarming ride. They spent the first two nights partially clothed and ready for the lifeboats. They had rough weather in the first days and Bob was ill, forcing himself on deck so as 'not to take any chances' with Phyllis by being sick anywhere near her. Phyllis wrote delighted letters about him to Nancy, as if she had discovered him for the first time. He 'always makes me laugh. I must say he is a delightful crittur and as good as gold to me and I am very happy with him . . . It has been a happier week than I ever thought I could have.'

A month after their wedding Bob Brand wrote to Phyllis, 'I shall always love you as if I were on a honeymoon. I never knew before what it was really to love anyone. Isn't it strange that something inside told me what the deepest want of my life was the very first time I met you? I didn't change because it was right.' He added, 'I shall certainly never forget the Adelphi Hotel. We must go back there someday.'

17

The Men in the Room

Peter was waiting for them in the lobby of the Biltmore Hotel in New York. He rushed to embrace his mother – he was now half a head taller than she – and burst into tears. Bob reflected to Nancy that the news that his mother was actually married had been 'at first very unexpected & a great shock to him in a sort of way but I am sure he is very pleased to see his mother happy & I think he likes me. I certainly like him.'

But Nancy Lancaster remembered it differently. 'Peter adored her and he was furious when she married Bob. He was very jealous. I was with them in Islesboro when they arrived that summer and they were all sitting in Phyllis's room while she was dressing and she said "Oh get out you all. There are too many men in this room." And I'll never forget Peter's face. He was devastated.' Phyllis had taken Peter to Mirador first, before Bob arrived to be presented to servants and neighbours. She wrote to Bob, '. . . Darling Bob, you have made me so VERY VERY happy, and I am so grateful. I never thought I could ever be perfectly happy again. It is as much a joy to love you as it is to be loved by you, and even the cloudiest days will seem now to be filled with sunshine.'

Chillie wasn't there at first for Phyllis's arrival. It was a deliberate protest, for the benefit of the neighbours, at Phyllis not having asked his permission to marry. He came back from Islesboro in a restless state, wobbly on his feet, his memory failing. 'At the moment all is harmonious,' Phyllis wrote to Bob, 'and I tread very lightly for fear of causing an explosion. I agree with every preposterous suggestion which completely reverses my old form and quite disarms him.' But when Bob came for a short weekend visit at the beginning of July 1917 Chillie was affable. 'For the first time in our married career we had two breakfasts and two dinners alone,' Phyllis wrote to Nancy. 'I do appreciate his goodness to father. He ambles about with him & listens attentively to his ruminations & has taken to Virginia like a native. All real people however do take to Va – I never saw it fail.'

On that Sunday Chillie Langhorne got out the cellar key and made his mint julep for the near teetotal Bob. They sat and drank under the trees, the minted sugar, the iced syrupy bourbon. Chillie watched his glass and said, 'Now come on. Bird can't fly with one wing. Have another.' But it was Chillie Langhorne who couldn't hold his bourbon. He would have the occasional 'turn' – weak spells. When he came back from dinner one night he forgot where he had been, which caused him great distress. Phyllis put it down to overeating and too many toddies.

Mrs Virgil Homer Brown, 'Callie', Phyllis's maid, pronounced on the balding, lanky Bob Brand (the phonetics are Phyllis's): 'Miss Phyllis, you cerny is got a puddy man.' Callie and Bob had been conversing freely on the porch, possibly on their shared admiration of Virgil and Homer. Bob had also been talking to Buck who had become, to the amazement of everybody, a member of the Virginia legislature.

Everybody from the neighbourhood came to inspect Bob during his short stays at Greenwood, between his bouts of work. Irene told Phyllis that she liked Bob Brand greatly, 'but I feel in my soul she doesn't a bit,' Phyllis wrote to Nancy. 'He hasn't got half enough gush for her. She will ask him the most personal questions and then when he gives her a straight answer I can see a look of surprise in her eyes.'

There were early skirmishes with the Brooks family over Peter's Southampton visits. The Brookses had wanted him there the whole summer, but he went only for the month of July, to please Phyllis. It was Reggie's mother who ran the Brookses' campaign – a fierce old lady who consulted her lawyer for every decision and whom Peter disliked. That was a card in Phyllis's hand. After one visit to her in New York, Phyllis reported Peter saying, 'Oh mother you ought to see their apartment, all gold and velvet and they don't even know there's a war going on.' On the other hand, Peter realized that he was now expected to vote with his feet since there was no legal remedy, and one of the choices he was expected to make was to 'ask' to go to boarding school in England, a prospect which he dreaded. He began to dig in and to resist his mother, developing a protective loyalty towards his father as the battle heated up. Once again there were difficult returns from Southampton to Mirador.

Bob Brand, of course, had no experience of child-rearing. He had been distant from his parents, but then there were no surprises in his childhood regime. Like other boys of his class he was brought up in a masculine world, in male-dominated institutions from the age of eight, separated from his mother as if by tribal practice, removed from Oedipal confusions.

In this awkward situation he toed the Phyllis line, which meant that Peter must do what he was asked, whatever his feelings. Bob complained to Nancy that it was all wrong that Phyllis should 'have to let Peter go' to Southampton, as if the legal requirements were the sole reason for his visits. It was upsetting for Phyllis, he said. It distressed Peter too, but in a different way: 'While he is there everything that money can give is showered on him,' he wrote. 'He lives in luxury, has golf professionals to teach him, 12 cylinder Cadillacs to drive, motor cycles given to him etc etc. It's hard on Peter, as it upsets him.'

So why did the 'easy life' to which Bob Brand thought Peter 'inclined' also upset him? Was it simply the contrast of the two ways of life or two kinds of money? Bob Brand didn't reflect on this. He believed that Peter must be removed from Reggie to save his character. He was 'easily led & influenced . . .' It was indeed a rare example of humbug from Bob, engaged as he was in a propaganda war to get his

family to England, in which only the Brands could protect Peter from
'the influence of money' (something that had never, apparently, influenced the Langhornes).

Secretly, the Brands began preparing a legal war. There was talk
of kidnapping Peter and taking him to England. But the main plank of
their campaign was to humiliate Reggie by proving that he was drunk
around the clock, 'to get into the position where we can prove R's
drinking habits & have evidence of them sufficient for a court'. But,
Bob wrote to Nancy, 'that is easier said than done. We haven't yet
found any good way of doing this but we are not going to leave any
stone unturned.' If they succeeded they could take a strong line and
remove Peter to England after Christmas. If not, and Peter still refused
to come, the Brands would return to England in 1918 without him,
leaving him with Irene. They could see no alternative. Bob had to live
where he was most needed and Phyllis wanted to begin her married life
with him. Moreover she was now pregnant.

Peter's unlikely defender was once again Nancy. She wrote to
Bob, not to her sister, whose 'poor judgement', in Nancy's view,
had been the cause of these problems with Peter. 'I see the trouble
and it seems to me very clear,' she wrote. 'That Phyllis must stop
with Pete until she gets him, until she makes him want to come over
and failing that I think she should keep Mirador for Peter & be there
during his holidays. If Peter refuses to come over here then her only
way of keeping hold of him is by keeping Mirador – & letting him feel
that it is his home . . . I feel it is so critical the next few years of
Peter's life and I feel Phyllis's first duty is to him. If Phyllis doesn't
bear that in mind she will lay up trouble for you both. Just the fact of
giving up everything for him will have a tremendous effect. If she sails
away and breaks up his home and leaves him to Irene then the
Brooks's & everyone have a perfect right to get hold of him and say
"Well she married again. Pete never came first." I turn cold when I
think of Peter being left there. It would be most unwise and a really
selfish act on Phyllis's part. Just put yourself in Peter's place. What
would you think?'

Furthermore, she wrote, if Peter took up with Reggie and Phyllis wasn't able to return to him it would break her heart and destroy their marriage. 'Remember if she lost him 10 little or big Brands would not make up. Women are that way especially Langhornes – we are maternal first & that's why you like us!'

Despite the fact that she gave birth that year to her fifth son John Jacob, known as 'Jakie', Nancy couldn't resist adding a general swipe at the wearisome business of love, this 'error' that interfered with everyone's lives. 'It was the Captain that did this,' she wrote. 'I always knew that Phyllis made a fatal blunder to divorce R at the time she did . . . I look on you as two old things that have fallen in love and lost your heads in yr old age! & feel yr judgement can't be straight when it comes to the idea of separation.'

In September 1917, soon after she had dropped Peter back at Hill School ('I simply hate the partings now more than ever'), Phyllis had a miscarriage. It may have been the effect of this, as well as what she described as 'the bursting of a dam inside' – the release of years of chained-up emotions – that put Phyllis back into a serious bout of autumnal melancholy. With Bob away in Washington, and badly missing Winkie, she could hardly bear to be alone at Mirador. Part of her inhabited the place, she said, like a ghost, or like someone living backwards. 'It is desperately lonely now,' she wrote to Bob, 'I am again left with only the shell of myself lying here, like those big locust bug shells that one finds empty clinging to the bark of a tree – I cling to the bed instead, but I feel as if all my inside workings, heart and soul, had gone to W [Washington] with you.'

Somehow, by the following spring of 1918, Phyllis had prevailed and Peter agreed to go to school in England. Phyllis described the crucial, painful meeting between Peter and his grandmother, in which he finally spoke the lines required of him, heavily briefed by Phyllis who had 'warned him of their overtures'. 'She [Mrs Brooks] then began about me, opening up with "Well, Peter, I see the Langhornes have got you"; she told him a pack of fabrications about me. Peter, however, stood his ground and said he didn't mind a bit. She was for keeping him there the whole afternoon but I rang him up at 3 and told him to come out with me. When he got back he said "Mother, they can't change me now".'

By the time they sailed for England in April 1918, Phyllis was pregnant again, expecting her child in September. The school chosen for Peter, now aged sixteen, was Bob's old public school, Marlborough College in Wiltshire. At first sight it must have confirmed all Peter's fears of England: the high, dark red walls, the mysterious bridge of sighs, the prison grimness of the buildings rising from the road. Phyllis found Bob Brand's name carved into a desk in the Upper VI form.

Phyllis managed the trick of the boarding-school mother of reassuring herself that all was well with her son. On her first visit, she was surprised to find him on 'quite intimate terms' with some of the boys, which she put down to a Langhorne trait. 'I can tell quite plainly,' she wrote to Bob, 'that he is not unhappy.' The fact that Peter found the system overwhelming she took in the same spirit. It was a natural part of his induction.

After a few weeks Peter reported home: 'I am way behind in my class in German. In History I'm in the midst of a book which I know nothing about. In French I'm doing private tuition. As for geometry I never had it.' He couldn't figure out the algebra or the way geography was taught or the English money system in arithmetic. 'I'm in quite a mess standing at the bottom of each respective form,' he wrote. Bob was a little concerned when Peter announced that he had taken up gardening instead of cricket, which he found unfathomable. 'Peter anyhow shd play some games,' Bob advised. 'It makes a lot of difference in a place like an English school, where games are what mainly determines your position. That may be wrong but it's true.'

Peter's father, Reggie, would have agreed. A year earlier he had written to Peter, 'I am grieved beyond words to learn that your tennis is not what it should be. You must learn to play good lawn tennis somehow . . . you don't know how, when you grow up, you will regret it.'

Peter began to be afflicted by eczema, his skin covered in welts 'like chicken-pox', that itched so badly he couldn't concentrate on his work. His classmates laughed at his face which had to be covered in bandages because of infection; the doctors, he said, laughed, too, at his incessant scratching. He wrote pleading letters to Phyllis in secret during class, describing his agony in miniature handwriting: 'It's as though I'm gradually being tortured to death . . . For heavens sake come up,' he wrote. Phyllis, at least, wrote to him every day and he responded: 'As soon as I get up every morning I look forward to the joy of seeing your letter downstairs on the table.'

The Brands had rented a house at 37 Great Cumberland Place in London. Nancy had also lent them a cottage on the Cliveden estate. In September Phyllis gave birth to a daughter, Virginia. By October Peter's letters began to express an obsessive homesickness for America: 'I get so lonely here sometimes for USA that I feel desperate . . . America seems the only place in the world. I love it more every day.' He asked his mother to understand his wish to return there in two years' time to go to college and 'that you won't put it in a way which will practically mean that I'm making it very hard for you and that it's breaking up your family. I know it's going to be hard for you but please make that sacrifice for me.'

The previous summer, soon after her marriage to Bob, Phyllis had bought Peter an old 'Ford racer' motor car to drive around the clay roads. 'I thought it would be an interest to root him closer to Mirador which he already loves devotedly,' she had written to Bob. Peter had taken to it with a passion, both the driving and the mechanical side of it. Now from Marlborough Peter wrote an earnest, begging letter, asking her for a motorcycle, 'that would mean everything in the vacations . . . something to clean, oil, grease, touch, something to replace the joys we had in America with the Ford and the electric light plant in the cottage'. Phyllis replied: 'Read your IVANHOE and like it – give up the idea of squandering money on a motorcycle.' Peter got around his aunt Nancy, who sent him a cheque for his birthday to buy one, 'but I made him give it back to her', Phyllis wrote to Bob, 'as I particularly told him if he got it it was entirely his own affair and he would have to pay for it and keep it up . . .'

In November, on leave from school, Peter and Winkie watched the Armistice celebrations with their mother. Soon after the New Year Chillie Langhorne died, of 'paralysis' as it was described in the *Richmond Times-Dispatch*, in his flat in Monroe Terrace where he had been living for the last year. He was seventy-five.

Nancy, afflicted with guilt at not having seen her father for so long, wrote to Irene (having discovered that she, too, had not been at his bedside). 'I feel almost bitter towards Waldorf. He should have realised and helped me to go over . . . I can't write. I feel as though this blow has made me sort of daft. Only I feel with 4 daughters it was tragic not one of us was with him. Tragic for us not father for I know it's best for him but for us its awful.'

The obituaries hailed him, primarily, as the father of 'the famous Langhorne girls', who were noted for their beauty and accomplishments. The *Times-Dispatch* named all the sisters and their husbands ahead of any list of Mr Langhorne's own achievements. But this in a sense was his achievement, except that he was 'said to be the handsomest and most likeable man of the Old Dominion'. He left a trust of just over a million dollars for his children.

18

Writing from School

Bob Brand and the economist John Maynard Keynes first met in the cold, bright sunny days of the Peace Conference in Paris in March 1919. They were on the same side in the lost battle to prevent the Allied politicians from demanding, as they saw it, punitive — and calamitous — reparation payments from the Germans. They also fought together to get a scheme accepted that would save the disintegrating European financial system. These twin failures of the Versailles Treaty, which were to have such dire repercussions for Europe, were the subject of *The Economic Consequences of the Peace*, Keynes's most brilliant, splenetic piece of writing. The book, with its acid profiles of the major figures, Clemenceau, Wilson and Lloyd George, made him world-famous and influenced the thinking of the next generation: the counterblast of the practical economists against the politicians, although since then, historians have returned their own counterblasts against the damage they perceived it to have caused.

Keynes was head of the British Treasury delegation. Bob Brand had been lent by his bank to be financial adviser to Lord Robert Cecil, a British government minister and, in Paris, Chairman of the Supreme Economic Council of the Allies. It was the Council's notional task to get the economies moving again after the Armistice.

The collaboration, and friendship, that began between Brand,

the cautious City banker and currency expert and Keynes, the revolutionary theorist, and which would last for over twenty years, got off to
a shaky start. 'An infernal fellow' was how Bob Brand described
Keynes to Phyllis from the Hotel Majestic after Keynes had 'coolly'
taken his dinner guests away to play bridge. 'I simply couldn't work
long with him,' he wrote. Almost the entire Round Table were in Paris
including Milner, Curtis (in the League of Nations section) and most
prominently Philip Kerr, the indispensable, and now highly praised
secretary to Lloyd George.

The news that arrived in Paris, day by day, confirmed just how far
the Round Table's old moorings were slipping. The reign of
Conservative Liberalism was over. The economic system of Europe was
in ruins, its energy consumed by inflation, chronic food shortages,
strikes, rebellions, ultra-nationalism. Britain, the world's largest cred-
itor before the war, had now become one of its major debtors. Italy and
France were pouring in weapons; revolution was seen to be moving
westwards 'like a prairie fire', Bob wrote at the time. The slogan in
France, 'L'Allemagne paiera' (the French wanting to destroy Germany's
military capability for ever) was matched by the vindictive 'squeeze the
German lemon till the pips squeak' in England: Lloyd George, his
political fortunes wobbling, was faced with a British electorate tuned up
to a fever of predatory expectation. Many years later, Bob put it simply:
'What did the victorious countries do, urged on by France under
Clemenceau and Poincaré? They demanded from Germany huge reparations which could only be paid out of Germany's surplus balance of
payments. But Germany's balance was in fact greatly in deficit. It was
mad.' Bob said it loudly at the time, too. For several frustrating weeks
he and Cecil and Keynes tried to get the Big Four powers (Britain,
France, Italy and the United States) to 'listen'. They never did.

It was exhilarating at first, Bob wrote, to be at the centre of the
world's reconstruction, to be among the assembled brain and talent,
until the chaotic meetings actually began. The financial commission in
Paris was a 'monkey house'. 'It's almost impossible to get through any
business and a vast waste of time.' None of the governments were

addressing the only vital issue, 'namely how to prevent Europe from complete collapse and revolution'. 'If peace is not made at once,' Bob wrote to Phyllis, 'Europe will fall into an abyss. The whole world seems to be moving to a crash.'

The 'burning question' of German reparations dominated the political agenda. The British Cabinet had appointed Lords Cunliffe and Sumner, the 'Heavenly Twins', respectively the Governor of the Bank of England and a distinguished judge who had little idea of finance, to fix the schedule of payments. The wild figures they came up with bore no relation to Germany's ability to pay. Bob Brand remembered that Cunliffe was asked by a colleague how he had reached the figure of £200 million in gold that he was suggesting Germany should hand over immediately. He replied, 'Because it's twice as much as they've got.' Cunliffe wanted to set a figure of £25 billion, several billion more than even the French were demanding, but agreed to recommend £8 billion, subject to the Americans' approval.

Asked for his view, Bob Brand told the commission that by the time he was eighty (he was then forty), Germany would still be paying £400 million a year, and that this was obviously nonsensical. But Lloyd George and his assistant, Philip Kerr, were saddled with the Twins, fearing that their opposition would 'crucify' the prime minister in Parliament. When the Americans suggested £6 billion, the Twins refused to budge. Brand and Keynes were called in by Lloyd George to work out a compromise.

Brand wrote later of his 'violent arguments' with Philip Kerr, mostly about the 'absurd' French demands: 'I remember Philip asking me to come to dine with Lloyd George and him to discuss the question. When I got to the villa Philip met me at the front door and said, "Cock it as high as you can," meaning reparations, "He is having great diffi-culties with the French." I said, "I can't cock it higher than I think right." None the less I think I did cock it too high.' The issue was fudged and shelved for a decade, for Brand and Keynes, but any hope of a magnanimous settlement had already disappeared by the end of March. By 1921 the sum demanded had risen to £33 billion.

Keynes had his own 'Grand Scheme for the Rehabilitation of Europe', a bold and imaginative plan which would scale down the demands on Germany, and enable her export industry to recover. Had it been carried out, in his biographer Robert Skidelsky's opinion, 'it is unlikely Hitler would have become German Chancellor'. But he was opposed by the Americans, who wanted the revival of Europe to be achieved through normal banking practice. One year later, as Keynes predicted, German credit had collapsed and inflation had begun to spiral – mostly the fault of the overlending banks. The questions – whether Keynes, and therefore Brand, were right in their assessment, and the ability of the Germans to pay the reparations demanded of them – are still controversial among historians.

The endless frustrating round of meetings that went on from morning until midnight, the rich food, the overheated rooms, the frazzled, neurasthenic atmosphere, claimed its victims. 'I'm sorry to say Lord Pembroke was quite drunk at the Ambassadeurs,' Bob Brand wrote. 'It's time he went home.' Chronically overworked, like everyone else, Bob found that he dreamed of financial problems at night, just as he had had sleepwalking nightmares of impossible mathematical puzzles as a schoolboy. Philip Kerr, staying in the prime minister's villa at 23 rue Nîtot, spent his spare hours in the Christian Science Reading Room.

The strain famously took its toll on Keynes, too. Bob described him turning on the Comte de Lasteyrie, the French Treasury delegate at an Inter-Allied committee meeting. 'The minutes had been read and the chairman asked whether anybody had any comments. Mr. de Lasteyrie, the French representative, held up his hand and said he had a reservation to make. Keynes turned to the secretary and said, "You need not put that down. Just say that Mr. de Lasteyrie made his usual reservation on all subjects."' If Bob occasionally found Keynes exasperating – he often had to cover up for his venom – he also said of him: 'Maynard was different in the flashing character of his intelligence & its many-sidedness from anyone I have ever met. I felt always when I was with him like the boy at the bottom of the school talking to the boy at the top.'

The Paris Conference was also an important excursion for women who considered themselves on the inside of politics and power. Margot Asquith came, Nancy came too, putting Philip Kerr to enormous trouble finding her a room and a driver 'as she demanded', in the overcrowded city.

Bob Brand's immense powers of concentration and calm were threatened by a chronic homesickness for Phyllis as his stay looked like stretching through April and into May. After years of bachelorhood he was now not only besotted by Phyllis but totally dependent on her affections. This was their first long separation since their marriage. 'I hate it . . . I really do hate it,' he wrote to her, 'I wonder if I am too wrapped up in my wife. But nothing whether fame ambition or wealth seems to be anything compared to the intense happiness I feel at our mutual love . . . There's no one in the world like you.' Phyllis, too, had come to love Bob with equal adoration. The way she ended her letters must have convinced him: 'Goodnight my blessing. I see very clearly you are my blessing and I do love you so very deeply. How nice it is — I love it'; 'Don't overtire and if it helps to know I love you take it all and be happy.'

He expected a letter every day. He would hang around the desk in the lobby of the Hotel Majestic, 'asking the ladies for a letter until they are sick of me'. The telephone had now become a new, frustrating factor in their relationship. He wrote, 'I was overjoyed to hear your voice down the telephone. It was like finding something one had been long looking for. I wanted to tell you how I adored you but there was a wretched fat vulgar Englishman at my elbow, who wouldn't go. The Frenchman there had the good taste to leave at once but not so the specimen of our dull witted race, damn him.'

The Brands had bought a large new house at 20 New Cavendish Street, London, whose furnishing expenses drove the parsimonious Bob Brand into further, remote anxieties. 'It is a glorious house and I am too delighted,' wrote Phyllis. Bills arrived at the Majestic for crêpe de Chine and black satin to be sent back to London. This was a late education for Bob Brand, which he didn't take to easily.

Soon after he arrived in Paris a domestic crisis erupted in their lives. It took them both by surprise, although the warnings had been there for some time in Peter's letters. Phyllis had tried to ignore – and had concealed from Bob – Peter's growing complaints in the year that he had been at Marlborough. These were never about the obvious drawbacks, the spartan discomforts, the freezing rooms, the corporal punishment. It was Englishness that he was rebelling against – that quality his mother liked so much. He had been reprimanded, in a school where grades of uniform and the status they conferred were taken seriously, for walking about with little American flags pinned to his coat. He had already broached the subject of finishing his education in America, and Phyllis had refused, but in early March he suddenly demanded to go back immediately.

His letters have a clarity and a determination about them, an almost weary, patronizing authority that Phyllis must have found shocking from a sixteen-year-old, bypassing as they did all the normal parental roadblocks. 'What I'm about to tell you I'm afraid is going to be a miserable blow,' Peter wrote. 'I wish to heaven I didn't have to say it but it's going to come out sometime so I might as well tell you now. I'M GOING BACK TO AMERICA! In the first place if I stay here much longer I shall BECOME ENGLISH and I'd rather "break my neck" than BE LIKE an Englishman . . . The reason why I said you could marry Bob was because I wanted to see you really happy and well provided for for the rest of your life and with somebody Mother dear, whom I knew would really love you and live to make you happy . . . Remember at Hill School when I told you I'd leave America, come and STICK by you and try to make everything easy for you? Well, from that moment on it has been a real struggle for me. I tried to be happy even if I only looked happy. But Mother, gosh, I honestly wasn't. When we got to England the school question came up. In the bottom of my heart I dreaded the idea more than poison but I was DETERMINED to do my part so I stuck it out for you. Now things are looming up . . .'

The most difficult subject for Peter to bring up, in this letter, was that of his father. It is clear that Phyllis had tried to bar Peter from communicating with him, and even receiving communications from him. Peter confessed that Reggie had sent him a birthday telegram and added that he hadn't wanted to tell her 'because you weren't really well and I've waited until now so the shock would not be as hard'. He wrote, 'Barring you I like Father better than anyone in the world and I think he is very fond of me too and I'm not afraid of saying that to anyone even if people hate me for it and say I'm not loyal. I think if I went back to father it would give him a chance in life if he drinks, to stop it. It would make him happy after all these years he has lived by himself without us. You'll probably say I'm going to father because he has some money . . . As far as that is concerned I wish he was poor.'

He ended his letter, 'It's awful to think that after you get this . . . you'll hate me and so will many, many other people who see what I do to hurt you. But Ma, I love you. I always shall and nothing will ever stop me. I just can't live over here any longer. Oh Ma I have got some feeling . . . if you could only understand my ambition . . . you might not think me heartless.'

Phyllis went down to the school immediately and wrote that night to Bob: 'Do please come back soon – I have had such a beastly Sunday at Marlborough with Pete; I don't believe he could begin to know how miserable he has made me and just about broken my heart. I can forgive anyone anything except a heart of flint, but that I can't forgive. He says he is determined to go back at any cost; when I told him that it meant spoiling your life, mine, Winkie's and Va's [Virginia's] too, he still said he was determined. Truthfully, Bob, I would rather have gone to Peter's funeral than to have gone through what I have this week-end – it has been a hideous revelation to me.' She added under her signature, 'Why was I ever born?'

But Bob Brand couldn't get back. Instead he wrote to Peter to reprimand him for 'prejudice' against England. Peter wrote back denying it. The problem came down, he said, to 'a fact which hardly anyone on this side of the family will agree . . . If I was not fond of father and found out that he wasn't really fond of me the whole thing would be easy. It's awkward and the more I think of it the more I feel that I'm making it 4 times as hard for mother. It tears away that much of our love. I love mother "tons" but somehow it does not seem as it used to. The fact seemed to creep up and stare me in the face more than half a dozen times during the holidays . . . It seems in my mind a blooming mess.'

Ten days later, Phyllis received another letter from Peter, a classic of its kind — the chilly, powerful, absolutist voice of the besieged adolescent. Peter was prepared to do anything, as his mother said, to get back to America. What might he do if he was prevented? The letter undoubtedly implied, among other threats, that of suicide.

Dear Mother,

I've thought over everything and decided to come to a definite decision and stick to it.

I hold my decision to three points namely:

1. That I'm going back to USA the very first moment I can and I am not coming back to Marlborough next term no matter whether I'm dragged back.

2. That my life is not going to be cut off from my Father.

3. Half my holidays are due to be with father and half with you.

This is what I have absolutely decided. I mean what I say and bar all argument. I shall not change. That's what's in my heart.

Everybody I know can hate me, kick me out of the front door and call me anything under the sun. But I shall stick to my point to grim death.

You can get Aunt Nancy, Uncle Waldorf, Bob or anybody to do or say anything to me. My point is my point and I mean it & I really mean to stick to it.

Argument — weeping — suggestions etc will only muddle. If you refuse I'll prove to you that I can mean it . . .

I realise it's hard for you and I wish to heaven things
weren't the way they are but they are unfortunately.
These days of my life are valuable and cannot be had over
again. I'm American and before it's too late I'm going to
take my last opportunity to be like one etc. Goodbye. I
love you just the same no matter what you think but I
must be <u>AMERICAN</u>. Pete

'Oh Bob I never dreamt a child cd give me so much pain,' Phyllis
wrote, 'it will leave a wound in my heart for the rest of my days.' Bob
replied from Paris, 'I always thought his father was writing to him,'
showing how far the Brands had demonized Reggie and, short of any
other explanation, blamed him for Peter's actions. Phyllis was further
shocked to discover that Peter had nearly called his father to get money
to finance his escape. They convinced themselves that there must be
some other influence behind this adolescent stubbornness and the *command* it could muster. Children, in Phyllis's experience, never wrote to
their parents in this manner. 'I never dreamt that Peter could possibly
take things like this,' wrote Bob, '& I thought we would all be happy
together.'

Lacking any understanding of Peter's desperation the Brands saw
the issue as a test of their authority as grown-ups over children, eclips-
ing any hope of a wise or pragmatic solution. Peter was behaving in a
'heartless' and 'cruel' manner. How could he 'remove his feelings'
from his mother? When he managed to express his own pain and regret,
he wasn't believed. If he felt like that he would surely change his mind;
he was acting out of guilt at his own ruthless behaviour. Only Phyllis's
hurt feelings were weighed in the balance. Never in all the correspondence is the question asked why Peter had gone to such extremes. It
was this lack of imagination – the phrase they used against Peter – that
led the Brands and the Astors to compound their mistakes with further
tragically poor moves. Peter was now put under immense moral pressure, and one can either admire his heroic resistance or commiserate
with the anguish that drove him to such a traumatic confrontation.

Bob was obliged to write again to Peter, risking his relationship with a stepson he barely knew. It began as the blueprint from the concerned housemaster about responsibility, duty, sacrifice and submerging one's own desires to the common good. It contained the lines that every chastised schoolboy knew by heart. What did he owe to his mother (or the school, the team, his country) 'who loves you so much and has given you so much?'

'Your letter, and what you said in it have hit her like a stab in the heart,' Bob wrote. 'You know what trouble she has had in the past and now you hold out the prospect of wrecking her life again.' As before it was all put in terms of Phyllis's pain. The message was that the only happiness under discussion must be hers. She was special, unlike his father, and Peter's duty was to make sacrifices. Bob Brand appealed to him to think of his responsibilities 'as an elder brother' and he ended, 'I want you to believe I will do anything which is in my power to make things happier for you.'

But Phyllis had already given way. She reported to Bob in Paris, 'I wrote to Pete this aft. and told him I wanted him to go back now . . . When I told him I should have to come over this summer and leave Winks and Va. he said: "Mother, I really do hate to make you do this, I know what it means", but nevertheless he is not going to change his mind, I fear.' The date for Peter's departure was set for 12 April 1919. Peter left Marlborough and was sent to see Nancy and Waldorf for more persuasion, their temporary sympathy for him having now evaporated. But even Phyllis thought that Waldorf had been 'pretty strong' in telling Peter that if Reggie had 'behaved himself' there would never have been any of these problems. He and Nancy advised Phyllis simply to refuse to let Peter go; that he could never do it without her consent. But Phyllis realized that if she took this advice she would lose all connection with her son. And Peter might eventually influence Winkie, too, to cross the Atlantic for the motorcycles in Southampton.

It had been a bad spring for Phyllis. Chillie had died in February, Bob had been away in Paris, and Nancy's attitude to the drama about Peter – which Phyllis felt as she might about a death in the family – had convinced her that she had finally lost her for good. Phyllis could rarely get to see her sister these days. She was too busy. 'Nannie goes to France on the 5th or 6th,' she wrote to Bob, 'She might as well be in France as far as I'm concerned. The only thing I now depend on is you and Va.'

When Phyllis did see Nancy, she was excluded by the combination of Philip Kerr and Christian Science. 'Mrs Eddie holds supreme sway here,' she wrote from Sandwich. 'I can discuss it [Christian Science] with Philip and enjoy doing so but it is quite impossible with N. She begins with condemnation for those who won't agree, and there we split; she only thinks now what Philip tells her to.'

Phyllis had until now been the most elevated figure in Nancy's life – precious, protected and certainly more special than anyone else. It was perhaps this that made her feel unconsciously that wrongs could only be done *to* her, not *by* her, or that she could emulate Nancy's power in blasting her way through obstacles. She was applying this force in Peter's case, without careful thought, and without Nancy's close protection.

Phyllis wrote to tell Irene, who would have charge of Peter in America, that she still hoped he might change his mind before the boat sailed. 'I don't blame him a bit for <u>wanting</u> to go back but I do blame him for going and leaving me. Nothing could be worse could it than to have one's first born turn away from his mother as if she were a thing of wood.'

The night before his departure, Peter broke down and wept, telling Phyllis how much he hated hurting her, how he couldn't bear to see her cry. Unable, until this moment, to see beyond the flint wall that Peter had erected and her own rejection, she wrote to Bob: 'At last I think his heart was touched. I felt this morning as if I were sending a baby out into the world. As the train pulled out I felt oh! such a tiny spec in the world, and oh! so absolutely deserted, but the worst is over. Poor Winks just sobbed and looked so pathetic trying to keep a straight face . . . But there it is – one pays very dearly for a youthful mistake.'

Meanwhile there was even less chance of Bob leaving Paris for the

moment. The conference with the Germans was about to begin.
Brand, Keynes and Cecil were still struggling to get the attention of the
Big Four, drafting financial plans day and night. So Phyllis came to
Paris instead. They rented a small flat near the Bois de Boulogne. The
day after she left, in early May, the Peace Treaty – in effect the diktat to
the Germans from the Allies – was handed over at Versailles with great
ceremony. The Germans would give their counter proposals. There
would be a reply from the Allies, turning most of them down. It was a
formality that would last for weeks – fateful weeks in which the Allies,
offering no grain of reconciliation, added what the Germans saw as vin-
dictiveness and further humiliation to a conquered enemy, whose
population was already suffering from a crippling Allied blockade.

On the morning of 7 May, Bob joined the crowds of tourists at
the château of Versailles and watched his friend Philip Kerr arrive in the
motorcade behind 'Woodrow Wilson alone in his car with its blue silk
flag and white American eagle; then Lloyd George and Bonar Law . . .'
After Japan and Italy came Liberia, Haiti, Siam. The reorganization of
Europe was like an Olympic Games in which all nations would play
against the Germans. 'If I were a German I shd be both proud and
ashamed,' Bob Brand wrote to Phyllis, 'proud to have fought the whole
world and ashamed to have made them all my enemies.'

But this was a brief respite, followed by dementing pressure,
almost literally for Keynes, who soon retired to the Bois de Boulogne
on the edge of a breakdown. The sense of powerlessness in the face of
disaster was compounded by the fact, as Bob wrote, 'that financial
leaders . . . are the only ones who understand what is happening in the
world'.

At any moment Bob Brand could have packed his bags and left
Paris, as he so desperately wished to do, without guilt or blame. He
was an adviser, unlike Keynes or Robert Cecil; he'd given unheeded
advice for four months and now his bank needed him back. His partner
at Lazards was also close to a breakdown from overwork. Versailles had
generated a huge volume of banking business: loans to Czechoslovakia,
Finland, Poland, as well as Germany. 'Lazards ere long will be bankers

to every government in Europe.' But Bob's attempts to get home for a few days' break were cruelly frustrated. On Saturday 10 May, he waited in his room at the Majestic, a place he now hated, with 'passport & ticket etc and a light and joyful feeling in my heart'. At midday Robert Cecil told him that their trio – Brand, Cecil and Keynes – had been asked to put together a financial package for the Big Four and to meet the following day.

It was duty that kept Bob Brand in Paris. Yet at this moment duty seemed to be something that belonged to the old values of nineteenth-century liberalism, to which the war had signalled an end. For Bob those values – order, stability, honour, consensus, even decency in war – were a far cry from cynical mass slaughter, poison gas and the deliberate starvation of civilian populations for political gain. The old pre-1914 culture, which he was vainly struggling to put back into place, included a belief in the balance of power instead of these arbitrary schemes to unbalance Europe and create little nationalisms, ignoring the commercial realities.

The Americans were, as usual, the only hope even though, Bob wrote to Phyllis, 'they are very ignorant of the troubles of poor old Europe'. That was a further reason for Bob to stay: 'Keynes isn't very popular with anyone just now & its very important there shd be someone here with whom the Americans get on.' Bob tried and failed to see Woodrow Wilson directly, writing memos, and lobbying his special envoy, Colonel House. 'If I find there is nothing to be done to get American help, I don't know whether I shall stay long. What's the good if there is nothing any human being can do?'

One of the shocks felt at Versailles by Brand and his colleagues was the realization that they had all been so badly informed. The makers of foreign policy and public opinion were quite ignorant of the forces that had allowed the world to blow up in their faces. Foreign policy had been something closely guarded by foreign offices before 1914, excluding the public and even party politics. The problem was first discussed at New College and Magdalen dinners in Paris during the peace talks. Then, under Round Table auspices, meetings were held at the Hotel Crillon and the Majestic in June between the British and American delegations and the press. (Walter Lippmann was there too.) The aim was to create institutes in both countries which would 'act as a telephone exchange' between all those involved in the foreign affairs process from civil servants to academics to journalists. It led, the following year, 1920, to the formation of the Royal Institute of International Affairs, or Chatham House, under the direction of Lionel Curtis. It was the first think-tank of its kind in the world (later copied by America and Russia) – a non-governmental institute of specialists studying foreign affairs. It was set up with large financial contributions from Waldorf Astor and Abe Bailey from South Africa, among others, and had a rapid and, to this day, lasting success.

When Bob did eventually get home, in late May 1919, he was summoned back almost immediately by telegram. Keynes had taken to his bed in despair and exhaustion. Bob lunched with him and found him 'pretty knocked out'. Soon afterwards Keynes resigned from the Treasury and left in disgust, writing to Lloyd George '. . . the battle is lost. I leave the twins to gloat over the devastation of Europe.' Three days later, coming to the same conclusion, Brand returned to London. There had been no workable plan made to stabilize the currencies or to settle the war debts, merely some vague hope that Germany would eventually pay for everything – indefinitely.

But the last act of Versailles – with its momentous consequences – belonged, extraordinarily and almost singly, to Philip Kerr. He had followed the devious twists and turns of his master Lloyd George with chameleon artistry and devotion. When Lloyd George began to see the wisdom of conciliation with Germany, Kerr drafted the elegant Fontainebleau Memorandum for him, pleading for a moderate settlement, noting the danger for the future of surrounding Germany with small states with large German populations. When the Unionist diehards in the coalition in England howled with rage, he set about writing the harsh words and phrases that appeared in the Treaty to appease them, or, as A. J. P. Taylor wrote, 'talking "hard" with the intention of acting "soft"'.

It was Kerr who, on behalf of Lloyd George, included the famous 'war guilt' clause in Article 231, the most damaging part of the Treaty, which said that the war had been caused solely by German 'aggression' thus justifying the inflated reparations claims. He would later say that this was a mere technicality, that cooler heads would sort out more realistic reparations later. But there was also his 'last note', which was to be remembered by the German delegation for years to come. This was the Allied reply to the German observations on the Treaty, as it was handed back to them for signing. It was drafted solely by Kerr and agreed to by Clemenceau and Wilson without a word being altered. It seemed to the Germans to taunt them further for their guilt, reminding them, as one historian saw it, 'that they alone were responsible for planning and causing the war and that they had carried it out in a savage and inhumane manner'. Whereas they not only felt they had acted defensively but that they had now overthrown the Kaiser and instituted democratic government. They saw the note and the war guilt clause, particularly the word 'aggression' as merely cynical, vindictive and needlessly insulting. These were the clauses and phrases that provided the main focus of German anger at the Treaty in the 1920s, so effectively exploited by Hitler.

The brilliant but impressionable Philip Kerr was certainly overworked like everybody else, suffering from extreme brain fag, and to judge from eye-witness accounts, possibly losing his mental grip. Jan Smuts, the South African general appointed by Lloyd George to the War Cabinet, spent his weekends with the Quakers; Philip Kerr spent his spare time in the Christian Science Reading Room, from which he emerged, apparently, with the opposite of meditative calm. One member of the German delegation, the economist, Professor M. J. Bonn, described Kerr at the negotiating table, in an unpublished letter, as 'shrill in manner' and 'unstable' with the look of a 'fanatic ascetic'. Kerr, he said, 'was driven by a kind of apostolic fervour denouncing German wickedness' which helped the French to make their unworkable reparation claims. Kerr's health would, in fact, soon force him to retire from Lloyd George's service.

A few weeks after the conference and long before Keynes's book had appeared, Phyllis wrote to Bob: 'Philip said the Peace Treaty would some day be looked upon as a great and splendid piece of work! It's high time he was leaving L.G.! He is the most impressionable person I have ever met.' She added, echoing Lloyd George's public regrets, 'I wonder if these Germans will sign or if these drastic terms will unite the nation and only make them prepare again for another war in another 25 or 50 years.'

The international impact of Keynes's book certainly rattled Philip Kerr, and, to a lesser extent, Lloyd George. Kerr's doubts deepened when the French occupied the Ruhr to force reparations payments in early 1923, ensuring the collapse of what remained of the German economy. From then on he became haunted, increasingly 'obsessed', according to his family-appointed biographer, that Germany had been badly treated, that she needed to be released from her 'straitjacket', that the Treaty should be torn up. Ever prone to conscientious inner conflict, he felt his own actions were part of the cause of the growing instability in Europe. He developed a sense of guilt about his responsibilities and a desire to make amends, which was to lead him – before he became Britain's Ambassador to the United States – into fatal misjudgements about Hitler in the 1930s.

When Bob finally returned home he and Phyllis were still unable to meet. Phyllis had taken Winkie and Virginia away to stay with some Astor cousins; Bob had to go to Oxford to sit on a committee to prevent 'radicals' taking over All Souls and couldn't join her. Then, in mid-June, Phyllis pursued Peter across the Atlantic, wearing a trace of martyrdom and unable to see further than the 'heartlessness' of Peter's disobedience. 'I am not sure . . . you will do much good,' Bob had warned.

Phyllis can't have been thrilled to read, before she set off, Peter's ecstatic report of his return to America. 'Literally I believe that the happiest day in my life was on the day I sailed into New York Harbor,' he wrote, a little callously. Getting back to Hill School, he said, was 'like a blind man suddenly receiving sight. All my friends greeted me as though I had only been away for a week end only.' His eczema had instantly cleared up 'like you wipe a black board off with a sponge and the dryness has almost completely gone and my head has stopped itching so life in general has greatly improved.' He added a ps: 'I love you although you may never believe it.' Soon Peter was reporting: '97% in algebra and 98% in French' and 'I haven't felt blue once.'

When Phyllis docked in New York she saw no sign of Peter at the pier. In those days, and certainly in the Langhorne family, meeting the boat was a basic convention. She immediately regretted having come at all. She travelled to Mirador, expecting to see him at Charlottesville, but he wasn't there either. She found a letter from him, sent days earlier, saying that he was going to Southampton to see his father before coming to Mirador. But no word since. There was a telegraph strike. It was almost impossible to get through by phone. Phyllis was stung by the coolness of his lack of communication. 'It's impossible for me to love anyone who can do this,' she wrote. She took to her bed, with a temperature of 103, and waited. Peter arrived at the end of June, his hair burnt to a copper colour by the Long Island sun. 'He rushed in and gave me two very fervent kisses,' she told Bob, 'but never once mentioned not having come to meet me or written to me since I arrived.'

Her relief was eclipsed by her irritation at his stories of Southampton where he had been given a new motorcycle and where, as Phyllis said, 'they treated him as a sort of hero who has come to save his father'. Reggie had taken another 'cure' since Peter's return, she wrote, and Peter loved the idea of reforming his father. 'It's a difficult battle for me with the B's. He seems to see absolutely no difference in what he owes me and what he owes his father,' she complained. 'In fact he is more ready to give to his father than to me . . . I am afraid when I return to England he is going to look upon his father's house as home, whoever lives at Mirador.'

But Peter had returned to Mirador to discover that his mother was in the act of selling the house to her niece Nancy Lancaster who, widowed from Henry Field, had recently married the millionaire

Ronald Tree. Another tie with his mother was being cut without any warning. Eighteen months earlier, just before Peter had been brought to England with Phyllis and Bob, he had written to his mother from Hill School to say that he had dreamed of Mirador burning down. His letter came after Phyllis had 'wept all night (in my sleep) dreaming of Mirador and saying goodbye to it and then your letter arrived. I hope it is no evil omen we have had!' She added, 'It does make me fearfully homesick when I think of leaving Mirador . . . However we shall always come back to it and think of no other place as Home, but Mirador.' In her letter to Reggie, announcing her engagement to Bob Brand, she had promised the same thing.

Now Phyllis was making her life in England and demanding that Peter cut himself off from his father altogether. This was the only way he could acknowledge what he 'owed' her – the frequently used word – for the years of unhappiness and neglect when Reggie was drinking. 'I honestly don't believe his affection for his father amounts to a thing but he loves comfort and approval,' Phyllis wrote. But Peter did love his father, as he repeatedly told her, although this was taken as a betrayal. He also felt sorry for him, responsible for his happiness, worried about his drinking, guilty for the break-up of his parents. He refused to be hustled out of his father's life. Peter began to button up. He would confide in Irene, but not Phyllis. Phyllis had set up a pointless battle for possession, one she had already lost. It never occurred to either Phyllis or Bob that Peter felt it heartless to abandon his father and that it had now become impossible for him to alternate between the two homes.

Bob had to subscribe to the *force majeure* of the Langhornes, since it was taken for granted in the battle and it was indeed a powerful and attractive force. Nevertheless, he wrote to Phyllis, advising some caution: 'I think the trouble is that Peter never felt really that he belonged wholeheartedly to the Langhornes.' He had other strong feelings which couldn't be 'eradicated'. Even now, when a terminal showdown was certainly coming, there was still no mention of Peter's own pain and unhappiness. The effect of all this parental confusion on a

sixteen-year-old adolescent could have driven him deeper into
secrecy, stubbornness and outbursts of verbal violence but in fact
Peter seems to have behaved remarkably well, with what Phyllis
described in a calmer moment as 'attentiveness and politeness'.

But, since Peter's demands were intractable, the result was tragic.
Peter had suggested to Phyllis that he should have tutoring during the
holidays to catch up with his form at Hill School. She had arranged,
from England, for him to go to summer camp school instead of going
to Southampton. Peter decided instead that he would arrange to have
the tutor at his father's house. Phyllis reported the rest of their conversation. 'I then said, "You mean you are quite willing . . . to leave me
and go to your father?" But he said, "It isn't that. If I have got to go away
anyhow from you I am going to him. I want to be with my father." So
then I let him have it and told him what an ungrateful little brute he
was . . . and if he attempted to go to Southampton I would raise the
greatest row that ever was . . . and he said, "I'm sorry, but I am going
to go."'

Phyllis wrote to Bob that Peter had 'openly' defied her and
'proposes making his home with his father when I am not here . . .
He says he is doing it because he loves his father, and feels he owes it
to him. I've always thought of Peter first & given him more affection
than anyone else in the world & he now puts his duty to R before his
love or duty to me. He doesn't feel he owes me anything, I suppose.
He said the other night, "But mother you have a nice husband and
Winkie and Virginia and Father has nothing."' An 'easy summer' and
the corrupting gift of a motorcycle in Southampton was, to Phyllis,
still the only explanation. The Ford Racer she had bought him in
Virginia 'to root him closer to Mirador' was not regarded in the
same light.

By 21 July, with time running out, Phyllis realized that she had
been beaten and that 'coercion is not going to be much use', although
she was frightened that if she didn't 'assert her rights' now the
Brookses would never listen to her again. It was Legh Page, the lawyer
from Richmond and Phyllis's old beau, who stepped in and tactfully

persuaded Phyllis 'not to make an issue out of Peter's visit to Southampton', pointing out that by the age of eighteen, in almost a year's time – his birthday falling in late summer – 'he could probably choose his guardian anyway'. And now Phyllis wrote to Bob contritely: 'I felt all along that to fight Pete would be a mistake – I don't want to make him feel antagonistic towards me, and I must remember that he is young and perhaps some day may see his mistake.'

When Phyllis left again for England, Peter turned to Irene for support, asking her directly for her friendship, writing to her in an invented grown-up style. Trying to intercede for his father, and trying to explain his own behaviour, he wrote, 'He has proved himself to me and I suppose only to me to be a friend. That means really a friend and who will see you through no matter what it is. He's "got a heart" which only those who know him <u>really well</u> can thoroughly appreciate.' He ended his letter, 'I remain always an admirer of your thoughtfulness and I hope you'll always love me if you have to search out the most extreme rung of your heart. Goodbye. Pete.'

Too late Phyllis's eyes were opened, as she put it in a letter to Bob, but not until 1920: 'Poor soul he has got a complex, but he can't help that and it is born there, and I'm sure the thing to do is to ignore all that and just pour out affection.' The opportunity, however, had passed.

Nora and Paul Phipps had emerged from the war with their marriage in the same troubled state as it had been in 1914, when Nora had dealt it the two solid body-blows: the 'engagement' in Richmond and the jaunt with Lefty Flynn. Scatter punches of various kinds had followed until Paul was almost on the ropes by 1919. The difficulty was that Nora admired Paul, she didn't want to hurt him, but she was out of control, off on a romantic agenda and quite unable to weigh up the consequences of her actions. Paul's response was to try and reassert his authority through low-scale domestic tyranny and to regain Nora's love by demanding it as his right, thus making matters worse. By 1920

Phyllis was describing Nora's behaviour as 'flabbergasting'. Irene's letters chart her departure from the narrow path that Nora genuinely intended for herself each time she made one of her 'fresh starts': 'Nora's behaviour grows more and more utterly hopeless'; Nora was 'leaving those she loves all scared up'; and 'Nora must be mad'.

Much had been hoped for from Nora's conversion to Christian Science, by Nora herself, by Nancy, who always reported improvement on its account, even after serious backsliding, and by her fellow convert Paul. He had tried to excuse Nora's earlier behaviour in America 'as bad as the business was' to the sisters. The separate life that Nora had led, coming and going as she pleased in New York, seemed almost acceptable in Paul's eyes; forgivable compared to the rest, which he blamed on the war and its 'great illness which has affected so many phases of life'. 'Now it is all over,' he predicted to Nancy when she was back in England, 'and there has come (thanks to CS once again!) a real awakening – I only wish you were here to see it.' Such wishful thinking only irritated the likes of Irene and Phyllis and particularly when it came from Nora: 'It is a wonderful thing,' Nora wrote of CS, 'and when honestly applied, too, it never fails. But,' she warned, 'it is not easy to get it. It means work and a desire to be right which I don't always have. I think I do but I don't.'

After the war Nora and Paul moved into a very small apartment in Burton Court, Chelsea. In another fresh start testimonial to Irene, Nora wrote, 'We have just moved into our flat and are just beginning to settle down. CS is helping me now as it did before when I was very unhappy . . . I know I must stick to Paul if it is possible and I am going to but it isn't easy.' There were special factors which explained her waywardness in America, when she had run off with Lefty. 'It was just after a very hectic four years of strain and excitement,' Nora wrote 'and I had been practically on my own all the time and when Paul came back (to England) it made me nervous and unsettled and got me down – in many ways – but I know my one job on earth is to try and make things go with Paul and myself which I am honestly trying to do.'

Phyllis wrote to Bob: 'She is a pathetic crittur at times to me, it is very sad to be young & attractive & not love your husband . . . Paul is an ass to behave as he does & demand affection . . . & nothing freezes her up like that.' Bob visited them and found Nora 'v restless and agitated, cooped up in her little flat and longing and panting for all the things she wants and for self expression, anyhow to feel herself expanding and not contracting. It's almost like Nancy living with Paul in one room. Just think of that.' Paul he described as 'terribly sententious and boring . . . he allows no contradiction'.

Waldorf now called in Bob (who was managing some of his investments) to try to solve the Nora debt crisis. In July 1920 Paul went to see him in the City. Nora's spending had finally hurtled out of control. Perhaps she had taken literally the Christian Science doctrine of the unreality of matter. She had already run up debts that year of £5,000 (at $4 to the £1, near to £48,000 or $192,000 allowing for inflation). He now needed another £2,000 to raise on Nora's share of Mr Langhorne's legacy. So reckless was Nora's plundering of their joint account that for Paul, as Bob remarked, it was like living with a burglar.

Further shocking details of Nora's pathology came to light. Bob wrote to Phyllis: 'N buys on the average 2 pairs of silk stockings at Woollands every 3 days; at the rate of £365 a year. Her bill at Enos [a fashionable couturier run by two American women near Mount Street, Mayfair, and one of Nora's favourites, which she would enter 'on tiptoe'] is about £1200. And so on. Poor Paul the thing is quite impossible. She is a dipsomaniac in clothes. It is no good lending her money. She will simply pour it out . . . They only let her have things because they know she is Nancy's sister.' Had he been her husband, he said, he would 'tear them to pieces' each time she bought a pair of silk stockings. 'She must somehow be brought up with a round turn.'

It was arranged that Waldorf and Bob Brand would guarantee a loan from the insurance company of which Bob was a director. But he laid down strict conditions. One of them, written in a letter to Paul, was that if the Eno's and Woollands' debts continued he would have to

give Brand and Astor an undertaking to make a public announcement
in the newspapers that he wouldn't pay his wife's debts. They were to
give up their flat and live in future at the cottage at Cliveden.

Nora protested violently. She became hysterical. She fainted
once or twice, but finally she promised to abide by the conditions.
'Nora is now at the cottage and getting on I believe very well,' wrote
Phyllis, who thought Nora had also sold her pearls to help pay the
debts. In fact she had hocked them. She managed to charm the sternly
principled Waldorf into redeeming them for Christmas that year, an
event repeated annually just before each Christmas in a ritual of debt
and forgiveness.

Meanwhile if Nora was temporarily forced to curb her clothes
spending, there was nothing she could do about taxis. Taxis were
Nora's oxygen. Many of the drivers who worked the ranks at Sloane
Square and Knightsbridge were her friends and part-time chauffeurs.
She would keep them sometimes all day — waiting outside the department stores. The twinkling tradesmen were her friends too,
particularly the one-legged gardenia-seller at the Berkeley Hotel and
the doorman at the Ritz where Nora spent many hours, as Phyllis put
it, 'dashing about with her stage friends who are a poor lot'. From
there, heartlessly, she would have her bills sent back to Paul, just as she
sent her dressmakers' bills to Nancy at St James's Square.

Once again the family found work for Paul. Phyllis needed some
alterations on her home, 'but he is difficult to do things with', Phyllis
wrote to Bob, 'Not very alert. However when I went up the little
narrow stairs to his office of two little rooms it almost made me weep.
The little sign "Paul Phipps — Architect" on the door and Paul inside
struggling & Nora outside spending . . . I sh have throttled her long
ago.' Paul was a man of sweetness, affection and considerable erudition
but he 'lacked drama', according to family lore. And he couldn't begin
to handle Nora. Waldorf in some ways couldn't handle Nancy either,
but the difference was that nobody else would have stayed married to
Nancy. Optimism and a belief in personal improvement had carried
Paul forward, latterly with Christian Science, but the days were long

gone since Paul had described Nora, soon after their marriage, as an 'excellent economical housekeeper'.

When the sisters laughed amongst themselves at Nora's stories about having been unhappy at home, they were treating it as just another breathtaking lie. Any deep unhappiness was disguised by Nora's magic, her supreme enjoyment of life. 'She simply <u>cannot</u> tell the truth,' wrote Phyllis. 'I really don't know what to do about her. She told Anne Islington she never spent a penny on clothes, made everything she wore, never had been in love with Paul & only married him to get away from home where she was very unhappy. How can you cope with that! . . . Nora solemnly talks about the spirit and soul when all she is really interested in is her body & the telephone!'

19

The Right Hon.
Nancy Astor, MP

One night in early October 1919, after a solitary dinner of mutton and burgundy in his house in Brighton, Waldorf's father succumbed to a heart attack and died. (Ever concerned with his privacy, despite the absence of guests, he had locked himself in the lavatory.) Waldorf became Viscount Astor and his political career in the House of Commons came to an end. The by-election for the Sutton division of Plymouth would have to be fought within a few weeks. Apart from their emotional attachment to Plymouth, Waldorf and Nancy were by now so enmeshed in the constituency — their institutions and acts of charity provided its only credible social security system — that it was decided by the local Conservatives to put Nancy in his place. It was not a bold move towards feminist politics, but for the times it was just as imaginative and risky. Waldorf believed that he would be able to drop his peerage through legislation. Nancy in the meantime would be a stop-gap for Waldorf for the period of only one Parliament. Nancy, therefore, was not chosen, nor was she elected by the committee as a feminist, but as an active supporter of her husband. Nancy and Waldorf were not prepared for this. Nor was it at all certain that Nancy would be adopted and then elected. Votes for women over thirty had been enacted only the previous year, and following that the eligibility of women to stand as candidates. In the 1918 election the

Countess Markiewicz, Yeats's beautiful street-fighting friend from Dublin, had been elected as the first woman MP at Westminster but, like the seventy-three other Sinn Feiners, had refused the oath of allegiance. Voting for women candidates in a conventional contest was untried. There was intense speculation as to whether Nancy would stand: she and Waldorf considered it for many days before she accepted on 26 October 1919. She knew the city backwards by now, and the voters knew her for her dedication: she had taken over many of Waldorf's constituency tasks while he was working at the Ministry of Foods. But she had never put her own political profile on the line, or stood up to the heckling and harassment of a full-scale campaign. These were rowdy days in politics and the Barbican, at the heart of the constituency, was considered by most Plymothians outside it, a 'no-go' area. Tories, certainly, were not welcome. Waldorf had never canvassed in the tenements, at street level.

Nancy had had little direct contact with the women's suffrage movement and its often violent campaigns of looting and bombing that had outraged middle-class voters. She was not the vision its members had of their first representative. They imagined an activist, possibly a social worker, or at least a student of politics, who would almost certainly be Labour. Instead here was a social reformer from America — a 'Virginian aristocrat' as they saw her — bent on acts of charity, with a whimsical idea of some spiritual bond between Plymouth and its slums and the Virginia settlers; who spoke of herself as the returned Pilgrim.

It was indeed an odd choice of role for Nancy. Intelligent and intuitive as she was, she was badly informed; she had little grasp of the major issues of the day and neither the inclination nor ability to concentrate her mind on them. Her general ideas were largely based on emotional prejudice, or what seemed to her blindingly self-evident truths bolstered by her brittle religious dogma and sense of moral certainty. She was to swipe at Catholicism, for example, bluntly and with blind prejudice all her life. Protestantism, from her Virginian point of view, meant 'freedom'; Catholicism, the 'despotism' from which her ancestors had escaped. Particularly on the subject of foreign affairs she was capable, Bob Brand wrote, 'of coming out with the most surprising and unverified assertions'. She once wrote to Irene, forbidding her to support a Catholic candidate for the US Presidency, telling her 'America is founded on Protestantism' – ignoring the precepts of its Founding Fathers. After Catholics in her demonology came the French, partly because she believed – and no one could tell her otherwise – that France was a Catholic country and therefore benighted, and partly because of her dislike of 'the Latin mind' with its 'different set of moral values . . . which permits them to . . . boast of things that no other man could be anything but heartily ashamed of'. 'France,' she once told Bob Brand in summary, 'is just one big brothel.' Lower down on her list, '*generally* speaking, but not individually,' as Bob Brand wrote – a dispensation that also applied to Catholics and Frenchmen – came the Jewish race, although here Nancy's attitude varied little from the 'casual and endemic' anti-Semitism that existed at the time in the English circles in which she moved. Bob crossed out these two sentences from his short unpublished memoir that described her handicaps (Nancy was still alive): 'You could not say she was remarkable for judicial fairness, impartiality, strong reasoning power, capacity to reflect, capacity for philosophic doubt. For Nancy everything is black or white.' Even though these might not be disadvantages in a populist politician, it seemed that Nancy would inevitably be caught out.

Bob believed that nobody had a better understanding 'of human nature in the mass' than Nancy. The voters had seen signs of this during Waldorf's campaigns but Waldorf played down the performing side of her nature in the adoption meeting at Plymouth: 'I want to tell you straight away,' he said, 'if anybody thinks she is going into this contest in a lighthearted spirit not realising the responsibilities that will be hers, that person is mistaken.' He was proved right. 'I am not standing before you as a sex candidate,' Nancy declared in her first speech. 'If you want an MP who will be a repetition of the 600 other MPs don't vote for me. If you want a lawyer or if you want a pacifist don't elect me. If you can't get a fighting man take a fighting woman. If you want a Bolshevist or a follower of Mr. Asquith don't elect me. If you want a party hack don't elect me. Surely we have outgrown party ties. I have. The war has taught us that there is a greater thing than parties, and that is the State.' Her first opponents were Isaac Foot (father of the future Labour leader, Michael Foot), standing on the Asquithian Liberal ticket, and William Gay the Labour candidate. Waldorf was forced publicly to retract Nancy's opening broadside against the latter, as the campaign got under way. She strayed from the script, libellously suggesting that Gay was a failure in his profession, as a manager of the Co-op.

At the height of the campaign Nancy was driven by a well-known cab driver, a fearsome Plymothian called Churchward, in his horse-drawn vehicle decked with Tory red, white and blue rosettes, with Waldorf, her chief of staff and speechwriter, often by her side. She looked wonderful in her pearls, her hat at a tilt, with immaculate shoes and white gloves. She deliberately dressed up, rather than down, judging correctly that this was what was expected of a millionaire's wife. Under stern advice she kept to broad issues where possible. Although Waldorf had tried to train and brief her on the more techni-cal topics, she would quickly lose the thread in favour of basic attitudes. 'I am sick and tired of hearing about the common man,' she declared, her voice high, musical, insistent. 'I want the uncommon man. It's the uncommon man who has been responsible for every step this country has taken,' or 'the Socialists believe in equality; the man who starts from scratch and gets to the top they now tell us is a public danger. I suppose they want the man who starts from scratch and keeps on scratching.' She quoted from the Bible freely. Wild cheering was reported when Nancy used it to attack the opposition, 'And do not forget our Lord said he preferred a harlot any day to a hypocrite . . .'

Nancy was naturally skilled at evasion and turning an awkward-ness to her advantage. 'I have so often watched you manoeuvre a heckler slightly off his question and then reply to and score off a question which in fact he had never put,' Waldorf wrote to her many years later. She wrote to Dana Gibson at the start of the campaign, 'This honour has been thrust upon me. I didn't want to do it but

Waldorf wanted me to & our 11 years work would have gone fut . . .
Only one thing was queer and v funny. The woman who asked me if I
would make divorces as easy here as in the USA. She did it to insult me
& she looked like nothing on earth. I leant forward and with a most
sympathetic smile said "Madam I am sorry that you are in trouble.'"
(One newspaper reported it, perhaps more accurately, as 'Sister, are
you in trouble too?') 'It was no answer,' wrote Nancy, 'but the whole
audience laughed for fully 5 minutes. Old Sir Henry Jones the
Professor of Moral Philosophy at Glasgow nearly rolled off the platform. It may not sound funny but it was. I am thankful to God for
having put the answer into my mouth. It came as a bolt from Heaven
both to me and the audience. Oh Dana I don't want to go to the House
of Commons. I wd far rather have a baby – perhaps I shall do both. "Mr
Speaker I beg leave to adjourn. I feel that I am doing a double duty to
this country."'

What startled the voters and the press ('Lady Astor has voters
gasping by the pepness of her campaign' one sub-headline ran in the
USA) was Nancy's extraordinary courage on the hustings, her wading
into slum areas where she was not welcome and winning over audiences, and above all the speed and wit of her rejoinders. They lose their
impact translated on to the page now. They miss her particular inflection, the comic timing, the surprise, the cheekiness. They miss too, the
image of Nancy, small and alert, looking beautiful in her challenging
soap-box pose, her hands on her hips, in a sea of faces, all of whom
seem to be laughing or smiling, rapt in attention. She was natural and
direct with her audiences and it was this that blew down their defences.
They had never seen anything like it from politicians of the ruling class,
certainly never from a Tory wife. Contemporaries describe the electric
effect of these meetings. It is hard to imagine a politician now, wagging
her finger at a persistent heckler and saying, 'Now just you shut up' and
taking the audience with her.

Most people saw immediately the comedy beneath the half-insults
and provocations with which Nancy greeted people, shouting across
the street, 'I want that baby!' 'Buzzard' or 'goose' were appellations of

endearment. But not to everybody. For most of her career her constituency minders had the task of trying to muzzle Nancy when she got
carried away; using codes if she was treading on toes, swiping at
Catholics to a Catholic constituent, for example. 'Tell Mr Smith how
you and Bernard Shaw got stuck in the lift in Moscow,' they would butt
in. Much time was spent on the telephone, calming ruffled feathers,
drafting letters of apology and conciliation, which Nancy willingly
signed, oblivious of the damage she had done.

Phyllis helped canvass the voters and wrote to Bob Brand on 10
November: 'The campaign seems to be going well, always overflowing
meetings, but the Liberal opponent has hit Nancy's weak spot when he
asks her to state what she stands for, Tariff Reform etc . . . Last night
Nannie . . . was not at her best, and there was a large gathering of
middle-class serious-minded people out to hear facts, and facts are not
her strong point. However they all say she will get in − she stands
campaigning like General Lee's old horse Traveller, who switched his
tail furiously at the smell of gunpowder. She is excellent with the
hecklers in the poorer districts and flattens them every time.' Phyllis
dreaded that Irene might give interviews in America: 'It really makes
me almost seasick to see the Langhorne sisters in print now. I despise
it and always have.' The reputation for charm and beauty would no
doubt seem frivolous now that Nancy was discussing issues of state.
'I'm sure if N is elected,' Phyllis wrote to Bob, 'it will be both her and
Waldorf's work here these last ten years; without it she wouldn't have
a ghost of a chance, nor would any woman.'

The declaration came on 28 November: Lady Astor 14,495
votes; Mr Gay 9,292 votes; Mr Foot, 4,139 votes. There was wild
cheering and Nancy was hauled off through the streets in the hired
carriage pulled by her supporters. She appeared on the balcony, wise-
cracking, but buckling with emotion. At Cliveden the staff lit bonfires
along the drive to welcome her home.

On the morning of 1 December Nancy went down to Parliament
with Waldorf to be introduced to the House by the prime minister, Lloyd
George, and Arthur Balfour. She took Bobbie, now aged twenty-one

and standing several inches taller than his mother, extraordinarily good-looking, dressed like a young blade in a pin-striped suit and white shirt, his hair slicked back with oil. Nora and Phyllis came and sat in the spectators' gallery.

Nancy, aged forty, had designed the sober costume, the one she would wear with variations for twenty-five years, to suit this parliament of men, where at least one of them, Austen Chamberlain, still wore a top hat in the House. She wore an elegantly cut black suit, long in jacket and skirt, her white shirt-collar spread across her shoulders, and a three-cornered hat. She looked serious and demure for the photographers, eyelids lowered in humility. Waldorf had been doing some strenuous instructing and lion-taming on the subject of procedure and etiquette, but at the first pause in the ceremony, after Lloyd George, Arthur Balfour and Nancy had bowed in ragged formation to the Speaker, she began chatting to her Cliveden weekend friends on the front bench. When she reappeared to take her seat, having spent some time looking for a lavatory that she could use, Austen Chamberlain, the Chancellor, was denouncing a scheme for Premium Bonds. Nancy began clapping his performance until someone on the bench restrained her. She was heard saying 'Hear, Hear'. She cast her first vote for the party.

She made her maiden speech the following February, 1920, opposing a bill to relax the wartime drinking restrictions. 'I am not pressing for prohibition,' she said in the House, 'I am far too intelligent for that.' Even so it was political dynamite — and Nancy realized this. She told the House, 'I know it was very difficult for some honourable members to receive the first lady MP,' (Hon. Members: 'Not at all'), 'but I assure you that it was as difficult for a woman to come in. To address you now on this vexed question of drink is harder still. It takes a bit of courage to dare to do it. But I do dare.'

Prohibition had been instituted in America in 1918, and Nancy and Waldorf approved of it. For Britain they advocated state purchase of liquor, not prohibition. But she was passionate on the subject — Chillie, Harry and Keene Langhorne had a lot to answer for. They could scarcely have imagined that their drinking bouts would lead to restrictive legislation in the mother of parliaments. But this – to raise the pub-drinking age to eighteen – was to be Nancy's only legislative achievement. She managed to position herself by saying that it was parental drunkenness that she was against, and its effect on the children. Even so, for an American couple to wade into English politics on the drink issue at all, with all the Tory distiller interests of their own party lined up in the House of Commons, was considered politically crazy by almost everyone else. But Waldorf backed Nancy and the principle at the risk of losing voters. They both believed that the distillers' representatives – who Nancy called 'The Beerage' – were, like the peerage, standing against progress.

The feminists had assumed that it would take all their considerable energy to get their first member elected. Instead Nancy had arrived almost by chance, and many of them regretted it. They couldn't make her out. Some of them saw the election in Plymouth as a circus, in which Nancy had made no more than generalizations about her commitment to bettering the lot of women and children. And since women had acquired the vote there was a great deal of legislation, specialized and otherwise, to put through Parliament. But she quickly attracted their attention, partly because the press was mesmerized by every move she made.

Then, early in 1920, she came up against Horatio Bottomley. It was largely a defensive battle, but Baroness Stocks, the educationalist, then a leading feminist, remembered it as a major moral victory and the moment that Nancy became their champion. 'One of the first unexpected things she did,' she wrote, 'was to engage in open, savage warfare with the most corrupt element in the House of Commons.' Bottomley, proprietor and editor of a reactionary, muck-raking journal called *John Bull*, and himself a paragon of unpleasantness, had cowed many MPs into a state of timidity through his litigiousness. Sullen, jowled, with a furtive expression and often inebriated, he was a man most of his colleagues avoided. He was a particular *bête noire* of the feminist movement. 'It really needed great courage to get in his way,' wrote Lady Stocks, 'and that courage Lady Astor, it seemed, did not lack.'

Like other diehards in her own party, Bottomley wanted to see Nancy fall flat on her face. Nancy's first vote, against the Premium Bond scheme, which Bottomley supported, gave him bad publicity which irritated him. He had also appointed himself exclusively as the 'soldier's friend', a role that Nancy had usurped as the Florence Nightingale of Cliveden.

Later that year, Bottomley saw his opportunity in a debate on the Divorce Law Reform Bill, which sought to extend the grounds for divorce to desertion after three years, in cases involving cruelty, habitual drunkenness, incurable insanity and life imprisonment. It was opposed by one of the leading right-wingers, Ronald McNeill. It was also opposed, to everyone's surprise, by Nancy. She voted against easing the divorce laws without consulting her women peers or the evidence, asserting arbitrarily that women did not want it; that they saw it as inimical to the preservation of the family, and as something that would be exploited only by men. A Labour Party women's conference passed an immediate resolution declaring that Nancy had no right to speak for women in this manner. Despite her own and Phyllis's divorces, Nancy was to be merciless about divorce in her own family and outside it. It was the Bible again. Perhaps, too, she remembered the disgrace she had felt in America; and how it had brought both Phyllis and herself across the Atlantic, looking for absolution. If Robert Shaw had not committed adultery would she still be married to him? Or would another way have been found?

Bottomley had dug up two embarrassing items. The first was a false entry in Debrett's under Waldorf's name, claiming that in 1906 he married 'Nancy . . . widow of Robert Gould Shaw'. It was unlike Waldorf to have forsaken his stern principles in this manner. It was never explained, but looked as if it had been inserted to help his career. Bottomley repeated a report from the *New York Herald* of 1903, which suggested that Nancy and Robert Shaw had illegally colluded in their divorce. It was untrue and certainly actionable. Bottomley hammered at these points in *John Bull* and put out street posters proclaiming 'Lady Astor's Divorce'.

He waited for the Astors to sue. Instead Nancy said nothing. When she came into the House for the first time after Bottomley's broadside she was applauded. Two months later she addressed her constituency, where she was given a vote of confidence. Bottomley renewed his attack but he had already lost the publicity battle and the story died. Two years later he was sent to jail for financial improprieties. It was seen by the feminists as a rout. He had picked on Nancy and lost. Lady Stocks wrote, 'If this particular embroilment must have occasioned Lady Astor a measure of distress, it must have also brought its consolations. It delighted the feminist organisations.' The Divorce Bill was dropped. Nancy's throwing her weight against it was considered, at the time, a deciding factor in its demise.

But Bottomley had affected Nancy more than he realized. The incident triggered in her a severe bout of depression similar to the kind that had assailed her soon after her marriage to Waldorf. In those days she had taken to her bed; now she fought it with a furious programme of travel and public speaking, with Christian Science and, her other anti-dote to fear, rigid self-discipline.

The real root of Nancy's crisis, and one that none of her biographers have detected, was the almost overwhelming effort of courage and will needed to stand up to the hostility – petty, persistent and often vicious – from her male colleagues in the House of Commons. And it came mostly from her own party. She was lying diplomatically when, after twenty-five years in Parliament, she said in her farewell speech: 'I don't think any assembly in the world could have been more tolerant of a foreign born woman, as I was, who fought against so many things they believed in.' She certainly hadn't forgotten the bullying animosity. Shortly before she died, sitting with her son David, 'soliloquising' and thinking it was obvious what she meant, she said, 'If I'd only known I never would have done it.' What was she referring to? 'The House of Commons, of course,' she said, 'If I'd known how much men would hate it I never would have dared do it.'

The early days were the worst, a time, she admitted, of 'unbearable strain'. There was an unwritten consensus among the Tories that a female MP was by nature wrong. The idea was to freeze her out, cause the maximum embarrassment and humiliation, and so discourage constituencies from adopting other women candidates. Tories that she knew well turned away from her, including her two brothers-in-law, John Astor and Bertie Spender Clay. The males in the House would prove that Nancy – and by implication all other women – would be unable to stand the work. They refused to give her a seat at the corner of a bench, forcing her to climb over the men's legs. At first they pretended that they couldn't find a lavatory for her and made her walk to the far end of the building. Before a debate on venereal disease they put the most graphic photographs they could find in the lobby, hoping to embarrass her. They made speeches that they considered unsuitable for a woman's ears. 'She realized what they were doing,' said David Astor. 'So she decided she would sit through this debate to the end no matter what they said or did. She would be damned if she would let them shock her into leaving. But it was one of her toughest tests.'

In the early 1990s Margaret Thatcher unveiled a plaque to Nancy in St James's Square, on behalf of a group promoting more women MPs. She said, in her speech, that it was hard enough for her as opposition leader and prime minister to put up with the hostility in the House, and she knew how much worse it must have been for Nancy; that had she not been a 'fighter' she could never have done it. Margaret Wintringham joined Nancy as a Liberal MP in 1921, taking over her husband's seat, after he died, in a by-election. The second woman in the House later told David Astor that the feeling of hatred in the chamber was so great that if Nancy wasn't there she couldn't sit there alone and had to leave. She couldn't imagine, she said, how Nancy had borne it by herself for two years.

Winston Churchill was her famous antagonist. Their exchange: 'If I was your wife I'd put poison in your coffee.' 'And if I was your husband I'd drink it' is quoted almost as often as Harold Macmillan's 'Events, dear boy, events' by people who know nothing else about her. Such prejudice in the House of Commons was still thriving in the 1950s when Lord Hugh Cecil, one of Lord Salisbury's younger brothers, wrote: 'My experience as I say, is not large enough to make me sure, but as at present advised, I should say they [women] are neither good at ratiocinative argument nor emotional appeal . . .' They made men self-conscious, he said, and 'banished the instincts of combat'. Towards the millennium, women MPs in Britain, despite their large numbers, are still protesting about their rough treatment by their male colleagues in Parliament. The tactics, it would seem, have not changed.

Nancy was undoubtedly an irritant beyond the fact of her gender. However much she tried she never got used to, or obeyed, the rules of the House of Commons, or its etiquette. Two years after her election she wrote to Irene: 'Well I am certainly a worker. It really almost means slaving for the time being. I sit for hours in the H o C. trying to learn its ways and precedents and trying to get the old gentlemen used to me! It takes great patience but it's not boring one bit.' She found it impossible to get used to addressing the Speaker and not the members. One exasperated Member, borrowing her direct approach, shouted across, 'Mind your manners'. 'I won't,' she said. 'The noble Lady ought to withdraw,' said the Speaker. 'He asked for it,' she replied. To another fellow Conservative, who opposed her drink bill, she said, 'You're the village donkey and the House of Commons is the village where you bray.' She was forced to withdraw the remark.

Nancy's technique of 'debate' was usually an audible commentary on a speech she disagreed with and continual interruptions until the Speaker gave way. She was proud of this and once told Bob, 'I got in a good interruption last night. You should have heard it', making him wonder whether that was really the point of being an MP. When a pompous backbencher got up to say, 'My opinion, for what it's worth . . .', Nancy interrupted: 'Well, what do you think it's worth?' Another MP was telling the House, 'When I was walking in my garden, this is the question I asked myself . . .' when Nancy interrupted, 'And I bet you got a silly answer.'

Nancy felt that these guerrilla tactics were what was expected of a Virginian – a 'born fighter'. She once got up to say that she had been listening for some time to the Honourable Member, who replied, also breaking the rules, 'We heard you listening.' Her own speeches, according to a former clerk to the House, 'were often so persistently provocative that they became dialogues with a series of interrupters'. 'Unlimited effrontery' was what one campaign worker observed of Nancy's technique on the hustings, and she brought it to the House of Commons where, to make any impact, wrote John Grigg, 'she had to avoid at all costs being assimilated into the system and so becoming, in effect, an honorary man'. No other political woman of her time, wrote Grigg, possessed these skills: '. . . her capital achievement was to defy the conventions without forfeiting, indeed while enhancing, a popularity that was by no means confined to her own sex'.

But this aggression, with its added air of unqualified moral certainty, further annoyed some of the Members, infuriating them in the second half of her career. Churchill, in particular, took every opportunity to rebuff her. She in turn intensely disapproved of his style and values; the braggadocio, the militarism, the cult of drink. But Churchill was quick enough to get the better of her. One day Nancy untypically asked Churchill why he kept up his hostility to her. He replied: 'Because I find a woman's intrusion into the House of Commons as embarrassing as if she burst into my bathroom when I had nothing with which to defend myself, not even a sponge.' Nancy replied, a little feebly, 'Winston you're not handsome enough to have worries of that kind.'

'It was Lady Astor,' wrote Harold Nicolson, 'who from the very day of her introduction [to the House of Commons], taught her contemporaries that the expansion of women's liberty could be achieved not by mute acquiescence, but by voluble pugnacity. She taught her sex to fight . . . she made no distinction at all between Prime Ministers or back-bench mutes, between Conservative magnates or young Socialists from South Wales; to her friendly banter they all fell victims although her chaff often irritated, and occasionally wounded, it was directed impartially to all sides.'

According to Lady Stocks, at the end of her first three years, Nancy had come to be seen as a most unlikely prize by the feminists. She had won favour, to their surprise, with her stance for 'a good feminist

puritanism', on the question of drink and sex and 'all the right ideas
about an equal moral standard for men and women'. 'Fate,' wrote
Lady Stocks, had 'improved on their own limited imaginations . . . they
were by now awake to the fact that Lady Astor was really doing all the
work they dreamed a woman MP would do, and more than one woman
could have been expected to do.'

What her feminist observers saw was a tornado – hopelessly
undisciplined and unconcentrated, but extraordinarily effective in the
House on behalf of the issues they cared about. Nancy had the advantage of a large, privately financed secretarial staff. She was also wise
enough to take expert advice, especially from her political secretary,
Mrs Oliver Strachey, an astute politician and Parliamentary Secretary
to the National Union of Women's Suffrage Societies. It was not only
Nancy's gall that fascinated the feminists but also her ability to stand up
to the battering she took in the House. They were impressed that she
was embarking on an independent programme of social reform, often
opposing the Tories. When it came to legislation she behaved more like
a socialist than a liberal Tory.

Nancy later boasted that the *only* clever thing she had done in her
life was to invite some of the leading political women, most of them
Labour, to tea at St James's Square soon after her election. 'Sitting at their
feet' she told them that she was ignorant when it came to the details of
politics but that she would act as their mouthpiece in Parliament, if they
would tell her what she should be advocating. By harnessing herself to
these Labour intellectuals Nancy said she had acquired 'the best brains
trust of any M.P., including the Prime Minister'.

In Parliament she agitated for basic reforms: for nursery schools,
votes for women at twenty-one, the subsidized provision of children's
footwear, improved treatment of juvenile offenders and women in
prison, the protection of married women (who lost their citizenship if
they married a foreigner), equal guardianship for mothers and fathers,
the abolition of the death penalty for expectant mothers (she was also
against any death penalty), and slum clearance. She believed in state
health-care and town planning, advocating a massive housing programme

'as important as building battleships in 1914'; she also advocated raising the school-leaving age. She supported the Trade Boards, to protect workers from exploitation and employers from being undercut; she supported the international eight-hour day. She tried to bring in a bill preventing prostitutes from being convicted on the evidence of a single policeman. She also answered all appeals from her constituents, or from anyone who came to see her in the lobby. Nothing was too much trouble. 'I don't like people I can't do anything for,' Nancy declared.

Nancy won four elections at Plymouth in the 1920s. One of the bitterest, in 1922, was won by 3,000 votes, as the Lloyd George coalition broke up and the Liberals went into temporary eclipse, giving the Tories their first overall majority since 1906. In 1923, in a straight fight with Labour, her majority was reduced to 2,500 and produced the first, short-lived minority Labour government in 1924 under Ramsay MacDonald. Most of the Conservatives in the West Country lost their seats and Nancy was exasperated that her party had, as she saw it, given away power by standing in the way of social reform. 'I'm not a conservative really & am sick of the whole lot of them,' she wrote to Irene, 'They are as stupid as owls.'

In the Tory landslide of late 1924, she regained her 5,000 majority. The closest she came to defeat, with a majority of only 200 votes, was in the turbulent 1929 election, after which Labour, again under Ramsay MacDonald, formed a government without an overall majority.

Many of the political meetings, which provided riotous popular entertainment, were held in the open on the fish quays next to the Barbican. Nancy would set up like a street preacher, standing on a box, and draw in the crowds. A *Daily Express* reporter recorded one of her rougher moments in the 1929 election, held in the wake of the General Strike: 'She stood completely alone in the courtyard of the worst tenement of the worst street in Plymouth, a Communist stronghold, and glowered at balcony on balcony above her packed with more than a hundred shouting, shrieking, hostile women. "So you are a pack of Bolshies eh?" she challenged, waving her umbrella threateningly.

"Better get away Lady Astor," I warned, for a hefty woman with sacking over her head was reaching for a cabbage. She spun round fiercely. "Leave this to me." A man caught her roughly by the shoulder, and she raised the umbrella. He ran like a hare, and then she faced the crowd. "Too proud for the working woman, am I?" She laughed merrily and struck an attitude, nose perked comically, and danced affectedly up and down outside the tenement.' Nancy then harangued the Labour candidate in front of them, 'Twenty years you have known me and this man is brought against me . . .' The *Express* reported that, after a moment's silence, 'they cheered her, cheered her like mad and as her car left the place roared and roared again: "Good old Nancy!"' The triumphant farewell seems far-fetched – this was the right-wing Beaverbrook press reporting. But the strutting about was pure Nancy – it went with the tap-dancing and the somersaults.

She was joined in Parliament that year, 1929, by fourteen women MPs, ten of whom were Labour. On the first day of swearing-in Nancy invited them to lunch. They discovered to their amazement that, as one of them put it, 'We were there to be told what we had to do. And what we had to do was to forget that we had been elected as representatives of the Labour Party, and its ideals and plans, and act, henceforth, as part of a Feminist phalanx. We were to form the backbone of a Women's Party.' It was an odd, slightly scatty idea and when Nancy discovered she wasn't putting it across successfully she began shouting. Some shouted back. She took it well, and they discovered that this headlong, bullying mode of attack was Nancy's way of making friends.

Women, she told her colleagues at that meeting, should act independently of men. Women were innately superior and prepared to be unorthodox and unconventional, to flout the rules to get what they wanted. Men, by contrast, hated stepping out of line, preferring to 'stand in rows together like soldiers'. Her audience, however, found it hard to accept Nancy's attempt to batter them into conformity with the blazing intensity of her convictions, and her passionate idea of Goodness.

Dedicating another monument to Nancy in 1995, Michael Foot, left-wing Labour intellectual *par excellence*, made many generous tributes to Nancy from across the party divide. He talked of 'the excitement and loveliness of Lady Astor, which is a unique thing in this century'. He had in mind, to a large extent, Nancy's extraordinary relationship with Plymouth. Perhaps no one in this century has had a more intimate relationship with a British constituency. She knew, or had memorized, an astonishing number of the faces and names of its 250,000 inhabitants and once she was on their side she was ruthless in pursuing their interests, applying all the authority of her wealth and powerful connections on their behalf. Her 'terrible' crusading desire to help people found infinite scope in Plymouth. It was the abiding passion in her life and a place where she felt completely at ease. This relationship may have stemmed from her romantic imagination: Devonians were really Virginians in need. But it translated into solid political fact. For this diminutive bejewelled figure to have held such a rough constituency for twenty-five years in those volatile inter-war years of capital versus Labour, of coalitions, landslides and watersheds, is proof of the success of the relationship. But it required unique qualities and no British woman or Tory man could possibly have achieved it.

The real key to Nancy's success was her unique ability to break down the British class barriers, particularly in a 'service town', a big naval base where, as one resident told me, 'people were used to standing to attention and saluting'. It had never happened before, and has hardly happened since. The memory of this explains why, as Nancy's great-nephew, I was treated to a visit of what was almost an all-party delegation of local politicians, dressed as if for an official occasion, and all of them too young to have known Nancy really well. None of them had lived through the campaigns of the 1920s. They came to talk to me for half an hour and, quite simply, to pay their respects.

In Plymouth in the late 1990s the memory of Nancy is as indelible and as vivid as the bombing that pulverized the city for seventeen months in 1941–2. The city has two icons: Sir Frances Drake and Lady Astor, although strangely no statue exists of their first woman MP. There are remaining monuments, particularly the airy complex of walkways and malls that fills the bombed-out city centre, a 1950s style of British 'modern' architecture — now looking worn and depressed — that seems to banish the residents to the edges of the city. This is Waldorf's odd legacy. He was elected the all-party Lord Mayor throughout the war — local politics were suspended — and fought with the local shop-owners, while the war was still going on, to get the city rebuilt on a new model to be drawn up by Sir Patrick Abercrombie, the leading town planner of the time. Waldorf can hardly be blamed for the result. There are place-names like Mirador Lane. There is Virginia House, the first community centre in Plymouth built in 1925, where women could meet together on neutral ground, outside their homes. It was hugely popular with its dances and movie shows. The nursery school Nancy built in the same year, on the fresh-air principle and without central heating, is still so popular that parents put their children's names down at birth. It was so well made that almost all the fittings, including the rows of miniature lidless lavatories in their separate cubicles, and toddler-high hand basins, are still in perfect working order. Nearby is the first football field Plymouth possessed — an Astor donation. Nancy's house at Elliott Terrace, on the Hoe, now belongs to the city, complete with all its furniture; and one of her huge diamond necklaces hangs from the necks of succeeding mayoresses.

On a hill overlooking the sea stand the ninety-six houses the Astors built — the Mount Gould estate spread widely over the land, their biggest visible achievement. Although they gave large donations and bought buildings, the Astors didn't pay directly for these projects. After 1919 the Exchequer provided subsidies to housing associations for the first time and the rest of the money was raised by what Nancy called 'agitatin'' the local authority and bullying her rich friends for low-interest loans. Nancy believed in harnessing private initiative, not depending on the state for social security, except for health-care for women and children. That was where she stopped seeming like a socialist. Despite her constant chiding of Conservatives for their diehard attitude to social reform she was shocked by the welfare state of post-1945.

Fred Brimacombe was born in the Barbican and remembered, as a child, leafleting for Nancy in her later elections. He remembered, through his father, too, how 'you would find she had organized a way out of people's troubles'. Coal, bedding, food was provided. But the reason that she was so popular in the working-class districts, he said, was that 'she talked our own language'. 'She was a speaker who could hold a crowd,' he said. 'She'd toss the talk back and forth; she was never serious or solemn. No one else was like that in those days.' Before her, people didn't have the opportunity to meet the politicians who would help them. Such informality was an utter novelty. 'I've never seen the like of her,' he said, 'and I never will.' Only an American, according to Fred Brimacombe, could have ignored the class distinctions, or treated them with such a lack of self-consciousness.

Undoubtedly Nancy was a different person in Plymouth. She led there a separate life to that at Cliveden and St James's Square. In Plymouth she had, by her standards, almost no staff. She rarely wrote anything down. Most of her work was done on her feet, walking the constituency. And it was on these walks, she confided later, that she would have to screw up her greatest courage – not against verbal or physical assault but against cats. Nancy had a deep, pathological phobia about cats. An approaching cat would take on the menace of a poisonous snake or a rabid monkey. At Cliveden the gamekeeper was instructed to shoot feral strays, and caterwauling, copulating felines at the back of St James's Square would be attacked by Nancy throwing lumps of coal at them and shouting. She described the terror of walking up narrow staircases in the Barbican, feeling cat fur brushing against her leg, and the exercise of will required to stop herself screaming. Going down to a hostile House of Commons, wrangling a hostile crowd, was nothing, she said, compared to that ordeal.

Meanwhile one of the most obscure political elections had taken place in Virginia. Buck Langhorne, by 1919 Chillie's sole surviving son, and the only one of his children left in Virginia, had been elected to the Virginia State Legislature. Buck's education had ended as a young man when he was expelled from the Virginia Military Institute for some prank involving taking a pig on to the parade ground. He was now thirty-five but 'really a child of about 3', according to Phyllis. He was also extremely popular, even famous in rural Virginia, which was how he had won this election. Nancy was outraged and was quoted publicly saying so. How could Buck Langhorne be elected to any assembly, when her Aunt Liz Lewis, Chillie's sister, the highly educated suffragette, still didn't have the vote?

Buck lived on a farm, and in a flaking colonnaded house his father had built him when he married Edith Forsythe. It was forty miles from Mirador at Esmont, along the James River. Later Chillie reflected on Buck, this patrimonial gift to him and his absences: 'Dammit he's the only man I ever met who inherited a self-running farm.' Buck, too, had the touch on his lung that had killed his elder brothers, aggravated in the same way by a fondness for moonshine whisky and for taking off into the mountains in his broken-down Ford on sprees and sleepless hillbilly trips that lasted days at a time. While Chillie was alive, his sisters accused him of exaggerating his illness to their father and called him 'Poppa's little boy' although his illness was irreversible. But they loved Buck and so did almost everybody else: he was known all over the state 'from the Shenandoah Valley to Buckingham County, from Richmond to Lynchburg' as a result of his terrible restlessness and his passion for company.

He had a long face, a large, loose mouth, freckled skin, light blue eyes and talked in a country Virginian dialect that was often indistinguishable from the accents of his black farm workers. 'He used to come by Mirador for lunch,' his niece Nancy Lancaster recalled, 'and yell as if he was calling cattle "OOOH Nancy"'. He even told Civil War jokes from his parents' generation (about his friend Sam Goodloe's Uncle Silas surrendering to the bull frogs in the Chickahominy swamp, for example, 'because he'd been raised too high on the mountain to ever hear a bull frog and thought they were Hessian soldiers [German mercenaries from the War of Independence] hired by the Yankees'). Buck would open up with phrases like 'I betcha a million dollars', or 'I declare 'fore Gracious'. Phyllis described his talk 'exactly like Amos and Andy particularly when Amos was making excuses to his wife about why he couldn't come home'.

'Buck simply couldn't bear to stay at home,' said Nancy Lancaster. Not only were his wife Edith and his four children left alone for long periods while Buck was visiting, but when he was at home he was quarantined from them in an adjoining bungalow because of his tuberculosis. He was therefore a remote figure in their early life. Buck had to live with the story, everyone loved to tell, of the night Edith began reading to the children 'Our Father which art in Heaven,' when one of them asked 'Where's Daddy gone now?' Phyllis claimed he had an excuse: 'Edith weighs easily 175 pounds & looked so fat and hot I honestly had a feeling of sympathy for Buck & his wandering habits.'

Usually Buck had gone with his bosom friend Sam Goodloe, one of four brothers, 'the Goodloe Boys' who lived at Acton, at the eastern end of Rock Fish Gap in the Blue Ridge. Buck and the Goodloe brothers were united by a love of hunting — as well as talking and drinking. They had a hunt club in Buckingham County — 10,000 acres under lease with a many-bedroomed hunting shack — where they would chase deer with hounds, shoot quail and wild turkey. Buck and Sam Goodloe would go up there for days with their friends. Buck knew every bootlegger and mountaineer for miles around and would defend their interests as a witness in the local courthouse since, of course, he knew all the judges. They also travelled far and wide in the pursuit of female company. Holman Willis, a Senator for Virginia and a patron of Buck's political career, recalled that they both 'rode like Arabs and attended all fox hunts and as many of the places where there were good looking women assembled as they could reach'.

Sam's nephew Goodloe Saunders, who still hunted in Buckingham County when I met him, said of Buck: 'He just had a personality you couldn't beat. He was the most outgoing fella I have ever known and he was a good hunter, he was a good friend. He was a very poor poker player. Terrible. He just didn't know how to pike or how to quit. But anyhow everybody loved him and he had a world of friends.'

Buck stood for election to the Legislature for Albemarle County

because he believed that public service was the duty of a country gentleman. He campaigned with another boon companion, Laurie Pitts.
Fired up on applejack (brewed from the Albemarle Pippin) they ended
their blazing campaign in neighbouring Nelson County outside their
constituency, where many of the locals voted for Buck anyway, adding
his name to their ballot paper on the grounds, as one of them said, 'I
always wanted to do something for Mr. Buck.'

The only recorded political exchange from the cut and thrust of
Buck's campaign was about a tricky area of taxation in which Buck
promised, 'Taxation is a matter that every man must decide for himself.'
Perhaps because of this Buck became a member, and at one time
Chairman, of the Finance Committee in his district – spending and
levying the money for his community. Goodloe Saunders remembers
the benefits that accrued to the taxpayers: 'We used to give him hell
'cos when he first started he was the first legislator to have proved and
fought for a bond issue on roads, and he got the road from Scottsville
[where Buck lived] to Charlottesville built under a bond issue. That
hurt him a lot because people don't like bond issues. He had a road to
Richmond, to the Legislature, but he wanted to get out of his place to
Charlottesville! Nothing else. And he got it through and we've been
years paying that thing off. But that was quite a feat for a blond headed
boy.' Otherwise Buck was often absent from the legislature. Senator
Willis remembers covering up for him many times, in return for which
he got crucial support from Buck on House Bills. When canvassing, said
Willis, 'Buck's answer to the question of what the Bill was about was
"How in the hell do you expect me to know? Holman Willis wants it."'

Clinton Harris, Buck's delightful valet and butler of many years'
service, was still living in Charlottesville, aged eighty-five, when he
recalled his time with Buck. He went into service as a bow-legged
orphan of eleven; his grandmother had handed him over on the steps of
the Green Mountain Post Office in 1912 for $1.50, and Clinton and
Buck were inseparable from then on. 'He was uncle Buck's personal
servant, you might say,' said Goodloe Saunders. 'He didn't do a damn
thing but everyone liked Clint.' Clinton agreed with the first half of the

assessment. He was proud to have been part of an era during which, he claimed, there was nothing for *anybody* to do. 'It was just like a big homecoming all the time.'

His own personal duties were a little more onerous. 'Keep the porches clean. Keep his shoes clean. Take a tray to him and see that the liquor decanter was always filled up. It was a dry State, wasn't nobody allowed to have a *Coca-Cola*, but Mr Buck carried a five or ten gallon keg o' liquor in the car with him wherever he went.' (This was often moonshine liquor, pure white whisky, also known as 'Squirrel's milk', brewed in the mountains.) Clinton claimed that Buck was so gregarious that whenever they saddled up horses and went touring the district, the horse would stop whenever another human being came in sight. 'The horse knows it's time for a conversation and would just pull off and stop. He didn't have to *tell* the horse.'

When it came down to what Clinton called 'the real nitty gritty' they were all friends: 'Miss Nancy, Miss Irene, Miss Nora, Miss Phyllis. We were all the same. It was just the feeling of a personal relationship. Everybody respected each other, respected the ladies and the ladies respected the gentlemen. There wasn't any playboys back in those days.'

Some people, especially in the Legislature, thought of Buck as a playboy, but Clinton didn't see it that way. When Buck went on sprees he was working: 'Mr. Sam Goodloe and Mr. Gordon Smith and Mr. Hawthorn Goodloe, they would get together two or three times a week, play cards and just have a good time, drinkin' and talkin' and passin' laws concerned about the State.' Businessmen from the Dupont powder company would come down to the Monticello Hotel – the centre of Buck's social life – and 'take a little drink. They started around lunchtime and would go on throughout the day. Everybody was happy and there wasn't any problem, wasn't any *strain*.' Clinton remembers carrying the local judge home after a cocktail party organized by Buck outside the local courthouse where Clinton had put up a card table for the drinks. 'It was just like a big family.'

Clinton remembered the dust storm in the early 1930s that lasted for three or four years. It was like a continual heavy fog and the drought curled up the stunted crops in the fields. 'That's when Mr. Langhorne started looking after the poor people. Chestnut Grove, Blenheim, Esmont and a portion of Buckingham County. He take care of them. Mr Langhorne used to send me to the James River market and the Scottsville flour mill to load this huge truck up with all kinds of food.' (Much of this charity was, in fact, a direct donation from Nancy and Waldorf Astor.) 'And he says "Clint, use your own judgement, we don't want nobody to be hungry."'

20

Nancy the Ringmaster

Bernard Shaw said that Cliveden 'was like no other country house in the world . . . you meet everybody worth meeting, rich or poor at Cliveden'. For Shaw it was more like a public theatre and it became, as did Nancy, a rich source of material for his plays. Compared to conventions of English upper-class life Waldorf and Nancy, 'a violently radical conservative, a recklessly unladylike Lady', as Shaw described her, were a very unconventional couple. They were high-minded, religious, Anglo-American in outlook, teetotallers, bent on the public good, with, in Nancy's case, a mania for entertaining. Nancy's personal maid, Rose Harrison, soon to appear on the scene as a major player in this spectacle, wrote in her memoirs that Nancy's two main pleasures in life were 'meeting people and telling off drunks'. English guests at Cliveden were struck by the 'sheer foreignness' of Nancy as well as her beauty – an attribute often submerged in the anecdotes of her volcanic behaviour – her fair hair and 'sapphire-blue eyes'.

Nancy's ambition was not just to meet people but, wherever possible, to enslave those about her; for a long time, and with the most unlikely candidates, she succeeded. This was Nancy the Good – one side of the coin – applying her gifts for genuine friendship, curiosity, compassion and hospitality. She went for the most obscure people as well as the stars. She believed that social snobbery was just not possible for the colonial gentry of Virginia, although she never got over her weakness for royalty and the guest list always had a solid weight of the titled and landed. But even old friends, the Cecils and the Cavendishes, for example, were judged according to a Virginian standard, as she often jokingly reminded them, of whether their forebears had crossed the water in wooden boats.

Except when it came to Christian Scientists – where her judgement often failed her – Nancy had an intuitive eye for moral and intellectual qualities that she admired, for her 'betters', as she called them. The gatherings at Cliveden or St James's Square mixed up, at tables of thirty or forty, not only rich and poor but Cabinet Ministers and temperance marchers, US Generals and Bolsheviks, municipal officials, tennis players, débutantes, schoolboys or what Irene, once feeling swamped, called 'every old rag-tail critter'. But her supreme skill, as ringmaster, was to get these inter-tribal gatherings to work as entertainment.

Nancy had an overriding quality, 'a grain of genius', her son Michael called it, for which her children forgave her almost everything else, including her near criminal record as a parent. It lay, he wrote, 'in the refutation of dullness in all its dreary forms'. 'The two most important things about my mother', said David Astor, 'was first that she was the funniest and most compelling entertainer. No one could touch her in our family. She was also socially fearless – something a lot of people claim to be but few really are – and there she was in a championship class. She would take your breath away by what she would dare to do and not be frightened to say.'

David Astor remembered his mother's first meeting with Mahatma Gandhi at St James's Square. Gandhi, who had struck awe and incomprehension into the Empire, was waiting, cross-legged in another room. Nancy walked in, with David, and said, 'So you're the wild man of God. I know all about you. Everybody thinks you're a saint. But I know what you really are. You're just like me, you're just an old politician.' Gandhi dissolved in laughter, relieved for once from the adulation and politicking that surrounded him, and the bond was instantly made.

Nancy was equipped with all the comedian's attributes: fearlessness, lack of caution, comic timing, deadly mimicry. She applied them to dominate these gatherings at her houses, talking down the table, singling out a guest, usually with some personal or provocative remark. It had the effect of exploding a series of dreary conversations like a firework, instantly changing the atmosphere, turning it, one guest remembered, from a debate into a 'riot' or at least a general conversation. It was alarming for the victim – it was a prototype of Dame Edna Everage's audience strikes – and Nancy expected her guests to perform in return, to stand up to her. Some were, at their first encounter, rendered 'speechless with indignation, reduced to stunned and respectful silence', one regular Cliveden guest remembered, by what seemed to them her sudden 'outrageous onslaught on themselves, their friends, everything they held sacred'. Like much comedy it could conceal an element of cruelty and it was for this that she was accused of being a bully by those who got hurt. Nancy got the reputation of being frightening, not because these were direct attacks, but because the comic techniques could make the person singled out appear clumsy or foolish; because she could turn the crowd for or against you. And she had no shortage of enemies who found her behaviour objectionable.

Nancy's ability to connect instantly with individual people was based on a similar riskiness – the directness that Phyllis called 'poking people up', like a child with a stick, rattling a monkey's cage. 'If there was a nerve on a tooth she'd find it,' said Nancy Lancaster. 'And then she'd turn them. They always ended up her slaves. She started by punching you in the stomach and then she'd wheedle you and you'd end up staying the night. I said to her "Why don't you think before you speak?" She said "How do I know what I think until I've said it?"'

By the mid-1920s Nancy could cold-call anyone who took her fancy, asking them, untried, for the weekend. Many of her conquests were tricky customers – it was part of the attraction – who would have walked away immediately if Nancy had tried to bully or manipulate them: A. J. Balfour, Ramsay MacDonald, Bernard Shaw, Charlie

Chaplin, Sean O'Casey, the Irish communist playwright with whom she corresponded for forty years. T. E. Lawrence, whom she befriended in his reclusive years, who 'worshipped' her and took her for rides on his fated motorbike, was similarly exonerated from playing and performing like the others and rarely spoke at Cliveden. These were people with whom she wanted to get on to intimate terms and to whom she would defer and treat with caution. And in most cases she held on to them forever. She pursued them out of genuine curiosity because they intrigued her, and because she venerated in them what she saw as improving virtue and wisdom. It was the directness, the cheek, that often first attracted these men, while she was cleverly befriending their wives. Many of them had never been treated like this before; she made them feel that they had achieved a rare intimacy with her, although, as the historian A. L. Rowse, another long-term acquisition, pointed out, it was impossible to be *un*intimate with Nancy.

One of Nancy's earliest conquests was the devoutly Catholic Hilaire Belloc with whom she struck up a friendship around 1911. Belloc's lively, versatile mind, his brilliance as a conversationalist, his fame as a writer, made him, Nancy told Phyllis, 'splendid company, v. mad but I like him'. They hit it off best on a level of farce and humour, and he loved her company, called her a 'dear friend'. He sent her volumes of attentive, slightly dotty letters, full of his rhythmic, beautifully turned prose — another example of Nancy's uninhibiting effect on her male admirers, at least on their correspondence. Like everybody else Belloc couldn't read her letters and complained, 'if your handwriting was as limpid as your eyes I could read every word of your note . . . It is your vast occupation and good-deed-buzz that so hastens your pen. I have leisure. I do nothing. Therefore I write elaborately.'

But there was also a serious underpinning to their friendship. Nancy was impressed by the force of Belloc's religious feeling, which was evident in most of his writing, despite her prejudice against Catholicism. Without this the relationship might have been impossible or even alarming to Nancy. Belloc's mother, also, was a leading figure in the suffrage movement and his wife was American. His French birth and naturalized Englishness qualified him as an outsider. Yet there were crazed flaws in Belloc's make-up. There is hardly a single letter to Nancy that doesn't somewhere display his rabid hysteria about Jews, referred to, in at least one letter, as 'Yids'. His other hatred, ironically, was for the rich nobility and the mercantile classes, who he blamed, from centuries back, for England's economic woes: the two hatreds often combined. Nancy said later that it was Belloc's 'mania' about the Jews and the rich that forced her to break off their friendship. Belloc's version was that he had found Nancy at Cliveden trying to convert his daughters to Christian Science and broke off immediately from 'that dangerous woman'. When, some years later, Nancy ended the silence and wrote to Belloc to commiserate on the death of his wife, he replied, 'It is such a delight to get a letter from you after all these years that I will swallow all & kiss respectfully the tips of your claws.'

Nobody in her pantheon was treated with greater care by Nancy than Bernard Shaw. From the late 1920s until he died in 1950, he became, for Nancy, her closest friend after Philip Kerr. It was some achievement; an improbable alliance, unimaginable before the event for Shaw's socialist friends and at first vexing for them. Nancy captured him at the height of his fame between his plays *Saint Joan* and *The Apple Cart*, by sheer persistence. Shaw wrote in 1926: 'The inimitable Nancy has laid many snares for me but never the right one. She thinks I want to meet people but I don't but Charlotte sometimes does . . .' A year later it was Charlotte who accepted an invitation for Christmas at Cliveden, where they found themselves snowbound for eighteen days. Awkward, unsociable, unused to luxurious surroundings, Shaw and Charlotte spent, from then on, a great deal of time at Cliveden and corresponded frequently with Nancy. Nancy wasn't interested in Shaw's ideas, or his plays; in fact by now she hardly read anything other than Christian Science pamphlets. They agreed on little except puritanism, teetotalism, a wariness of sex, a love of wit and a belief in speaking your mind. Nancy disliked socialism; the evolutionist Shaw mocked her Christian Science. One thing they had in common, though, was their exhibitionist fame.

Nancy developed a deep affection and respect for Shaw, although it was never spelled out or articulated. Shaw liked the 'fighting woman' side of Nancy, the fact that she was engaged in the public good in a foreign land and the fact that she wasn't bound up in political careerism and could therefore, as he thought, say unfashionable and silly things. He liked the way she forced him on walks, telling him once, 'Come out of there you old fool. You've written enough non-sense in your life!' Nancy had similarities to his mother – a forceful, powerful, fortress-like woman – and to T. E. Lawrence's mother too. Both men shared, as did other male friends of Nancy's, a liking for the fact that the relationship was devoid of sexual innuendo. As with Sargent, and others, it gave safe boundaries to the mock flirtation and the games.

'He saw her as a heroine in one of his plays,' said Shaw's biographer Michael Holroyd, 'and Cliveden was the setting for them – a place of grand rehearsal.' Shaw, according to Holroyd, found the mixture of people at Cliveden with their opposing ideologies – the liberal Kerr, the communist Charlie Chaplin – truly democratic, 'an Arcadian alternative to Parliament'. 'They could talk things out as if it were the House of Commons and this helped him with the dialogue for his plays,' said Holroyd. 'It had a surreal quality as if something in his own work had actually come into being.' After fifteen years of friendship he was describing Nancy as 'a unique and amusing phenomenon . . . whose philosophy begins and ends with her being a good sort'. Bobbie Shaw, for one, didn't see Shaw's presence in such theatrical terms. 'It was like having an old dog around,' he said, 'one that you were very fond of but should have put down years ago.'

There were others in Nancy's inner circle who were valued and protected and especially well treated. Tom Jones, socialist son of a Welsh mine foreman and Professor of Economics, was brought from Wales by Lloyd George, and became an adviser and *éminence grise* to Baldwin and Ramsay MacDonald, a quiet and cultured man who Nancy revered and loved and who became one of the Astors' closest confidants over the years. A prized guest was Dame Lilian Barker, the first woman prison commissioner, large, loud-voiced and blatantly lesbian, a woman of moral courage and, Nancy perceived, deep goodness of character. Dame Lilian wore a pork-pie hat, smoked cigarettes and talked back to Nancy, addressing her, occasionally, as 'old dear'. Every Christmas for thirty years Nancy invited 'Judy' Judge, for example, a provincial journalist from Plymouth, barely known in his own city, an agnostic and a fellow saint, who became almost a relation to Nancy's children. It was watching Nancy, and her idea of people having merit outside the social categories, said David Astor, that influenced him in much that he did as editor of the *Observer* later on, particularly in his unconventional choice of staff. When he met, and hired, George Orwell, he felt at once that he was 'morally strong and with a remarkably independent mind'. Orwell was hardly known at the time but David had learned from Nancy, he said, to trust his instincts and value above all else qualities like those.

There was a large, invisible group of people who Nancy quietly supported or helped with money, a group that included impoverished Virginian relations, whose children she educated, distressed non-royal Russian *émigrés*, and soldiers long gone from the Cliveden hospital. In such matters her loyalty and attention to detail seem to have been faultless. There were some characters living on the Cliveden estate – a large village run on a paternal basis by the Astors – who Nancy adopted in moments of spontaneous generosity and housed for the rest of their lives. There was the shell-shocked Mr Dance, whose job was sweeping the drive, who suffered periodically from bad depression. When he disappeared one day Nancy, instead of calling the police, drove around the countryside looking for him, found him in Maidenhead and persuaded him to come home, promising to look after him. There was the old travelling woman Mrs King, too old, Nancy thought, still to be on the road, whom she persuaded to come in through the gates. Mrs King died some years later in a spare room in a cottage on the estate. These were people Nancy treated with deference and respect – Mrs King was treated 'like the Queen' and often visited – and with whom she never took liberties.

Both Nancy and Phyllis also had the ability for finding the most talented servants, and converting them, as best they could, into their 'relations', Virginian-style. The Astors had the luck of inheriting from William Waldorf, at first as a footman, one of the great butlers of his time, Mr Edwin Lee, who ran the whole enterprise in five different houses for over fifty years. Born into a farming family in Hereford, Mr Lee, whose underlings called him 'Sir', and who Nancy came to call 'Lord Lee of Cliveden' was a kind, wise, flawless man of great balance, who treated everyone alike, with tact and respect.

For myself, as a teenager, Mr Lee had the face of some grand European statesman of the stature of Adenauer or de Gaulle – he was impressive – and if you met him on one of his walks in the Cliveden grounds, dressed in his tailored tweed suit and carrying his stick, you might have mistaken him for one. Born into a different class, Mr Lee could have commanded a regiment or governed a province with distinction, such was his natural authority, his fairness, and his talent for administration. But even Mr Lee succumbed to the status of relative on some level. He quickly acclimatized to Nancy's ways, to the semi-familiarity with the staff that was unheard of in English service. 'One never felt that you were the underdog,' he said, 'or anything like it. One minute she would make you feel you could nearly kill her but the next time you saw her she would be full of fun and life and as if she was one's own sister. One day after I had said plainly what I thought she declared roundly, "Really Lee, you talk to me more like a husband than a butler".' Once, exasperated by the number of guests Nancy had suddenly invited, and the impossibility of making space between the chairs for serving food, Lee announced that after that lunch he was resigning, that he didn't feel he could perform his duties properly. Nancy told him, 'If you're going Lee, take me with you.'

The most extraordinary relationship of Nancy's life, inside or outside the family, began in the late 1920s when Rose Harrison came to work at Cliveden as Nancy's lady's maid. The two women engaged from that moment in a titanic love–hate struggle that lasted thirty-six years, one that only gradually developed into an undeclared mutual admiration and dependency and ended, from Rose's point of view, in an honourable draw. Rose had come from Ripon in Yorkshire to work as Wissie's maid, and before Nancy claimed her, Rose had little idea of the dangers of proximity to Lady Astor, despite Mr Lee's warning: 'She's not a lady as you would understand a lady, Miss Harrison.' Nancy had the reputation of someone 'who couldn't keep a maid': in the fashion of the time they had mostly been French – a foregone disaster given Nancy's dislike of 'French manners'. None of them understood Nancy's petulant outbursts, or her mocking imitations of their accents and most were dismissed before they had time to resign. Nancy had taken a liking to Rose's character, to her stocky appearance and the way she spoke: loud and straight in her Yorkshire accent.

The extraordinary communications between the two women from then on were known and marvelled at only by the immediate family and some of the staff – the sheer volume of some of the exchanges could hardly be ignored – until Rose published her ghosted memoirs after her mistress's death. Rose's ghost-writer omitted the enjoyment both women got from their unguarded intimacy and close combat, and gave an impression of relentless maid-bashing on Nancy's part. He left out, too, the fact that nobody except Nancy would have put up with the way Rose talked back to her as she was expected to do; that Rose had become a 'relative', an honorary sister, and that Nancy had no other relationship in her life as familiar as that with Rose. But there's no doubt that from the first day Nancy launched into what appeared to be 'sadistic and sarcastic' attack. 'She mimicked me, not out of fun but to hurt. She shouted and rampaged . . . I don't think anyone knew at the time how bad it was,' Rose recalled. Rose began going to pieces. Then, as she described it, she went into a 'trance' one day in her bedroom, and emerged armoured and resolved, ready to fight back. She recited a short declaration of rights which began 'My lady from now on I intend to speak as I'm spoken to . . .' A startled Nancy apologized. One morning soon after this, Nancy said, only half in jest, 'Rose, it's my ambition to break your spirit.' 'I know it is, my lady,' Rose replied. 'There's two of you trying to do it, you and the devil. And neither of you will succeed.' 'And I got an understanding of her,' Rose told me, when she was in her nineties, 'how I don't know. And after that my life was fine. I thought I can stand anything now.'

From then on the verbal sparring, which sometimes led to shouting matches, would begin each morning after Nancy had had her cold bath and performed her physical exercises, punctuated with cries of 'Shut up, Rose.' 'Their rows were unbelievable,' said Nancy's great-niece, Elizabeth Winn, 'I remember once I was watching her dress for dinner, she said, "Rose, I'm not taking that to London tomorrow, put out another dress. I don't like it." Rose said, "I'm very sorry my lady, I've packed the suitcase. It's finished and you'll have to go in your nightdress." And Aunt Nancy used to say, "Shut up talking Rose." "I can't help it my lady, I've got to say something sometime."'

Nancy was unable to give praise or to show she was pleased, either to Rose or to any of her children. And yet Rose declared, 'I can honestly and truthfully say that I enjoyed every minute of the 35 years I was living with her and I was never afraid of her.' So much so that Rose had to be forced to take days off and holidays. She was immensely proud of her work, of the immaculate way Nancy was turned out. She was a consummate lady's maid of a kind that has now disappeared – she was a hairdresser, dressmaker, seamstress, dog-handler, confidante. Nancy sometimes wore five sets of clothes a day, including her golfing outfit, all of them kept in a long room devoted entirely to her wardrobe, which included the hats and shoes and gloves she would order in multiples. And Rose was the keeper of Nancy's huge collection of jewellery, the only one apart from Waldorf who knew the combination of the safe. Jewels were the one item of dress that Nancy could get wrong; her diamond rings had always looked a little too big for her miniature hands. Rose stepped in on one occasion when Nancy was invited by Queen Mary – almost the only person, according to Rose, able to intimidate her mistress. 'One night she put this tiara round her waist,' said Rose. '"Oh," I thought. "Don't she look awful," and she says, "What do you think I look like?" She was just going off to

Buckingham Palace plastered in diamonds. I said, "I don't know what Queen Mary will think, I'm sure." She said, "Well what do I look like?" I said, "Cartiers." I said, "You're not going with that round your waist.""

Rose claimed that Nancy underpaid her all her life, but compensated her with arbitrary hand-outs of jewellery which eventually paid for a large and airy seaside house in Worthing, on the Sussex coast. 'I loved her ladyship, but not as I would love anybody,' she told me. One birthday, having nothing to give her employer, said Rose, she decided to give her a kiss. 'She let me kiss her, so I knew the affection was there. Only she couldn't *give* it. She was so kind and that but she couldn't demonstrate it, she couldn't show it at all.'

For Nancy the real and fierce exercise of power lay not in politics but in the intimacies of her life, particularly in her dealings with her own family. Her inability to show affection, which laid a gunpowder trail of unhappiness around her, was matched by her powerful desire to be first in the attentions and affections of her family; as Irene put it, 'she yearns for people to love her <u>best</u>'. She would often go to shameless lengths to get proof of it, exercising a relentless drive to control and correct everyone close to her. Inevitably this possessiveness began to shake loose her family relationships, but Nancy was never aware of the dangers. Her highest ambition for herself from childhood was to become a saint, so that, as she told the writer Freya Stark, 'everyone can feel my influence when I walk into a room'. In her own case this was already a *fait accompli*, in some part of her mind, at least in vocational terms, after she had taken up Christian Science. Having declared, when it suited her, the material world unreal, she was only dimly aware of the yawning gap between her saintly ambition and her behaviour. The problem was that Nancy never understood her religion, such as it was. She recited its ideas and then did exactly what she wanted, including, for example, always fixing the scores at golf and tennis to her advantage. Mr Lee once told Rose Harrison, 'Lady Astor is not a religious woman, she's all the time looking for a light she can never find.' 'She was by instinct a gangster,' was how one of her nephews put it, 'who was always trying to be good.' You couldn't really separate Nancy the Good from her gangster shadow; they were intertwined and both formidable, both fuelled by the same impulse. She was sometimes on the rails and sometimes off.

Nancy always longed to be like Irene, 'who knew how to live without fighting', and who had Nanaire's qualities of peace-making. She had always seen her father, by contrast, as a 'rough character' and was shocked at the way he behaved, especially to her mother. And yet more than any of her sisters, his was the character she had inherited. 'Every day I pray that I shall be really spiritual and that I'll be able to raise the dead,' Nancy told a clergyman friend in her later years. 'Then I go out and all I do is raise hell.' Bob Brand described how she took a 'ferocious joy' in attacking her sisters, brothers-in-law, even their babies ('I hear he's chinless but don't worry Jakie was too, and he's very intelligent'), and interfering in their lives. She launched her raids face to face, by telephone or letter, in what she believed to be a justified crusade to keep them on the narrow way – to stir them up to moral improvement. It was mostly possessiveness, jealousy and selfishness masquerading as goodness. Nancy never for a moment doubted that she was *always* right, as she battled against the tide of human feeling, love, sex, 'sin and suffering'. Cocooned in her personal version of Christian Science, she behaved subliminally as if she were acting on behalf of a higher being, as if, said Rose Harrison, 'she had invited Our Lord to one of her parties, he had accepted and sat at her right hand.'

Even the innocent and elevated figure of Irene, once beyond criticism, came in for some of the worst attacks. 'How cruel Nancy is,' Irene wrote wearily in the mid-1920s, 'her ability to hurt those she loves is paramount.' Nancy loved and revered her elder sister, the queen of New York, but she could no more resist dusting her up, and sometimes reducing her to tears, than a terrier could resist harassing an elegant swan. It originated in various jealousies, in Nancy's irritation at Irene's 'dependence' on Dana and vice versa, and in her peculiar notions of

'unselfish love'. 'You serve,' she wrote to Irene, 'and that's why you are
so happy but I wish some of those you serve would learn a lesson! I
know I am jealous but mother was before me.' But it also came from
the intimate tribal relationships between the Langhornes. Irene
belonged to Nancy and so she could say what she liked.

Irene was a tempting target for Nancy since she was officially a
non-combatant as a Langhorne sister; the family stabilizer. She was
slower-witted than the others and lacked the steely qualities of Nancy
and Phyllis. Serenity was her trademark. Her life had been plain sailing,
apart from a few financial ups and downs in Dana's career, to the point
of being almost eventless in terms of drama. The state of calm was
maintained by a constant drip of admiration, the drug to which she had
become addicted in her teens. Nancy wrote to Phyllis in 1911, 'Irene
and I have been shopping and I gave her two of Worth's evening gowns
and a black walnut daygown from Jay's and she is just like a child. I tell
her she is just like Pa. She hums to herself all day long . . . I think Irene
is much more Southern than we are. She is still a Southern Belle. Today I laughed at her about asking everyone if they thought her clothes
the smartest they had seen, and later on she attacked me and wept but
I am glad I stopped her asking what must appear to people an idiotic
question. Its all very well for Wissie [Nancy's daughter, then about
three] but really, Phyl, in Irene its so grotesque. Her nature is so different from ours, and her spirit so young, that I feel like Socrates.'

Like some great athlete or ballerina Irene had been living on the
past since the days of her cotillion triumphs at the turn of the century,
depending on this sustained chorus of compliments or 'dewdrops' as
she preferred to call them. 'Fifty one today, but I look very pretty,' she
wrote to Nancy in 1924. 'I hope I will have a long time yet. Life is very
full and very sweet and very kind to me and mine has been all happiness
except where those I have loved have gone.' She added 'Isn't that nice?
and of course any suffering you all have had has been mine too. I think
I ought to carry some of the burdens.'

She was like a popular monarch in her later years, revered and
beyond reproach. She had become the curator of her own monument –

to the last Southern Belle – keeping alive the memory of a vanishing institution with formidable energy. In the business now of being 'attractive and amusing', in New York social parlance, as her beauty faded, she had also become a little vain. This was not unexpected in New York and in that generation where exaggerated forms of admiration were a convention of society. There were other latterday Southern Belles at large in the city between the wars: Mrs Cole Porter, formerly Linda Lee Thomas, Mrs Harrison Williams (later Countess Bismarck), both from Kentucky, and Nanneline (Mrs James B.) Duke from Georgia. '*Elegance?*' the *cognoscenti* would say, 'Just watch the way Nanneline gets up from a *chair*,' – a mysterious arrangement of the arms and legs unknown to Yankees. Irene became senior *grande dame* among them; someone very important to have at your coming-out ball. 'There's Irene Gibson,' they would say, 'doesn't she look wonderful?'

At 'Return of the Belle' parties Irene would carry the American flag, her chin slightly upturned, leading with the bosom – a touch of Margaret Dumont in the Marx brothers' films. Bob Brand described her at a party in Washington in the 1920s 'looking flowing and glowing, particularly after a cocktail or two'. She would preside over Gibson Girl revivals, where she would sing 'Why do they call me the Gibson Girl?', sitting at the piano, throwing back her head, or read the Uncle Remus stories of Joel Chandler Harris. Even in ordinary conversation she was not averse to turning up her Virginian accent a few degrees.

The publicized appearances were often for charity, for which Irene worked tirelessly. For twenty-five years she was chairman of the Child Planning and Adoption Committee for the State Charities Association. She was a member of the Society for Prevention of Cruelty to Children, founded the New York branch of the Southern Women's Educational Alliance, and was a director of the Protestant Big Sisters. At the time she was quoted as saying that she found philanthropic work 'exciting'. In addition, she was a major mover in the campaign to restore General Lee's birthplace at Stratford Hall in Virginia.

If admiration didn't come to Irene, she sought it out. She liked what she called 'a bit of yearning'. She would hold flattering tea parties; she would flirt, as she had always done, although she had never been unfaithful to Dana, who understood her need for admiration. 'If you have a canary,' he would explain, 'you've got to let it sing.' She had a habit of standing in front of an open fire slightly raising the back of her skirt, apparently to warm her legs, secretly to show off their fine form. She held tightly to her beaux and admirers, past and present – the *raisons d'être* of the Belle. 'I dashed to the races in Boston for 2 days,' she wrote to Phyllis in 1928, aged fifty-five, 'and it did me good to see my old friends and old beaux and they fed me up with compliments and I love them.' At the Kentucky Derby she said that her old beaux were 'most attentive and enthusiastic, making me feel quite perky'. If you sat next to Irene she might lower her husky voice and ask, 'Did you ever know Prince Arthur of Connaught?' She would boast of the many men who had been in love with her, like Clemenceau, the old French states-man and radical and friend of Dreyfus – who had once given her instructions on where, in which room, along which corridor, to find him in heaven. She dined with him in New York in the mid-1920s and wrote to Nancy, 'The old tiger wired from Chicago. He wanted to see me. He was fine & really <u>very</u> nice to me. Says he is in love with me. That shows he is a man of intelligence. I really love the old boy. He is <u>so</u> witty. I have just returned from bidding him farewell at the steamer. He could hardly let me go.'

In 1925 Nancy wrote: 'I hear that your ol' deaf sweetheart fol-lowed you from Boston to New York. You really are the limit. I had hoped that when the change came in your life you would have changed your views about the gents!!' Some of them were indeed wearing out, like Irene herself. 'Gordon (the faithful) has been here for 3 days. Oh! the beau has aged. He is falling all about the chin, mouth and neck. Oh. It makes me feel sad. I don't dare think that I may be doing the same. But Paris built up the face & neck. I roll it pat it, & caress it. Cream & powder it & some time a little ssh shh! O you know (Rosy Posy). I sound senile & maybe I am.'

Twenty years after this letter, at the age of seventy-five, Irene was still an object of wonder – for her looks as much as her manners. She visited the White House in April 1945, a few days before Roosevelt died, on her way from Mirador to New York. In her newspaper column, 'My Day', Eleanor Roosevelt wrote, 'The younger members of the family were fascinated by her, because she is still the Gibson Girl of her husband's drawings; and though some of the youngsters had never heard of the Gibson Girl, they fell a victim to her charm of manner and beauty. All of the Langhorne sisters are people one has to notice!'

When she came to Cliveden each year Irene was at first treated 'like Garbo', — as someone of supreme importance — and she was happy to act the part. She had long felt assured of her immortality, like some great movie star, even making sly references to it in her letters. David Astor recalled being fascinated by Irene as a child 'because she used to sort of hold court . . . She had an Edwardian queenliness about her . . . But Aunt Irene gave a lovely gentle atmosphere, a sense of well being and ease and she was sweet with children.' But the peace Irene hoped to bring when she visited Cliveden, or when Nancy visited her in Dark Harbor, Maine, never lasted long. After a while Dana declined to come to Cliveden, unwilling to put up with the cycle of rows and tears and repentant distribution of jewellery. But he would allow Irene to go alone, with the cautionary advice: 'Fruit and flowers, honey. Just keep to fruit and flowers.'

Once, after Irene left Sandwich a little battered and bruised, Nancy wrote to her, as if nothing had happened: 'Last night you were with me & tonight I am here by the sea alone. Its a strange thing life — I look out on the sea and realise that you are on it & happy at going home & that home for me is over & gone! Home for me was my Ma! & oh Irene how I miss her & how I love you & hate you leaving, you seem more like home to me than anyone. Perhaps I am too fond of the people I love. I believe I am.'

Deep down what Nancy couldn't bear was Irene's happy marriage, her contentment with life, while she, struggling with her soul and her Science books, was unable to find peace. The fact that Irene wouldn't even engage in the struggle of 'prayer, watching and working, combined with self immolation', as Mary Baker Eddy put it, and was still finding life fulfilling and pleasurable, was irritating. And Nancy therefore periodically loosed off what Irene called 'rip shooters', letters of general abuse, striking 'like a rattlesnake', particularly at Dana. Reacting to one of these, Irene wrote to Phyllis, 'Nannie is crazy! . . . She has paranoia. She attacks us all and then always encloses the letters she gets from her friends who write her how wonderful she is and her children and her happy atmosphere at Cliveden so she must appreciate how cruel it is to have those things said to <u>her</u>. But she rarely thinks of our feelings. Poor critter. She must feel mighty <u>poorly</u> inside some time . . .'

One of the major skirmishes of the mid-1920s was unleashed when Irene asked Nancy and her children to spend part of the summer in Islesboro, Maine, where Irene held sway on Seven Hundred Acre Island. Either out of nerves or competitiveness or fear of staying in other people's houses, Nancy wrote several letters to relations and friends before the visit saying she was afraid to go to Islesboro on account of the 'worldly' life Irene led, throwing in, as well, some more general abuse of the Gibsons. It all got back to Irene, including the line, 'Irene's so romantic, she wants everyone to adore her.' This stirred Irene to a rare fury. She wrote to Phyllis: 'Lordy! Mercy! Pon my soul! What can we do about Nannie's complete lack of humour & taking herself so seriously! There are so many 'pretty ways' of putting things over & getting it to you. But Nannie's letter telling me <u>how</u> they must be treated and the Hermit life for her & her children for 2 weeks is done <u>so</u> clumsily . . . She asks us to a <u>cozy</u> family life at Cliveden. We sit down <u>30</u> & are made to entertain every old Rag Tail Critter Nannie has there while she reads C. S. with Philip & <u>then</u> takes the floor & says anyone else is talking twaddle & nonsense <u>showing</u> that its self, self! . . . All the real joy & fun has gone — she has hurt me unspeakably. How stupid of Nannie not to write & say in a graceful way I know you all want to give us a nice time etc etc but let's be quiet!! . . .'

Phyllis replied, advising Irene that it would blow over: 'Darling Sis. your letter steam blowing has just arrived. Don't worry about

Nannie, her letters thank heavens, are always worse than her bite . . .
I believe she has forgotten by now she said it. Of course she can't do
anything like anybody else and it is almost impossible for her to put
herself in anybody else's place. That particular talent has been left out
of her composition. We cannot blame her for what she hasn't got.'

But Phyllis was wrong. The summer turned out disastrously.
Soon after she arrived Nancy opened a new front against Irene, under
an old and bloodied banner: 'criticizing other people's children'.
Irene's daughter, Babs, had recently divorced and was planning to
remarry. Nancy would not have it, even though, of course, it was none
of her business. She had taken an open dislike to Babs – her looks, her
personality, her attitudes – and communicated this directly, and fatally,
to Irene who wrote to Phyllis, after a savage anti-Babs attack, 'Nannie
hopes they (the Gibsons) will all die & called Babs flat-faced.' The Babs
row was still simmering two years later when Irene retaliated again by
refusing to come to Cliveden. '"My heart goes out to you." That's one
of Irene's favourite expressions,' Nancy wrote to Phyllis, 'only she
doesn't follow her heart.' Nancy then apologized but managed to take
it back by putting the blame on Babs. 'Darn Babs & her wrecking of yr
love for me,' she wrote, 'You could disapprove of every child I had and
it wouldn't shake my love for you . . . Please write to me you do
understand and not blame me if I don't see Babs' point of view. I am
not a pleasant person I fear but I do love you better than any Gibson
ever could because you are flesh of my flesh and we are different.'

The first major relationship to come adrift in Nancy's life was that
with her closest sister, Phyllis – a relationship that once seemed sacred
and unassailable. Irene had once written to Phyllis, after a Nancy
attack, 'Mrs Astor [sic] is curious. If we cut her up we would find only
Bobbie and you next to her heart.' Several forces were splitting them
apart: the wall of Christian Science, Philip Kerr – elevated even higher
as adviser and guru – and Nancy's constant sniping at the Brands' marriage. In Phyllis's eyes, Nancy had become almost completely a 'public
character' – no longer reachable on a sisterly level.

'Phyl is completely Branded,' Nancy wrote to Irene. 'I feel she's never really happy away from Bob and the children. I wish she would come to me quietly when I get quiet but she seems to be satisfied as she are!' By 1924 Phyllis was complaining, 'The Astors can no longer entertain by the tens or twenties. It is now thousands! . . . Nannie has really completely forgotten what a private family life means which is very sad . . . She always taunts me with leading a selfish life with Bob and the children but I wd rather die than lead one like hers.'

'Kiss the Banker,' Irene wrote to Phyllis. 'Nannie loves him but is very jealous of him. I think she is jealous of happiness in a funny way.' Nancy unconsciously confessed this to Irene in 1922. 'BB seems either weighted down with responsibility or happiness. I think and pray the former.' It was almost Bob's most famous remark about Nancy that if she saw two doves flying together, she would try to separate them, and in this respect Bob had committed the unforgivable sin. He had married Phyllis, removed her from Nancy's power and, worse still, made her happy. The Brands were in love with each other. They seemed to have achieved an ideal of marital happiness and intimacy, sharpened, undoubtedly, by their long separations. Bob seemed to think so too, writing to his wife in 1922, 'When I look around I think we are the happiest couple in England.'

What Nancy found impossible to tolerate was the strength and support that Phyllis had found in Bob, as well as their material prosperity. The combination suggested a heresy against her, and a proof against her influence. It cut across her ruling instincts. 'I know Bob has got you away from me!' she wrote to Phyllis, two years after her marriage, 'Please remember my love and how much nearer a mother's love it is than anything Bob can give you!'

The wisest man in the Empire was living up to his name; Bob Brand was even becoming a celebrity. Now on almost permanent loan from Lazards, he made the opening speech at the League of Nations financial conference in September 1920, just before the birth of their second daughter, Dinah, that same month. He gave the delegates grave warn-

ings on the fate of Europe; that unless the governments took the risk of
mutual trust between them to solve the foreign debt crisis, they might
as well prepare for another war. 'Everybody has congratulated me,' he
wrote to Phyllis afterwards, 'I am to be interviewed by numerous
journalists . . . So your husband is getting a great deal of réclame.'

Two years later in October 1922, Bob and Maynard Keynes
crossed the Channel together once more on their way to Berlin. They
went to advise the German government on the stabilization of the
mark which, with the collapse of German credit, was hurtling out of
control – as both men had predicted. Bob wrote to Phyllis that Philip
Kerr had warned him of '"the most terrific financial and economic
crash ever known in the history of the world." I told him that I had been
warning him since the Peace Conference to pay attention to these matters & he wdn't and now he is in a panic & much more pessimistic than
I am.' The German government waited for the committee of experts to
tell them how they could continue to pay reparations when their credit
was collapsing. It was a dire moment for Europe – the beginning of the
headlong slide into German hyperinflation. Brand and Keynes were
both agreed that there must be a moratorium on reparations payments,
that Germany must be made strong again and above all that the
German banks must stop printing money. Brand and Keynes's minority view seemed simple enough, as Bob put it: 'If you want to be
prosperous, you mustn't ruin the countries you do business with.'

Bob was consequently amazed at the message waiting for him at
the Kaiserhof Hotel on his arrival in Berlin. It came from Dr
Haverstein, the old Prussian president of the Reichsbank. The bank,
wrote Dr Haverstein, was aware of the scarcity of money in Germany
and was preparing to remedy the situation. They had just bought new
factories where bank notes could be printed, hired employees and
were poised to print a great deal of paper currency. The Germans
were selling their ever-inflated marks, borrowed on three-month loans
from London banks such as Lazards, to pay for reparations as the Allies
had insisted. When Brand and Keynes arrived in October 1922 the
mark stood at 40,000 to the pound. By the following year, after

Poincaré invaded the Rhineland, one pound sterling was worth twenty thousand million marks. Obstructed, as ever, by the French, there was almost nothing the committee of experts could do to avoid a total collapse of the mark. And, as usual, there was Keynes's temperament to deal with. 'Keynes is rather upsetting the other members of the cttee,' Bob wrote to Phyllis. 'He is so arbitrary and critical in his views that he rather loses the effect of his extraordinary cleverness. They get distrustful of him. He always wants to rush everyone.'

The press photographs showed Bob staring out over the gloomy Bismarckian interiors in his rimless glasses, arms folded, weighing up the prospects of European survival. But as his letters, written in committee meetings, show, he was thinking about his new wife much of the time, as his colleagues droned on, and of his desperate desire to get home: 'I don't thank you, as you wd say, for having bewitched me. I am so restless away from you that I can hardly contain myself . . . I am bored, awfully bored!!' His letter included descriptions of the 'peculiarities' of hyperinflation, something not experienced until now. You could buy anything made in Germany for almost nothing, the exchange rate always tumbling faster than the prices the Germans charged for their goods. Bob Brand bought a pair of Zeiss binoculars for the equivalent of £1, almost the same price as his ten-day stay at the Kaiserhof. He had to take a knapsack to the bank each day to get his basic living expenses in the wads of German bank notes inflated by Dr Haverstein.

Later Bob believed that nobody in the 1930s could fully understand how inflation had led to the rise of Hitler and the Second World War unless they had seen its dramatic effects at first hand. One weekend in the spring of 1923 he saw the devastation that it was already causing, especially to the middle class. He went to the Black Forest, stayed in a vast hotel of pre-war glory, the Zommer Zarhlinger Hof and visited his old friend Dr Martin, his attentive practitioner and spiritual adviser, in his house in Schulsee. The two men hadn't met since before the war, when Bob was writing love letters from this same place to Phyllis in Mirador. Bob's description of the meeting is as poignant as any photograph of that interlude in Germany. The two men sat on the hotel terrace, sheltered from the cold spring wind, their shirtsleeves rolled up in the hot sun. Dr Martin told Bob Brand that he, his wife and two teenage sons, were now obliged by law to share their wooden house with a railway contractor and his family, the village tailor and his wife, a small mechanic and his family. 'How would you like that? Think of New Cavendish Street!', Bob wrote home. 'Mrs Martin', he added, 'overwhelmed me with gratitude for sending them white bread just after the Armistice when they cd get nothing here.' He found it hard to fathom the conditions in Germany. 'The peasants and farmers are well off. The workmen not as well off as before the war. Other whole classes ruined. There has been an enormous redistribution of wealth. Nobody has money . . . working capital is diminishing. Unemployment is beginning . . .'

That year, to Nancy's further irritation, the Brands bought Furneux Pelham Hall, near Buntingford in Hertfordshire, Bob's home county, out of reach of Cliveden. It was a small 'squirearchy' house in red brick, with a fine garden, a tennis court, and a farm with a shoot alongside. It was bought mostly with Phyllis's patrimony and her divorce settlement. The hunting wasn't equal to her prowess or ambition, but Bob could get back there from the city on weekdays. To own land for the first time, near his father's house, gave Bob much happiness. He wrote to Phyllis a year later, 'The garden is just bursting out with flowers, and I have two huge vases of red poppies in the drawing room and they look lovely . . . The farms are being tidied up, and the hedges put right and the yards cleaned up and the wheat and barley looks wonderful. I have lots of stock and there is plenty of grass. George Patten apparently says that my crops are the best in the neighbourhood. They ought to be for what they have cost.'

On their wedding anniversary in 1922 Phyllis had written to Bob: 'This is just a little extra unnecessary note to tell you how much I love you, and how happy these five years have been for me, and how it fills me with joy to think of the two treasures I have gained thereby . . . I could write you pages of "dewdrops" about yourself as a perfect spouse, but it might be bad for you, but you are a perfect one.'

In 1924, their last child and only son, Jim, was born at Furneux Pelham. But there was always the shadow of Peter on Phyllis's happiness and Nancy was merciless in reminding her of it. 'If only you hadn't married that Jew!' Nancy, the original promoter of the match, had written when Phyllis was at her lowest ebb after Peter's departure, 'I should feel you could demonstrate more the <u>Christ</u> which you believe in. However he has fine Human qualities but you need more than that now. Mortal mind is trying to rob you of peace & joy & its not right.' The underlying message, to be spelled out more clearly later, was that Phyllis should never have remarried, but instead devoted herself to her sons' welfare as Nancy claimed to have done with Bobbie. 'If I had not put Bobbie ahead of Waldorf and all the children, I should never have had him at all,' she told her. It was a sore point. In the background was Nancy's guilt about her own divorce, and Phyllis's annoying resistance to Christian Science.

Another anxiety for the Brands was the onset of their daughter Dinah's prolonged ill-health, in the mid-1920s. She suffered from chronic eczema, asthma and severe allergies; she contracted bronchial pneumonia twice between the ages of three and five. Until Dinah reached her teens in the mid-1930s much of her parents' time was centred around trying to get her well, requiring further separations. She was often sent away from home, to Torquay for the sea air, to St Moritz for eighteen months with Virginia at the age of seven, finally to boarding school at Fetan, from where she was rarely able or allowed to return home for the holidays. The hardness of the winter in Switzerland was wholly antipathetic to Phyllis's sun-loving nature. There were a series of painful partings as Phyllis left for home after her visits, walking away to the railway station at St Moritz. Dinah recalled later, 'I remember thinking, as my mother turned to go that I was actually dying. That this was what it was like to be dead.'

Dinah, who Phyllis thought an 'entrancing' child, got used to the many partings, and to being alone with nurses, governesses or headmistresses. Phyllis wrote one day from Torquay: 'I can't go off to Furneux Pelham on Wednesday and leave her, as I am afraid she would be so lonely — she clings to me; she is <u>very</u> pleased at having her meals with me, but oh! how I wish she could get rosy and well, those sad blue eyes haunt me. She tried to dance to the gramophone tonight, but her legs were very wobbly.'

Another source of separation — and major expenditure — were the many trips Bob and Phyllis made to European health spas and clinics for their own health. Phyllis went for various water cures, Bob returned to Dr Martin and the Kurhaus-Sanatorium Hoven, or Dr Dengler's clinic at Baden Baden to service what seemed an ever-more elaborate hypochondria. He was fascinated by the workings of his body. 'Referring to your letter,' one of Dr Martin's assistants wrote, '. . . I beg to say that I cannot see any connection between the bladder irritation, the fibrositis in the shoulder and your teeth'.

Nancy, meanwhile, demanded Phyllis's presence continually. 'I can't get used to yr life apart from me!', she wrote to her in 1922 when she was forty-three years old, 'It comes always as a shock!' One weekend, on an increasingly rare visit to Cliveden, Phyllis left early when Bob returned unexpectedly from Berlin. Nancy wrote that she was 'hurt and dazed' by her departure: 'I knew you weren't very keen to come here & were coming as a sense of duty. Mother always said I was a fool about you & I am seeing that & it hurts like hell but I believe it's the Christ way & we must look away from the material.'

Phyllis's main problem with these visits now was her awkwardness with the ever-present Philip Kerr. 'N is hypnotised by P . . .' Phyllis wrote to Bob from Rest Harrow, 'I told her last night that Philip was fast absorbing all her independence of thought and could make her believe blue was pink! Her usual retort was, "But look what Bob has done to you!"' Phyllis came to the painful conclusion that there was no pleasure to be had now in Nancy's company. It was almost as if she had invaded 'the honeymoon', as she described it, of her sister with Philip Kerr. 'I must say N. makes me feel de trop when P. is about,' she wrote to Bob, 'I can't help being terribly hurt. Philip has so obviously taken my place and he is making flint out of her and developing all the qualities in her that religion should have killed . . . I don't

fear for Nancy as she's got too much of her Pa and the love of this world
in her, but it's astounding to see what Philip can make her believe . . .
He used to be Nancy's tin God. Now he's the Golden Calf.' According
to Phyllis, at one point she was so overcome by Christian Science
'jargon' that she had to walk out on to the Deal golf course and lie flat
on her back 'to let the breezes blow it out of my system'. She warned,
'If N goes on denying all the human instincts her religion is bound to
make a great gap between our lives, which grieves me sadly . . . I shall
never make fun of them again as they are in such desperate earnest.'

In 1924, having held out for ten years, Waldorf was converted to
Christian Science during a bout of sciatica. Phyllis described the effects:
'So long as I see him bent double with pain I cannot believe in the miracle. However so long as Nannie (+Philip) are CS I am glad W is one
too as he will not be left out in the cold any longer & I am sure it is
best.' But it was a genuine conversion. Waldorf was never one to act
with a shred of intellectual dishonesty.

When Phyllis refused Nancy's summons, preferring to stay in
her own home, Nancy turned on Bob, calling him at his office in the
City and telling him that Phyllis was 'infatuated' with him, but would
soon get over it – that things would soon return to normal. This was
comic enough and Bob was not easily perturbed. But she managed to
penetrate his defences on their wedding anniversary when Phyllis was
sailing to America, chasing Peter. 'She chose this morning of all mornings to ring me up in my office & blackguard me on the 'phone in the
grossest way,' he reported. 'I never heard anything like it. I had separated you from your boy & made you very unhappy . . . I deliberately
refused to let her see "your" children & kept them with my own family
when you were away. I filled them with fear. I really don't know what
she said. I tried to stop her and said she was talking madness. Finally I
had to ring off. I cdn't do anything else.' Nancy rang again that afternoon to apologize.

Nancy attacked Bob on several fronts, but she particularly liked
getting at him on the subject of money – 'money bags' now being her
epithet for him, as well as 'jew banker'. Both she and Phyllis shared

some deep old prejudice that 'moneylending' was a low profession, one without 'uplift'. 'I like your saying you had to help the poor by stealth!' Phyllis wrote to Bob in the early days of their courtship. 'How easy to persuade oneself that one's mode of life, no matter how bad, is the right and unselfish one.' Nancy was always conscious of money and always insecure about it. Both she and Bob Brand shared, in different ways, fundamental worries about its supply. Bob was concerned about his powers of obtaining money and he was careful with it, parsimonious, always conscious of starting from nothing as the younger son of a peer. Nancy's fears went back to Danville days; she was always aware of the possibility of poverty. The fairy gold could disappear at any moment; she felt she had no control over it. It amused Waldorf when she thought she was running out of money, as she always did, no matter how much she had; and the fact that she never told him how much money she had received from the Shaw settlement and kept it, all her life, in a secret account. 'I didn't marry an Astor,' she said, 'to spend my own money.' And she could never have enough jewellery, even at the end of her life: it made her feel safe, despite the fact that she was married to one of the richest men in the world. Nancy told her children that she had planned exactly how to survive when her money was removed from her: she would run a hotel, and with great efficiency.

'Bob likes his comforts,' she would say, in front of him, to taunt him when he was her guest, 'but he doesn't like paying for them.' One day, on holiday in Jura, when Bob had had 'to listen constantly to gibes about my stinginess, my richness, my neglect of my children', and to accusations that Phyllis was forced to go to cheap shops, Bob temporarily lost his patience and sent her a cheque for £100 to pay his rent, telling her to send it to charity if she didn't want it herself. The cheque was torn up.

Nancy's nerve attacks almost always exploited some grain of truth. 'Don't you dare arrive here with a long face over finances!' Phyllis wrote to Bob, 'I couldn't stick it!! I'll willingly let New Cavendish Street, or anything, but I won't talk poor! So there.' Langhorne-like she had had to train him carefully in the giving of gifts, educate him in post-poverty thinking. Bob was amazed by the bursts of expenditure his married life required: two fully staffed houses, enormous fuel bills, motor cars, the cost of entertaining, the trips to the spas. The prices of the furniture and the antiques that the Langhornes were so brilliant at finding, with their Virginian taste, made him 'tremble' and he worried constantly that their spending was out of control. He kept a fierce grip on the household bills – the smallest purchases for the nursery were recorded in ledgers. 'I hear there is a wonderful fur shop in Berlin,' Phyllis wrote to him, to bring him back in line, 'so do look around if you get the chance for a Russian sable stole, a large ample generous one!!'

But Bob learned never to meet Nancy's reckless attacks against him head-on. After one of their clashes he sent a chiding letter, but of statesmanlike forbearance, refusing to engage. 'As you know I am never going to quarrel with you . . . there is no one except your sister of whom I am fonder or to whom I am more devoted. And therefore, as I say, I can never quarrel.'

Very few people, except her son Bobbie and her youngest son Jakie, would be able to outplay Nancy or trip her up, using her own weapons. Yet Bob was the most skilful of her relatives in dealing with Nancy – he was her biggest challenge. He was sceptical, detached and usually amused by her antics. It was light relief for him the way she would sometimes barge into political conversations among the heavy-weights, throwing in a few personal remarks, and a little rampant prejudice. 'You're talkin' like a lunatic' was a favourite rejoinder. She told Bob in 1923 that the proper settlement of foreign affairs was that England and the US as well as France should all take a bit of Germany and keep it; that this would at least keep the Germans from having it. 'She has been telling us how they "o'ganise" politics in Danville,' he wrote to Phyllis.

Bob applied a method with Nancy that David Astor described as a 'sort of cool, intelligent way of making her look slightly silly'. As a child I would go into Nancy's bedroom at Sandwich, the bed covered with bibles and CS literature, her face covered with cold cream. Fixed between her eyes was a triangular plaster, designed to prevent wrinkling. Bob would tease her about these little vanities – which didn't change over thirty years – and ask her if God had noticed this, and whether this meant that the outside of her skin 'existed' but not the inside. Nancy would call him 'Anti-Christ' and say that some day he would find the truth. In fact, Nancy, had a whole range of standard criticisms of Bob and would tell his children repeatedly in the same unbroken sentence: 'Be good to your father, he's wrong in many ways.' Fifteen years after the Brands' marriage Nancy was still unable to hide her jealousy as Phyllis recounted to Bob: 'Nannie wrote this a.m. but chiefly chiding me about all my affections going to you and the children etc. She really does not seem to like me liking my family!'

21

The Boy Problem

Navigating their way through the 1920s and into the 1930s with their well-regulated households, their model husbands and their many children, Phyllis and Nancy couldn't escape the past, their Achilles' heel: the early departures from Mirador and their failed first marriages. The past began, perversely, to acquire a sharper focus as the years went by, even though the events themselves were deliberately blurred in their memories or publicly airbrushed from their histories.

The 'stepchildren' — as they had now become in their own minds — cast a shadow first on Phyllis's life. She could never come to terms with Peter's departure, and his silence towards her. It caused her unrelenting pain. By the early 1920s he was clinging on at Harvard, an awkward, distant personality, 'so pathetic and odd', as Nancy described him, unsure of his place in the world, with no real parent to turn to, and now racked with doubt about his treatment of his mother. Phyllis not only feared that Peter's influence might take Winkie away from her, she also feared the influence of Bobbie Shaw, the oldest and pioneering stepchild. When Winkie went to Eton in 1923, Bobbie was twenty-five, an officer in the 'Blues'. The Royal Horse Guards was the social regiment *par excellence*, sporting and unserious, favoured by the débutantes and the society beauties. Winkie was impressed and nicknamed him 'Mon Capitaine'.

Nancy once criticized Phyllis for letting Winkie go off in the summer holidays. 'Boys are so curious and if you miss this time with them,' she wrote, 'you will never get it back again.' Bob made a rare counter attack: 'I wrote Nancy that I thought by her methods she had sucked Bobbie's vitality away – & that you didn't want boys to grow up as namby pamby men who can't leave their mother's apron strings.' Phyllis saw how Nancy's enslaving techniques were ruining Bobbie, who had developed a resentful, destructive streak in his personality. He was obsessed with his mother and could certainly never leave her, but he was also acutely aware of the difficulties of their relationship.

In his own perception, Bobbie understood that this domination of his life by his mother had its origins in Nancy's trauma and loneliness in Virginia after her divorce, and her insecurity in England before her second marriage, when she never let him out of her sight; he was forever associated with these painful emotional experiences which had bonded them like twins. 'They were the two closest people I've ever known in my life,' said Nancy Lancaster. 'He kept saying, "She's my arm, she's not my mother. When I go into the bathroom she covers herself up, as if her body mattered to me. It's my own leg.' After she had borne three more Astor children Nancy wrote, 'Oh Phyl they are wonderful children, David so robust, Wis so winsome and Bill all a companion should be but Bobbie has my heart.'

Nancy ruled her family partly by favouritism and Bobbie never concealed his resentment of the younger competition, of siblings or cousins. He took on the role of a semi-outsider and concealed his hurt feelings with wit and self-ridicule, sometimes casting himself as the family ogre. He would make faces at the babies in their prams, only half playfully, and when they burst into tears he would exclaim with surprise, 'Why is it crying?' He made a play of frightening younger children to tease them and he imparted unsuitable information, what Phyllis called 'loose talk'. Except for his Astor siblings, children, especially threatening cousins, became wary, even frightened of Bobbie. Phyllis, for one, forbade her children to be alone with him.

Bobbie resented, among many other things, that he had been sent to Shrewsbury School instead of Eton, perceiving it as a relegation to the second eleven. He minded that the decision had been made by a committee which included Lloyd George and Tom Jones, his parents' socialist confidant. In fact this decision may have been made (according to Nancy Lancaster) on the grounds of Bobbie's undoubted beauty and Eton's reputation for homosexuality, of which Nancy was leery without knowing much about it. Bobbie used to claim that he had already been handled, before this decision was taken, by Lord Kitchener on one of his visits to Cliveden, and that Kitchener's pointing finger in the recruiting poster was really aimed at him.

Bobbie hadn't liked his school, but he loved every aspect of the army. He was a superb rider, by far the best in his family. His enforced demobilization in 1918 left him the option of returning to the Horse Guards as a career later on, but for the moment he did nothing except ride and go racing. He lived at Cliveden close to his mother.

Signs of dissolution and of suspected vices were seized upon by Phyllis in 1919 when Bobbie was twenty-one, and Peter was about to cross the Atlantic. 'Nannie must have fearful moments about Bobbie,' she wrote. 'He dined here last night, and I just wondered as I looked at him if I would rather have Peter all smelling of scent and useless and stay here, or go as he is going. I should rather have him go I think.' In her eyes Bobbie didn't have the ragging terrier spirit that was her model for all young men. Winkie had had some of that spirit as a boy, but Bobbie was now Winkie's idol and Bobbie seemed to be developing into an apprentice Boston layabout. She noticed, too, beyond the smell of scent that of whisky and this, combined with his 'tight brown suits', she found repellent. Phyllis sensed wickedness in Bobbie but confided only in Bob. 'We will go to Cliveden for Xmas but Bobbie always takes all the pleasure away from that visit,' she wrote. 'He does not look his best just now, but praise be! Nannie doesn't seem to see things as I do.' In her sister's child it was easy for Phyllis to recognize Nancy's mismanagement in her over-doting love, since Phyllis believed fervently in the opposite course. With Bobbie there was never to be a struggle for independence, of the kind that nearly crippled Nancy's eldest Astor sons. How could you separate yourself from yourself? There was no leverage. Instead Bobbie settled for a struggle for equality inside the cage.

There were fights, stand-offs, trial separations. And Bobbie was independent-minded and uncompromising. No one else, except for David, many years later, had dared to tell Nancy that her Christian Science was hokum. Bobbie did it very politely in his ungrammatical letters in the 1920s: 'You must admit you are an autocrat and you seem always to be urged to rule, to tell people what they should and shouldn't do and more often than not to see the error of their ways. In fact I feel that none of your thoughts about people could possibly be called the thoughts of any genuine CS. Please do not think that I am trying to abuse you only I like CS people and I like CS minds. Can you say or pretend you have a CS mind? Surely not . . . until you are stronger at the carrying out of your religion than the letter it is useless our going any further.' Bobbie was trying to convey, in his hopeless syntax, that 'vain repetition' was all that Nancy's Christian Science consisted of in practice.

In another letter he wrote in a similar vein, 'You are always hoping that I will what you call "wake up" and do this and that. You say you don't want to see me until I have changed. I am afraid I shan't change very much from now till my death. It is unfortunate from your stand point but it can't be helped. Miracles don't happen today and leopards can't change their spots. You always know where to find me if you need me and if you ever want to see me I will always come round.'

At twenty-two Bobbie still had to respect family wishes. Nancy and Waldorf decided that he would go, with a family friend, Peter Lindsay, to work on a farm in Rhodesia – for a little character-building in the bush. Bobbie began to prepare the ground for his early return as soon as he arrived in Cape Town. 'Darling Mummie You can never know what we have been through. Of all the awful places in the world I think Africa the worst . . . what wouldn't I give to be back in England.'

But the remote farm near Umvuma, Southern Rhodesia, was worse. He wrote to Waldorf, 'It is a sort of prison without prisoners. One never sees anyone from morn till night, day after day. Anyone who we talk to would jump at any opportunity to get out.' Waldorf replied with warnings against 'throwing up the sponge and failing', but Bobbie wasn't impressed. He ended one of his letters to Nancy, 'Your shrivelled by boredom, heat and longing to return son . . . Oh for the 2.5 from Paddington to Taplow.' He got his way in less than eight months by rejoining his old regiment, the Royal Horse Guards. This, he said from Rhodesia, had always been how he saw himself: looking good on a horse, dressed in the uniform of the Blues.

Bobbie turned into an excellent officer, a natural leader, quick-thinking and competent, 'good at standing up to Generals', and popular with his fellow officers. In 1925 he was mentioned in dispatches for showing initiative and intelligence in army manoeuvres, and congratulated by Earl Haig. 'I can't tell you how it surprised me,' wrote Nancy to Phyllis. 'I never take the view about my children that you do about yours. I am always amazed when they show any of my qualities!!!' He won many steeplechases while in the army, including the most prestigious of all – the Grand Military Gold Cup, which he won twice, falling off ahead of the field on his hat trick. They were the happiest days of his life.

One day at school in the mid-1920s, David happened to see Bobbie, who was stationed with his regiment at Windsor, riding through Eton high street on a chestnut thoroughbred racehorse, stepping sideways through the traffic, in a smart khaki uniform. David signalled him into a side street and said breathlessly, 'Bobbie you look wonderful.' Bobbie put on a mock bashful look and replied, 'It's only at home I'm the onion.'

Bobbie's acceptance of his homosexuality came only gradually and, in the end, traumatically. While he was an officer in the Blues he had many women friends and admirers, all except for one opposed by Nancy, who didn't notice his friends of the same sex. He was in love for a time with Lady Alexandra ('Baba') Metcalfe, youngest daughter of the then foreign secretary Lord Curzon and wanted to marry her. They had been likened to a couple in a musical comedy, he superbly handsome, she a great beauty, both immaculate-looking 'as if they'd slipped onto the stage and were about to go into a dance routine'. Alexandra's mother had died when she was eleven and she had stayed often and for long periods at Cliveden, looking on Nancy as a surrogate mother. She recalled, aged ninety-three, Bobbie's glamour — so different from Phyllis's contemporary descriptions. 'Bobbie was immensely amusing and entertaining, frightfully funny, very attractive,' she remembered. 'He was very popular in his regiment and with all the Blues that used to come to the Ascot parties. He was very much in love with me and he was told by Nancy and Waldorf that there was nothing he couldn't have if I made him marry me. It was the last thing I wanted to do. I wasn't a scrap in love with him. He never actually said "will you marry me" because I would have said "No I don't want to marry you. I'm not in love with you." So I give very good marks to Bobbie for realizing that. He, as it were, opted out because he knew that he couldn't make a good husband to anyone. I don't suppose I knew then he was homosexual. I was only nineteen.'

But Bobbie, of course, did know of his homosexual inclinations and had also realized that a conventional life of marriage to a Marquess's daughter was not for him.

In the mid-1920s he had a riding fall that nearly cost him his life. An operation was performed to remove part of his skull; his mental faculties were undamaged, but his tolerance of alcohol was noticeably lowered. He would drive back from Ascot, weaving up the drive and come to a halt 'with a crash of brakes', according to Baba Metcalfe. 'We were alerted to these arrivals. We used to get Bobbie through the side door on the wing, put his head under the tap to try to sober him up before dinner.' Either Nancy never noticed or she forced herself to turn a blind eye to these mortal errors.

Bobbie did have a taste for wickedness and risk but Phyllis saw only the superficial corruption of his appearance and didn't notice other sides to his character. Bobbie also believed in goodness and propriety, and was almost beginning to separate the two parts of himself as if preparing to lead two physically separate lives. There was no blurring of good and bad, no lies or pretence. He had a rock-like integrity and self-possession – you couldn't get around Bobbie. 'He had more moral courage than anyone. There's no doubt about it,' said Nancy Lancaster. 'I was devoted to Bobbie. I always told Nannie he was the best bred of all her children.'

As the Astor children grew up they became deeply fond of Bobbie. They regarded him with some awe for his cheek and his nerve in standing up to people, and for his unique ability to turn the family laughter against their mother. He became the chief wit of the family, the scourge of visiting dignitaries. It was other children's parents who had an exaggerated fear of him, particularly Phyllis.

Bobbie had many gifts, some of them inherited directly from Nancy. He had her gift for comedy and for connecting with people, her ability to say unspeakable things, knowing how to time it to make it funny instead of offensive. They shared an unrivalled ability to play on the emotions. And yet Bobbie's taunts could be more wounding and astringent and sometimes crueller than Nancy's impulsive outbursts.

Only Bobbie could penetrate Nancy's defences and reduce her to tears by probing knowledgeably into the past. 'Why did aunt Nancy marry uncle Waldorf?' a cousin once asked, with wicked intent. 'Mother wanted a multi-millionaire who would act as first footman and they weren't easy to come by, were they?' Bobbie replied. Only he could turn Nancy's attacks back on her. Once, after a severe scolding at the lunch table from Nancy, he began primly reciting the words of the hymn, 'Could a mother's tender care/ Cease toward the child she bear?/ Yes she *might* forgetful be . . .' – the equivalent of Nancy making the face of a madwoman when she was subjected to complaints.

It was their closeness that made their double act so fascinating to outsiders. David Astor recalled Nancy 'saying dismissively, as she often did, "Oh you Astors are all this and that . . ." and Bobbie saying "I think you're right about the Astors. I think we should go back. You get out my little sailor's suit and we'll go back to America." They had a sort of incredible intimacy, based on total devotion on his part and long ownership on hers. They could read each other's thoughts.' Bobbie knew the Christian Science jargon backwards and enjoyed deceiving the practitioners who came to stay – a particularly humourless bunch – into believing he was one of them. Bob Brand wrote to Phyllis of a weekend at Cliveden in 1926 where a Mr Dorley, a Christian Science practitioner, had been staying for some days: 'Bobbie said that Mr. Dorley said last week that Waldorf was ill because he had roused so much "hate" in the (Drink) Trade & the evil thought was making his heart bad. I asked which it was, Worthington, Bass or Whitbread. I said too that if I knew Nancy, some of the brewers must be feeling sick too. I asked Bobbie if Waldorf was going to play golf today. He said "It depends on how he has met Mr Bass's thought during the night." The whole thing seems to be quite fantastic.'

Many of their dramas were played out in the dining room and I remember them well in Eaton Square in the late 1950s when they had become a little rough but always funny and quick, two people talking past each other, with an undercurrent of needling observations from Bobbie. 'Mother and Nancy [Lancaster] married five millionaires between them, *completely* by mistake' was one of the mildest.

It was Irene who had kept Phyllis in touch with Peter's troubled odyssey after his return to America in 1919. He had written infrequently, adding to his mother's pain; the letters he did write reopened the wounds of their bitterest mother–son fights. Peter remembered each intemperate word his mother had used and recycled them years later to refresh her memory.

In autumn 1920 he wrote rapturously to Phyllis about his summer in Long Island: 'Father is a different man today and is the wonder of my existence. [Reggie did go on the wagon periodically at this time, but would slip back in the winter months at Aiken and Palm Beach into bouts of bottle-throwing alcoholism.] I love everything about him and thank God I came over when I did. I regret not one thing

I have done in the position I was in, for I feel that it was for the good of everyone that I undertook what I did. To me the whole thing is a great success except the very fact that in what I did I have generated in <u>your</u> heart a feeling towards me that my heart is of stone, that I have <u>no</u> soul, that I am a hypocrite of the most poisonous type, that my sympathy for anyone is nothing concrete, that I have neither <u>character</u> or backbone, and that I am, as you once told me . . . a "Damn little son of Hell" and that you hoped I would "weep my soul out someday for what I had done." Yet a mothers love burns on and she naturally wonders and wonders for her eldest boy as you for me. I wonder how much you'd hate me if you saw me now. I wonder if your first meeting would be <u>real love</u> or whether some kindling fire of previously aroused "Langhorne Spirit" would press forward a new wounded issue of feeling that would render a touch which would make our meeting so different from "ye auld days".' He ended 'About how much I wonder could we love each other again or do you think I'd make a mess of the whole thing. Best love Pete.'

When Dinah, Phyllis's second daughter, was born in 1920 he added some avuncular congratulations. 'It gives me a warm spirited chill of "soul joy" when I realise that your prayer has been fulfilled and you have been blessed with a "cute little Dinah". God Bless everything about your little family.'

Until he reached Harvard in 1922, Peter had been buoyed up by his triumphant return to America (this, at least, was how he saw it in the late adolescent epic in which he starred) and the mission to save his father. But what little there was of his underlying self-confidence, always threatened by his dislike of his own looks and his personality, began to evaporate in the social shakedown of college life. His desire to be 'American and concurrent with American ideas', which he loftily expected Harvard to satisfy, was less simple to achieve than he had imagined. Harvard brought all his confusions into sharp focus.

Peter wanted to please his father, for whom the Porcellian, the most snobbish of Harvard clubs but also the alcoholics' boarding card, had really been the only point to his Harvard days. Perhaps Peter couldn't enter wholeheartedly into the series of backslapping lunches and dinners and drinking marathons that would-be members were invited to as part of the election process. Having a father as a former Porcellian gave you extra points. Even so Peter's membership was not sought. He confided in his Aunt Irene, telling her that he wouldn't try again. Many a rejected applicant for the Porcellian never got over it in their later lives, as Irene knew. But instead of dismissing the idea as a waste of time, given that Peter was unlikely to be elected, she advised him to 'think about that carefully', so compounding his sense of failure.

Slipping lower on the social scale Peter took part, instead, in the same sophomore year, in a traumatic fraternity initiation which lasted for three days. He was hoisted by rope to the top storey of a high building, suspended while blindfolded in mid-air, and then dumped in a tank of muddy water, half-concussed.

He was by no means friendless. In his desperate desire to succeed and somehow vindicate his father and show up his English relations, he trained exhaustively in athletic track. But the academic work was beyond him and he felt sure he would fail. 'Since I last saw you,' he wrote to Bob, 'my intelligence remains about the same. It really is a sorry thing because I find myself very stupid . . . Bob I talk a great deal about my athletics but compared to Winks or others I'm a perfect "flat-tire".' This was characteristic self-effacement. In fact he was one of the fastest runners on the campus, winning a crucial race against Yale. The papers, which covered these events, mentioned his connection with Lady Astor and nicknamed him 'The Freshman Flier'. A photograph showing the Harvard team of four running towards the camera confirms Peter's image of his physical self; he appears much smaller than the others, pixie-like with a disproportionately large head. It was somehow typical of the way life wrong-footed him that he was judged to have come second in the most important race of the year at Harvard: a race that the published photograph of the finish line shows him to have won by several inches.

Phyllis visited him in the summer of 1922: it was a disastrous expedition. Whatever new affection he was showing in his letters, apparently expressing a great desire to see his mother, he couldn't match it in his meetings with her. The visit was plagued by omissions and thoughtlessness on his part. He displayed a coldness and emotional paralysis of which he was partly and painfully aware, writing to his mother that he felt 'as though I'd committed some cruel deed and that pathos was reigning everywhere'. He heard the fog horn after she left and 'pictured you weeping and the whole thing seemed terrible'. Phyllis wrote to Bob in July: 'I haven't yet told him what a trick he played on me . . . I shall never be led astray by his letters again.'

By the following year Peter was suddenly full of regrets for the way he had behaved to Phyllis. On her next visit their meetings were more successful and he wrote to her after her departure: 'It was a dream come true to see you just the same sweet Ma unchanged because you can't be different or better in your unique self at your home with the children. The only regret I have is that my narrowness gave way to possibly unbalanced prejudice and that I didn't receive criticism in at all the right spirit. I'm sorry but I appreciate it all now and hope you'll forgive.' Phyllis had had her third child with Bob Brand, completing a family from which Peter understandably felt excluded. But he tried hard to please, writing to Bob, 'How I long to come over and see you all . . . Bob you must look quite like the "Rat's rubbers" with your little family . . .'

In 1924, consulting no one, Peter left Harvard without completing his exams. Phyllis had written to Irene, asking her to 'talk to him about leaving Harvard', hoping it was untrue. 'I haven't had a letter for nearly two months. I wish he wouldn't go around telling everyone how much he loves me and admires me & etc & then treats me as he does. It reminds me so of his Pa & makes me feel sort of sea sick.'

Peter went to New York and took two brief jobs, one as a law court reporter on the *Herald Tribune*. He decided that office life was bad for him, partly on the grounds that it made him 'pale and constipated' and by 1926 he was unemployed. He was only seeing his father in the summer and then barely once a fortnight. On these occasions Reggie was drunk but still managed to communicate his disappointment to Peter, driving him to a 'frenzy', as he confided to Irene. Peter, who received only irregular hand-outs from Reggie and a mysteriously diminished allowance from his grandmother's trust, was now living in a cheap New York flat and going out to a Child's restaurant (slot-machine food) for breakfast. He complained to Phyllis, 'When you see me you'll find that I'm about the same, if anything a bit uglier, a terrible disappointment for the son of a personality plus Langhorne sister.' He suffered bouts of loneliness and homesickness for his childhood: 'Do you still cold cream at night, Mother? The hot water in the morning and your bracelet knocking on the bed post and your slippers that made that characteristic sound on the floor are really missed a great deal and I must hear them again.' He became obsessed with marriage — the enticements and the fear of it — and often wrote to his mother of his romances, in particular with a débutante called Mimi Brokaw, adding clumsily embarrassing details about other girls he had slept with: '. . . we will "love" for hours and fall asleep in each other's arms'.

On a business trip to New York in 1926 Bob reported back on Peter's condition. 'Nancy [Lancaster] says her friends tell her he is v reserved and queer and lives too much by himself . . . I gather he seldom sees his father, who is living with a woman. Undoubtedly he feels v homeless and longs for home life and to come over to England.' He also discovered that Peter had broken off his relationship with Mimi Brokaw, who had subsequently become engaged to Peter's best friend, Dick Tucker, who shared his apartment. 'He lets Dick Tucker have his bedroom for nothing & he sleeps in a bed which in the day is hidden behind a screen in the sitting room!' Bob was mystified by this and much else in Peter's life, but paid his debts with a cheque for $1,000. 'His passion is now to do something with aeroplanes,' he reported. 'He says it is full of romance and will be something big. You know how he always deludes himself with dreams.'

But it was indeed flying that saved Peter. He turned out to be a natural mechanic. Even before Lindbergh's flight in May 1927, which spawned an army of gentlemen aviators flying powerful 'monocoupes', he had caught the bug. He told none of his family that he had been spending his days at Curtiss Field, New York, offering his services for nothing as a 'grease monkey', preparing planes for record-breaking, long-distance flights. He found new companionship in the camaraderie of the hangar, where he was known as 'Pete', and acquired his pilot's licence. He wrote to Phyllis, '. . . I'm afraid Mother dear your son is just not cut out for social success with the intelligentsia . . . the sound of lathes in a good machine shop is music to my ears.' In August 1927, three months after the Lindbergh flight, Peter took delivery in Dayton, Ohio, of a Waco biplane with a 200-horsepower Wright Whirlwind engine. He had sold his Isotta Fraschini motor car and his flat to pay for it and Reggie had made up the difference. He had a hair-raising journey flying it back to Long Island, losing his way in fog and getting his bearings, at 50 feet, only by recognizing his parents' old house at Westbury. He was immediately in the gossip columns of the *New York Times*, as an aviator and as Lady Astor's nephew. Nancy told him he was 'trying to be a hero'. Peter couldn't get it right with his family, even though in less than a year he had become a fearless stunt flier, a daredevil, and the 'personality' he had always wanted to be. That September, he said, he intended to go in for the Trans-Continental Derby. He was elected a member of Lindbergh's Quiet Birdmen Club.

In 1928 he wrote to his mother, 'I'll bet I'll be someone yet because I'm now in something I love with heart and soul and there's a demand for people like that.' He added, 'Flying seems the only real way to escape the horrors of getting tangled up in a marriage . . . where I could worry myself straight to hell & experience all the godawful things that you and Father went through.' Peter could now nurse his loneliness in the hours alone in the cockpit, roaring across America like Saint-Exupéry, delivering aeroplanes. It was no accident that Peter had chosen flying as his obsession. The rich and dashing gentlemen aviators were a close fraternity with a strong image of themselves. They shared a code of chivalry and a sense of omnipotence derived from their mastery of the air and the god-like power of their machines.

In that summer of 1928, Peter scribbled a letter on the back of an envelope in the cockpit of his aeroplane, the handwriting shaking with the thermals and engine vibrations. 'Dear Mother I am up in the air at

1000 feet on a 66 degrees heading, motor roaring, headed from New York to Boston. I've "pulled up" through the ceiling and clouds just a few feet below my landing gear are whisking by at 130 miles per hour. Hello I see New Haven Connecticut through a hole in the clouds but Oh Oooh! it looks sort of dark ahead towards Newport and I wouldn't be surprised if there was some pretty bad ground fog around Pt. Judith. I'll cut inland a bit and see if I can get round it.' 'It's wonderful,' he told her, 'how flying literally reduces the world to a place about the size of an olive.'

Winkie had been sent to Eton in 1923. In contrast to Peter, he was an engaging and much adored boy, passionate, in his teens, about ragtime music and smart clothes, and a talented games player. His closest ally among his English cousins was David Astor, two years his junior. However, Peter was Winkie's American hero and they corresponded across the Atlantic. Winkie would arrange the hit jazz records Peter sent him in a pile and place above them reverently a picture of Peter's car, the Isotta Fraschini.

Nancy believed that Phyllis loved Winkie above all her children, and she, too, recognized his charms, writing pointedly to Phyllis, 'I do so love Winkie. I've had a good try at the Brands, but they are as strangers compared with Winks.' Phyllis was fascinated by Winkie. She loved his looks, his 'delicious laugh' and his companionship. 'I miss Winks dreadfully,' she wrote to Bob in 1923, 'and I hope he did not find letters from Peter at Eton.' But desperate not to spoil him, she had begun, as with Peter, to treat him severely. She wanted to wean him away from 'that type' as she now described the house of Brooks. 'So instead of giving him a good pony,' said Nancy Lancaster, 'she'd give him a bad one to make things hard for him. She was terrified he would become like his father.'

Winkie never took up riding, perhaps deliberately, thus severing one crucial bond with his mother. Phyllis wanted what she thought of as a plain 'natural' world for Winkie – the opposite of the luxury that fascinated him. 'I fear Nannie has forgotten what simplicity means,'

Phyllis wrote captiously to Bob Brand. 'She told me last night she thought I ought to send Winkie back to Eton by motor instead of train! If I had ten motors I wdn't do it.' As she became more methodically strict and denying, Winkie began to believe in adolescence, that he was losing his mother's affections. He had a sweet nature and he liked his siblings, but at the age of fourteen, when his half-brother Jim Brand was born, he wrote bitterly to his mother from Eton: 'You will have to use a heavy hand with him when he gets bigger as you do with me!!'

Phyllis believed it was her trainer's hand, with the lunging rein to which he was attached, that would bring out Winkie's breeding. She often used animal images. She described him delightedly, when he came home for the Easter holidays at the age of sixteen, as 'strong and muscular as a little bull'. David Astor remembered Phyllis 'saying she liked little boys who were like fox terriers'. 'And Winkie was exactly that,' he said. 'He was full of life and energy and fun and he was just about the best balanced person. He couldn't play a game without doing it beautifully . . . He was her type and Phyllis adored him. I think she was, therefore, trying to hold on to him all the more and trying to make him do what she wanted.'

Phyllis was able to accept Winkie's interest in girls – something that Nancy formally forbade her sons in her unashamed possessiveness: 'It makes me feel a little ancient when he says he is going out to dine with some girls and boys at a restaurant. It is very hard to "let go" I find,' she wrote to Bob, 'but he is now 17 and a half & I spose I must.' In fact, like Nancy, Phyllis couldn't let go when it came to Winkie asserting real independence by pursuing his own tastes and allegiances.

Winkie was obsessed with his light-blue gramophone – his most precious possession. He would write to his mother from school, 'Do, I beg of you take care of the gramophone.' He came back for the holidays one summer, when Phyllis was elsewhere, to find a new consignment of twenty of the latest ragtime records from Peter in America. Bob wrote to Phyllis, 'He was thrilled & it was with extreme reluctance he cd tear himself away. I have arranged he can take them & his gramophone to Rest Harrow . . .' adding defensively, 'He wd be

miserable otherwise as he says by Xmas they will be out of date!' But
the jazz records touched a nerve in Phyllis. Nora's son Tommy Phipps
remembers her bursting into the room one day in the guest cottage at
Furneux Pelham, where Winkie was playing 'Black Bottom Stomp',
and losing control as she confiscated the records – Peter's gifts. 'It was
as if he'd been shooting cocaine. It was something extraordinarily
immoral.'

Winkie complained to his cousin David about his mother's severity, as well as her bad and sparse food. He thought she kept her house
'deliberately' dark and uncheerful and preferred the grandeur of
Cliveden, while David preferred staying at Furneux Pelham with his
sympathetic Aunt Phyllis. Phyllis gave David solace although she would
never let him criticize, or complain about, his mother. Winkie couldn't
understand David's problems with Nancy who treated Winkie, as
Phyllis's son, with special favouritism.

While Phyllis insisted on 'simplicity' Winkie continued to
develop a love of dandyism and overspending, a yearning for grand
hotels and first-class travel. His clothes, which he regarded as an art
form, became more extreme. He owned many pairs of shoes and
dreamed of a valet to iron their laces. His suitsleeves clung to his arms,
sealed at the wrist with eight buttons. Dressing took up a great deal of
time and effort. 'This morning,' wrote Bob to Phyllis, 'Winkie arrived
down in what I told him was a ridiculous suit with a double breasted
waistcoat, very cut in, a terribly "shaped" coat & extremely pleated
trousers. He also said he was going to Peal's [of Jermyn St, one of the
most expensive men's shoe shops in London] to order a pair of tennis
shoes. I got quite angry with him . . . His passion for clothes is astonishing.'

Bob Brand had discovered that on a holiday in France with a Mlle
Vignand, hired by the Brands to teach him French, Winkie spent his
allowance taking her to the St Regis Hotel, to a restaurant and the theatre. 'He gets into extravagant ways v quickly,' wrote Bob. 'He is going
to be a difficult problem so far as expenditure is concerned.' Bob was
kind and attentive to Winkie, and more tolerant than his watchful

mother. The two were close in a way Bob Brand never managed with
Peter. Winkie signed his letters to Bob Brand, 'Your aff. son Winkie'.
He was proud of Bob's *réclame*, enclosing a cutting with his neat and
dutiful letters, describing Bob, 'whose reputation as a financier is
world-wide'.

But Winkie's natural ally was Nora. Just as Bobbie had been
Nora's false chaperone, Nora, now aged thirty-seven, acted as Winkie's
secret agent for metropolitan pleasures. They shared the same tastes for
glamour, high spending and, particularly, for musicals. An unsuspect-
ing Bob Brand offered Winkie a theatre outing with his Aunt Nora one
night in 1926, while Phyllis was in Plymouth. 'I thought she wd dine at
home & go quietly to a theatre,' he told Phyllis. Instead Nora took
Winkie to the Savoy Grill where they dined with a popular actress
called Betty Chester, who was appearing in a musical comedy at the
Shaftesbury Theatre, and 'a man called Seabright'. Bob happened to be
dining nearby himself and called in at the Savoy where, to his amazement, he saw the party: 'Winkie lolling back in a chair taking his coffee
and puffing a cigarette. You sh have seen his face. The cigarette suddenly disappeared under the table . . . Nora was resplendent in the
most brilliant golden dress.' Bob later discovered she had taken a box at
the theatre to accommodate Mr Seabright and the modest evening had
turned into a spending bonanza. Winkie got a dressing-down the next
morning. As for Nora, 'She really is foolish,' Bob wrote, 'I suppose I
shall have to pay for the whole entertainment. She isn't fit to send
anyone of Winkie's age out with.'

At Eton Winkie's school work was poor to atrocious. 'He shows
himself a shirker when he is faced with difficulties,' reported his classics master. 'He could do better if he could set his teeth . . . But he is
too well satisfied with himself and self indulgent to do so.' In French
he was bottom. Nevertheless, added the master, 'I like him.' Winkie
was good at Maths, however, and his contemporaries never thought of
him as a dim boy or a 'laggard'. His dandyism and his excellence at
sport made him popular but he was in constant trouble with the
authorities. He was often beaten (corporal punishment administered

by the senior boys) and in 1926 at the age of sixteen he was 'swiped' or birched by the headmaster for repeated cribbing – the most serious punishment at Eton short of being expelled. This was a deliberately intimidating and painful ritual, and it made Phyllis's 'mother's heart fly up in rage at the vision of Winkie being held down by hired help (a school official received 5 shillings for the task) and leathered by Alington [the headmaster] but I am prepared to stand anything to make a man of him.'

There was evidence of Winkie drinking and playing hooky to slip off to London. He always seemed to have a little extra money – possibly provided by Peter, who had come into some of his inheritance at the age of twenty-one. Winkie had made a glamorous young friend in Margaret Whigham, later Duchess of Argyll, whose name was soon to be included in Cole Porter's song, 'You're the Top'. Her memoirs describe her father sending the Rolls to Eton to collect a group of boys, including Winkie, who were 'not only good looking but tremendous fun', to play tennis and dance.

Nora, the promoter of romance in any form, took Winkie and Margaret, on the weekend of the Eton–Harrow match, to see *Show Boat*, which had just opened in Drury Lane and starred Paul Robeson. 'Nora Phipps', wrote Margaret Whigham, 'turned out to be more fun than the rest of us put together, and no young girl could have had a more enchanting chaperone.'

Winkie in turn took Margaret, aged fifteen, to lunch at Cliveden, where she had a 'shattering' experience. 'I remember being overawed even at the sight of Cliveden and by the stone staircase that led up to the house and seemed to be never ending. Once in the hall I met Lady Astor looking just as formidable as she was reputed to be, and she did nothing whatever to put me at my ease.' As soon as lunch began, Winkie left the dining room. Nancy signalled Margaret Whigham to leave as well. It turned out that Winkie, the worse for drinks before lunch, had thrown up on the carpet in the hall outside. The couple were made to leave the house 'without lunch' in disgrace. The source of pre-lunch drinks was undoubtedly Bobbie, 'Mon Capitaine', who had a speakeasy in his rooms upstairs – a fact known to the staff but not to his parents.

Towards Easter 1928, Winkie begged his mother to be allowed to go to America, 'which I've been longing to do for five years', to see Peter and his father. Phyllis was particularly worried by this reasonable request because Winkie's housemaster had suggested that Peter had been trying to persuade Winkie to leave early and to emigrate permanently to America. Winkie had just taken his Oxford exams but, even with the easy requirements for a boy of his background, and with Bob's influence, had little hope of getting in. Winkie left Eton – for mysterious reasons but with his mother's approval – before the end of the Lent term.

A classic valedictory of its kind was sent to Phyllis by Winkie's housemaster, the Rev. J. C. Chute: 'He just <u>isn't</u> and never has been an Etonian,' he wrote, 'nor has he reacted to the ordinary Eton stimuli . . . He is of a type to which I am not accustomed – I suppose it is American blood. I've always liked him but realized that he did not "fit" here. I wonder what he will fit into?'

Phyllis must have wondered where she had failed in her programme of character-building as she read: 'He is just a visitor, mildly interested in our ways, submitting with a fair grace to our customs but wholly lacking in enthusiasm. It is not unfitting [Chute meant 'it is typical'] that he should leave finally before the end of the half, when he could have been a great help to the House Rugger side in the Final of the House matches: I know the reasons for his going – and they were quite valid – but the ordinary English boy just <u>couldn't do that!</u> I had a very interesting talk with him just before he left. He seems very unsettled, & inclined to seek his fortune in America . . .'

By June 1928 Winkie was aboard the *Majestic* bound for America. 'It's marvelous!!!' He wrote to his mother, 'This is certainly a wonderful boat it is enormous the restaurant is exactly like Claridges, just what I like, and everything is de luxe.' Phyllis was right to fear his departure; Winkie never came back to live with his mother.

*

David Astor, who saw Winkie as an icon of style and fashion, also had a special insight into his predicament. David was devastated when Winkie, his family ally, left him behind at Eton and went to America. It triggered off a severe emotional crisis at the age of sixteen, whose real cause, he discovered, was the same as Bobbie's self-mocking explanation for his own condition: 'As you might have guessed, it's Mother.'

David suffered, along with his siblings, the indelible, and in some cases tragic, effects of what Harold Nicolson described as the 'stupidity' with which Nancy brought them up. David judged that Nancy's first three children — Bobbie, Bill and Wissie — were 'shockingly treated' by Nancy, leaving his own scarred childhood and adolescence out of this assessment.

Nancy believed that family affection was a given fact like blood, or tribal loyalty. It didn't need affirming or demonstrating, just, from time to time, 'poking up'. 'Conceived without pleasure, born without pain' Nancy would say proudly to her children. 'Is that why we're all so odd?' Jakie once replied. When her younger sons were in their teens and one of the playful-but-rough verbal battles was taking place, with Nancy ahead, as always, on points and footwork, she said, 'I suppose you all think you're misunderstood.' Bobbie replied, 'There's no question of being understood. We've given up hoping for that long ago. All we want is a bit of civility.'

The closeness and warmth that Phyllis and particularly Nora gave to her young children were not to be had from Nancy. For the Astor children emotional nourishment came not from their mother but from Miss Gibbons, the nanny who occupied the nursery floor, survived thirty years and died at Cliveden, unconverted to Christian Science. She was a paragon of affection and understanding and gave praise where it was due. In this last respect, Nancy was especially lacking; it was when things were going well that her children had the least chance of attention. If they were sick she might come, at least, and massage their head. On rare tea-times or evenings when she wasn't busy with the guests that poured through the doors of Cliveden, she would read Uncle Remus, performing the characters in their Southern voices. She

would invent fables from Mirador, working in the characters of her
brothers Buck, Harry and Keene, recreating her mythological childhood world. This was the closest she would get to intimacy before
restlessness would bewilderingly change her mood. She would switch
to an admonitory tone; battle often followed and then tears and an
order to stop crying, 'an order so perplexing', wrote Michael Astor,
'that it occasionally worked.'

The Christian Science lessons that took place in her boudoir provided rare moments of closeness. But they were not quiet moments of
instruction. There was so much talking, commanding and telephoning
that Nancy would get lost in the texts and the children would lose
whatever concentration they had mustered. The 'lesson', which was
punctuated by Nancy repeating the Christian Science slogans with great
earnestness: 'Man is made in the image and likeness of God', sometimes ended in loud arguments. On one such occasion Bobbie Shaw,
who was normally excluded from these sessions, came in during a
lesson that had broken down in disorder and quickly withdrew again.
He was found sitting in the hall, shaking his head with mock contrition
and saying 'I should have known, I should have known, when I heard a
noise like a bullfight that it was the Bible lesson.'

Nancy's eldest Astor son, Bill, said that in order to maintain any
close relationship with her you had first to kill your love. 'Mr. Billy was
frightened of her,' said Rose Harrison, 'he would turn white when she
came in the room [a description also given by Bill's third wife,
Bronwen]. When I was in the Westminster Hospital, Mr. Billy turned
round to me and he said, "You know Rose I've never had any mother's
love." I said, "Don't you talk so silly" . . . I knew it was the truth. She
couldn't. I don't think she ever took them in her arms and held them,
kissed them or gave them any affection. It was a routine. Get up, go to
bed, dress for tea . . .' David claimed that admiration had to be substituted for two-way love – a quantum leap for a child – and he often
longed for his mother to be more like Nora. Nancy, however, dismissed
all Nora's qualities: she thought such affection was a soppy quality in a
mother, and somehow misguided and bad, like Nora herself.

Nancy's unfavourable comparisons of Bill as an infant with Bobbie, and her disappointment in him, was transmuted over the years into a form of loveless possession. Bill belonged to the early days of the marriage to Waldorf, when Nancy regarded 'those Astors' as a foreign tribe that she didn't belong to, and he remained stuck with the Astor label, never wholly accepted by Nancy. He grew up when Waldorf and Nancy were in their sternest and most earnest period of Christian Science and political idealism, when it was unclear in David's view, 'what they wanted their children to be'. They were not able to be as generous and easy-going with these first children as they were, by comparison, with the later ones. There is a photograph of Nancy and Bill together at Henley Regatta in 1925, Bill dressed in the pale blue flannel of the Eton eight, of which he was cox, his face pinched with anxiety. What Bill chiefly remembered of that day, in which the Eton crew were beaten in the second heat, was Nancy gloomily blaming it on the fact that he hadn't been working hard enough at his Christian Science to assure victory.

A little encouragement from Nancy would have gone a long way to keeping her children off the casualty list. Instead she would criticize, correct and comment unfavourably on their appearances and achievements. Bobbie was fond of the warm and homely wife of the Cliveden coachman who lived above the stables. When he was at Cliveden he would always go and have a cup of tea with her. 'He really felt at home with her,' said David Astor, 'Once he came back and said, "It's very strange. When I come home Mother says 'Where have you been? Look at you, look at your face, your trousers are too long. You look all wrong.' But when I go and see Mrs Brooks she says, 'Oh, Mr. Bobbie you do look well. Where have you been?'" He said, "It makes a difference, doesn't it?"'

It was at the onset of adolescence that Nancy's children began to be battered by the whirlwind of her domination. By 1924 the nursery was closed: Bill was seventeen, Wissie, fifteen, David, twelve, Michael, eight and Jakie, six. 'Never tell me that a divided household doesn't mean agony and misery for the Mother,' wrote Nancy to Phyllis on the

Phyllis Brooks

*Phyllis Brooks, Nora Phipps
and Nancy Astor*

Henry Douglas Pennant

Bob Brand (right)

Phyllis and Bob Brand

Bob and Phyllis Brand

Winkie Brooks, Phyllis and Bob Brand

Bobbie Shaw

Nancy and Bobbie

Winkie Brooks

Phyllis Brand and Winkie at Sandwich

Phyllis Brand, with Winkie, Dinah and Virginia

Winkie Brooks

Waldorf, Nancy and Astor children in Scotland

Waldorf and Nancy Astor with Phyllis Brand and children

Phyllis Brand and Fountain Winston at Mirador

Nora Phipps, David Lloyd George
and Bobbie Shaw at Cliveden

Nancy Astor at Plymouth

Nancy Astor at Plymouth

Phyllis Brand with her sons, Winkie (left) and Peter Brooks

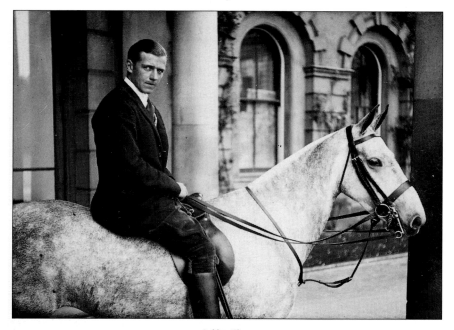

Bobbie Shaw

David Astor

Winkie Brooks at Eton

Peter Brooks with Monocoupe and flying trophies

Winkie and Adelaide Brooks, 1936, at El Morocco soon after their wedding

Left to right: *Bill Astor, Bobbie Shaw, Wissie Willoughby de Eresby,*
Nancy Astor, David Astor, Michael Astor, Jakie Astor

Wissie and James Willoughby de Eresby
on their wedding day

Waldorf Astor as Lord Mayor of Plymouth

Bob Brand at Eydon

Bob Brand and Nancy Astor at Sandwich, early 1960s

Waldorf Astor

*Nora at the wedding of Dinah and
Lyttleton Fox, 1943*

Nancy Astor

Nancy Astor

subject of Peter's departure. 'It's simply laying up trouble for your old age, and Heaven knows there is enough trouble without laying it up.' Nancy didn't imagine that a household could be divided when all its members were present. Neither she nor Phyllis had any notion of dealing with adolescence — what Phyllis called 'the boy problem' — even though they gave each other much advice on the subject. A rigid — and selfish — idea of what they wanted their children to be, based on some view of themselves and some fear of the past, was to be the real, but invisible, layer-up of trouble. In Nancy's case, her children were her exclusive possessions to the point where even their friends were seen as a threat to her ownership.

Michael Astor remembered Nancy as a 'lively, dancing, sparkling figure' in his childhood before the bitter battles for independence took over. David Astor recalled, at the age of eighty, 'My mother's voice coming down stairs now would move me more than any other sound. It was as if the light was going on and everything was coming to life and I felt alive. I would have gone anywhere to spend time with my mother when I was young. I can only tell you that in spite of everything, the thought of my Ma still brings more joy and comfort and courage to me than the thought of almost anyone else — even though the thought of her can also bring feelings of discouragement and of emotional betrayal.'

Wissie, the only girl in the family — highly strung, nervy and beautiful — was a main sufferer from Nancy's ruling method of blowing hot and cold, raising and demoting her favourites. She was ruthlessly put down by her mother, as if she presented some kind of competition to Nancy, and her confidence never recovered. Willing, friendly and admiring of her mother, Wissie was nevertheless subjected to 'unmerciful teasing' and 'snubbing' and continuous correction. She was also 'drowned' by the presence of her cousin, Alice Perkins (later Winn), Lizzie's daughter, who was treated with special favouritism by Nancy as a Langhorne, and a true Virginian, and who could never do anything wrong. As part of the family Alice shared holidays with the Astor children, Nancy and she 'speaking the same language', all of which put

Wissie out on a limb. Alice was understandably unpopular with her cousins at that age and became a particular victim of Bobbie's cruellest humour. Joyce Grenfell, another cousin, brought up affectionately by Nora, was also strong and confident by comparison with Wissie, despite her own fear of Astor gatherings. Generally, Nancy liked to promote other cousins above her own children. Writing to Irene about Jim Brand, she declared: 'I honestly never met a more attractive or more brilliant child. He puts my young ones in the shade.'

But David, born in 1912, was Nancy's special case. Nancy was relaxed enough to make a big fuss of him in his first four years – her letters are full of praise for him; he was a gift, a pleasant surprise. Then, confusingly, after Michael and Jakie were born in 1916 and 1918 she blew cold, scarcely bothering to visit David when he was sent away to his first prep school. He was taken instead by Mr Lee, the butler at Cliveden, who walked him up and down and told him of his memories of not wanting to return to the trenches, until he was ready to go in.

David had the feeling he had been abandoned, sent into exile for no apparent misdemeanour. His trust in his mother was fractured and would never mend. By the time Nancy suddenly blew warm towards him again, in the late 1920s when he was in his teens, it was too late. She then restored him as her favourite, after Bobbie, claiming him as her property, and denying him any other important relationship. She had marked out his future and wrote mysteriously to Phyllis that he had 'the makings of a Virginia Captain'. He would be trained up as a Christian Science practitioner, the standard bearer of the family faith. He belonged, in her mind now, in a trio with herself and Philip Kerr, which for David was an embarrassing relationship in any case. Despite the early damage to his self-confidence and his apparent diffidence, David was becoming the most critical and independent-minded of her children. Nancy sensed the danger: 'I wish you'd been born an ugly girl,' she told him, 'then you couldn't leave me.'

'My mother would always bring things to the point of a row. She would criticize people to the point where they'd protest. You couldn't avoid being drawn into combat. But she did it as a form of affection,' said David. He added, 'It's very difficult to talk about my mother truthfully without making her sound hateful, which she really wasn't.'

David tried, at first, to reason with Nancy and persuade her to grant him independence peacefully. But Nancy never understood what he was talking about. In the holidays they would often argue, Nancy putting on her demoralizing funny 'mad' wall-eyed look when cornered. With some honesty Nancy admitted that the only real power she had over her children was that she could check them, even bring them back by making them laugh. It was her last weapon; the one that ended all argument.

At other times the fights would end inconclusively in a tearful, and rare, embrace. Often the rows were about sex: 'My mother made it impossible to bring home girlfriends . . . She tried to convince me that falling in love was "a snare and illusion",' said David. At around the age of eighteen David began to warn his mother that he couldn't fit in with her wishes; that he would be a disappointment to her. He told her, with some courage, that he had doubts about Christian Science, which had no emotional content for him; that he wanted to live an independent life, had no wish to be celibate and certainly no ambition to be the ugly girl at home. Nancy was to write: 'He thinks CS has failed him. Needless to say it never occurs to him that he has failed CS.' 'I can remember her saying to me much later,' recalled David, '"Philip agrees you have seen the light of Christian Science and so you'll come back one day."'

The long fight cost David dearly. He claimed to the author of *David Astor and The Observer*, Richard Cockett, that he 'wandered through youth in an anxious and unsatisfactory confusion, being neither good nor bad, neither at home with my parents nor able to leave them'. He suffered an adolescent crisis at Eton – a collapse that left him feeling lonely and demoralized, and 'shaky'. But oddly, the first trigger for this sense of loneliness and depression, he remembered, was his ally Winkie's departure to America. His housemaster alerted Nancy who sent Philip Kerr, familiar with the traumas of apostasy and a veteran of depression, to counsel him. On their afternoon walks he sold David on reading, telling him 'if you can read you can really choose your company and meet much more interesting people than you can meet otherwise'. But Philip wouldn't listen to complaints about Nancy, which angered David. 'He also told me', David remembered, 'that people who have a happy upbringing often end up about as interesting as a sausage on a plate; those who have to solve their own problems often do better. And all that was kindly and reassuring.'

In the end David was saved by an inspired and attentive teacher, the historian Robert Birley, later headmaster of Charterhouse and in the 1960s of Eton, who recognized his ability. He began to win prizes and school sports events, as Birley steered him towards Balliol, fighting off Nancy's suspicious attempts to remove him from the school altogether.

Phyllis, writing to Irene in 1929 to commiserate with her after a Nancy attack, remarked that Nancy 'must feel what she has missed from her children but she is still far too cocksure she is always right & this gets all her children's goat, as she is 50 now. I wonder sometimes if she will ever learn.'

In the background was the ever patient, fastidious and kind Waldorf, a man of heroic character. It was he who kept the family together, even though thus far, because of his austerity and reserve, the children could never come to him as a court of appeal against their mother. Waldorf's life was in large measure devoted to the help and protection of Nancy and her talents, to keeping her on the rails politically and steering her out of trouble. Nancy knew she couldn't win elections at Plymouth without Waldorf and in the earlier years she listened to him. Only occasionally do Waldorf's letters to her protest at the endless criticism he received. 'You always seem to be so understanding with everyone else and with me to be sitting just trying to find fault,' he wrote to her from Jura in 1913. Nancy treated Waldorf as if he was a rock that could never be shifted or cracked, resenting, at the same time, the fact that she depended entirely on his support.

Waldorf's saintliness, his innocence and straightness had its greatest proof in his dealing with Nancy's relationship with Philip Kerr.
Nancy never regarded Waldorf's feelings when she embarked on her
long-term *coup de foudre* with Philip. Innocent though it was, the
panache and intellectual brilliance of her platonic friend was clearly a
substitute for the drama that Waldorf lacked. 'How I wish I was with
you. I long to have someone to talk to,' Nancy had written to Phyllis
some years earlier. 'Waldorf can't. There's no use he simply can't. So
away from my public life there's no one. You can't think how lonely it
gets. You don't know. However I've no right ever to complain . . .' And
Philip was always there, a constant companion, intensely engaged with
Nancy in their new religion, in a permanent 'honeymoon' or so it
seemed to Phyllis. It was disturbing for the rest of the family too —
hence David's embarrassment when Nancy tried to bring him into a
trio. But Waldorf never let it touch him. And Waldorf was by no means
incapable of jealousy. Phyllis was constantly reminding Nancy, in the
early days of her marriage, to beware of ignoring such feelings in him.
Writing about one of Nancy's society women friends she said to her in
1909: 'I am afraid W is worried about yr & A.'s intimacy. It seems to
annoy him, & I really can see how it would. So don't be foolish &
overdo it . . . remember that W comes as near being an angel as the
male can possibly do.'

The children cringed when Nancy turned her guns on him, talking him down and embarrassing him, mocking his old horsey friends.
His technique was not to react, to ignore it, to treat Nancy as a precocious child. One of her cruellest jibes was to imitate his secretary,
Miss Kindersley, who came from the Lazard banking family, and ran
the family finances with great efficiency. The fact that Waldorf
regarded her so highly annoyed Nancy, who worked up her devastating
imitation into a major performance. Miss Kindersley had a large
mouthful of teeth and Nancy could somehow make her own teeth
grow to match them, adding in her 'matter of fact upper class
voice . . . bringing everything down to common sense'. It became
impossible to see Miss Kindersley without remembering it. The

children thought it outrageous, but Waldorf ignored that too. If she went too far he would grip the back of her neck and shake her gently, the lion with the cub, saying 'easy, steady'. And Nancy never objected to this. The children didn't like to see their father pushed around and found it 'thrilling' to see her taken down a peg, however subtly. Waldorf never once gave into the pressure, never lost control and, incredibly, never uttered a hurtful word.

Without his farming interests and his racing stable, Waldorf would have suffocated. He would take the children to his training stable at Manton, on the Marlborough Downs, where they would spend the night. There they were 'on Tom Tiddler's ground', where 'we had left Mama and where Papa was the boss and where he did what he wanted. And we enjoyed it,' David recalled. Waldorf had become a highly successful breeder without investing much money, which was the grander way to do it. With three mares, one of them the hunter he had bought at Oxford, he came second in the Derby five times between 1917 and 1924. In the same period he won the Oaks five times, the 2,000 Guineas three times, the 1,000 Guineas twice. At the 1919 Derby, when Waldorf's horse Buchan, lost by a neck, Phyllis was amazed to see Nancy reading her Bible in the grandstand, 'holding the right thought and forgetting to look at the race'. When he came second in the Derby for the fifth time Nancy softened her usual indifference and said she was sorry for him. She often quoted, with admiration, his answer: 'What matters is that all the children are well.' But Nancy never let up on her antagonism to racing. Many years later, long after she had given up even reading her Bible in the grandstand while Waldorf's horses raced, she shouted to her son Jakie as he left Cliveden, 'Don't forget racing brings out the worst in all classes.' 'Just like the House of Commons,' he shouted back.

In June 1929 Bobbie was reported drunk on duty by the adjutant, who ordered him to his room and appointed another officer in his place. Bobbie was made to accept the commanding officer's suggestion that he resign his commission rather than face a court martial. This was not only a disgrace it was a disaster for Bobbie, whose life was constructed around the army.

Worse still, the real reason for his resignation was not drink – that was nothing new among officers – but that Bobbie was guilty of a homosexual act with another soldier. Like Edwardian adultery his homosexuality was accepted by his close friends as long as it was never mentioned and never discovered. The law was still much the same as in Oscar Wilde's day. The drink story was put out by his commanding officer to save Bobbie's reputation and that was the story Nancy and Waldorf, and the rest of the family, believed.

The effects on Bobbie – his demoralization and remorse, his greater dependence on his mother, and his bewilderment at the prospect of finding some alternative life – only became apparent slowly. Nancy had little idea of Bobbie's predicament, although she did write to a trustee of the Shaw family, warning against giving Bobbie money. Since he had left the Guards, she wrote in November 1930, one year later, 'as far as we can make out [he] does not one single thing, except sit in cinemas and visit his friends. He takes no exercise of any kind and has even given up riding. I shouldn't mind [giving him money] if he would work, but he won't.'

That same year Bill was at New College, Oxford, whose warden was the historian H. A. L. Fisher, Bob Brand's old tutor, now a figure of great prestige. Bill was a promising undergraduate at New College, but in his first year he fell gravely ill. Fisher considered that Nancy had actively prevented him from receiving medical attention and that his life had been put at risk. In a book called *Our New Religion*, Fisher produced a blistering and weighty attack on Christian Science. But Nancy and Philip Kerr simply dismissed it as an unwarranted outpouring by an unbeliever.

It was perhaps this mood of defiance which led Nancy to make her gravest and most lasting mistake with her children's health in December 1929. Wissie, aged twenty, was seriously hurt in a hunting accident at Kelmarsh, while staying with her cousin Nancy Lancaster. She fell at a fence, her horse rolled on her and the pommel of her side-saddle broke her back. A radiologist, called in by Ronnie Tree, brought a portable X-ray machine that showed that Wissie had severely injured her spine and that it should be 'rearticulated' immediately by an orthopaedic surgeon. Nancy and Waldorf then arrived with a Christian Science practitioner. After much argument, Nancy conceded that a doctor should be called but that only the surgeon who had operated on her abscess in 1914 would be acceptable. He arrived at midnight, knowing nothing about the true nature of Wissie's injuries, and 'flew into a rage', pointing out that as an abdominal specialist he was unqualified to treat Wissie. Nancy and Waldorf backed down and agreed to let him call a leading orthopaedic surgeon, who arrived the following morning. He too expressed some dismay at the delay of twelve hours, and insisted that Wissie be put in plaster immediately. Nancy objected. There was further fierce argument, but the surgeon prevailed and went ahead with the treatment.

Contrary to Christopher Sykes' account in his biography of Nancy, but confirmed by that of John Grigg, Wissie never made a full recovery. For the rest of her life, she could not sit down without pain. Whether or not the delay in treating her made a clinical difference, Nancy's behaviour was generally judged to have been outrageous, certainly by her sons. Nancy's description of the event, writing to Irene a few weeks later, is fascinating for its omissions and for her astonishing assertion that no doctor had been present. 'Wis has had no pain since the second day & looks well & cheerful & everything goes splendidly . . . I have never in my life been more grateful to "my curious religion" than this last fortnight.' Philip supported the party line, seeing Wissie's recovery as 'a real step in advance; the right answer to the Fisher book & the new attacks on CS'.

When Wissie made her own bid for independence four years later, she was subjected to further insulting behaviour. Deriding her marriage to a wholly admirable young man and one of the richest landowners in England, Nancy pronounced him, publicly and mistakenly, 'a bore', and mocking his name, as she repeated it, 'Lord Willoughby de Eresby'. The photographs show Wissie's extraordinary beauty and her happiness, walking down the steps of the Cliveden terrace in her long bridal dress on her wedding day, into her new life. When it came to the younger children, the parental regime relaxed a little, and their problems were not as great. Waldorf called Michael and Jakie 'The Chicky Boys', like two junior outlaw characters out of a *Beano* comic.

22

Nora's Garden of Roses

Nora's behaviour took several dramatic turns for the worse in the 1920s. Yet even in the estimation of her own family Nora's magic was great enough to outweigh her faults, grave and exasperating as these were. 'We'll just have to go on forgiving Nora,' ruled Irene, 'otherwise we wouldn't be able to enjoy her.' All children, in particular, adored Nora. If Nancy treated you roughly and inconsistently, Nora treated you with a mesmerizing interest and attentiveness. Her approach would signal an hysteria of excitement and anticipation. At Cliveden it was only for Nora that the children would go out and wait anxiously on the gravel for her arrival. Dinah, Bob and Phyllis's youngest daughter, said that waiting for Nora to come down the bedroom passage 'was like looking forward to paradise . . . She could get down to playing on your level in 5 seconds and make you die of laughter or die of sadness.' She looked wonderful too, 'sort of pretty and pert and well dressed'.

One of Nora's tricks, unforgettable for children, was playing the fairy tailor. The child would shut its eyes and Nora would measure for a suit, lengthening it here, taking a tuck there, choosing material. If it was a girl she would be got ready for the ball. The final act, by which time the child was either delirious with pleasure or half-asleep, was to slip the ring on her finger. Or the child would be a chicken that Nora would prepare for the oven; a bay leaf under the shoulder, salt, pepper, a little butter. The child would willingly fold itself into a ball, trussed and ready to roast. She invented a memorable family called 'The Buttonhooks', whose summer holidays were a long series of disasters.

Nora's daughter Joyce was unaware, until her teens, of the delinquent side of her mother's personality and of her chronic unfaithfulness to her father. The childhood she remembered and held on to was the one that became part of her celebrated stage performance in its odd mixture of class sentiment and satire: a cosy, idealized upper-middle class world with some Church of England and a little Virginia, in which Nora was the talented, rather whimsical mother; Paul the quiet, instructive father.

When Joyce was thirteen the family moved to an eighteenth-century red-brick house in St Leonard's Terrace, Chelsea. It looked across the Guards' cricket ground to Wren's Royal Hospital, one of the greatest views in London. From her windows Nora could monitor the cab rank in the Royal Hospital Road, and have one of her devoted drivers around within the minute to take her the few hundred yards to Peter Jones.

At the back of the Chelsea house was a large studio and this was the centre of Joyce Grenfell's cherished childhood: a pre-war world of Fuller's walnut cake, Tiptree Little Scarlet strawberry jam, and Nora's flower arrangements set against 'bright white walls, and strong pinky red' curtains. There was a Decca gramophone and a piano which Noël Coward would come to use. Ivor Novello brought Nora bunches of Parma violets.

There was much sharing of clothes among the Langhorne sisters and between the aunts and the nieces – a vestige of domestic life in *post bellum* Virginia. Joyce remembered the high moments when the suitcase would arrive from Nancy filled with Lanvin, Victor Stiebel, Schiaparelli. Nancy ordered these clothes in multiple quantities and gave many of them away. Nora was as generous as any of them, even with her debt-financed costumes (although it became more difficult when, in her mania for new clothes, she took to wearing mail-order dresses for a day and then sending them back, unwanted, with uncharacteristic punctiliousness). Later on, Nora radically changed her style of dressing and shocked one of her nephews by revealing the secret behind her own simple style, which was to become her trademark – a navy blue pleated skirt, a white blouse, and usually a tam o'shanter. Most women, said Nora, took the trouble to dress up fancily in bright colours and new fashion, thinking that this was what impressed men. In fact what men really liked was navy blue and white, pleats and simple blouses: they were frightened by anything else. Since flirtation was Nora's stock-in-trade these were the clothes she adopted.

Joyce was a conventional, physically unprepossessing teenager, awkward with the world and often embarrassed by Nora's comic turns and public clowning. Nancy, Nora and, to a lesser extent, Phyllis would think nothing of acting 'mad' in front of their children to keep the railway carriage to themselves. Joyce described herself as a 'narrow minded, prejudiced, self centred and self righteous' young girl and her mother couldn't resist teasing her for her conventionality and fear of embarrassment. In a railway carriage (a favourite forum for comedy) with one other woman passenger Nora would be French or *Mittel*-European. She would see a cow through the window and ask 'Eez set a gee-gee?' The woman passenger would smile and nod. Nora would attempt to drop a piece of paper on to her hat without the woman noticing. Mixed with Joyce's helpless sniggering was always the excited terror that Nora would be bored, give up and revert to her normal voice.

For many years Joyce was aware of Nora's admirers only as voices on the telephone. She accepted merely that Nora liked going out in the evenings, and her father preferred staying at home. Despite her hectic social life Nora's unswerving principle was to put her children ahead of everything and everybody else. Later Joyce discovered that she would even rush home in the middle of a matinée, dumping her beau, to be with them at bed-time.

Cuckolded and reduced, Paul had decided not to fight Nora. He found there was nothing he could do to improve her or check her excesses. He was fastidious about money and always concerned with treating people decently, but there was no appealing to Nora's conscience; she was without one and without any sense of cause and effect when it came to relations between adults. When things got out of hand, she put her faith in the 'fresh start', unilaterally declared and immediate in effect. Paul was still in love with Nora and deeply unhappy. He decided to accept an uneven marriage as the only way to preserve it, and in the meantime he was obliged to scramble around, borrowing from relations. This produced a predictable reaction from the sisters – who had no solutions of their own beyond paying Nora's bills and then complaining, especially when the next time they saw her they found her dressed 'in a superabundance of chiffon'.

As Nora continued to collect admirers, Paul became ever more patient as well as exasperated. He even complained to Bob Brand that when Nora's young men took her to the Ritz, the bill always came to him. Her affairs were becoming obvious to the younger generation. Her niece Phyllis Draper, Buck's daughter, remembered a visit to England in her teens: 'Nora had a boyfriend called Kroll who had black hair and a black moustache. He was so lickin' in love with Aunt Nora, you could see it written over his face. He didn't have to tell you. Even I knew what it was all about. Joyce caught on too. She knew. So I said to Aunt Nora "What does Uncle Paul say?" and she said "Not very much". I said "Well does he approve of it?" She said "Surely". She said "Paul is so sweet."' Among her other conquests was the Earl of Sefton, then a dashing officer in the Royal Horse Guards, a Maharaja and Waldorf's own brother, Colonel John Jacob Astor, who, said Phyllis Draper, 'sent her the most beautiful jewels to St. Leonard's Terrace you've ever seen in your life and I wonder to this day why Uncle Paul didn't raise hell'.

Nora began to lead her own separate life from Paul quite publicly and without pretence. Phyllis wrote to Bob as early as 1924: 'Nora is off for a visit for a week with some people none of us know, but Paul seems quite calm and happy about it – I hope he will get his reward before long, for I have never met such patience. It is so selfish of Nora to go on hurting him, and I know it really hurts him, though he never says a word against her. "Treat her rough" is the only kind of language Nora would understand — I wish he wd try it once . . . it is really uncomfortable being with Nora when you know she is deceiving everyone.'

Her infidelities were not solely to do with sexual passion. There was a part of Nora that was, simply, 'mad about romance'. Other people's affairs were almost as exciting as her own and at the first sign of it 'she would be around in a flash'. She would present her own admirers with a sentimental picture, her '*idée fixe*' of a cottage, covered with roses and hollyhocks, 'where she could go with just herself and whoever she wanted to be with'. It was the 'cunning cottage' of the Gershwin song of the period 'I've Got a Crush on You'. 'Nora always believed,' said her niece Dinah, 'that everything would have a happy ending.'

Joyce's débutante season was not a success. 'Flat-footed and staid', as she described herself, as well as 'large' and too tall, she had an air of gawkiness and felt uncomfortable and unattractive. In later years Nora would perform an irresistibly funny imitation of Joyce and herself at gatherings, with Nora smiling and beaming and nodding, trying to unstiffen her daughter and push her to the centre of the room. This was exactly the sort of skit Joyce performed later — the awkward schoolgirl in smocks and pigtails, or 'Lumpy Latimer', who turns up years later looking for her former school friends. Nora would also cajole Joyce into singing duets with her in public — which Joyce found intensely embarrassing.

When Joyce became engaged to Reggie Grenfell in 1929, Nora chose almost the very same day to embark on the most scandalous as well as the longest entanglement of her romantic career. Lizzie's daughter, Alice, was living in St James's Square with Nancy when Nora invited her to lunch on the day Joyce's engagement was announced. 'And she suddenly said to me: "You know Alice, I'm in the most terrible state. I'm very, very worried. A man I used to know very well who was awfully in love with me in America just before the war, I've just had a letter after not having heard from him for seven years to say he's coming over to England to get me and I'm terribly worried.'" Nora's 'correspondent', she then revealed, was Lefty Flynn, the Yale football star, and glee singer. Nora was 'obliged' she said, a word she bandied about a lot in the next few days, to see him. But there was one crucial omission in Nora's story: Lefty was already in England and he and Nora had also secretly resumed their affair.

Lefty had had an exciting fifteen years since his elopement with Nora. After the war, in which he had served as an aerial navigator with the Navy, he had been noticed by the director William Wellman singing with the Yale Glee Club in Los Angeles. Wellman was struck by his life-guard good looks, the 'broad shoulders' that had so attracted Nora in 1914, and by the early 1920s Lefty was starring in silent pictures. He had made five films: *Omar the Tentmaker* (1920), *Bucking the Line* (1921), *Salomy Jane* (1923), *The Drums of Fate* (1923) and *Open All Night* (1924). The last film had an appropriate title for Lefty's Hollywood swansong. Success had turned him into a genial but advanced drinker, who would disappear into his own world of comic fantasy for days on end. During the shooting of *Open All Night* Lefty had asked to go to the lavatory. Eight days later he was tracked down to a hotel in Oklahoma City where, according to his friend, the actor David Niven, he was 'sitting up in bed playing a guitar and painted bright blue from head to foot. In the room with him was a six-piece Hawaiian orchestra which he had picked up en route to San Francisco.'

His romantic career had been equally reckless. In 1915 the news-papers announced his second marriage to Miss Blanche Palmer, a Denver society beauty. 'Mr and Mrs Flynn will make their home in Colorado where Mr. Flynn owns a ranch at Craig,' it was reported. By 1925, Lefty was ready to marry again, although the announcement was made only by his fiancée, a film actress called Grace Darmond. Possibly Lefty had forgotten all about it, or was blotto at the time, because in the same year he married Viola Dana, who was a fairly well-known Hollywood star, aged twenty-seven. She was a very small woman, which would have appealed to the towering Lefty, one of

whose pranks was to stop small women in the street and bow to them
for comic effect. In 1927 Viola Dana obtained her divorce from Lefty,
claiming that her husband had been 'intoxicated for two and a half
years in our three years of married life'.

Two years later Lefty, described in a biography of the period as a
'dipsomaniac', was at a loose end. He had cabled Nora from Honolulu
and received an encouraging reply. The situation was irresistibly romantic to Nora. Like Nancy, she also had a soul-saving and proselytizing side
to her nature, much bolstered by her new belief in Christian Science.
Nora was deeply against drink and no doubt believed that she could save
Lefty. She saw only one option – to run away with him to some imaginary
cottage with roses where everything would have a happy ending. And so,
in early 1930, while Tommy was at Eton and Joyce newly married, she
and Lefty fled to the South of France. She left without a word to Paul.

A search party was formed once again, this time under Nancy's
command and with Rose Harrison and Joyce Grenfell. Reggie Winn,
Alice's husband, was included in the posse that boarded the Blue Train.
He was not the right man for the job. Charming, excitable, happiest in
White's and on the golf course, Reggie had shown promise of brilliance
at school until a cricket ball had struck him a debilitating blow and
although the effects were not obvious, Reggie could no longer lay
claim to a first-class brain. Deeply embarrassed by his errand, Reggie
tried to disguise it by taking along his tennis racquet and golf clubs. It
was a hopeless mission and Reggie ended up making friends with the
irresistible Lefty, who was found in the hotel restaurant putting golf
balls into a tooth-glass. Nora refused to return. She and Lefty had
resumed their close harmonies. Love had returned; the soufflé had
been successfully reheated.

Nora's relations believed that this was just another escapade, but
they were wrong. This time Nora would not come home. Lefty was her
destiny, she declared, and she intended to divorce Paul and marry him
as soon as possible. Nobody believed that this would actually happen.
It was presumed that the romance of life with the hard-drinking Lefty
would soon wear off and that a homesick Nora would return in time

for Tommy's school holidays. By March 1930 the couple had arrived in Paris – Nora declaring she would stay there and 'wait to be divorced' – and Nancy was writing that Nora was 'sticky about returning', and that 'Paul has taken Tommy to the country to steady him. Oh Irene try to wake poor little Nora up.'

Phyllis went to Paris that month and wrote to Bob, 'It seems so strange that I should be here & Nora not far off living as she is. What wd my poor mother say – I am sure she would be compassionate and indignant too.' Paul meanwhile sat in the background, believing that Nora would see reason and return. 'Paul seems to have great faith in Nora's judgement,' wrote Nancy, sarcastically.

Then Nancy played another card. She sent sixteen-year-old Tommy to Paris to try and lure Nora back. Tommy, who later became a successful Hollywood scriptwriter, wrote a play about the episode. He remembered it as a traumatic experience and questioned the 'curious lack of morality' that allowed Nancy to expose him to such a difficult situation. Lefty tried unsuccessfully to win Tommy over, asking him on automobile rides and outings in Paris. Tommy's dislike for Lefty deepened, as did his loyalty to Paul. Nora was unmoved.

In the spring the couple came to England and took a cottage in Deal, a village half a mile along the coast from Sandwich Bay and Rest Harrow. This was a deliberate ploy by Nora: she longed to have Lefty accepted by the family, and was prepared to risk Nancy's attacks. It was Phyllis who first recognized the *fait accompli*, writing to Irene: 'I feel if she really is to marry then we must see him & try to forget the rest. She seemed so pleased when I asked [to meet her] that I almost wept.'

Mystery surrounds Paul's acceptance of the divorce, and the speed with which it went through. But then Nora delayed her marriage plans and Phyllis seemed to have changed her mind about meeting Lefty. She reported to Irene her meeting with Nora at the Ritz Hotel in August: 'She looked very sunburned & healthy but her eyes looked puffy & not right . . . she was hurt that none of us had written a line to Lefty to say we had no ill feeling. Can you beat it?' The correspondence reveals that Phyllis's disapproval of Lefty had been reinforced by his shameless publicizing of their engagement. Lefty had taken Nora to Le Touquet 'where everyone that she knows goes & subjected her to more & more talk & one wd think a decent man would want to protect her from that sort of milieu. I came back home & had a nightmare thinking about Nora. It's so terrible to see her living as she is.' A month later, in September 1930, Phyllis doubted whether the marriage would happen after all. 'I somehow feel it is all over. It is now so strained seeing her & her values are all messed up & I am sure that she feels we ought to see Lefty but I shall not do this unless she marries him. No one tries to stop her & I think it has made the whole thing lose its kick.'

St Leonard's Terrace was sold. Paul moved into a gloomy furnished flat off Sloane Square and avoided his friends. Lefty returned briefly to America. There was a drifting eighteen months in Nora's life while she waited for Tommy to leave Eton, before joining Lefty. She went to Paris in February 1931, where she started mixing up letters and envelopes. Irene wrote to Phyllis: 'I received from her in Paris a letter <u>completely</u> covered with blots, only 6 lines & not signed & in it was another letter of the same kind saying Darling Lefty I have just come in to dine with (unreadable) & want to write a line (that was not signed either). Poor little thing <u>where</u> is she?'

Men in general liked Lefty enormously and instantly. Women found his relentless schoolboyishness tiresome. Phyllis imagined signs of regret and homesickness in Nora in the autumn of 1931 when she was on the verge of leaving England to join Lefty at Greenwich, Connecticut, a bohemian community with cheap accommodation where he had rented a house: 'I feel her large lump of clay is becoming heavy and sticky in her hands.'

To Irene, however, Lefty was anathema. She found him 'tacky' and called him 'The Man from the Golden West'. 'I can't abide Lefty. He turns my insides up in a knot . . . that fat mouth & pointed ears & they both acting as if they had done nothing & when I hear of the close harmony & the guitars I get sick.' Lefty had even taken to explaining, with photographs, the family trees of the Mirador servants. 'I could have rung his neck!! The idea!' wrote Irene. She rallied the family against him. Irene's plan was to keep Nora away from Virginia, where Buck had refused to speak to Lefty and the neighbours were gossiping viciously. Nevertheless in November the couple were finally married in Richmond in a blaze of publicity. Nora gave detailed and expansive interviews to any reporter who approached her.

Irene wrote to Phyllis: 'I do think Nora might have gone elsewhere to wed – poor old Paul!! . . . the utter lack of feeling she has shown is dreadful & so selfish.' In 'An interview with Mrs Paul Phipps', Nora had told the full story of her first elopement with Lefty in 1914, including descriptions of her life with Paul in Ottawa. She was quoted as saying, 'My duty to my children called me home . . . When I met him again all my old love welled up. I knew I must have him. Then a divorce was gotten in the pleasantest and kindliest fashion and ahead of us lies . . . *a garden of roses*.' It didn't seem to occur to Nora that she had broken Paul's heart. He never recovered from the trauma of Nora's betrayal, retreating into a shell of melancholy and loneliness until his death in 1956.

23

Winkie and the Jazz Age

Winkie sailed to America on the SS *Majestic* in June 1928 for what was intended to be a three-week holiday. Bob had arranged for him to return to work at a small private bank in Germany for six months, starting in July. Winkie's reaction to America was identical to that of Peter nine years earlier: bedazzlement mixed with anger against Phyllis that he had been deprived of it for so long. Winkie was a natural child of the jazz age and he had forever longed to join the grown-up world. He even looked the period part with his sharp fashions and his slicked-back hair. In addition, as if his life was being written by Scott Fitzgerald, he had a father who was very rich and lived in a large house on Long Island, 'the most marvellous place I have been', he reported. There the eighteen-year-old Winkie quickly discovered his confidence and his success with girls.

After two weeks in America his boyish letters to Phyllis contained the familiar signals that she dreaded. 'Father is in the very best form and I like him terribly,' he wrote, piling on the bad news, echoing Peter's 'discovery' of the martyred Reggie. And he had fallen for America: 'There is an awful lot of pep in everything that is going on. Everyone is free and on an equal level and you have to learn to be a man. There are lots of ways of getting on out here. Much more so than in England. People get on quicker. Things happen. Well I won't go on boring you.'

Phyllis walked into this minefield like a somnambulist. Neither her programme of disciplining Winkie and inducing mother-loyalty nor that of cleansing him of Reggie and America's influences, seemed to have worked. Once off the lunging rein Winkie was relishing his independence. Phyllis now began to repeat, almost exactly, her behaviour with Peter, which had caused her such lasting pain, as if this time, with her favourite son, the sanctions would succeed. She was blinded to Winkie's needs, never seeing beyond the threat of outside influences. Focusing as always on money she had managed to communicate with Reggie to try and clip Winkie's wings on what was still, as far as she knew, a three-week summer holiday. Reggie, for some reason, had complied.

'I think you did rather an underhand trick by writing to Father & telling him not to give me any money,' Winkie wrote to her from Mirador. 'It seems absurd to me and very narrow minded. How am I to get down here or anywhere for that matter. However if you must do that!!!! You make me very angry with you . . . I believe the heat is affecting me so I don't think I'll stay here more than a week.'

There were exciting tennis matches on Long Island to get back to. He went to many balls there including one given by Mrs Winthrop where 'The band was better than I have ever heard & the girls prettier than I have ever seen.' He had fallen deeply in love with a débutante called Isobel Henry. 'She gets more beautiful every time I see her,' adding, in his up-to-the-minute jargon, 'She is what I call "the berries".'

Winkie was taken to the Tunney versus Heeney fight and to the Cotton Club in Harlem to see Duke Ellington's band. Winkie's great interests were pleasure-seeking and money, style and glamour. He didn't seriously believe in anything else and from this point of view America was intoxicating; it was like a continuous Broadway show. He had been welcomed like a returning hero by Reggie, who showered him with gifts and garlands: 'He is having everything he wants,' Irene confirmed, 'on the top of a wave of admiration from Reggie.'

It is clear that Winkie decided to stay in America soon after he arrived. A talk with the Brookses' family lawyer revealed that if he remained in England he would inherit only one third of the money he was due when he was twenty-one. Reggie offered him $5,000 and an apartment above Peter's if he stayed. His grandfather presented him with a new car. Like Peter he felt sorry for his father, who was sober for a while after Winkie arrived in New York. They walked around the reservoir each morning and lunched at Reggie's club. Following in Peter's identical footsteps Winkie wrote to Phyllis: 'I find that all the time I have been living in England with you I should be allowed to see father by law three months in every year and this is the first time in twelve years. Also there are many other small facts that you never told me about. It makes me think that you have been rather selfish about letting father see me and he has not complained. So I think it is my duty to stay with him for at least another month or two.'

As to the job in the bank, he wrote, 'I don't think I could face going to Germany for 6 months all alone. I should probably go mad . . . I feel that this is the place I belong, after all I am an American and it is just coming out in me.' He was shedding his dandy English collars, getting American shirts with loose collars, getting 'tough' — 'You should see me now.' 'And anyway,' he added defiantly, 'I don't care what Aunt Nancy or anyone says about father he is a great friend and has a big heart. I like him very much. He may have his weak points but every one has those even you may have although you think you haven't.'

Irene was sent in to mediate. She called Winkie to her house and reported back, advising Phyllis, 'Darling Phyl it just had to come. There is no use getting hurt or worried, boys are made differently. Yours are charming. But you must realise — the other parent can't be eliminated and under the circumstances it was natural to occur this way. He finds his Pa in a most attractive house & I hear Reggie is sober and I suppose has just done all he could to make Winkie happy & therefore he likes it. How to advise you I do not know. But if you come to get him, Heaven knows I long to see you, it might just be agony . . . Pressure is the very worst thing.' In her next letter she wrote more forcefully, 'Leave him alone and he will come home bringing his tail behind him.'

But Phyllis rejected Irene's good advice. She sent Winkie a cable, ordering him home. Irene saw Winkie again, and discovered that he had indeed dug in; he refused to return. 'I did my best. I used tact, firmness & kindness. I could not touch him . . . He feels everyone has lied to him about his father. Someone has filled him with some kind of talk painting his father as a "badly treated man." Winkie said "Grandfather Langhorne loved my father." I explained what a hard time you had trying to keep the peace . . . You would find him combative now and he would say things he would regret all his life. Winkie will come to his senses one day I hope (and find out the truth about R). Oh I am so sorry for you.'

Winkie sent a telegram to Bob's office. 'REALLY BELIEVE BEST FOR BOTH WAIT AWHILE TO SEE EACH OTHER. PLEASE DON'T FEEL UPSET. LAST THING I WANT TO DO HURT YOU . . .' He followed this with a touching letter to his mother, pleading for his independence and saying that he feared returning to her 'strict eye': 'I have reached the age where I must be on my own and fend for myself . . . Mothers also have hard times when their children grow up they have to face it . . . Please do not think that I don't love you any more because I do more than anyone in the world and I shall always be thinking of you. Explain everything to Bob for me. I am sure he will understand. He always does in matters like this and I do appreciate it.'

Somehow, by September, Bob had fixed Winkie up with a place at Harvard. Phyllis came over in October and met him early one Saturday morning in New York at the Copley Plaza Hotel. She had calmed down enough to spend a happy day with him on Long Island: 'He seemed really pleased to see me . . .' Winkie told her he had to go back early to catch up with his work and that he was worried he wouldn't be able to get through the Harvard curriculum. Revealing how little she had grasped the situation, Phyllis wrote to Bob: 'Winkie looked really homesick when he had to say goodbye . . . I'm perfectly sure, if he had not seen the rosy prospects of a motor car and a fat allowance, he would never have wanted to stay over here. It may do him a lot of good. I hope and pray so. He is far more communicative and cosy with me than Peter, who I never feel is natural with anyone but himself.'

Winkie lasted barely two months at Harvard. Scared that he would fail his November exams, he simply walked out, reclaimed his motor car and headed for California. A flurry of letters followed. Nancy wrote to Irene, 'We are now reeling under Winkie's having left Harvard. It is an amazing thing. I simply cannot understand it. Phyllis doesn't know yet what to do.' Before Christmas 1928, Phyllis wrote to Irene, 'I am just longing for some news of Winkie, so far only the cable saying he had left H. and was going West . . . Why oh why do my boys seem to be so thoughtless. They wouldn't I know if they only half realised what it all means to me.'

Winkie's first communication arrived in January 1929, a letter written in late December from a hotel in San Diego. He seemed to have travelled alone across America, driving long, sleepless stretches, 'stopping only for food and gas' – south to New Orleans, West through El Paso. Winkie's letters were never reflective. He didn't intend to be ironic when he wrote: 'I am doing what Aunt Nancy thinks she's doing when she goes down to Sandwich: getting right away from everything and taking a complete rest.' He added, 'Don't think too harshly of your 2nd born. He may be a nit wit but he's still going strong.'

They were to meet again in spring 1929, when Phyllis brought the Brand children to Mirador for three months and enticed Winkie down for a weekend. He had, by then, agreed to take a menial job in Wall Street, working as a runner for the broking firm of Clark Dodge & Co. She wrote, after he left: 'Dearest Winkie, I hate saying goodbye to you. I love to see you come & hate to see you go.' She apologized for being 'a meddlesome old thing' and for having told him 'some truths you might have to know'. 'Nobody else on earth is going to do this but me & someday maybe things I've tried to tell you will percolate. If I did not love you very much I just wouldn't bother.'

Winkie telephoned in mid-June to say that the job was 'lousy'; 'but I believe he likes it' Phyllis wrote, deluding herself again. Winkie's letters were rare from now on. 'I do so long to hear; sometimes it gnaws at my heart,' Phyllis confided to Irene, 'but I deliberately try to put him out of my mind sometimes now.'

By September Winkie had bolted from Wall Street. He wrote to Phyllis from Southampton, 'Trouble at the office and I am now once again a free man . . .' Three months into his job, the office manager, 'a man whom I had seen nearly every day', summoned a runner and Winkie was sent in. 'He asked me if I was one of the new fellows who had just come in. This made me sick. You work for three months and your boss does not know you at all. I got furious and quit . . . Anyway I hold that it is up to you to do what you want and not to do what other people want you to do . . . I am with Father . . . I shall secure a job in two weeks.'

Phyllis wrote to Bob: 'Peter I see has inculcated him with his philosophy — of doing exactly what he wants and then putting it on almost moral grounds that what he has done was right. I can't do anything I suppose and Winkie must now help himself — I am so sorry and disappointed. Reggie and Peter are not much of an incentive for sticking to one's job. I can't help feeling very sorry for Winkie as he needs help so much, though he thinks he doesn't. I could cry my eyes out but I <u>am not</u>. I can't go on living and letting these things get at me, and I want to live very much. I just mustn't think too much.'

But Winkie was true to his word. By October he was working for a family friend's broking firm, 'counting stocks', and still in love with Isobel. Peter knew that he would be blamed for Winkie's defection to America. A visit to Aunt Irene confirmed 'within ten minutes' that he was 'a bald headed ass that has ruined Winkie's life . . . been terribly selfish (which undoubtedly is true) . . . and that I have crazy blood direct from Grampa.'

'When I read the tail end of your letters to Winks, "with love from Mummie",' he wrote to Phyllis in January 1929, 'my heart (. . . made purely of stone) bleeds . . . when I think of what you have gone through and the miles that separate you two I almost go blind.' But it was inevitable, he said. He asked her to look for 'greater happiness in understanding and deeper sympathy. I'm strongly of the opinion that you and I and Winkie are very selfish and that we ought to spend more time allowing for our differences and not feel each one must follow closely the plans of the other . . . Bob I think is the only satisfactory member of the family. If it wasn't for him the whole structure would collapse.'

Phyllis bought Peter and Winkie an apartment in Beekman Place, New York, in May 1929, bringing Winkie, who had been living in his father's apartment, closer to his dream of a valeted existence. 'Persuade Peter that they must keep a permanent servant in their new flat,' she wrote to Irene. 'I will willingly pay for it as I think it so important for Winkie to feel he can go home for his meals when he wants them . . . I feel Peter is sufficient unto himself but I don't feel that about Winkie. I feel he would really like a home & how I wish he wd come & share mine.' Peter described the butler, who Winkie had immediately installed, in a letter to his mother: '"Tombs" our gentleman's gentleman, visits for a few hours each day to comfort our Peal shoes [of which Winkie had amassed a large collection] and see that our clothes are perfectly pressed.'

That year Reggie Brooks married again, breaking Peter's normally defensive silence about his father's behaviour. The telegram Reggie sent him read, 'HAVE JUST BEEN MARRIED TO A MOST CHARMING WOMAN. WISH ME LUCK.' 'I have no idea who this charming woman is,' Peter wrote to Phyllis, 'but it's not hard to have grave suspicions. There may be a tragic side to this situation which may point to a very definite turn for the worse.' Phyllis wrote in turn to Bob: 'I had a really peculiar feeling when I heard the news. I really can't explain it! I have no regrets!' Later she reported, 'Larry Waterbery told me the woman R married is a real terror and had been about with various men for years. It's all rather disgusting for the boys.'

Peter wasn't sure how to deal with his new stepmother. He wrote to Phyllis from Southampton, 'My mind was buzzing with the awful feeling that any even civil relation to my new Ma "step" would be doing to you something that you described in a flood of tears and a lot of deep feeling as being "the greatest public insult" to you and also something about proving to the world that I was without standards of any kind. The result was I was on the horns of a dilemma, had a very unpleasant feeling inside, swore to myself at the general arrangement of life and then felt very hopeless.'

As it turned out, there wasn't much he could do to be nice to his new stepmother: 'With Father and his lantern jawed blonde staging a pitched battle with beer bottles my background in Florida was very weak,' he wrote. Peter had predicted the violence to Phyllis, 'given my old man's condition of health', revealing just how badly Reggie had slipped into dipsomania. It was also the end of any proper relationship between Peter and his father. The marriage was to last less than a year. The *New York Times* reported the divorce proceedings: 'Mrs Brooks asserted that Brooks secreted alarm clocks about their Palm Beach home setting the alarms at one hour intervals. She also charged him with parading through the house ringing cow bells and with other acts which she said caused her health to break and necessitated her going to a hospital. The recommendation gave the opinion that the defendant had been guilty of "extreme cruelty".'

That Christmas of 1929, feeling lonely, with Winkie away in England, Peter decided to fly to Mirador. He 'zoomed' Greenwood at 170 m.p.h., as he proudly reported to his mother. But Peter would never let up on the reminders of their own fights, as he probed for signs of love and reconciliation. 'My dinner was served on your little folding table. Fried chicken, beaten biscuit, lemon pie and apple jelly. In small baskets about the room are piles of crab apples. Callie or Aunt Ann are coming into see me soon and that "stone heart of mine" will certainly bleed for your presence – you bet.' He called Uncle Buck, he told her, who ended the conversation with the simple words: 'I love you Pete, come on over and see me.'

'You probably wonder what I'm doing in Chicago,' Winkie wrote to his mother in August 1930, when she imagined he was working in Wall Street. It was the first letter she had received from him for three

months. The letterhead was from the Drake Hotel on Lake Shore
Drive. 'I am going up to Alaska and British Columbia on a shooting trip
with a fellow called George Ryan,' he told her, adding for reassurance,
'I think you met him once at the Winthrops' down on Long Island.'

Once again Winkie had quit, this time it seemed, for good. 'My
experience of working in Wall Street was enough to put me or anyone
against work of that sort for the rest of my days,' he explained. 'And
unless I am forced to go back I never shall. I got so depressed and miserable that I am sure if I had continued I would have either died or
committed suicide.' He only had a year to wait before he came into his
trust fund. The love affair with Isobel, who had encouraged Winkie to
work, but whose ups and downs had caused him to feel 'very low', was
now apparently over.

But the real reason for his Alaska trip was that Reggie had gone on
a drinking spree that summer, making his house in Southampton unin-
habitable for both his sons. Peter confessed this to Phyllis, describing
how Reggie would bang on the doors of the bedrooms at 3 a.m., getting Peter and Winkie and all the servants up 'to talk to us about
himself'; how he would embarrass them by appearing at parties and
trying to dance with their girlfriends. 'You have no idea how disturbing
it is to me to have the disorganization of an insane parent,' Peter wrote,
'part sober and part drunk so I have to be highly skilful at adjusting
myself to a myriad of changing situations.' Winkie, he told her, had a
tendency to drink too much, but 'father is teaching him a lesson'.

Winkie subsequently returned to New York, with nothing to do.
The depression that had hit the stock market in 1929 was not mentioned in Winkie's sporadic letters, despite his keen interest in money.
Not until March 1931, when he heard, to his amazement, that the
Astors had temporarily shut down Cliveden for economy reasons, did
he write: 'Times must certainly be hard!' Winkie decided that it would
now definitely be a selfish act to go out and look for a job. He told his
mother: 'The unemployment situation is very bad. I feel that if I took
a job I would be preventing some other poor fellow from making a
living. This is my good deed for the year!!'

Winkie now declared that he was unsuited to business; all that American robustness and pep that he had admired was not for him. 'I propose to become a traveller and see the world and then some day maybe I'll find something,' he told Phyllis. First he had to find a girl-friend – Isobel was 'off my hooks for a long time now' – who wasn't under her family's influence and who would like him 'even though I don't work'.

It was a cool, provocative snub; a declaration that he was now finally beyond Phyllis's reach. But it also revealed Winkie's chronic workshyness and his avoidance of people who might question him about what he did or pressurize him into getting a job. 'Straight laced people make Winkie nervous,' Peter told Phyllis. 'He's very fit and has absolutely no desire EVER to do any kind of work . . . He finds he's better treated when people are worried about him than when he's in an office . . . where everyone overlooks him.' From now on Winkie's life was devoted to pleasure and the pursuit of women – and to golf which he often played with his new friend and semi-lookalike, Bing Crosby, then a crooner with Paul Whiteman's orchestra. Crosby was seven years older than Winkie and a couple of years away from fame.

Winkie became a feature in the gossip columns as an escort for the fashionable débutantes of New York. Like almost everybody else in those speakeasy days, he drank more than he should. He was preoccu-pied by money – 'I hear Bobbie Shaw is very rich now,' he wrote carelessly to his mother. Winkie was waiting for the magic age of twenty-one and his regular income. He had six months to go when Peter wrote to Phyllis, 'Winkie has developed so much sweetness and charm and his sex menace has increased so much that my eyes start and my jaw hangs in surprise more and more every week. My very brother under my very roof is sought after by the most stunning and attractive girls in New York – girls that I would fly across stretches of water at night for in sleet storms to get a smile out of. These ravishing creatures NEED Winkie. Their hearts ache for him and what does he do? I ask you? HE turns 'em down.'

Peter, now twenty-eight, felt responsible for Winkie and had taken on the roles of 'adviser, nurse, mother and father' to his younger brother for whom he often expressed his deep affection. 'Wink is GOING to be a smart man about town — a gentleman of leisure just as long as there's a chance of getting away with it,' he wrote to Phyllis on the eve of Winkie's twenty-first birthday. 'If the money doesn't happen to turn up SUICIDE has been definitely elected as the alternative. Winkie has decided long ago to be a P. G. Wodehouse character or die in the attempt and that's what his soul craves. Given the fact why not then help him . . . stop wasting time trying to get him to do what he'll never do and help him accomplish something which he really wants to do? . . . I beg of you as long as you can't easily discipline him and get away with it find some way of getting "pally" or "cosy" or something with him. He loves you Ma but I don't know what it is — he's afraid of getting the third degree or too many reminders.'

'Peter is certainly a wonderful pilot,' Winkie wrote to his mother. 'Down at Curtiss Field he is considered as a really big bug and no one really appreciates it.' He meant, in the family, and he was right. Clearly Phyllis had never tried to make her peace with Peter, whose insecurities about his looks and his failure with women grew by comparison with Winkie's charms. Somehow his success as a flier — he was now collecting trophies for stunt-flying, featuring in the aviation magazines, making a good living demonstrating and delivering airplanes — didn't make up for all this. He wrote to Phyllis to remind her that his Aunt Nancy had told him, to his face of course, that he looked like 'a cross between a duck and a monkey'. 'During the great part of my life,' he wrote, 'people seemed to have asked me whether I hadn't lost a great deal of weight. My eye is shifty, my colour is pale. I appear to have lost a great deal more weight than I actually have. My hair commences to drop out. Therefore the question which I ask myself while standing in front of the mirror is "Why has God given me such a hell of a break?" No self-respecting woman would be making a wise move in marrying me. I'm far too absurd.' Phyllis, for her part, never ceased to blame him for breaking 'your mother's heart' and 'when I'm in England I have been reminded what a cad I've been all my life', Peter wrote to her. He wondered whether he would ever be forgiven for what he had done.

Peter was still going to Newport for weekends and trying to keep up with the Porcellians, 'three rasping cocktails before lunch' then backgammon, 'and towards tea time all the Porcellians come in and sing songs and get absolutely plastered'. He knew he didn't conform in either looks or social status and he was losing his nerve. He wrote to his mother in 1930, 'The disorganization of my family background without that assistance of a delightful home and attractively organised relations has been something that made my position weak compared to the other beaus. A detachment from family environment has made me a shade more like a taxi driver than an aristocrat.' It didn't help Peter that whenever he was mentioned in the gossip columns it was first as Lady Astor's nephew, and second as 'the well known sportsman flier'.

A 'delightful home' was what Peter longed for and felt excluded from. All the news of the Brand family was of a happy enterprise — stable, loving, underpinned with success — something Peter felt he would ruin with his awkwardness if he came back to visit. Peter's letters of congratulation on the appropriate occasions strained to be generous and grown-up, but a tone of forced jauntiness always betrayed his sadness, even before he reverted to old conflicts and wounds. In late 1929, the Brands bought Eydon Hall in Northamptonshire, which was, indeed, one of the most delightful houses in England.

Phyllis's niece Nancy Lancaster, who had married Ronnie Tree in 1920, now kept Mirador as a holiday home for only short return visits. Nancy had hoped that Ronnie would pursue his political ambitions in America so that she could hold on to the Mirador life, but it hadn't worked. Instead, when they moved to England, Ronnie was offered the post of Joint Master of the Pytchley hunt in Northamptonshire, which was considered the 'ideal training ground for politicians'. Not only was this the grandest and smartest high society hunt in the shires, but Nancy Lancaster, making the usual Langhorne transition, had turned their great James Gibbs house, Kelmarsh, near Market Harborough, into the central stage of its entertaining. Backed by Ronnie Tree's great wealth she had already begun to make her revolutionizing mark on English houses and gardens. Kelmarsh, with its pink painted hall, Nancy's bright yellows and greens, flowers and wood fires – as well as her unparalleled levels of hospitality – stunned the local gentry, who were unused to pint-sized glasses of orange juice for breakfast.

Phyllis would often visit and hunt with the Pytchley. 'She would say, "If only I could pick up Mirador and put it in the Pytchley,"' said Nancy Lancaster. When he was looking for a country house in 1920, Bob Brand had written to Phyllis that he wanted to find her 'somewhere that would in some degree compensate you for the loss of Mirador'. Phyllis longed to be in better hunting country. Hunting in the winter months was the real business of life and that meant, ideally, Northamptonshire and the Pytchley, two counties and 100 miles or so away. The 1920s were the last golden decade of hunting in the shires, the supreme moment of high confidence in rural life, of wealth and display and high society for four or five days a week, until the Depression brought it to an end. And Phyllis was considered by the hunting fraternity – and this claim seems unchallenged – the best horsewoman in England.

Nancy Lancaster was particularly fond of her aunt Phyllis, seventeen years her senior. When Nancy came to England, Phyllis instructed her niece 'how to be the smartest turned-out sidesaddle rider'; how to put on her liquid lipstick and to show a long neck, with the hair bun meeting the back rim of the hat; how to tilt the hat forward at an angle; and how to wear white linen waistcoats. She passed on the old lessons in how to dazzle within the rules of hunting etiquette. Apart from hunting they both liked shooting, a rarity among women, and both shot well.

If Nancy wanted to return a favour to her aunt, her chance came in 1928 when she was out hunting with the Pytchley. She saw Eydon Hall, near Banbury, with its warm brown stone and tall Doric columns, sitting in a perfect position at the summit of a low sweeping hill. It reminded Nancy of Bremo (an *ante bellum* house on the James River in Virginia) and it was in the best possible situation for hunting, within striking distance of the Bicester, the Grafton and the Pytchley. It was also for sale.

Eydon Hall was, and still is, one of England's finest smaller country houses. It was designed by James Lewis, a pupil of Adam, and built of rust-coloured ironstone from the local quarry, quite unlike the icy beige limestone of the neighbouring Cotswolds. Each block of stone was a slightly different colour, giving a rosy softness to its walls. Instead of the usual massive stone balustrade, ornamental wrought iron had been substituted in the original design, giving it extra lightness. This, and the widely spaced Doric columns on its rear elevation, gave it its *ante bellum*, Bremo feel. Sitting up on its hill, it had the compactness of a grand Virginian house – tall, self-contained, almost isolated from the land around it. It was set in a five-acre park and surrounded with its own rich arable farmland. But the real magic of the house came from the light inside it; it poured in through the enlarged Palladian windows reaching from floor to ceiling, and from a central glass dome on to the staircase. The classical proportions and the scale of the house, midway between intimacy and grandeur, meant that the light was carried from room to room. Nowhere was there a hint of the dullness or darkness of Furneux Pelham. It was a graceful house, simple and restrained to suit Phyllis's taste in decorating and furniture. On the drawing-room wall was a plaster frieze of Diana, goddess of the chase, balanced with one of a fox's mask. The hall was laid with black and white flagstones. It had a garden of many walled enclosures, a kitchen garden with high walls of red brick and a fine semi-circular stable yard with many horse boxes. Whatever Winkie's adolescent views on his mother and her severity, this house better suited her personality. It was a house that seemed to invite happiness. Nancy Lancaster decorated it, painting the hall pink like Kelmarsh; Phyllis's bow-fronted sitting room she painted 'yaller'.

Eydon was run on intimate, Virginian lines, which had much to do with Phyllis's talent, equal to that of Nancy's, for finding servants of exceptional niceness and making them, at least in her imagination, into 'family' — even in Northamptonshire. The contrast between the two households at Cliveden and Eydon and their different attitudes to life, dictated only in some ways by their different means, is well marked in the characters of their two respective butlers: the familiar and jolly Mr Blyth and the upright Mr Lee. 'As a butler Bill Blyth was a rough diamond,' said David Astor. 'My mother couldn't make out why aunt Phyllis was so devoted to him until she realized that she had found the only butler in England who was as informal as the coloured butlers in Virginia. Nobody else in England, said my mother, would have kept a butler who talked the whole time and treated the children as if they were his.' Blyth would indeed interrupt conversations at table, correcting facts, counting numbers aloud and giggling at jokes.

When not on duty, Blyth was usually horizontal, summoned only to man the switchboard in a pantry down the long corridor from his room, a journey — Blyth was 'a very bad mover' — that often took many exasperating minutes. Once there his homely ways extended to sharing conversations with the parties on the line as if they were a matter of public or family property. The farm manager at Eydon, whose telephone was on an extension of the switchboard, would have the topics summarized in advance by Blyth before he was put through: 'It's your mother and she says she can't come up Sunday.' Phyllis was once heard shouting at Blyth down the telephone: 'Blyth Blyth get off the phone. I can hear you breathing.' Sweets and chocolates, for which he had a great weakness, he also considered rightly shareable. When a jar of special lemon drops, sent over from America, began to disappear from the drawing room, Phyllis asked him, 'Blyth is there anyone else eating these except you and me?' Bob collected Blyth's homely phrases. Unable to find some white shirts after a trip to Le Touquet, Blyth had advised him, 'I think they must have found their way to Le Tokyo, Sir.'

Eydon took Phyllis further away from her sister Nancy. Behind her back Nancy had now taken to blackmailing relatives to stay with her instead of Phyllis — with the threat that they would never be asked to Cliveden again. Nora, for one, took this threat seriously and stayed away. Nancy waited two years to visit Phyllis at Eydon, and only did so after Phyllis had complained bitterly. 'The Viscountess in company with the Marquis [Philip Kerr, now Lord Lothian] has just arrived,' Phyllis reported finally. 'As she came up the steps she said: "There's no doubt about it, I am the most unselfish woman to come to do this." . . . Nannie has been in the house just one hour, half of which she was eating dinner and now she is swamped in newspapers. She is panting to get away and it's not exactly restful. Oh my! Oh my! She will never be a private visitor again, I fear!'

24

Nancy to Moscow,
Bobbie to Jail

In July 1931, with Nora and Lefty Flynn in Greenwich, Connecticut, and Winkie, in the high summer of his twenty-first birthday, golfing at Southampton with Bing Crosby, the German banking system began to disintegrate. Bob Brand was sent to try and save it, believing, with Keynes, that capitalism (and western civilization) was possibly coming to an end.

This was the month of Nancy's visit to Moscow with George Bernard Shaw. It was the month, too, that Bobbie was sent to Wormwood Scrubs prison.

Despite his self-appointed role as a missionary for communism, and his status in the Soviet Union as a popular hero and playwright – *The Apple Cart* had recently been a big success in Moscow – Bernard Shaw had never been to Russia. He had turned down many invitations, holding back, according to his biographer Michael Holroyd, 'until the chaos of the Revolution was over and the communist state fairly launched. He feared what he might see.' Even in the late 1920s he felt it was too soon to go 'because people were expecting miracles from Soviet Communism'. In his seventy-fifth year he evidently thought this was his last chance, but even then he denied that the initiative was his despite his official invitation. 'The Astors suddenly took it into their heads to see for themselves whether Russia is really the earthly paradise I had declared it to be; and they challenged me to go with them.' It was all 'a bit of an accident'.

The departure was planned for Saturday, 18 July. Along with Shaw, the Astors had invited Philip Kerr, now the 11th Marquess of Lothian, and David, aged nineteen, who was studying briefly at Heidelberg in the months between Eton and Balliol, Oxford. There was another Christian Scientist, Maurice Hindus, the Russian-American author, and others, later eclipsed in the glare of publicity, to make the ballast.

Five days before the planned departure, Bobbie Shaw was warned by the police that he was about to be arrested for a homosexual offence. It was two years since he had been banished from the army. Waldorf and Nancy had been generous and forgiving over his expulsion, still believing that drink had been responsible.

In fact it was Bobbie's closeness to Nancy, to whom he spoke every day, that had kept him going. Out of uniform he felt he didn't belong anywhere; and his life had quickly begun to unravel. A short-lived job had been found for him in a London firm called Service is Shipping, token work of no interest to him, and Bobbie quit. ('Is that a proverb, like Silence is Golden?' Paul Phipps had asked him. 'That's enough Paul, that's quite enough,' Bobbie had replied.) His life became increasingly dissipated; his face 'puffy', as Phyllis had noted. He had begun to drink heavily, and become careless in his sexual encounters. 'The sad thing about Bobbie,' observed Baba Metcalfe, 'was that he never wanted his own class, you see. It would have been safer if he'd gone with his own class but he wanted what you call the batman soldier class.'

The police had already warned Bobbie twice about importuning guardsmen. There had always been pubs near the London barracks where these liaisons could be made and Bobbie knew them well. This time the police had enough evidence to charge him. They let him know that the warrant would not be issued for four days, giving him the chance to leave the country. After a year or so, the charges would almost certainly have been dropped. But Bobbie decided that he would prefer jail to exile, which had its own particular horrors for him, and he stuck out the next four days in London, waiting to be arrested. The worst part of this for Nancy was the total surprise. She had no idea of this separate sexual side of his life and of what it entailed. David was telephoned in Germany by his brother Bill, to be told that Bobbie had been charged with something 'that only schoolboys should get up to'. Nancy was told the news on Monday night after a church meeting. Those present saw the unfamiliar sight of Nancy losing control, weeping hysterically, 'clinging and pulling at the curtains'. But then her courage rallied.

Nancy was unable to describe these events to Irene until Bobbie had been in jail for almost a month, and she had returned from Moscow. 'I hated your having to know,' she wrote, 'I wish no-one could know except me . . . Bobbie has more good than evil & such courage & strange strength. He was amazing when it happened – wanted to do what was best for us either kill himself disappear or face it. Of course we said face it – if he wanted to be clear of it. He said "Mummie its a horrible disease. I have never dared tell a living soul – it has been a tyranny & now I can feel I can face you and start fresh."' Bobbie wrote to Nancy, 'Darling Mother, For the first time in my life you know everything and what I have been up against. Now thank God it feels dead. I can just get thro if I see no one I know that is the only way. Your thoughts have saved me from suicide. I got a letter from Baba which I enclose. It was hard receiving it. Your love for me passes all understanding . . .'

Baba Metcalfe, now six years into her marriage, sent a note of loyalty and friendship on a plain scrap of paper: 'Bobbie dear, I hear you are in trouble. I have tried to find you everywhere but failed. If I can help in anyway let me see you. I am in London tonight and all tomorrow.'

'God only knows how we bore those days but Bobbie bore up and so did I,' Nancy wrote to Irene. 'The next morning at 10 I had to go to Plymouth – the big hospital fete was opening at 3!' she wrote. 'I was met by the Mayor & Corporation – in pouring rain. They remarked all wd be well now that Lady Astor with her gaiety and courage had arrived!!! I ask you. That night the Lord Lieutenant to dinner. Wednesday the Prince of Wales arrived & I had the whole day of functions. Took the night train to London & there we had to settle things. I saw Bobbie late Thursday & on Friday – he was taken. Waldorf and I left for Sandwich & Saty [Saturday] went to Russia. Philip & Waldorf thought I couldn't go. But I realised it had to be done otherwise what would they all have said. I wd rather face Russia than people at home. It turned out a Godsend I will write you some more about it.'

The Prince of Wales wrote to Nancy a few days later, 'Baba and Fruity have told me you knew all about it . . . at Plymouth and so I should like to say how absolutely marvellously I think you behaved & bore up . . . during that long day of presentations. It does seem a cruel shame that a minute's madness should be victimised when we know of so many who should have "done time" in prison years ago.'

Baba Metcalfe, who called round to St James's Square, described how surprised she was that Waldorf knew so little about homosexuality. 'What do you suppose they *did*?', Waldorf asked her. 'I thought that was rather strange,' she remarked. 'He must have at least heard about it at Eton.'

The press was squared. No mention of the case ever appeared in print, either in England or abroad – a minor example of the solidarity of the press barons, British and American, that was to be seen working most spectacularly in the Duke of Windsor abdication story a few years later. The gentlemanly rule at the time was, according to David Astor, that newspaper proprietors 'didn't bomb each other's headquarters'. Waldorf, of course, owned the *Observer*, and John Jacob Astor owned *The Times* – he had bought it in 1922. J. L. Garvin, the *Observer* editor, leaned on Lord Beaverbrook of Express Newspapers. Harold Harmsworth of the *Daily Mail* and *Daily Mirror* complied. The editor of the *Western Morning News* in Plymouth wrote to Waldorf: 'Your Lordship will realise, of course that such an item from the strictly newspaper point of view, is important, and that we have a heavy sense of responsibility in the matter. Mr Harmsworth said at once, however,

that all reports were to be suppressed in all our papers, no matter
what other people might do, and guarded instructions have been given
accordingly.' Communications of this nature were made 'by pre-
arranged code', in the case of the Harmsworth papers, and through
intermediaries, so great was the fear of a leak, 'which might be used as
a lever in future cases'.

Nancy reported to Irene that 'Every one has been so good even
Lord Beaverbrook [a declared enemy of Nancy] spent a whole day
keeping it out of the papers. The Prime Minister had the case hurried
on & not one single soul has failed us. Bobbie's friends seem outraged
at the law & forgiving of him.' Most of the letters of sympathy from
Nancy's friends put the catastrophe down not to Bobbie's sexuality but
'bad associations', 'bad people', 'bad friends', the 'evil influences' of
other people. Philip Kerr wrote to Nancy, 'It is only in the rarest cases
that we get healed of sin without suffering, without deep ploughing of
our inmost being . . . He has some pretty deep evils to get rid of.'

Ellen Wilkinson, the socialist woman MP, who had been elected
to Parliament in 1924, was staying in the guest cottage at Cliveden, and
wrote to Nancy that 'this thing is all through the public schools (and as
an ex teacher I can assure you in the elementary ones too). Mostly it is
left behind like any other silly bad habit (biting nails etc). It is only all
this furtive mystery, & the vague horror of prison & all the blackmail
that drives it deep into secrecy and so prevents teachers or decent
older friends saying in perfectly calm tones, "don't be a dirty little
pig." That would be so much more effective than all this hysterical
horror about the habit that goes deep into our biological history.'

On 15 July 1931 Bernard Shaw wrote Nancy a letter that has
never been published:

Dearest Nancy,

Why is Providence so jealous of your high spirits that
it deals you these terrible BIFFS at your most hopeful
moments? What can one do to comfort you?

I hope the Press will have the decency to say nothing about poor Bobbie's step-connexions. In his case I think I should plead technically Guilty, admitting the facts but not the delinquency. The natural affections of many men, including some very eminent ones (Plato and Michael Angelo, for instance) take that perverse turn; and in many countries adults are held to be entitled to their satisfaction in spite of the prejudices and bigoted normality of Virginians and Irishmen like our two selves. Bobbie can claim that he has to suffer by a convention of British law, not by Nature's law. At the other side of the channel there would be no case against him, and no disgrace attached to him.

I must go to Russia, sadly enough now. If I did not, people would ask why; and that must not be.

Oh Nancy, Nancy, something is wrung in me by your sorrows. I supposed you would call it my heart.

Better tear this up

ever & ever

G.B.S.

Philip Kerr was on the point of becoming Under-Secretary of State for India, and offered Scientific and headmasterly advice in the days before Bobbie's arrest. 'I've no doubt that the right thing is for Bobbie to face the music — which I think means a period in gaol. It is really exactly what we have all known he needs — a period when he will have to work & be kept from idleness & false pleasures. It's just the charm of sensuality destroying itself. From the Science point of view it is a blessing for him & but preparation for healing. Scientifically you can rejoice in it.' But he went on, 'I don't see how you & Waldorf can go to Russia on Saturday whatever happens . . . Gosh mortal mind has planned a good one this time — But it can only work for the greater good of everybody, Bobbie, yourself, W. & the family & Science itself.'

Bernard Shaw countered this advice from Nancy's chief counsellor in a further thoughtful and sympathetic letter about 'our friend Bobbie', in which he said, 'In this matter Mrs Eddy, bless her, is no use. The Bible, with its rubbish about Lot's wife, is positively dangerous . . . a man may suffer acutely and lose his self respect very dangerously if he mistakes for a frightful delinquency on his part a condition for which he is no more morally responsible than for colour blindness.'

Just before his arrest, Bobbie wrote to Nancy from Brown's Hotel: 'Darling Mother . . . Just a line to say I have never been so happy or free before. Thank God we both understand each other now. I am glad we do before either of us die as I feel happy that you know my love for you as I know your love for me. Have a good trip and rejoice. Bobbie.'

Hurried on by the Prime Minister, Bobbie's case was heard the morning after he was arrested. Baba Metcalfe recalled waiting in a room in St James's Square, with Nancy, Waldorf and Nancy Lancaster, as Bobbie was sentenced in the Magistrates Court. He received four months' imprisonment. 'It was a long two or three hours, and Nancy suffered so much. It is engraved on my memory for ever. She made noises almost like an animal. She couldn't control her emotion.'

Somehow Nancy got herself on to the train the following day at Victoria Station with the rest of the Moscow party. Her later letters suggest that Bobbie's imprisonment set off fits of panic of the kind that had rarely afflicted her since her conversion to Christian Science. It was a depression more manageable than Bobbie's suicidal feelings in prison, but evidently devastating nevertheless. And yet her letters show that her concern was solely for Bobbie – there is never a hint of worry for her own reputation.

For anyone less used to public attack than Shaw or Nancy, or less stoical and philosophical than Waldorf, the trip to Moscow might have been a severe embarrassment, and a public relations disaster. The arch capitalist Nancy and the arch socialist Shaw hand in hand, touring the country as semi-official guests, the one loudly eulogizing the Soviet system, the other telling the communists that they had taken the wrong path, the path of the Anti-Christ. 'I am a Conservative. I am a Capitalist. I am opposed to Communism. I think you are all terrible,' Shaw recorded Nancy saying at one point. Her head, he said, 'is full of Bolshevik horrors'. Nevertheless it was courageous of Nancy to go. Very few people visited Russia in those days and the Left in Britain was itself increasingly divided in its attitude to Soviet communism.

The expedition was a reporter's delight. It received daily coverage in Britain and the US and much ridicule from both political poles: nothing that Shaw didn't expect, or even welcome — the trip promised nothing if not theatricality. Underlying his buffoonery and his extravagant praise of the Soviet system and Stalin too was Shaw's Irish-born disdain for the British and American establishment, who had condemned the Soviet 'experiment' from the very beginning. While Bob Brand was in Berlin trying to save capitalism, Shaw, disillusioned by the failure of the Labour government of the late 1920s, sought to recharge his batteries with any sign of hope he could find in the only real experiment of the socialism he had been advocating for forty years. There was already much evidence against the Soviet experiment, less so in 1931 than 1936, but this Shaw decided to ignore. David Astor observed that in Russia Shaw 'looked at nothing, took nothing in. He behaved as if he knew it all already . . . It made one wonder how he experienced life in general. Did he perhaps do so like a dreamer-cum-entertainer who was sharply interested in ideas and dramas but not very close to ordinary life?' Shaw's biographer, Michael Holroyd, believes, however, that Shaw didn't ignore everything, 'but rather he tended to disperse anything unsavoury into the generalities of history'.

Nancy meanwhile wrote to Bobbie from the Metropole Hotel in Moscow, 'I can't tell you what a world we have jumped into. Just as great a change as yours. Perhaps we both needed it, who knows. In some ways my change is as painful as yours. I hope we will grow. Oh dear. Oh dear. Life is like a dream. That's all it can be until we awake.'

They saw nothing of the mechanics of Soviet life, of labour camps, or collectivization, or the famine then beginning in the

Ukraine. Instead, there were the predictable showpiece events, scrubbed and glowing workers arranged, literally, in their thousands. Shaw realized that he was in the middle of a comedy. It amused him to see Nancy, like the heroine of one of his plays, coming out with her forthright views, denouncing the system, and being applauded for the mistranslations offered by her trembling interpreters. This was almost certainly why he brought her along. 'Nancy jollies them along until they do not know whether they are head up or heels.' Shaw wrote to his wife, Charlotte, 'her stock accusation being that they are all aristocrats which does not wholly displease them.'

Shaw made a fool of himself on his seventy-fifth birthday, when he delivered a speech praising the Five Year Plan, and earned even the forbearing Waldorf's impatience. Pointing to his friends, the Astors, he said that they couldn't help being rich capitalists; they had found themselves in that situation. But it was one that would soon be remedied by the British proletariat. 'Bad effort,' Waldorf responded. This didn't stop Nancy, charged by Charlotte Shaw to watch over her husband, from the caring and grooming of Bernard Shaw, meticulous cleanliness being another of their bonds. She washed his wispy white hair in Lux at the Metropole Hotel.

Winston Churchill was to write later in *Great Contemporaries*: 'The Russians have always been fond of circuses and travelling shows. Since they had imprisoned, shot or starved most of their best comedians, their visitors might fill for a space a noticeable void. And here was the World's most famous intellectual Clown and Pantaloon in one, and the charming Columbine of the capitalist pantomime. And Stalin, . . . pushing aside his morning's budget of death warrants and *lettres de cachet* received his guests with smiles of overflowing comradeship.'

Churchill omitted to tell how Nancy, unintimidated by the surroundings of the Kremlin and the beast himself, spent two and a half hours attacking Stalin for his repressive policies, going at him, according to Shaw, 'like a steamroller'. At first the interpreter would not translate her questions, but Shaw insisted that he should. According to her son David, Nancy asked Stalin, 'How long are you going to have to go on ruling by Tsarist methods?' When Stalin asked her what she meant Nancy spoke of death warrants, secret trials, political prisoners in Siberia and the stifling of criticism. 'I don't accept what you say, that I rule by Tsarist methods,' Stalin responded, 'but insofar as we haven't yet achieved the aims of the Revolution that's a matter of time. Surely you know that was the same with Cromwell.' Waldorf wrote drily in his diary, 'Stalin . . . assured her that the need for dealing with political prisoners drastically would soon cease.' Stalin told his daughter Svetlana that he found the whole visit a most disagreeable experience and that Shaw was a truly 'awful person'. In retrospect, the visitors were impressed by Stalin's self-control.

'Then the homecoming,' wrote Nancy to Irene from Jura in August, '& I saw Bobbie. That was difficult but I wd not have failed him as you can imagine – he wanted to see me. He is having the most ghastly time but I won't dwell on that – a month is over & on Nov 22 he comes out and starts fresh . . . I have "fits" literally fits. But they pass. This won't kill me . . .' Nancy's misery about Bobbie was sharpened by the discovery, on her return, that he was on the verge of a breakdown in jail. Bobbie felt 'absolutely destroyed in prison. He thought he was going to die,' David Astor recalled. For most of his four months in Wormwood Scrubs Bobbie suffered a horrendous level of anxiety, dominated by the belief that he would never come out alive. It was triggered, in part, by the separation from his mother, compounded with guilt – the fear that he had done her a terrible injury and shamed her, that by concealing this 'sin' from her he had broken their symbiotic contract. Bobbie was fixated on reunion with his mother. He described the distant moment in terms of a glorious resurrection, of love everlasting, purified of sin: 'Pray God we may be united in peace for ever,' he wrote to her.

Early on in his sentence he circumvented the rules by sending Nancy a note written on the flyleaf of a library book: 'I do not intend to write any letters in here as the warders think I have no relations and I want it to remain that way as long as possible.' Only the Governor, Colonel Johnson, and the Deputy Governor, Commander Foster, knew of and agreed to conceal Bobbie's identity. In this sense he already had privilege and protection. They allowed Nancy's friend Lilian Barker, the prison commissioner, to visit him officially. Through her Bobbie was able to send mail unscrutinized by prison officials – a crucial lifeline for Bobbie and for Nancy too. Great care was taken to conceal these irregularities. Foster and Johnson wrote to Nancy and Waldorf from their home addresses, never mentioning Bobbie by name.

The Astors corralled into their network all available officials including Lieutenant Colonel Cecil Bevis, the Honorary Probation Officer at Marlborough Street Magistrates Court. Ex-Indian army, blue-eyed, moustached, Colonel Bevis was a gent who, according to a profile in the *Evening News*, 'despite his having means which could enable him to have a life of sport and leisure . . . has chosen to give his time to helping people who stray'. Bevis visited Bobbie three times a week and co-ordinated news security. Flowers were sent from Cliveden to Borstal, apples to Wormwood Scrubs. Lilian Barker was sent on holiday. Wissie took the prison governor and his wife to the theatre. Lilian Barker passed on to Nancy, without comment, Bobbie's request in August, to send 'some grouse, lobster and venison' from Scotland to Colonel Johnson and Commander Foster.

But it was the manly Lilian Barker who, Bobbie said later, saved his sanity. Two weeks into his sentence Lilian revealed to Nancy – writing to her in Moscow – that Bobbie had been recognized, at least as Robert Shaw, by a prisoner who had placed a bet on him at the racecourse. Now he could get no favours, 'as at once the men would take it out on him'. Visits would have to be taken in the regular way, which meant that if Nancy came to see him it would have to be in the presence of a third party, 'and this I think would be unbearable for you and Bobbie'.

'I hope you won't go to see him when you come back,' she had written. 'You really don't quite know what it is like & I know he would hate you to see him in prison clothes & with all the formalities which are bound to be in a prison.' She described him dressed in 'fustian trousers and grey, rough coat with a wispy tie'. She warned Nancy, 'He is naturally feeling very much the surroundings & companions he has because he comes in contact with no one at all in his own class. The men are rough and of unclean tongues which revolts him very much.' He seemed, she added, 'more like a boy than I have ever seen him'. This was also something that David noticed and remembered sixty years later – that in his depression Bobbie had regressed, all the courage stripped away, his vulnerability laid bare. 'He became very intimate almost like a little boy and I felt he was clinging to our correspondence. He kept saying the people in prison were so low; he couldn't raise any human feeling. Bobbie suffered agony in prison . . . His fear and hatred of things was quite extraordinary.'

A further description of Nancy's first visit to Bobbie was written to Irene later from Jura, which neither of them liked visiting. 'I feel I want to mortify the flesh . . . Bobbie clung to me and said, "I feel Mum you may take me away." & I said "not to Jura Bobbie, you can't want to go there" – he smiled & said "Jura sounds like paradise" & so it has been as I can read my Bible & prayer [sic] & oh God how good he is.' She added, 'Bill has been so nice & Wis & David but they adore Bobbie & love will heal & help, won't it? David is a tower of strength. As for Waldorf no one ever lived quite like him. Never one word & only one thought how can he help Bobbie. Its amazing.'

Nancy could have arranged to make a backdoor visit to Bobbie in jail. Instead she decided to go through the public visiting procedures. But her visit plunged Bobbie into a deeper anxiety, according to Lilian Barker, who now sent telegrams to Nancy after her visits. Soon after her own visit Nancy received a 'piteous letter' from him. One of the prisoners' wives had died. 'That did the trick as far as I was concerned,' Bobbie wrote. 'I had kept saying what a wonderful time we were going to have together and in future nothing but death could part us whereupon a little voice said, "yes and death may part you. Something may happen to your mother before you get out. What then?"'

Bobbie now pleaded for daily bulletins of his mother's health, seized with the fear not only that she would die while he was inside but that this would make him insane. He told her that he was reading

Science and Health — anything to connect him to his mother, to repair the damage: 'I have not got very far,' he wrote, 'but I have seen sin uncovered and all the ghastliness of following self and evil . . . Don't worry the terrible past is over and I can start with joy in my heart a new life of peace and I hope unselfishness . . . One thing leads to another and I trust with the cancer gone all must be well . . . I only want to do what is right . . . I hope only now I can practise what I preach.' Nancy went along with it, reporting that Bobbie had 'been so sunk in selfishness & materialism that nothing but a bomb could have stirred him & that bomb had been cast!'

But the real 'cancer' that was growing inside him was that of self-loathing for what he and everyone else considered to be a perversion. It was already evident as he prepared for his release, while Nancy fought the roughest election of her career in Plymouth in October 1931.

That summer there had been an unprecedented run on the pound and the gold reserves — the worst financial crisis ever known in Britain. Ramsay MacDonald offered his resignation when his Labour cabinet refused to endorse his draconian spending cuts — which included slicing 20 per cent off unemployment benefit — but then agreed to lead an all-party coalition, a National government. Britain was forced off the gold standard and into a 30 per cent devaluation of the pound. There were riots and strikes. MacDonald went to the polls again for a vote of confidence for the government's economic recovery programme. Believing that this fight would be too much for her, with the strain of Bobbie's imprisonment, and secretly knowing that she had passed her peak as an effective Member of Parliament, Nancy's friends and relations urged her to stand down and let her son Bill, aged twenty-four, take her place. Waldorf stood on the sidelines. Nancy said she would listen to God, not to her advisers; that she must stand again 'to fight class consciousness and bitterness' and to 'weaken the forces of hate'. Phyllis wrote to Irene from Plymouth on 22 October: 'I am happy we are getting nearly to the end of this election. Nannie had a very bad day yesterday after receiving a letter about Bobbie who has been through a bad time lately mentally, and I think she is afraid he will lose his reason – she was terribly upset and weepy. Everyone seems to think she will be returned, but the ones against her are very bitter.' The Labour Party lost almost all its seats in the election that followed. The Tories won a landslide victory, giving them a majority of almost 500 in the House of Commons. The Plymouth electors returned Nancy with a 10,000 majority.

As Bobbie's release date approached Commander Foster began to persuade him that he had best make himself scarce for a while. 'The less he is seen about, the quicker people will forget,' he wrote to Nancy, adding the extraordinary suggestion that 'A trip abroad would meet the situation and if he were to get presentably married in the process, the forgetting business would probably be accelerated.' Bobbie, he claimed, was seriously considering France or Germany – 'an advance', said Commander Foster, 'on the part of the most insular person I have ever met'. He was right. Bobbie, who had a horror of enforced separation and foreign countries in general, was trying, nevertheless, to play the game with the Deputy Governor. Alternatively, Commander Foster helpfully suggested the Antipodes and 'something in wool'. It was the prospect of Umvuma again.

But Bobbie had a different vision. He wrote to his mother in the spirit of a beleaguered couple starting over again, united against the world through their adversity: 'I won't start making plans but I think that you and I will just have to go to our house at Sandwich. We will be out of the way and yet anyone who wants to can come and see us there and from there we can go anywhere or do anything that we decide. No one can say anything about us going there and we both adore it. We would be so cosy there. All my love mother darling.'

Bobbie had felt 'woozy' the first time he walked across the parade ground unchaperoned by a warder. 'This is an indication of how much mental adjustment is required,' wrote Foster. In the last three weeks of his confinement Bobbie became afraid that his 'torn nerves' would collapse within minutes of his release and that he would never retrieve his confidence. The commander warned Nancy of the exit syndrome –

the prisoner's fear of the gate and freedom. Above all, said Bobbie, Nancy must not come to meet him. 'I could never stand the memory of you being at the gate, that horrid gate.' If anyone he knew came to meet him 'like a bird just out I might fly into the fire through fear or get muddled . . . I know you will be patient with me.'

In the end it was his devoted Baba Metcalfe who he agreed should come to the gate at 7.30 a.m. She took him to the Basil Street Hotel where they had breakfast. From there Bobbie was taken to Sandwich where he stayed for some weeks. There was a family Christmas without guests, which David remembers as a happy moment, marred only by Nancy's nervous and inept handling of Bobbie. She couldn't provide the patience he had asked for. 'She upset Bobbie, who was shattered and terrified, by jumping on him if he did anything that you could interpret as being self indulgent in any way.' They were small things – some treat, some scented soap for his bath. 'And at once she would say "watch out this is the slippery slope."'

Whatever the sympathy and the goodwill from friends and relations, Bobbie couldn't show himself at his old haunts – the racecourse, the clubs – where he might be slighted. The first time he went to lunch at St James's Square he was faced with his uncle, Bertie Spender Clay, a colonel-ish figure of reactionary opinions who took a dim view of homosexuals. He ignored Bobbie throughout the meal. Bobbie made a joke of it, saying to David Astor afterwards, 'I'm not *certain* whether Uncle Bertie has insulted me or whether I've insulted Uncle Bertie.' Above all Bobbie had to keep away from London.

From some branch of the Astor network a couple called Courtland Taylor were found, who had a large family and lived on a farm in Wrotham, Kent. He was a stockbroker, she was the farm manager, and they took on Bobbie as an apprentice farmer. To help keep him on the farm, Waldorf had provided the Courtland Taylors with a herd of prize cattle, Bobbie's only declared interests in life being 'cattle and horses'. Nancy wrote to Irene, 'I have just come from seeing Bobbie in his new job & oh I am so happy about him & it all. He has a nice big room which he has made cosy. At first he was very discouraged

– and it was all so different but now he's settling down & looks so well & almost happy so I do thank God & oh Irene its such a relief – you never saw anyone who made friends quicker than he does or who keeps them longer – every kind of person writes & wants to see him & that of course helps him. He's only an hour from London so I can easily go down to him.'

Bobbie put up a picture of Nancy in his room. 'You remember the one,' he wrote to her, 'It is really very pretty with the gold bracelets, tight waist and Ava Ribblesdale [formerly Astor] poise of the hands.' Nancy held on to the belief that, once Bobbie had 'paid for' his mistake, the stigma would vanish; that it was only a matter of time before his friends rallied round and restored him to his old life.

When the Duchess of York (later the Queen Mother) was visiting Kent, Nancy had the idea that she might call in on her son, whom she knew, and asked her niece Nancy Lancaster to suggest it. 'Nannie was very peculiar. It was quite extraordinary for her to think that the Duchess of York would go out of her way to see someone just out of prison for homosexuality. Do you see what I mean? Something was dead in her like that. Bobbie wouldn't have wanted it to begin with. And all his friends tried to see him and he would never see them.'

In April 1932, a letter from a Christian Science counsellor assigned to watch over Bobbie, told him, 'Your father and mother are coming to the end of their tether . . . since your recent lapses they live in terror of your being arrested.' In May, now six months after Bobbie's release, Sir Reginald Poole, the family lawyer, who clearly had a reliable police source, warned Bobbie that 'by the strangest possible coincidence I have received information that you were seen to enter a particular Public House, have a drink and apparently look for someone who was not there . . .' To the Astors he wrote that 'others may have been watching' and that the police were accumulating evidence for a fresh case. Waldorf had already temporarily banned Bobbie from Cliveden under any circumstances. Bobbie, said Sir Reginald, should immediately go to France. 'I do not think any time ought to be wasted.'

Within two days Bobbie was in a *pension* at Ville d'Avray near St

Cloud, outside Paris. Nancy had alerted Mrs Caroline Getty, a friend of some grandeur from the CS network, who lived nearby at Sèvres, and was part of the racing world. She would be Bobbie's minder and instructor. Christian Science was now forced on Bobbie: he agreed to instruction, to embracing Mrs Eddy wholeheartedly.

However, Bobbie's options were dwindling — he was faced with exile, but with nothing to occupy him. There were some feeble suggestions to work in a stables, or in banking in Paris, 'which you could see would be impossible', he wrote. As he hinted in his letters, all this was pointless lip service to an idea now long moribund — that of working at a job. Yet Nancy and Waldorf were faced with the disastrous alternative of Bobbie going back inside for a long prison term. Any form of exile seemed preferable. Under the heaviest pressure Bobbie's natural authority began to assert itself. He wanted to return to the Courtland Taylors, despite Nancy and Waldorf's refusal to let him go back. 'I hope after I have done some reading here with Mrs Getty and have got a fair idea of Science to be able to return to the Taylors and carry on there with CS.' London, in this plan, would be given 'a very wide berth'.

The routine of his days in Paris, he threatened, couldn't last. How long could he go on trying to answer the question, posed at Mrs Getty's dinner parties, of what he was doing in France? But worse than that, of course, was France itself. 'As you realise my feelings towards the French, it would be impossible to live among them. I can not mix with the French. I cannot tell you what they do to me . . .' he wrote to Nancy. It was an irony that France, the source of all vice, in Nancy's book, had to be the place of Bobbie's exile and redemption, and it was easy to play up the point. Bobbie now added blackmail: 'As you see I could stay here and loaf and do what I like with impunity.'

Finally he got his way by simply declaring that he was fed up with the prescriptions of all the CS practitioners, the suspicion of his motive for returning and the anxious condemnations of every move he made. He begged his mother not to be talked around. Mrs Taylor wrote inviting Bobbie back; he had been in France only three weeks.

Nothing, of course, had been resolved. By August Phyllis had told Bob that she was going to try and persuade Bobbie to go abroad again as he was having a terrible effect on Nancy. 'She is in a bad state and weepy and upset all the time, and he is killing her. What a terrible trial he is.' Phyllis hadn't thought clearly about the reality of Bobbie living abroad – a 'solution' promoted by others in the family. Exile from his mother and close relations like David would certainly have killed Bobbie.

Nancy began to realize that Bobbie wanted to excommunicate himself for ever: to live as an exile in his own country. Unable even to visit a racecourse without embarrassment, preferring not to see old friends and more than ever dependent on his possessive mother, Bobbie's life was effectively ruined. Each weekend Nancy visited him in Kent. 'Deep and heartrending' was how Baba Metcalfe accurately described their love for each other many years later in a letter to *The Times*. A year after his release, Nancy reported to Irene that he was 'in a depressed mood but plays up like anything. He says his life is just outside of anything & he must accept it & only time can help. God only knows what it means to see a life smashed – yet God doesn't know & in his eyes man is perfect. I wish I could see with God's eyes.'

Since her return from Moscow and the jail sentence Nancy, like Bobbie, had found it difficult to go out in 'society'. She felt 'unsafe' and suffered a rare and debilitating lapse in her self-confidence. Just before a dinner party she was giving for Bill in January 1932, she wrote to Irene that she 'nearly backed out at the last moment . . . not having been anywhere since July, but I managed to get through it although I confess that I felt bluer than I thought it possible for anyone to feel!'

Bobbie had become very fond of the Courtland Taylors, now the 'C.T.'s', but he quickly tired of apprentice farming. Within a year Nancy had built him a house at Wrotham with large Georgian windows. Bobbie specially requested that it be built near the main road. 'Don't forget in my heart I am half suburban,' he told her. He filled it with fine furniture for which he had a sharp eye; developed the garden,

collected dogs and peacocks and often invited his beloved Mrs C.T.,
who had become Bobbie's surrogate mother, to visit him. He made
many trips from Kent to London and spoke to his mother each day.
Phyllis went with Nancy to see the house and reported to Bob, 'Bobbie
is lavish in his hospitality, with roaring fires in every room. If this house
had been shown to me by a newly-married bride I would say how
charming it all was, but to be owned by Bobbie rather makes me feel
sick – thank heaven Nannie doesn't see or feel about him as I do.' She
reported him later looking 'dreadfully fat and dissipated' and, again,
smelling strongly of whisky. 'I could hardly sit at the table with him,'
she wrote, 'and certainly couldn't talk to him. He really is beyond the
pale.'

But Bobbie had his sympathetic allies. Replying to a goodwill
letter from Lilian Barker, he wrote, 'Dear Miss B, I am afraid I shall
never be what they call happy again. As when you are married to a past
like mine it does not lead to happiness. However I am not unhappy,
merely a complete neutral. I know I have a lot to be thankful for but if
all the gilt has been knocked off the gingerbread I know I have only
myself to blame.'

Bob Brand and Maynard Keynes had joined up again in the dark days of
the great Depression in 1930, for what turned out to be the most his-
toric and momentous economic debate of the century. The response on
the part of most governments and economists to the slump and unemployment that were destabilizing the world was to keep applying the
old *laissez-faire* orthodoxies: to let wages and profits fall until they
found their 'natural' level when employment and production would
pick up, weeding out, according to their view, only the inefficient and
the lazy. To the bafflement of the old orthodoxy this strategy continued
to fail, both in impoverished Europe and in the affluent United States.
It merely increased unemployment and decreased profits, as well as
causing much human suffering.

In 1929, the British government had set up the MacMillan

Committee on Finance and Industry to examine the banking system and the causes of unemployment. Keynes, concerned as much as anything with the social consequences of unemployment, devoted most of his time to it. The committee represented all extremes of opinion and sat for eighteen months, in exhausting and argumentative sessions in which Keynes displayed his most imaginative brilliance and, again, nearly ruined his health. It was in these hearings that he began to expound his 'New Theory' – the central insight of Keynesian economics. Robert Skidelsky once usefully simplified this in a lecture to sixth-form students as 'The more people tried to save, the more unemployment there would be unless the government stepped in to spend the surplus savings itself,' and therefore 'thrift, the great Victorian virtue became a vice'. (Put another way: saving removed from the economy the spending power to buy what was produced at prices sufficient to cover the costs of production, the results of which were bankruptcies and unemployment.) Instead of the consumer leading the cycle, it should now be investment, private or public, that stimulated growth.

Before this revolutionary theory had become the majority view (it was the genesis of Roosevelt's New Deal) there was perplexity and fierce rearguard action. Keynes could be complex, difficult to understand. And it was at least heterodoxy in the City of London to bring in the state to regulate their business; a mixing of socialism with capitalism. Bob Brand had turned his back on *laissez-faire* politics; he represented the City, to the right of Keynes. But he was also sympathetic; he was by temperament a Keynesian now, a reformer and stabilizer, whose idea was that money should be organized in the interests of the whole community. He was therefore uniquely able to calm discussions, to draw out Keynes, to establish clarity and to find a meeting point between Keynes's ideas and city orthodoxy.

Bob wrote to Phyllis in April 1931. 'This committee meeting is killing me . . . I feel really tired & know the symptoms well. However the worst will be over in a fortnight or so.' But in early June, the day the committee's report was signed, when the Kreditanstalt in Vienna

closed the doors on its depositors, the whole exercise suddenly seemed
obsolete. It was the triggering of a crisis which might well, in Bob's
view, have caused the collapse of the whole capitalist system. 'Things
are extremely bad,' he wrote to Phyllis, as he packed his bags for
Berlin, still exhausted from the work with Keynes. 'It is worse than
August 1914 almost.' He was about to witness, close at hand, the set of
events that would bring down the Weimar Republic in less than two
years and install Hitler in power.

Bob arrived at the familiar rooms of the Esplanade Hotel and
next day wrote a letter home which he might as well have written
from Paris in 1919. 'I really think the Govs are mad . . . If only the US
would loosen up I daresay something could be done. But the ignorance and obstinacy of Congress [insisting on debt repayments] really
breaks ones heart. How frightfully stupid human beings are and selfish
and jealous. The politicians, stirred on by the ignorance of the masses
are ruining the world . . . These French are certainly not good
Europeans. How they have stuck like leeches to Reparations.' And
everyone he spoke to, he said, 'says that no German government wd
ever dare again to pay one penny of reparations. So we are in for a
pleasant time.'

Phyllis was now in Vichy, taking a cure ('I have changed my bath
from the douche couche to the douche de Vichy which is delicious. You
lie flat in warm water while two women massage you, then a spray.').
To her amazement one of her fellow guests was May Handy, the greatest of all the Southern Belles, the revered goddess of the White Sulphur
Springs. Phyllis, alas, recorded no conversation, observing simply, 'She
was of the queenly type, which looks comic with about 50 extra
pounds. It's 20 years since I saw her.'

The banking crisis began to accelerate towards the end of July.
The US and British bankers, who had once scrambled to lend money to
Germany under the Dawes plan of the mid-1920s – at high interest
rates – were now falling over each other to pull out their short-term
credits. Millions of dollars were draining away daily, drying up
Germany's liquidity, intensifying the political crisis. Bob calculated

that, soon after his arrival, the Reichsbank was down to £20 million worth of gold deposits in its vaults. The loans had assumed the German economy would revive, but it had been hit harder than any other in the Depression and depended now almost entirely on these credits, with which it had to pay reparations and service its debts. Brand telephoned his partner, Sir Robert Kindersley, urging him to get the British banks together first, then the Americans, to persuade them not to withdraw any more money. This led to the setting up that July of the Stillhalte (Standstill) Committee whereby all the international banks put a freeze on further short-term withdrawals, negotiating future dates for their eventual redemption. In many cases this was as late as the early 1950s. These Standstill arrangements brought Bob back to Berlin many times over the next five years, enabling him to watch developments close at hand, and placing him in a unique position compared to his circle of friends and colleagues in Britain to monitor what he called 'the lunatic development of the Hitler craze'.

By December 1931, unemployment in Germany had reached 6 million and there was no progress on reparations. Towards Christmas Phyllis wrote, 'Please come back, and insist on a good holiday – I just couldn't face life if anything happened to you – I know quite plainly that you are my rock of Gibraltar and my true love.' But Bob decided he would have to stay in Berlin over Christmas. Phyllis wrote: 'The children are terribly sorry . . . and I am bitterly disappointed, but in this black year of 1931 we must lump everything. I am sure you will be sorry too, and I hate even to contemplate your being in Germany alone for Xmas – you know how sentimental I am about that day!'

By mid-January 1932, Bob was reporting 'nerves and tempers are going . . . The work is so v heavy and complicated that we all get so tired we can't make decisions. The wretched Germans are nearly at the end of their resources . . . It is essential to get rid of political debts but that is only a small stop now to salvation.' The conference on reparations was presided over by the German Chancellor Heinrich Brüning, with whom Bob had struck up a crucial relationship in recent weeks. Brüning, installed the previous year by President Hindenburg, had been governing by decree over the heads of the Reichstag, the first breach in the Weimar constitution that Hitler was later to exploit. His deflationary policy, intended to prove to the world that Germany couldn't pay further reparations, had, however, a devastating effect on the population and certainly hastened the end of the Republic. Bob admired the courage with which Brüning stood up to attack and intrigue from all sides, from Social Democrats, Communists, Nationalists and Nazis in the chaotic days of 1931. The conference was brought to a standstill by the French and postponed until June.

This was the decisive moment for Brüning and the Republic. Denied success on foreign as well as domestic policies and known now as 'The Hunger Chancellor', he was abandoned by President Hindenburg, lost the support of the army and resigned on 30 May. In March, Hindenburg had defeated Hitler for the Presidency and had banned the Nazi paramilitaries. In July all the reparations payments were suspended, under Franz von Papen as Chancellor, but it was too late to restore stability. Hitler, waiting in the wings, held all the cards.

In September 1932 Jim Brand went to boarding school, taken, aged eight, by his father along the road of grief to Cothill, near Oxford, dressed in a uniform of plus fours and crêpe shoes, 'like a weekend golfer . . . He was full of tears, but very brave and then he disappeared from sight. How well I remember the feeling of desolation at the same moment. When I said goodbye to my father I was left alone among absolute strangers. But Jim will soon be alright, I know, and the plunge had to be made.' Jim Brand was an uproarious, gay, singing child of whom Bob wrote to Phyllis, 'I don't know a human being with more attraction.' In contrast to Peter and Winkie, he felt 'that Jim has that truly and deeply loving heart that will never forsake you'.

Phyllis had written to Bob from Freiburg in April 1931 where she had gone for a cure: 'Winkie's twenty first birthday is on the 30th. Will you send him for me the following cable – "My best love and congratulations for your twenty first birthday, come and get your present. Love, Mother."' She next heard from Winkie in October when he wrote her a letter of airy mindlessness, describing his playboy's progress. Winkie had by now come into his inheritance. 'It is a long time since I have written you and I feel quite embarrassed sitting down and trying to explain why I haven't. That is really one of the reasons why I haven't. I have had a marvelous summer down here this year. Played a great deal of golf and have really improved my game . . . I have a Cuban valet called Carlos who does almost everything for me . . . I have a Duizenberg car which goes 125 mph and is 265 horsepower . . . There has been a terrible depression here in the financial world and we are all about ½ as rich as we were before which is an awful blow. I'm a member of the Racquet Club now and my name comes up for Knickerbocker this month. So life in New York will be pleasanter than it was before.'

Peter drily wrote to his mother, 'Twenty-one so long looked forward to has turned out splendidly. He has spent all his money already and nothing awful has happened.' But this wasn't the whole story. Peter had dropped hints in his letters about Winkie's developing alcohol problem, and at the age of twenty-one he was taken into a nursing home suffering from delirium tremens. While he was drying out, Winkie persuaded a nurse to take him for a drink. At 2 a.m., driving back along the East Drive, Central Park, he skidded near 87th street, hit a guard rail, crashed into a tree and overturned. Neither Winkie nor the nurse was seriously hurt, but the story made the papers. Only then did the alarm spread. Irene wrote to Bob describing how upset everyone, including Reggie (now on the wagon) was about Winkie. 'He drinks continually. I think he is now in Palm Beach. His father sent for him at Peter's request . . . He is entirely without ambition & keeps company with many he should not . . . Peter realises Winkie is heading for a fall & he believes he will never do anything worth while . . . They never come near me & I tell you quite truthfully they don't give a hang for any of us.'

Nobody in the family noticed that Peter, early in 1932, had won the top trophy in America for aerobatics at the annual national convention at Miami: 'The lure of flying has still GOT me' he wrote to Phyllis, 'It's the extreme expression of adventure, romance and action and I'll sell my soul for it anyway.' Only with his flying friends in Florida did he feel he had 'a complete world' of his own, with people 'who regardless of anything will be FOR me'. He told her he was coming to England to show off his Monocoupe 'with a Warner 110 Horse Power Motor that will race, stunt and land in back yards'.

But as always, there was that fear of reunions across the water, particularly at Cliveden. '. . . I can well remember the days when I had been quelled for so long I gave up talking altogether,' he wrote. '. . . In England I feel tolerated and terribly nervous rather like a chicken wandering around with all its feathers plucked out.' Peter tried to impose advance conditions: 'I want to see you very much but I have decided not to come over without something up my sleeve with which to get away from sitting around and saddening over all the terrible things I've done in the past which have broken your heart . . . With a chance to fly about England, it would make all the difference. I don't ride and I am terrified and dumbfounded by highbrow society. I don't know, I just can't seem to sleep in the bosom of the family in England. Too many things prey on me. I like England really but I don't fit in . . . Now with an interest there I think it would be possible to come over and take a chance at not going to pieces within a month.' After commiserating about Bobbie he ended that letter: 'Goodbye mother. You are sweet. I miss you so much sometimes that I just make myself force myself to put you right out of my mind until I can think smoother . . . the subject's too difficult.' Phyllis never offered Peter any reassurance of her love in return; like Nancy she remained oblivious to the effects she had upon her children.

Dangerous daredevil stunts were now Peter's speciality. He had recently been dragged out of Long Island Sound when his amphibian plane had overturned. And in October 1932, at an air exhibition at the Long Island Aviation Country Club, attempting an 'upside down' landing – which meant flipping the plane upright again fifty feet above the ground – he landed unevenly and skidded into a telegraph pole, somersaulting the plane into the ground. His head hit the instrument panel with great force, fracturing his skull, and he was pulled out of the wreckage unconscious. He had a broken jaw, a dislocated shoulder, a broken ankle and was some weeks in hospital.

The following year he was back in the air again, part of the time on active duty with the Marine Air Squadron at Quantico Virginia, as a reserve lieutenant. He wrote, 'I now get up regularly at 4 a.m. and fly off on a sort of "dawn patrol". The air at that hour is full of the kind of magic that dreams are made of, the sky is a wondrous blue and with the May foliage all blossoming out, the view is a vision sublime and infinite. You must come up with me sometime in a May dawn into the Kingdom of the Air and I'll show you where MY castle is. Then perhaps you might understand why flying means everything to me and why I'm selfish in putting my privilege to fly ahead of everything else . . . That hospital experience terrified me especially when Aunt Irene said, "I'm glad your aeroplane (the love of my life) is all smashed up so you can't fly it anymore."'

25

Papa Wants a Little Gun

Phyllis was often alone at Eydon in the early 1930s. Her younger children were away at school; Bob was in London in the week or on prolonged foreign trips, often to the USA. Dinah was at home for a brief period attending a day school nearby but in 1934, aged fourteen, she went into another lonely exile in *pensions* in Switzerland, her health never seeming to respond to the cures and regimes of the specialists, who had been consulted from Geneva to Vienna. Phyllis had to split the precious school-holiday time between St Moritz and Eydon. Neither Bob nor Phyllis were in robust health themselves. The strain of his work sent Bob back to Dr Martin at Freiberg for many days, more for spiritual therapy than physical cure. Phyllis took cures in Vichy or Baden, suffering from back pain and rheumatism, the legacy of old hunting falls. The Thomas Cook representative at Boulogne had become as good a friend as any of their family servants.

Phyllis yearned for the warmth of the Mirador sun and the Virginian voices and hated the English cold and the dark early evenings. Hunting, her greatest pleasure, was one sure protection against the melancholy and morbidity that dogged her increasingly as the years went by. After fifteen years of marriage, Phyllis and Bob still longed for each other's company, expressing their undimmed love, and their luck, in almost every letter. But the departures and near misses sometimes left Phyllis feeling deserted and she would occasionally snap at Bob, imagining a lack of attention, annoyed at the overwhelming demands of his work, and then instantly apologize by letter, often writing minutes after he had left. 'I have a cold dread of this busy life of yours filling up every crevice of your time and leaving no room for the cozier happier things of married life, so if I am disgruntled at times you will know it is that. I don't profess to pretend that I would like you an idle man strolling about but there is a half way. I long to have my family at home together,' Phyllis wrote. 'I have been torn apart too long and it's getting on my nerves. Come on home as soon as you can. I do <u>not</u> like being a widow woman.'

On another occasion, she exploded in rage at a plan Bob had made to meet mutual friends of theirs in Paris on one of his trips. In apology she explained a deeper cause for her 'bruised soul'. 'I am sure I was over sensitive about it all but Winkie and Peter have made that "not wanted" complex <u>terribly</u> sensitive, . . . It nearly crippled me up to feel even the shadow of a doubt to cross my mind that you would prefer to go jaunting without me! But I am an ass . . . The boys have made me feel at times so terribly deserted and lonely, and I really believe if it hadn't been for Eydon and hunting at the moment when it came, I should have gone off the deep end.'

But Phyllis was beginning to take bad falls out hunting which 'horrified' Bob, and he begged her to give it up, although he was aware of the state of mind that drove her to these excessive displays of courage: 'The boys have given you a terribly sore spot which won't really heal,' he wrote, 'I think your trouble is that sometimes you brood on the past too much . . . I don't know how to tell you how I hate bringing this trouble on you. But I feel like a rat in a trap and don't know how to help . . . I am glad you have some small children who will always love you.'

Insomnia often kept Phyllis up in the early hours before dawn when she would write to Bob and to her distant sons. Letters were now the only conduit for any kind of relationship with Peter and Winkie, and Winkie had stopped writing. As late as 1935, when Peter was thirty-three, his letters still contained unbearably hurtful barbs: 'Please write more. I love your letters. They are so darn nice that I actually get homesick for you for the twinkling of a second before I realise the problem that you are to me, then I have very nice but very, very MIXED feelings. Isn't love the strangest thing after all?'

Bob left again for Berlin in the middle of the crisis that brought Hitler into the cabinet in January 1933. The previous July all the reparations payments had been suspended, but that, also, was too late. Now the German government found itself in the position of having to offer Hitler the chancellorship, needing the support of the Nazis to 'restore stability' and to block the communists – hoping at the same time to contain Hitler in a coalition cabinet.

Phyllis followed Bob's departure with a melancholy letter written by lamplight at lunch-time when Eydon was hemmed in with ice and fog. 'Your white slave (that's me) feels like a detached lonesome atom when you go away – but I mustn't tell you these things as you'll begin to strut about like all men do when they think they've got their wives!' To which Bob replied, 'I am more in love with you than I have ever been. You know there's something in you that compels me [to love you] as it always did since the day I met you . . . So this is what you have done after 16 years.'

Phyllis usually went to Virginia in the autumn, before the English hunting season got under way, to stay with her niece Nancy Lancaster, steeling herself against the absences of Peter or Winkie when she got there. On one of these trips she revealed to Nancy Lancaster the grip that her love for the Captain still held on her imagination. 'I said to Phyllis,' said Nancy, ' "Isn't it wonderful the way everything has worked out. Here you are with this nice young family and so happy with Bob." Phyllis replied "Yes I am happy but if Captain Pennant came down the road today, I'd be gone." I thought that was so extraordinary. You know I think that was a *romantic* love. But she adored Bob.'

Despite his contacts – especially with President Brüning – Bob Brand, like almost everyone else outside Germany, had no sense of

alarm or fear of impending change at Hitler's appointment. He
assumed that Hitler would be tamed and fenced in by high office and
that this was simply yet another turn in the chaos of Germany's politics.

His old friend Brüning predicted that Hitler would become
President. 'Don't repeat this as from him, as he was talking privately,'
Bob wrote to Phyllis. 'He says the Germans are in a quite abnormal
state; that the nerves of the war and <u>post war</u> generation just growing
up have never recovered. He says if the Communists had a great leader,
which they haven't, they would easily be in power in 6 months. He says
he pities Hitler since he always looks absolutely at sea & confused when
one talks of finance or economics but that he is a great organiser.
Anyhow it is the only thing now between Germany and Communism.
So we had better all hope for its success.'

A few days later, from his hotel window, Bob witnessed massed
Nazis marching in a funeral procession. 'The youth are in a state of wild
exultation. Their leader is almost divine . . . The poor Germans are
like children with their politics, parading & uniforms etc. But they
shoot one another every day. They are getting quite used to it. Really
there is a sort of madness in this people. I just don't understand them.'
At the house of another friend, the Jewish banker Jakob Goldschmidt,
Bob sat next to a woman who 'declaimed to me passionately how right
the Germans were to hate the Jews as a race & this in J.G.'s house! It
gave me a good light into German mentality. She was very sincere and
modest but felt very deeply that the Jews disintegrated German life.'

In January and February 1933 Adolf Hitler, with the help of
Hermann Goering, seized the instruments of state across Germany,
particularly in Prussia, as Brüning had predicted. Bob left Berlin a few
days before the Reichstag fire on 27 February, which led to the round-
up of 4000 communists, the assumption of dictatorial powers of arrest
and censorship and the suspension of all basic civil rights, followed by
anti-Jewish legislation.

Bob returned briefly in May and went to the Berlin horse show
where he 'sat quite close to Goering and Goebbels. There is an air of
suppressed excitement as none of the creditors know what Schacht

[President of the Reichsbank and later Hitler's Minister of Economics, credited with controlling German inflation] is going to say. Everywhere you see Nazi flags . . . I don't suppose there is any censorship of letters but perhaps it is better for me not to express any political opinions while I am here.' He did report, though, that Jakob Goldschmidt's brother was 'beaten up and that his family couldn't recognise him. However I will tell you about conditions when we meet.' He was surprised at the airport to find the Lufthansa aircraft, which was taking him back to Rotterdam to change planes, now painted with Nazi crosses.

In the same month, May 1933, Phyllis received a cable from Peter telling her that he had married his girlfriend Aline Rhonie, whom Phyllis had met only once. She was the daughter of Arthur Hofheimer of Warrenville, New Jersey, who owned the Bamberger department store. Aline, too, was a high-profile flier and something of a star. She was also a painter, who had spent some time as a pupil of Diego Rivera, and had painted a mural in the clubhouse at Roosevelt Field aerodrome in the Rivera style, a homage to aviation and progress.

'I was swept off my feet by Peter's cable,' Phyllis wrote, in shock and disapproval, to Bob from Lausanne where she had been taking Dinah to school. 'I can't say it was exactly a surprise as that is the sort of thing Peter would do, but to this particular person I am surprised, as he told me he would never think of marrying her as she was a Jewess . . . Poor Pete — I hope he hasn't married because he was lonesome . . . I hope and pray he has done the right thing. There was something independent about the girl that I liked and she was certainly very pretty, and she must by now know Peter.'

Aline then wrote to Phyllis, 'Peter is the most wonderful person — I've tried for two years to find every reason for not getting married. Now I'm the happiest girl in the world. Have been worried a long time about bringing my Jewish blood into your family, but Peter and I have the same views on this subject. As it hasn't been in my life he doesn't want it to seem important . . .'

Their honeymoon was an aviation publicity stunt with major news coverage – a 17,000-mile flight around the American continent in their separate planes, communicating to each other, in the absence of radios, with flapping wing signals.

Winkie came over to England on a sudden whim in the summer of 1933, went briefly to Eydon to see his mother, and arranged with David Astor to visit Bobbie. Phyllis wrote to Irene in August, 'Winkie has not seen him yet . . . I dread the contact as Bobbie is such a diabolical character but Winkie I think sees how really useless he is.' But it was, instead, Bobbie and David who saw a side of Winkie's character that Phyllis could never have imagined.

By now he was 'handsome, wealthy but profoundly alcoholic', as a New York contemporary, the designer Oleg Cassini, described him. Winkie had arrived in England straight from a second detoxification in New York. When he and David went to visit Bobbie they went to the pub. 'He didn't tell us that he shouldn't be touching alcohol,' said David, 'We discovered later that they'd had a terrible time drying him out. He was already drinking somewhat but not much. At Bobbie's house we had a couple of lagers and suddenly Winkie couldn't walk; he was falling about.' They had great difficulty in getting Winkie upstairs, but managed to undress him and put him to bed. 'As he lay there and we were trying to get him ready to sleep, he started saying, "Give me a little gun",' David remembered, 'and he talked in broken English as if he was a Frenchman. "Papa" – he called himself – "Papa wants a little gun, give him a little gun." Gradually we realised Winkie was talking suicidally. Bobbie was shocked and was really severe with him. Winkie just repeated, with an odd smile, "I'm no good." We said "Don't be silly, why do you think you're no good?" and he said "Well my mum thinks I'm no good". He talked meanderingly of his mother's disapproval of him; that he'd never liked horses, only golf. We said "That's no reason. You're no worse than we are." It was terrible to hear it said: "She thinks I'm no good, so give me a little gun."' David and Bobbie were utterly surprised.

Winkie had never seemed to care what his mother — or any older person — said and had always defied her. David had always admired Winkie as an independent character who had gone his own way and who seemed to be enjoying life. 'I had no idea that his self-esteem was so low,' David said, 'I would never have believed it if I hadn't heard him talk.'

The next morning Winkie shrugged off the incident, saying, 'Maybe that was nature's little warning.' To which Bobbie replied, 'When you go mad, you call it nature's little warning?' But Winkie had expressed a deadly truth, in his delirium, about his relationship with Phyllis.

Winkie largely avoided his mother in England after his visit to Eydon. He went to Paris in October 1933 and there met up with Bob, who was on a business trip, thus showing some desire for family contact. A short letter from Phyllis which read, 'I simply am flabbergasted at your never even sending me a line since you left. It takes all the kick out of me. aff Mother' was returned, stamped '*Non Reclamé*'. Winkie had made one communication with his mother's maid to have clothes sent to the Ritz in Paris. But just before he returned to America he rang her and they met. 'It's curious [that] when I am with Winkie I also long to have him <u>want</u> to be with me, but when I know he doesn't then I long not to be with him,' Phyllis wrote to Bob. 'It's a terrible feeling of failure for me for both of my boys to grow up not caring a rap really if they ever saw me again. It really has been a terrible blow. I don't blame <u>them</u>, money's done it more than anything else, and no imagination has helped too.'

Of the three young men — Bobbie, David, Winkie — who met together that summer weekend at Bobbie's house, each with his different crisis, it was David's that was perhaps the most acute. David's difficulties with Nancy had pushed their relationship to breaking point in 1931. Bill and Wissie, in less obvious ways, were also on the casualty list, partly as a result of Nancy's domination and deafness to their needs. Nancy had certainly not learned from her own past. She missed the irony, and any recognition of herself, in the paragraph she wrote later in her memoirs about her father: 'He was not so good with his sons. He never let them go. From time to time he would say: "You ought to get out and earn your living."'

Soon after David went up to Balliol in 1931 he began to suffer bouts of depression worse than any he had experienced at Eton, culminating in a paralysing emotional breakdown. Looking back he believed it was caused by 'a kind of self contempt' brought on by his unhappy relationship with his mother. He was torn between his love and loyalty and the need to break from her completely. His work was reduced to a trickle of half-written essays, and early in 1933 his tutor gently advised him to withdraw. The most intellectually gifted Astor son would not sit his finals.

He went to see his father, asking for a confidential talk. He had carefully rehearsed his lines on a subject that he believed could never be broached between them. He told Waldorf that he could no longer get on with Nancy for whom he had lost his respect. He went further, accusing his mother of hypocrisy; that what was dressed up in great acts of unselfishness was always driven by a personal motive. He told him that he would have to make the break. Waldorf listened in complete silence and 'at the end he said he was sorry to hear it. He just looked a little pale but he never contradicted me. From then on we had a secret pact. It was the beginning of an unspoken bond between us that lasted all his life. I think it was tremendously to his credit.'

Nancy was aggrieved at David's departure, but reverted to Christian Science-speak to claim that she had no doubts or regrets. Replying to a letter from Irene, who urged her to calm down the furious restlessness of her dealings with the world, Nancy wrote, 'I am not the kind that can just sit and rock . . . I have a flame inside me so I can't rock that way. The boys one moment think I never stop trying to meddle in their lives & won't let them alone & the next I have neglected them for public life. They can't both be right – so I am really unmoved by their criticism & know that they will be sorry that adolescence took them that way.'

It took David six years to recover and to become fully active

again. These were years of preparation for his role as the most independent-minded of British newspaper editors, at the *Observer*, which he
ran with great success for twenty-five years after the war. Bob gave him
a temporary job at Lazard Brothers; Phyllis comforted him. He
returned only occasionally to Cliveden to see his mother. On one of
these visits Nancy implored him to stay on over Sunday night. David
invented an excuse to go back to London, but only to prove his independence. There was an argument, and then, putting on a voice of
mock politeness, Nancy said: 'If you see your mother, do give her my
regards. I hear she's a perfectly charming woman.' Disarmed again by
her wit, David left all the same.

Phyllis had little, if any, advance warning of the infrequent arrivals and
departures of either of her own eldest sons. In Winkie's case communication took the form of an occasional apology. Peter also discovered
that he was drifting away from Winkie, partly because of his marriage
and partly because Winkie now inhabited a world that Peter didn't
belong to. Peter was shocked when Aline told him, 'You can't wear
that suit if you're going out with Winkie', as he was leaving for a lunch
date with his brother at the Racquet Club. 'What do I amount to if I
can't even dress right?' Peter complained to Phyllis.

Peter's apartment was not the sort of place Winkie could have
brought his friends, nor indeed, one would have imagined, a new
bride. It had been turned into an aviation museum: the curtains were
made from parachute silk, the bar from the side of a bi-plane, the
wastepaper basket from a petrol tank, the desk supported by pro-
pellers, the ashtrays from cylinder heads and lamps from a crankshaft.
He had a sound system which produced the noise of engines roaring
and idling, even a device to put out different smells, 'dear to the heart
of the flier'. Suspended from the walls and ceiling were pictures of the
dog-fights of Richthofen's flying circus.

When Winkie came over, Peter wrote to Phyllis, 'We make him
a fine drink just the way he likes it then we talk about money which
has always been his favourite subject . . . we discuss ties and shirts . . .

but we're not quite as cosy as we used to be, Winks & I; he's a man of great importance, moving with people of vast incomes that sleep during the day and live at night. However he does play good golf and keeps fairly fit.' He ended the letter with a sad, and bitter, survey of their lives: '. . . I'm sorry that your heart is tired and I do feel that a high percentage of the blame can be fairly placed on me. You had a tough break with your first two sons . . . you didn't draw a real leader in me and it will hit you a little hard when you see me and dream of what I might have been but you missed and so now let's turn our thoughts to Jim. He'll make up for Winkie and I from what I hear everywhere.'

In February 1934, von Schleicher, Hindenburg's army appointee as Chancellor and the last man to get close to outmanœuvring Hitler, was murdered in the Night of the Long Knives. He had been a friend of Jakob Goldschmidt and Bob Brand had met him in the course of business. Brüning would almost certainly have been killed too had he not left Germany the previous June. Bob wrote to Phyllis: 'A procession of soldiers passed me and 3 men standing just by me saluted. I did not and one of them looked as if he wd have liked to have kicked me . . . I feel as if the tension here were not nearly over. I'm not sure the world isn't going into many years – a generation or two – of trouble & chaos & autocracy and maybe war. I hope not. But human beings are mad and stupid.' Phyllis replied, 'Look out for the Nazis and give them the salute whenever they want it, as I do not wish you to be battered up while away from home.' She added, 'Tilly [the cowman at the Eydon farm] tells me to say to you that the report on the cow (the abortion one) is quite alright. He was very anxious for you to know. Tell the Standstill Committee. It may interest them too.'

Meanwhile, at home in England, Phyllis met Neville Chamberlain at Cliveden, three years before he became prime minister and reported: 'He is a poor looking little man and by rights ought to be selling *woollen* goods at Birmingham! though I must say is very nice to talk

to. I sat next to him at luncheon; Mrs is like a powder puff, nothing
more or less.'

She visited Dinah and her nursemaid in St Moritz, writing a week
later to Bob: 'Dinah is a treasure, so cheerful and sweet and kind and
never a word of complaint; and she is so full of a sense of the ridiculous. I do love her. When I think what a disposition I have given that
child, it comforts me!'

Winkie returned to England for Christmas 1934, lured by the
glamour of Cliveden, but spent little time with Phyllis. Then in January
he agreed to go with her to Estoril in Portugal. It was a strange
moment of peace between them. For companionship Phyllis invited
Leila Hampden, an attractive young woman recently married to Bob
Brand's first cousin, Thomas Hampden. Winkie's drinking appeared to
be under control. 'He is docility itself,' said Phyllis. 'He went gambling
at the Casino a few nights ago and like an ass lost about £30 and is now
cabling America for more. It's not a bad thing as he has none now to
buy so many cocktails with.' The signs again were misread. Drink was
clearly one of the reasons that Winkie had avoided his mother and her
stern eye. Phyllis attributed the 'so many' cocktails, as ever, to the
ready availability of money.

Bob had a brief holiday in August that summer in Jura with the
Astors, and with his son, Jim Brand. These moments of pure pleasure
in the Western Isles – Colonsay, Oronsay, Mull – were mixed with
gloom at the collapse of democracy in Europe: 'What a place the world
is,' he wrote to Phyllis, 'Mussolini has killed the League of Nations. The
only good I see is that it will waken the English from their dream.
When one thinks of Mussolini and reads of gas masks & all the horrors
of civilisation, what are we to do? What a horrible place the world is
becoming for our children. Is the human race so mad that it can't stop
the rot? I fear not.'

By October 1935 Bob had convinced himself that England would
have to defend herself against Hitler's aggression. He began to urge his
view on his contemporaries, who were either disbelieving or unwilling
to listen. Some of Bob's information came from his European business

contacts. In Copenhagen, in September that year, he wrote of a lunch with a shipping millionaire, A. P. Moller: 'You shd have heard him on the risks England is taking [in not re-arming]. He thinks it is hardly possible that Hitler will resist the temptation of attacking us. He thinks we may very well share the fate of Abyssinia. But he says you can never change the English.'

There were days of unseasonable midsummer heat in October 1935 when Phyllis returned to Mirador for her autumnal visit. She waited by the telephone for news of Winkie. She had seen him briefly at a dinner in Long Island soon after her arrival in New York, and wrote to Bob: 'I thank goodness I am no longer stabbed to the quick by his indifference – I don't really much mind now – I feel as if that heart wound had been tied up with a string to stop the bleeding!'

Three weeks passed without a message and Phyllis prepared to return to England. A birthday lunch was given for her at Mirador the day before she left, but she complained, 'neither Peter nor Winkie have sent me a birthday greeting and yet I borned them [sic] not long ago'. Then, three days before sailing back to England from New York, Winkie came in from Long Island to see her. She reported simply: 'He looks dreadfully, has a heavy cold, is still on the wagon and says it is <u>why</u> he feels so badly! He is going to Florida soon to join his father.' It was a chilly, standoffish meeting, but it was all Phyllis was to hear of Winkie until June 1936, the following year, when she discovered, at second-hand, that he too was married.

26

Scott Fitzgerald's
Intimate Strangers

Lefty Flynn – football star, prankster, and now Nora's husband – had gradually begun to wear down the family resistance. Dana Gibson was one of the first to crack. Irene wrote from Dark Harbor, 'Dana says he is our safeguard and keeps Nora straight. But how Joyce and Tommy can stop with him I cannot see. I mean their sense of <u>loyalty</u>.'

Tommy, Nora's son, was sharing an apartment in New York with his friend, the actor David Niven, before he embarked on his Hollywood career. Tommy took him to Connecticut for a weekend and Niven described in his autobiography, *The Moon is a Balloon*, how he immediately fell in love with Nora and Lefty. Lefty and Niven had a similar sense of humour, equally high spirits, and a love of practical jokes. Lefty was continually thinking up schemes of the schoolboy-inventor type to make his fortune. Once he came up with a device that Nancy Lancaster remembered as 'a sort of lamp that you stick on your head'. She described Lefty as being 'like Nora, like a child. I mean he would cry one minute and then get quite satisfied with something that he could put on his head.'

In 1934 Lefty and Niven got involved in a project with some grown-ups which ended in full-scale disaster. That year Niven had met a man named Doug Herz, a promoter of extravaganzas and a part-time cowboy, when he tripped over his spurs in a bar and fell into Niven's arms. Niven, Lefty and Herz decided to set up a rodeo act, horse relay races, lasting fifteen minutes, in which the jockey would change mounts each minute, riding bareback, then turn back to front and swing under the horse's belly. Fired with the certainty that they would soon be rich men they raised many thousands of dollars from friends, including Damon Runyon. They gathered a large herd of polo ponies and an army of cowboys and set up the American Pony Express Racing Association, which opened to wild applause and success in Atlantic City. But they had ignored the local mafia, who took revenge by pulling the plug on the floodlights on three successive nights. Very little was salvaged from the wreckage. 'Lefty could take all the disappointments,' wrote Niven, 'except the desertion of the cowboys.'

Perhaps the greatest proof of Nancy's generosity and magnanimity, faced with the flood of Nora's bills that still arrived at St James's Square, was her acceptance in 1935 that Lefty was staying and that they must have somewhere to live. They had rented a house in Tryon, an unfashionable but relatively cheap little town in North Carolina, at the foot of the Smokey Mountains, whose mild climate attracted retired Northerners and convalescents from tuberculosis. Nancy wrote to Irene, 'Will you get someone in South Carolina or get Legh [Legh Page, the Richmond lawyer] to secretly buy that bit of land that Nora wants for a house . . . and he can put the deeds in a Xmas stocking.'

Nora built a timber-frame house in hunting country north of Tryon and soon, playing the role of 'rural duchess', she and Lefty dominated the social life of the community. Nora was already an honorary celebrity as a Langhorne sister and now with her visitors and dinner parties and charity benefits, she managed to establish a cosmopolitan outpost in the Smokey Mountains. 'She organised benefits and judged fashion shows,' wrote Andrew Turnbull in his biography of Scott Fitzgerald, 'and when she walked down the street at Tryon people of all ages and descriptions clustered around her.'

One night in February 1935 there was a new visitor to the enclave. Scott Fitzgerald arrived in Tryon, unannounced and unexpected. At thirty-nine years old, 'half crazy with illness and worry', as he described it, he was tens of thousands of dollars in debt. He took a room in the Oak Park Hotel, overlooking Tryon's main street, ordered innumerable drinks and started trying to churn out some stories for the popular magazines. 'One harassed and despairing night,' he wrote of his flight to Tryon, 'I packed a brief case and went off a thousand miles to think it over. I took a dollar room in a drab little town where I knew no one and sunk all the money I had with me in a stock of potted meat crackers and apples.'

Fitzgerald had finally come to realize that his wife Zelda, confined in the Sheppard-Pratt hospital in Baltimore, was never going to recover from her own breakdown; he had lost his life's companion. The 'death-dance', as Hemingway had described their marriage, was ending in an exchange of tragic letters, full of love and longing, and in vacant, sometimes embarrassing meetings.

This realization, combined with his brooding disappointment at the mixed reception of *Tender is the Night* the year before, had helped to raise Fitzgerald's drinking rate, aggravating the damage to his lungs. He believed that his talent had left him and he was finished as a writer. 'Then I was drunk for many years and then I died,' he wrote mournfully in his notebook. Although he still had five years to live, he was experiencing what he thought was a terminal breakdown. He carefully watched and recorded the signs of his disintegration and managed to write about them in 'The Crack-Up' – the series of public confessions published by *Esquire* magazine in 1936.

It wasn't long before news of Fitzgerald's presence reached Nora and she sought him out in his dingy hotel room. He took immediately to the Flynns. In Lefty, as Henry Dan Piper has pointed out, he found the type he most admired – the athletic college hero, the handsome football player that he had written about, for example, in 'The Bowl' in 1928. As a couple he saw them as 'the unorthodox rich' – another of his favourite subjects. He was instantly charmed by Nora. He found her 'gay brave stimulating'. He loved her attitude, Arthur Mizener wrote, of 'tighten up your belt baby let's get going. To any Pole.' 'I am astonished sometimes by the fearlessness of women, the recklessness, like Nora, Zelda,' he wrote. 'But it's heartening when it stays this side of recklessness.' But he added that there was little Nora could do to lift him out of his depression. 'Of all natural forces vitality is the incommunicable one,' he wrote. 'You have it or you haven't like health or brown eyes or honor or a baritone voice . . . I could [only] walk from her door holding myself very carefully like cracked crockery and go away into the world of bitterness where I was making a home with such materials as are found there.'

Nora gave him an open invitation to their house, and Fitzgerald spent much time there. He was fascinated by their double act and soon he and Lefty were acting in a comic playlet, *Love's Melody*, written by Fitzgerald. Nora had no helpful advice about finances but she did try, using Christian Science methods, to wean him off the drink. She had done so successfully with Lefty, and her house, Little Orchard, the setting for Nora's famous parties – and her delicious food – was a dry house where 'nobody ever brought a drink or hid one'.

By the end of the month in which he had met Nora, Fitzgerald had stopped drinking almost completely. Nora buoyed him up, encouraged him, flattered him, hugged him in his lowest moments of depression and, according to Andrew Turnbull, 'threatened to spank him if he didn't cheer up'. Nora must have told Fitzgerald the story of her life in some detail as part of her therapy course – how to overcome life's enormous difficulties and keep smiling. Fitzgerald, by now, was plundering any sources close to him for copy for his magazine pieces and immediately used Nora and Lefty in a story called 'The Intimate Strangers'. Turned down by the *Saturday Evening Post*, the story was bought by McCall's for $2,700 and published the following June.

By Fitzgerald's standards it is a poor piece of work, although given the condition he was in it is extraordinary that he could summon the energy to write at all. It nevertheless provides an insight into life at Little Orchard. Nora must have told him of the phrase 'a heart like a hotel' and Fitzgerald wrote, '"To Let" or not her heart poured into her voice as it soared through the long, light music room . . .' In the story the couple, who are renamed Sara and Killian, had run away together just before the First World War, singing close harmonies and spending several blissful days in the mountains, while Sara's husband had returned to Europe to join up. Killian is described as 'adolescent', fond of going on binges, 'yearning for the society of friendly policemen'.

One of Fitzgerald's biographers speculates that he also had an affair with Nora. Certainly Fitzgerald was looking for love and approval. According to Scott Donaldson, he told Laura Guthrie, a palm reader, who became a confidante of Fitzgerald's, 'that Nora was deeply in love with him and wanted to go off with him as she had done with Lefty. Scott said he wouldn't because he didn't want to be the last bus that Nora took. He told her, "Nora's passion lingers so long because nothing has happened."' Nora later said, 'Scott always said he was terribly in love with me, and it was so foolish. I cared so much for Lefty, and he did too. And it was such an obvious relief to Scott when I finally told him off and we could forget the sex and just be friends. He was so charming and such fun to talk with.' And Zelda told Henry Dan Piper in 1947: 'He loved her I think. Not clandestinely but she was one of several women he always needed around him to stimulate and to turn to when he got low and needed a lift.'

In 'The Intimate Strangers' Fitzgerald described some of the Flynns' skits (some of them exact Joyce Grenfell prototypes): the dancing master teaching the Turkey Trot; the French woman giving English lessons; and 'the Russian gibberish song.' 'Not knowing a word of the language they had yet caught the tone and ring of it,' wrote Fitzgerald, 'until it was not burlesque but something uncanny that made every eye intent on their faces, every ear attune to the Muscovite despair they twisted into the end of each phrase. Following it they did the always popular German band, and the Spanish number and the spirituals . . . their faces flushed with excitement and pleasure like children's faces.'

Fitzgerald returned to Baltimore in March, where proximity to Zelda and her worsening condition led to another drinking spree. By now tuberculosis had been diagnosed and he was ordered by his doctor to return to North Carolina. He moved into the luxurious Grove Park Inn in Asheville. For the next two years he moved about in the area between Asheville, Hendersonville and Tryon. Fitzgerald's depression worsened towards the end of 1935; as did his debts and his stories.

Nora continued to look after him. Zelda entered the Highland Hospital in Asheville in April 1936. He would take her out on visits to Little Orchard, where Zelda would dress in the clothes of the 1920s, her hair down to her shoulders. Nora told Henry Dan Piper that Zelda came one day, looking old and ill. 'After walking about and touching things for a while she started to dance. I shall never forget the tragic, frightful look on Scott's face as he watched her . . . They had loved each other. Now it was dead. But he still loved that love and hated to give it up – that was what he continued to nurse and cherish.'

In October 1936 Fitzgerald wrote: 'During the mood of depression that I seem to have fallen into about a year ago she [Nora] was a saint to me; took care of Scottie [his daughter] for a month one time under the most peculiar circumstances, and is altogether in my opinion, one of the world's most delightful women.'

When Fitzgerald made his third and last visit to Hollywood, in 1937, he wrote to Nora and Lefty from the Garden of Allah, a letter unpublished until now:

> What you meant to me during those bleak years can't be
> expressed in words . . . You were the bright spot in an
> existence that seemed to have touched bottom
> permanently and always I can fix my mind on lovely
> pictures of you, of Lefty's kind and <u>interested</u> promenades
> along State Street and Nora's gay entry into the drugstore,
> just <u>slithering</u> along, sideways sometimes, with that
> deathless determination that life could be somehow fun
> and maybe you could <u>edge</u> into it – and your parties with
> Lefty carving what was somehow the best meat in the
> world, and Nora showing the big window with her
> beloved self reflected in it, faintly like an artist's signature.

The drugstore referred to here – Misseldines – had been immortalized by Fitzgerald in a song he had written on a napkin, to be sung to the tune of 'Tannenbaum'.

Oh Misseldines, dear Misseldines
A dive we'll ne'er forget.
The taste of its banana splits
Is on our tonsils yet.

Its chocolate fudge makes livers budge
It's really too divine
And as we reel, we'll give one squeal
For dear old Misseldines.

When Fitzgerald met Nora again in January 1940 he asked her whether he should divorce Zelda and marry Sheilah Graham, the columnist he had met in Hollywood in 1931. Sheilah had met Nora in London before the war and she remembered being 'intimidated' simply by the fact that Nora was one of the Langhorne sisters. Nora wrote to Fitzgerald: 'I am sure you are doing the right thing – about Zelda – I know you have been beyond words wonderful to her – I also know the time has come for you to have a life of your own – to choose your own life, not for Zelda or Scottie but just for you . . . I have a strange feeling that—— [Sheilah] is the right person for you – I feel she knows the real you – and that's what counts.' But before he could do so, he died of a heart attack in December that year.

27

A Shovel in the Post

'Winkie's news has just reached me a day or so ago,' Phyllis wrote to Irene in 1936 when she heard of Winkie's marriage. 'As you can imagine I was taken off my feet & felt as if I had been hit below the belt, but I am glad to hear she is a nice girl & I think it may be the best thing for him . . . I thought I was shock proof about the boys but after all mothers never can be shock proof about their children. Well, that's that.'

Winkie's bride, Adelaide Moffett, was twenty-three years old and already a celebrity. She was a Park Avenue, East Hampton society girl who had flouted the conventions of the *Social Register* to become a nightclub singer – unheard of for an ex-deb. Her father was a Standard Oil executive and a millionaire, who had been Federal Housing Commissioner; her mother had died the year before, jumping or falling from her apartment window soon after her divorce. Adelaide made her début at the Embassy Club in Miami, singing under the pseudonym Diana Dorrance to appease her father. Her career had been carefully followed by the press: 'Jimmy [her father] vowed he'd give her the spanking of her life if she ever uttered another note in a nightclub. And thata was thata. For the moment,' wrote the *Daily News*. A little later *Variety* described her as 'tall, blonde and niftily groomed, she's got what it takes to score on that end. Not quite so much can be said for her pipes, which lack flexibility and fluidity.' Oleg Cassini, who later had a 'nice, light, sophisticated affair' with her, described Adelaide as 'striking with dark (now) hair and enormous dark eyes, though perhaps a little too voluptuous. She was very lively and had lots of friends.'

Winkie, now well known to the gossip columns, was described on his wedding day as 'lady killer and man-about-town'. His last girl-friend, another popular society belle called Gloria Baker, was reported to be conveniently 'abroad with her mother, Mrs Margaret Emerson, visiting Il Duce'.

The papers reported the marriage as an elopement, although Adelaide's father gave them lunch at the Colony Restaurant that day, and the reception was held in Winkie's temporary apartment at the Hotel Pierre. The wedding cake was sent up by room service. Winkie was dressed in a beautiful double-breasted suit, his shirt collar slightly pinched in over the tight knot of his tie, with a handkerchief in the top pocket and his hair slicked back. He looked nearer to thirty-five than his real age of twenty-six. The couple were photographed, looking like two movie stars, sitting against the blue zebra stripes of the ban-quette at El Morocco.

In a moment of yearning for Mirador, back in 1915, when Phyllis was nursing wounded soldiers at the Cliveden hospital and grieving for Henry Douglas Pennant, she had written to Irene, 'I wish with all my heart we were all together there now like a covey of quail.' In fact she had to wait twenty-one years, until October 1936, for the four sisters to be reunited at Mirador. It was the last public appearance of 'the famous Langhorne sisters'; it was also the last time the remaining four would all be together. They went in a chartered bus from Mirador to the New Green Mountain Baptist Church in Albemarle County, a coloured church as it was called, for the wedding of their brother Buck's black valet and factotum, Clinton Harris. They turned what might have been an intimate occasion into the biggest social event the community — black and white — had witnessed for many years.

Phyllis had been the first to arrive for this reunion, bringing with her Virginia, now aged seventeen. Dinah was in Switzerland, Jim at Eton. Peter had written to her but there was no sign of Winkie. She wrote to Bob: 'Once more I feel folded in the arms of my first love, Mirador. We arrived this a.m. a beautiful blue sky and bright sun and the place is looking lovely. Buck was at the station to meet us looking very well. I heard "Hi Phyl," before I left the train. How I wish you were here . . . Callie [Phyllis's old nurse] is simply lovely. When she saw Virginia she said, "Miss Phyllis she cerny do favour you." I of course revel in being here, and had a sleep this afternoon in the sun, with my long chair turned towards the mountains.'

Nancy arrived by car from Washington, firing off commands and admonishments, ready to erupt. A crowd of people came to the door to get a glimpse of her but were told by the butler that she wasn't there. 'I feel Nannie is now a complete alien in Virginia,' Phyllis wrote a few days later, 'I really can't get over how completely removed she is from the spirit of this place . . . She cannot forget she is a public character. Woe betide the day she became one. She gets VERY impatient with Buck's somewhat lengthy conversation. I sit in fear and trembling that she will hurt his feelings; and as for Irene when she arrives next week, I dread the contacts!'

Phyllis was hurt that Nancy, even at Mirador, insisted on going to the Christian Science church instead of to 'our little church built in mother's memory, where both father and mother worshipped – but no! imagination and sentiment play no part in her life I fear'. Otherwise Nancy played golf as often as possible, missing the meet of the Albemarle Hunt, and further upsetting Phyllis. 'I think it is such a strange lack of imagination to come to Virginia and do exactly the same as if you were in England or Long Island.'

The only shadow of which the sisters were aware at this reunion was that incredibly, given their combined wealth and the sacredness of the ground, Mirador had been put up for sale by Nancy Lancaster. A potential buyer from Chicago had already offered $225,000. It seems that it was being abandoned almost by default and that its significance had dwindled to that of public myth. Nancy was the only sister who could afford to buy Mirador but whatever she said on the hustings at Plymouth, Phyllis reported to Bob, 'I'm afraid Nancy is not going to buy it, she just doesn't love it enough.' She added, 'I can't tell you how sweet Mirador looks now and it just seems to be like pulling my insides out to think of us all deserting it — it seems almost disgraceful to me that we can't somehow manage to keep it.'

Phyllis wrote to Nancy Lancaster in England, 'Oh Nancy don't leave this place, you can't live without your roots and you know perfectly well they are here where everyone loves having you so much. I wish to heavens I could afford to buy it. I swear I would not hesitate. I am afraid you may regret bitterly if you sold it.' It emerged years later that the 'sale' was in fact an elaborate wheeze on the part of Nancy Lancaster, who was having some difficulty justifying the expense of keeping Mirador, to get Nancy Astor to buy the house. Knowing that she wouldn't often go there, Nancy Lancaster could continue to be its *de facto* owner. She had gone so far as to arrange stalking-horse buyers to establish a price, and had kept the secret from all the others.

The entire neighbourhood had been alerted by Buck to Clinton's wedding. Cousins and friends came from Richmond in their hundreds, mainly to get a look at the sisters. There had been nothing like it since Nancy's barnstorming return in 1922, when she was faced with relations screaming out their family trees to claim kinship and force on her some self-aggrandizing hospitality. The bridal couple were overwhelmed. 'Buck has given him a dress coat to be married in at 4 o'clock,' wrote Phyllis, 'but his "mommer" thought it would look nicer if she cut the tails off a bit, so he is going to the altar with his wings clipped . . . The sunshine is trickling through the trees and the grass and we are in for a hot day, and I rejoice.'

'I was so short,' Clinton recalled almost fifty years later, 'it looked like I was walking on my knees . . . I was scared to death. Lot of people want to see Miss Nancy, Miss Phyllis and them. Lot of people know them when they're growing up. I never saw so many people, all wanting to see these famous ladies.'

Phyllis wrote early the next day: 'As he stood at the altar waiting for his bride he looked scared green and streamed with sweat, and the best man evidently had fleas as he never stopped scratching.'

On 16 October, she wrote to Bob that Winkie had arrived in New York but had not contacted her. 'I talked to Peter tonight on the telephone and he is coming down on Monday, and said Winkie was coming too but I know nothing more of him. I feel if his wife were any sort of a girl she would have made him write or something . . . I shall be very sad to leave Mirador, in fact, I can't bear to think it may be for good.'

In the meantime the sisters travelled back with Nora to Tryon to visit her house. 'Nora lives in a perfectly LOVELY untouchable country, I mean, untouched by money and Yankees,' Phyllis wrote. 'She seems perfectly happy there, and it is gratifying to see how much all the people love her . . . Nannie spoke for her at the Town Hall, and the whole countryside turned out, and Nora says she is now set up for life in that community. Lefty is like a Newfoundland Dog around the place, very kindly and harmless; he does a good deal of physical work, clearing the woods etc . . . as he appears to make Nora so happy I suppose we ought to be grateful, but how she could have married him I shall never know. You should see Irene trying to like Lefty – she cannot succeed to save her soul . . . He still makes her almost sick. Nannie managed it much better and presented him with a pair of gold link cuff buttons. Nora was so happy to have us, and so relieved that the visit went off without any fireworks! It made me sad to wave farewell to her, she looked sort of pathetic . . . she has let her looks go to pot, but doesn't seem to care.' Nancy, reported Phyllis, 'is fairly peaceful these days with a little bust loose here and there. I long to get her out of politics but at the same time I hate to think what she would do in our lives in her spare time.'

Knowing that Winkie had been in New York for four days without sending word, Phyllis had begun to feel that she would rather not see him. Then, two days before she was due to leave, 'Winkie walked into the house as casually and calmly as if he had left here yesterday and been married all his life. He is completely indifferent to me and so I am to him . . . Peter is far more affectionate.' At least, she remarked, Winkie and his bride, 'seem very happy'.

A little less than a month later, on the night of 15 November, Winkie and Adelaide went to the Colony Restaurant to dine, then to a dance at the Hotel Pierre, where Howard Hughes was among the guests. They returned to their suite at the Mayfair House at 3.30 a.m. Winkie, according to Adelaide, telephoned a friend to cancel an appointment later that morning, saying that they were leaving early for Long Island to play golf. Adelaide went into the bedroom to take off her coat and came back into the sitting room to find Winkie gone. The window, which had a low sill, was wide open. Screaming for help, Adelaide went down in the elevator and found him on the pavement outside. Winkie's body was seen falling by several taxi drivers on 67th Street; he was killed instantly.

Dinah was at school when she picked up the newspaper and read the headline: 'LADY ASTOR'S NEPHEW DIES IN FALL FROM PARK AVE BRIDAL SUITE'. The news reached Eydon soon after Sunday lunch. Phyllis's niece Alice Winn, Nancy Lancaster's sister, was staying in the house and Bob sent her to find Phyllis. Alice couldn't hold back the news that something terrible had happened to Winkie and remembers Phyllis repeating, as she went to find Bob, 'I have such regrets, such terrible regrets.' 'I had to tell Phyllis as best I could,' Bob wrote to Nancy. 'She often told me that she had learned to forget, that she had grown a hard skin over the wound. But she never had . . . How deep the wounds are is evident in her terrible anguish.' Bob had heard that Winkie had been drinking again, but he kept this from Phyllis, who at first announced 'it was a complete accident'.

It was a blow to Phyllis, from which it was almost impossible to recover. There was too much guilt mixed in with the grief and sadness, with her sense of failure as a mother, regrets at the separations and the consequences of her remarrying in England. For weeks after his death she would burst into anguished tears. And there was a further horror for Phyllis to suppress: that Winkie's death had not been an accident. Bob later revealed his secret thoughts, and subsequent information when he wrote, 'Winkie escaped from a world he suddenly couldn't face.' Nancy let slip in a letter that it was, at least, a consequence of Winkie's life, rather than an accidental fall. David, his friend and cousin, was sure that Winkie had committed suicide. Four years earlier, he and Bobbie had witnessed Winkie's suicidal outburst and had seen the real nature of his depression — the lack of self-esteem, the compulsive drinking.

David discovered later that Adelaide's father had sent Winkie a shovel in the post shortly before he died — a brutal reminder that he considered it indecent for Winkie not to have a job. He had reproached him about this many times, and the reproaches had finally turned to insults. Adelaide, too, had been leaning on Winkie, since their marriage, to take up some employment. But she had clearly not yet understood Winkie's pathological fear of working; and his fear of people who tried to force him into it. It was not a great exaggeration when he had written to his mother, after his 'shattering' experience of working in Wall Street five years earlier, that if he was forced to continue 'I would have either died or committed suicide.' Peter's semi-joking letters had contained a prophetic warning. Winkie had also told his mother around that time that he was looking for a girl-friend 'who would like me even though I don't work'. And now Adelaide was taking sides against him. When the shovel arrived, said David Astor, 'Winkie was so shattered by this and felt humiliated and I think this was what finished him.' It was merely an echo of his mother's disapproval, as he complained to David in his alcoholic ramblings: 'She thinks I'm no good.' And it was too much. Winkie's death was a tragic copy of the way Adelaide's mother had killed herself the previous year. The *post mortem* never revealed how much alcohol he had had in his blood at the time. It was only later that Adelaide, the only one in the apartment with Winkie when he fell, pieced together his true psychological state.

Phyllis wrote to Nancy: 'My gay young Crusader has gone so they all tell me but the Winkie that I know and love is <u>still</u> here with me as he used to be as a little boy. I can't and won't believe he has just passed out of life without leaving me all the things I loved about him. I once said I was shock proof & had grown an extra skin & all that sort of thing but Oh! Nannie it <u>is</u> a misery this earthly parting & Winkie so loved life & just now too when his sort of grown up life was beginning. He had so many attractive qualities, his honesty, lack of hypocrisy & snobbery & oh! that delicious laugh . . . I can't bear to think of those years from 18 to 26 when he was floating about without a real home. He didn't feel he needed me then but I always knew I needed him. Oh! Nannie it does hurt so terribly.'

'I can't stop weeping inside & out,' Nancy wrote to her, 'Winkie somehow was so much a part of your & my life, the last thing on earth one supposed was to outlive him.' At the Mirador reunion, the last time she had seen him, she had said: 'He was so like his old self, giggly and watching to see if I liked Adelaide & if she liked me, you know how he looked out of the corner of his eye . . .' Nancy, somewhat tactlessly, saw Winkie's death as further proof of the worldwide evils of alcohol: '. . . If that cursed devil drink had not got him. How oh how can you all be so indifferent to a poison which ruins so many young lives.' She now suggested that she and Phyllis go on a world tour asking people 'to sign the pledge and deny themselves because so many are possessed and ruined by it. Oh Phyl we must wake up. But Phyl don't grieve, remember we can't. It's cowardly and we are Virginians.'

Phyllis was further 'bruised and hurt' when Nancy stirred up enmity against the Brooks family, furious that they had 'taken over' the funeral, which she tried to get postponed for four days so that she could attend. Nancy's grief also led her to attack Irene for allowing Winkie to be buried in Woodlawn cemetery, which she considered a Brooks domain, claiming that she was interpreting Phyllis's wishes. In fact, Winkie was buried there next to Phyllis's son Jackie, who had died in infancy. But Nancy was alone in wanting to attack the Brooks family; all of them had turned up to mourn Winkie. Irene wrote to Bob, complaining of Nancy's attack, 'Imagine me making things difficult or unpleasant when every heart was broken.' But Nancy was beyond understanding such sentiment.

Peter, too, had somehow hurt Phyllis's feelings. His letter, which hasn't survived, was sent on to Bob with the note, 'This from Peter astounds and hurts to the core, but I suppose he doesn't mean to. Do you think he can possibly know what all this terrible month has been like? How did I produce boys so heartless? I pray Jim may never be so unimaginative.' Peter, equally crushed by the death of his younger brother, had almost certainly written words to the effect that it had all been avoidable.

Phyllis locked herself away in her room at Eydon Hall and surrounded herself with Winkie's photographs. She developed strange patches of colour on her face as if a cancer was eating away at her. She wrote to Irene, 'I know if you were here you would say "don't let Phyllis be alone," but you can't think how precious I find it being alone with Winkie. He seems to exist and I know God has taken him to protect him and to keep him safe until I come, so don't worry that I am worrying, I'm just waiting . . . Poor Pete, I will have to give him the comfort I wanted to so many years ago.'

28

Alone in the Universe

Barely a month after Winkie's death, Peter, his wife Aline and Winkie's widow Adelaide all sailed over to England for Christmas. There was to be a big house party at Cliveden. Phyllis was growing to like Aline and wrote to Irene, 'I shall be so delighted to see them. Peter has never seen Eydon. I shall put all the Xmas decorations up & ready for them and we will have three days here before we go to Cliveden. That I am afraid I dread but all the children will like it. Thank heavens they are totally unconscious of my misery or heartaches like little birds that sing away at everything.'

Joyce Grenfell, not yet launched on her own career, reviewed the family performances that Christmas in a letter to her mother, Nora: 'Aunt N. wore false teeth and her hair in a frizz on top and was any very rich old woman in the Ritz in any country. Quite uncanny and terribly funny . . . Jakie and David did their famous ventriloquist act and Adelaide crooned. She's got a really low radio voice oozing with S.A. (Sex Appeal) and she sang songs like 'How Deep is the Ocean' without turning a hair while Aunt Phyllis wept and Alice [Winn] and Bobbie fidgeted with embarrassment. Most extraordinary. But she's quite unhypocritical about it and I don't doubt she misses Wink awfully at times, but between whiles she's quite natural and normal and just exists.'

Phyllis left early, around 28 December and wrote to thank Nancy: 'I am certainly glad I was there for I should probably have expired anywhere else. I came away because I just had to & I know you will understand. I feel more smoothed out, I went out for an hours hunting and it was like lifting a load off my mind. I wish I could do it all day, all night . . .' She planned to go to London to see Peter and Aline before they left again, taking Jim with her.

Instead, Phyllis caught flu just before the New Year. By Monday 4 January, she seemed to have recovered. She wrote that day to Nancy. 'Dearest Sis, Well I'm just emerging from my bed after a nasty go of the flu. It really is a horrid thing to have and I am left feeling like a locust shell – nothing inside but air! . . . As the days go by the terrible realisation that Winkie has gone is like being knocked backwards every morning when I wake up . . . I know there is no hope in looking back so I'll turn my eyes to the far horizon beyond and maybe just over the border he will be there. Send him yr prayers each day he mustn't feel lonely wherever he is.'

On Thursday, 7 January, she made a hurried journey back to Cliveden to see Peter and Aline, who had spent only three days at Eydon during their stay in England. She sent a note to Bob, 'I'm sorry to be leaving but I feel must see all I can of Pete now as the time is so short.' She was back at Eydon on Friday night.

Usually Phyllis was wary of going out hunting with a cold but now, for a few hours of mental relief, she sacrificed caution. She went out with Dinah the following day, Saturday, with the Grafton Hunt.

It was a particularly cold, wet day. Phyllis led the hunt in a very fast run, getting very hot and then, because the car was late in finding them, very cold. 'We rode towards home quite a long way,' said Dinah, 'and I remember her saying "Oh I'm so cold."' To Crisp, the chauffeur, she repeated that she had never felt so cold in her life. Before she went up to bed, 'She came and rested herself on my shoulder as I was standing before the fire,' Bob wrote, 'All that evening when we were with others and when we were alone she seemed particularly anxious to show me the love she felt for me. I have so often thought of this since; did she subconsciously foresee the future?'

Bob, who thought that her flu had been 'a very mild attack', stayed at Eydon until Monday to shoot with Jim, before he left for his first term at Eton. The following morning he left for London. Phyllis, already beginning to feel ill again, stayed in bed but then got dressed to go to a Women's Institute Meeting in the village in the evening. Hilda Smith, the children's nanny, remembered: 'We were walking back up the drive and she was perfectly alright. We were laughing and singing. She was always so jolly. In the night her bell went and she could hardly breathe.' Bob was called in London at 4.30 a.m. on Wednesday morning and told that she had pneumonia. It took him three or four hours, until after until 8 a.m., ringing around to find a nurse in the middle of what he later discovered was a flu epidemic. 'The first words your mother said to me as I went into the room were, "Well I've done for myself this time,"' he wrote to his children later. Doctors arrived. Bob sent for Nancy, who came with Rose Harrison. Philip Lothian came, bringing a Christian Science nurse. For the first three days of her illness Phyllis talked, even joked, to Bob and Nancy. The doctors had told Bob that to avoid sapping her strength, he must not spend too much time with her. He complied and regretted it for the rest of his life. He recalled, 'She whispered to me one day "Kiss me and don't leave me. I don't like these professional ladies." And I had to leave her. She said to me "Bob do you think I'm going to pass away?" I said "Of course not." But she knew her danger and she longed for me to be by her. And then she became delirious and it was too late . . . I never said what I wanted.'

Over the next few days Bob hardly spoke. Dinah described him as paralysed with fear and trauma and remembered the 'grim almost unbearable' meals, the bewildering atmosphere lightened only by Nancy's efforts to keep the children entertained. They would eat and separate. The lights in the house blazed for many nights. Dinah remembered the bright glow that came from under her mother's door as they passed it to walk downstairs, the doctors and nurses coming and going.

On the evening before the last night of her life Phyllis had revived enough to ask to see the children. Bob knew that they would find her greatly changed in looks and begged them not to show their feelings. Virginia and Dinah thought she just recognized them. To Jim she managed to say, 'Well young man I must get well quickly or you'll be slipping out of my clutches.' They each stayed a minute. Dinah remembered her 'frantic' Aunt Nancy, walking the children around in the snow, holding on to them tightly and saying, 'Your mother's going to live. I know she's going to live.' By Saturday Phyllis was delirious again. Bob and Nancy sat with her alternately but they were together with her just before dawn on Sunday morning when she died. Dinah and Virginia were in bed on the top floor of the house, both knowing, from all the activity, that something terrible had happened and neither of them had slept. Bob Brand came in and sat on the bed, his face in his hands. It was the only time he broke down in front of his children. When they were taken to see Phyllis, lilies of the valley had been placed on either side of her head. 'It was all very quiet,' said Dinah, 'and she looked serene. But I don't think we quite took it in.' Dinah described Nancy walking in the garden that morning and hearing her 'utterly desperate. She let out a terrible wailing, almost an animal noise.' Her maid Rose Harrison remembered that Nancy was 'crying and screaming and praying'. 'I went to her and I hugged her – it was the only time I'd ever done that and I said "Now stop this my Lady, nothing on earth will bring Mrs Brand back. For goodness sake stop yelling and screaming." And she did. She did.'

Joyce Grenfell described the funeral to Buck: 'There were about 125 wreaths and none more touching than the white narcissus horseshoe with violets for nails – which Smith the groom sent with a card, "From F. Smith and the hunters." How aunt Phyl would have *loved* that . . . The service was at 11.45 and through the blinding rain and high wind cars began arriving and soon the church was full up completely with neighbours, villagers, London friends, family, hunting friends and the household. Jim stood it all pretty well but when we got beside the grave he couldn't bear much more and poor little boy he cried hard. The service in the church was simple and very moving,

ending with one of Aunt P's favourite hymns 'Abide with Me.' (That
quite finished me I can tell you!) Out in the rain we processed to the
rather cheerful little cemetery which is some 200 yards up the road and
there a great bank of flowers shone in the greyness like jewels and at
once I forgot the gloom and saw again Aunt Phyl's lovely vivid little face
and remembered how much she loved flowers — especially the brave,
gay almost clashing ones . . . At 3 aunt N and Waldorf drove away with
Uncle B to Sandwich. Jim went to Eton.' Hilda Smith, his nanny,
remembered this as 'almost the saddest thing'.

The full flood of his grief, the *physical* pain of it, broke over Bob
Brand when he got to Sandwich. Bob was uninstructed in loss. He had
never been close to a parent, a brother or sister, and had hardly
received any affection until he had married Phyllis at the age of forty.
His celibate bachelor life was then transformed, as he saw it, into one
of unimaginable happiness. In all the twenty years he could never quite
believe his luck. Hardly a letter he wrote her omitted his expressions
of deep love and gratitude to her. As the years passed he had elevated
Phyllis to an almost surreal plane in his estimation, believing that there
was no one like her in the world. Now he was abruptly condemned to
a mental solitary confinement, without any adequate language to
express his heartbreak. The letters and notebooks he left in the trunk
give an account of the treadmill of his grief and depression.
Abandoning his well-practised scepticism and rationality he reverted to
atavistic images of simple religious faith: clinging to the hope of meeting her again in human form, searching for any shred of evidence that
could take the edge off his torment.

Having no faith of his own, Bob had to invent his own rituals of
mourning, applying his intellect to try and relieve his feelings. He
wrote many letters to Nancy, his partner in grief; he read nothing but
works of philosophy, searching for any hints of the immortality of the
soul, or 'some ultimate purpose in the universe'. He knew such certainties were never to be had without an unquestioning faith but that he
could never achieve. And yet he refused to believe that we are 'destined
to be born and die like the Mayfly', or that the universe was just a

'farce'. 'Alone in the universe. I am content with that,' he wrote to Nancy, 'but it meets in no way the need of my heart. Taken in an ordinary sense, love then does not conquer death . . . The young are so different. They love and regret. But it doesn't cut them in half. I'm glad it is so. I feel I'll always have this pain in my heart.'

Less than a month after Phyllis died, Bob had to return to his work with the Standstill Committee. He wrote to Nancy on the eve of his departure for Berlin: 'I think the only thing to do, when you can, is to do work. But I find it sickens me . . . I feel I must have time to work out & think of this problem that just obsesses me all the time. Can I hope to see Phyl again in some other world? When I am not working I think of nothing else.' He found it difficult to take an interest now in what might happen in the world over the next ten years (Bob was now almost sixty years old) but he forced himself to do so. It came back to his sense of duty, 'because there is no other way one can help'.

Nancy, whose letters at this time do not survive, had clearly reverted to Christian Science homilies, the only language of consolation she knew, advising Bob not to give into mortal mind and the 'self'. Bob took this patiently. He wrote to her, 'You see Nancy, I think it is only human to be full of sorrow. Resignation will come but I am only human . . . How can I help longing for the happiness I had for so many years? I don't think that selfish.' He was tormented, he told her, by not being with Phyllis more towards the end. 'She begged me to stay & I let the doctor force me not to . . . to think that somehow dimly & deep down she might have felt I had failed her is dreadful to me. It is no good thinking these things. It was Winkie's death and the whole sequence of events after that that lost her to us.'

Bob carried a small blue notebook around with him now, in which he recorded his thoughts. 'How far Have I Got?' he wrote on the opening page, three months after Phyllis had died. Below he wrote, 'The religion of humanity is useless to me. I want some absolute purpose.' He held on to the philosophical idea that the only true reality was that of the spirit, of truth, beauty and goodness. Phyllis embodied these qualities of the spirit; like matter itself they were indestructible.

Mind was as real as matter, or more so, and so he had hope. He was 'comforted a good deal by the thought that <u>I can never know for certain I shan't see Phyl again.</u>'

Elsewhere he wrote: 'I think it was Nietzsche who said that human beings could not live unless they could forget. I cannot forget. In any case I am too old for that. Since Phyl's death everything has changed for me . . . I feel somehow I took a creature from another sphere from warmth and sun & love and stuck her down among the cold English climate & cool English hearts. It didn't affect the warmth and love of <u>her</u> heart but I know it played havoc with her poor body.'

He returned to Eydon Hall for the first time since Phyllis's death in the middle of March 1937. He found himself fighting depression 'with great difficulty'. 'I find the loneliness bad,' he wrote, 'I feel half of me has been torn away. You can't be happy when you know your happiness in this world has gone for good . . .'

A letter arrived from Peter in April, his first communication since the death of his mother. With his relationship with Phyllis now unresolvable, and hearing, no doubt, the old imagined voices of blame, even possibly for her death, he couldn't bring himself to mention it. In reply to Bob's letter he wrote, merely, 'It has meant a lot to me to hear from you . . . Yes life is difficult to understand.' He wrote to tell him that he and Aline were divorced. 'Something about different friends . . . a different sense of humour,' he wrote. It was 'a very friendly divorce', postponed because of Winkie's death and then that of Phyllis. It would, he said, 'preserve the niceness and fineness of our four years of marriage which is more than I ever thought I'd carry off successfully . . .' He ended the letter, 'I crave the companionship of my friends and family. I'd love to come back to England and see you all and have you know me better and under no strain . . . so complicated have been my problems that it has not been easy to write . . . Bob remember you have my deep love and I really want to see you soon.'

Bob visited Mirador on a business trip to America in September and wrote to Nancy, 'When one looks out at the Blue Ridge, as I am doing now, with the sun getting ready to sink behind the hills, the beauty of it makes me want to cry . . . I live all day as if I were already a part of another world . . . I feel much more like a spectator waiting for the play to finish. It sometimes occurs to me that I might live till I was 80 i.e. as long again as from the time I married Phyl. But that seems impossible and ghastly and I am sure won't be so.'

Bob was never to get over his grief. Three years later, in 1940, he made a solitary wartime visit to Mirador from where he wrote to Nancy: 'Not a soul here. The house shut . . . I have never felt such a ghost. When I think of two generations of gaiety, laughter, beauty here and now silence. This morning early the dove was softly mourning. This is a sound that whenever I hear it brings back to me hot mornings at Mirador when I first was in love with Phyl and when there was warmth and love and ease and happiness before me, and the smell of honeysuckle, an indescribable mixture that marks this time out from any other in my life and when Virginia became, as it remains, the truly romantic spot in the whole world. Everything passes, everything changes and God knows what we are or why we are here. Some moments have made life worth living. But they are all gone except in memory and when I think of the names in the Mirador visiting book I wonder why I am still alive.' There was not a day in the next twenty-six years that he didn't think of Phyllis. Seven years after she died, in 1944, he was writing to Nancy from Eydon, on a brief return trip from Washington: 'My life is terribly full now and nearly all my waking hours are filled with endless problems. Nevertheless underneath I find one thought possessing me which it has done ever since Phyl left, this wondering whether I shall meet her again, almost an obsession with the question of life and death & the mystery of the world. As the day I lost Phyl slowly recedes, her loveliness of character grows clearer and purer in my mind.'

29

Cockburn's
'Cliveden Set'

'The Baldwin and Neville Chamberlain period is a very curious one.
We so happened to have two Prime Ministers who knew nothing
whatever about the Continent of Europe.'

BOB BRAND

'If ever that silly old man comes interfering here again with his
umbrella, I'll kick him downstairs and jump on his stomach in front
of the photographers.'

ADOLF HITLER after their meeting at Munich
with Chamberlain, 29 September 1938
(from *The Collapse of British Power* by Correlli Barnett)

Waldorf was one of the few foreign visitors to Hitler, perhaps the only
one, who provoked one of his sudden fits of rage, the black-comic
tantrum. The other English emissaries – Lothian, Simon, Halifax, Lloyd
George (who described Hitler as 'The Resurrection and the Way' for
Germany), Chamberlain himself – with their emollient offers of peace
and territory, or the aristocrats, the Angleseys, the Londonderrys, the
Duke of Buccleuch or the Windsors, elicited nothing but empathy and
reasonableness. Meanwhile they were being sized up, flattered and
deceived, Hitler having done his careful homework on each of them.
But then none of them had mentioned the predicament of the Jews in
Germany, whose persecution had begun almost the day Hitler became
Chancellor in 1933. 'Excitable' is the word so often mentioned in the
British diplomatic documents of the appeasement strategy; that one
should avoid topics that might make the dictators *excitable*.

It was not expected that Lord Astor would bring up that subject. He had come, in some part, to ask for tolerance for his co-religionists — the issue of persecution was already established. Hitler received him in a private meeting as a newspaper publisher, a member of the House of Lords, and therefore, in his mind, a policy-maker. Ribbentrop, his ambassador, the former champagne salesman, remembered as an absurd figure, had understandably reported that the gatherings at Cliveden, the lobbying activities of the Round Table and Chatham House, of which Waldorf was chairman throughout the 1930s, and the person of Lord Lothian, whom Hitler had met twice, were at the centre of British power. Among these high-minded internationalists and imperialists Ribbentrop had reported much apparent pro-German sentiment, and a need to make amends for the injustices of Versailles, as well as hostility to France and Russia. Indeed, Ribbentrop had on one occasion discussed the possible outlines of an Anglo-German deal, a revision of territories, with Lothian and others at Sandwich in 1936, where he had been invited by Tom Jones.

Hitler gave Waldorf his assurances about Christian Scientists, a negligible claim on his attention, and quickly turned to politics, asking Waldorf why relations between their two countries were not better? Why should the Anglo-Saxons interfere in the Pan Germanic destiny, in its eastward-looking *Lebensraum*; they could share the spoils, reorganize the strategic balances between them to their mutual advantage? Waldorf told Hitler that it would be impossible to have good relations until he changed his policy towards the Jews. 'I've heard other people say that this was perhaps the only time it was said to Hitler,' said David Astor. 'And Hitler got a spasm, an actual spasm. The conversation stopped, he paced around the room, he had to be comforted by his aides, and my father said he really thought he was beside himself, as if he'd had a fit of some sort and he was eventually calmed down, and sat down, and they continued the conversation.'

This incident, if indeed it was ever known about, was obliterated by the tide that gradually overcame Waldorf and Nancy in the days before, and long after, the Munich crisis of September 1938, when

Neville Chamberlain, bamboozled by Hitler, made the tragic concessions in the years before the Second World War. The Astors acquired the reputation of being pro-Hitler, pro-Nazi, 'friends of the Third Reich', a reputation enshrined in the unkillable myth of the 'Cliveden Set'. They were clearly none of these things, and the historians' verdict, although largely ignored, has declared the 'Cliveden Set' story a fiction and the accusations baseless. There were Nazi sympathizers and Hitler admirers in the British ruling class, but the Astors were never among them.

Partly because of the neatness of the title, the mud stuck to the Astors and Cliveden and still sticks – they became a scapegoat for a shameful and bewildering moment in British foreign policy when everybody, with a few famous exceptions, got it disastrously wrong, following Chamberlain's policy of seeking accommodation with Hitler. What started as Marxist kite-flying in a cyclostyled news-sheet grew into a myth that helped to end Nancy's political career, damaged her reputation irreparably and closed down Cliveden as a social and political powerhouse. So indelibly had the tag become the official symbol, especially in America, for wrong-headed British appeasement of Hitler under Chamberlain that Waldorf's friend, President Roosevelt, was using it himself in 1942, and then apologizing after protests from Nancy ('I am really distressed that you as a friend should have given such widespread publicity to a really cruel lie . . .'). Roosevelt drafted a reply for Eleanor to sign which said, 'Of course when Franklin spoke to the press, he was speaking generically – in general terms and certainly without reference to you and your husband . . . *rightly or wrongly* [my italics] the term Cliveden Set has become a symbol in the country of not just appeasement but a failure to evaluate the world situation as it really was.' By then, in 1942, Nancy and Waldorf had been battling to set the matter straight for five years.

The phrase, the 'Cliveden Set', was coined almost by accident by Claud Cockburn, a brilliant journalist and a Marxist who had formerly worked for *The Times* of London under Geoffrey Dawson, and who was later the English correspondent for *Pravda*. He had started his own newsletter – *The Week* – in the early 1930s, four pages of foolscap on an ancient Gestetner machine, distributed by post to government departments, Members of Parliament, embassies, diplomatic correspondents of newspapers, City of London and Wall Street institutions. The Cliveden Set made his name. In Cockburn's memory, 'it exercised an influence and commanded an attention grossly, almost absurdly, out of proportion to its own resources'. Part of the reason for this was Cockburn's own ability combined with his extraordinary network of sources and contacts, which expanded with his success. He was an extremely funny and attractive man, and almost mystically alert to the conflicting, paranoid *Zeitgeist* of the time. If you wanted to leak something, as a diplomat or as a conspiracy freak, you leaked it to *The Week* and were assured, because of its attentive readership, of an impact the national press could never match.

The Week also flourished because of the extraordinary self-censorship of the British press, at the time of the appeasement strategy. When Lord Halifax, as Lord Privy Seal, returned from Berlin in October 1937, having met the Nazi leaders, he brought back their message that the press attacks against Hitler in Britain were the main obstruction to useful dialogue. Hitler had talked of almost nothing else, Goebbels too. Philip Lothian had heard the same thing from Ribbentrop. Nancy wrote to Bob Brand, on 10 February 1937, 'Ribbentrop [said] that Hitler was getting very restless and thought England was always snubbing them.' Ribbentrop had also told Hitler that the newspapers that were snubbing him were owned by the men who dictated British policy.

The big newspapers obeyed. 'The Press,' wrote Richard Cockett, in *Twilight of Truth: Chamberlain, Appeasement and the Manipulation of the Press* 'had become not so much the watchdogs of democracy as the harlots of democracy – at every level forfeiting their independence for power and fortune (and frequently a peerage).' But, in fact, they also went along with the Chamberlain line because they believed it. Lords Kemsley, Beaverbrook, Camrose and Rothermere all fell in line. So, patriotically, did the *Observer*, owned by Waldorf and edited by J. L. Garvin. But the arch example was Cockburn's former employer, and

Round Table member, Geoffrey Dawson, editor of *The Times*, owned by
Waldorf's brother John Astor, who became Chamberlain's most loyal
mouthpiece. Dawson simply suppressed all the sinister news from
Germany and Italy, or doctored the copy, causing one of his correspondents in Berlin, Norman Ebbutt, to have a nervous breakdown
after which he never worked again. Dawson wrote, 'I do my best night
after night to keep out of the paper anything that might hurt their [the
Germans'] susceptibilities,' while writing in a *Times* leader defending
the Cliveden Set, 'The hidden mainsprings and the secret wires are
poppycock. The march of events in the world today . . . are accessible
to every newspaper reader.' In this vacuum of information, at a
moment of great danger and unease in Europe, allegations in *The Week*
of a great conspiracy found a ready audience.

   Almost everybody in Britain believed in appeasement in some
form, as the only means of avoiding war, until Hitler marched into
Prague in March 1939. And almost everyone in British politics had failed
to 'evaluate the world situation', as Roosevelt had charged, or had found
it unbearable to do so – the government as well as the opposition, who
favoured disarmament until the last moment, most of the population
and, with rare exceptions, the national press. The conspicuous handful of
anti-appeasers, who had urged rearmament, warning that Hitler was
bent on military conquest and would have to be fought, had also been
guests at Cliveden: Winston Churchill, Duff Cooper, Anthony Eden,
Lord Cranbourne, Harold Macmillan. Some were relations, like the MP
Ronnie Tree, married to Nancy, Lizzie's daughter, and Bob Brand was
always there. Three members of the Round Table – Bob Brand, Lionel
Hichens and Edward Grigg – were strongly opposed to appeasement.
The most convincing refutation of the 'Cliveden Set' myth is that the
inner circle of regular guests at Cliveden, all powerful and influential,
were divided almost exactly down the middle on this issue. 'Brand is
always negative,' wrote Dawson of his Round Table colleague and friend,
and in 1939 he described Bob's 'repetition of the case for a Continental
army which he had poured out to me at Eydon and on many occasions'.

   It is hard to believe the descriptions of the wild euphoria in the

House of Commons, the cheering in the streets, when Chamberlain came back from Munich with precisely no concessions from Hitler — having, to Hitler's further irritation, offered him Czechoslovakia before he had even asked for it, apparently depriving him of a victorious invasion. (Chamberlain's single-handed diplomacy by now seemed even to members of his loyal cabinet to have been dangerously out of touch with reality.) To read about it now jolts one sharply into a climate of opinion, easily lost in reconstruction — the enormous popularity of Chamberlain in the late 1930s and the feeling that avoidance of war was worth almost any concession, however humiliating or shameful, however many allies it betrayed or treaties it broke. Nor can one read in any newspaper — you can only get it by verbal account — of the subsequent sense of psychological shock at the Prague invasion — the terrible sense of having been asleep for all this time and waking to find oneself in a position of utter danger. There had to be an explanation beyond the ability and willingness of the entire population to be deceived: it was unbearable to live with, difficult to admit to. For the politicians, too, unable to accept their own naivety and lack of perception, a scapegoat was required. How else could they explain away British behaviour?

The 'Cliveden Set' was ready to hand. It had become almost a cliché by late 1937. Claud Cockburn had begun to target the Astors in early 1936 for their 'extraordinary concentration of political power' and undue influence on the government. He had to wait eighteen months before the story, to his great surprise, took off.

The Astors, from his point of view, were a far better target for a witch hunt than the popular Chamberlain. He saw in them a foreign capitalist cabal — the 'Cliveden Set' accusations always contained a tabloid whiff of xenophobia — who wanted an accommodation with Germany as a bulwark against the Bolsheviks, and who were able to exert through their wealth and their newspapers a manacling influence on the government.

He had disliked them on several other counts, according to the memoir of his wife Patricia Cockburn. He found them 'pompous, hypocritical and treacherous'. He had taken, she said, great pleasure in the snobbish tag he repeated for them, 'the ex-furriers from Lower Broadway'. But mainly Cockburn needed a focus for the Marxist line that the crisis in Europe was being concocted by the capitalists, a conspiracy to protect their own interests; that in Britain a pro-Hitler group inside the cabinet wanted to make an Anglo-German alliance, to accede to Hitler's foreign ambitions, to swing the German menace to the east and south-east, and let Hitler loose on Russia. Believing, like the Labour Party, in disarmament, Cockburn wanted an Anglo-Soviet alliance against fascism – an option which ended with the shock of the Nazi–Soviet pact of August 1939. Before this Cockburn's line implied that if only the appeasers would stop appeasing, fascism might somehow be checked without the need for rearmament and conscription. He was clearer than most on Hitler's true intentions, but as much as anyone on the left he was lost for a policy against the Nazis.

Nancy was at sea in European politics. She knew nothing about them. She ardently followed the popular Chamberlain line but unwisely aired her prejudices in public to support him. 'Surrounded by such men,' wrote her old protégé A. L. Rowse, meaning particularly Lothian and Dawson, 'how could Nancy be blamed for the nonsense she thought about Germany? It fitted in with her emotional prejudices.' In Nancy's eyes, according to Rowse, 'the French were immoral, and Catholic when they weren't atheists, the Germans were moral and largely Protestant. After all this was the dominant point of view in nineteenth-century Britain, of such asses as Carlyle.' Nancy would say that Germany had a right to rearm because it was 'surrounded by hostile Catholic powers'. But stronger than her general prejudices was the all-pervasive influence of her co-religionist Philip Lothian.

The underlying view of Waldorf Astor and Philip Lothian, and perhaps most of the pro-Chamberlain Tories, was that communism was the serious threat – to Christianity and capitalist civilization. Nazism was not unthreatening but if you could get on good terms with them and quieten them down the communist danger would be greatly reduced. There was no talk of the partnership that the Russians feared – merely of an understanding. Lothian would say in conversation that if you had to choose which was the greater danger in the future, the fascists were nearer to our world; they were easier to talk to than the communists. And here – in the idea that the fascists could be talked down – they made their worst miscalculation.

Europe's stability, meanwhile, depended on a strong and peaceful Germany. If Germany could achieve this, went the theory, she could live in harmonious equilibrium with France and Italy. For this, Lothian and Waldorf Astor believed that the Treaty of Versailles must be reversed 'before drawing a line on German expansion'. Lothian hoped that as soon as Germany realized that no further accusations of guilt were directed at her, she would calm down and take her rightful historical place as a great power. 'I believe,' he wrote, 'if we assist Germany to escape from encirclement to a position of balance in Europe, there is a good chance of the 25 years peace of which Hitler spoke.' There was a strand of Victorian liberal, reforming – and, when it came to Germany, patronizing – Christianity in the ranks of the Round Table, mixed with the old public school principles of fair play and forgiveness. Justice for Germany, Lothian claimed, was a greater motivation for him than anti-Bolshevism. To seek friendship with Germany was moral and 'realistic'; it set aside prejudices. Waldorf declared in *The Times*: 'History shows that on the whole nations like individuals, react to the treatments accorded them and that generosity and justice will bring their reward.' This, after all, had been the theme of Maynard Keynes after Versailles, in his *The Economic Consequences of the Peace*. Halifax, Dawson and Chamberlain too were sincere Christians brought up in this tradition, who could not believe that the leaders they dealt with could be inherently evil. Bob Brand wrote, 'Although Edward [Halifax] was very clever the world was an innocent world to him. To live in it during Hitler's epoch with the ideas his father had planted in him was extremely difficult.'

But Lothian had his own special atonement to make. His highly tuned conscience had increasingly nagged him in the 1920s, with a sense of guilt and an 'intense regret' about his part in the Treaty of

Versailles. He had continually expressed shock at what he saw as Lloyd George's abandonment of principle for vote-getting, and bitterly regretted how easily he had fallen in with Lloyd George and Clemenceau to punish the Germans. By 1935 he had become 'obsessed', according to Bob Brand, with undoing the damage he felt he had caused, feeling that he had been an accomplice in a wrongful deed. Almost every aggressive action of Hitler up until Prague – the tearing up of treaties, the persecutions inside Germany, reported glee-fully in the German newspapers – he ascribed to the injustice of the Treaty and its consequences. He managed to convince himself, as late as 1937, that Nazi atrocities were 'largely the reflex of the external persecution to which Germans have been subjected since the War'.

Lothian had described Hitler variously in the 1930s as 'a visionary rather than a gangster', even 'one of the creative figures of this genera-tion'. In 1935 Bob Brand wrote to Phyllis, 'Philip told us all about his meeting with Hitler. He described him as rather a naive little carpenter prophet. But his strength lay in the fact he was a prophet. Hitler declaimed to him without a stop for an hour.' Lothian's biographer, the Oxford historian J. R. M. Butler, commissioned by the Lothian family, wrote in airy excuse, 'He was not acquainted with the criminal type . . .' In Philip Lothian's two interviews with him, in 1935 and 1937, Hitler, passionately agreeing with Lothian on most issues, seemed so utterly plausible and reasonable. The first talk was interspersed with Hitler's 'Certainly I agree', 'Certainly. Most absolutely correct'. To Lothian's request that the Austrian question should not be settled by force, and that a treaty should be made with Poland, Hitler replied 'Force absolutely ruled out.' On his return Lothian wrote in *The Times*, 'The central fact [in Europe today] is that Germany does not want war and is prepared to renounce it absolutely as a method of settling her disputes with her neighbours provided she is given absolute equality.' He may have been right that Hitler didn't want war – Churchill said the same – but he was wrong that he didn't want illegal conquest. It wasn't until April 1939 that Lothian, the tireless information-gatherer, read *Mein Kampf*, in which the plans for the racist onslaught were clearly laid out.

While Lothian was writing to *The Times* that Hitler wanted anything but war, Bob Brand was watching the 'craziness' in the streets in Berlin, 'the endless processions down the Unter den Linden, the two armies, the Germany Army and the Hitler Army – each in different uniform'. It seemed to Bob that every German was in uniform, that 'most Germans one met would give one a military salute instead of shaking hands'. He began to develop a feeling of 'violent hostility' to the Nazi regime and sensed a 'terrible disaster'. He spent much time at the Reichsbank, doing business with Schacht, the Weimar official who became the financial architect of the Nazis' rearmament programme. Apart from Bob Brand's government business, Lazards had invested heavily in Germany and he could therefore could see the immense scale of the expenditure on arms. He wrote to Geoffrey Dawson with suppressed astonishment that he could write leaders saying that Germany was 'starved of raw materials'. How, in that case, had she managed to arm herself to the teeth? Already by 1935 Bob Brand had judged that it was too late to offer satisfactory terms to Germany, and that, as he wrote later, 'Hitler could only remain head of the Reich if he were a conqueror in war and the momentum to war couldn't be stopped. The last chance was the Rhineland and we couldn't get French support,' (a point historians will dispute), although the *real* last chance had been in the 1920s when Bob was struggling to restore Germany's economy and end reparations. 'Bob was the most clear sighted,' remembered David Astor, 'He was continually saying: "Don't listen to what's being said, just look at what they're doing."' In retrospect Bob Brand, in a generous understatement, thought that Lothian 'didn't face facts'. Lothian, in turn, thought his friend 'often reactionary and unimaginative'.

As a director of *The Times* Bob Brand had had a hand in appointing Dawson as its editor. Now, whenever he came back from Germany, he would tell Dawson and Halifax that 'we must be able to meet the Germans in the field of battle, which was surely coming, if we did not prepare. Geoffrey Dawson was always reluctant to listen to me, as was Barrington Ward his Assistant Editor.' Bob Brand told Barrington Ward, in addition, that you couldn't have an ally twenty-four miles away (the French) and 'leave them absolutely without any protection from us. He replied to me, "All I can say is there must never be another Passchendaele."' He meant, there must never be another massacre for no good reason.

Bob Brand would sometimes write to Dawson on successive days. He complained in July 1936, soon after the Rhineland invasion, that *The Times* was 'unduly pro-German'. 'I wish you had been present at our discussion with Philip last night. We were unanimous that he was going too far in the direction of trying to appease Germany. I feel it is extremely dangerous to encourage the present German leaders at this moment . . . I would not encircle Germany but I wd make it absolutely clear that as regards the whole of Western Europe we should fight . . . But I believe it is quite a hopeless policy to try and make concessions to Germany at the moment in the hope of satisfying her or to do what Philip does too much, namely keep on saying that she is hemmed in and ought to have more freedom and so forth. He was unable to answer last night what he meant by being hemmed in . . . We shd do nothing to encourage them [the Germans] to think that . . . we are prepared to smile on schemes of aggrandisement that she no doubt has in view. We have to remember that those in authority in Germany are extreme, ruthless, entirely regardless of their word and that their whole men-tality is something that we cannot understand.' Hitler's one aim, he repeated to Dawson, was to dominate Europe and his pretended inter-est in the former German colonies – which Lothian, among others, had offered him – was 'just a blind' to draw attention from what he really intended to do.

Lazards had employed a young Austrian Jewish *émigré* called Erwin Schueller in the 1930s, who had intimate intelligence of what was going on in Germany and was helpful in getting some of Lazards' money out of the country. One night in 1937, when Brand and Schueller were together in Berlin, Wilhelm Furtwängler came to con-duct a charity concert at the Esplanade Hotel where they were staying. They bought tickets and went down to take their seats. Bob wrote later, 'When we got in, to my surprise I saw within 20 feet of me in a box only just raised above floor level, Hitler, Goering and his wife, Goebbels and his wife, Blomberg and one or two more. I said to my young friend. "If I had a hand grenade I could get them all." He was terrified. He said "For God's sake don't say that here." I have often thought "Would I, if I had had a hand grenade have thrown it?"' David Astor, who heard Schueller's version of this story, remembered Bob Brand saying to him at Cliveden soon after this that he regretted not having done it. 'He said a thing I've never heard anybody else say: "There's only one reason why I don't try to assassinate Hitler and why you and other people don't, and that's vanity. We have this ludicrous belief that there's something more valuable that we can do than give our lives in that effort but there's nothing more important."'

Claud Cockburn's strong point was never accuracy. He believed in high risk, scatter-bombing, smoking out his prey. But he was usually at least half right on the facts, if not the interpretation, and from late 1937 he acquired an extraordinary new source in Sir Robert Vansittart, permanent under-secretary at the Foreign Office. From then on, he wrote, his tips 'had that particular zip and zing which you get from official sources only when a savage intramural departmental fight is going on'. He also had, according to Patricia Cockburn, 'astonishing' contacts inside the Third Reich. So, too, had Vansittart.

The secret fight was between Downing Street and Vansittart and his few friends in the Foreign Office. Chamberlain is remembered fondly, for the most part, as the honourable, naïve, if exhausted-looking, Christian shopkeeper from Birmingham, with the sad face, waving his piece of paper with Herr Hitler's peace guarantees at the airport. But he had another less familiar persona: the vain, duplicitous political manipulator, capable of dirty tricks; of ordering phone-taps on his cabinet colleagues in order to stab them in the back; of great susceptibility to flattering attention from his grandee admirers. Chamberlain had confided to Nancy at Cliveden soon after he became Prime Minister, for example, that he intended to take most of foreign policy into his own hands. In his self-appointed, near divine mission to seek a *rapprochement* with Germany, Chamberlain had to bypass the Foreign Office, which under Vansittart, took a pro-French, anti-German, anti-appeasement stance. Chamberlain ended up conducting Britain's entire foreign policy in secrecy even from his own Cabinet colleagues.

Vansittart had his own secret intelligence operation to keep him informed of goings on inside Germany. With an acute sense of the Nazi danger, he mockingly disapproved of the unofficial peace feelers to Hitler by 'amateurs' like Lothian, whom he described as 'an incurably superficial Johnny-know-all'. Resentment against Lothian in the Foreign Office had originated in his meddling in foreign affairs when he was Lloyd George's private secretary. Vansittart, like Cockburn, but for different reasons, thought the 'Cliveden world' of appeasers harmful, even dangerous. And he knew they saw him as an unreconstructed warmonger, who must be got rid of. Cliveden became the centre of his suspicions. 'I told Eden, who was welcome there,' he wrote in his memoirs, 'that his visits were unfair to me while animosity ran so high.'

Part of Vansittart's complaint was that he knew a lot more than they did – he knew what the Germans and the Italians were saying in private. The fact that Dawson was deliberately keeping news out of *The Times* each night convinced him of the harmful undemocratic power of his rivals in the Cabinet. In his biography of Lord Halifax, *The Holy Fox*, Andrew Roberts quotes from a letter Halifax wrote to Baldwin: 'Nationalism and Racialism is a powerful force but I can't feel that it's either unnatural or immoral!' On the eve of his departure to meet Hitler in 1937, Halifax wrote, 'I cannot myself doubt that these fellows are genuine haters of Communism, etc! And I daresay if we were in their position we might feel the same.' And there exists an extraordinary letter from Chamberlain to Sir Abe Bailey, the South African mining magnate who funded the Round Table, written on 10 May 1937, less than a month after Hitler's bombing of Guernica. Chamberlain ends his letter: 'I agree that things look bad on the continent; public opinion seems to be in the process of being exasperated deliberately. But one must not take it too seriously.'

The 'Cliveden Set' entered mythology (and Vansittart's career ended) at the time of the visit by Halifax to Berlin in October 1937 — the starting point of Chamberlain's highly personal direction of the clandestine appeasement strategy. Vansittart, who wanted to wreck the visit, had seen a natural ally in Cockburn and began leaking information to him. Cockburn duly reported that the purpose of the Halifax visit was to 'discuss an Anglo-German bargain whereby Germany would offer a 10-year "colonial truce" to Great Britain in exchange for a free hand in eastern Europe'. This was very close to the bone. Nancy had written a letter to Bob Brand earlier that year, in February 1937, after one of Lothian's German visits, that would have been devastating had it come to light at the time: 'Philip reminded him [Ribbentrop] that England had said she would not interfere with Germany in the East, and gave it as his view that Hitler had quite a chance of getting colonies in the Cameroons if he did not go throwing his weight about.'

Vansittart thought he could stop the Halifax visit by blowing the secrecy that Hitler had insisted upon. And he nearly succeeded. Then Cockburn added in *The Week* that the plan hadn't come from Germany, but from England: '. . . the plan as a concrete proposal was first got into usable diplomatic shape at a party at the Astors' place at Cliveden on the weekend of October 23 and 24th'. Here was a conspiracy. And yet Cockburn was wrong on almost all the details. Halifax wasn't there. His German visit had been arranged before the guests met that weekend. And there could hardly have been a conspiracy when Anthony Eden, then considered an arch anti-appeaser, had been a guest that weekend, together with Bob Brand. But this time *The Week* used the 'Cliveden Set' headline and it hit a nerve.

'Within a couple of weeks', wrote Cockburn of the 'Cliveden Set' headline, 'it had been printed in dozens of newspapers, and within six had been used in almost every leading newspaper of the western world. Up and down the British Isles, across the United States, anti-Nazi orators shouted it from hundreds of platforms. No anti-Fascist rally in Madison Square Garden or Trafalgar Square was complete without a denunciation of the Cliveden Set . . . People who wanted to explain everything by something and were ashamed to say "sunspots", said "Cliveden Set".' A damaging cartoon by Low of the *Evening Standard*, owned by Beaverbrook, the Astors' ally at the time of Bobbie Shaw's jailing, sealed the fate of the Cliveden group. It showed 'The Shiver Sisters' – Lothian, Dawson, Garvin and Nancy herself – dancing in a chorus line to the instructions of their ballet master, Joseph Goebbels.

By December, a month after the piece came out, Nancy wrote to Philip Lothian, 'Apparently the Communist rag has been full of the Halifax–Lothian–Astor plot at Cliveden, and then Time and Tide has taken it up; people really seem to believe it.' Because the tales were untrue, Nancy had no suspicion of the damage they were causing. She wrote to Irene after the 'Cliveden Set' story had broken, in December 1937: 'We are delighted over Neville Chamberlain's trying to get on with the Germans. It may keep off a European war.' And in February 1938, also to Irene, she wrote, 'I believe he is perfectly right to leave no stone unturned with those disgusting Italians, whom we should all like to fight if it would not involve a world war but we know that it would.'

Despite Lothian's invitation Nancy had refused to visit Hitler in Germany, but invited Ribbentrop to lunch at St James's Square along with many other guests – at Philip Lothian's insistence. The lunch began badly. David Astor remembers his surprise at his mother's mockery of Ribbentrop's mission; her bad judgement, given Ribbentrop's 'utter humourlessness and self-importance'. Nancy asked him how anyone in England could be expected to take seriously a man with a little Charlie Chaplin moustache. Tell him, she said, 'he's got to take it off'. Ribbentrop was flummoxed by Nancy and obviously rattled. For a moment it looked as if he might leave the table and walk out. At the end of the war, Nancy was found to be on the Nazi blacklist for immediate arrest if the Germans had successfully invaded Britain, an honour apparently given in memory of this slight. At the Nuremberg trials Ribbentrop had the sense to exclude her from the list of his character witnesses. He requested Lord Dawson of Penn, the old Royal doctor, and Geoffrey Dawson, both of whom were by then dead; Lords Kemsley, Londonderry and Vansittart to testify that he had tried to promote an Anglo-German entente.

Waldorf tried to ignore the 'Cliveden Set' slurs, but when the term became common currency in the House of Commons and Nancy was jibed at as 'the member for Berlin' he attempted a counter campaign in the correspondence columns of *The Times*. The emotions widely aroused by the Prague occupation in March 1939 ensured that he never succeeded. The idea had lodged deeply, particularly in America, as Philip Lothian wrote from there to Nancy in January 1939, 'The Cliveden Set yarn is still going strong everywhere here. It symbolizes the impression spread by the left and acceptable to the average American that aristocrats and financiers are selling out democracy in Spain and Czechoslovakia because they want to preserve their own property and privileges. Chamberlain is their tool.'

The historian's verdict was to be put succinctly by Martin Gilbert and Richard Gott in *The Appeasers*, still a classic work on the subject, published in 1963, a year before Nancy's death. 'The disposition to appease was widespread,' they wrote. 'It needed no half hidden cabalistic social gathering to enforce it. The talk at Cliveden was certainly of appeasement, but it was a sideshow.'

If Cockburn had wanted to focus on a real story about *éminences grises* and power behind the scenes and outside the cabinet, instead of slandering Nancy – who had nothing to do with the appeasement strategy – he would have targeted Philip Lothian alone. Nobody, except perhaps Chamberlain, emerges as a more fascinating touchstone of the self-delusion of the time – and in Lothian's case of a mixture of intellectual high-mindedness with fatal misjudgement. Bobbie Shaw would put it differently in his slight cockney accent, 'They were the best minds of their generation, and *look* what a mess they got us into.' Bob Brand's friend had been wrong with passionate intensity at Versailles, and then partly out of guilt at his actions, wrong again at Munich with even greater certainty. Once again, he refused to take in Bob's highly informed evidence or advice. Philip Lothian was appeasement's most skilful and dedicated publicist, tirelessly lobbying Dawson, Garvin, Chamberlain, Halifax, Smuts, Roosevelt, making speeches, writing articles. Winston Churchill had also said of him in the 1920s when he was working for Lloyd George: 'No one who did not hold a leading position in the state should be allowed to exercise so much influence as Philip Kerr.'

Lothian's influence had, if anything, increased, by the time of Munich. After Chamberlain had moved against the Foreign Office, Lionel Curtis wrote Philip Lothian a letter of congratulation: 'Your long and persistent efforts were largely responsible for the replacement of Vansittart-Eden, by Halifax. Though Chamberlain and Halifax may have diverged from your lines [Lothian was for rearmament and appeasing from 'strength'] you will exercise the most powerful influence on their policy outside the Cabinet.' This was the view shared by Ribbentrop who told Hitler that Lothian was 'the most influential Englishman outside the government'. More significantly, Jan Masaryk, then the Czech Minister in London, reported back to his government that Lothian 'had been the most dangerous, because the most intelligent friend of Germany in England'. Lothian's official position at this moment, and since 1929, was no more than secretary to the Rhodes Trust and a contributing editor of the Round Table, but he often spoke in the House of Lords. Lothian's charm, as well as his opinions, affected many people of his generation. Tom Jones described him as 'positive, assertive, he conveyed a fallacious lucidity of one who had done the thinking and solved the difficulties for you'.

But he was still the chameleon Bob Brand had first met in South Africa. Seizing on the abstract idea of justice for Germany, Lothian worked backwards and forwards to make the pieces fit his scheme, always confusing the grievances of Germans with Hitler's motives. As a starting point, Christian Science dealt with evil by denying its existence altogether. Threats of aggression for six years would be met with the 'moral case' for setting matters right. His biographer, Butler, was forced to the conclusion that Lothian fatally misjudged the situation because 'he knew neither the language nor the people . . . and altogether failed to comprehend the mentality of Hitler and his crew'.

The puzzle for historians and reviewers when they come up against Philip Lothian, apart from the question of his shadow role, is how such a clever man – in other words, one who could be expected to see past the conventional views of his class and tribe – could have been so deluded. A key to this may be that he could only pursue his theme if he turned a blind eye to what was going on in Germany, although he wasn't alone in this. It caused him anguish and he tried to reason his way out of it. The optimistic blind eye saw the persecutions as window-dressing, crowd-pleasing, something that would settle down. Refusing to recognize the evidence, Lothian, reading *Mein Kampf* too late, grouped the Jews equally with others who had offended the Nazi regime.

He had written to Lord Allen of Hurtwood in 1935, 'Every time I see Ribbentrop, and every time I know anybody going to Nazi headquarters, I tell him to tell them that the present obstacle to Anglo German relations today is the persecution of the Christians, Jews and Liberal Pacifists . . . I do not believe that individual protests under existing circumstances will have any effect except to salve our own consciences. The solution lies in the fundamental causes . . . If only we can get into conference with the Germans . . . we could influence them, I think, to moderate the brutality of their practice.'

Yet Ronnie Tree, whom Philip knew well from Cliveden, millionaire and master of the Pytchley Hunt, went on a visit to Germany in the early 1930s with a Jewish member of Parliament and was outraged when his friend was excluded from their audience with Goering. He saw the violence against the Jews in the streets, the bricks through the shop windows, the laughing, clapping onlookers. He joined, as a result, the small band of Tory rebels – Eden and Churchill and Macmillan. It caused a major family row. His wife Nancy (Lancaster) refused to see or speak to her aunt, Nancy Astor, and wouldn't have her in the house for two years before the war, so violently did they disagree.

Nancy Astor's views on the Jews were in line with the general, passive anti-Semitism of the British public but even so Jews came a long way below Catholics in her bad books. Throughout the world at that time there was an indifference, with a slight edge of hostility, towards Jewish people, reflected in the unwillingness of any country to allow more than very small numbers of Jewish refugees in from Germany. The underlying thinking at Cliveden, despite Waldorf's direct protest to Hitler, was that his ill-treatment of the Jews, although disgusting, was irrelevant to the great European crisis; it was not worth another world war to protect Jewish civil rights in Germany, which was all that seemed at stake in the early Hitler years. If the Jews were being roughly treated they may even have asked for it by the way some of them had behaved during Germany's inflation. For the Germans to be hostile to them, to want them to go abroad (as it was perceived at that time) wasn't all that dreadful in itself. They had always survived, moved on from one country to another.

Nancy was at least aware of the Nazi brutality and wrote to Irene in February 1938: 'Chamberlain is having a hard fight as Hitler is behaving so despicably cruel to the Jews and Jewish communist propaganda as you know is so bad.' But her main concern here was that the Jews wouldn't mess up the hope of preserving peace by arousing intense hostility to Germany. She made a typically rash remark in a speech in America in 1938, saying that the backers of anti-German feeling there were overplaying their hands and 'militating against peace'. 'If the Jews are behind it,' she said, 'they are going too far, and they need to take heed.' She claimed later that she meant Jews mustn't fall into the communist camp with their anti-German feeling, but when the story reached England it was seen as Lady Astor simply going on about Jewish communist propaganda and was taken as further evidence of her pro-Nazi leanings.

Lothian, with his stubborn blind eye, was the last person in that band of influence, apart from Dawson and Chamberlain, to admit the true nature of the disaster. He had accepted Hitler's re-entry into the Rhineland, feeling this was a necessary preliminary to a settled peace. He became a little alarmed after the *Anschluss* in March 1938 when Hitler marched into Austria (and arrested 76,000 people). Was it necessary to make such a show of strength when it was a territorial claim that was justified? Nevertheless it was done and there remained 'only one or two minor matters to be adjusted'. When Hitler marched again, into the Sudetenland in October, a pretext for invading Czechoslovakia which he described as 'a French aircraft carrier sitting in the middle of Europe', Lothian wrote, on this minor adjustment, 'I'm not very sorry for the Czechs. [Edward] Beneš [the Czech President] has been the Quai d'Orsay's [The French Foreign Ministry's] principal tool in Europe since 1920 and if C is saved it is not because of Beneš. His policy led inevitably to world war in which Czecho-Slovakia would have been far more deeply mutilated or destroyed altogether.'

Then came the occupation of Prague in March 1939. Lothian wrote, 'Up till then it was possible to believe that Germany was only concerned with the recovery of what might be called the normal rights of a great power, but it now seems clear that Hitler is in effect a fanatical gangster who will stop at nothing to beat down all possibility of resistance anywhere to his will.' Of Czechoslovakia's total destruction Butler, his biographer, wrote that Lothian 'had the grace to admit later that "the way in which Czechoslovakia was thrown to the wolves at the last minute has left a nasty taste everywhere".'

One day soon after this Lothian ran into Mauritz Bonn in Lower Regent Street in London, the man he had faced across the table at the Paris Conference in 1919, who had remembered him as 'shrill' and 'fanatical' on behalf of Lloyd George. Bonn had settled in London after being kicked out of Germany in 1933, and had met Lothian only occasionally in the 1930s. He wrote in 1963 to Michael Astor, 'He stopped me in the street and said, "I have been wrong. I never imagined that they were scoundrels."'

In August that year Lothian was offered the ambassadorship of the United States. In December he was to say, with serene unselfconsciousness, 'The USA is becoming realist once more. Munich has been the most salutary shock. It has shaken her out of Baldwinite complacency in which she has been dreaming since 1920. Her own vital interests are at stake. So I think the democracies have woken up just in time, but I am not yet sure.'

In the debate in Parliament when Churchill delivered his famous line on Munich: '. . . we have suffered a total and unmitigated defeat, and . . . France has suffered even more than we have', Nancy interjected, shouting 'Nonsense', and later 'Don't be rude about the Prime Minister'. By this time Nancy's public image was shattered. So damaging was *The Week* story that everything she said and did was interpreted in the light of an arrogant, rich and rude woman who fraternized brazenly with Hitler's friends. When she entertained Lindbergh — which she had done many times before — she was now seen as consorting with a devotee of National Socialism who had been decorated by Hitler. A friend from America wrote to one of Nancy's friends, 'The Cliveden set has come in for much reviling and Lady Astor is not much cherished in her native land these days. Tonight she and Lindbergh are being fantastically united to the whole Hitler-Chamberlain combination.'

With the invasion of Czechoslovakia the wool also fell from Nancy's eyes. She wrote to Bob Brand a month later, 'Everyone seems to feel that something will happen in the next fortnight [after Britain's guarantees to protect Poland] and Philip says that Hitler is bound to hit back. However I have come to the conclusion that Philip does not understand Hitler as well as he thought he did.'

Three months later, when Britain's first military conscripts were enrolled and when several hundred Polish Jews were deported from Germany to Poland for extermination, Brand wrote again to Dawson with barely disguised sarcasm, '. . . I heard the P.M. a very short time ago sing a Paean of Praise in honour of Munich as a great success, so he may want another. The Government must have willed the means with the end.' He made the heretical suggestion that the government should be strengthened 'by bringing in men like Winston, who will make a firm stand and will be known throughout the world to be ready for a firm stand. As at present constituted the Cabinet seem either "career" men or hopeless mugwumps.' Again Bob Brand was ahead of the game. Churchill was currently still unpopular and discredited on both sides of the House and had few political supporters.

But now Nancy and Waldorf also set about replacing Chamberlain and promoting Churchill, their old enemy, when Chamberlain wouldn't listen to their demands for Churchill to be in the Cabinet. (As Prime Minister they wanted Halifax.) The bitter debate on confidence in the government a year later in May 1940 — after Hitler had overrun Norway and the Low Countries — was followed by rowdy scenes in the voting lobbies when thirty-three Tory backbench MPs voted against Chamberlain and with the Labour Party, defying a three-line party whip, thus ensuring his resignation. One of them, courageously, was Nancy. Another was the youngest MP in the House, Jack Profumo.

It didn't do Nancy much good. Back in March 1939, when Czechoslovakia was gobbled up by Hitler's army, Nancy had asked in the House: 'Will the Prime Minister lose no time in letting the German Government know with what horror this country regards Germany's action?' A fellow Conservative shouted, 'You caused it yourself', neatly illustrating the fate to which she had been condemned.

Ten years after the story first broke, and with a world war in between, Nancy walked down the gangplank in New York in 1946 towards the waiting reporters. The *Herald Tribune* reported: 'She sidestepped the inevitable question about the "Cliveden set" with all the skill of an experienced fighter pilot getting into an emergency air strip.'

'It is an extraordinary thing that my mother never understood the "Cliveden Set" view of her,' said David Astor. 'She never understood it because she was sure it was completely untrue. But the damage it did her was huge. And it affected the whole family's reputation. The only thing most people seem to remember about our family is the Cliveden

Set and the Profumo scandal. Both stories were untrue but I think they'll be there for ever.'

Perhaps the only satisfaction Nancy got out of the affair occurred a year or so later when she met Claud Cockburn and made the gesture of spitting in his face. He later said how much he admired her for that.

30

Fort Augustus

Philip Lothian was installed as Ambassador to the United States a few days after Hitler invaded Poland in September 1939. It seemed an incongruous and controversial appointment – Lothian was a non-career diplomat with old enemies in the Foreign Office, and closely identified with the 'Cliveden Set' smear which had become almost more of a deep-rooted myth in America than in Britain. Yet it turned out to be his finest hour. He brought off a political and diplomatic coup that would have eluded any other British civil servant, an act of persuasion that amounted almost to genius and arguably changed the course of the war for Britain – desperate for ships and dollars – and for America too.

America – Congress, the voters, and President Roosevelt himself, facing renomination and an election in 1940 – did not want to be drawn out of neutrality and into a war. Nor, at first, did they want to give money and materiel to a nation that might soon be defeated. Even as late as May 1941, a year after France had fallen, a Gallup poll showed that 79 per cent of the American public were opposed to voluntary entry (although they didn't mind being forced into it).

It was Halifax who appointed Lothian, shrewdly calculating that someone who had gone the last mile in trying to get on with Hitler would be the right person to persuade an insuperably cautious, neutral

America, entrenched in isolationism, that it was in its own vital interest to support Britain. Lothian also had an unparalleled range of
contacts on Capitol Hill, in the press and across America, from his
many trips there for the Round Table and more recently as Secretary to
the Rhodes Trust.

Roosevelt had met Lothian several times and took much pleasure
teasing him, in the early days of his appointment, about his pre-war convictions. Lothian's first achievement was to find a way through the
mutual suspicions of Roosevelt and Churchill, who was reluctant to put
himself at the mercy of the United States and admit a possible British
defeat. At a moment of real danger for Britain Lothian suggested a deal
that was to form the basis for future reciprocity and co-operation and
didn't seem to be begging America for money. The idea originated in the
old Round Table belief in an Atlanticist alliance to keep world peace.

The 'Destroyers for Bases' agreement offered British landing
rights and territorial leases in various strategic possessions in the western Atlantic and the Caribbean in exchange for fifty destroyers and
other goods. It was the first move in Lothian's seduction of American
public opinion and had much to do with close contacts with the hawks
in the Roosevelt office, particularly the secretary of the Navy. But
more urgent than this was Britain's need for dollars and munitions.
Lothian's skill as a diplomat and publicist was to manoeuvre American
opinion into believing that the fates of Britain and the United States
were indivisible, and to forecast the dangers America faced if Britain
lost the battle. Roosevelt saw the need to come to Britain's aid, but it
was Lothian who provided him with the freedom to act by creating a
public debate which put the issue squarely before the American people
and Washington's opinion-makers.

Lothian came back to Britain during Roosevelt's election in
November 1940. Even though Churchill had disagreed with Lothian on
every issue from Versailles to Munich, he had come to like him in the
days of Lloyd George. He wrote later of their meetings that winter,
'Lothian seemed to me a changed man. In all the years I had known him
he had given me the impression of high intellectual and aristocratic

detachment from public affairs. Airy, viewy, aloof, dignified, censorious, yet in a light and gay manner he had always been good company. Now under the same hammer that smote upon us all, I found an earnest deeply stirred man. He was primed with every aspect and detail of American attitude. He had won nothing but goodwill and confidence in Washington by his handling of the Destroyer-cum-Bases negotiations. He was fresh from contact with the President, with whom he had established a warm personal friendship.'

Lothian persuaded a reluctant Churchill, who was loath to give away secrets, that Britain must put all its cards on the table to show that, if America didn't help, Britain would be up against the wall. In November 1940 Churchill accordingly wrote his famous letter to Roosevelt, 'one of the most important I ever wrote', candidly setting forth Britain's predicament. Candour was required because, said Lothian, 'there was an idea that we were asking for more than was necessary'. (Bob Brand had written to Nancy, 'It's a terrible pity that the British are regarded here as always "out smarting" the U.S. It is a profound superstition on the part of the American public wh. will take a generation or two to eradicate.') Lothian gave an equally famous press conference in which he is alleged to have said, although it's now disputed by historians, 'Well boys, Britain's broke. It's your dollars we want.' Lothian leaked information, made unauthorized pronouncements and took many risks to create the public debate that enabled Roosevelt – who had been working on his own comprehensive plan to help Britain – to act on it. Lothian's initiative obliged him to act quickly. The result was the Lend-Lease Act passed by Congress the following March 1941, which enabled the immediate supply of arms and equipment to Britain and launched US industry into war production.

On his last trip to Europe in the summer of 1940, friends had noticed Lothian's bouts of drowsiness. In the first week of December in Washington these became more pronounced, but were put down to overwork. Lothian called a Christian Science nurse and a practitioner, but on the night of 11 December, he died of uraemia, a build-up of toxins in the blood due to kidney disorder. It would have been a relatively simple matter to cure with proper medical treatment, and he would almost certainly have survived. Bob Brand was on a mission in Uruguay when he heard of Philip's death. Lionel Hichens, his other Kindergarten and Round Table colleague and fellow anti-appeaser, had also died recently, killed in the Blitz. All this crowded in on Bob, laid low with melancholy, thinking, still, every hour about Phyllis. He wrote to Nancy: 'It is a terrible loss to the country. But it is the personal loss that hits us so deep down. Everything that holds me to life, except my children & you & Waldorf and my friends seems to be going. I cannot believe Philip has gone I always expected a long life for him. I deeply grieve for you as I know how much you loved him. The Old RT group has lost its two best. To them it is a shattering blow.'

Churchill said of Philip Lothian in the House of Commons, 'I cannot help feeling that to die at the height of a man's career, the highest moment of his effort here in this world, universally honoured and admired . . . is not the most unenviable of fates.'

Nancy was devastated, although she stoically claimed that given their beliefs the death of her closest friend and mentor was no cause for grief. 'I know you cannot agree. But he shd have seen a doctor,' Bob wrote to her. 'Clearly for many months this poison has been in him. His work wasn't done.' Letters of condolence by the hundreds were written to Nancy in recognition of their special and exceptional relationship. Rose Harrison claimed that Nancy was spared some of the shock because of the continual state of crisis in her own and everybody's lives since the outbreak of war.

The bombing of Plymouth had started late in 1940 and Nancy and Waldorf had moved there almost permanently, lending St James's Square to the Free French and converting Cliveden, once again, into a war hospital. Before their move in October, St James's Square suffered a direct bombing hit and the same night a bomb fell on the pub in Wrotham, Kent, which Bobbie was visiting. Almost everybody was killed but Bobbie escaped with severe wounds. He was hospitalized for many weeks, followed by three months of convalescence at Cliveden.

Nancy wrote to Irene: 'The shock to his head seems to be deeper than we thought & he gets really panic stricken at the thought of my ever leaving him. It is so unlike him but I know he will soon be better of that.' Bobbie was concerned, he said later, to persuade his mother that he had only gone to the pub 'to get a packet of cigarettes'.

The first sustained German blitzkrieg on the city of Plymouth began on the night of 20 March 1941 and flattened the centre of the city. Over two nights 293 planes dropped incendiaries, time-bombs and mines on the town and the docks, aiming to cut the transatlantic lifeline that the U-boats had failed to close. In late April there were five further raids, the bombers coming in waves of 100 strong, an unprecedented attack on a small town of less than a million inhabitants. Almost as bad as the terror, the fires and the deaths were the lulls, of days, sometimes weeks, between the raids and the constant anticipation, the many false alarms and, what many residents remembered as one of the worst sensations, the claustrophobia. Plymouth was unprepared, either with anti-aircraft batteries — almost useless anyway in raids of these size — or with fire-fighting equipment. Nor, until many more raids had taken place, was it declared an evacuation zone. There were, at first, no canteens, no hot food and, since this was a cash economy in which most people were permanently in debt, no hard currency.

Nancy, by now unpopular in the rest of the country, with her new demonized identity, became a heroine in Plymouth. She was immensely brave, outwardly fearless, undoubtedly putting heart into the weary and frightened inhabitants. She walked the streets tirelessly and climbed the rubble often in highly dangerous circumstances, arranging shelter, food, clothing, evacuations, bullying the local authorities, talking to the remaining residents, the soldiers and sailors. Once again it was Nancy's defiant presence, her high spirits, her identification with the people of Plymouth, that endeared her to them. She was there and she was always visible. She used the same old techniques of cheering and entertaining that she had used in the Cliveden hospital in the First World War. She did her cartwheels, aged sixty-two, in the shelters to create a diversion when things were going badly.

This time, like everyone else, she was under the stress of permanent fear as the bombs fell, the glass flew, the masonry collapsed and
the city burned. Rose Harrison accompanied her and came to 'idolize'
Nancy for her bravery and example. They huddled together in the
shelters, picking bits of glass out of each other's hair, and once even
hugged in a moment of relief, with Nancy exclaiming, 'I'll never leave
you Rose.' Elliott Terrace was hit, with Rose and Nancy scrambling
from the basement to douse the flames licking along the roof. Waldorf,
the all-party Lord Mayor, spent hours on trains to London forcing the
Home Office to help rebuild the city, or at least to protect it with adequate fire-fighting facilities. Nancy persuaded the council to hold
dances on the Plymouth Hoe in the daylight before the raids – the
most famous picture of her in the war shows her palais-gliding with a
sailor beneath the Plymouth monument. When General Montgomery
came on a visit to Plymouth, he said, 'I must tell you, Lady Astor, that
I disapprove of women politicians,' to which she replied, 'The only
General I have any respect for is Evangeline Booth (of the Salvation
Army).' Churchill came and spent much of the day in tears at the
destruction. 'Men are so emotional,' said Nancy.

In the middle of the bombing, Nancy wrote to her sister, 'Oh
Irene I ache to see you really ache & get oh so home sick. I feel sometimes I must have you to lay my head down and weep on your lap. You
know the feeling. Its like a nightmare yet I am fortunate & despise
myself for even getting blue. I don't often just some times. Phyl's going
leaves such a gap. I feel like a one legged woman yet you can't give in.
It would be cowardly. Don't tell anyone what a coward I am. They
think me so brave. There's no one on earth I should rather see & I do
long for you. I find my family very remote really. But war so near all
around, the only place you can keep it out is your heart & I try hard to
do that.'

One luxury Nancy craved to keep her spirits up was chocolate, to
which she was undoubtedly addicted. 'I have sent you some candies,'
Bob Brand wrote to her. 'I could not get any chocolates but hope you
will like what I have sent. Your passion for them surprises me. I can

understand your berating me for not sending them to some materially minded poverty-stricken women and children in England but chocolates are material things and I thought for you, therefore, they didn't exist and therefore I always assumed you didn't know whether anybody sent you such things or not. Now I know that you are not as firm in the faith as I believed, I will try and do better — but I feel I am enticing you along the downward path.'

One morning Nancy's addiction got the better of her with nearly catastrophic results. A parcel of chocolates arrived from America for the people of Plymouth. Nancy wanted to sample one. The high-principled Waldorf refused to let her. They were intended, he said, for those in greater need. Rose described the 'tantrum' that followed and how Nancy 'was rude and spiteful to him in front of the guests'. Rose found Waldorf in another room 'in a dreadful state', his face high-coloured, his breathing difficult, and decided he had had a heart attack. He was removed to the countryside outside Plymouth for several weeks.

The stress, the 'heroic excess', according to Plymothians who witnessed it, to which Nancy pushed her courage and the effect of the deaths of Phyllis and Philip were taking their toll in other ways. On her visits to the House of Commons Nancy began to make alarmingly reckless and stupid remarks, without caution or apparent thought. She had lost the edge of wit that had saved her in the past, and had become hard and autocratic as if some inner chemistry had changed. Her performances were often rambling, the prejudice tuned up a few degrees; her interjections often rude and insulting. She talked, in a debate in March 1943, of the Foreign Office being 'dominated by the Latin point of view . . . that is why the policy is dominated by France. The Latin point of view is dangerous. What is wanted is the British point of view.' Harold Nicolson, who was present at the debate, described her mind 'spreading sideways with extreme rapidity . . . further and further did she diverge from the point'. Nancy restarted after an interruption, 'Well I come from Virginia . . .' She attacked the Russians, now British allies, as being as bad as the enemy we were fighting and attacked our allies, the French. Bob Brand wrote to her from Washington an alarmed letter, warning her that she was regarded in America as English and not American and that the British Government might ban her from travelling there. She made several astonishing assertions about the Eighth Army — some of them in Parliament. The troops in the Middle East, she said, were riddled with syphilis and the womenfolk of England must beware of men with sunburnt knees. One day in Parliament, she claimed that the troops in Italy, who had fought their way north to Rome in 1944 with terrible casualties, were now lying about in the sun on the Mediterranean, bathing and taking it easy, avoiding taking part in D-Day. In the old days she might have got away with this — it was clearly an ironic jibe. She knew as well as anyone what horrors had taken place at Monte Cassino. But what Nancy never took in or understood was her new stigmatized identity beyond Plymouth, and to the outside observer her unbalanced behaviour confirmed the story. By now her enemies were out to catch her: one mistake and the Cliveden Set was raked up again; her bossiness was put down to 'fascist' behaviour from Hitler's friend. The stigma wouldn't go away. A popular anti-Nancy song, 'The D-Day Dodgers', was sung to the tune of 'Lili Marlene' and included the verse:

> Dear Lady Astor you think you're pretty hot
> Standing on the platform talking bloody rot
> You're England's sweetheart and her pride
> We think your mouth's too bleeding wide
> We are the D-Day dodgers in Sunny Italy.

It was evident that Nancy, among other mistakes, had cast herself loose from Waldorf's restraining, managing influence, even before the war. There had been sudden political differences as Nancy moved, or jerked without any particular process of thought, to the right. There had been divisive family rows. Waldorf wrote to Nancy on the very day of Germany's capitulation at Rheims, 7 May 1945, revealing, significantly, that they had also fallen out over Munich. 'I may be wrong but

I feel you did better in public life when you took some notice of my opinions . . . unfortunately from the Munich period on not only did you not listen, but, to an ever-increasing extent, you took the opposite line . . . consequently I often shut my mouth because by opening it I only created an automatic opponent . . . so it is not I who have temporarily loosened our earlier harmonious collaboration . . .'

All Nancy's sons had seen some form of military service by 1944: Bill in naval intelligence, David in the Marines and on the military staff of the Free French Army, Michael and Jakie in 'Phantom' reconnaissance units. That year David, flown into France with the Special Operations Executive (SOE) to make contact with resistance groups, was wounded in a fire-fight. He managed to escape and return to hospital in England. When the war broke out Bobbie tried to join up with the Scots Greys – the only regiment he could find that still used horses. Having been ejected from the army, he would volunteer as a private soldier. He travelled to Edinburgh where his head wound, discovered in the medical examination, disqualified him. Instead he joined the barrage balloon squadron of the Home Guard in Kent. Bored with the wartime countryside he then went to London and became a volunteer ambulance driver, and was highly popular with a group of ex-taxi driver volunteers. Finally Bobbie became a waiter in a service canteen at the back of the church of St Martin-in-the-Fields near Trafalgar Square. Wearing an apron Bobbie would serve the food and clear away. He told David Astor, 'It's funny. In the First World War I was an officer in the Horse Guards, riding down Whitehall on a charger. The second world war I'm a charlady.' It showed, said David, Bobbie's 'mobility and his guts. There was nothing defeatist or snobbish about Bobbie.'

By the late 1930s Bob Brand had achieved an almost unique position as a major broker behind the scenes between the City financial establishment and the Government. With his Anglo-American credentials, he travelled to Washington in April 1941 as chairman of the British Food Mission and then of the British Supply Council, to organize the equitable distribution of food among the competing Allies. Lord Halifax had succeeded Philip Lothian as Ambassador to the United States, and it was with Halifax in the British Embassy that Bob Brand at first stayed. Halifax had also been lent Mirador by Nancy Lancaster for the duration of the war, and it was ironically as Halifax's guest that Bob now returned there on occasional visits. Bob's eldest daughter, Virginia, had travelled to America soon after the outbreak of war, and was married to an American, Jack Polk. Dinah, my mother, had spent the early war years driving mobile canteens in the bombed city of Coventry, and by 1942 she too had joined her father in the USA, acting as his housekeeper. By 1943 she was married to my father, Lyttleton Fox, and living on the other side of the continent in Seattle. Bob's son Jim, aged eighteen, was soon to join up with the Coldstream Guards.

Work, as ever, was Bob's way of preventing his grieving thoughts from overwhelming him, even seven years after Phyllis's death. He would occasionally return to Eydon for brief rests, 'but what's the good of returning without Phyl . . .?' His one great pleasure was seeing his beloved son Jim and in 1943, on leave from training at the Coldstream Guards depot in Yorkshire, Jim came to spend ten days at Eydon.

Bob wrote to Nancy, 'I can't tell you how much I, & I think he, enjoyed the holiday. But it has gone like a flash. He is so cheerful a companion & as Blyth said to me tonight constantly reminds one of Phyl. I can hardly bear to think how happy she wd have been to see him. He has everything she wd like, courage, gaiety, mixing with all love of reading, music & when he sets to at a job he really carries it out, which I think a good sign for a useful life. I am so glad I had a chance to have this week. He loves you & I am deeply grateful for all you do for him.'

The ending of Peter Brooks's marriage to Aline, the deaths of Winkie and then of Phyllis, all within a year, induced in Peter a breakdown from which he had barely recovered when the war began. Aline, too, appeared confused and uncertain. She would turn up at Mirador, 'looking unhappy' and needing to talk to Nancy Lancaster or Irene.

She also came to England during the war where she developed an 'extravagant' adoration, an unrequited love for Bobbie, who managed to keep her at arm's length without hurting her feelings. Peter wrote to Bob in 1939, wanting information about Aline. 'It would be a great relief for me to know the truth as I've been getting something else from the various sources here. When will she marry Bobbie?' Peter was lonely and also physically ill. He had an ulcer which hospitalized him and drained his now scarce resources as well as causing him 'pain so mean that it frightens me . . . I get pretty lonely at times curled up in my corner wondering when I can get well and what's going to happen'. The Brooks family had been hit hard in the 1929 crash. Peter described himself as the 'residuary guy in a nest of trusts'. His aeroplane had been wrecked in a hurricane and the insurance company had refused to pay up. He had sold his spare plane for $750 to pay his hospital bills.

Then in 1940 he wrote again to Bob from Miami Shores to say that he had remarried. He was flying again and had taught his new wife Mary, who, according to family legend, was 'very cute' and whom he had 'met in a brothel', to be a pilot and she was now – like Peter – training pilots for Roosevelt's military build-up in Miami. 'Letters seem inadequate,' wrote Peter. 'I'm happy. My wife is humorous, lovely, charming, sweet, not mercenary, simple in her tastes and of English & Scotch descent. And 26. I've left New York for good & have 2 spaniels, a nice house . . .' And, then contradicting his claims of happiness he added, 'The sun dazzles . . . I prune and weed. It's the only way to get over terrible ulcers and nerves. My past frustrates me mentally. I shudder to think. Here I have peace of mind & a chance I hope, to get well, though I've suffered incredible pain . . . My father, whom I adore, has his ups and downs & the complications that go with it all have been hard on my nerves and so now I'm trying desperately to achieve peace . . . My wife, Mary, is a life saver to me. A year & I'll be better. Strangely though you'd never know it I have real love for you & deep sympathy and understanding. Aff. Pete.'

But Peter was never allowed a lucky break. Mary died within two years of their marriage of a terminal disease and Peter's depression deepened. He gave up flying. A severe motorcycle accident in early 1944 broke his skull, ribs and shoulders, and left half of his face paralysed. In July 1944 he married again, writing to Bob in August: 'I am now settled into home life with good resolutions for the future. She's half Spanish and half Danish, 28 years old and has beautiful red hair.' Her name was Racquel, or otherwise Saga, a woman remembered in the family as 'really low life'. Miami acquaintances remember the couple fighting and Peter drinking excessively. There are letters from Peter refusing invitations to come and meet Bob in Washington. At the end of October, just two months after he had written to Bob, Peter's picture was again in the New York papers under the headline, 'Lady Astor's Nephew Dies; Believed Suicide.' He had shot himself in the head in the garage of his house at Miami Shores.

There are very few details surviving, beyond newspaper quotes from friends saying that he had been depressed since his divorce from Aline. Bob reported to Nancy a call from Peter's wife who 'wired me 24 hours ago to tell me Peter had died the day before. I rang her up in Miami at once. She sounds very upset indeed. She said he had shot himself the evening before after having several drinks. But she was pretty incoherent.' Bob tried to get a plane reservation but there was nothing for a week; the twenty-four hour train journey was also booked up. 'There is nothing I can do. But the thought of Phyl made me want to go if I possibly could. Irene and Dana thought it foolish. But I felt Peter far away alone there & thought of the past. It is all a dreadful tragedy & it had awakened all sorts of memories in me since I always felt I was responsible for most of Peter's difficulties. I was v fond of him as you know & I know he was fond of me too. What caused this act I don't know . . . I heard rumours once or twice lately that he had got in the habit of drinking too much. Something always made him a pathetic figure. Yet he achieved absolute supremacy in one thing, flying, and not many people do that . . . Thank God Phyl doesn't have to bear this final blow. But there is something too sad in the thought of her deep love and early joy in her two boys & then the end of both to be what it was . . . I know you will feel very unhappy about this. I feel one hasn't any right to be living. But Phyl's little grandchildren are, at any rate, the most smiling, gorgeous little things. Pray God they will always stay so. Perhaps Peter had in mind how Winkie escaped from a world he suddenly couldn't face and decided to follow him. It is all beyond me.' Peter's cremation was attended by his father Reggie Brooks, who also lived in Miami. He died not long afterwards.

Back in Washington, separated from his children and they from each other by 'so many thousands of miles', Bob wrote to Nancy, 'Jim is always now in my mind. Wd that I cd see him. But like Jim I am in another sense my country's soldier. My work may not be v glamorous but I know it is important. Nevertheless to wish to see him tugs at my heart. Do keep in touch with him. I really love him deeply.'

Jim was now a lieutenant and a tank commander in the 4th Battalion of the Coldstream Guards. In February 1945 the Allies advanced to the pre-war German frontier. Bob confided to Nancy, 'My thoughts are full of the attack on the Rhine by the 2nd Army which I imagine has begun or is just beginning. I feel sure Jim will be right in it, as I suppose the Guards are certain to be on the front line. There is nothing to do but to wait and it is no good talking about it. I suppose Michael will be there too. I have no idea where David and Jakie are.'

At the end of March, a week or so before the end of the war, Jim's battalion crossed the Rhine and joined up with a US parachute regiment. Eight days after Bob wrote that letter to Nancy, Jim's squadron met heavy German resistance, roadblocks, tanks and snipers near the village of Buldern in Westphalia. His tank, leading the troop, topped a small crest on the road and came under heavy fire. Jim, standing in the turret, as was necessary and so often fatal for tank commanders, was hit directly in the head with 9mm cannon. A report Bob received many weeks later said 'the rest of the crew were untouched, and one man still inside, who started up and drove away the vehicle'. Jim was taken to a farmhouse where he died without regaining consciousness. 'Jim had always been the same,' the report continued, 'We all loved him – officers and men alike – and in battle he was the best.' He was buried by the padre, said the report, along with other guardsmen, outside Buldern.

Bob was brought the message on 5 April in Washington by his friend Dorothy Halifax, wife of the Ambassador. His daughter, Dinah, who happened to be with him, remembers him receiving it in complete silence.

Bob wrote to Nancy the following day, 'I knew and he knew the danger but I had at least always comforted myself with the thought that the odds were against it and the end of the war near. But the blow has fallen and there is nothing but that final fact . . . It is inevitable that since I am human and still living I should grieve at the loss of a son I deeply loved and who loved me. Most of all I hope that death was instantaneous and without suffering and that he went through no moments of agony . . . But I grieve deeply also that so young, strong, gay, generous, affectionate and intelligent a life should have been so prematurely cut off by the tragedy of this dreadful world . . . I would more than gladly have given my old life for his. It is this destruction of the youngest and the best that is so terrible. I am glad Phyl had not to bear what would have been for her this crowning tragedy. She could not have borne it.'

He then described to Nancy the touching memorial that he, Dinah and Virginia held in Washington. They got up at 5.30 a.m. '& went to our church near here so that we sd be there during the Memorial Service at Eydon & think of Jim & you. We had told them to keep the church open but unfortunately we cd not put the light on. So we sat in the dark or almost dark & prayed & thought of Jim & talked of him for ½ an hour. Then we tried to get into the Cathedral just by. But it was locked so we sat in my car & read the lessons and hymns. I hope and believe the Pilgrim's Progress passage was the wonderful one about Mr Valiant-for-Truth & the trumpets sounding on the other side. I read it to Dinah afterwards, but I couldn't really get thro. Jim was certainly valiant-for-truth. What a blank life is. In the Church I must say the girls brought some joy by remembering a lot of the funny things which had happened to Jim & them . . .'

A month later he wrote to Nancy, 'I can understand how mothers and fathers feel so well . . . I know now what Phyl went through with Winkie tho I didn't then. But men don't burst into anguished tears as Phyl did weeks after still. Fate however gradually beats down everyone into acquiescence. There will always be a pain now. He was so dear to me. How I hated VE day.'

There was no rest for Bob Brand when the war came to an end. When Truman succeeded the Presidency on the death of Roosevelt in 1945 he abruptly cancelled the Lend-Lease agreement. Twenty-five years after their first collaboration in Paris, Brand, now chief representative of the UK Treasury, and Keynes were working together again. They co-operated in the difficult and acrimonious negotiations that followed, and after that in the setting up of the huge American and Canadian loans to replace the Lend-Lease agreement – Keynes's great achievement. Both men had played a leading part at the Bretton Woods conference of 1944 and the preparations for the formation of the International Bank for Reconstruction and Development and the International Monetary Fund. The work finally broke Keynes's health and he died in 1946. That year Bob Brand finally accepted the barony that he had refused when his son Jim was alive, not wanting to burden him with a title. When it was announced the *Washington Post* took the exceptional step of writing a leader on him with the title 'Honoring Mr Brand' – praising him not only for his achievements. 'Even more outstanding and precious,' it read, 'is his record of friendships made . . . Americans who have come into contact with Mr Brand prize his friendship. It is restful to meet a man who is so sweetly reasonable, so devoid of dogmatism, so willing to learn and to share what he knows, and is so unobtrusive.'

He returned to Eydon, welcomed by Mr Blyth and Ethel, the two surviving members of the staff. In 1943 he had written to Nancy, 'I tell Blyth and Ethel my whole existence depends on them. It does. They are the link between my present life & my life with Phyl. I suppose I shall go on here even if I live in two rooms.' He had thought of selling Eydon. But his happiness was restored to an extent by the presence of his grandchildren – both his daughters had now returned to England. Virginia's youthful husband had died of cancer; Dinah was divorced. Bob sat in his study reading science and philosophy, the world seeming 'every day more queer and dreamlike', looking at it, 'as if I was a newcomer, a visitor from Mars'. Its window overlooked the park that led to the church where he had put up a plaque to his wife and son, listing their shared qualities, 'Gay, generous, valiant, thoughtful, loving'. He wrote letters to *The Times*, presided over the Royal Economic Society, visited All Souls, spoke in the House of Lords on the burning questions of socialism and nationalization and returned to merchant banking to try to revive a momentum of finance and commerce from the ruins of the war.

I remember my first sight of Bob Brand, standing tall at the top of the stairs at Eydon to welcome me, aged three, when my mother had brought my sister and me over from America. I said, apparently, in my American accent, 'How do you do, Lord Brand.' A decade later, after all he had been through, I nearly did for my grandfather. Playing tag with cousins and other children I jumped from one roof of the pump house, forbidden because of its large cylinder tanks, onto a lower roof which gave way and landed me in a water tank. Bob came running – something no one had ever seen – his heart, whose weakness had kept him out of the First World War, pumping to my rescue. I had fallen only into a shallow feeder tank, the roof had broken my fall and I was unscathed. And Bob lived on, writing me encouraging letters at school, punishing me for smoking in the holidays, winning our hand-squeezing competitions with an iron grip.

The state of family relationships had shocked Nora when she visited Cliveden soon after the war. 'She said "What's wrong with this family?"' recalled David Astor, '"There's no love in it. You don't talk to each other nicely. What's up?" She was taken aback but we'd got used to it by this time.'

Nora had been hearing such news from her daughter Joyce, who had been lent Parr's cottage on the estate by Nancy. 'There is no ease, no rest, no peace up there . . .' she wrote in 1941. She had observed this before the war too, at a lunch at St James's Square in 1938, at which most of Nancy's children were present. 'You know how it is. Awful! (But don't say I said so!)' wrote Joyce. 'Everyone was very nice and the whole unreality of the atmosphere flowed over me to suffocation point and I was glad to get out into the air again. I wonder what it is. Money? Not really; complacency? – yes and a sort of stark cynicism that turns all beauty to sawdust.' Yet Joyce was a biased onlooker. She felt swamped by her Astor cousins; she felt 'bolshy', as she described it, about all the wealth and consumption – much of which, she admitted, came her way too. She hoped socialism would put an end to it all. There were times, wrote Joyce, 'when the atmosphere of C [Cliveden] strikes me as being so darned poisonous that I have to get out at once'. Ironically, and despite the laughter she provoked with her later stage persona, Joyce was strangely lacking in humour; she rarely had the confidence to join the spontaneous performances at the family gatherings.

It was Bobbie Shaw who always brought the house down at the Christmas parties with his impersonation of a vicar, taking as his text, 'Is there an after-life on the moon?' Michael Astor wrote of the memorable '. . . the Very Reverend Robert Gould Shaw, his refined, drawn-out, ecclesiastical tones, his anguish, his doubts and his expressions of faith while addressing himself to the subject of his text'. Joyce reported to her mother, 'Bobbie Shaw was the same old curate and he made a little speech that was quite funny and I'm glad to say clean.' And yet the disapproving Joyce was watching all this carefully. The skit that launched her own career – in which she played a member of the Women's Institute instructing her charges how to make boutonnières out of dried nut clusters – employed cardboard teeth, a direct steal from her Aunt Nancy.

By 1945 any visitor to Cliveden could have sensed tensions in the family. A comparatively minor issue, compared to the pitched battles later, had been Nancy's attempts, using every method available to her, to demolish the engagements and then the marriages of three of her

sons — Michael, Jakie and David — during or just after the war. The fact
that she admitted that she couldn't control her jealousy or hostility
didn't modify her behaviour at all. The most offensive to Nancy of her
sons' marriages was that of Jakie to Chiquita Carcano, the extraordinarily beautiful daughter of the Argentinian ambassador, in 1944: Jakie
was marrying a Catholic. After a long war of nerves, Nancy refused to
go to the wedding and persuaded Waldorf to refuse as well. Bob Brand,
now trying to modify Nancy's increasingly immoderate behaviour by
letter, had tried to suggest to her that it might be better to be a Roman
Catholic than to have no religion at all. Jakie could never forgive his
mother. He told her in return, that he would not go to her funeral.

   Trying to bury the hatchet, Jakie took Chiquita to Cliveden for
the first time some months later and some weeks after Chiquita's
grandmother had died, an event which had greatly upset her. At a
crowded party Chiquita, feeling her English was inadequate, sat shyly
in a corner. She watched as Nancy put in her false teeth and took the
floor: 'This is the way Chiquita's grandmother dances,' said Nancy,
shaking her head. Chiquita's fury overcame her fear, 'and I looked at
her and I said "You . . .!" And she came up and she said, "You . . ." And
it was like a bullfight. The whole room stopped and you could hear a
pin drop and we looked at each other like that, just like a cowboy film,
and I said, "You bitch." And she couldn't believe it and that was the end
of Aunt Nancy. I mean that she never dared again, like all bullies. I was
horrified by what I said. I nearly died. But I realised it was the best
thing I've ever done in my life. Things were easier after that but she was
such a bore. She kept on saying "You're a Catholic". I used to say
"Thank God you're not a Catholic because you'd be even more of a
bore if you were. You'd be eating saints."'

   Nancy gave Barbara, Michael's wife, a woman of great charm and
good nature, 'a bloody time', according to family consensus. David had
kept his relationship with his wartime fiancée a secret from his mother
until shortly before he set off to marry her in Paris in 1945. Again Bob
Brand got news of Nancy's intended rampage and David's fear of her
'violent reaction' and warned her in one of the only admonitory letters

he ever sent, 'I shd <u>never</u> suppose that a man and a son of over 30 sd ask his mother whether she approves of him marrying the girl he loves. It is <u>his</u> business not <u>hers</u> . . . So I beg you to be kind and helpful. In some ways you are a wonderful Christian. In other ways you find it difficult to be one . . . You must forgive this letter. But I love you and David also.'

Her sons' wives were subsequently insulted at every opportunity. Only Rose Harrison was able to dissuade Nancy from having a lunch party for all her sons, deliberately excluding their wives. In the event of divorce, which occurred in three of the four marriages, Nancy would convert the ex-wives into lifelong friends and pour out kindness and attention.

One of the biggest causes of division in the family, that would rankle for many years, emerged during the war when Waldorf decided that he would entrust control of the *Observer* to David, over the head of Bill Astor who had always imagined it would be his. Waldorf consulted many of his colleagues, but the decision partly hinged on the fact that Bill, who had first entered Parliament in 1935, was somewhere on the right of the Tory party, while David was liberal and left-leaning, like Waldorf himself. (It turned out to be wise decision. David Astor later became, in journalistic terms, the most distinguished newspaper editor of post-war Britain and the *Observer* an exemplary, enquiring activist newspaper, allied to no political party but certainly with a liberal out-look.)

But Nancy's mysterious change of personality included a politi-cal mutation. Her new right-wing instinct perceived a left-wing conspiracy between Waldorf and David. Socialism was in the air. The Beveridge Report, published in 1942, the blueprint for the post-war welfare state and for the new Labour Government of 1945, was exactly what Waldorf had always been advocating. Not so Nancy. She now turned against everything Waldorf and David stood for, every institution they supported, many of which she had herself helped to put in place. Nancy didn't understand the issues but she was still good at the labels and sound-bites and was delighted with her remark, 'They call it the Welfare State. I call it the Farewell State.' 'It was almost unbearable for her,' wrote Bob 'that in a paper like the *Observer*, owned by Waldorf, David should espouse many causes to which she was thoroughly antagonistic.'

Worse was to come. It was clear in late 1944 that Nancy shouldn't stand for re-election in Plymouth. Waldorf couldn't bear to see her rudeness, her lack of ability to argue reasonably and consequently the punishment she was beginning to receive, especially in Parliament. Nancy still had no idea how she was perceived in the public imagination. When Waldorf told her that the whole family thought it was unwise for her to stand again and that he therefore couldn't support her, the effect was tragic and volcanic. He never told her that all her parliamentary friends as well as the Plymouth constituency party agreed with him. He wanted, as usual, to protect her, taking the blame himself. Chiquita Astor, who happened to be at Cliveden soon after Nancy and Waldorf had made the joint announcement, remembered Nancy's acute depression, her 'walking up and down the terrace at Cliveden, tears streaming down her eyes. And she'd been walking all day.' Nancy saw it as a male conspiracy. 'I have said I will not fight the next election because my husband doesn't want me to,' she said in Plymouth. 'Isn't that a triumph for men?' She wrote to Bob Brand, 'I am in the most awful jam. I am sure Waldorf has made a fatal mistake about making me resign. At this moment it's knocked me out completely and I feel I cannot go down and speak for a pukka soldier from Burma [the new candidate] and tell people that I want him to take my place – because I don't.' Nancy went everywhere for advice, trying to get the decision overturned. She would quote anyone who would denounce Waldorf's judgement and aired the whole business in public.

Waldorf warned her to be careful, to say 'nothing which may mar the historian's account of yourself as an MP, of your life in Parliament, of its beginning and its ending. You have a responsibility to all the women and to all the movements which have supported you . . . I ache to see you safely through because I do love and admire you. But you have made me so sad . . . do wake up my darling Nance.'

Nancy turned on Waldorf, whose health was weak, with truly

ferocious venom, which would not cease until his death in 1952. She saw nothing but loss, humiliation, the removal of the purpose of her life, as if Waldorf had finally reminded her of her place and her dependence on him. 'There were open wounds all over her,' wrote Bob Brand, 'which couldn't bear to be touched.'

So startling was the opening attack that Waldorf retreated to Jura in May 1945, 'just to get outside the turmoil'. He was pursued by letters in almost every post. Nancy had decided that she was unable to live with him, her tormentor; that she was, effectively, abandoning him. Only Waldorf's painstaking, sometimes desperate responses, always addressed to 'Darling Nance', give an idea of the wildness of Nancy's letters, which do not survive.

He wrote that May from Jura, 'I was so distressed by your recent letters that I put on my praying cap and tried to apply all the understanding I had to pierce this dreadful fog of mesmerism – When Nancy says that Waldorf is unloving, arbitrary, misguided, weakminded, selfish: that in consequence he must be punished by her for all (mortal) time for his errors: that never must he be listened to or receive any affection or be treated as a rational well intentioned being (for that is your attitude) who is saying or writing or thinking all this? Is mind thinking it? Or is an idea of Divine mind saying it? . . .' He added the postscript: 'Are you really going to leave me deserted in my old age? – I am a good deal older – up here I can't do as much as two years ago and am only 25% of my pre-war self in walking capacity – I know also that in London my working day capacity is considerably reduced. I'm so sorry for myself I could almost weep – Well you can discard me if you like – after years during which in spite of many blunders my main concern has been yourself.'

He tried reason, sympathy, praise and explanation in his replies and efforts to calm her: 'I know how you adored the actual combat and the cut and thrust, the noise of electioneering,' he wrote, 'I am terribly sorry for you . . . no one has done so much as you for certain causes. It is because I care for you that I speak out to you – others either don't care or are unwilling to face your onslaught and resentment by telling you what they feel inside . . . When you accuse me of driving you out so that I could satisfy my ambition you prove how unbalanced your judgment is just now . . . whether I made mistakes now or 5 years ago or 10 years ago or 15 years ago nevertheless my overwhelming desire has been to back you, to support you, to publicise you, to defend you.'

It didn't work: 'It shows that its vain my attempting to reason,' Waldorf wrote, '– you dispute every point and go in circles like Gandhi and go over old grievances like de Valera.' He described, aphoristically and pertinently, the old Nancy problem: 'When you say that "honesty is spiritual power" you really claim that you are entitled to say exactly what you think about others regardless of their feelings . . .'

In this vein Nancy managed to make Waldorf feel guilty about his continuing frail health. It was irritating to her that he had so succumbed to mortal mind and error. He apologized that he had indeed 'failed' her by 'breaking down', 'but you contributed to my physical failure by continuous embroilments, by increasing your disagreements on policy and by "hitting me over the head" – as I got older and more strained I could not stand up to the "come back" – I was in a constant state of worry and soreness – this was wrong on my part as a CS – but I just state facts. I know that my public service is enormously diminished in value without your help – but I know equally that it could not have continued and in fact cannot now continue if I am continually battered or if I am deserted . . .'

Waldorf never gave up expressing his love, and his longing for Nancy. He never allowed himself to give into the pressure. In 1946, after a year of continuous warfare, he wrote to her: 'Darling Nance – I have thought so much and often of you – of all our happiness for which I am so grateful . . . I have been so proud of you. I wish you were here and that I could hold your hand and put my head on your shoulder and get words of cheer and wisdom from you (for you do also speak them).'

Two years later there had been little change. Nancy had still not come to terms with the loss of Plymouth. Her travel and speech-making in the United States and elsewhere had been fraught with blunders and embarrassments. She and Waldorf spent very little time together in the same house. Waldorf wrote to her that she had choices open to her, including co-operating with her sons 'as they wish you to co-operate – as they need you. But that does not mean directing them.' Or, he said, 'you can continue to be the suppressed ex-heroine – misunderstood by your family – misjudged by the world and unfortunately achieving little . . . I do look forward to your awakening from the dream – I look forward to your becoming once again good natured and being filled with love for others encouraging us all with your jolly vitality – but dont wait too long – time is slipping by and I resent the recent waste of valuable years – I do love you. It has been hard enduring this most uncomfortable physical suffering without having you close at hand.'

Waldorf's words were ignored as Nancy drove her children further away, blaming and criticizing, ordering and cajoling. David was forced to write to her with a rare ultimatum. 'When something goes wrong . . . you look aggrieved, are very upset, hurt, downcast – then you recover & go ahead <u>much as before</u>. A little non Langhorne <u>restraint</u> a little non Langhorne <u>patience</u> a little non Langhorne <u>humble study of other people</u> is what her ladyship lacks . . . you say "no I won't face thwarting resentment and opposition. If I can't alter it all, I will just go away." No no dear lady, alter yourself; accommodate, live and let live, play second fiddle sometimes. As I've said to you dozens and dozens of times dealing with grown-up children is something quite new to you & you've got to alter your style; the old style won't do.' He ended the letter: 'Now dear Mother rest assured that we all love you, that you are very valuable to us & important in our lives – but that you've got certain qualities that are either going to bust the family or be restrained.' He said he could praise her for her great qualities, which he supplied in several lines, 'But I don't think it would do any good. If there are difficulties they had better be faced.'

Whenever Nancy came back to Cliveden from trips abroad or to their other houses, she would soon start off 'lambasting' Waldorf, even though he was by now extremely frail. The topics were the same, including David and the *Observer*. Four years after this argument began,

Waldorf wrote, 'I never said that I thought you <u>hoped</u> David would make a mess of the *Observer* — what you have said to me and others even almost to strangers was that you thought he would make a mess or conduct it badly and that you would oppose his being given a chance.' The saddest evidence of Waldorf's declining strength in this battle is the gradual weakening and shakiness of his hand-writing and the shortening of his letters. Still he declared his love, never giving up. He was in some pain by 1950, taking no medication for his heart trouble and his rheumatism and confined to a wheelchair.

But finally Waldorf could take no more arguing and attacking. Without ever giving his reasons, although they were obvious to his children, he went to stay with Bobbie at Wrotham. He chose Bobbie to make the protest as friendly as possible: he was going to Nancy's side of the family, not into the Astor camp. He took his valet Arthur Bushell, who had once done such brilliant drag impersonations of Lady Desborough at the staff Christmas pantomimes. Bobbie was honoured, flattered, 'tickled to death' that 'Papa' should come to stay. He changed the house about to make it seem as familiar as Cliveden and entertained Waldorf for four happy months. Not once did Waldorf mention his difficulties with Nancy.

Then Waldorf took the risk of moving on to David's house at Sutton Courtenay near Oxford. He would sit most of the day in a deck chair in the garden, in an open-neck shirt, resting and relaxing. When Bobbie arrived one day, Waldorf was clearly delighted to see him. Bobbie was the only one in the family who could manage to tease Waldorf; the others had never dared to challenge his austerity and authority. Bobbie said to him, 'I don't know what Mama would say if she could see somebody now. She thinks somebody's in a very bad way, but I think somebody's having rather a good time.' Waldorf started giggling, delighted by Bobbie's familiarity. Not many days later Waldorf had a minor heart attack. He decided that he would have to go back to Cliveden. Because of Christian Science he could never speak about death, but he made it clear that he felt it would be wrong for him to die away from Cliveden, that it would embarrass Nancy, and publicly reveal the trouble between them. He went back knowing that she would go on attacking him and knowing that he couldn't stand it. David thought this 'a heroic act', similar to that of Captain Oates.

Back at Cliveden, Waldorf occupied the Sutherland room, the most ornate and one of the darkest rooms on the ground floor, which gave him access to the garden. He would tour the grounds in his electric wheelchair, an invention which gave him a new mobility and freedom, reminding him of his younger days and reviving his interest in the forestry of the Cliveden woods. One evening the wheelchair broke down and Waldorf was stranded, far from the house, for many hours until he was found. After that it was fitted with a loud hooter. These were the days, in 1950 or 1951, that I remember at Cliveden, when I was posted there with a nanny while my mother went back to America to sort out her affairs. I remember the darkness of Waldorf's part of the house, and the silence, and the occasional appearance of Waldorf in his chair, wrapped in a blanket. When Waldorf died in 1952 Nancy showed no outward signs of grief. She remained unrepentant, continuing to insist that she had been right and Waldorf had been sadly led astray in his judgement by listening to bad advice. She merely regretted, as she wrote to a friend, 'so many wasted years'. It was only gradually that she came to realize that her main point of stability had disappeared.

There was a gathering soon after his death at Cliveden, when all her sons were present. Nancy was in a calm mood. She asked what they all thought of her: would it be, as usual, that she had never understood them? Jakie took the initiative, held her affectionately and said, 'No Mama, I don't think that at all. I think the final verdict on you will be guilty on all counts, but insane.' Nancy took this lightly and responded by striking a funny, 'insane' face.

Nancy was soon negotiating with her son Bill to move out of Cliveden. In future she would divide her time between a house in Hill Street, London, and Rest Harrow in Sandwich. In the late 1950s she moved into a flat in Eaton Square.

*

Soon after the war, Nora's 'garden of roses' at Tryon, North Carolina, was looking a little bedraggled and untended. Nora had not managed to tackle her pathological extravagance, nor, as Joyce Grenfell put it, 'the backlogs of unpaid bills, engagements forgotten or cut, fibs told, mistakes that were regretted never fully rooted out'. Lefty's 'pathetic' schemes, such as the 'candlegrippers' – an invention 'to keep the candle in the candlestick' ('for some reason best known to himself he thought that this was going to be big business. I think he sold three and gave away 8,000' said Tommy Phipps) – had further depleted their borrowed credit or the outright gifts that often came from Nancy. Even so, Nora would run up debts and conceal them from Lefty. Buck's daughter remembered fierce rows between Nora and Lefty when she went to stay. Bob Brand, called in to advise on urgent credit, discovered that security for their last loan of $2,000 from the local bank consisted of 'jewels, a horse, future peaches etc'.

Then came Chuck. No one remembers much about him except his name, the fact that he offered to ghost-write Nora's memoirs and the story of the Langhorne sisters, and that Nora had first taken him under her wing, like Fitzgerald when he, too, came for a detoxication cure. Nora fell in love with Chuck, who was then in his twenties. She couldn't help it. Nancy Lancaster remembers her taking out his photograph from her bag 'and she showed me a picture of a baby boy about the age of her son Tommy. Nora was older than Chuck's mother.' Nora told Lefty she wanted to leave him and marry Chuck. Upset and broken-hearted Lefty headed for Newport. On his way he stopped off at Charlottesville to stay with Buck's daughter, Phyllis Draper. 'I said, "Lefty what are you doin' drinking?",' said Phyllis, 'and he said "because I have left your Aunt Nora, and I've been wanting a drink for nigh on eighteen years." And he said "I'm on my way up to Newport to see this girl who I met there last year and I've written her a postcard."' The woman was an heiress called Lesley Bogert who was married with three young daughters. Within a year she was divorced and married to Lefty, who lived with her quite happily until he died in 1950.

Chuck didn't last long with Nora and for the first time in her life she experienced real loneliness. She wrote to her sister-in-law, Buck's widow Edith, after Lefty had disappeared, 'The reason why I am writing to you in pencil is because I am sitting at a table strewn with pencils and sheets of papers writing on my book about the family. I am working really hard and my agent in New York is very enthusiastic. I am going to England in June and want to finish it before I go. I long to read you the part I have written about your wedding. There is so much Edith that I would like to talk to you about and things that I want you to know, but they will have to wait until we meet. I do want you to know that I am all right. It's been a great shock to me but I have no bitterness towards Lefty and the Divorce will I hope be soon. Much much love to you Aff. Nora.'

Nora developed cancer in 1955 but because of Christian Science and the persuasion of the practitioner to whom she had assigned herself, she let it go untreated for many months. She suffered acute pain until her son Tommy persuaded her to see a doctor, against the advice of the practitioners who assured him: 'the healing is complete'. Nora was almost dying when Tommy brought her to hospital in New York. Tommy sent bulletins to Nancy about her decline, some of them showing irritation with Nancy's efforts to surround Nora with more Christian Science practitioners who sent her glowing reports of Nora's operation and cure. Tommy's bulletins, however, spoke of Nora's relapse after the operation. 'Her nerves are very bad and it just seems as if she can't stand another injection. Her whole body is black and blue from where she has been stuck for this and poked at for that . . . she is still under the tent but breathing easier . . . I'm sorry if I sounded petulant and annoyed. I had just come from an around the clock sitting at my mother's bedside — and didn't want to get involved in a lot of CS talk.'

Nora survived a few more weeks. In her last letter to Nancy she wrote, 'You say to me "your life has been amazing, mixed and sad" and that only my fortitude has brought me through the things I have been through. C.S. alone has done this. I think I have had a wonderful life, and I couldn't be more grateful for it. The hell that I have been through has been because of the things I have done and every bit of suffering that

I have gone through I have learned something from. The past three years I have learnt more than I have ever learnt in my life. I found myself alone. Absolutely alone – not even a servant to say good morning to. At first I felt I couldn't stand the silence and loneliness of it but I had to stand it and now through the understanding that I have such as it is, I am able to be alone, and this is really something to be grateful for. You say you know that you have failed to help me and you have tried so hard to do so. Your kindness to me is something I will never forget – and nobody could have been more generous. I don't believe that anybody can help you but yourself but kindness always helps. The thing that I know has helped me now is that I have had to face the things that have been difficult in my life alone – I never talk about C.S. to you for I always feel you think I know nothing about it. When you write and say you hear I am leading a gay life and going to night clubs etc I just don't answer you, either to deny it or say that I do . . . There is no time left for judgement or misunderstandings. Much love dearest Nannie, I do want to see you. God bless you. Nora.'

Joyce Grenfell wrote that Nora had 'an innate honesty that she refused to use until late in her life and it built into remorse. Remorse is bad company and she came to know it well.'

Nora went back to Tryon to die. Phyllis Draper spoke her epitaph. 'She's the most loved member of the entire family, without any doubt. Young, old, everybody. You couldn't help love Aunt Nora. She was the funniest woman that ever lived, I think.'

Irene lived mostly in New York after Dana Gibson died in 1944. Her happy days as a much-loved grandmother, presiding with Dana over the summers at Islesboro, ended with the war. She remained, until she was very old, the family peacemaker and stabilizer although her broking skills were mostly confined to the only other contestants, Nancy and Nora. She died on 21 April 1956 after a long illness and some years of loss of memory, at the home of her daughter-in-law Parthenia Gibson, near Greenwood in the Blue Ridge Mountains. The headline in the *New York Times* read: 'Mrs Charles Dana Gibson Dies; Original Model for

Gibson Girl.' The sub-title read, 'Widow of Artist Was One of Five Langhorne Sisters – Symbol of Nineties.'

In the early 1950s, Bobbie abandoned his country life at Wrotham for London where his official headquarters was a Queen Anne house in Seymour Walk off the Fulham Road. Bobbie had what some considered exceptionally fine, if conventional taste in decoration and furniture – dark red Turkish carpets, dark green sofas – and the interior of the house, whose name was Pineapple Priory, appeared from time to time in the glossy magazines. He called it 'my little worker's cottage'.

Bobbie Shaw was in his early sixties, and I was fifteen, when I saw him that day in 1960, at lunch with Nancy at Eaton Square. I barely recognized him from childhood visits to Sandwich, or from the many photographs of a handsome, worldly-looking cousin. He was sitting halfway down the table between about a dozen relations. In front of him was the large gold Fabergé cigarette case, containing his Woodbine cigarettes which he smoked constantly – the cheapest and worst quality of all, known to all schoolboy smokers – a noticeably eccentric touch. His face was now creased and crumpled; he looked weary and a little fed up. His clothes were a version of those I aspired to myself in my fashion-conscious adolescence. Bobbie, who belonged to the Edwardian age, was, ironically, paying homage in his dress to a version of the eponymous Teddy boy style of the late 1950s, or so it appeared to me. He wore a well-tailored long jacket. On his feet were a pair of thick crepe-soled shoes. His trousers were narrow. He wore a knotted silk tie, for me a convention-breaking item at the time. His hair was dyed black. He was by no means dressed up or showing off. Clearly this combination was what made him feel comfortable, and reflected the different worlds he inhabited, or had adopted, although I had never seen any grown-up relation dressed remotely like this, certainly none over sixty, and I admired it.

More surprising was the cockney inflection in his voice, as he delivered a series of cutting asides to Nancy's conversation, producing cries of 'Shut up Bobbie.' It was funny and shocking to my ears in its irreverence and — at one point, when he told Nancy in turn, 'Mother do shut up' — in its rudeness. The rough banter between them didn't seem to bother anybody else.

Bobbie had a young friend in Grey Gowrie, later Lord Gowrie, Minister for Arts in Margaret Thatcher's Government. Grey's war-widowed mother had been befriended by Nancy, who lent her Parr's cottage on the Cliveden estate. Grey, a 'precocious', performing child, was taken up by the Astors and he, in turn, took strongly to Bobbie whom he found 'worldly, amusing and funny'. It was to his mother's credit, Grey said, that she ignored the criticism she received for letting her son go around with a middle-aged man who had been jailed for homosexuality, that she 'didn't fall into the trap that many heterosexual people made that because one is homosexual one is automatically pae-dophiliac'. Grey recalled Bobbie's 'great affection and sweetness of nature' towards him and later his palpable sadness. 'People used to say it was because of prison, but it was clearly more to do with his terrifyingly close and impossible relationship with his mother.' Between Bobbie and Nancy, he remembered, in these later years, the 'steady stream of bitch-ing, but rather obsessive bitching, coming from the old attachment. Their actual words weren't meeting; he was providing a slightly camp chorus to her sentences, dropping little bits of acid on what were occasionally her soupy ideas and values . . . He was very clever and very quick-witted, worldly, cynical, disillusioned, and I should think an unhappy man.'

Bobbie had always been an elegant and careful dresser. His later style, said Grey Gowrie, was 'aiming off being a gent, although you could see that he was one. He looked like a mixture of a society person and an ex-con — he looked a bit like Sid James. He was rather a period piece of the late forties and fifties London *demi-monde*.'

Bobbie's life had evolved by now into three separate but well-bal-anced compartments and he moved easily between them: his 'overground' life at Cliveden and Seymour Walk, the restaurants (particularly his favourite, Chez Victor, in Soho), the minor race-courses — 'a very full empty life' as he described it; his adopted working-class family life in London; and the dangerous — because criminal — underworld of 'rough trade'. This was the world in which Bobbie was known by the name of 'Woodbine Jack'. 'Jack' was the pseudonym Bobbie had given himself for this other life, although others took it as code for his conspicuous wealth in that low-life world — 'Jack's alive' being the rhyming slang for a five-pound note. It was a world that suited Bobbie's particular love of danger, risk and awkward situations, but the excessive risks he took were often triggered by drink and his lowered resistance to it. He had been arrested for the second time in Canterbury in the early 1950s, for a trivial episode with a local character, who was declared to be mentally deficient. The offence, for this reason, was considered particularly heinous and Bobbie was offered, at Maidstone Crown Court, the choice between prison and psychiatric treatment, which also meant internment. This, too, had escaped the tabloids. David Astor, by now Bobbie's official rescue squad and devoted friend, described the psychiatric hospital as 'a hideous place', where you couldn't see out of the windows. Bobbie was so horrified by his surroundings that he asked to be transferred to prison. David, with great difficulty, managed to get Bobbie to attend as a reporting out-patient.

But quite separately from the world of brief encounters, Bobbie had established his own alternative and highly respectable quasi-working-class life. He had built up some long-term family relationships and steady friendships which were the reverse of the danger-seeking world of rent boys and certainly a universe away from Cliveden. He had a boyfriend from before the war whose foster mother, Mrs Carr, lived in a quiet Victorian terraced house beyond the Elephant and Castle in London where Bobbie had rooms. 'She was a homely, very warm-hearted cockney lady who adored Bobbie,' said David Astor, who got to know Mrs Carr and her family well. It was a world, he said, of 'steadiness and regularity and respectability. Bobbie had his feet under the table, having his meals there, and was treated as a member of the family. They didn't find anything odd in Bobbie or his interest in Mrs Carr's foster son.'

The most important and the longest lasting of these friendships was with Frank Goody, whose 'bossy' mother had also adopted Bobbie. Goody was a strong character, tall, 'not at all handsome', with a fierce nervous tick. 'He was very intelligent and he understood Bobbie well,' said David Astor. 'He was a wonderful character and very amusing, and he treated Bobbie severely. But Bobbie liked that.' Bobbie of course was consistently unfaithful to these friends. But it was Frank Goody who became his protector and minder. He had become such an accepted part of Bobbie's life that Nancy was bound to meet him. Bobbie wrote to his mother, 'I am glad you like Frank as he is really a true friend to me and looks after me like a watchdog.'

Bobbie's penchant for working-class life went beyond his liking for boys. He came to believe, according to David Astor, that its members 'were nicer, more human and had better family relationships and he thought they enjoyed life more'. He preferred the lifestyle, the dress, even the vocabulary. He began to insist that 'portion' was the correct term for a plate of food; that 'zebra' was better than the conventional 'zeebra'. Seymour Walk was where he would often sleep, but he would never eat his meals there, rarely had visitors and never used it to entertain boy-friends. Bobbie had an exceptional skill for mixing in any circle but 'How he did it I cannot imagine because you would have thought he was either condescending to them or exploiting their relationships but he clearly wasn't. They were honourable equal relationships.'

Bobbie's letters to Nancy towards the end of her life show, nevertheless, that hers was the only relationship he really cared about and thought about, obsessively, each day. Bobbie was thwarted, all his grown-up life, from achieving his strongest desire – to return to an intimate relationship with the mother who totally possessed him, but yet had put her other children and her public career between them. His letters show that he still hoped the time might come when she would drop everything and return to live with him again. For fifty years, ever since he had been displaced by 'those Astors', he had felt homesick for the exclusive love of his early childhood when he was the epicentre of her life. For most of his adulthood he saw Nancy as somebody perfect; his love for her was unconditional and he was merely puzzled when any of her other children criticized her, or found serious fault with her behaviour. Only gradually and very late in her life, did he begin to accept that hers was a selfish, one-sided love; that he could never command her full love in the way she commanded his.

He wrote to her in an undated letter, sometime in the 1950s, 'I wish you liked a quiet ordinary life and we could be so happy living together but alas a public life seems to captivate you.' When they did manage to spend a weekend together he wrote afterwards, 'I thought just you and Rose [Harrison] and May [a housemaid] at Sandwich was perfect. If you would live at Sandwich with only Rose and May and perhaps Arthur [Bushell, Waldorf's valet] I would quite willingly sell my house and join you. Then you could endow Rest Harrow to the Nation should you go before me. Really no one means anything to me but you. I may go thro phases, but in the end it is always the same conclusion.' Bobbie telephoned his mother every day. When she was away he would write despairing letters to her wherever she was, often one-liners, especially later in his life, such as 'Darling darling mother you are my life I am dead without you.'

He wrote to Nancy just before she left for a trip in the late 1950s: 'Just went over to Eton [a few miles from Cliveden] and I had such nostalgia for Cliveden as we have always known it, I thought I would die – the Hall, your boudoir with the sweet smells, I just broke down and wept. I can't believe it has gone. I just could not go up to Cliveden . . . I hope you will never be as unhappy as I am. I really don't know how I stand my existence. It is one unending hell. I will be pleased when you get back. I only hope this gets you before you sail. With best love from Bobbie.' And shortly before she returned, he wrote, suggesting that he had nearly lost his mental balance without her: 'Darling mother I say in real earnestness Thank the Lord you will be boarding the boat home on the 10th of this month (April). Some day you may know how difficult it has been for me without you. I can promise you once or twice it has been a near thing. But I seem to have come out Victor by a hair's breadth. It seems a miracle.' He added ironically, 'I am getting too old for you to disappear for so long.'

And Nancy would reciprocate these feelings. Bobbie went to Copenhagen, an almost unique post-war trip abroad, in 1960. He was shocked by the expense of it, writing to his mother, 'I wish I was an Astor like you.' Nancy wrote, 'Dear Bobbie, I was delighted to get your telegram but I hope that you won't be taken by Copenhagen. If you are you must reserve a room for me because I certainly can't live without you in London. Remember if you are in trouble to get in touch with Queen Ingrid and tell her who you are.'

Still, Bobbie had a clear insight into his own predicament, and for many years, while Nancy herself was responsive, he managed to sustain some kind of equilibrium. But as she began to lose her own balance, Bobbie's letters showed signs of frustration. After Nancy had written, announcing her return from another trip, Bobbie wrote back, 'Yes you must come back but when you say for the children don't <u>kill</u> yourself. There are no children they are all grown up with children of their own. You must think of birds that fly from the nest. Then they grow up and have nests of their own. And they have children. That is nature and that is what has happened but you have no children. I being different from the others cling, I have no nest and no children of my own only a mother.' He was infuriated to be included, even late in life, in the Astor grouping: 'You certainly don't write any letters. Don't send me the one starting "Dear Children" I am <u>not</u> one of <u>the 'dear children'</u>. So don't forget they have nothing to do with me.' Bobbie was wrong: despite his casting of himself as 'the foster', the Astor children saw him as the crucial link between them all, the one who understood each of them best. It was partly this that inspired their deep devotion to him.

Money was a frequent cause of complaint in Bobbie's letters. He was convinced that he was so poor he could barely exist and bitterly compared himself to his half brothers. After a lunch with Michael Astor he wrote to Nancy, 'I can't understand why I am so poor when my brothers are all <u>so rich</u>. Some day you better explain how that is.' 'I am <u>sick</u> of poverty,' he wrote in another letter, '62 years of it has been too much for me.' In fact Bobbie wasn't poor; his house was full of beautiful possessions. He was looked after by his devoted maid, Lottie, who had been a housemaid at Cliveden. But Nancy had always kept him on a tight rein, controlling his money until she died, buying the big items for him and keeping him, as he thought, short of cash. The motive was partly fear of blackmail – and there she was justified.

A bleak depression began to seize Bobbie towards the end of the 1950s as his relationship with Nancy deteriorated. He began to understand her selfishness for what it was, as she herself declined into resentment and brittleness. Bobbie felt bitter; he was openly rude to her, deliberately trying to inflict pain.

His despairing letters were always mixed with wit: 'I like tottering around the London streets, very poor, not much in my pockets with my little pack of corgis waddling beside me their eyes full of love and admiration.' 'Do you realise I am over sixty next year,' he wrote to Nancy in 1958. 'Poor Bobbie all his life spent looking forward to nothing. Over sixty is past enjoying anything but resting or sleep I should imagine. So all the pleasures of cars, bobtail sheepdogs, Cartier wrist watches and things that used to thrill are dead. Such is life.'

At other times the letters expressed a more alarming note: 'At times I get so down. I feel so hard up with not a penny to spend, it really all hardly seems worth it. Why do I go on? You seem ok without me. I mean <u>nothing</u> to anyone else. So I ask you?' He requested Nancy not to ask anyone to ring him up or visit him. 'People upset me too much I simply can't stand it so do remember this – I am only well when quite alone . . . It is awful today the only nice things one has to make oneself – one's house, dogs, birds – all else makes one shudder.'

Even David Astor didn't suspect how serious Bobbie's condition was until he got a call from Frank Goody, who shared a house with Bobbie in Deal, Kent, asking him to check on Seymour Walk after a worrying conversation with Bobbie. David went there with his wife, Bridget, and found Bobbie preparing to commit suicide and angry at being interrupted. In the early 1960s he made his first serious attempt, with pills and whisky, but was found early enough to be revived at St Stephen's Hospital. David gave in to Nancy's repeated questions, 'Where's Bobbie, where's Bobbie?' and took her to see him, although by now she was 'pretty gaga herself', and never really understood what had happened. Bobbie barely revived. He spent days staring at the wall, not

shaving, sunk in gloom. A bout of electric shock treatment was administered which lightened his suicidal depression, but numbed him otherwise.
For a while he returned, nevertheless, to some sort of normal routine.

Nancy Lancaster took in her increasingly erratic Aunt Nancy almost
every weekend in the late 1950s and early 1960s, at her famously beautiful house, Haseley, near Oxford. Baba Metcalfe who had loved 'aunt
Nancy' as she called her, deeply, described how she had become 'a
very bitter, rather cruel person and you never knew where you were
with her'. 'She did rub people up the wrong way,' said Nancy Lancaster.
'I loved Nancy and the thing I liked about her was she could give hard
hits but she could take hard hits. Someone came here and said "How can
you stand it? She's so rude to you." And I said "I don't mind a bit."'
Every weekend, said Nancy Lancaster, her aunt would say the same
thing as they walked to the garden and inspected the borders. 'She
really didn't know a thing about gardens and she was always trying to
be appreciative and one thing she always said was "Old Mr. Shaw said
that you must always have a bit of red," – that the whole basis of the
Barbizon school was that there was always a touch of red in the pictures
to bring out the other things. She said it every Friday.'

The interminable battle with David and the *Observer*, now almost
fifteen years old, became ever more repetitive and, from Nancy's point
of view, bitter. Nancy's weapons were direct – she would insult David
publicly, buttonhole his correspondents and ask them why he 'put so
many black men on the front page', furious at the leading egalitarian
stance of the paper over the apartheid issue in South Africa, or over
Africa in general in the independence period. Nancy believed quite
genuinely in a paternalistic Virginian solution. She talked of the
migration of Southern blacks to the Northern factories in the early part
of the century, where nobody cared for them and no one offered them
friendship. And Nancy took action. Thinking it would hurt David, she
made a special effort to befriend the South African High
Commissioner. She went to Rhodesia, where the independence issue
was on the boil, and bought land; she got mixed up in local Rhodesian

politics. Nancy would address black audiences on the theme of knowing a good master when they saw one – and somehow got away with it. 'She saw the whites in Rhodesia as the equivalent to the Virginians,' said David Astor, 'a gallant minority living a civilised life and keeping the blacks doing what they ought to do.' When Nancy died the property was sold, with great difficulty and at a fantastic loss, as Ian Smith began on the doomed path of independence under white rule.

There were many recorded incidents of Nancy's cranky behaviour in this period. One day she was walking through the bar of the Hyde Park Hotel in London and noticed the writer Caroline Blackwood, sitting with her mother Lady Dufferin, and her husband, the painter Lucian Freud. Nancy, an old friend of Lady Dufferin, stopped, approached, shook Caroline Blackwood's shoulder, tugged at her hair and said 'Mrs Frood. You're a frump.' In his rage at this offence Lucian Freud sent a letter to Lady Astor, which read:

Dear Lady Astor,

Does it never occur to you how despicable are old women who make a point of insulting young girls whom they do not know?

My wife was most surprised at the vulgarity of your behaviour in the Hyde Park Hotel today; but she was even more amazed (so she tells me) at actually seeing you since we had both imagined you to have been DEAD for a number of years. Lucian Freud.

Nancy wrote a reply, profusely apologizing, astonished that she should have caused such offence.

Towards the very end of her life, anxiety got the better of Nancy's warrior spirit and she began calling David, almost each day, simply to tell him that she felt bad, unhappy, troubled. What she could never understand, she said, was how she had finally alienated herself from her children. She complained that she had wanted to grow old like her mother Nanaire, with her children coming to visit her and look after her and that because of this she had been a failure. 'And she said it without self pity,' said David Astor, 'and it was tragic.'

For her eightieth birthday she had asked for a diamond ring. 'We gave her one and it killed Bobbie that at 80 she still wanted diamonds,' said David. 'At the birthday party he called it her "Monroe Ring".' Jewellery remained her insurance against ancient insecurities, and the fear that the Astor millions would run out. Now when Nancy promised cheques for a thousand pounds, despite attempts to confiscate her cheque book, the recipient would get a call from her secretary saying 'Lady Astor is very sorry, she doesn't have enough money in her account to cover it.'

When Bob Brand was eighty-two and I was seventeen we lunched, to my great delight, at the Athenaeum club. He had always liked only the plainest food, and here the meal was ordered by writing items on a card. This he did with his fountain pen, the hand shaking, but the principle as firm as ever – poached halibut, boiled potatoes, boiled carrots. For a time Bob had lived, on an experimental basis, with Nancy, when he was in London, in her house in Hill Street and then at Eaton Square, but the noise quickly drove him away. Bobbie speculated that they would have lived like two old tom cats on a wall, eyeing each other, their ears torn from fighting. Nancy couldn't resist the odd attack, another reason why he moved away. But Bob was still imperturbable, writing to her: 'Please think kindly of me. I am not different. However much you "lambast" me I shall love you just as much. But you must fill your heart with love. You mustn't expect perfection in those you love. We are all together lost in this great unyielding universe & want one another's sympathy.' In London he found peace and rest, staying with his daughter Virginia and her second husband, Edward Ford, then assistant secretary to the Queen, at their house in Stable Yard, St James's Palace. My mother, Dinah, had also married again. Bob Brand now had eight grandchildren, their ages spread between infants and school-leavers, and Eydon was back again in full operation for weekends and holidays.

The bad heart that had first been diagnosed in his schooldays began to falter. One day at Sandwich, Nancy went too far repeating by rote the old gibes about meanness and money-making. Bob suddenly left the table in disgust and rage. He retired to his room and wouldn't be spoken to. Nancy immediately felt a desperate sense of guilt and remorse. Rose had to be summoned to calm her. But Nancy and Bob never met again after that weekend.

In August 1963 Bob, aged eighty-three, stayed with us in my mother's house in the village of Firle, East Sussex. One evening I began to ask him about South Africa. He became animated, talking of his treks in the high veld, the politics, his youth. His face was flushed. I remember him saying, 'Smuts was a very stubborn man.' Because of his heart condition I had given him my bedroom on the ground floor. That night he died. My mother summoned me at 6 a.m. It was the first time I had seen his face without spectacles – waxy, drained of age, contented. At the memorial service, after the priest had intoned the prayer of thanksgiving, Nancy turned to Dinah and said, 'I could kill your father for dyin'.'

Bob Brand's ashes were buried next to those of Phyllis, under a flat stone in the Eydon graveyard on which, twenty-six years earlier, his tribute to Phyllis had been carved with lines from Milton: 'Love, sweetness, goodness in her person shin'd so clear.'

Nancy herself died a year later, aged eighty-five, unconscious enough of her surroundings not to have taken in the Profumo scandal that had put Cliveden, now under the tenure of Bill Astor, back in the headlines, because of an innocent friendship of Bill Astor's with one of the protagonists. John Profumo was Secretary of State for War, a young and already risen star in the MacMillan Government, and a frequent guest at Cliveden where Bill had revived the old-style gatherings. Stephen Ward, a social-climbing osteopath, who treated Bill for back injuries, was given rent of a cottage on the estate. Ward collected girls as instruments of his social-climbing, and possibly, in his mind, for future blackmail, and their presence no doubt amused Bill Astor, unmarried at the time. Ward was given access to the swimming pool, but rarely to the gatherings. At this pool one day in July 1961 Profumo was introduced by Ward to Christine Keeler, a nineteen-year-old call girl. It was two years later that the revelation of

Keeler's parallel friendship with Captain Ivonov of the Soviet GRU nearly brought down the MacMillan Government – in those paranoid, Cold War, spy-ridden days – caused Ward's suicide as he was hounded by the state on trumped-up charges and led to Profumo's lifelong banishment from politics. Christine Keeler's tabloid 'confessions' centred, as did the tabloids themselves, on Cliveden and Bill Astor. Bill's worst, and only, crime in family memory, was to have had the bad judgement to have had someone like Ward, who everyone could see was trouble, close by, and therefore bringing down shame on the family name. Cliveden had been tainted again,and again unfairly. In the very last phase, staying at Grimsthorpe with her daughter Wissie, who had looked after her attentively in her last years, Nancy's mood and demeanour changed radically. David could tell that she thought she was back in Virginia in her youth. Their relationship also changed abruptly: 'I was a very welcome visitor. She was happy, light and charming and in a holiday mood. She treated me as an equal. It was a complete transformation, and it was delightful.'

Three years later her eldest Astor son, Bill, died, the heart attack that killed him undoubtedly hastened by the stress of the Profumo affair. Bill's heir, William, was fourteen, and the Astors told the National Trust that they were leaving Cliveden for good. Bobbie managed to hold out for six years after Nancy died, suffering terrible depression. He ended his life at Frank Goody's house in Praed Street in Paddington, but not without dignified ceremony. 'He had the nerve and the decency to ring up and thank everybody,' said David, 'I've never heard of that. He was quite himself and very touching. He just said "I'm terribly grateful and I'm just ringing to say goodbye."' When David tried to dissuade him, Bobbie replied, 'You wouldn't be so unkind would you, to make me stay on?' This time, David made no attempt to stop him.

At the coroner's inquest, an unknown young man, who had been staying with Bobbie, gave evidence. He said that Bobbie had told him he would have to leave because he, too, was leaving. The boy asked where he was going. Bobbie had replied, 'Fort Augustus' – the place in Scotland where he used to spend summers with Nancy when she first came to England, before any siblings disturbed their relationship.

Acknowledgements

My deepest thanks to Frances Coady, whose skills as a publisher are equally matched by her talent and dedication as an editor, an increasingly rare combination and one in which she has few rivals. The first draft that she saw, much of it necessarily raw material, was twice the length of the published text and I am grateful to her for divining a book in it and for never wavering in her encouragement and her belief in its outcome.

I am extremely grateful to Ed Victor, my agent, who launched the project in the first place, in a dramatic week of auctioning and telephoning, before a line was written. His friendship, patience and encouragement since then I greatly appreciate.

For her help in the preparation of this book I owe a great debt to Kate Hubbard, the main researcher from the earliest days of letter reading and transcribing. The sheer volume of letters, their everincreasing mass seemed at moments overwhelming and required a steady nerve. For this and for her other hard and careful research, as well as for her feats of memory, and her unwavering moral support, I am extremely thankful.

I am enormously indebted to David Astor, a witness to many of the events in this book, whose information and guidance provided over many hours of interviews gave me the key to interpret much of the correspondence and the relationships within the extended Langhorne family. He also showed me unseen and unpublished documents and letters that greatly expanded and illuminated the story. For his continuous encouragement, his confidence and trust in my handling of this material, and his rigorous objectivity — unchanged since his days as editor of the *Observer* — I am deeply grateful.

Above all I thank Bella Freud for her love and companionship, severely tested, as ever, by the dire process of book-writing. My further luck lies in her talent as a reader and editor, her sharp eye and ear, and her sure-footed discrimination. I could not have written this book without her.

Of the highly skilled staff at Granta Books I would particularly like to thank Ben Ball, Peter Dyer, Margaret Halton, David Hooper, Gail Lynch and Isobel Rorison for their friendliness and always attentive help, and for their making the process of publishing so enjoyable. My very grateful thanks, too, to Jane Robertson, who edited the final manuscript so expertly and with such meticulous care.

At my former publishers, Jonathan Cape, I would like to thank Tom Maschler for first commissioning the book for the UK and Dan Franklin for his generous help to me at a later stage.

I was honoured that John Grigg, whose many works include the best book on Nancy Astor, agreed to read the manuscript and I am grateful to him for his very helpful corrections and comments, as I am, too, to Sir Edward Ford, and John Peake for their own careful reading and their informed observations and suggestions.

My heartfelt thanks to Susannah Clapp who, as an extra benefit of friendship, has always and unstintingly provided me with her wisdom and expert advice.

The University of Reading is a main depository of the correspondence of Nancy Astor and other Langhorne papers and I would like to thank its Librarian, Michael Bott, and his staff for their never failing help and courtesy during the many hours I spent there. My greatest source of family correspondence was Bob Brand's trunk, stored at Eydon under the care of my Aunt Virginia and my uncle Sir

Edward Ford. I am extremely grateful to them both and latterly to Sir Edward Ford for allowing me access to this store of material and for allowing me to reproduce many of the letters in this book. I am similarly grateful to Viscount Astor for showing me letters between the Langhorne sisters in his archive at Ginge Manor and for his permission to reproduce them. My thanks, too, to Nancy Astor's literary executors for permission to reproduce her letters. My thanks to the Marquess of Lothian for permission to use the letters of Philip Kerr, 11th Marquess of Lothian and to Nigel Nicolson for permission to quote from a letter by Harold Nicolson. My retrospective thanks, too, to the late Lady Douglas Pennant for permission to quote from the letters of Henry Douglas Pennant. Among my own relations in the extended 'Langhorne family' and its descendants I would also like specially to thank my mother, Dinah Bridge, Langhorne Gibson Jr, Nancy Lancaster, Harry Langhorne, Phyllis Draper, Tommy Phipps, George Post, Michael and Lady Anne Tree, Alice Winn and Elizabeth Winn for providing me variously with letters, stories, information, goodwill and encouragement. Some of these relations have not survived to see the finished work, but I salute them all the same.

There are a great many others who have helped me in various ways with the preparation of this book and I give them my warmest thanks. To those whose names I may have inadvertently omitted, my apologies and my thanks too:

Emily Anderson
Neal Ascherson
Brooke Astor
Mickey Astor
Judy Astor
Sir John Astor
Jim Bailey
Ruby Baker
Paul Bareau
Robert Becker

Ean Begg
Carmen Callil
Virginius Dabney
Marie-Laure de Decker
The Librarian and the Keeper of Collections, Chatsworth
The Duchess of Devonshire
Phyllis Draper
Vernon Edenfield
Faith Evans

Marlowe Fawcett

Mr and Mrs FitzGerald Bemiss

Genevieve Fox

Phyllis Fox

Thomas Fox

Lucian Freud

Diane von Furstenberg

Rene Gooddale

The Right Honourable the
Earl of Gowrie

Vanessa Green

Clinton Harris

Kenneth Harris

Henry Hodson

Michael Holroyd

Robert Hughes

Victoria Hughes

Heather Jarman

Joanna Jenkins

Freddie Knox

Elizabeth Langhorne

Philip Mansell

Derek Marlowe

Alexander C. May

Alice Mayhew

Alexander and Cecilia McEwen

Romana McEwen

George Melly

Diana Melly

Karl Miller

Mrs Beatty Moore

Karma Nabulsi

Nigel Nicolson

Elise Paschen

Lady Douglas Pennant

Mary Phipps

Stuart Preston

David Renton

Tomos Roberts, the Librarian,
Bangor University

Norman Rose

Stanley Rosenthal

Anthony Sampson

Goodloe Saunders

Fred Seidel

Robert Skidelsky

Mary Smith

Gerald Studdert-Kennedy

Sir Peter Thorne

Hugo Williams

Bibliography

Argyll, Margaret Campbell Duchess of, *Forget Not* (autobiography), London: W. H. Allen, 1975

Ashe, Dora Jean, *Four Hundred Years of Virginia 1584–1984, An Anthology*, University Press of America, 1985

Asquith, Lady Cynthia, *Diaries 1915–1918*, London: Hutchinson, 1968

Asquith, Margot, *Autobiography*, edited by Mark Bonham Carter, London: Eyre & Spottiswoode, 1962

Astor, Michael, *Tribal Feeling*, London: John Murray, 1963

Baker Eddy, Mary, *Science and Health*, Boston: The Christian Science Publishing Society, 1875

Barnett, Correlli, *The Collapse of British Power*, Gloucester: Alan Sutton, 1972

Becker, Robert, *Nancy Lancaster, Her Life, Her World, Her Art*, New York: Alfred K. Knopf, 1996

Birkenhead, F. W., *The Earl of Halifax*, London: Hamish Hamilton, 1965

Brand, R. H., *Correspondence and Papers*, Oxford: Bodleian Library

Brand, R. H.(ed.), *The Letters of John Dove*, London: Macmillan, 1938

Brand, R. H., *The Union of South Africa*, New York: Negro Universities Press, 1969

Brookes, Pamela, *Women at Westminster: An Account of Women in the British Parliament, 1918–1961*, London: P. Davies, 1967

Bruccoli, Matthew J., *Some Sort of Epic Grandeur, The Life of F. Scott Fitzgerald*, New York: Harcourt Brace Jovanovich, 1981

Butler, J. R. M., *Lord Lothian 1882–1940*, London: Macmillan, 1960

Cash, J. M., *The Mind of the South*, New York: Alfred A. Knopf, 1941

Cassini, Oleg, *In My Own Fashion*, New York: Simon & Schuster, 1987

Chisholm, Anne, and Michael Davie, *Beaverbrook, A Life*, London: Hutchinson, 1992

Churchill, Winston, *Great Contemporaries*, London: Odhams Press, 1937

Cockburn, Claud F., *Crossing the Line*, London: Macgibbon and Kee, 1958

Cockburn, Patricia, *The Years of 'The Week'*, London: Penguin, 1971

Cockett, Richard, *The Twilight of Truth, Chamberlain, Appeasement and the Manipulation of the Press*, London: Weidenfeld and Nicolson, 1989

Cockett, Richard, *David Astor and The Observer*, London: André Deutsch, 1992

Collis, Maurice, *Nancy Astor*, London: Faber and Faber, 1960

Connolly, Cyril, *The Evening Colonnade*, London: David Bruce & Watson, 1973

Cowles, Virginia, *The Astors*, London: Weidenfeld and Nicolson, 1979

Craig, Gordon, *Germany 1866–1945*, Oxford: Oxford University Press, 1978

Crankshaw, Edward, *The Forsaken Idea, A Study of Viscount Milner*, London: Longman, 1952

Curtis, Lionel, *With Milner in South Africa*, Oxford: Basil Blackwell, 1951

D'Abernon, Lord, *An Ambassador of Peace: Pages from the Diary of Viscount D'Abernon*, 3 vols, London: Hodder and Stoughton, 1929

Dabney, Virginius, *Virginia, The New Dominion*, New York: Doubleday, 1971

Dawson, Geoffrey, *Correspondence*, Oxford: Bodleian Library

Donaldson, Scott, *Fool for Love*, New York: Longdon and Weed, 1983

Downey, Fairfax, *Portrait of an Era as Drawn by C. D. Gibson*, New York: Charles Scribner's Sons, 1936

Edel, Leon, *The Life of Henry James*, 2 vols, London: Penguin, 1977

Fest, Joachim, *Plotting Hitler's Death*, London: Weidenfeld and Nicolson, 1996

Foote, Shelby, *The Civil War, A Narrative*, London: The Bodley Head, 1991

Fraser, Caroline, 'Mrs Eddy Builds Her Empire', *New York Review of Books*, 11 July 1966

Fussell, Paul, *The Great War and Modern Memory*, London: Oxford University Press, 1975

Gibson, Langhorne Jr, *The Gibson Girl, Portrait of a Southern Belle*, Richmond, Virginia: The Commodore Press, 1997

Gilbert, Martin and Richard Gott, *The Appeasers*, London: Weidenfeld and Nicolson, 1963

Graham, Sheilah, *Confessions of a Hollywood Columnist*, London: W. H. Allen, 1970

Graham, Sheilah, *The Real F. Scott Fitzgerald Thirty-five Years Later*, New York: Grosset & Dunlap, 1976

Grenfell, Joyce, *Darling Ma – Letters to her Mother 1932–1944*, edited by James Roose Evans, London: Hodder and Stoughton, 1988

Grenfell, Joyce, *Joyce Grenfell Requests the Pleasure*, London: Hodder and Stoughton, 1988

Grierson Edward, *The Imperial Dream*, London: Collins, 1972

Grigg, John, *Nancy Astor*, London: Sidgwick & Jackson, 1980

Harrison, Rosina, *My Life in Service*, London: Cassell, 1975

Harrod, Roy, *The Life of John Maynard Keynes*, New York: Harcourt, Brace, 1951

Holroyd, Michael, *Bernard Shaw, Volume 3, 1918–1950*, London: Chatto & Windus, 1991

Jones, Thomas, *A Diary with Letters 1931–1950*, London: Oxford University Press, 1954

Kavalier, Lucy, *The Astors, A Family Chronicle*, London: George G. Harrap, 1966

Keynes, John Maynard, *The Economic Consequences of the Peace*, London: Macmillan, 1971

Lamb, Richard, *The Ghosts of Peace, 1935–45*, London: M. Russell, 1987

Langhorne, Elizabeth, *Nancy Astor and Her Friends*, London: Arthur Barker, 1974

Lavin, Deborah, *From Empire to International Commonwealth. A Biography of Lionel Curtis*, Oxford: Clarendon Press, 1995

Lees-Milne, James, *Ancestral Voices*, London: Chatto & Windus, 1975

Lehr, Elizabeth Drexel, *King Lehr and the Gilded Age*, Philadelphia/London: J. B. Lippincott, 1935

Levy, David W., *Herbert Croly of the New Republic*, Princeton, NJ: Princeton University Press, 1985

Lindsay, Jean, *The Great Strike. A History of the Penrhyn Quarry Dispute of 1900–1903*, London: David & Charles, 1987

Lloyd George, David, *The Truth About Reparations and War-Debts*, London: William Heinemann, 1932

Lothian, Lord, *The American Speeches of Lord Lothian*, London: Oxford University Press, 1941

McAllister, Ward, *Society As I Have Found It*, New York: Cassell Publishing Company, 1890

McPherson, James M., *Battle Cry of Freedom, The Civil War Era*, Oxford: Oxford University Press, 1988

Marlowe, Derek, *Nancy Astor*, London: Weidenfeld and Nicolson, 1982

Masters, A., *Nancy Astor, A Life*, London: Weidenfeld and Nicolson, 1981

May, Alexander C., 'The Round Table 1910–1966', Ph.D. thesis, Oxford: St John's College, 1995

Mayer, Arno J., *Politics & Diplomacy of Peacemaking, Containment and Counterrevolution at Versailles 1918–1919*, New York: Vintage, 1969

Mitchell, Margaret, *Gone with the Wind*, London: Macmillan, 1939

Mosley, Nicholas, *Julian Grenfell*, London: Weidenfeld and Nicolson, 1976

Myers, Jeffrey, *Scott Fitzgerald*, London: HarperCollins, 1994

Nicolson, Harold, *Curzon: The Last Phase 1919–1925*, London: Constable, 1934

Nicolson, Harold, *Diaries and Letters 1930–1964*, edited by Stanley Olson, London: William Collins, 1980

Nimocks, Walter, *Milner's Young Men: The 'Kindergarten' in Edwardian Imperial Affairs*, London: Hodder and Stoughton, 1970

Niven, David, *The Moon is a Balloon*, London: Hamish Hamilton, 1971

Page, H. S., *Over the Open*, New York: Charles Scribner's Sons, 1925

Page, Thomas Nelson, *In Ole Virginia*, New York: Irvington Publishers, 1986

Pakula, Hannah, *The Last Romantic, A Biography of Queen Marie of Roumania*, London: Weidenfeld and Nicolson, 1985

Piper, Henry Dan, *F. Scott Fitzgerald. A Critical Portrait*, New York: Holt, Rinehart & Winston, 1965; London: Bodley Head, 1966

Reniers, Perceval, *The Springs of Virginia*, Chapel Hill: The University of North Carolina Press, 1941

Reynolds, David, *Lord Lothian and Anglo-American Relations 1939–40*, Philadelphia: The American Philosophical Society, 1983

Riddell, Lord, *Lord Riddell's Intimate Diary of the Peace Conference and After, 1918–1923*, London: Victor Gollancz, 1933

Roosevelt, Eleanor, *The Autobiography*, London: Hutchinson, 1962

Rose, Norman, *Vansittart. Study of a Diplomat*, London: Heinemann, 1978

Rowse, A. L., *The English Past: Evocations of Persons and Places*, London: Macmillan, 1952

Rowse, A. L., *All Souls and Appeasement*, Basingstoke: Macmillan, 1961

Rowse, A. L., 'Nancy Astor', in *Memories of Men and Women*, London: Eyre Methuen, 1980

Sinclair, David, *The Astors and their Times*, London: J. M. Dent, 1983

Skidelsky, Robert, *John Maynard Keynes, The Economist as Saviour 1920–1937*, London: Macmillan, 1992

Sloane, Florence Adele, *Maverick in Mauve, The Diary of a Romantic Age*, New York: Doubleday, 1983

Stampp, Kenneth M., *The Era of Reconstruction: America after the Civil War, 1865–1877*, London: Eyre & Spottiswoode, 1965

Stark, Freya, *Over the Rim of the World. Collected Letters*, London: John Murray, 1988

Sykes, Christopher, *Nancy: The Life of Lady Astor*, Frogmore, St Albans, Herts: Granada, 1979

Taylor, William R., *Cavalier and Yankee*, London: W. H. Allen, 1963

Thornton, A. P., *The Imperial Idea and its Enemies*, London: Macmillan, 1952

Turnbull, Andrew, *Scott Fitzgerald*, New York: Scribner's, 1962

Turnbull, Andrew (ed.), *The Letters of Scott Fitzgerald*, New York: Scribner's, 1975

Vansittart, Robert Gilbert, Baron, *The Mist Procession – the Autobiography of Lord Vansittart*, London: Hutchinson, 1958

Williams Smith, Ella, *Tears and Laughter in Virginia and Elsewhere*, Virginia: McClure Press, 1972

Willis, Holman, 'Buck Langhorne and Sam Goodloe', unpublished MS

Wilson, Derek, *The Astors*, London: Weidenfeld and Nicolson, 1993

Wilson, Edmund, *Patriotic Gore: Studies in the Literature of the American Civil War*, New York: Farrar Straus & Giroux, 1966

Wilson, J., *CB: A Life of Sir Henry Campbell-Bannerman*, London: Purnell Book Services, 1973

Winn, Alice, *Always a Virginian: The Colourful Langhornes of Mirador, Lady Astor and their Kin*, Lynchburg: Kenmore Association, 1982

Wrench, John Evelyn, *Geoffrey Dawson and Our Times*, London: Hutchinson, 1955

Index